CHURCH AND SOCIETY

CHURCH

and

SOCIETY

---◈◈◈---

The Laurence J. McGinley Lectures,

1988–2007

AVERY CARDINAL DULLES, S.J.

FORDHAM UNIVERSITY PRESS
New York *2008*

Library of Congress Cataloging-in-Publication Data

Dulles, Avery Robert, 1918–
    Church and society : the Laurence J. McGinley lectures, 1988–2007 / Avery Dulles. — 1st ed.
        p.   cm.
    Includes bibliographical references and index.
    ISBN-13: 978-0-8232-2862-1 (cloth : alk. paper)
    1. Catholic Church—Doctrines—History—20th century.   2. Catholic Church—Doctrines—History—21st century.   3. Christian sociology—Catholic Church.   4. Church and social problems—Catholic Church.   I. Title.
BX1751.3.D85   2008
282—dc22
                                                                        2008003277

Printed in the United States of America

10   09   08   5   4   3   2   1

First edition

Contents

FOREWORD

Avery Dulles, *Vir Ecclesiasticus*

ROBERT PETER IMBELLI

O ne of the most heartfelt accolades the early Fathers could bestow on a theologian was to praise him as a *vir ecclesiasticus*: an ecclesial man. I can think of few theologians of our day who so merit the title as Cardinal Avery Dulles. He merits it not merely because of his rank as a "prince of the Church," or even because his primary theological focus has been ecclesiology, the theology of the Church. Rather, his whole theological and priestly existence has been in service of the Church, dwelling in its midst, nourished by its tradition, seeking to extend that life-giving tradition to meet the questions and challenges of our time. The Introit for the Mass of a Doctor of the Church surely summarizes his life's commitment: to speak and write "in the midst of the Church"—*In medio ecclesiae aperuit os ejus.*

THE CHURCH IN LIGHT OF VATICAN II

However, the earthly Church is not some Platonic idea, floating free of history. Like its incarnate Lord, Christ's Church is immersed in history as it pursues its pilgrim journey to the fullness of the Kingdom, the heavenly Jerusalem, the City of Peace. Every theologian inhabits a specific historical context, speaking and writing a distinctive language within a given social and cultural setting.

For the contemporary Catholic theologian a defining characteristic of the context in which he or she labors is the ongoing reception of the Second Vatican Council. In the introduction to his book *The Resilient Church* (1977), Dulles wrote:

There are some events in church history so decisive that they set the agenda for an entire historical era. For Catholic ecclesiology the Second Vatican Council seems to have been such an event. More than a decade after the Council the Catholic ecclesiologist has no choice except to frame his questions in the light of what the Council initiated.[1]

What he wrote in 1977 he doubtless would repeat in 2007. The council continues to set the agenda for our day into the foreseeable future. Few have contributed so magisterially to the elucidation and appropriation of the council's ecclesial vision as has Avery Dulles.

One acknowledges his unparalleled familiarity with the entire range of the council's documents. One admires his knowledge of the prehistory of the council: from Vatican I through neo-Scholasticism to the *nouvelle théologie* and the pioneering encyclicals of Pius XII. One appreciates his refusal to countenance a facile separation of the council's supposed "spirit" from the manifest teaching of its texts.

Dulles holds together the creative tension that characterized the labors of the council itself: the dynamic of *ressourcement* and *aggiornamento*. *Ressourcement* was the return to the sources made possible by the flowering of scriptural and patristic scholarship in the decades prior to Vatican II. It uncovered the wellsprings of the Catholic Tradition, much deeper and more nourishing than the relatively constricted forms of post-Tridentine Catholicism. *Aggiornamento* was the recognition that one could not merely remain in the fifth century with Augustine or even the first century with Paul but had to bring their life-giving words into the present in a way that is intelligible and transforming for men and women of our day.

In his book *The Reshaping of Catholicism* (1988), Dulles has a significant chapter entitled "Vatican II and the Recovery of Tradition." He articulates one of the council's key accomplishments thus:

> Getting away from an excessively rigid, conceptual, and authoritarian view of tradition, the Council emphasizes that tradition arises through a real, living self-communication of God in grace and revelation, that it is rooted in the life of the community of faith, and that it adapts itself and develops in changing historical situations.[2]

This rich, multidimensional sense of tradition permeates Dulles's work. It owes much to such thinkers as Newman, Blondel, and Polanyi. It stresses that tradition embraces both content and process; that it is both conservative and innovative.

This persuasion lends Dulles's theology both firmness and flexibility. One turns to it confident of finding utmost fidelity to the Catholic substance joined to creativity in the employment of the Catholic imagination. To my mind the deepest reason for this is that, for Dulles, the ultimate anchor of tradition is the person of Jesus Christ himself, the living Lord of the Church. He affirms: "The true content of Christian tradition is nothing other than Christ, who is the same yesterday, today, and forever (Heb 13:8)."[3] To foster and sustain this encounter with Christ, ever ancient and ever new, is the whole purpose of the tradition. Beyond propositions and process, the person of Jesus Christ constitutes the very heart of Catholic tradition.

Another manifestation of Dulles's rigorous espousal of the Catholic "both/and" appears in the article "Institution and Charism in the Church" in his book *A Church to Believe In* (1982).[4] The article is vintage Dulles: a clear exposition, historically informed, respectful of colleagues, decisive in affirmation. One is not surprised to find the avowal:

> The Church, then, would not be truly Church without both the institutional features, whereby it manifests its own abiding essence, and the charismatic features, whereby God efficaciously transforms the interiority of concrete persons. The relation between institution and charism is a particular instance of the general relation between sacramental signs and the spiritual realities to which they point.[5]

One delights to follow his elaboration of the reciprocal relations of these two constitutive dimensions of the Church's life, which often live in creative tension with each other.

Noteworthy is the ample scope Dulles brings to the understanding of these two inseparable dimensions of the Church. He does not limit the "institutional" merely to Church office, however important that is. The institutional dimension of Church embraces its Scriptures, its sacraments, and its creeds. These all precede the believer, and he or she derives life from them.

But that life is always appropriated personally: for "grace was given to each of us according to the measure of Christ's gift" (Eph 4:7). The charismatic is not merely an attribute of the early Church, but perdures in the body of Christ. Moreover, it cannot be restricted to the extraordinary gifts of the Spirit. The forms it takes are as manifold as God's bounty. Dulles rises to almost homiletic fervor when he writes:

> Since charisms, in the widest sense, are simply concretizations of the life of grace, a Church without charisms could only be a Church without grace. Such a Church would be a false sign; it would betoken the presence of what is absent; it would be a pseudosacrament, and for this reason it would not be truly Church.[6]

Perhaps Dulles's best-known work in the theology of Church was *Models of the Church* (1974). I vividly recall the impact it had and the pedagogical and pastoral purposes it served. In the aftermath of the council it seemed to provide a theological way forward by indicating the plurality of possible approaches to the mystery of Church. At the same time it helpfully delineated the relative strengths and weaknesses of each model, and its need for completion by other perspectives. Moreover, in the face of increasing polarization among Catholics, both in religious communities and in parishes, it offered a way that differing visions might be brought into fruitful dialogue with one another.

However, I think it significant that he subsequently added to the original five another model, that of Church as "community of disciples." A sketch of this approach appeared in *A Church to Believe In*, under the title "Imaging the Church for the 1980s." There he lamented that "for some reason the Catholic Church seems unable to capitalize on the yearning for religious commitment and spiritual experience felt by so many of our contemporaries."[7] He goes further, even to suggest that Vatican II itself bore some of the blame for the postconciliar confusion and crisis. "The Council intensified the dissatisfaction or the Catholic intelligensia with the hierarchical ecclesiology that had been dominant since the Counter Reformation, but failed to propose an alternative image that proved truly viable."[8]

Without pretending that the community-of-disciples model represented a "supermodel" capable of synthesizing the legitimate theological perspectives of the others, I suggest that it offered a starting point that gave concreteness to the community that is Church, while also evoking the "cost of discipleship" (in Bonhoeffer's phrase), that may require of Christians a countercultural stance.

In addition, the community-of-disciples image served to call into question, in some measure, the ecclesial-fixation that was monopolizing and polarizing so much of Catholic discussion in the 1970s, by pointing to the one who alone was "the light of the nations," the Lord Jesus himself. In the more fully developed statement of the model that Dulles published in the expanded edition of *Models of the Church*, he wrote of the model: "It precludes the impression that ecclesial communion exists merely for the sake of mutual gratification and support. It calls attention to the ongoing relationship of the Church to Christ its Lord, who continues to direct it through his Spirit."[9]

READING THE SIGNS OF THE TIMES ANEW

One of the expressions of Vatican II that has passed into everyday currency is that of reading and interpreting "the signs of the times." It occurs in *Gaudium et Spes*, the "Pastoral Constitution on the Church in the Modern World." The council teaches:

> The Church has always had the duty of scrutinizing the signs of the times and of interpreting them in the light of the Gospel. Thus, in language intelligible to each generation, she can respond to the perennial questions which men ask about the present life and the life to come, and about the relationship of the one to the other. We must therefore recognize and understand the world in which we live, its expectations, its longings, and its often dramatic characteristics.[10]

Dulles has always echoed this call of Vatican II to read the signs of the times; indeed it is but the extension, to the Church as a whole, of the Ignatian urgency for discernment of spirits. However, it is self-evident (or at least ought to be) that not all "adaptations" are faithful to the gospel, which must ever be the measure. The subtitle of Dulles's book *The Resilient Church* is, as we have seen, "The Necessity and Limits of Adaptation."

After a prolonged period of stasis and uniformity, the council unloosed a theological whirlwind that threatened to sweep away not merely the dry wood but the very life-giving roots of the Tradition. Dulles does not defend the "excessive uniformity" that prevailed prior to the council.

But he deprecates what at times appears to be an almost anarchic plural-ism. In the introduction to his award-winning book *The Craft of Theology* (1992), he comes close to issuing a cri de coeur:

> The different theological schools have drifted so far apart that what seems false and dangerous to one school seems almost self-evident to another. Theologians lack a common language, common goals, and common norms. Civil argument has ceased to function, and in its absence opposing parties seek to discredit one another by impugning the motives or compe-tence of their adversaries.[11]

In effect, Dulles has scrutinized the theological and ecclesial signs of the times and found them tempestuous.

Rather than contenting himself with lament, Dulles charts, in *The Craft of Theology*, a constructive way forward—one that his McGinley Lectures of the next fifteen years since the publication of that book will illustrate in a dazzling range of topics. Indeed, two of the early lectures, in revised form, were incorporated into the book.[12] Far from sounding a retreat from the requirements of *aggiornamento*, he voices the conviction that "theology can never be static." He further explains:

> [Theology] must deal with new questions put to the Church by the course of events and by the circumstances of life in the world. Continual creativity is needed to implant the faith in new cultures and to keep the teaching of the Church abreast of the growth of secular knowledge. New questions demand new answers, but the answers of theology must always grow out of the Church's heritage of faith.[13]

As a help in furthering this program, Dulles devotes a pivotal chapter of *The Craft of Theology* to a fruitful dialogue with the distinguished Lu-theran theologian George Lindbeck. In his important book *The Nature of Doctrine*, Lindbeck identifies three styles of theology which he called "propositional-cognitive, experiential-expressive, and cultural-linguistic." To a great degree, the first two approximated, in Catholic theology, the approaches of neo-Scholaticism and modernism.[14]

Dulles agrees with Lindbeck concerning the shortcomings of these ap-proaches to the task of theology; and he espouses the third approach, which Lindbeck also favors. But, in a crucial change of terminology, Dul-les calls this third approach "ecclesial-transformative." Let me indicate what I take to be some of the salient features of his suggested approach.

First, in the face of a widespread exercise, in scholarly circles, of a "hermeneutics of suspicion" toward the Church and her Tradition, Dulles urges a "hermeneutics of trust," especially in the Church's constitutive symbols. Second, these symbols are not merely affect-laden. They bear significant cognitive content. However, this content cannot be exhausted by conceptual analysis or propositional statement. The symbols lead, in mystagogic fashion, to the depths of the community's lived encounter with its Lord, especially in its liturgical celebration. Third, the encounter, thus realized, effects a real transformation in the participants, a purification of the human spirit. Finally, all of this transpires, of course, within the Church, whose reality is not instrumental, but sacramental. As Dulles writes:

> As a great sacrament [the Church] extends in space and time the physical body of the Lord. It is not a mere pointer to the absent Christ, but the symbolic manifestation of the present Christ. The members of the Christ, insofar as they are remade in Christ's image by the power of the Holy Spirit, represent Christ to one another and to the world. He identifies himself with them. Especially is this true of the saints, those who allow themselves to be totally transformed in Christ. The Church, in its most basic reality, is a holy fellowship built up through the self-communication of the triune God.[15]

It is surely in keeping with his commitment to an ecclesial-transformative understanding of the theological task that Avery Dulles chose as the topic for his inaugural McGinley Lecture, in fall 1988, "University Theology as a Service to the Church." I would like to suggest further that Dulles's ecclesial-transformative theological program has a particular congruence with his Ignatian heritage.

THE IGNATIAN CHARISM IN THEOLOGY

Dulles entitled his spring 1997 McGinley Lecture "The Ignatian Tradition and Contemporary Theology." The lecture remains one of my personal favorites. In it he draws generously on the work of four prominent theologians to illustrate dimensions of the Ignatian vision. These four are Pierre Teilhard de Chardin, Karl Rahner, Henri de Lubac, and Hans Urs von Balthasar. I would add a fifth representative figure: Avery Dulles him-self. One may profitably read the present collected essays as so many soundings of the Ignatian charism brought to bear on crucial theological and societal issues of our day. Let me single out some features of the Ignatian charism that govern Dulles's writings.

The first I draw from his fall 2006 lecture, "The Ignatian Charism at the Dawn of the Twenty-First Century." There he identifies salient fea-tures of the distinctive Ignatian vision, the first of which he formulates thus: "Dedication to the glory of God, the 'ever greater God,' whom we can never praise and serve enough." The motto of the Society of Jesus, "for the greater glory of God," is here joined with the profound Ignatian sense of God's transcendence as the one who is "ever greater:" *Deus semper major.*

In this light, it comes as no surprise that Dulles was actively involved in the epoch-making and controversial "Appeal for Theological Affirma-tion," commonly known as "The Hartford Appeal" of 1975. The eighteen theologians who participated in its drafting and dissemination were pri-marily moved by their concern regarding the "loss of a sense of the tran-scendent," a loss that risks undermining the very mission of the Church.[16] It is in keeping with his commitment to the vision of Ignatius that Dulles places the ever greater God as the principle and foundation of his theolog-ical labors.

However, if this were the unique note, we would have a totally other God, awesome in majesty yet ever distant from human encounter. And so the Ignatian charism embraces, as every authentic Christian vision must, the drawing near of the Transcendent in the mystery of Incarnation. Ignatius insisted that the Society he founded be designated by the name *Jesus.* Thus the second feature that Dulles associates with the Ignatian charism in his fall 2006 lecture is "Personal love for Jesus Christ and a desire to be counted among his close companions." Toward the end, he remarks pointedly: "Above all, it needs to be mentioned that the Society of Jesus is primarily about a person: Jesus the Redeemer of the world. If the Society were to lose its special devotion to the Lord (which, I firmly trust, will never happen) it would indeed be obsolete. It would be like salt that had lost its savor."

Dulles clearly concurs with von Balthasar's view that Ignatius's *Spiri-tual Exercises* are "the great school of Christocentric contemplation, of attention to the pure and personal word contained in the gospel, of life-long commitment to the attempt at following." Since, in the Ignatian vision, spirituality and theology are inseparable, Christocentric contemplation and Christology complement and mutually nourish one another. Thus Dulles quotes von Balthasar again: "The *Spiritual Exercises* provide 'the charismatic kernel of a theology of revelation that could offer the unsurpassed answer to all the problems of our age that terrify Christians'" ("The Ignatian Tradition and Contemporary Theology").

It is well known that Vatican II did not produce a document exclusively devoted to Christology; and this fact may have led, in certain quarters, to a certain Christological reticence and even neglect in the years following the council. But Dulles, with his profound knowledge of the conciliar documents, sees clearly that they are permeated with Christological conviction and commitment. In his fall 2001 lecture, "Christ Among the Religions," he writes:

> Vatican II proclaimed a very high Christology. It taught that God had established Christ as the source of salvation for the whole world (*LG* 17) and that he is "the goal of human history, . . . the center of the human race, the joy of every human heart, and the answer to all its longings (*GS* 45).

And he continues:

> As a consequence of its high Christology, Vatican II took great care to insist on the unique mediatorship of Christ and to emphasize the abiding importance of missionary activity. Acknowledging Christ as the Redeemer of the world, the Council called on Christians to disseminate the gospel as broadly as possible.

If evangelization is the responsibility of all the baptized, it seems especially incumbent on the Society that bears the name of the Savior as its very own. Hence Dulles concludes his fall 2006 lecture by recalling Pope John Paul II's charge to the Jesuits to engage in "the new evangelization." After invoking the exemplary witness of St. Francis Xavier, Dulles affirms: "Evangelization is at the heart of all Jesuit apostolates in teaching, in research, in spirituality, and in the social apostolate." And he voices his own conviction: "The figure of Jesus Christ has not lost its attraction. Who should be better qualified to present that figure today than members of the Society that bears his name?"

The third and last characteristic of the Ignatian charism that I draw from these presentations is its ecclesial nature. I have already commented on Dulles as *vir ecclesiasticus*, on his scholarly and pastoral dedication to expounding a theology of Church in the light of Vatican II, on his espousal of the one Church as inseparably institutional and charismatic. I need now only underscore the Ignatian inspiration of this persuasion. Dulles quotes the *Spiritual Exercises*: "I must be convinced that in Christ our Lord, the bridegroom, and in His spouse the Church, only one Spirit holds sway, which governs and rules for the salvation of souls." Moreover, this commitment is not to some abstract idea or Platonic form, but it is rooted in the very concrete reality of the "the hierarchical and Roman Church, the true Spouse of Christ our Lord, our holy Mother."

Such conviction is not naïvely innocent, either for Ignatius or his spiritual son, Avery Dulles. True spiritual discernment discloses how the Church of saints and sinners stands ever in need of purification. But it is the recognition, with Vatican II, that "this Church, constituted and organized in the world as a society, subsists in the Catholic Church, which is governed by the successor of Peter and by the bishops in union with that successor, although many elements of sanctification and of truth can be found outside of her visible structure" (*LG* 8). Like so much in Vatican II and in the theology of Cardinal Dulles, the two affirmations present in that teaching of the council do not stand in contradiction but in creative union, indicating both the concrete embodiment and the breadth of the Church's catholicity. The affirmations, for the council and for Dulles as well, serve as spur to ecumenical exchange and commitment, since (as *Lumen Gentium* continues) "these elements, . . . as gifts belonging to the Church of Christ, possess an inner dynamism toward Catholic unity."

CONCLUSION

In his preface to this volume Cardinal Dulles speaks of his ever growing trust in the great Tradition of the Church. I have endeavored to suggest that his appropriation of that Tradition is marked by a distinctive Ignatian sensitivity to such foundational themes as the ever-greater Mystery of God, the Christocentric concentration of that Mystery, and its ongoing ecclesial discernment. Though Cardinal Dulles disclaims aiming at "originality" which he considers "a quality frequently overrated in theology" (why can I hear that wry chuckle?), the following essays are the splendidly crafted offerings of one who is, in every sense, an "original." They exemplify his trademark clarity and balance, his generous reading of the works of others, his forthright taking of a position of his own.

And they are frequently seasoned by the inimitable, often dry, Dulles wit. In closing, I cannot forbear calling attention to the quote from John Wycliffe that he cites in the very first paragraph of his inaugural McGinley Lecture, "University Theology as a Service to the Church." Wycliffe, with the one-sided zeal of the reformer, denounced universities as "products of vain heathenism," "as much good to the Church as the devil is!"

Dulles informs us that this proposition taken from Wycliffe's writings was condemned by the Council of Constance in 1415. We might add: happily so! Otherwise we might not have the pleasure of reading these lectures delivered at Fordham University, by the Laurence J. McGinley Professor of Religion and Society, Cardinal Avery Dulles of the Society of Jesus.

NOTES

Robert P. Imbelli, a priest of the Archdiocese of New York, is associate professor of theology at Boston College and a former director of its Institute of Religious Education and Pastoral Ministry. He is the author of many articles and the editor of *Handing on the Faith: the Church's Mission and Challenge.*

1. Avery Dulles, *The Resilient Church: The Necessity and Limits of Adaptation* (Garden City: Doubleday, 1977), 1.

2. Avery Dulles, *The Reshaping of Catholicism: Current Challenges in the Theology of Church* (San Francisco: Harper & Row, 1988), 77.

3. *Ibid.*, 89 and 90.

4. Avery Dulles, *A Church to Believe In: Discipleship and the Dynamics of Freedom* (New York: Crossroad, 1982).

5. *Ibid.*, 31.

6. *Ibid.*, 32.

7. *Ibid.*, 3.

8. *Ibid.*, 6.

9. Avery Dulles, *Models of the Church* (New York: Doubleday, 1987), 206.

10. "Pastoral Constitution on the Church in the Modern World; *Gaudium et Spes*" (Boston: Pauline Publications), 4.

11. Avery Dulles, *The Craft of Theology: From Symbol to System* (New York: Crossroad, 1992), viii.

12. *Ibid.*, 219 and 220, "Sources."

13. *Ibid.,* 10 and 11.
14. *Ibid.,* 17 and 18.
15. *Ibid.,* 35.
16. The Statement is printed as appendix 1 of Dulles, *The Resilient Church.* "The Critique of Modernity and the Hartford Appeal," chapter 4 of that book, is Dulles's commentary on the Statement.

PREFACE

U pon my retirement as a professor of theology at The Catholic University of America in 1988, Father Joseph A. O'Hare, S.J., President of Fordham University, invited me to be the first oc- cupant of the newly established Laurence J. McGinley Chair in Religion and Society at Fordham. He offered me a choice between accepting for two years or for one year, renewable. Being of a cautious mentality, I decided to accept only for one year, so as to see how things worked out before committing myself to a second. The mutual satisfaction was suffi- cient so that I was appointed for the following year and, as it happened, for many others, so that as a result I am still sitting on the McGinley Chair almost twenty years later. As part of my assignment I am required to deliver one public lecture each semester.

Both Father O'Hare and his successor, Father Joseph M. McShane, S.J., have been uncommonly supportive of the McGinley Lectures. They have almost always accommodated their schedule so as to introduce me. I should add that the former president of Fordham for whom the chair is named, Father Laurence J. McGinley, S.J., was present for the first few lectures, and gave the benediction at the beginning of the entire series.

The lectures do not have any set theme beyond being in the general area of Church and society. I simply dealt with issues that seemed to be of current interest and in need of theological clarification. The theme of the Church and politics was suggested by the presidential campaign of 1992; the lecture on human rights was presented to mark the fiftieth anni- versary of the Universal Declaration on Human Rights (1996). Many of the lectures deal with perennial topics keenly debated at the time: for instance, those on forgiveness, religious freedom, the death penalty, and evolution.

The majority of the lectures focus on ecclesial themes. The paper on John Henry Newman was composed for the centennial of that cardinal's death (1990). The publication of the *Catechism of the Catholic Church* in English translation occasioned the lecture for the fall of 1994. I spoke on the travails of dialogue to deal with certain questions regarding the "common-ground initiative" launched by Cardinal Bernardin and others in 1996. I lectured on justification to take part in the discussion of the Lutheran-Catholic Joint Declaration on that subject in 1999. The United States bishops' statement on lay ministries inspired my talk on that subject in 2006.

Many of the lectures pick up initiatives of the Holy See. I spoke on the "new evangelization" in 1991 to carry forward a favorite theme of John Paul II. The lecture on priesthood and gender was delivered shortly after the papal declaration on the ineligibility of women for the Catholic priesthood. I spoke on Mary in 1997 in view of the pope's proclamation of the Marian Year. The paper "Should the Church Repent?" (1998) was motivated by John Paul's many "apologies" (as they were called) for the sins of Catholics. My lecture on Christian philosophy (1999) was inspired by the recent encyclical on faith and reason. I spoke on the Eucharistic Church and the Real Presence during the Year of the Eucharist proclaimed by John Paul II for 2004–5. The lecture on Benedict XVI in 2005 was intended to introduce the newly elected pope.

Two of the lectures deal with more properly Jesuit concerns: those on Ignatian theology in the twentieth century (1997) and on the Jesuit charism for the twenty-first century (2006). These topics, celebrating different Jesuit anniversaries, were appropriate in my judgment because Fordham is New York's Jesuit university. In these two cases Presidents O'Hare and McShane respectively proposed the subjects to me.

Readers familiar with my work will be aware that I do not aim at originality, a quality frequently overrated in theology. Practiced without regard for continuity, originality creates confusion and doubt in the Church, rather than clarity and conviction. Tradition attunes us to the greatest religious thinkers of the past and, when creatively retrieved, serves to correct the biases of our own day. From my studies in history I have become convinced that the greatest danger for the Church and theology is to accommodate excessively to the spirit of the times. In my sixty-seven years as a Catholic I have had a constant and ever growing confidence in the great tradition of the Church. For this reason I seek to adhere to the consensus of the Fathers and Doctors of the Church. But, avoiding any unhealthy traditionalism, I try to make the adaptations necessary to render the wisdom of past ages applicable to the world in which we live. The tradition by its very nature stands open to homogeneous development, which must be distinguished from disruptive change or reversal. The spirit of the age is often contrary to the Holy Spirit. Following the Ignatian principle of "acting against" seductive temptations, I sometimes set myself in deliberate opposition the spirit of the times.

These lectures, of course, contain only a fraction of the articles I have written in the past twenty years, but they give a representative sample of my way of approaching current issues. I hope that they can provide helpful examples of the interaction between the Catholic tradition and the turbulent world of our day.

I was delighted when Father McShane told me that he was asking the Fordham University Press to publish a collection of all the McGinley lectures to date. As appears from the list of sources, almost all the lectures have been previously published in pamphlets or periodicals, but many of them are now difficult to find and acquire. In some cases editors have abridged the text or omitted the footnotes. While profiting from the opportunity to make some minor improvements, I have refrained from updating the lectures, since that would have involved substantial rewriting. This edition of the lectures may perhaps be considered definitive.

In preparing the current collection Robert Oppedisano, director of Fordham University Press, and Nicholas Frankovich, the managing editor, have been models of cooperation and efficiency. I am also deeply grateful for the assistance given by Dr. Anne-Marie Kirmse, O.P., Mrs. Maureen Noone, Michael M. Canaris, Katelyn Moore, Gregory McNamee, Nicholas Taylor, Timothy Clifford, and Thomas Lay. Special thanks are due to Father Richard J. Regan, S.J., for preparing the index.

December 3, 2007
Feast of St. Francis Xavier
Avery Cardinal Dulles, S.J.

ABBREVIATIONS

AA	*Apostolicam actuositatem.* Vatican II's Decree on the Apostolate of the Laity
AAS	*Acta Apostolicae Sedis.*
AG	*Ad gentes.* Vatican II's Decree on the Church's Missionary Activity
APD	*Aperite portas Redemptori.* Bull of Indiction of the Jubilee for the 1950th Anniversary of the Redemption, John Paul II.
AS	*Acta Synodalia Sacrosancti Concilii Oecumenici Vaticani II*
CA	*Centesimus annus.* Encyclical, John Paul II
CCC	*Catechism of the Catholic Church.*
CD	*Christus Dominus.* Vatican II's Decree on the Bishops' Pastoral Office in the Church
CELAM	Consejo Episcopal Latinoamericano
CL	*Christifideles laici.* Apostolic exhortation, John Paul II
CT	*Catechesi tradendae.* Apostolic exhortation, John Paul II
CTH	*Crossing the Threshold of Hope,* John Paul II
DH	*Dignitatis humanae.* Vatican II's Declaration on Religious Freedom
DS	Denzinger-Schönmetzer *Enchiridion Symbolorum*
DTC	*Dictionnaire de Théologie Catholique.*
D&V	*Dominum et vivificantem.* Encyclical, John Paul II
DV	*Dei Verbum.* Vatican II's Dogmatic Constitution on Divine Revelation
EA	*Ecclesia in Africa.* Apostolic exhortation, John Paul II
EB	*Enchiridion Biblicum.*
ECE	*Ex Corde Ecclesiae.* Apostolic constitution, John Paul II
EE	*Ecclesia de Eucharistia.* Encyclical, John Paul II
EN	*Evangelii nuntiandi.* Apostolic exhortation, Paul VI
EV	*Evangelium vitae.* Encyclical, John Paul II
EWTN	Eternal Word Television Network.

FC	*Familiaris consortio*. Apostolic exhortation, John Paul II
FR	*Fides et ratio*. Encyclical, John Paul II
GE	*Gravissimum Educationis*. Vatican II's Declaration on Christian Education
GS	*Gaudium et spes*. Vatican II's Pastoral Constitution on the Church in the Modern World
HV	*Humanae vitae*. Encyclical, Paul VI
ICEL	International Committee for English in the Liturgy.
LD	*Letters and Diaries*, John Henry Newman.
LE	*Laborem exercens*. Encyclical, John Paul II
LG	*Lumen gentium*. Vatican II's Dogmatic Constitution on the Church
MD	*Mulieris dignitatem*. Apostolic letter, John Paul II
MF	*Mysterium fidei*. Encyclical, Paul VI
NA	*Nostra aetate*. Vatican II's Declaration on the Relationship of the Church to Non-Christian Religions
NCCB	National Conference of Catholic Bishops.
NEP	Prefatory Note of Explanation to the third chapter of *Lumen Gentium*.
NMI	*Novo millennio ineunte*. Apostolic letter, John Paul II
OA	*Octogesima adveniens*. Apostolic letter, Paul VI
OL	*Orientale lumen*. Encyclical, John Paul II
ORE	*L'Osservatore Romano*, weekly English edition
PG	*Patrologiae Cursus completus, Series Graeca*.
PO	*Presbyterorum ordinis*. Vatican II's Decree on the Ministry and Life of Priests.
PP	*Populorum progressio*. Encyclical, Paul VI
PT	*Pacem in terris*. Encyclical, John XXIII
PTM	*Papal Teachings: Our Lady*. Benedictine Monks of Solesmes.
QP	*Quas primas*. Encyclical, Pius XI
RH	*Redemptor hominis*. Encyclical, John Paul II
RMat	*Redemptoris Mater*. Encyclical, John Paul II
RMis	*Redemptoris missio*. Encyclical, John Paul II
RP	*Reconciliatio et paenitentia*. Apostolic exhortation, John Paul II
RSV	*Revised Standard Version*.
SC	*Sacrosanctum concilium*. Vatican II's Constitution on the Liturgy

SD	*The Scripture Documents*. Edited by Dean Béchard.
Sp. Ex.	*Spiritual Exercises*. Saint Ignatius of Loyola.
SR	*Sources of Renewal*, John Paul II.
SRS	*Sollicitudo rei socialis*. Encyclical, John Paul II
TMA	*Tertio millennio adveniente*. Apostolic letter, John Paul II
UN	Address to the United Nations of October 5, 1995. John Paul II.
UNESCO	United Nations Educational, Scientific, and Cultural Organization.
UR	*Unitatis redintegratio*. Vatican II's Decree on Ecumenism
USCC	United States Catholic Conference.
UUS	*Ut unum sint*. Encyclical, John Paul II
VS	*Veritatis splendor*. Encyclical, John Paul II

CHURCH AND SOCIETY

1

University Theology as a Service to the Church

December 6–7, 1988

The title of this lecture could be an occasion for some surprise. University theology is not always considered a benefit to the Church. In the light of certain well-publicized cases of recent memory some might be inclined to repeat the proposition: "Universities, with their programs of study, their colleges, their degrees, and their professorships, are products of vain heathenism; they are as much good to the Church as the devil is."[1] This proposition, taken from the writings of John Wycliffe, was condemned by the Council of Constance in 1415. The condemnation, approved by Pope Martin V in 1418, may be taken as evidence, at least indirect, for the Church's appreciation of universities and their theological faculties.

DIFFERING STYLES OF THEOLOGY

The concept of university theology is necessarily somewhat vague. No sharp opposition can be drawn between theology done at the university and that done in other forums, but theology does tend to take on different hues depending on the environment in which it is practiced. Patristic theology, for instance, had a particularly pastoral character since it was closely linked with the preaching of the bishops to their flocks. In the early Middle Ages theology, chiefly practiced in monasteries, became more contemplative; it was closely bound up with the pursuit of holiness and with prayerful reading of sacred texts, both biblical and patristic. In the high Middle Ages the universities emerged as the chief centers of theological productivity. Theology became more academic and scientific. Then, in early modern times, when the universities became secularized and nationalized, theology moved by preference to the seminaries, and there it remained for the most part until about a generation ago. Seminary theology has usually been somewhat clerical and doctrinaire. Since the mid-1960s there has been a notable shift back to the university but in a situation quite unlike the Middle Ages. As yet few theologians have reflected seriously on what should be expected from university theology as a service to the Church in our day. The answer to this question will depend in part on how one appraises the changing character of the university itself.

Contribution of Medieval Universities

The golden age of university theology was no doubt the high Middle Ages.[2] The earliest medieval universities grew up spontaneously as expansions of preexisting schools and were subsequently recognized by papal or royal charters. Later medieval universities were founded directly by popes or, in some cases, by kings and emperors. The university faculties of theology, especially at Paris and Oxford, produced the greatest speculative theology of the age, and perhaps of any age. Bonaventure, Albert the Great, Thomas Aquinas, and Duns Scotus composed philosophically sophisticated articulations of Christian doctrine that still remain vital elements in the heritage of Catholicism. When new problems have arisen in later centuries, Catholics have found light and guidance in the work of the medieval masters.

It is not easy to summarize the manifold contributions of medieval universities to the life of the Church. Most obviously, they provided Europe with some learned clergy. Many of the popes, cardinals, and bishops were former students or even professors of theology or canon law. Viewed in historical perspective, the intellectual probings of the medieval Scholastics have given the Church of later ages an invaluable doctrinal resource. The theology of Thomas Aquinas guided the Council of Florence in its teaching on the Trinity and on the sacraments; it was used by the Council of Trent for its teaching on justification and the Eucharist, and again by Vatican Council I for its decrees on faith and reason and on papal primacy. Modern developments in Mariology, and notably the doctrine of the Immaculate Conception, gained impetus from the speculations of Duns Scotus at Oxford and Pierre d'Ailly at the University of Paris. The theology of grace and of salvation history, as developed by many modern authors, is indebted to Bonaventure.

The medieval universities, especially from the fourteenth century on, cooperated with popes and bishops in the formulation of doctrine and maintenance of orthodoxy. The university theologians were considered to have quasi-hierarchical status as members of what was called the *ordo doctorum*. The Decrees of the Council of Vienne (1311–12), by order of Pope Clement V, were not promulgated until they had been reviewed by the universities.[3] The university theologians attended councils such as those of Constance and Basel and were entitled to a deliberative vote within their "nation" or "deputation"—a right of some importance because the *doctores* frequently outnumbered the bishops themselves. At Paris in the fourteenth century, the theological faculty had an acknowledged privilege to pass judgment on its own members before any ecclesiastical authority could censure them for doctrinal deviations. When controversies arose, the theological faculties pronounced on questions of orthodoxy and heresy. Thus the University of Oxford condemned the eucharistic teaching of Wycliffe and the University of Prague censured certain errors of Jan Hus. The theological faculties of Cologne, Louvain, and Paris drew up lists of errors culled from Luther's writings, so that Rome had little more to do than to ratify what the universities had previously done.

In certain crises the university faculties of theology were of direct assistance in matters of church governance. Robert N. Swanson in his 1979 book *Universities, Academics, and the Great Schism* has shown in some detail how the eyes of Europe turned to the universities, especially Paris, to provide a remedy for the constitutional problem created by the rivalry of two, and eventually three, claimants to the see of Peter.[4]

THEOLOGY IN MODERN UNIVERSITIES

The contribution of the medieval universities was in some ways unique because of the dominance of the Catholic faith throughout Western Europe and because they antedated the rise of the modern national state.

Later the subjection of Oxford and Cambridge to the British crown, and that of Paris to the king and *Parlement*, severely damaged the value of the universities to the Catholic Church. But even after the Reformation and the rise of nationalism, Catholic universities continued to serve the cause of Catholic orthodoxy in regions known to us as Belgium, Spain, Portugal, Germany, Austria, and Italy. These universities, staffed principally by Dominicans, Jesuits, and Carmelites, produced updated syntheses of theology and philosophy, modeled on the great summas of the Middle Ages, and laid the groundwork for a vigorous proliferation of controversial literature, catechetical literature, and seminary handbooks. Besides responding to the new challenges of the Protestant Reformation, rationalism, and skepticism, the university theologians of the sixteenth and seventeenth centuries attempted to deal with social and moral problems arising from the modern nation-state and the colonial expansion. Spanish and Portuguese authors such as Francisco de Vitoria, Francisco Suárez, Juan de Lugo, and John of St. Thomas added luster to their age.

Crushed by the secular spirit of the Enlightenment and the oppressive tactics of absolutist monarchs, Catholic university theology suffered a severe decline in the eighteenth century, but it revived by the middle of the nineteenth. The Gregorian University, in close alliance with the papacy, promoted a new vintage of Scholasticism, which survived down to Vatican Council II. This theology, heavily apologetical in tone, became the basis of seminary textbooks and controversial literature throughout the Catholic world. The German universities developed several creative strains of theology. The professors of Tübingen and Munich entered into fruitful dialogue with German idealism and with German historical scholarship, thus paving the way for major developments in the twentieth century.

It seems fair to include under the caption of university theology the work of John Henry Newman, who developed the main principles of his thought during his years as a tutor at Oriel College, Oxford. Later Newman served briefly as the first rector of the Catholic University at Dublin and in that capacity published his eloquent and balanced proposals for the pursuit of theology in a Catholic university. In other works Newman drew richly from patristic sources and from the Anglican divines in order to respond to the challenges posed by agnosticism and secularity.

The mention of Newman's work at Oxford serves as a reminder that the Catholic Church, as well as other confessions and communions, owes a great debt to the university research not conducted under Catholic auspices. As I have already suggested, the philosophical, philological, and historical scholarship of German universities in the nineteenth century, especially at centers such as Göttingen and Berlin, was destined to have an enormous impact on all Christian theology. Biblical studies at Cambridge and patristic studies at Oxford were likewise of momentous import. The biblical and patristic *ressourcement* that took place in the Catholic Church between World War II and the Second Vatican Council relied heavily on the pioneering work of these non-Catholic scholars.

With a few notable exceptions, such as Tübingen and Rome, Catholic higher education in the nineteenth century was relatively weak. In many parts of Europe it labored under laws that discriminated against Catholicism or even against all religion in higher education. In laicist France, no Catholic university faculties survived, but some of the functions of university theology were performed by Catholic institutes of higher studies and by houses of formation in which religious orders educated their own members.

In the United States it became possible for Catholics to erect their own colleges and universities, but until after World War II these institutions were small and poorly endowed. Graduate programs in theology, where they existed at all, were designed for clergy and religious. In the late 1940s a women's college, St. Mary's in Indiana, opened a school of theology for sisters and laywomen. In the 1960s, doctoral programs in theology, offering civilly recognized degrees, came into existence at a number of Catholic universities, including Notre Dame (1961), Marquette (1963), Fordham (1967), and St. Louis (1969).[5] Catholic institutions also entered into joint theological programs such as the Graduate Theological Union at Berkeley, California. Today, therefore, there exist many doctoral programs in Catholic theology, some of them having a serious research component. A glance at the membership lists of theological associations, at publishers' catalogues, and at the tables of contents of learned journals strongly suggests that Catholic theological leadership has in recent years passed from the freestanding seminaries to the universities and graduate schools. A similar shift would seem to have taken place in many European countries. The Catholic university faculties of Germany, Belgium, and Holland have produced much of the most creative theology of the past few decades. The fact that a former university professor has been elected pope (John Paul II) may be of more than symbolic significance.

THE CONTRIBUTION OF UNIVERSITY THEOLOGY

In view of the contemporary preeminence of university theology, it becomes important to inquire what kind of benefits such theology can be expected to confer on the Church in our day. The question can be approached by considering the typical characteristics of university theology as contrasted with seminary theology. The two would appear to be mutually complementary. The seminary, generally speaking, is oriented toward the formation of future clergy. For this reason it puts the accent on teaching rather than on pure research. The seminary professor can normally assume that the students are already convinced believers and, in Catholic seminaries, accept the doctrines of the Church. Seminary theology is specifically aimed to equip the students for the tasks of the ordained priesthood—especially preaching, counseling, and the ministry of the sacraments. Seminaries generally operate in comparative isolation, feeling little need to expose their students to intellectual challenges coming from other disciplines. The intent is to transmit safe and established doctrine. Proof frequently takes the form of an appeal to authoritative texts—Scripture, councils, papal utterances.

University theology, by contrast, is oriented more heavily toward research. In order to make new advances it maintains, or should maintain, close contact with other disciplines, such as history, literary criticism, sociology, psychology, and philosophy. It makes use of reason not only deductively but also critically. It may address a widely diversified audience, including persons who are adherents of different religious traditions, or even of no particular religion. It concentrates on open and unsolved questions that cannot be settled by a simple appeal to authority. For all these reasons university theology can become the seedbed of new and exciting developments.

The reentry of Catholic theology into the universities is no doubt providential. Since the Council of Trent theology had become too far removed from the modern world with its ebullient secularity. Skillfully as the traditional Scholastic questions continued to be pursued, the vibrant movements of the day were not addressed with sympathy and understanding. The Church confronted the secular world too much as a judge, too little as a participant. The kind of careful attention that Thomas Aquinas gave to Aristotle, Maimonides, and Averroes was rarely given to modern thinkers such as Newton, Kant, Hegel, and Heisenberg, mentioned as adversaries but scarcely read in Catholic seminaries. The products of the seminary system, staffing the Roman congregations and other sensitive positions, maintained and defended the Catholic tradition but seemed ill at ease in the modern world. The new shift back to the university corresponds to the call of Vatican II for openness and dialogue. Reminding Catholic Christians of their involvement in the problems common to all humanity, the council strongly endorsed the teaching of theology in Catholic universities. It called for research in the sacred sciences so that the Church might make its presence felt in the enterprise of advancing higher culture and might form citizens capable of witnessing to their faith and shouldering social responsibilities in the world of our day.[6]

The revival of university theology cannot make its expected contribution unless lessons are drawn from the past. Precisely because it encourages independent thinking, such theology can easily be a source of error. Nearly all the major heresies since the twelfth century have been associated with university theology. One thinks in this connection of Wycliffe, Hus, and Luther, of Averroism, Conciliarism, Gallicanism, Jansenism, and various forms of rationalism.

Even when it escapes the trap of heresy, university theology exhibits certain weaknesses as compared with the typical seminary theology. It tends to become rather detached from the Church and from pastoral concerns. It easily adopts methods more appropriate to secular disciplines. It frequently becomes tinged with skepticism, positivism, historicism, relativism, and similar errors. Discouraged by the failure of the German universities to stand up against the Nazi ideology, Dietrich Bonhoeffer resigned from the University of Berlin in 1934 and in the following year founded a kind of religious community for seminarians and newly ordained ministers. In a letter to a friend he explained: "the whole ministerial education today belongs to the Church—monastic-like schools in which pure doctrine, the Sermon on the Mount, and the liturgy are taken seriously. In the university all three are not taken seriously, and it is impossible to do so under present circumstances."[7] Bonhoeffer, of course, was speaking of ministerial formation in state-controlled universities in Nazi Germany, but his words may be read as a warning to any university that undertakes to treat theology as an objective science independent of faith and ecclesiastical authority. If a faculty did not take the gospel, worship, and sound doctrine seriously, could it claim to be teaching theology at all?

A certain tension has always existed between the Church and scientific university theology, as may be seen from the struggles with the Averroists in the Middle Ages and with the Gallicans in early modern times. In a form that comes closer to home, the conflict broke out in Germany in the middle of the nineteenth century. In 1863 the Catholic historian Ignaz Döllinger presided over a Congress of Catholic scholars and intellectuals at Munich.[8] In his presidential address Döllinger questioned the adequacy of traditional Scholastic theology and called for greater attention to biblical criticism and scientific history. True theology, he insisted, must not panic when scholarly inquiry threatens to demolish what had previously been regarded as unassailable truth. The received opinions of Scholastic philosophy and theology, he maintained, should not be accorded the kind of authority that belongs to defined dogma alone.

Döllinger's address was widely interpreted as an effort to liberate Catholic scholars from the Scholastic heritage and to exempt Catholic universities from the vigilant supervision of Roman congregations. Pius IX felt it necessary to react to this challenge. In a letter to the archbishop of Munich (December 21, 1863), he warned that Catholic scholars cannot regard themselves as entitled to contest whatever falls short of defined dogma. They are bound to accept the ordinary teaching of the magisterium throughout the world as a matter of faith. In addition they must reverently submit to the doctrinal decisions of the Roman congregations and respect the authority of the Scholastic theologians of previous centuries.[9]

The clash between the Munich Congress and Pius IX in the mid-nineteenth century is instructive because the issues then were much the same as in several contemporary collisions between the ecclesiastical magisterium and university theologians. The situation in the United States today is further complicated by two themes that have greatly developed since the nineteenth century—academic freedom and religious pluralism.

ACADEMIC FREEDOM OF THEOLOGY

Vatican Council II asserted that the various branches of knowledge are to be pursued according to their own principles and methods, with appropriate freedom for scientific investigation.[10] The revised Code of Canon Law, following up on the council, recognizes that theologians must have freedom for competent research and for communicating their own ideas.[11]

These principles make it necessary to inquire what kind of academic freedom is suitable to Catholic theology. If academic freedom meant that theologians were entitled to teach as true whatever seemed to them to be suggested by purely rational methods of inquiry, without any deference to Scripture, tradition, or ecclesiastical authority,[12] theology would sacrifice its status as a reflection on the corporate faith of the Church and would cease to render the kind of service that the Church expects from it. Whatever may be the case with regard to other academic disciplines, theology requires a living relationship to a community of faith and to the official leadership of that community.

Since popes and bishops have an indispensable role in specifying the contents of Catholic faith, their authoritative proclamation has a positive and normative function for theology. Before such proclamation theologians may by their study prepare the way for the judgment of the Church.[13] After the ecclesiastical magisterium has spoken, theologians have the tasks of interpreting the statements and fitting them into the total self-understanding of the Church. They may continue to raise questions arising from their personal study and reflection and in this way prepare for further refinements of the official teaching. But theologians cannot simply disregard the teaching of the pastors. They cannot responsibly substitute their own opinions for the official teaching. Pope John Paul II, speaking at New Orleans on September 12, 1987, summed up the matter in these words: "The bishops of the Church, as *magistri et doctores fidei* (teachers and doctors of the faith), should not be seen as external agents but as participants in the life of the Catholic university in its privileged role as protagonist in the encounter between faith and science and between revealed truth and culture."[14] The university status of a theologian, therefore, must not be understood as placing that theologian outside or above the Church.[15]

John Henry Newman in his lectures on *The Idea of a University* suggested that the university is related to the Church somewhat as reason to faith and nature to grace.[16] Because there can be no real contradiction between faith and reason, true progress in the academic realm is never a threat to the Church. New developments in the secular sciences may seem to conflict with faith, but in the long run it will appear either that the developments were unsound, or that there is no real conflict, or that the conflict is not with faith itself.[17] But to find out which of these answers is correct may take time and discussion. The magisterium of the Church should not be pressed into deciding the issues before the debate has matured.

Theology as an academic discipline gathers evidence, sifts it, frames hypotheses, and tests them. Often enough the hypotheses prove faulty and must be amended. To succeed by its own methods theology must be given its due measure of freedom. It cannot serve unless it is free to make its own specific contribution (*Non ancilla nisi libera*). Scholars who are striving to grasp some new truth often fall into error in matters of detail. Such was the case, Newman concedes, with Malebranche, Cardinal Noris, Bossuet, and Muratori. Yet the service of these thinkers to religion, Newman holds, was too great for them to be molested on account of their occasional deviations.[18]

In many cases the progress of science and scholarship has required painful revisions in the understanding of the faith. This was true in early modern times, when the Dionysian corpus, the Donation of Constantine, and the Isidorian Decretals were exposed as unauthentic. Then came the major shifts in astronomy, geology, and archaeology, followed by biblical criticism, which radically changed the previous state of church teaching with regard to the dating and authorship of the biblical books. All these discoveries, heralded by progressive university theologians, were initially disturbing to churchmen. But in the long run they proved acceptable, even beneficial to the understanding of the faith. Faith is solidified when it is liberated from time-conditioned human opinions that have attached themselves to it in the course of history.

Only where theologians operate in dialogue with other academic disciplines can there be a vital and stimulating interchange between faith and reason. Theology can be invigorated and purified by interaction with the human and natural sciences. The scientific community can profit from the comprehensive vision of theology and from theology's integration of truth with values. In a recent letter to Rev. George Coyne, S.J., Pope John Paul II has illustrated this interaction with regard to anthropology, Christology, eschatology, and cosmology.[19] Without such an exchange, he suggests, theology can profess a pseudoscience or science can become a spurious theology.

While pleading for restraint and tolerance on the part of church authorities, Newman laid down four conditions for scientific investigation.[20] Adapting these conditions to the subject matter of theology, we may paraphrase Newman's principles approximately as follows: it must not collide with dogma; it must not issue pronouncements on religious matters in competition with the official magisterium of the Church; it must not indulge in brilliant paradoxes but rather propound serious views; and it must take care to avoid shocking the popular mind or unsettling the weak. If these four conditions had always been observed by university theologians, many bitter conflicts with ecclesiastical authority could have been avoided.

It is often imagined that the popes and bishops are forever trying to shackle university theologians in their scholarly pursuits. In point of fact the ecclesiastical authorities have often acted to restrain intolerant believers from recklessly accusing scholars of heresy. Increasingly this seems to be a problem today. Many non-theologians who want simple and secure answers to every conceivable question are urging church authorities to clamp down on the freedom of theologians to raise uncomfortable questions. Good communications between the ecclesiastical magisterium and university theology can be of great assistance in resisting the assaults of anti-intellectual bigots. At New Orleans in 1987, Pope John Paul II called attention to the close relationship that has always existed between faith and the love of learning. He then added: "Religious faith itself calls for intellectual inquiry; and the confidence that there can be no contradiction between faith and reason is a distinctive feature of the Catholic humanistic tradition as it has existed in the past and as it exists in our own day."[21] Applied to the question of academic freedom, the Holy Father's words may be taken as meaning that Catholic faith is a powerful safeguard of the just liberty of responsible scholarship.

IMPACT OF RELIGIOUS PLURALISM

In addition to the problems arising from conflicting views of academic freedom, university theology in the United States is troubled by questions arising from religious pluralism. I shall touch on the problem only briefly and with specific reference to the nature of theology. Occasionally it is said that the pluralistic character of the society in which we live makes it impossible for theology to be taught in a university.[22] By its very nature, we are told, a university must avoid taking a stand in the sphere of faith, which is viewed as purely a private matter. If anything is to be taught about religion, therefore, this must be a matter of objective scientific study, free of value judgments. Departments of theology should consequently be dismantled in favor of departments of "scientific" religious studies.

Because religious studies are not pursued in the light of faith and are not intended to contribute to the understanding of faith from within the believing community, the substitution of religious studies for theology on a large scale would notably impair the kind of service that the Church has traditionally received from university faculties. Without denying the legitimacy of religious studies, I would contend that theology still has a place on many campuses even in a pluralistic situation. Pluralism consists in the coexistence of several living faiths, no one of which can be well understood except from within its own framework. In a university that is Catholic by tradition and has a large proportion of Catholic students, courses should be offered in theology from a Catholic point of view. A Catholic university would fall short of its mission if it failed to present its students with the possibility of gaining a mature and sophisticated understanding of their faith, developed in proportion to the general state of their intellectual culture. Training in theology should make the students judicious and ecumenically sensitive. It should equip them with a free and honest commitment to values and beliefs tested by inquiry and reflection. Without exposure to university theology many students would never develop their faith with the help of rigorous intellectual discipline.

In a pluralistic situation, allowance must of course be made for faculty and students who do not profess the Catholic religion. Non-Catholics should presumably be offered options other than Catholic theology. Even in Catholic theology it would be inappropriate to demand a profession of faith from the student. Here again a certain difference appears between university theology and seminary instruction that is intended to qualify students for ordained ministry.

In these remarks I have in mind, first of all, private universities with a Catholic affiliation of some kind. Parenthetically, however, it may be noted that in many other religiously pluralistic countries, such as Germany, Holland, Australia, and Canada, there seems to be no difficulty about teaching Catholic and Protestant theology in publicly funded state universities.

In our own country the relationship of university theology faculties to the Church varies enormously from one institution to another.[23] Some universities have canonically established faculties that confer ecclesiastical degrees in courses of study approved by Roman congregations. Others confer civilly recognized degrees in Catholic theology. It is possible also to have joint theological programs with faculty members from a variety of religious traditions. There is nothing in the nature of theology that precludes any one of these arrangements. The choice is to be made on pragmatic grounds: which is the most feasible and best adapted to the needs of a given constituency?

The kind of service rendered to the Church varies according to the type of faculty and program. Ecclesiastical faculties, generally speaking, collaborate more directly with the Church's magisterium and enjoy a stronger ecclesiastical certification. But even a nonecclesiastical faculty that is free of juridical controls by church authorities will ordinarily strive to transmit the Catholic tradition in its purity.

REMAINING CHALLENGES

The Catholic universities in the United States have already performed a signal service in forming several generations of theologically literate graduates. The relatively high degree of theological education enjoyed by many Catholic lay persons in this country has greatly enhanced the vitality of American Catholicism. Large numbers of clergy and religious in this country have benefited likewise from university programs in theology.

Until recently the focus of Catholic university theological education in the United States has been more on instruction than on research. The professors of theology were in many cases priests handing on simplified versions of their seminary course. In the past generation this situation has been rapidly changing. We are beginning to get respected graduate departments of theology that can hold their own in comparison with the renowned faculties of Western Europe. It must, however, be confessed that the Catholic universities in this country have not as yet produced the kind of creative scholarship associated with Rome, Strasbourg, Louvain, Innsbruck, Fribourg, Nijmegen, Tübingen, Münster, and Munich. Time is needed to develop a theological tradition. Many of our universities are still hampered by the lack of adequate funding.

While taking some legitimate pride in the quality of their teaching and in the loyalty of their graduates, our American theological faculties are today challenged to make further advances. In living dialogue with contemporary culture and technology, university theology must bring the full resources of Catholic tradition to bear on major questions regarding belief and conduct raised by other disciplines. These answers, inevitably somewhat tentative and exploratory, must ultimately be tested by the faith of the whole Church and by its official leaders. But theology alonè has the responsibility to open up new lines of reflection and new styles of systematization. University theology, which has so ably served the Church in centuries past, is urgently needed in our day. It still has much to contribute to the renewal of Catholic intellectual life.

NOTES

1. Denzinger-Schömetzer, *Enchiridion Symbolorum*, 32nd ed., 1179.

2. For an informative survey see Jacques Verger, *Les Universités au moyen âge* (Vendôme: Presses Universitaires de France, 1973).

3. See Yves Congar, *Vraie et fausse réforme dans l'Eglise*, 2nd ed. (Paris: Cerf, 1968), 461.

4. Robert N. Swanson, *Universities, Academics, and the Great Schism* (Cambridge: Cambridge University Press, 1979).

5. For data concerning the erection of such programs see Claude Welch, *Graduate Education in Religion* (Missoula: University of Montana Press, 1971), 230–31.

6. Vatican Council II, Declaration on Christian Education, *Gravissimum educationis*, 10.

7. Quoted from Eberhard Bethge, "The Challenge of Dietrich Bonhoeffer's Life and Theology," *Chicago Theological Seminary Register* 51 (February 1961): 23.

8. Döllinger's address is reprinted in *Ignaz von Döllinger*, edited by Johann Finsterhölzl (Graz: Styria, 1969), 227–63. For an account in English see Wilfrid Ward, *The Life of John Henry Cardinal Newman* (London: Longmans, Green, 1912), 1:562–67, 641–42.

9. Pius IX, letter *Tuas libenter*, December 21, 1863, *ASS* 8 (1874–75), 438ff.; excerpts in Denzinger-Schönmetzer 2875–80.

10. Vatican II, *Gravissimum educationis*, 10.

11. Vatican II, *Lumen gentium*, 37; *Gaudium et spes*, 62; Code of Canon Law (1983), can. 218.

12. Sidney Hook defined academic freedom as "the freedom of professionally qualified persons to inquire, discover, publish and teach the truth as they see it in the field of their competence, without any control or authority except the control or authority of the rational methods by which truth is established. Insofar as it acknowledges intellectual discipline or restraint from a community, it is only from the community of qualified scholars which accepts the authority of rational inquiry" (*Heresy, Yes—Conspiracy, No* [New York: John Day, 1953], 154). Bishop Donald Wuerl in his "Academic Freedom and the University" (*Origins* 18 [September 8, 1988]: 208) characterizes this definition as typical of the current secular model. Richard P. McBrien in his "Academic Freedom and Catholic Universities" (*America* 159 [December

3, 1988]: 455) accuses Wuerl of giving a caricature. This difference of opinion indicates some lack of clarity in the current American concept of academic freedom.

13. Vatican II, *Dei Verbum*, 12.

14. John Paul II, "Catholic Higher Education," *Origins* 17 (October 1, 1987): 269.

15. Wuerl, "Academic Freedom," 210.

16. John Henry Newman, *The Idea of a University Defined and Illustrated* (Notre Dame, Ind.: University of Notre Dame Press, 1982), 345.

17. Ibid., 351.

18. Ibid., 360.

19. "A Dynamic Relationship of Theology and Science," *Origins* 18 (November 17, 1988): 375–78.

20. Newman, *The Idea of a University*, 354–56.

21. John Paul II, "Catholic Higher Education," 269.

22. Christopher Driver paraphrases the British professor of comparative religion Ninian Smart as "arguing in effect that in today's pluralistic society, the comparative approach was the only possible one for a university" (*The Exploding University* [London: Hodder and Stoughton, 1971], 181). Driver explains how Smart's proposals and arguments, based on his conception of the secular university, were accepted by the University of Lancaster in 1970.

23. See Ladislas Örsy, *The Church: Learning and Teaching* (Wilmington, Del.: Michael Glazier, 1987), chap. 4, "Teaching Authority, Catholic Universities, Academic Freedom," esp. 113–21.

2

Teaching Authority
in the Church

March 16, 1989

I n its full scope the problem of authority and freedom in the Church is much broader than what I propose to cover in this brief paper. Under the rubric of authority I shall limit myself to the teaching authority of those who hold pastoral office in the Church—the pope and the bishops in communion with him. Under freedom I shall consider the right of theologians to follow what they understand to be the requirements of their own discipline. I shall present a Catholic point of view, leaving it to my distinguished respondents to provide the ecumenical dimension.[1]

THE PROBLEM

The problem I am addressing is a lively one today. Theologians all over the world have developed a kind of class consciousness and show a new eagerness to protect their legitimate autonomy. Some resent what they regard as the authoritarianism of Rome and the bishops. As an example of this tendency one might cite the "Cologne Declaration," issued in January 1989 over the signatures of 163 German-speaking theologians.[2] This was in large measure a protest against the undue extension of hierarchical control over theology, especially on the part of the pope, and an assertion of the autonomy of theology and the rights of personal conscience in the Church. In our own country also, many statements have been issued, both by bishops and by theologians, describing the doctrinal responsibilities of these two classes of teacher.[3] Unless harmony of views is achieved on this important question, the Church will be weakened, as it already has been to some extent, by internal division and polarization.

Most parties to the discussion appeal to Vatican Council II. The council said little about the role of theologians but a great deal about the teaching office of the hierarchy. "The order of bishops," according to the Dogmatic Constitution on the Church, "is the successor of the college of the apostles in teaching authority and pastoral rule" (*LG* 22). Elsewhere in the Constitution on the Church it is asserted that the judgments of the pope and of individual bishops, even when not infallible, are to be accepted with religious submission of mind (*LG* 25). The living teaching office, said the Constitution on Divine Revelation, speaks with authority in the name of Jesus Christ (*DV* 10). The bishops, and they alone, establish the official doctrine of the Church, and as pastoral rulers they see to it that the faith is rightly taught in the churches under their care.

Even when all this is recognized, an important task still remains for theologians. The Church needs them because its members are human beings—that is to say, animals who ask questions. When something is proposed as a matter of Christian faith, reflective believers ask, quite legitimately: What exactly is the revealed datum? Where and how is it attested? How can things be as faith says they are? What logically follows from the truths of faith? People who try to answer these and similar questions in a methodical way are called theologians.

THE GROWING DISTINCTION

The functional distinction between the hierarchical magisterium and the theologians has been gradually clarified in the course of centuries. In the early Church most of the great theologians were bishops; for example, Irenaeus, Cyprian, Athanasius, the two Cyrils, Chrystostom, Basil, Gregory Nazianzen, Gregory of Nyssa, Hilary, Ambrose, Augustine, Leo, and Gregory the Great. They engaged in what we may call episcopal theology. Theologians who were not bishops, such as Justin, Clement of Alexandria, Origen, Tertullian, and Ephrem, wrote in a style not radically different from the bishops just mentioned.

In the Middle Ages the distinction of functions became clearer, especially as university theology came into its own. Only a few of the medieval theologians were bishops, and only a few of the bishops were theologians. The theologians of the time immersed themselves in highly technical questions about the processions in the blessed Trinity, the nature of the afterlife, the causality of the sacraments, and predestination. They debated such questions with the tools of Aristotelian logic and metaphysics. Thus theology became a well-defined enterprise, somewhat removed from preaching and pastoral instruction.

As theology took on its distinctive identity, the hierarchical magisterium underwent further development. It became less pastoral and more judicial. The popes and bishops in the Middle Ages were under great pressure to endorse the theological positions of one school and to condemn rival schools. Yielding somewhat to this pressure, the magisterium became embroiled in speculative questions of little concern to the average worshiper.

From the sixteenth century on, the magisterium has taken on a clearer functional identity. It has increasingly sought to stand above purely theological disputes, while keeping these disputes from becoming divisive. The Council of Trent was careful not to commit itself to any of the reigning theological systems, whether Thomist, Scotist, or Augustinian, but to pronounce only on matters of Catholic faith. In the following century, when the theological schools gave different interpretations to Trent's teaching on grace, the Roman magisterium declared that each should be free to hold its own theoretical positions provided that it did not accuse the other schools of heresy.[4] The magisterium did not abandon its judicial role, but it sometimes chose to exercise that role in a permissive rather than a restrictive way. While upholding the doctrinal tradition, the magisterium also protected the freedom of theologians to speculate within the limits of that tradition.

CONTEMPORARY MEANING OF *MAGISTERIUM*

In the nineteenth century the term *"magisterium"* took on a more precise meaning than before. Whereas previously it had meant simply the office or function of teaching (and thus applied as much to theology professors as to bishops), the term—often spelled with a capital *M* and accompanied, in English, by the definite article—now came to mean the *public* teaching authority of the Church. Magisterium became a collective noun meaning the class of people who are institutionally empowered to put the Church as such on record as standing for this or that position. The theologians, by contrast, came to be regarded as private persons in the Church. Unlike popes and bishops, they could not speak for the Church as an institution, nor could they oblige anyone to accept their views. As a result of this clarification, the term "magisterium" came to be used almost exclusively for the hierarchical authorities. It is rarely used in our day to designate the teaching function of theologians.

In the late nineteenth and early twentieth centuries a further clarification of the terminology occurred. Until that time the teaching power of the hierarchy was not clearly distinguished from its power of jurisdiction or government. Thanks to the labors of theologians such as Yves Congar, that distinction has been clarified and has been canonized, so to speak, in the documents of Vatican II. Even when the teachers are the same persons as the rulers, the magisterial role is different from the power to govern. To teach is not simply to command or to forbid a course of action. Teaching is addressed to the intellect and calls for internal assent. Commands are addressed to the will and call for external obedience.

This clarification has had some practical effects. The popes and bishops no longer confine themselves, as they generally did in the Middle Ages, to judging between opposed theological schools. They are increasingly disposed to originate or develop doctrine in their own name, especially doctrine that is closely connected with the pastoral government of the community. This kind of teaching is illustrated by Vatican Council II and by the encyclicals of recent popes. The very abundance of magisterial teaching can today be seen as posing a problem. How much of it calls for the assent of the faithful?

SOME COMMON OBJECTIONS

Some might question whether there is any need for a continuing magisterium. After all, the revelation by which Christians live was completed long ago, and it has, in substance, been committed to writing in the canonical Scriptures. Scripture alone, however, has not proved to be a sufficient rule of faith. From the early centuries it has been supplemented by creeds and doctrinal declarations. Popes and councils were called on to decide doctrinal questions that arose as the faith became rooted in

Hellenistic soil and interacted with the culture and philosophy of the ancient world. For the same reason, a living magisterium continues to be needed in every century. The message of Christ must be proclaimed in new situations. The ecclesiastical leadership must decide whether new hypotheses and formulations are acceptable in the light of Christian faith. On occasion the Holy Spirit may enable popes and councils to speak with full assurance in the name of Christ and to settle some grave question definitively.

The objection can be made that it is the theologians' role to study current questions and that the magisterium, if it speaks at all, must follow the guidance of theologians. The historic experience of the Church, in my estimation, shows that theologians are often unable to resolve their own differences, still less to establish doctrine for the Church. They are, by training and temperament, suited to gather data, to ask questions, and to speculate, rather than to make doctrinal decisions for the Church. Some theologians regard doctrinal decisions as an unwelcome intrusion on their own freedom of inquiry. As scholars, theologians dwell in a somewhat rarified atmosphere, remote from the world of the ordinary believer. For all these reasons, the Church needs a living voice other than those of the theologians to preserve continuity with the apostolic faith and to maintain communion throughout the Church. We may be grateful, then, that Christ has equipped the Church with a living body of pastoral teachers, competent to decide what is to be preached and to set the limits of theological debate.

For fruitful relationships between themselves and theologians, it is desirable for popes and bishops to be theologically educated. According to the present Code of Canon Law (can. 378), every bishop ought to have a licentiate or doctorate in biblical studies, theology, or canon law, or at least be truly skilled in these disciplines. But the same canon requires that bishops be outstanding in strength of faith, moral probity, piety, zeal for souls, wisdom, prudence, and other human virtues and gifts needed for their office. Professional theologians do not necessarily make the best bishops. If they are raised to the episcopal office, they must learn to separate their theological positions, which are personal and private, from the doctrine of the Church, which it is their responsibility to promote. For good reasons, therefore, the Church generally selects its bishops from priests experienced in preaching, counseling, and active ministry who have, in addition, shown a capacity to delegate and to govern.

In their magisterial role, residential bishops have a primary responsibility to judge what should be preached and taught in their particular church at a particular time.[5] Even popes and councils, speaking to the universal Church, do not escape the conditions of their own age and culture. The bulk of official teaching is correlated with particular historical contingencies, but is not for that reason less authoritative. The magisterium has a pastoral mandate to direct the Church's response to new challenges and opportunities.

MUTUAL ASSISTANCE

Although the functions of the magisterium and of the theologians are distinct, each group requires and profits from the work of the other. The theologians depend on the magisterium because the creeds and dogmas of the Church are constitutive for their own enterprise. Theology is a reflection on the faith of the Church as set forth in the canonical Scriptures and in the official statements of the Church's belief. If the magisterium were not trustworthy, the foundations of theology, including even the canon of Scripture, would crumble. The more abundantly theology draws on the teaching of the magisterium, the richer, generally speaking, will it be. To ignore or dismiss magisterial teaching is to neglect resources that are at hand. It is possible, of course, to disagree with the magisterium on some point or other or to wish to nuance its declarations, but the first instinct of the theologian should be to accept and build on what is officially taught in the Church. It is a great benefit for theology to have a magisterium that is committed and qualified to safeguard the apostolic faith.

Just as theology depends on magisterial teaching for its data and security, so conversely the hierarchical magisterium depends on theology. Pope Paul VI acknowledged this in an address of 1966:

Without the help of theology, the magisterium could indeed safeguard and teach the faith, but it would experience great difficulty in acquiring that profound and full measure of knowledge which it needs to perform its task thoroughly, for it considers itself to be endowed not with the charism of revelation or inspiration, but only with that of the assistance of the Holy Spirit. . . .

> Deprived of the labor of theology, the magisterium would lack the tools it needs to weld the Christian community into a unified concert of thought and action, as it must do for the Church to be a community which lives and thinks according to the precepts and norms of Christ.[6]

By their preliminary research theologians help to mature the judgment of the Church. When such judgments are made and promulgated, theologians are often the drafters. They provide the exact technical language and make sure that what is said takes into account the latest findings of sound scholarship. Vatican Council II has provided within recent memory a splendid example of fruitful collaboration between bishops and theologians.

The services of theology to the magisterium are manifold. Most of them are positive, for, as just stated, theology prepares the way for the magisterium to speak, and after it has spoken, theology explains and, as necessary, defends what has been taught. To perform these various services, theologians must have the freedom to follow the principles of their own special discipline.

LEGITIMATE CRITICISM

The service of theology to the magisterium can, on occasion, involve criticism. Scholarly investigation may indicate that some reformable teaching of the Church needs to be modified or that the concepts that have been used for the communication of the faith are unsatisfactory in terms of contemporary science or knowledge. If so, theologians have the right and even the duty to make their views known.

In the past century or so we have seen many examples of theological criticism, some justified and some unjustified. At times the criticism has been bitter and intemperate and has produced alienation in the Church. An example might be the work of certain Modernists such as Loisy, Tyrrell, and Buonaiuti at the beginning of the present century. On the other hand, other thinkers of the same period, such as von Hügel and Blondel, very close to the Modernist movement, exerted a strong positive influence on the official teaching through their intellectual probing.

More recently, in the pontificate of Pius XII (1939–58), several of the most eminent Catholic theologians, such as Henri de Lubac, Yves Congar, John Courtney Murray, and Karl Rahner, cautiously advocated doctrinal positions that were, for a time, resisted by the magisterium. They made their proposals without rancor and, when rebuffed, submitted without complaint. After they had proved their loyalty and obedience, they were rehabilitated and invited to take part in Vatican Council II, where they made immense contributions to the official teaching of the Church. In view of cases such as these, it is difficult to deny that critical questioning of current magisterial teaching may sometimes be legitimate.

Just as the theologian may sometimes be entitled to raise questions and present doubts about current official teaching, so the magisterium has the right to keep dissent from impairing the unity of the Church and integrity of the faith. The hierarchy has an inalienable responsibility to see to it that the Christian faith is transmitted without diminution or distortion. It therefore has a right of supervision over theology, insofar as theologians engage in teaching Christian doctrine. This right of supervision is exercised in a variety of ways. The bishops can insist on prior censorship of books on certain sensitive subjects, such as catechisms, liturgical texts, and manuals of doctrine. The bishops can require, and on occasion refuse, ecclesiastical permission to publish books and articles (*imprimatur*). The hierarchical authorities can control the appointment of seminary professors and members of ecclesiastical faculties who teach with a canonical license (*missio canonica*). They can issue warnings against books that misrepresent or attack Catholic doctrine. Controls such as these are considered necessary to prevent the true teaching of the Church from being obscured and to protect the faithful from being confused about whether certain teachings are in force. Some restriction on the freedom of theologians may thus be necessary to enable the magisterium to be free in the performance of its task and to give the faithful freedom in their access to the approved doctrine of the Church. These restrictions, when prudently exercised, are a positive benefit to sound theology.

The question of academic freedom is far too complex to be treated within the framework of the present paper. In any such discussion it would have to be made clear that the rights and powers of the hierarchy differ greatly according to the nature and canonical status of the university or faculty. The Vatican has a measure of direct control over ecclesiastical schools that grant degrees in the name of the Church. For the magisterium to intervene in the operation of nonecclesiastical faculties that grant only civil degrees, provision must be made in the statutes of the university, which must be drawn up with a view to the laws and customs of the place. Even when they have no power to control the institution, ecclesiastical authorities may be able to give orders that are binding on the conscience of the individual professor, but the efficacy of any such command would depend on its conscientious acceptance by the professor in question. Canon 812, which requires certain professors to have a mandate to teach (*mandatum*), binds the professor, not the institution in which he teaches.

Recommendations for Each Group

Theologians and hierarchical leaders alike have a responsibility to avoid destructive collisions between them. The theologian should normally trust and support the magisterium and dissent only rarely and reluctantly, for reasons that are truly serious. Dissent, if it arises, should always be modest and restrained. Dissent that is arrogant, strident, and bitter can have no right of existence in the Church. Those who dissent must be careful to explain that they are proposing only their personal views, not the doctrine of the Church. They must refrain from bringing pressure on the magisterium by recourse to the popular media of communication.

The magisterium, for its part, can take certain steps to minimize dissent and conflict about doctrine. The recommendations I shall make are, in fact, commonly followed.

In the first place, the hierarchical teachers can use their influence to moderate the charges and countercharges exchanged among adherents of different theological tendencies. The magisterium should discountenance reckless and unsubstantiated accusations of heresy.

Second, the magisterium can avoid issuing too many statements, especially statements that appear to carry with them an obligation to assent. In doctrinal matters, as in legislation, freedom should be extended as far as possible and restricted only to the degree necessary.

Third, before issuing any binding statement of doctrine, the magisterium would do well to consult widely with theologians of different schools. The sense of the faithful should likewise be ascertained, with care to discriminate between an authentic sense of the faith and mere opinions that happen to exist among church members.

Fourth, the hierarchy, before it speaks, should anticipate objections and seek to obviate them. The faithful should not be caught by surprise, and convincing answers should be given to honest difficulties.

Fifth, the magisterium should take care to be sensitive to the variety of cultures in the world. Often the rejection of doctrinal statements is occasioned not so much by their substantive content as by the thought forms and rhetoric. Advance consultation with episcopal conferences can be, and has often proved to be, of great assistance to the Roman magisterium.

THE NEED FOR CLEAR TEACHING

In the final analysis, popes and bishops cannot be infinitely permissive. They have the painful duty of setting limits to what may be held and professed in the Church. There is no guarantee that the true doctrine will always be pleasing to the majority. Jesus uttered hard sayings, with full awareness that in so doing he was alienating some of his own followers. Peter spoke for the believing minority when he exclaimed: "Lord, to whom shall we go? You have the words of eternal life" (Jn 6:68).

Christianity, and perhaps especially Catholic Christianity, requires an element of trust in those who are commissioned to teach officially in the name of Christ. Theologians, like other members of the Church, have no right to demand that the magisterium always follow their own opinions. In fidelity to Christ and the gospel the magisterium may be obliged to utter hard sayings of its own.

Under such circumstances it is easy to protest that the hierarchy is being autocratic. The dissenting theologian will be acclaimed in some quarters as the champion of freedom, the model of courage and independence. But this reaction only raises more acutely the questions: What is true freedom? What are the proofs of courage and independence? When the current of public opinion is flowing against the official teaching, its acceptance, I suggest, may require a greater exercise of freedom and courage than would contestation.[7]

The abuse of authority is a real danger in the Church as in any other society. In our day, however, it is not the greatest danger. Christianity is threatened by the demonic power of a public opinion that refuses to submit to the discipline of faith. The tide of public opinion pounds incessantly against the rock of faith on which the Church is built. If the Church allowed herself to be carried away, or even materially weakened, by this demonic force, the prospects of Christian faith in the modern world would be less favorable than they are. The hierarchical magisterium, generally speaking, has been more effective than the theological community in safeguarding the purity of the faith against the trends and fashions of the day.

Notes

1. This lecture was delivered at an ecumenical symposium at which the respondents were Bishop William H. Lazareth of the Evangelical Lutheran Church in America and Father John Meyendorff of the Orthodox Church in America.

2. "The Cologne Declaration," *Origins* 18 (March 2, 1989): 633–34.

3. "Doctrinal Responsibilities: Approaches to Promoting Cooperation and Resolving Misunderstandings," *Origins* 19 (June 29, 1989): 97–110.

4. Paul V, "Formula pro finiendis disputationibus. . . ," Denzinger-Schönmetzer, *Enchiridion Symbolorum* (32nd ed.), 1997.

5. See the statement of the National Conference of Catholic Bishops, "The Teaching Responsibility of the Diocesan Bishop: A Pastoral Reflection," *Origins* (January 2, 1992): 473–92.

6. Paul VI, Address to International Congress on the Theology of Vatican II, *AAS* 58 [1966]: 892–93; English translation in *The Pope Speaks* 11 (1966): 352.

7. A wise philosopher of science has observed: "Admittedly, submission to authority is in general less deliberately assertive than is an act of dissent. But not always. St. Augustine's struggle for belief in revelation was much more dynamic and original than is the rejection of religion by a religiously brought up young man today." (Michael Polanyi, *Personal Knowledge* [New York: Harper Torchbooks, 1964), 209.

3

Catholicism and American Culture

The Uneasy Dialogue

December 5–6, 1989

After several centuries of increasing centralization, Vatican Council II set the Catholic Church on a course of inner diversification. It depicted Catholicism in terms that were pluralistic rather than monolithic, multiform rather than uniform.[1] The Church of Christ, said the council, should be incarnate in many cultures, all of which were in a position to enrich one another and to bring the wealth of the nations to the feet of Christ the King.[2]

THE ENCOUNTER BETWEEN FAITH AND CULTURE

In the decade after Vatican II inculturation became a buzzword.[3] Although popes have used the word only with caution, they have said on journeys to Asia and Africa that the Catholic Church in those continents ought not to be a slavish copy of the European Church. As a consequence American Catholics began to conclude that Catholicism in this country should develop its own distinctive traits. In the past it had been a mosaic of importations from various "Old World" nations—Ireland, Germany, France, Poland, Italy, and others. Even if the efforts of Isaac Hecker and Archbishop John Ireland to Americanize the Church in the nineteenth century proved abortive, perhaps the time had now come for a new and

---

27

more sober effort. Would not such Americanization, far from undermining authentic Catholicism, serve to solidify and strengthen it? This question is being asked in many places at the present time.

The importance of an encounter between faith and culture has been a major theme of the present pontificate.[4] The meeting between the U.S. archbishops, the pope, and the heads of Roman congregations in March 1989 took as its theme "Evangelization in the Context of the Culture and Society of the United States."[5] Thus the topic of this lecture is one that the Holy See places very high on its agenda. It is also a subject that should concern Fordham, for every Catholic university, according to no less an authority than John Paul II,[6] is a place of encounter between faith and culture. As occupant of the Laurence J. McGinley Chair of Religion and Society, I feel a particular responsibility to address this question.

AMERICAN CULTURE

Our analysis must begin with a brief discussion of the nature of the American culture into which the Catholic faith might be inserted.[7] This country is extremely diverse. Catholics in the United States come not only from the various Western European countries already named, but some are American Indians, some are African Americans, some are Vietnamese or Filipinos, and very many are Spanish-speaking people from the Caribbean or Latin America. Thus we cannot easily find a common denominator.

Even the white, Anglo-Saxon, Protestant (WASP) culture that has played a preponderant part in shaping the habits of the nation is not all of a piece. It has gone through a number of major shifts in the centuries since the first settlers came to New England and Virginia. Four major stages may here be pointed out:

1. The Puritanism of Congregationalist New England, which underlies much of our history, was anything but liberal. The Pilgrims looked upon the New World as a promised land where the covenant people could build the City of God. The culture of seventeenth-century Massachusetts involved a rigorous code of belief and morality founded on the Bible as read in the Calvinist tradition. The Church dominated civil society in Boston as firmly as it had done in Calvin's Geneva.

2. This Calvinist heritage has been, for the most part, cast off. And yet it remains a living memory. It fueled many nineteenth-century exhortations about the "manifest destiny" of the United States, and it continues to reappear in Thanksgiving Day proclamations, in campaign oratory, and in anniversary celebrations of the Declaration of Independence or the Constitution. Because of this vibrant tradition it is still possible to speak of the United States, with Chesterton, as "a nation with the soul of a Church."[8]

3. By the time that the United States received its foundational documents (the Declaration of Independence, the Constitution, and the Bill of Rights), the Enlightenment was in full swing. The common faith of the founding fathers was no longer that of the Pilgrims but that of Christians profoundly influenced by the deistic religion of "nature and of nature's God." The religion of reason was, however, understood with clearly Christian overtones, as can be seen from the Declaration of Independence. There and in other documents God was depicted as creator and ruler of all. Human beings were considered to be endowed by their creator with natural rights that demanded universal respect. Among these rights was listed the free exercise of religion, which in turn required that that no one church be established as the religion of the State. The law favored certain generically Christian institutions, such as monogamous, indissoluble marriage. Commitment to these traditional religious and moral values gave a transcendent basis to the claim that the country should be free and independent. The influence of John Locke on the founding fathers disposed the nation for a major incursion of individualistic utilitarian philosophy in the nineteenth century. The common good was reconceived as the net result of a balancing of contrary interests. The pursuit of private gain by individuals and groups was seen as contributing, in the long run, to the prosperity of all. The Puritan moralism of the seventeenth century, and the cult of civic virtue in the eighteenth century, now yielded to a system in which material wealth became the dominant value. The role of the government was seen as that of an arbiter, laying down the conditions under which competition could be fairly conducted. At its worst, this new mentality spawned a kind of social Darwinism. The great capitalists amassed fortunes for themselves but, having done so, they were driven by their residual Puritan conscience to a pursuit of philanthropy, no less ardent than their previous self-enrichment.[9]

4. In the twentieth century still another major shift has occurred. A new mass culture, largely determined by technological advances, superimposed itself on the three layers already examined. The dominant trait of contemporary culture is well described by the term "consumerism." Each individual is seen primarily as a consumer, and heavy consumption is viewed as the key to social well-being. Wealth becomes a function of sales, which are increased to the extent that people can be induced to buy new goods. To provide such inducement, business sponsors a gigantic advertising industry, which in turn supports and dominates journalism and mass communications. Advertising is funneled into programs that have the widest popular appeal. Nearly everything, from sports to education and religion, succeeds to the extent that it can arouse interest and provide entertainment. The desire for pleasure, comfort, humor, and excitement continually intensifies. The traditional work ethic becomes tributary to, and is to some extent undermined by, the quest for affluence and sensory gratification. While the entertainment industries and business grow ever more fiercely competitive, alcoholism, drug abuse, and obsessive sex proliferate in large sectors of the consumerist society.

This fourth layer of culture has not totally displaced the previous three, but it threatens to modify them profoundly. The culture that the Church faces today cannot be understood as that of the previous three centuries, though some elements of the earlier American heritage still survive.

FOUR STRATEGIES FOR ENCOUNTER

In the Catholic literature on American culture published in the past twenty years or so, it is possible to detect four major strategies. For short they may be called traditionalism, neoconservatism, liberalism, and prophetic radicalism.[10]

1. Traditionalism is the posture of those Catholics who are highly critical of what they find in the dominant American culture and who wish to restore the more centralized and authoritarian Catholicism of the years before World War II. James F. Hitchcock[11] and Ralph Martin[12] are representative of this tendency at its best. Confusion in the Church, they lament, has resulted from attempts to make peace with contemporary culture. America today, in their judgment, is less hospitable to Catholic values than in the recent past, when John Courtney Murray wrote about

the American proposition. Today it is necessary to be more divisive and to make the Church a "sign of contradiction." True to its vocation to judge the culture of the day, the Church must run the risk of being considered a ghetto. Within their own families, parishes, and communities of prayer, Catholics must pass on their religion by providing an experience of living faith. Liturgy must be celebrated with dignity and convey "the beauty of holiness." The young should be familiarized with the Latin Mass and with time-honored devotions. Doctrine must be clearly taught, with authority and not simply as a matter of opinion. Moral norms, especially in the area of sexuality, must be strictly maintained. Ecumenical contacts should be sought especially with conservative Evangelicals, with a view to reinvigorating Christian influence on American culture.

In contrast to the moderate traditionalism just described, certain more extreme traditionalists such as Archbishop Marcel Lefebvre dismiss Vatican Council II as a capitulation to the ideals of the French Revolution. These traditionalists repudiate all forms of ecumenism and interreligious cooperation. Some American disciples of Archbishop Lefebvre have followed him into schism.

In either of these forms Catholic traditionalism is self-consciously countercultural. It seeks to maintain a Christian and Catholic culture alongside of a secular culture that it deplores.

2. The neoconservative strategy rejects as unrealistic the restorationism of the paleoconservatives. Thinkers such as George Weigel,[13] Archbishop J. Francis Stafford,[14] and to some degree Michael Novak[15] belong to this category. They exalt the powers of natural reason and the value of civility in argument. They espouse an optimistic, world-affirming humanism. While recognizing that the Church's first task is to proclaim and embody the gospel, these authors focus their attention especially on the second task, the renewal of American democracy. The culture-forming task facing the Church today, they assert, is that of "constructing a religiously informed public philosophy for the American experiment in ordered liberty."[16]

The American experiment, according to these writers, has its roots in the Catholic natural-law tradition. Several presidents of the United States, as John Courtney Murray pointed out, officially proclaimed God's sovereignty over the nation and urged the nation to make a public acknowledgement of its dependence on God.[17] Human rights are inalienable because they have their source in God's eternal law. For democracy to succeed, human passions must be guided by moral values. Rights cannot be safeguarded without public virtue and care for the common good.

The neoconservatives are confident that the Catholic Church, with its liturgical, personalist, and communal heritage, and with its long tradition of moral reflection on the proper ordering of human society, has unique resources for the renewal of the American experiment. By using these resources courageously, this policy hopes to bring about what the Lutheran (subsequently Catholic) theologian Richard John Neuhaus, in his 1987 book, hailed as the "Catholic moment."

The American experience, in the neoconservative view, is harmonious with some current trends in the universal Church. John Paul II has accepted the human rights tradition and has praised the American experiment of freedom. The Congregation for the Doctrine of the Faith, in its 1986 Instruction on Christian Freedom and Liberation, calls for political freedom, human rights, pluralism in institutions, private initiative, and the separation of governmental powers. Thus there seems to be some convergence between the present Roman agenda and authentic Americanism. Neoconservatives express optimism that the system of democratic capitalism is beginning to enrich official Catholic teaching on political economy.

3. The third option, Catholic liberalism, can be verified in the work of many leading scholars, such as Richard P. McBrien, Charles E. Curran, Daniel Maguire, and Jay Dolan. The Detroit Call to Action conference sponsored by the American bishops in 1976 was a triumph for liberal Catholicism.[18] Not satisfied to concentrate on what the Catholic tradition can contribute to the American experiment, Catholic liberals are primarily intent on showing how Americanism can help to modernize the Church. They propose to reform Catholicism along the lines of participatory democracy.

Dennis P. McCann provides a showcase exhibit of the liberal Catholic position. In his book *New Experiment in Democracy*,[19] he overtly aligns himself with the optimism of Archbishop Ireland. Americanism, he holds, was not a phantom heresy but a reality against which Leo XIII delivered a preemptive strike. Yet the strike was not fatal, because Americanism can never be extirpated from the soul of the nation. "What they condemned in Rome as the Americanist heresy is the key to our historic development within the family of Christian churches" (6). Vatican II, while it promoted religious liberty against state control, failed to address the question of religious freedom within the Church. Such freedom can eventuate if the Church democratizes itself on the basis of the "republican blueprint" drawn up by Archbishop John Carroll and the lay trustees of the early nineteenth century (166). The U.S. bishops in their recent pastoral letters on peace and the economy have introduced a dialogic method that promises to transform the Catholic Church into an open "community of moral discourse" (179). The same method of consulting the faithful, if transferred to other sensitive areas such as birth control, abortion, and divorce, could result in a broader moral consensus (119). In the name of the principle of subsidiarity, the hierarchy should be made subordinate to the people, and accountable to them (139). Whenever Rome or the bishops fail to speak credibly, the faithful are justified in adhering to Catholic doctrine on a selective basis (64). The Church, after all, is a voluntary association (68).

4. In the past, Catholics, generally speaking, have shunned the sectarian stances of American Protestantism. But as the Catholic Church has become more solidly rooted in American culture, it has begun to take on the characteristics of its new environment. It has made room for radical expressions bordering on the sectarian. Dorothy Day, a convert to the Church from Marxist Communism, founded the Catholic Worker Movement, which has inspired numerous Catholic pacifists and Catholic socialists. Daniel Berrigan, a leader of radical protest movements since the 1960s, has been relentlessly countercultural. The cross and the world, he maintains, can never meet otherwise than in conflict. Christ, he adds, cannot enter our sinful world except under a cloud that blinds the eminences and authorities. These power holders typically don the mantle of Dostoyevsky's Grand Inquisitor, hounding and crushing the authentic witnesses of the gospel.[20]

Berrigan's apocalypticism is only one variety of radical Catholicism. Some radicals espouse a theology of violence and revolution modeled on heroes such as Che Guevara. More recently we have seen the budding of New Age theology and of a creation-centered spirituality. Repudiating spiritualities based on the fall and redemption, Matthew Fox advocates a creationist paradigm.[21] Although he is far more optimistic about nature and creation than Berrigan, and far less oriented toward suffering and sacrifice, Fox speaks out with a similar prophetic vehemence against capitalism, consumerism, militarism, racism, and the genocide of native peoples. Like Berrigan, he champions the rights of homosexuals and other "oppressed" minorities. Berrigan and Fox alike, as radicals, though differing in their radicalism, agree in their antagonism to every establishment, whether secular or ecclesiastical.

While calling for the total conversion of Church and society, radical Catholics seek to legitimate their positions by invoking historical precedents, both religious and civil. Catholic pacifists point to the early Christians who refused to bear arms for the Roman empire; they make common cause with Quakers and Mennonites, and they praise the nonviolence of Gandhi. Catholic radicals draw inspiration from the Franciscan spirituals, from utopian socialists, and from the abolitionists of the Civil War period. Berrigan, besides looking to the crucified Jesus, sees himself as a disciple of the Jesuit martyrs of Elizabethan England. The creationist and Green movements[22] find their historical roots in Genesis, in the nature Psalms, in Francis of Assisi, and in Hildegard of Bingen. They find allies among the native Americans and the nature worshipers of many peoples, ancient and modern. Creationists also include in their roster of heroes writers such as Henry David Thoreau and Walt Whitman. Thus they are not totally countercultural. They identify with selected streams of the cultures they wish to reform.

ASSESSMENT OF THE STRATEGIES

The strategies I have examined are easily identifiable in contemporary American Catholicism. The four positions could easily be arranged in a logical square of opposition. For the neoconservatives both Catholicism and American secular culture are basically good; for the radicals, both are fundamentally corrupt. For the Catholic traditionalists, the ecclesiastical culture is holy, but American secular culture is demonic. For the liberals, the American experiment is fundamentally healthy, but traditional Catholicism is diseased.

In the square of opposition, therefore, the neoconservatives are diametrically opposed to the radicals; the traditionalists, to the liberals. The other pairs, though opposed on some points, can agree in part. For example, the neoconservatives can agree with the liberals on the value of the American experiment in democracy. Neoconservatives and traditionalists can agree on the importance of stability and on the need for authority in any society. Liberals and radicals can agree about the Church's need for continual self-criticism and reform. Traditionalists and radicals vie with each other in denouncing the evils of our pleasure-loving consumerist society. Militants of the peace movement and of the pro-life movement have more than a little in common.

None of the four strategies, I submit, is simply wrong. The realities of American Catholicism and of American culture are complex and many-faceted. American life has aspects that we can praise with the neoconservatives and the liberals, and other aspects that we must deplore with the traditionalists and the radicals.

Regarding the Church, I would hold with the traditionalists and neo-conservatives that it is basically healthy and that we should let it shape our convictions and values. The first loyalty of the Catholic should be to the Church as the body of Christ. But the liberals are correct in holding that the Church must accept sound developments in secular culture. Roman Catholicism, as it has come down to us, has been significantly shaped by the social institutions of medieval and early modern Europe, and this very fact suggests that the Church might have something to learn from the American experiment of ordered liberty. Liberal Catholics and neoconservatives alike insist that the Vatican II Declaration on Religious Freedom is due in part to the influence of the American system. Further influences of this kind might be beneficial to world Catholicism.

The radicals also have some valid points to make. The Church, like secular society, is continually tempted to settle for mediocrity. To the extent that it has adopted the values and attitudes of middle-class America, the Church deserves to be admonished by prophetic reformers. Repentance needs to be preached to those within the household of God.

Just as all four of the strategies have their strengths, so too, taken in isolation, they have weaknesses. Catholic traditionalism is on the whole too regressive. It looks nostalgically back to a past that can hardly be recovered. In its typically American expressions, moreover, traditionalism offers little guidance to Catholics who live amid the secular realities of our day. While adhering to the strictest canons of orthodoxy in their beliefs and personal morality, many affluent Catholic traditionalists want the Church to be silent about politics, economics, business, and professional life. They effectively divorce their religious convictions from their day-to-day activities.

The neoconservatives, with their patriotic attachment to the American heritage, are inclined to minimize the extent to which the tradition of public virtue has been eroded by the quest for pleasure and material gain. Intent on maintaining civility in the orders of law and politics, they neglect the urgency of renewing the faith commitment and devotional life of contemporary Americans. They could be understood as holding that some kind of generalized civil religion suffices and that personal commitment to a specific religious tradition is a purely private matter, even a matter of personal taste. To point out this danger is not to accuse all representatives of the model of falling into the error, but simply to indicate that the neoconservative model needs to be supplemented and balanced by other models.[23]

Liberal Catholicism, with its enthusiasm for participatory democratic models, runs the risk of introducing into the Church the ideologies and interest groups that compete for power in civil society. Americanist Catholics easily forget the New Testament warnings against personal ambition and partisanship. In their zeal for updating, the liberals too easily canonize the present. They seem to advocate that Catholicism do away with its traditional structures, its reverence for the sacred, its docility to authority, and its esteem for sacrifice, prayer, and contemplation.

Finally the Catholic radicals, with their strident apocalyptic denunciations, cannot hope to play more than a marginal role in Catholicism, which is and must remain an essentially incarnational faith. According to the famous phrase attributed to James Joyce, Catholicism means "Here comes everybody." Sectarian militancy lacks the broad popular appeal needed for it to be effective in such a large and traditional institution.

ACCOMMODATION OR OPPOSITION?

The most fundamental question raised by the preceding discussion is whether the Church in this country should become more countercultural, as the traditionalists and radicals would wish, or more accommodationist, as the liberals and some neoconservatives propose. The tide since Vatican Council II has been running heavily toward accommodationism. Middle-aged adults constitute the last generation of Catholics raised with a strong sense of Catholic identity. Most younger Catholics look on themselves first of all as Americans, and only secondarily as Catholics. Their culture has been predominantly formed by the secular press, films, television, and popular music. Catholicism is filtered to them through these screens.

Catholic schools are becoming less numerous and less distinctively Catholic. Catholic colleges and universities, while in some cases expanding, have lost much of their religious character. A certain vague religiosity perdures among the young, but it is that of "communal Catholics" not strongly committed to the doctrines and structures of their Church.[24]

Under these circumstances parents and teachers, fearful of being rejected as old-fashioned, are understandably reluctant to confront the young with the challenge of official church teaching, especially in the area of sexuality. Religious educators often feel powerless in the face of the sexual revolution and the passion for affluence that possesses their students. Bishops and pastors find it increasingly difficult to shape the convictions and attitudes of the faithful. Apart from the issue of abortion, on which they are willing to risk a measure of unpopularity, the bishops increasingly shift their attention to social issues, adopting agendas that in many ways resemble those of the liberal intelligentsia, notably in their teaching on peace and on the economy. They seek to appeal to a broad public that includes non-Catholics, non-Christians, non-believers.

Many sociologists of religion speak of a crisis of identity among American Catholics of our day. In the opinion of Joseph Fitzpatrick the strength and stability of the Catholic Church in this country has hitherto rested on the religious symbols and practices that the immigrants brought with them. "Now, as these supports weaken and disappear, there is nothing in the American culture which provides a similar support for Catholic belief and practice."[25] Another sociologist of religion, John A. Coleman, traces the current identity crisis to the jettisoning of many elements of Catholic tradition and disregard for historic Catholic sensibilities. "Today," he writes, "Catholic America, like the larger nation, is a land without adequate symbols."[26] Classical Catholic wisdom concerning asceticism, contemplation, and mysticism has been largely forgotten. "Finally and most importantly, the Church seems to have suffered pastoral bankruptcy in dealing with a specifically religious agenda at a time when a kind of religious revival of interiority is occurring outside the Church."[27] Fitzpatrick and Coleman alike recognize that the middle-class American values that have been accepted by most contemporary Catholics are not genuinely Catholic.[28]

In this context the problem of accommodation takes on rather concrete implications. There can be no question of simply rejecting accommodation as a strategy. It has always been an honored principle of pastoral and missionary practice. The Christian message must be presented, insofar as possible, in forms that make it intelligible, credible, interesting, and relevant to the hearers. Vatican II, in its Decree on Missionary Activity, recommended that the younger churches should borrow "from the customs and traditions of their people, from their wisdom and their learning, from their arts and sciences . . . all those things which can contribute to the glory of their Creator, the revelation of the Savior's grace, or the proper arrangement of human life."[29] Accommodation becomes a problem only when the hard sayings of the gospel are watered down, when faith is weakened, and when immoral or dehumanizing practices are tolerated.

As I have said, there are healthy elements in American society. Liberals and neoconservatives have good grounds for maintaining that the Church in this nation will be stronger to the extent that it builds these elements into its own life and makes them available for the universal Church. Our American traditions of freedom, personal initiative, open communication, and active participation can undoubtedly be a resource for the renewal of Catholicism in an age when authoritarian structures, repression, and conformity are in general disrepute.

On the other hand, it can be at least equally important to guard against the dangers of accommodation. To the degree that she adjusts to the dominant culture, the Church has less to say. By simply echoing the prevailing opinions and values, the Church undermines the credibility of her claim to present a divine message and weakens people's motivation for seeking membership. A Church that no longer issues a clear call for conversion is only dubiously Christian. Traditional Catholicism has convictions and priorities very different from those embedded in contemporary American culture. The more thoroughly Catholics become inculturated in the American scene, the more alienated they become from their religious roots and the hierarchical authorities. Accommodation, therefore, can increase the crisis of identity felt by American Catholics.

Because of all these factors there is reason to believe that the greatest danger facing the Church in our country today is that of excessive and indiscreet accommodation. Catholics will be well-advised to cultivate a measured, prudent counterculturalism. Traditionalists rightly insist on this. The first and most urgent priority, they would say, is for the Church to socialize its members into its own tradition by immersing themselves in the symbols and meaning systems of Scripture and Catholic tradition.

Only by so doing can communities be formed in which the gospel, the sacraments, and pure doctrine are taken seriously.[30]

Pope John Paul II, like Paul VI before him, repeatedly called on Catholics everywhere to evangelize their cultures. He recognized that faith cannot survive without cultural embodiment, and that faith can have no home in a culture untouched by the gospel. To carry out their assignment from these popes, Catholics must first of all become firmly rooted in their own religious tradition. They must, through their parishes, their families, prayer groups, or basic ecclesial communities, find an environment in which they can interiorize their religious heritage. In this way they can prepare themselves to become agents in the evangelization of the secular culture. Such cultural evangelization, in turn, may help to establish an atmosphere in which Catholic Christianity can be lived out more faithfully by greater numbers.

The neoconservative program, more outgoing than that of the traditionalists, has its proper place in the Catholic agenda. Neoconservatism, if it allows itself to be enriched by the sacramental piety and prayerful interiority of the traditionalists, has great potential for the evangelization of American culture. But these two strategies, even in combination, do not exhaust the possibilities. As I have already indicated, the Catholic Church stands to gain from a prudent introduction of certain American democratic values and practices as urged by the liberals. The neoconservatives do not deny this, and traditionalists would be well-advised to concede the point. Catholic radicalism, finally, serves as a needed gadfly. Both Church and secular society need to be challenged by the radicals' call to higher standards of evangelical perfection.

In summary, the four strategies are not reciprocally exclusive. They can and should be pursued concurrently. Although American Catholics can disagree about the extent to which each strategy is appropriate at a given time and place, they should be on guard against mutual hostility and recrimination. Each group should respect the intentions of the others and humbly recognize its own limitations. The internecine struggles between opposed factions are a scandal and a waste of energies that could more profitably be devoted to the common mission of the Church to minister to the salvation of the world. By generously recognizing the diverse gifts of the Holy Spirit, all can help to build up the body of Christ in unity and strength. Traditionalists and radicals, liberals and neoconservatives, by their joint efforts, can enable the Catholic Church to enter into dynamic and fruitful relations with American culture in its full complexity.

NOTES

1. Vatican II, *Lumen gentium*, 23; *Sacrosanctum concilium*, 37–40; *Unitatis redintegratio*, 16–17; *Orientalium Ecclesiarum*, 2–4.

2. Vatican II, *Lumen gentium*, 13; *Ad gentes*, 22; *Gaudium et spes*, 44.

3. Among the important treatments of this question one might list: Ary A. Roest Crollius, "Inculturation and the Meaning of Culture," *Gregorianum* 61 (1980): 253–74; Marcello de Carvalho Azevedo, *Inculturation and the Challenges of Modernity* (Rome: Gregorian University Press, 1982); International Theological Commission, "Faith and Inculturation," *Origins* 18 (May 4, 1989): 801–7.

4. See the useful survey of Hervé Carrier, *Gospel Message and Human Cultures from Leo XIII to John Paul II* (Pittsburgh: Duquesne University Press, 1989).

5. The texts of all the addresses at this meeting are published in *Origins* 18 of March 23 and March 30, 1989.

6. In his address at Xavier University, New Orleans, September 12, 1987, Pope John Paul II spoke of the Catholic university "in its privileged role as protagonist in the encounter between faith and science and between revealed truth and culture"; also of the universities as "privileged settings for the encounter between faith and culture." See *Origins* 17 (October 1, 1987): 268–70, quotations from 269.

7. Helpful for this purpose is Robert N. Bellah, *The Broken Covenant* (New York: Seabury/Crossroad, 1975) and the coauthored work of Robert N. Bellah and others, *Habits of the Heart* (Berkeley: University of California Press, 1985). For an earlier assessment see Jacques Maritain, *Reflections on America* (New York: Scribner's, 1958).

8. Quoted by George Weigel in his "Is America Bourgeois?" *Crisis* 4 (October 1986): 9.

9. For a powerful analysis of this syndrome see Bellah, *Broken Covenant*, 130–36.

10. Many typologies have been proposed since the seminal works of Ernst Troeltsch and H. Richard Niebuhr. Joe Holland, in his introduction to Joe Holland and Anne Barsanti (eds.), *American and Catholic: The New Debate* (South Orange, N.J.: Seton Hall University, Pillar Books, 1988), distinguishes three programs: integration, restoration, and regeneration. David O'Brien in "Join It, Work It, Fight It" (*Commonweal* 116 [November 17, 1987]: 624–30) likewise identifies three orientations, which he labels the republican style, the immigrant style, and the evangelical style. See also O'Brien's "Choosing Our Future: American Catholicism's Precarious Prospects," in *Rising from History*, Proceedings of the College Theology Society, 30 (Lanham, Md.: University Press of America, 1987), 17–45.

11. James F. Hitchcock, *Catholicism and Modernity: Confrontation or Capitulation?* (New York: Seabury/Crossroad, 1979). The following paragraph is heavily indebted to the last chapter of this book.

12. Ralph Martin, *A Crisis of Truth: The Attack on Faith, Morality and Mission in the Catholic Church* (Ann Arbor, Mich.: Servant Books, 1982).

13. George Weigel, *Catholicism and the Renewal of American Democracy* (New York: Paulist, 1989).

14. J. Francis Stafford, "This Home of Freedom: A Pastoral Letter to the Archdiocese of Denver," *Origins* 17 (June 11, 1987): 53–63; idem, "Virtue and the American Republic: A Pastoral Letter to the Church of Denver," September 14, 1989.

15. Michael Novak has written particularly on Catholic social thought, notably in his *Freedom in Justice* (San Francisco: Harper & Row, 1984).

16. Weigel, *Catholicism and the Renewal*, 8, 204, quoting from Richard John Neuhaus, *The Catholic Moment* (San Francisco: Harper & Row, 1987), 283.

17. John Courtney Murray, *We Hold These Truths* (New York: Sheed & Ward, 1960), 29–30.

18. See Joseph A. Varacalli, *Toward the Establishment of Liberal Catholicism in America* (Washington, D.C.: University Press of America, 1983).

19. Dennis P. McCann, *New Experiment in Democracy: The Challenge for American Catholicism* (Kansas City, Mo.: Sheed & Ward, 1987). Numbers in parentheses in the present paragraph refer to pages in this work.

20. Daniel Berrigan, *To Dwell in Peace: An Autobiography* (San Francisco: Harper & Row, 1987), esp. 347. For a more general survey of this strategy, see Francine du Plessix Gray, *Divine Disobedience: Profiles in Radical Catholicism* (New York: Alfred A. Knopf, 1970).

21. Among the many works of Matthew Fox, special mention may be made of his *Original Blessing* (Santa Fe, N.M.: Bear, 1983).

22. An American Catholic adherent of the Green Movement is Charlene Spretnak. See her "The Regenerationist Perspective: Catholic Exploration of a Post-Modern America," in Holland and Barsanti (eds.), *American and Catholic*, 99–113.

23. A severe critique of George Weigel from a traditionalist perspective has been mounted by David Schindler in a series of articles in *Communio* 14 (Summer 1987): 262–90, and 15 (Spring 1988): 92–120. See also his contributions to *30 Days* 2 (May 1989): 57–60, and 2 (June 1989): 55–59.

24. See Andrew M. Greeley, *The Communal Catholic: A Personal Manifesto* (New York: Seabury/Crossroad, 1976). This theme runs through many of Greeley's subsequent works.

25. Joseph P. Fitzpatrick, *One Church Many Cultures: The Challenge of Diversity* (Kansas City, Mo.: Sheed & Ward, 1987), 106.

26. John A. Coleman, *An American Strategic Theology* (New York: Paulist, 1982), 158.

27. Ibid., 159.

28. Fitzpatrick, *One Church Many Cultures*, 120.

29. Vatican II, *Ad gentes*, 22.

30. On the importance of resisting accommodation and adopting processes of intense socialization into communities of faith, see George A. Lindbeck, *The Nature of Doctrine* (Philadelphia: Westminster Press, 1984), especially the final chapter.

4

Faith and Experience

Strangers? Rivals? Partners?

March 14, 1990

MEANING OF THE TERMS

Philosophers cannot agree about what "experience" is, and theologians differ widely regarding the meaning of "faith." Since the very terms are matters of debate, I can hardly be expected to settle the relationship between experience and faith in the time at my disposal. Nevertheless I welcome this opportunity for proposing my own understanding of the two terms and their connection. Because the subject is highly complex, my presentation this afternoon will have to be compact and wide ranging. For this I beg your indulgence.

Experience originally meant the process of testing or trial. It has gradually come to mean actual observation or experimentation, considered as a source of knowledge. For the empiricists it frequently meant the cogent evidence given by hard facts, apart from free interpretation. I shall use the term somewhat more broadly to signify whatever is perceived in an encounter between a conscious subject and an immediately given object. The content of experience therefore includes both the object as a phenomenon and the subject as a conscious participant.

I shall use the term *faith* to mean the combination of conviction, trust, and commitment that the Christian is expected to have toward God. For present purposes the emphasis will be most of all on conviction, that is to say, on the cognitive dimension of faith. Although I shall not be exploring all dimensions of faith, I shall here presuppose that faith is not a sheerly intellectual act but a loving and fruitful assent. Our questions will be: How does experience enter into this intellectual acceptance? And conversely, how does faith, when it is present, affect experience?

In broad strokes we may distinguish three sources of knowledge: immediate apprehension, inference, and authority. Immediate apprehension, when it bears on concrete and present realities, is practically synonymous with experience. As the most basic mode of knowledge, it is presupposed by the other two. It gives rise to spontaneous factual judgments about the here and now, especially as given in sense perception. Inference, as I understand it, is the process of deriving new knowledge, without added experiential input, from things already known, through mental operations. Inference may take the format of scientific proof, but it may also be the kind of informal reasoning by which we interpret the meaning of signs. By authority, finally, I mean reliance on the testimony of trusted witnesses.

Experience and Religion

Applying these three modes of knowledge to the realm of religion we may say, in the first place, that God can in some way be known by inference from created realities. We can reason to God as the first cause or final goal of the things known by experience. The vastness and beauty of creation point to the power and goodness of the divine Creator. But this inferential knowledge of God is difficult to attain, often uncertain, and in any case fragmentary.

Living religions rely on a richer, more vivid knowledge of God. They depend to a great extent on the testimony of prophets or founders. The authority of religious leaders plays an important role but it cannot be the sole source of religious knowledge. For it does not explain the originality of the founders, nor does it tell us why people choose to rely on their authority rather than on some other authority or no authority.

Focusing for the moment on the great religious founders, we may observe that they are never completely original. Paul and the other apostles, like Moses and Isaiah before them, were formed in a definite religious tradition before they began to preach a new version of the faith of their ancestors. The same may be said of Jesus without prejudice to his divinity.

He was steeped in the Scriptures and religious traditions of Israel. As for the original element in the teaching of these leaders, the sources indicate that they underwent intense religious experiences that are often described in terms of seeing visions and hearing divine or angelic messages. Whether revelation came to them in verbal form, or whether the verbal component was supplied by the mechanisms of their own consciousness, may be disputed. Even if, as I suspect, their ears did not actually hear words miraculously spoken from heaven, and their eyes did not physically see supernatural objects, they must have had remarkable spiritual experiences that gave rise to such auditory or visual phenomena.

Does this mean that they had direct experience of God or the realities that they proclaimed? At this point we must ask whether it is possible for anyone in this life to have a direct experience of God. Can the human consciousness make direct contact with the divine? Both the Old and the New Testament repeatedly assert that no human being can see God and live (Ex 33:20; 1 Tm 6:16), though the Gospel of John seems to allow for an exception in the case of Jesus because of his divine origin (Jn 1:18).

It would seem impossible for the human mind to make contact with God as an object, because God is not an object in the ordinary sense. Every object of direct knowledge is a particular finite being perceived against a larger horizon or, if you like, a broader background. It stands within some class or category. God, as the actual infinite, bursts the limits of all categories. According to the classical theological tradition the divine essence, transcending as it does every genus or category of being, is not attainable as an object of direct perception, at least under the conditions of this present life.

Not all experience, however, is that of objects. When we act we perceive our own activity—the activity of knowing or willing. In some sense we experience ourselves as the subjects or bearers of our own activity. Even so, the action and the subject in question are finite. To imagine that God is perceived in this subjective manner would be to confuse the Creator with the creature.

Can God be perceived in some other way? We perceive ourselves, no doubt, as reaching out in knowledge and love beyond all finite realities toward the unconditioned Absolute. In some extended sense of the word we may be said to perceive the infinite as the ultimate term toward which the human spirit is oriented. But we perceive the goal only implicitly in the movement toward it. The goal is not directly perceived, for it is not yet present; we are still reaching out toward it.

On the other hand, precisely because the finite is perceived as not satisfying the cravings of the human heart and mind, the domain of our perception cannot be limited to particular finite things. The horizon toward which the human spirit reaches out is at least potentially unlimited. This drive toward the infinite, I believe, makes us capable of experiencing the divine. The reality of the absolute is not simply inferred from the conditioned beings we encounter but is immediately given, in a tacit or implicit way, insofar as we spontaneously judge that the source and goal of our spiritual dynamism must be real. In affirming the finite as finite we implicitly affirm (or coaffirm) the infinite.

Thus far I have made no mention of grace. According to Catholic teaching, God mysteriously bestows his grace on those whom he calls to union with himself. Theologians have debated for centuries about whether the presence of grace in the soul can be perceived or whether it is known only on authority, thanks to the teaching of the Church. Some argue that grace can be perceived, since it influences our minds and hearts, and that in perceiving it we in some sort perceive God, for grace, they say, is nothing other than God's self-communication.

Personally I am inclined to look critically at the idea of grace as God's self-communication. God does communicate a created participation in his own life, but the life of a creature, however elevated by grace, cannot be identical with that of God in himself. Furthermore, even those theologians who insist most strongly on the idea of grace as God's self-communication feel bound to concede, as I believe they must, that we cannot by mere introspection clearly perceive the presence and activity of God in our souls. They admit that we would not be able to speak about the reality of grace were it not for the teaching of the Church. Still, when the Church does give us that teaching, it serves to throw light on certain inner experiences that would otherwise be difficult to explain.

Saint Augustine wrote in the first chapter of his *Confessions*: "Thou hast made us for thyself, O Lord, and our hearts are restless till they find rest in thee!"[1] The sentence is constantly quoted because it tallies admirably with the inner experience of religiously oriented people. This inner experience of being attracted toward an ineffable union with the divine, even though it may not be adverted to, is a necessary condition, I believe, for the possibility of the spiritual experience of prophets, mystics, and religious founders. Less conspicuously, this attraction is an ingredient in the religious life of ordinary folk like you and me.

Sources of Christian Faith

It would be far from the mark, however, to imagine that the founders of public religious communities, such as the Christian Church, derived their insights exclusively, or even primarily, from turning inward and consulting their own private experience. For the apostles, who were in some sort the founders of Christianity as an organized religion, the crucial element was the life, death, and resurrection of Jesus Christ, interpreted against the background of Jewish messianic expectation. They regarded the teaching of Jesus concerning the kingdom of God as an external, publicly available revelation of the mind of God himself. Christianity, then, is founded principally on the person, actions, and teaching of Jesus Christ as attested by the apostolic Church. The focal element in the experience of the apostles was the meaning of what they saw with their eyes and heard with their ears—in other words, their external experience.

To understand the faith of the apostles, therefore, we must take account of three dimensions of their religious awareness—their inner dynamic orientation toward union with God, grounded in the nature of the human spirit and the impulses of grace, the beliefs of the Jewish community in which they were raised, and their outward experience of the presence of the divine in Jesus Christ. They saw the humanity of Christ and, thanks to grace, were able to interpret it as God's presence in the flesh. This I take to be the obvious meaning of the passage in Matthew's Gospel in which Jesus congratulates Peter on having recognized him as Messiah and Son of God not by means of flesh and blood but by revelation from the Father (Mt 16:17).

You might object, of course, that at the resurrection Christ's divinity became manifest, enabling Thomas to confess, "My Lord and my God" (Jn 20:28). But on closer reflection it becomes apparent that what Thomas saw with his eyes was the risen human body, and that that body, under the concrete circumstances, was a clue or pointer to Christ's divinity. Thomas was able to make a confession of faith in Christ as God because he interpreted the phenomena in the light of his previous acceptance of the Scriptures and the teaching of Jesus, as well as his inner religious orientations. The faith of the apostles therefore arose out of a combination of authoritative testimony, inner experience, and outer experience. They did not empirically perceive the contents of revelation, as God's Word, and if they had done so the experience would have removed both the need and the possibility of faith.

What I have said about the faith of the apostles gives the key to some questions we might have about the faith of later Christian believers. The prophets and apostles, as I have said, made use of a traditional faith and reformulated it in the light of their personal experiences and insights. Subsequent Christian believers likewise find it necessary both to submit to a tradition and to appropriate that tradition personally. In order to accept the teaching of the Church or of Christianity with personal faith, we need what the councils refer to as "the illumination and inspiration of the Holy Spirit, who gives ease and joy in assenting to the truth and believing it."[2] Many Christians feel this ease and joy in assenting, and in that sense they are conscious, in an obscure or implicit way, of the Holy Spirit at work within them.

In summary, then, the life of faith is a tantalizing combination of experience and non-experience. We can directly perceive persons or books that propose the faith, and we can assess the credibility of the teaching by reasoning on the basis of experience. We can perhaps perceive our own attraction toward the new life offered to us in Christ. But the realities in which we believe lie, for the most part, beyond the reach of experience. For our explicit awareness of the assistance of the Holy Spirit and of the contents of the creed we depend on the testimony of the Church.

THE RELATION BETWEEN FAITH AND EXPERIENCE

With this background we may turn to the three questions in my title. Faith and Experience: Are they strangers, rivals, or partners?

It might seem that they are *strangers* because they do not meet. Experience deals with inner-worldly realities, but faith deals with God as he freely turns toward us in love. Faith has to do with a realm to which experience gives no access—the inner nature of God, his saving plans, and the ultimate end for which we are destined after we die. Cardinal Newman was keenly aware of the gap between *experience* and *faith*. In one of his letters he represents his correspondent as saying: "To see and touch the supernatural with the eye of my soul, with its *own experience*, this is what I want to do." Newman then replies: "Yes, it is—You wish to 'walk *not* by faith, *but* by sight.' If you had *experience*, how would it be *faith?*"³

Going beyond the implications of this quotation, one could even argue that faith and experience are *rivals* contending for our allegiance. Martin Luther in one passage maintained that "experience is against faith and faith against experience." For example, experience indicates that the dead do not rise, that miracles do not happen, and that sin and death still rule the world, in spite of what faith affirms about Christ's victory over evil. The Christian, Luther concluded, must pay no heed to experience.⁴

Luther, like Newman, was making a valid point. It is easy to find tensions and apparent conflicts between faith and ordinary experience. And yet I would argue that, notwithstanding, faith and experience can be friends. Rightly used, they assist one another. Experience raises the questions that make faith meaningful, and impels us to reach out toward the God whom faith proclaims. Outer experience puts us in contact with the signs that make faith credible, and enables us to put our faith into practice in the world. Without experience, faith would be impossible, and even if it were possible it would be sterile.

Just as experience is the support of faith, so conversely faith contributes to experience. The success of Christianity in gaining adherents and perpetuating itself is due in no small measure to its capacity to enrich and deepen human experience. Faith enables us to see the world with new eyes and to encounter life in a new way. The image of Christ, as it lives in our hearts and minds, transforms us into its own likeness. By adhering to Christ and the gospel, we are able to perceive the good things of life as gifts from the hand of God and to find meaning in the riddles of suffering and death. Faith gives direction, purpose, and coherence to our lives. No one who has been caught up in the love of God as displayed in Jesus Christ should be content to say that faith is a mere stranger or rival of experience. Faith and experience are friends, and at times they are so closely conjoined that it is hard to draw the line between them. Faith itself becomes experience in the believer's encounter with the world.

Most Catholics, in my judgment, have too little awareness of the experiential dimension of faith. They tend to look on religion as a collection of doctrines and precepts imposed from on high, regardless of their experience. Some, who do hunger for religious experience, turn to other churches or religions, unaware of the tremendous resources for religious experience given in Catholicism as a mystical, incarnational, and sacramental faith. Without falsely claiming any direct perception of God and of the mysteries of revelation, people can have profound experiences, even prior to faith, disposing them to accept the Christian message. And once they do believe, faith itself, as a loving adherence to the person of Christ, transfigures the whole experience of living in the world. A successful synthesis of faith and experience is, I submit, the key to a joyful, stable, and rewarding relationship with God.

NOTES

1. Augustine, *Confessions*, book 1, no. 1.

2. The Second Council of Orange, canon 7 on grace, in Denzinger-Schönmetzer, *Enchiridion Symbolorum* 377. Cf. Vatican I, Dogmatic Constitution on Faith, DS 3010.

3. John Henry Newman, letter to W. R. Brownlow of April 29, 1871, in *The Letters and Diaries of John Henry Newman*, ed. Charles Stephen Dessain and Thomas Gornall (Oxford: Clarendon Press, 1871), 25:324.

4. Cited in Paul Althaus, *The Theology of Martin Luther* (Philadelphia: Fortress, 1966), 63.

5

Newman, Conversion, and Ecumenism

December 4, 1990

The centenary of Cardinal Newman's death, on August 11, 1890, has occasioned a large number of conferences and studies dealing with various aspects of his work. The present lecture is intended as a part of this commemoration. As one who came to the Catholic faith in adult life, Newman reflected long and deeply about his own religious pilgrimage and became the adviser of many companions and followers. He therefore deserves to be remembered as one of the great theologians of conversion. Because of his comprehensive vision of Christianity as a whole and his lifelong concern with overcoming Christian divisions, he has also been hailed as a forerunner of ecumenism.[1] His observations on Christian unity in some respects anticipate the directions of the Second Vatican Council. But there was in his thinking a tension between the convert and the ecumenist, the apologist for Catholicism and the friendly observer of other Christian communions. His efforts to be faithful to his dual vocation as a convert and as an ecumenist make his thought particularly relevant today, when a number of distinguished ecumenists, without loss of their ecumenical commitment, have felt the call to enter into full communion with the Church of Rome.

THE CONVERT

Newman's conversion was slow, deliberate, and painful, but by no means halfhearted. For more than five years, from 1839 to 1845, he felt

---

an increasing realization that the Church of England, to which he belonged, was not a part of the Catholic Church. But even so, he hesitated to sever his ties. In June 1844 he wrote to John Keble explaining his reluctance:

> As far as I can see, all inducements and temptations are for remaining quiet, and against moving. The loss of friends what a great evil is this! the loss of position, of name, of esteem—such a stultification of myself—such a triumph to others. It is no proud thing to unsay what I have said, to pull down what I have attempted to build up. And again, what quite pierces me, the disturbance of mind which a change on my part would cause to so many, . . . the temptation to which many would be exposed of scepticism, indifference, and even infidelity.[2]

In November 1844 he continued to dwell on the obstacles to conversion. He wrote to Henry Edward Manning, who was still an Anglican at the time: "I have no existing sympathies with Roman Catholics. I hardly ever, even abroad, was at one of their services—I know none of them. I do not like what I hear of them."[3]

A few months later, in a letter of January 8, 1845, he said that he did not know whether he was in favor of people moving from Anglicanism to Roman Catholicism, since "the state of the Roman Catholics is at present so unsatisfactory." He then added: "The simple question is, Can *I* (it is personal, not whether another, but can *I*) be saved in the English Church? am *I* in safety, were I to die tonight?"[4] Having answered this question for himself, he wrote to his sister Jemima on March 15, 1845: "I am giving up a maintenance, involving no duties, and adequate to all my wants. . . . I have a good name with many; I am deliberately sacrificing it. . . . I am going to those whom I do not know and of whom I expect very little. . . . Oh, what can it be but a stern necessity which causes this?"[5]

Newman became a Roman Catholic because deep study had convinced him that it was impossible to be in the one, holy, catholic Church without being in communion with Rome. This remained his position for the rest of his life. He frequently spoke of the Roman communion as "the only True Church, the Ark of Salvation,"[6] as the "One Fold of Christ,"[7] and as "the only religious body . . . in which is salvation."[8] The true Church, for Newman, must necessarily be a single communion and could not contain elements that were "independent of the whole, discordant with one another in doctrine and in ritual, destitute of mutual intercommunion."[9] Because Anglicans and Roman Catholics were not in mutual communion, they could not both be parts or branches of one and the same Church.

NEGATIVE JUDGMENTS ON OTHER COMMUNIONS

When Newman as a Catholic speaks of other ecclesial communities, he does not sound, by twentieth-century standards, very ecumenical. Yet he is far more positive than many of his contemporaries, such as Cardinal Manning and the fiery lay convert William George Ward. He is willing to grant that grace is given and received in such communities, partly because they have retained certain elements of the Catholic patrimony, and partly because they may be expected to benefit from God's uncovenanted mercies.

In speaking of the Orthodox (or, as he calls it, "Greek") Church, Newman admits that it has true sacraments, a valid sacrifice of the Mass, and authentic priestly orders.[10] But the priests and the flock of that Church are, he says, merely passive believers; their religion has become mechanical and superstitious.[11] Since both the Byzantine and the Russian Church were merely local or national, their existence, for Newman, constituted no serious objection against the catholicity of the Roman communion.[12] Newman dismissed the long period of separation from the West as "eight centuries . . . of religious deadness and insensibility."[13] Yet he maintained that in the Crimean War England should have supported Russia, as a Christian power, rather than Turkey.[14]

If Newman was reserved about the Orthodox, he was even more sparing in his praise for the Protestants and Anglicans. To some degree they too lived off the biblical and sacramental patrimony of the Catholic Church. They had a valid baptism and had picked up some scattered fragments of that "large floating body of Catholic truth" that had been "poured into all quarters of the globe," while being found "in fulness and purity in the Church alone."[15] Newman dared to hope that the Bible and the *Book of Common Prayer* retained enough Catholic truth for many Protestants to be saved.[16] In a letter of April 26, 1841, written in the latter stages of his Anglican period, he wrote to the Catholic theologian Charles W. Russell that the long duration of Protestantism was evidence that it must contain many and great truths, for so much piety and earnestness must be rooted in a measure of truth.[17] As a Catholic, Newman apparently adhered to this position. In one of his last letters he testified that he continued to cherish "those great and burning truths" that he had learned from Calvinist Evangelicals as a boy.[18] Nevertheless he denied that he owed anything religiously to Protestantism, for he held that the doctrines of the Holy Trinity, the Incarnation, grace, election, good works, and divine life in the soul, which he had imbibed from Evangelical authors such as Thomas Scott, were not characteristics of Protestantism but parts of the old Catholic truth that had come down from Christian antiquity.[19]

In his *Lectures on Justification* (1838), Newman vehemently attacked Luther for having left Christians in bondage to their feelings and for leading many to disbelieve in the efficacy of the sacraments. These lectures are in many respects quite polemical, being directed primarily against the Evangelical doctrine of justification by faith alone. But even here Newman did not repudiate what he himself had learned as a young Evangelical. Rather, he completed it by showing how faith brings the believer to obedience and sacramental life. Louis Bouyer remarks that Newman's thought on justification, as expressed in these lectures, holds

> enormous consequences for ecumenism. It means that reunion with Catholicism will not force Protestants to abandon anything in this their rightly cherished, most fundamental spiritual intuition. If anything, they will have to give it a more searching reappraisal and a more radical development than they have ever done heretofore. By the same token, if Catholicism is to be truer to itself and to its own proper principles, it must not only take this and other Protestant intuitions seriously, but, recognizing that they issue from authentically Catholic wellsprings, it must set about to reintegrate them in an effective way into both its theory and its practice.[20]

Regarding the Protestant and Anglican churches as cut off from the true communion, Newman was convinced that they were not true churches and that their ministrations could not be blessed with covenanted graces. He was doubtful—and increasingly doubtful as the years passed—about the validity of Anglican ordinations.[21] But he was optimistic about the abundance of the unpromised visitations of God's mercy. He compared dissident churches to the Ten Tribes after they had been separated from the kingdom of David and the Aaronic priesthood. Just as God had sent prophets such as Elijah and Elisha to the schismatic Israelites, so he might raise up holy ministers among Protestants and Anglicans.[22]

In a seemingly harsh judgment, Newman declared that the grace given in the Church of England did not come from that church, which was in his estimation nothing but "a tomb of what was once living, the casket of a treasure which has been lost."[23] Anglicans, he said, could no more receive grace from their own church than "an infant could receive nourishment from the breast of its dead mother."[24]

THE ANGLICAN ESTABLISHMENT

Newman's ambivalent attitude toward the Church of England becomes dramatically manifest in the series of statements he made over the years about the establishment of Anglicanism as the national religion. In three letters written in late 1850 and early 1851 to the Catholic layman J. M. Capes, Newman warned him against launching a crusade against the Establishment. Newman said that he looked on the Church of England as "a bulwark against infidelity," in the shadow of which all the dissenting churches lived. While the established Church existed, it served, according to Newman, as a witness to revelation and to dogmatic and ritual religion. If the Anglican establishment were to go, infidel literature would, so to speak, flood the market. The Catholic Church was not yet strong enough in England to take the place of the Establishment.[25]

In 1860 Newman declined to take part in building a new Catholic church at Oxford, on the ground that it might lead to controversy with the Anglicans there. In a letter to Bishop Ullathorne's secretary, Canon E. E. Estcourt, he explained his reasons at some length:

> While I do not see my way to take steps to weaken the Church of England, being what it is, least of all should I be disposed to do so in Oxford, which has hitherto been the seat of those traditions which constitute whatever there is of Catholic doctrine and principle in the Anglican Church. . . . Till things are very much changed there, in weakening Oxford, we are weakening our friends, weakening our own *de facto* παιδαγωγός into the Church. Catholics did not make us Catholics; Oxford made us Catholics. At present Oxford surely does more good than harm. . . .
>
> I go further than a mere tolerance of Oxford; as I have said, I wish to suffer the Church of England. The Establishment has ever been a breakwater against Unitarianism, fanaticism, and infidelity. It has ever loved us

better than Puritans and Independents have loved us. And it receives all that abuse and odium of dogmatism, or at least a good deal of it, which otherwise would be directed against us.[26]

In subsequent years Newman maintained approximately the same position. In a letter of June 7, 1863, to his Anglican friend Isaac Williams, he wrote: "The Anglican Church has been a most useful breakwater against scepticism," but in the same letter he expressed his fears that latitudinarian opinions were spreading furiously in the Church of England.[27]

In his *Apologia pro vita sua*, written the following year, Newman recalled his long-standing "firm belief that grace was to be found within the Anglican Church"[28] and he added an appendix on "The Anglican Church" in which he called it "to a certain point, a witness and teacher of religious truth."[29] In an autobiographical vein he said, "the Church of England has been the instrument of Providence in conferring great benefits on me." "While Catholics are so weak in England," he continued, "it is doing our work." It is therefore "a serviceable breakwater against doctrinal errors more fundamental than its own." For all these reasons he wished to avoid anything that would weaken its hold on the public mind or "lessen its maintenance of those great Christian and Catholic principles and doctrines which it has up to this time successfully preached."[30]

In a letter of November 1, 1864, to an unknown addressee, Newman observed:

With a violent hand the State kept down the multitude of sects which were laying England waste during the Commonwealth. The State kept out Unitarianism, not to say infidelity, at the era of the Revolution. It was the State which prevented the religious enthusiasm of the Methodist revival from destroying dogma. At this moment, destroy the establishment of Anglicanism, and the consequences would be terrible.[31]

Here Newman might have left the matter except that Edward Pusey, in a pamphlet, paraphrased Newman as holding that the Anglican Church was "the great bulwark against infidelity in this land." Cardinal Manning, in a response to Pusey, rejected this estimate. In his public *Letter to Pusey* of 1865, Newman felt obliged to deny that he had ever deliberately called the Anglican Church a bulwark; he repeated from the *Apologia* that he viewed it as a "serviceable breakwater against errors more fundamental than its own." Unlike a bulwark, he explained, a breakwater is not an integral part of what it defends and is serviceable if, without excluding error altogether, it detracts from the volume and force of error.[32]

ALTERNATIVES BETWEEN ATHEISM AND CATHOLICITY

As a convert, Newman had to ask himself whether he could make a definitive commitment to his new faith. This raised for him the further question whether certitude in matters of religion was reversible. In numerous publications he took the position that religious certitudes are, at least normally, irreversible.

We have already seen that Newman as a Catholic continued to affirm what he had previously believed as an Evangelical Christian. He also retained the convictions he acquired as an Anglican regarding the existence of a visible Church, the sacramental system, and the dogmatic decrees of the early councils. His conversion was therefore not a repudiation but an affirmation of his past; it was continuous, progressive, and incremental.

More precisely, we may say that Newman experienced in himself something analogous to the cumulative process that he attributed to the whole Church in his famous *Essay on the Development of Christian Doctrine*. He began, as did the Church at its infancy, with an indistinct global idea not yet articulated in dogmatic form. As a young man, he came to accept the great Trinitarian and Christological doctrines that were common to all major Christian denominations; then in his years at Oxford he perceived the major ecclesiological and sacramental implications and at length came to embrace the doctrines specific to post-Reformation Roman Catholicism. His earlier beliefs prepared the way for the acceptance of the later ones.

Already as an Anglican, in the last of his *Oxford University Sermons* (1843), Newman held that the Catholic idea is one and that it implicitly includes all the dogmas. "These propositions imply each other, as being parts of one whole; so that to deny one is to deny all, and to invalidate one is to deface and destroy the view itself."[33]

In a whole series of writings Newman spoke of the stages by which an individual comes to a fuller appreciation of the contents of the faith. In his *Discourses to Mixed Congregations* he taught that

> once a man has a real hold of the great doctrine that there is a God, in its true meaning and bearings, then (provided there is no disturbing cause, no peculiarities in his circumstances, involuntary ignorance, or the like), he will be led on without an effort, as by a natural continuation of that belief, to believe also in the Catholic Church as God's messenger or prophet.[34]

The most complete statement of Newman's position on this point is in the *Grammar of Assent* (1870), in which he analyzes the steps by which a sincere Protestant might find his way to Catholicism. A Protestant who assents to the doctrine of our Lord's divinity with a real assent, he concludes, is easily led to welcome the Catholic doctrine of the Real Presence and that of Mary as Mother of God (*theotokos*).[35]

Ten years later, in a new edition of the *Grammar of Assent*, Newman added an endnote explaining that the first principles, sentiments, and tastes that incline one to accept any revealed truth constitute an *organum investigandi* leading the mind by an infallible succession from the rejection of atheism to monotheism, from monotheism to Christianity, from Christianity to Evangelical religion, and from there to Catholicity.[36]

Corresponding to this theory of an ascending logic leading from theism to Catholicity, Newman postulated a descending movement. The disposition that inclines a person to doubt or reject any revealed truth will, if consistently pursued, terminate in total infidelity. Thus, in his *Discourses to Mixed Congregations*, he argued that when a person ceases to believe in the Church, there is "nothing in reason to keep him from doubting the existence of God."[37] "Unlearn Catholicism," he wrote, "and you open the way to your becoming a Protestant, Unitarian, Deist, Pantheist, Sceptic, in a dreadful but inevitable succession."[38] Already in 1845 Newman had read the autobiography of Blanco White, an Oxford friend who had forsaken the Catholicism of his youth and had ended as a pantheist.[39]

In the *Apologia* (1864) Newman gives a very succinct summary of his two-edged principle. He reports that by 1844 he had come to the conclusion "that there was no medium, in true philosophy, between Atheism and Catholicity, and that a perfectly consistent mind, under those circumstances in which it finds itself here below, must embrace either the one or the other."[40]

This double principle is perhaps Newman's most seminal contribution to ecumenical theology. Non-Catholics, to be sure, could hardly be expected to agree that the fullness of truth was to be found only in Roman Catholic Christianity. But the formula challenged Catholics to acknowledge the salutary value of the faith of non-Catholic Christians and motivated Catholics to help these other Christians to deepen their own faith rather than renounce it. By subordinating the acceptance of particular dogmas to personal adherence to the revealed idea, Newman provided an explanation of the existence of authentic faith among Christians whose doctrines were, by Catholic standards, deficient. As Newman knew from his own experience, it takes time and favorable circumstances to grasp certain doctrinal implications of the Christian faith commitment. But at the same time Newman's principle avoided any reductionism. He insisted that sincere believers must continue to explore the implications of what they believe and thus to progress toward the fullness of Catholic truth, even as the Church itself must continue to ponder the apostolic deposit and draw out its meaning and consequences. By the same token, Newman warned against the casual dismissal of any revealed doctrine, inasmuch as the totality of dogma is a single indivisible system.

REFORM OF THE CHURCH

While accepting without question the whole system of Catholic dogma, Newman was quite aware that the Church, as it existed in history, suffered from many human defects. He would not have become a Catholic unless he had learned to think critically of the Church in which he found himself. As a Protestant, Newman frequently reminded Catholics that their Church needed to reform itself before Protestants could be attracted to it. In a letter to an Irish theologian, he exclaimed: "O that you would reform your worship, that you would disown the extreme honors paid to St Mary and other Saints, your traditionary view of Indulgences, and the veneration paid in foreign countries to Images!"[41] Although Protestantism was itself an aberration, it was a reaction, Newman believed, to "some very grave errors on the side of Rome."[42] But as he drew nearer to Catholicism, Newman recognized that the Protestant Reformers had been disingenuous in attributing to Roman Catholics many tenets and practices that Catholics in fact condemned.[43]

Newman, in fact, came to realize that many of his own previous charges against Rome, especially his identification of the pope with Antichrist, were unjustified. In January 1843, more than two years before his conversion, he published a short retraction of some of his charges and epithets.[44] As a Catholic, he frequently asserted that the veneration and invocation of saints, including Mary, was not idolatrous or injurious to the sole mediatorship of Jesus Christ.[45]

Newman's whole career as a Catholic was marked by misunderstandings with hierarchical authorities and especially with Roman curial officials. Throughout these trials he remained remarkably patient. He never stridently protested; still less did he have any regrets about his conversion. He had come into the Church with open eyes, recognizing that on the human level it had many defects. As a quintessential Englishman, Newman felt a certain tension with the clerical culture of the Mediterranean world. In his diaries and personal letters he expressed the view that the Roman mentality was too abstract and doctrinaire to deal with the realities of the religious situation as he experienced it in England.

As a convert, Newman brought with him into the Church a critical spirit formed in the tradition of British philosophy. Nowhere does this appear so brilliantly as in his 1877 preface to the third edition of his *Via Media*.[46] Here he depicts the Church as a complex reality that preserves itself through the constant interaction of three principles—the rational, the devotional, and the political. The theologians, representing the rational or critical principle, tend to be cold, detached, even skeptical. The body of the faithful, representing the devotional, provide warmth and conviction, but they are inclined toward superstitious excesses. The hierarchical leaders, representing the political, provide unity and order, but they are tempted to make decisions based on mere expediency. Within the Church as a whole these three elements offset one another's weaknesses and thus provide a healthy equilibrium.

As a theologian, Newman greatly appreciated the importance of theological debate and reflection. His patristic studies gave him a sense of the slow historical processes by which errors are sifted out and corrected. He esteemed a measure of private judgment and local autonomy as one of the prerequisites without which no consensus could be genuine. It was Newman's vocation and destiny to oppose the excesses of Roman centralization. For this he earned some official distrust in his own lifetime but has won the acclaim of later generations. The ecumenical importance of Newman's principles for the self-criticism and self-reform of the Church was to be recognized by twentieth-century successors such as Yves Congar and Hans Küng.

ECUMENICAL STRATEGY

Some features of Newman's ecumenical strategy have by now become apparent. He rejoiced in the common heritage shared by all believers and sought to confirm Christians of every communion in those doctrines and practices that belonged to the general patrimony. In the attitude of faith itself Newman found an implicit commitment to the entire content of revelation and a promise of healthy growth.

One of the pillars of Newman's ecumenical policy was undoubtedly his conviction that everyone is subjectively obliged to follow the biddings of conscience. "I have always contended," he once wrote, "that obedience even to an erring conscience was the way to gain light."[47] Sensitive to the precepts of conscience, Newman was on guard against unsettling other Christians in their faith. On the very day of his reception into the Catholic Church, he wrote to his sister Jemima that his acceptance of the claims of the Roman Catholic Church was entirely "consistent with believing, as I firmly do, that individuals in the English Church are invisibly knit into that True Body of which they are not outwardly members—and consistent too with thinking it highly injudicious, indiscreet, wanton to interfere with them in particular cases."[48] While he wanted to urge those who were suitably prepared to take the step of becoming Catholics, he did not wish to undermine the piety of English popular religion. Far removed from fundamentalism, Newman was dubious about the historical accuracy of many biblical stories; but he lamented the reckless attacks of liberals on the reliability of the Bible because they deprived conservative Protestants of a needed support. "To unsettle the minds of a generation, when you give them no landmarks and no causeway across the morass is to undertake a great responsibility."[49]

Although Newman engaged freely in religious controversy when he felt it necessary to repel false charges, he observed certain ground rules. His published writings and his private correspondence alike are generally models of frank and courteous dialogue. Believing that "it does not mend matters for us to conceal our mutual differences," he held that real disagreements ought to be confessed "plainly though in charity."[50] He sought always to give a moderate exposition of Catholic doctrine that would not shock and repel the very persons whom one was seeking to persuade. He was particularly opposed to vituperation and personal abuse. Writing on April 13, 1866, to Henry James Coleridge, the Jesuit editor of the *Month*, on the occasion of that journal's response to Pusey's *Eirenicon*, Newman stated: "Abuse is as great a mistake in controversy as panegyric in biography."[51] Those who respond to Dr. Pusey, he cautioned, should bear in mind that their aim is to convince readers who respect and love that author.

For many years Newman was in correspondence with Ambrose Phil-lipps de Lisle, a Catholic layman who was enthusiastic about the prospects for reunion with the Anglicans. When de Lisle espoused the scheme of corporate union, Newman frankly appraised the project as unrealistic for reasons we have already seen. The Anglican Church, he believed, had never been more than partially Catholic, and its ecclesiastical organization was fundamentally Erastian. To make that Church genuinely Catholic would be to fashion a new creature: "It would be to turn a panther into a hind."[52]

In 1876 de Lisle favored a scheme to form an Anglican Uniate Church patterned on the Catholic Churches of the East. Newman expressed sym-pathy with this effort to draw good people into the Church, but he felt that this complicated plan would not commend itself to the Holy See unless there were a likelihood of bringing in a large part of the Church of England.[53] The plan soon collapsed because the Anglo-Catholics were unwilling to accept the recently defined dogma of papal infallibility and the proposal of conditional reordination.[54]

In some of his writings Newman expressed a clear desire for individual conversions. We must be anxious, he said, for all those who close their eyes to their heresy or schism and refuse to act on their knowledge of the divinity of the Catholic Church.[55] On the other hand, Newman as a Catholic refused to engage in a hunt for converts, and for this he was sometimes accused of a lack of zeal. In his journal for January 21, 1863, he wrote:

> At Propaganda, conversions, and nothing else, are the proof of doing any thing. Every where with Catholics, to make converts, is doing something; and not to make them, is "doing nothing." . . . But I am altogether differ-ent. . . . To me conversions were not the first thing, but the edification of Catholics. . . . I am afraid to make hasty converts of educated men, lest they should not have counted the cost, & should have difficulties after they have entered the Church. . . . [T]he Church must be prepared for converts, as well as converts prepared for the Church.[56]

The governing body of the Church, Newman surmised, were annoyed at his opinion that the Catholics of England were in need of a better education.[57]

While Newman was eager to receive individual converts who were properly prepared, he recognized that some might not have a personal call

to make this step. When his friend Samuel F. Wood died in 1843, Newman wrote to his sister Jemima: "I think he considered the Church of
Rome the true Church,—but thought God had placed him where he
was"—that is to say, in the Anglican communion.[58] Some decades later
Newman speculated that some Anglo-Catholics may have been providen-
tially "kept where they were, with no more light than they have, being
Anglicans in good faith in order gradually to prepare their hearers and
readers in greater numbers than would otherwise be possible for the true
and perfect faith."[59]

Newman does not seem to have had anything resembling an overall
strategy for restoring the unity of Christendom, much as he desired that
objective. It seems fair to say that he felt unable to visualize how this goal
could come to pass. He was therefore content to lay the groundwork and
to begin at the bottom. "Whatever tends to create a unity of heart between men of separate communions," he wrote, "lays the ground for
advances towards a restoration of that visible unity, the absence of which
among Christians is so great a triumph, and so great an advantage to the
enemies of the Cross."[60] Toward the end of his life he became increasingly
disturbed at the spread of atheism and irreligion, and as a result he came
to take greater satisfaction in the unity that already existed among religious minds. "I rejoice in it as one compensation of the cruel overthrow
of faith which we see on all sides of us, that, as the setting of the sun
brings out the stars, so great principles are found to shine out, which are
hailed by men of various religions as their own in common, when infidelity prevails."[61]

In these final years Newman sensed the rise of what we would today
call an ecumenical spirit: "Never did members of the various Christian
communions feel such tenderness for each other."[62] The first step toward
unity, Newman believed, must be "for religious minds, one and all, to
live upon the Gospels."[63] In another letter, written in January 1873 to the
same correspondent, he added that the result of the dawning movement
toward unity must be placed in God's hands. The differences are real and
beyond human power to solve. Nevertheless, Newman observed, "We
may hope that our good God has not put into the hearts of religious men
to wish and pray for unity, without intending in His own time to fulfill
the prayer. . . . [W]e may humbly hope that in our day, and till He
discloses to the hearts of men what the true faith is, He will, where hearts
are honest, take the will [to unity] for the deed."[64]

NEWMAN AND VATICAN II

Catholic ecumenism, properly so called, is almost entirely a twentieth-century phenomenon; it received its first real charter of legitimacy at the Second Vatican Council. In many respects, as others have said, Vatican II was Newman's council. It endorsed many of his general theological principles: for instance, his emphasis on guidance of conscience and the inner workings of the instinct of faith in the minds of believers, as well as his recognition of the value of theological pluralism and the need for gradual historical development in matters of doctrine. Ecumenically the recent council shared Newman's relatively optimistic assessment of the possibilities of saving faith among non-Catholic Christians who remain in good conscience outside the Catholic communion. It recognized the presence of grace, both covenanted and uncovenanted, in other Christian communities. It favored the kind of frank and open dialogue, unmarred by polemics or false irenicism, exemplified by Newman's letters, both private and published. The council also stressed, as did Newman, the intimate connection between the inner renewal of the Catholic Church itself and the prospects for broader Christian unity.

In one important respect Vatican II went beyond Newman. It held that the Orthodox churches and Protestant ecclesial communities have, as such, salvific importance.[65] Imperfect though they are, they in some way pertain to the mystery of the Church. The Church of Christ, in that sense, is more inclusive that the Roman Catholic communion. Yet the mystery of the Church is realized in institutionally complete form in Roman Catholicism and not elsewhere. The doctrine of Vatican II on the "subsistence" of the Church of Christ in the Catholic communion[66] differs in subtle but significant ways from Newman's teaching that the Catholic Church, and it alone, is the one ark of salvation. If Newman had anticipated that development, he might not have been at such pains to deny that other Christian communities utterly lack the attributes of the one, holy, catholic, and apostolic Church. But this realization would not, I think, have altered his insistence on the importance for individuals and groups to enter into full communion with the Roman Catholic Church. For Vatican II, like Newman, taught that God had made the Catholic Church necessary for salvation and that all who are in a position to know this have an obligation to enter that Church and remain in it.[67]

Newman, we may conclude, was a forerunner, standing on the threshold of a new ecumenical age. In him the convert spoke louder than the ecumenist. But he did succeed in combining a loyal adherence to the Catholic Church with a deep concern for Christian unity and a measure of appreciation for the workings of grace in other Christian communions. His frank and realistic appraisal of the obstacles to union can be a salutary corrective for a generation that is tempted to minimize the distinctive claims of every religious body.

NOTES

1. Heinrich Fries, "John Henry Newman: Ein Wegbereiter der christlichen Einheit," *Catholica* 15 (1961): 60–70. See also John Coulson, A. M. Allchin, and Meriol Trevor, *Newman: A Portrait Restored. An Ecumenical Revaluation* (London: Sheed & Ward, 1965); Johannes Artz, "Newman als Brücke zwischen Canterbury und Rom," *Una Sancta* 22 (1967): 173–85; Werner Becker, "Ökumenische Aspekte der Katholizität John Henry Newmans," in *Festgabe Joseph Lortz,* ed. Erwin Iserloh and Peter Manns (Baden-Baden: Bruno Grimm, 1958), 2:481–505; Matthias Laros, "Kardinal Newmans ökumenische Sendung," ibid., 2:469–79.

2. Newman to John Keble, June 8, 1844, in *Letters and Diaries of John Henry Newman* (Oxford: Clarendon; London: Nelson, 1961–2000), 10: 262; henceforth *LD*.

3. Newman to H. E. Manning, November 16, 1844, *LD* 10:412.

4. Quoted in Newman's *Apologia pro vita sua* (London: Longmans, Green, 1895), 230–31.

5. Newman to Jemima Mozley, March 15, 1845, *LD* 10:595.

6. Newman to Miss Rowe, September 16, 1873, in *LD* 26:364. Earlier, in *Certain Difficulties Felt by Anglicans in Catholic Teaching* (1850; Westminster, Md.: Christian Classics, 1969), Newman expressed his "intimate sense that the Catholic Church is the one ark of salvation" (1:4) and is "that Church in which alone is salvation" (1:5).

7. Newman to Edward Husband, July 17, 1870, *LD* 25:161.

8. Newman to Mrs. Christie, December 20, 1881, *LD* 30:33.

9. Newman, *Difficulties of Anglicans,* 1:170.

10. Ibid., 1:353.

11. Ibid., 1:351.

12. Ibid., 1:343.

13. "Lectures on the History of the Turks" (1853), in *Historical Sketches* (London: Basil, Montagu, Pickering, 1872), 1:192.

14. Ker, *JHN,* 403.

15. *Discourses to Mixed Congregations* (1850; London: Longmans, Green, 1909), 174.

16. Newman, *Difficulties of Anglicans,* 1:357.

17. Newman to C. W. Russell, April 26, 1841, *LD* 8:182.

18. Newman to George T. Edwards, February 24, 1887, *LD* 31:189.

19. See unpublished letter of November 1, 1864, in the archives of the Archdiocese of Philadelphia. This letter, to an unknown addressee, was quoted in full by Patrick T. Brannan in a paper delivered at the Newman Centenary Celebration at the University of Pennsylvania on May 15, 1990.

20. Louis Bouyer, preface to Thomas L. Sheridan, *Newman on Justification* (Staten Island, N.Y.: Alba, 1967), 12. In a recent article an eminent Anglican ecumenist remarks on the highly polemical character of the Lectures on Justification and on Newman's unfairness to Luther, but he concludes: "Like much else in Newman, the book is among the major muniments of the modern ecumenical movement." See Henry Chadwick, "The Lectures on Justification," in *Newman After a Hundred Years,* ed. Ian Ker and Alan G. Hill (Oxford: Clarendon, 1990), 287–308, quotation from 308.

21. In a letter to Ambrose Phillipps de Lisle, July 30, 1857, Newman takes the irreverence of the Anglican clergy toward the Blessed Sacrament as indirect evidence that they do not validly consecrate; *LD* 18:103–5. Writing to Edward Husband on July 17, 1870, Newman remarks that when he became a Catholic in 1845 he did not yet have "that utter distrust of the Anglican Orders which I feel in 1870," *LD* 25:160.

22. Newman, *Apologia,* 154, referring to four sermons preached at the end of 1843.

23. Newman to Helen Douglas Forbes, October 4, 1864, *LD* 21:249.

24. Newman to Mrs. Christie, December 20, 1881, *LD* 30:34.

25. Newman to J. M. Capes, December 24, 1850, and February 9 and February 18, 1851, *LD* 14:173, 207, 213–14.

26. Newman to Canon E. E. Estcourt, June 2, 1860, *LD* 19:352. This letter was not sent in exactly the same form as is here quoted from Newman's draft.

27. Newman to Isaac William, June 7, 1863, *LD* 20:460.

28. Newman, *Apologia,* 227, referring to a letter of September 1844.

29. Ibid., 340.

30. Ibid.

31. Unpublished letter in archives of Archdiocese of Philadelphia; see note 19 above.

32. Text in Newman, *Difficulties of Anglicans,* 2:1–170, esp. 9–11. Newman at this point had presumably forgotten having called the Anglican establishment a "bulwark" in the private letter to Capes of December 24, 1850, mentioned above.

33. "The Theory of Developments in Religious Doctrine," sermon 15 of Newman's *University Sermons,* ed. D. M. MacKinnon and J. D. Holmes (London: SPCK, 1970), 336.

34. Newman, *Discourses to Mixed Congregations,* discourse 13, "Mysteries of Nature and of Grace," 261.

35. Newman, *Essay in Aid of a Grammar of Assent* (1870; 7th ed., London: Longmans, Green, 188), 245.

36. Ibid., 499.

37. Newman, *Discourses to Mixed Congregations*, discourse 13, 261.

38. Ibid., 282.

39. Ian Ker, *John Henry Newman: A Biography*, reprint with corrections (Oxford: Claredon, 1989), 298.

40. Newman, *Apologia,* 198.

41. Newman to C. W. Russell, April 13, 1841, *LD* 8: 174.

42. Newman to C. W. Russell, April 26, 1841, *LD* 8:182.

43. Newman to R. W. Church, September 12, 1841, *LD* 8:266–68.

44. In Newman, *The Via Media of the Anglican Church* (London: Longmans, Green, 1896), 2:427–33; cf. Ker, *JHN,* 269, for the correct date of this retraction.

45. See, e.g., his "Letter to Pusey," *Difficulties of Anglicans,* 2:91–96.

46. Newman, *The Via Media of the Anglican Church* (London: Longmans, Green, 1911), 1:xv–xciv. See Avery Dulles, "The Threefold Office in Newman's Ecclesiology," in *Newman After a Hundred Years,* ed. Ker and Hill, 129–52.

47. Newman to Mrs. William Froude, early 1844; Ker, *JHN,* 284.

48. Newman to Jemima Mozley, October 9, 1845, *LD* 11:14.

49. Newman to Malcolm Maccoll, March 24, 1861, *LD* 20:488.

50. Newman to Principal David Brown, January 18, 1873, *LD* 26:234.

51. Newman to Henry James Coleridge, April 13, 1866, *LD* 22:211.

52. Newman to Ambrose Phillipps de Lisle, March 3, 1866, *LD* 22:170.

53. Newman to de Lisle of January 19 and January 27, 1876, *LD* 28:18, 20.

54. Ker, *JHN,* 695.

55. Newman, *Difficulties of Anglicans,* 1:358.

56. John Henry Newman, *Autobiographical Writings*, ed. Henry Tristram (London: Sheed & Ward, 1956), 257–58.

57. Ibid., 259.

58. Newman to Jemima Mozley, April 30, 1843; *LD* 9:321.

59. Newman to unknown correspondent, probably from early 1871, *LD* 25:260.

60. Newman to Henry Allon, January 28, 1868, *LD* 24:22.

61. Newman to Principal Brown, January 24, 1875, *LD* 27:188.

62. Newman to Principal Brown, October 24, 1872, *LD* 26:187.

63. Ibid., 188.

64. Newman to Principal Brown, November 3, 1873, 26:381.

65. *Unitatis redintegratio*, 3.

66. *Lumen gentium*, 8.

67. Ibid., 14.

6

The Uses of Scripture
in Theology

April 10, 1991

Over the centuries, the Catholic Church has accumulated a vast body of official teaching on the interpretation of Scripture.[1] The Council of Trent, warning against the dangers of private interpretation in matters pertaining to Christian doctrine regarding faith and morals,[2] declared that it is for the Church to decide on the true meaning and interpretation of Scripture and that Scripture is never to be interpreted contrary to the unanimous consensus of the Fathers (*EB* 62, *SD* 5).[3] Vatican Council I repeated the same warnings (*Dei Filius, EB* 78, *SD* 17).

The popes in their biblical encyclicals reiterated the same restrictions but also added positive encouragement for biblical scholars and theologians. Leo XIII in *Providentissimus Deus* (1893) praised the medieval interpreters for their care to preserve both the biblical texts and the patristic tradition of interpretation, as well as for the great precision with which they distinguished the various senses of the Bible, including those that were figurative or allegorical. While defending the primacy of the literal sense, Leo XIII pointed out the value of investigating the "other senses, adapted to illustrate dogma and confirm morality" (*EB* 108, *SD* 47, 49). Turning to theology, the pope laid down the principle, often repeated since his day, that "the use of Holy Scripture should influence the whole teaching of theology and should be practically its soul (*eiusque prope sit anima*)" (*EB* 114, *SD* 50).

Benedict XV in his encyclical *Spiritus Paraclitus* (1920) was understandably defensive against the recent incursions of Modernism, but in the positive portions of his encyclical he exhorted Catholic scholars to imitate the scholarship of Jerome in seeking out the literal sense and to see that any mystical interpretations are solidly based on the literal. "For all the children of the Church," he concluded, "we desire that, being saturated and strengthened by the Scriptures, they may arrive at the all-surpassing knowledge of Jesus Christ" (*EB* 495, *SD* 110).

Pius XII in *Divino afflante Spiritu* (1943) exhorted Catholic exegetes to take as their principal task the discovery and exposition of the literal sense, "so that the mind of the author may be made abundantly clear" (*EB* 550, *SD* 125). He reminded biblical interpreters of the need to take account of the various literary forms used by the ancient Semites so as to understand the texts correctly (*EB* 558–60, *SD* 128–30). Emphasizing the freedom of Catholic biblical scholars, the pope mentioned that "there are but few texts whose sense has been defined by the authority of the Church, nor are those more numerous about which the teaching of the Holy Fathers is unanimous" (*EB* 565, *SD* 132). At several points the pope exhorted exegetes not to confine themselves to historical and philological questions but to assist in determining the theological meaning of the sacred text, so as to be of assistance to professors of theology and to preachers (*EB* 551, 567, *SD* 126, 134).

The official teaching of the magisterium on the interpretation of Scripture was admirably summarized by Vatican II in its Dogmatic Constitution on Divine Revelation, *Dei Verbum*. In article 12, expressly devoted to biblical interpretation, the Constitution distinguished between two levels of meaning, the literal sense intended by the biblical writers themselves and the further understanding that may be attained thanks to "the content and coherence of Scripture as a whole, taking into account the whole Church's living tradition and the analogy of faith," that is to say, the harmony that exists among revealed truths. In later articles the Constitution encouraged Catholic students of the Bible to pursue a deeper penetration of the Scriptures based on the teaching of the Fathers and the testimony of sacred liturgies (*DV* 23). Repeating statements of Leo XIII and Benedict XV, the Constitution on Revelation declared that the study of the sacred page is, as it were, the soul of sacred theology (*DV* 24). At many points *Dei Verbum* made it clear that the theological interpretation of Scripture requires faith (*DV* 24), since "Sacred Scripture must be read and interpreted in the light of the same Spirit through whom it was written" (*DV* 12). In the perspectives of Christian faith, the council repeats the dictum of Augustine that "the New Testament is hidden in the Old, and that the Old Testament is manifest in the New" (*DV* 16).

One of the most instructive recent documents on the use of Scripture in theology is the statement of the Biblical Commission on *Scripture and Christology* issued in 1984.[4] This statement surveys eleven contemporary approaches to Christology and points out their respective assets and limitations.[5] While calling attention to what may be one-sided in these various approaches, the Biblical Commission adopts a basically positive attitude, accepting what is sound in each methodology. The commission concludes that an integral Christology must take account of the full content of the Bible and all aspects of the biblical witness.

In view of the profusion of approaches already current, the most pressing need is not for the elaboration of new methods but rather for a critical assessment of those already in use. The question is whether all the existing methods are legitimate, and whether they can comfortably coexist. Is the theologian compelled to choose certain methods and reject others? Although the methods could be multiplied almost endlessly, I shall try to summarize under ten headings the methods that seem most evident in contemporary theology.

1. *The Classical Doctrinal Approach.* For many centuries theologians, both Protestant and Catholic, have been using the Bible as a treasury of doctrinal statements or as an armory from which doctrines of the Church can be textually vindicated. Taking the Bible as an inspired and inerrant book, or at least as a normative source of Christian doctrine, theologians quote biblical texts that seem to support their own positions or the positions of their Church.

The Bible, for instance, states repeatedly that there is one God, Creator of heaven and earth, and that he is all-powerful, merciful, and faithful to his promises. It says further that the Word who exists eternally with the Father became incarnate in the womb of Mary, that Jesus Christ is the Son of God, that he died for our salvation and rose glorious from the dead. The Bible also tells us that Christ founded a Church, that he will be present with it till the end of time, and that participants in the Eucharist receive his body and blood. To a great extent, the creeds of the Church are a patchwork of citations from Scripture.

This use of Scripture was dominant in medieval and modern Scholasticism. Today it is much in use in fundamentalist and conservative Evangelical circles. No believing Christian will want to deny the value of scriptural affirmations for establishing or confirming points of doctrine. But in our time Catholic theologians, who have never accepted the idea that the Bible alone is the source of Christian truth, tend to be cautious about the conclusiveness of isolated "proof texts." Three main reservations may be indicated. In the first place, the real meaning of a text cannot always be rendered by a quotation out of context. Often it makes a great difference who is speaking, to whom, and for what purposes. The classical dogmatic use of Scripture tended to overlook the importance of context. Second, critical approaches to the Bible have shown that the understanding of the biblical authors developed gradually and that many statements in the Bible, especially those composed in the early stages of salvation history, fall short of definitive truth. Confessional statements that express the faith of the whole Church after Pentecost usually have greater doctrinal value than statements embodying the personal theology of an individual author. It needs to be recognized, in the third place, that the biblical language is often poetic, hyperbolic, or metaphorical. The language of exhortation and of love differs from the language of doctrine. Although the Bible does contain propositional statements, excessive concentration on this aspect of Scripture can lead to an impoverishment or distortion of the true meaning.

These reservations do not invalidate the method itself. But the need to state these reservations indicates the importance of other methods that will be examined as this paper proceeds.

2. *Biblical Theology.* A healthy reaction against the use of isolated proof texts came about with the rise of biblical theology, especially during the decade following World War II. Many biblical scholars at that time attempted to synthesize the teaching of the Bible in terms of biblical concepts such as creation and redemption, word and spirit. Some tried to capture the unity of the whole Bible under rubrics such as covenant (W. Eichrodt), the history of traditions (G. von Rad), or God's "elusive presence" (S. Terrien). Others produced studies on "biblical themes" (J. Guillet) or on key terms such as revelation (W. Bulst), work (A. Richardson), baptism (T. F. Torrance), and time (O. Cullmann). In the United States, Protestants such as Paul S. Minear and James D. Smart and Catholics

such as John L. McKenzie were prominent in the biblical theology movement. These scholars sought to do justice to the diversity as well as the unity of the biblical materials, and to exhibit how the Old Testament themes became enriched and progressively transformed as they found their way into the New Testament.

In the biblical theology movement it was rather commonly held that the terminology of the Bible reflected specific styles of thought that should be contrasted with nonbiblical thinking, especially with Greek concepts, which were viewed as alien to Christian faith. This thesis was defended, for example, in Thorlief Boman's *Hebrew Thought Compared with Greek*.[6] Oscar Cullmann in his popular *Christ and Time*[7] gave the impression of holding that the biblical concepts of time were normative for faith, and that classical Greek philosophies of time were to be rejected as unbiblical. Thus divine authority was given not merely to the teaching of Scripture but to the very concepts and terms in which the biblical authors expressed themselves. Catholic theologians objected, correctly in my opinion, that the biblical message could be translated into other idioms, making use of different philosophical frameworks.

3. *Spiritual Exegesis.* A number of Catholic theologians during the 1940s and 1950s, advocating a return to the biblical and patristic sources, revived the kind of "spiritual exegesis" that they found in the Greek Fathers and medieval monastic theologians. For Louis Bouyer the Christian reader must seek in the Bible "not a dead word, imprisoned in the past, but a living word, immediately addressed to the man of today . . . a word which affects him, since it is for him that it was uttered and remains uttered."[8] The spiritual meaning, for Henri de Lubac, interprets the Jewish past from the viewpoint of the Christian present. The contemporary Christian studies the Bible in order to live by it: "This is his own history, from which he cannot remove himself. This history interests him personally. It is a mystery which is also his own mystery, identically. . . . He 'searches the Scriptures' to discover God's thoughts and designs on him."[9] For de Lubac this point of view is not a matter of private devotion or spirituality but of theology properly defined. In patristic times, he contends, the so-called mystical meaning was always considered the doctrinal meaning par excellence, as the meaning that disclosed the mysteries relating to Christ and the Church.[10] He quotes Dom Célestin Charlier to the effect that exegesis, for the Fathers, "consists in drawing forth the

profound and objective significance of a text, in the light of the entire economy of salvation."[11]

Hans Urs von Balthasar holds that God's word in Scripture has an essentially Christological form. Christ delivers himself to the Church under two forms, as Scripture and as Eucharist. The Holy Spirit as primary author leads those who read the Scripture in the Church to understand the inner spiritual meaning: "Scripture therefore is *God speaking to man*. It means a word that is not past but present, because eternal, a word spoken to me personally and not simply to others."[12]

Yves Congar, whose interpretation of Scripture likewise deserves to be called spiritual, holds that "the meaning of Scripture must be communicated by the Spirit of God in a revelatory action whose fruit in us is Christian knowledge, 'gnosis.'"[13] Such gnosis, accessible within the Church, manifests the unity of the two testaments and enables councils to achieve unanimity about matters of faith. Scripture, therefore, must be read within the Church, within the tradition.

This "spiritual exegesis," in my estimation, incorporates some of the finest insights of the biblical theology movement. It also comes close to the "pneumatic exegesis" of Karl Barth, who will be considered in next section. It must be acknowledged, however, that an excessive enthusiasm for spiritual meanings led in some cases to fanciful allegorical interpretations, such as those developed by Paul Claudel, who exhibited an intemperate hostility to modern critical scholarship. A corrective may be found in historical-critical analysis, which, as we shall see, emphasizes the controlling importance of the literal sense.

4. *Word Theology*. A Protestant counterpart to spiritual exegesis is provided by Karl Barth, who made use of "pneumatic exegesis" in his theology of the word of God. By the "word of God" Barth meant not the dead letter of Scripture but the living Christ who speaks to us here and now through the inspired words of Scripture. The word of God, for him, was not simply the text but the event in which the reader encounters God today. The canonical books are those in which the Church has heard God speaking in the past and in which it hopes to hear his voice again.

Barth insisted that the exegete must be a believer. To gain any understanding of the biblical message and of God, who is its essential content, one must have a personal affinity with God through faith. The Holy Spirit actively inspires not only the authors of the Bible but also believers who read it in the Church today. Divine life encounters us only when it is pleased to do so: "Hence one cannot lay down conditions which, if observed, guarantee the hearing of the Word. There is no method by which revelation can be made revelation that is actually received, no method of scriptural exegesis which is truly pneumatic, i.e., which articulates the witness to revelation in the Bible and to that degree really introduces the Pneuma."[14]

Barth maintains, on the basis of Scripture itself, that God's self-revelation occurs principally in Jesus Christ, the incarnate Word of God. Through the Christ event God personally encounters humanity. Theology, seeking to explicate the character of God as agent, listens to God as he speaks to the Church today through the Scriptures. Not only the express statements of Scripture, but the patterns of biblical narrative, including saga and legend, can mediate an encounter with God's living and personal word.[15]

Barth's theology of the word, as already noted, harmonizes well with some tendencies in Catholic biblical theology and spiritual exegesis. His emphasis on the personal action of the living word seems to have influenced Bouyer, de Lubac, and von Balthasar. But Barth is more inclined than his Catholic colleagues to make a dichotomy between God's word and human understanding, and between the authority of the Bible and that of the Church. Questions can be raised about whether Barth himself succeeded in sealing the interpretation of Scripture off from his own philosophical presuppositions and from the influence of his own Church tradition as thoroughly as he claimed to do. But his summons to be attentive to the word of God, and to avoid imposing our own meanings on it, retains its pertinence.

5. *Existential Hermeneutics; Theology of Proclamation.* About the same time that Barth was working out his word theology, Rudolf Bultmann was attracting great attention with his existential hermeneutics. Influenced by the philosophy of the early Heidegger, Bultmann contended that the real intention of the Bible was to impart an authentic self-understanding to the human person struggling to attain authentic existence. The New Testament kerygma, according to Bultmann, speaks to man as a historical (*geschichtlich*), responsible, future-oriented being. The biblical message of the cross and resurrection of Jesus comes to the reader or hearer as a summons to radical obedience, detachment, freedom, openness, and trust. It rids us of fear and anxiety in the face of suffering and death.

The biblical message, according to Bultmann, is encased in ancient mythological structures of thought and language that make it difficult for contemporary readers, whose worldview is shaped by science and technology, to grasp the real meaning. Bultmann therefore instituted a program of demythologizing the New Testament. He tried to strip away the mythological structures in order to retrieve the existential meaning that lies hidden beneath them. As a scientific exegete he felt entitled to take a very skeptical position regarding the historical value of the Bible, including the words and deeds of Jesus as reported in the Gospels.

During the 1950s and 1960s some disciples of Bultmann, notably Ernst Fuchs and Gerhard Ebeling, somewhat modified Bultmann's positions under the influence of Heidegger's later philosophy. The Bible, they held, must be understood as a stage in the history of the word of God. The biblical word is efficacious; it produces a history of transmission and interpretation, and this "effective history," in turn, illuminates the original word. The word of God, as a living subject, challenges the reader and demands a response. Hermeneutics, as a study of the word event, aims to clear the way for effective proclamation of the word and removing obstacles to contemporary interpretation. Theology, as a hermeneutical discipline, must attend to the word of God and contribute to the effective proclamation of the word in the Church today, so that hearers are challenged to respond with trust and submission.

The hermeneutical theology of the Bultmann school proved helpful to many readers who wanted to remain Christians but found it hard to accept the miraculous and apparently legendary features of the Bible. Conservative Protestants, who based their faith on the authority of the Bible, regarded Bultmann as a dangerous heretic. Catholics, who believed that the Bible always had to be interpreted in the light of philosophical and scientific knowledge, saw some merits in the Bultmannian program, but they objected that its purely existential exegesis was too narrow. The Bible, they insisted, had a lot to tell us about God and not only about human self-understanding. The Bultmann school, I would agree, concentrated too narrowly on the existential categories of address and response. And many of members of the school, including Bultmann himself, had an exaggerated antipathy to the supernatural. Thus this school, like many others, was more valuable in what it affirmed than in what it dismissed or denied.[16]

6. *The Experiential-Expressive Approach.* A widespread trend in the use of Scripture may be characterized, in the terminology of George Lindbeck, as "experiential-expressive."[17] This approach, which may be traced back to Friedrich Schleiermacher, is a theological counterpart of the philosophical "turn to the subject" commonly attributed to Immanuel Kant. Karl Rahner, though he uses more than one approach, speaks of Scripture primarily as a historically and situationally conditioned deposit in which the utterly simple "experience of the divine grace of faith" comes to expression.[18] Scripture, he says, is "one of the ways, although a preeminent way, in which God's revelatory self-communication to man becomes explicit and thematic in history."[19] The theologian turns to the Bible to recover the foundational experiences of the early community, to make those experiences intelligible to men and women of our day, and to express them in ways that evoke and confirm the contemporary experience of grace, which, prior to all theological reflection "has already been experienced and lived through more originally in the depths of existence."[20]

This experiential approach is widespread in current theology. Gregory Baum, for example, writes: "The Bible is the test, norm, and judge in the church by purifying and reassuring Christians in their own experience of life."[21] David Tracy uses the concept of the religious classic as his point of departure for understanding Scripture. By classics he means "certain expressions of the human spirit [that] so disclose a compelling truth about our lives that we cannot deny them some kind of normative status."[22] The Scriptures are "the normative, more relatively adequate expressions of the community's past and present experience of the Risen Lord, the crucified one, Jesus Christ."[23]

Unlike the schools previously examined, theologians of this experiential school are reluctant to speak of the Bible as the word of God. They tend to place the locus of authority not in the text itself but in some prior experience that is regarded as compelling and therefore normative. Edward Schillebeeckx, at least in his *Jesus* volume,[24] is more concerned with reconstructing Jesus's "original *Abba*-experience,"[25] and the "Easter-experience" of the disciples[26] than with the biblical testimonies to the message of Jesus and the resurrection. These original experiences, for Schillebeeckx, are important insofar as they can serve as paradigms and catalysts for Christian experience today. The word of Scripture is brought into "critical correlation" with our own experience so that the relative adequacy of each can be assessed.[27]

A major difficulty in this approach is the ambiguity in the term "experience." It is widely recognized today that we do not have some pure experience prior to thought and word, but that our experience is largely molded by the presuppositions and interpretative categories we bring to it. Religious experience is not a mere matter of God being perceived in the depths of the soul. To classify any experience as "religious" is a matter of interpretation, and the interpretation is inevitably dependent on social and historical factors. The Bible may indeed intensify and direct our spiritual experience, but it can hardly do so unless we are prepared to accept the interpretation that the biblical authors put on their own experiences and on the tradition that had come down to them. Thus the experiential approach to Scripture cannot stand on its own.

7. *Authorial Intention.* A broad current of biblical scholarship still looks on the Bible as a trustworthy rendition of the truth that God intended to disclose through the inspired authors. Using all modern techniques of investigation, these scholars seek to establish the literal meaning, that is to say, the meaning that the inspired authors intended and expressed by their words. This method of interpretation is identified with notable Catholic exegetes such as Raymond E. Brown and Joseph A. Fitzmyer, who have recently written defenses of their approach against critics from within the exegetical community.[28] They do not contend that the meaning established by their discipline is determinative for tradition and dogma, but that it needs to be taken into account, and that the divinely intended meaning, at the very least, cannot contradict the literal meaning. Shared by many Anglican, Lutheran, and other Protestant scholars trained in the universities of Europe and North America, this approach has proved very useful in ecumenical dialogues for arriving at a measure of consensus about the meaning of the Bible as the basic document of Christian faith. Historical-critical biblical studies of this kind have been fruitfully used in ecumenical dialogues, for example, in the volumes on Peter, Mary, and righteousness commissioned or composed by the Lutheran-Catholic Dialogue in the United States.[29]

The method of interpreting texts by seeking out the intention of the authors has come under attack from new trends in literary criticism, which assert that the meaning of any text is separable from what the author intended by it. Texts, it is argued, take on meaning from the context in which they are handed down and from the perspectives of the readers. In the case of Scripture we have the additional problem that for many texts there may have been no author in the modern sense of that word. The so-called author is simply the redactor of an oral tradition or fragmentary documents that originated and grew anonymously. For other texts, which presumably have an author, we cannot identify the place and time of composition.

Admitting that these difficulties are not without force, defenders of the "authorial intention" position reply that for many texts one can say approximately what the author must have intended and what would presumably have been understood by readers in the Old Testament and New Testament communities. Besides, as Brown and others assert, the meaning intended and expressed by the first author is not terminal. Historical-critical study can identify trajectories of development within the Bible and thus point the way to later doctrinal developments in Church tradition.[30] The Church may well insist on traditional and dogmatic meanings that go beyond the intention of the first author, but the original literal meaning, which was divinely inspired, can be used to correct misinterpretations that may have arisen at a later time. Brown himself has written extensively on the "more-than-literal" meanings that flow from the text as taken up into the canon, the tradition, and the teaching of the Church. This series of hierarchically ordered meanings (which begins with the literal meaning but goes well beyond it) can be very helpful to the theologian; it harmonizes well with the teaching on the interpretation of Scripture in Vatican II's Dogmatic Constitution, *Dei Verbum*, article 12.

With these reservations and modifications, the method that seeks out the "authorial intention" merits approval. The more we know about the original text and the author's intention, the better shall we be positioned to propose and evaluate further interpretations that purport to go beyond the literal.

8. *Historical Reconstruction.* Another form of historical-critical study tends to probe beneath the texts in order to find a meaning anterior to them. Liberal Protestants such as Adolf Harnack believed that by identifying the earliest sources, those closest to the actual events, scholars could achieve a reliable historical reconstruction. In particular, Harnack tried to get to the words and deeds of Jesus by using a combination of the Gospel of Mark and a hypothetical source named "Q." This quest for the historical Jesus is carried on more cautiously today by theologians such as the Protestant Wolfhart Pannenberg and the Catholic Hans Küng. Their assumption is, or seems to be, that revelation is most clearly given when it

first comes, rather than in subsequent reflection. In the case of Pannenberg, the operative assumption is that revelation consists primarily in God's deeds in history, especially in the person and career of Jesus.

This approach to Scripture is not without value insofar as, by showing that the Christian story has a solid foundation in fact, it can serve to strengthen faith. In addition, believers cannot fail to have a keen interest in all that throws light on the dealings of God with his people, and especially on the words and deeds of Jesus, whom all Christians seek to follow. As contrasted with the experiential school, this school respects the objective givenness of the contents of faith and refrains from equating redemption or revelation with a direct experience of the transcendent. But still there are difficulties. The scholars who reconstruct the events of sacred history have not succeeded in achieving an agreed reconstruction of the past. It is all but impossible to prevent the bias of the historian from predetermining what will be found. All too often, the historians adopt methodological presuppositions that are alien to Christian faith and achieve only fragile hypotheses, incapable of sustaining the weight of faith or serving as the basis of a solid theology. The deeds of God in salvation history are not Christian revelation except as taken up into the inspired word of Scripture and the preaching of the Church, which treasures the Scripture as a privileged text.

9. *Narrative Theology; The Cultural-Linguistic Approach.* A number of contemporary theologians, dissatisfied with the dogmatic, experientialist, and historicist approaches, are returning to something like the biblical theology of the mid-twentieth century. Professing what they call a narrative theology, they hold that the Bible consists primarily of stories and that it should be accepted on its own terms rather than forced into alien categories by people who read it with an agenda formed by the contemporary secular world.

From the Catholic side, Johann Baptist Metz is prominent for his insistence that Christianity is a community that cherishes the "narrative and evocative memory of the passion, death, and resurrection of Jesus. The logos of the cross and resurrection has a narrative structure."[31] In fact, he maintains, Scripture has from beginning to end a fundamentally narrative character. As a consequence, Metz believes, theology must have a narrative and practical structure. While admitting that argumentation may have a legitimate place in theology, he insists that its primary function is "to protect the narrative memory of salvation in a scientific world, to allow it to be at stake and to prepare the way for a renewal of this narrative, without which the experience of salvation is silenced."[32]

In the United States the late Hans Frei of Yale University maintained that the meaning of the Bible can only be the fruit of the stories themselves, which communicate the subject matter to the reader by the interaction of persons and events. Interpretation must appropriate the narrative in its own right and not pose questions that arise out of a different horizon.[33]

George Lindbeck, influenced by his Yale colleague Frei, proposes a "cultural-linguistic" theology. From the patristic age until after the Reformation, he notes, Scripture served as "the lens through which theologians viewed the world" rather than as "an object of study whose religiously significant or literal meaning was located outside itself."[34] For the reinvigoration of Christianity, he maintains, the Scriptures must regain their position as canonical texts, in the sense that they create their own domain of meaning. "A scriptural world," he writes, is "able to absorb the universe. It supplies the interpretive framework within which believers seek to live their lives and understand reality."[35] For this cultural-linguistic approach it is not crucial to distinguish between certain biblical passages that are, and others that are not, historically or scientifically exact. The Bible can be taken seriously even when its history or science is challenged: "As parables such as that of the prodigal son remind us, the rendering of God's character is not in every instance logically dependent on the factuality of the story."[36]

These theologians are correct, I believe, in holding that the revelatory power of the Bible is diminished if one does not allow the stories to work in a symbolic way on the reader's affections and imagination. Modern rationalistic criticism has often neglected this dimension. But it must be asked what task remains for theology. Ronald Thiemann, who like Lindbeck is a follower of Hans Frei, holds that "theology is primarily concerned with the interpretation of text and tradition and only secondarily, if at all, with speculations about the true nature of the self and the deep structures of human understanding."[37] He goes on to say that the conception he espouses

> sees the primary theological task to be the critical redescription of the Christian faith in categories consistent with the church's first-order language. It eschews the systematic correlation of Christian concepts with

those of a philosophical anthropology and thus resists theology's "turn to the subject." Its primary interest in biblical narrative is in discerning God's identity as agent in the text and in the on-going life of the Christian community.[38]

Although I recognize real value in the narrative theology fashioned along the lines proposed by Thiemann and Metz, I am not convinced that the predominantly narrative structure of the Bible requires that theology retain the narrative mode. Theology, as a reflective discipline, cannot content itself with describing or redescribing the biblical story. It may be expected to explore the deeper implications of that story, as it has done in elaborating the attributes of God and the doctrine of the Trinity. Pheme Perkins wisely observes:

> Narrative analysis does not yield the kind of conceptual syntheses which might provide the introductory paragraphs to systematic expositions of Christology, ecclesiology, Christian discipleship, or ethics. . . . In the Christian tradition our stories have provoked theological and ethical reflection, but they do not hand us theology or ethics on a platter ready for consumption.[39]

While using a biblical framework, theology can ask questions not asked in the Bible itself, and in answering these questions it need not confine itself to biblical concepts and categories. Augustine and Thomas Aquinas can provide models of how to insert questions arising out of Platonic and Aristotelian philosophy into a domain of meaning established by the Bible.[40]

10. *Liberation Theology.* Metz's narrative theology already leans somewhat in a liberationist direction, since the "dangerous memories" of the passion of Jesus, in his view, provoke protests against the injustice and violence reigning in our world. A more specific and constructive social program is involved in Latin American liberation theology as typified, for example, in the work of Gustavo Gutiérrez, Juan Luis Segundo, J. Severino Croatto, and José Miguez Bonino.

In general, these authors may be said to adopt a kind of hermeneutical circle, which begins and ends with the existing social reality. Analyzing the situation in which they find themselves, these theologians consciously adopt a partiality based on a commitment to the poor and the oppressed. In light of that commitment, they adopt a "hermeneutics of suspicion," contesting all readings of Scripture that do not favor their own social orientation. Conversely, they select in the Bible passages that confirm their own options. Then they proclaim the gospel as they have interpreted it within the context of their commitment to liberation. Only in that context, they hold, is it possible to understand the implications of the gospel and give in a real impact.

According to Segundo, Latin American liberation theology "is known to have a preference and a partiality for the Old Testament in general, and for the Exodus event in particular,"[41] for in no other portion of Scripture does God the liberator reveal himself in such close connection with the political plane of human existence. On the other hand, Jesus and Paul seem to be almost unconcerned with, if not opposed to, liberation from political oppression.

An approach similar to Segundo's may be found in the black liberation theology of James Cone and in the feminist exegesis of Elisabeth Schüssler Fiorenza. Fiorenza, for example, starts with an analysis of the oppression of women today, then proceeds to unmask the oppressive patriarchal structures in the Bible, and finally calls attention to nonandrocentric elements in Scripture that can be used for grounding a theology of feminist liberation.[42]

In favor of liberation hermeneutics, one may say that a deliberately partial reading permits one to see certain implications that might otherwise escape notice, but at the same time this selective approach can blind the interpreter to lessons that ought to be gained from the text. Gregory Baum, in a sympathetic critique of Segundo, calls attention to the need for the originating experience to stand up under the verdict of Scripture. As Segundo analyzes it, the initial experience seems not to be subject to any critical examination at all. For this reason, says Baum, Segundo neglects the personal dimension of life in favor of the social. He has little to say about central features of human life such as birth and death, friendship and love.[43] In an official critique, the Congregation for the Doctrine of the Faith in 1984 called attention to the danger of radically politicizing the affirmations of faith and thus reading the Bible in too narrow a framework. More specifically, liberation hermeneutics tends to overlook the transcendence and gratuity of grace and to secularize the kingdom of God.[44]

I am aware that the ten categories in this paper do not exhaust all the possibilities of hermeneutics. Other approaches are in use among historians and literary critics. I have attempted to keep my eye fixed on the theological literature and to ask how systematic theologians have in fact been using the Bible.

All ten of the approaches described in this paper are in my opinion verifiable on the contemporary theological scene. It would be a mistake to dismiss any of them as worthless. All have their distinctive values and would defy incorporation into a single unified methodology. The coexistence of different styles or "models" is healthy and desirable. Different methodologies may be useful, depending on the precise questions being asked.

A given theologian, pursuing a particular project, may legitimately adopt one approach or another as a primary tool of investigation. My own present leaning would be toward a method that makes use of historical critical studies to assure a solid foundation in the biblical sources themselves but does so under the continuous guidance of tradition and magisterial teaching. An adequate theological use of Scripture, I believe, would build also on the achievements of biblical theology and the kind of spiritual exegesis described above. An interpretation that limited itself to the historical-critical phase would overlook the tacit meanings conveyed by the biblical stories, symbols, and metaphors. A comprehensive approach, combining scientific and spiritual exegesis, would do better justice to Catholic tradition and the directives of Vatican Council II. In addition, such an approach best serves the needs of systematic theology.

NOTES

1. For a concise survey, see Raymond E. Brown and Thomas Aquinas Collins, "Church Pronouncements," in *The New Jerome Biblical Commentary*, ed. Raymond E. Brown, Joseph A. Fitzmyer, and Roland E. Murphy (Englewood Cliffs, N.J.: Prentice-Hall, 1990), 1166–74.

2. *"In rebus fidei et morum,"* DS 1507. The word *morum* can also be translated "of customs" and is so translated in *Decrees of the Ecumenical Councils*, ed. Norman P. Tanner (Washington, D.C.: Georgetown University Press, 1990), 664.

3. The letters *EB* in this paper stand for *Enchiridion Biblicum*, 4th ed., Rome: A. Arnodo, 1961). The numerals stand for the paragraph numbers in the margins. For

English translations see *Rome and the Study of Scripture*, 7th ed. (St. Meinrad, Ind.: Grail, 1962), and *Official Catholic Teachings: Bible Interpretation*, ed. James J. Megivern (Wilmington, N.C.: Consortium, 1978). The letters *SD* followed by numerals stand for page numbers in *The Scripture Documents*, ed. Dean Béchard (Collegeville, Minn.: Liturgical Press, 2002).

4. See Joseph A. Fitzmyer, *Scripture and Christology: A Statement of the Biblical Commission with Commentary* (New York: Paulist Press, 1986).

5. These methodologies may be roughly designated as follows:

(1) The classical approach based on dogmatic texts and sources;

(2) Revisionist approaches based on historical consciousness;

(3) Efforts to reconstruct the life and teaching of Jesus through historical probing;

(4) A refinement of this latter approach with data from the history of religions;

(5) Study of Jesus in light of Palestinian Judaism;

(6) Approaches through salvation history;

(7) A variety of anthropological approaches;

(8) Existentialist interpretations;

(9) Sociological and liberationist perspectives;

(10) Constructive systematic approaches;

(11) Further refinements of these constructive approaches in Christologies "from above" and "from below."

Some of these approaches are strictly exegetical; others involve larger hermeneutical programs. This lecture was published too early to take into account the document of the Biblical Commission on "The Interpretation of the Bible in the Church" (1993).

6. Thorlief Boman, *Hebrew Thought Compared with Greek* (London: SCM, 1960).

7. Oscar Cullmann, *Christ and Time* (Philadelphia: Westminster, 1950).

8. Louis Bouyer, "Liturgie et exégèse spirituelle," *La Maison-Dieu* 7 (1946): 30. Cf. Henri de Lubac, *Sources of Revelation* (New York: Herder and Herder, 1968), 73.

9. De Lubac, *Sources of Revelation*, 27–28.

10. Ibid., 12, 49.

11. Célestin Charlier, *The Christian Approach to the Bible* (Westminster, Md.: Newman, 1958), 255–63; cf. de Lubac, *Sources of Revelation*, 13.

12. Hans Urs von Balthasar, "The Word, Scripture, and Tradition," in *Word and Revelation: Essays in Theology* (New York: Herder and Herder, 1964), 1:9–30, quotation from 26–27.

13. Yves M.-J. Congar, *Tradition and Traditions: An Historical and a Theological Essay* (New York: Macmillan, 1967).

14. Karl Barth, *Church Dogmatics* (Edinburgh: T. & T. Clark, 1956), 183. See Thomas E. Provence, "The Sovereign Subject Matter: Hermeneutics in the *Church*

Dogmatics," in *A Guide to Contemporary Hermeneutics,* ed. Donald K. McKim (Grand Rapids, Mich.: Eerdmans, 1986), 241–62, at 251; also Mark I. Wallace, "Karl Barth's Hermeneutic: A Way Beyond the Impasse," *Journal of Religion* 68 (1988): 396–410, at 408.

15. For a compact account of Barth's use of Scripture see, in addition to the articles already cited, David H. Kelsey, *The Uses of Scripture in Recent Theology* (Philadelphia: Fortress, 1975), 39–55. Kelsey finds in Barth a "narrative theology" similar to that of Kelsey's Yale colleague Hans W. Frei, which I shall take up in my ninth category.

16. In these paragraphs I summarize a longer exposition and critique in my article "Hermeneutical Theology," *Communio: International Catholic Review* 6 (1979): 16–37. See also Anthony C. Thistleton, "The New Hermeneutic," in *Guide to Contemporary Hermeneutics,* ed. McKim, 78–107, and Joseph Cardinal Ratzinger, "Biblical Interpretation in Crisis: On the Question of the Foundations and Approaches of Exegesis Today," in *Biblical Interpretation in Crisis: The Ratzinger Conference on Bible and Church,* ed. Richard John Neuhaus (Grand Rapids, Mich.: Eerdmans, 1989), 1–23.

17. George Lindbeck, *The Nature of Doctrine* (Philadelphia: Westminster, 1984), 16, 31–32, and passim.

18. Karl Rahner, "Theology in the New Testament," *Theological Investigations* (Baltimore: Helicon, 1966), 5:37–38.

19. Karl Rahner, *Foundations of Christian Faith* (New York: Crossroad, 1978), 370.

20. Ibid., 17.

21. Gregory Baum, "The Bible as Norm," *The Ecumenist* 9 (July–August 1971): 75.

22. David Tracy, *The Analogical Imagination* (New York: Crossroad, 1981), 108.

23. Ibid., 248.

24. Edward Schillebeeckx, *Jesus: An Experiment in Christology* (New York: Seabury/Crossroad, 1979).

25. Ibid., 256.

26. Ibid., 379–97.

27. For criticism see George Lindbeck in his "Scripture, Consensus and Community," in *Biblical Interpretation in Crisis,* 74–101, esp. 87–88; also Garrett Green, *Imagining God: Theology and the Religious Imagination* (San Francisco: Harper & Row, 1989), 119–23.

28. See Raymond E. Brown, "The Contribution of Historical Biblical Criticism to Ecumenical Church Discussion," in *Biblical Interpretation in Crisis,* 24–49; Joseph A. Fitzmyer, "Historical Criticism: Its Role in Biblical Interpretation and Church Life," *Theological Studies* 50 (1989): 244–59.

29. Raymond E. Brown et al., *Peter in the New Testament: A Collaborative Assessment by Protestant and Roman Catholic Scholars* (Minneapolis: Augsburg and New

York: Paulist, 1973); Raymond E. Brown et al., *Mary in the New Testament: A Collaborative Assessment by Protestant and Roman Catholic Scholars* (Philadelphia: Fortress and New York: Paulist, 1978); John Reumann, *"Righteousness" in the New Testament*, with responses by Joseph A. Fitzmyer and Jerome D. Quinn (Philadelphia: Fortress and New York: Paulist, 1982).

30. Brown, "The Contribution," 28–29.

31. Johann Baptist Metz, *Faith in History and Society* (New York: Seabury/Crossroad 1980), 212.

32. Ibid., 213.

33. See Hans W. Frei, Preface, *The Identity of Jesus Christ: The Hermeneutical Bases of Dogmatic Theology* (Philadelphia: Fortress, 1975), vi–xviii; also Frei's earlier work, *The Eclipse of Biblical Narrative* (New Haven, Conn.: Yale University Press, 1974).

34. Lindbeck, *The Nature of Doctrine*, 119.

35. Ibid., 117.

36. Ibid., 122.

37. Ronald F. Thiemann, *Revelation and Theology: The Gospel as Narrated Promise* (Notre Dame, Ind.: University of Notre Dame, 1985), 83.

38. Ibid., 84.

39. Pheme Perkins, "Crisis in Jerusalem? Narrative Criticism in New Testament Studies," *Theological Studies* 50 (1989): 296–313, quotation from 312–13.

40. Lindbeck himself concedes this in *The Nature of Doctrine*, 117.

41. Juan Luis Segundo, *The Liberation of Theology* (Maryknoll, N.Y.: Orbis, 1976), 110.

42. An excellent example is Elisabeth Schüssler Fiorenza's *In Memory of Her: A Feminist Theological Reconstruction of Christian Origins* (New York: Crossroad, 1986). For a helpful survey of the various trends see Phyllis Trible, "Five Loaves and Two Fishes: Feminist Hermeneutics and Biblical Theology," *Theological Studies* 50 (1989): 279–95.

43. Gregory Baum, "The Theological Method of Segundo's *The Liberation of Theology*," *Proceedings of the Catholic Theological Society of America* 32 (1977): 120–24.

44. Congregation for the Doctrine of the Faith, "Instruction on Certain Aspects of the 'Theology of Liberation,'" *Origins* 14 (September 13, 1984): 193–204.

7

John Paul II and the New Evangelization

December 4–5, 1991

T he majority of Catholics are not strongly inclined toward evangelization. The very term has for them a Protestant ring. The Catholic Church is highly dogmatic, sacramental, and hierarchical in
character. Its activities are primarily directed toward the instruction and
pastoral care of its own members, whose needs and demands tax the institution to its limits. Absorbed in the inner problems of the Church, and
occasionally in issues of peace and justice, contemporary Catholics feel
relatively little responsibility for spreading the faith.

EVANGELIZATION IN HISTORY

The Catholic Church has, of course, a long history of missionary involvement. In the early Middle Ages the Benedictine monks evangelized much
of Europe. Since the sixteenth century the extension of Christianity beyond Europe was considered to be the special vocation of missionary
orders and societies rather than the responsibility of all members of the
Church. Even in these restricted circles Catholics before Vatican II spoke
rarely of evangelization. They used terms such as missionary activity, the
propagation of the faith, and the planting or extension of the Church.

In predominantly Christian territories Catholics showed no lack of
interest in convert making, but again the thrust was not evangelical; the
gospel was hardly at the center. This apostolate was mainly directed to

showing, against Protestants, that Christ had founded a hierarchical Church, which was to be accepted as the organ of divine revelation. The focus was more on authority than on content. Catholics were instructed to believe whatever the Church taught precisely because it was Church teaching.

The terminology of evangelization came into Catholic literature toward the middle of the present century, partly through the influence of Protestant theologians such as Karl Barth. In the face of dechristianization, many pastoral theologians and religious educators in Western Europe became convinced that the best remedy was a confident proclamation of the basic message of salvation through Jesus Christ.[1] The kerygmatic sermons of Peter and Paul, as reported in the first chapters of the Acts of the Apostles, were studied as models.

Some religious educators and missiologists of this period distinguished three stages of initiation into the faith.[2] The first, called pre-evangelization, was concerned with arousing interest in religious questions and disposing people to hear the Christian message. Then came the stage of evangelization, the proclamation of the basic Christian message. After faith in this message had been elicited came the stage of catechesis, or elementary doctrinal instruction, which in principle should precede the reception of the sacraments.

Building on the kerygmatic theology of the preceding decade, Vatican Council II made use of evangelical terminology. A comparison with Vatican Council I, which reflected the nineteenth-century mentality, is instructive. Vatican I used the term "gospel" (*evangelium*) only once, and then only to mean one of the four Gospels. It never used the terms "evangelize" or "evangelization." Vatican II, by contrast, mentioned the "gospel" 157 times, "evangelize" 18 times, and "evangelization" 31 times. When it spoke of evangelizing, Vatican II seems generally to have meant what the kerygmatic theologians meant by the term: the proclamation of the basic Christian message to those who did not yet believe in Christ.

In the very first sentence of its Constitution on the Church, Vatican II affirmed that Christ had sent the Church to preach the gospel to every creature (*LG* 1; cf. Mk 16:15). Because the Church is missionary by its very nature, evangelization, according to the council, is a duty of every Christian (*LG* 16–17; cf. *AG* 23, 35). The bishops, in union with the pope, are charged with leading in the process (*LG* 23; *CD* 6; *AG* 29, 30); priests are to stir up zeal for the evangelization of the world (*PO* 4; *AG* 39); and all the laity are expected to cooperate in the work of evangelization, especially in the environment of their work and family life (*LG* 35; *AA* 2–3, 6; *AG* 41). Without slighting the ministries of sacramental worship and pastoral leadership, Vatican II gave clear primacy to the preaching of the word among the responsibilities of bishops (*LG* 25) and priests (*PO* 4).

PAUL VI

Following the lead of the council, Paul VI (1963–78) gave even greater emphasis to evangelization. In choosing the name of Paul he signified his intention to take the Apostle of the Gentiles as the model for his papal ministry. In 1967, when he reorganized the Roman curia, he renamed the Congregation for the Propagation of the Faith the Congregation for the Evangelization of Peoples. He was the first pope in history to make apostolic journeys to other continents—first to the Holy Land (1964), then to India (1964), then to New York (1965), then to Portugal, Istanbul, and Ephesus (1967), then to Colombia (1968), then to Geneva and Uganda (1969), and finally (1970) a long journey including Tehran, East Pakistan, the Philippines, West Samoa, Australia, Indonesia, Hong Kong, and Sri Lanka. For good reason he was often called the "pilgrim pope." At his burial an open book of the Gospels was fittingly laid on his coffin, a sign of the evangelical quality of his ministry.

Wishing to orient the Church more toward the dissemination of the gospel, Paul VI chose as the theme for the synod of bishops in 1974 the evangelization of the modern world. From materials provided by that synod he composed in 1975 his great apostolic exhortation on evangelization, *Evangelii nuntiandi*.[3] That document proposed a comprehensive concept:

> Evangelization is in fact the grace and vocation proper to the Church, her deepest identity. She exists in order to evangelize, that is to say in order to preach and teach, to be the channel of the gift of grace, to reconcile sinners with God, and to perpetuate Christ's sacrifice in the Mass, which is the memorial of his death and glorious Resurrection. (14)

Paul VI's notion of evangelization is more inclusive than that of the kerygmatic theologians. In his view proclamation and catechesis, while occupying an important place in evangelization, are only one aspect of it (22).

Evangelization, moreover, should be directed not simply at individuals but also at cultures, which need to be regenerated by contact with the gospel (20). The tasks of human development and liberation, according to the apostolic exhortation, are profoundly linked with evangelization. But they are not the same thing. Against all secularizing tendencies, Paul VI warned that evangelization can never be reduced to a merely temporal project (30–34). It must always include a clear and unequivocal proclamation of Jesus as Lord (22). It must be directed to eternal life in God (26, 35).

JOHN PAUL II

John Paul II at the opening of his pontificate attended the general conference of the Latin American bishops at Puebla, near Mexico City, in January 1979. The theme of that conference was "Evangelization at Present and in the Future of Latin America."[4] While accepting Paul VI's identification of evangelization with the very mission of the Church (4), Puebla emphasized that through evangelization the Church intends to "contribute to the construction of a new society that is more fraternal and just" (12).

In his opening address at Puebla John Paul II quoted extensively from *Evangelii nuntiandi*.[5] Like Paul VI, he warned against acceptance of secular ideologies and sociological reductionism, but at the same time he declared that the Church "does not need to have recourse to ideological systems in order to love, defend, and collaborate in the liberation of the human being" (3:2). An indispensable part of the Church's evangelizing mission, he said, "is made up of works on behalf of justice and human promotion" (ibid.). "We cry out once more: Respect the human being, who is the image of God! Evangelize so that this may become a reality, so that the Lord may transform hearts and humanize political and economic systems, with the responsible commitment of human beings as the starting point" (3:5). In March 1979 the pope sent the Latin American bishops a letter with a ringing endorsement of the conclusions of the Puebla conference.[6]

Beginning with the Puebla conference, John Paul II has made himself the principal evangelizer in the Catholic Church. In his arduous apostolic journeys, in his annual messages for World Mission Sundays, and on many other occasions, he has continued to build on the themes articulated by Paul VI. He speaks of the evangelization of cultures and a "synthesis between faith and culture."[7] While insisting on the priority of eternal salvation, he maintains that human promotion is integral to the process of evangelization.

On March 9, 1983, John Paul II first mentioned the "new evangelization."[8] Speaking at Port-au-Prince, Haiti, to the bishops' council of the Latin American churches, he observed that the year 1992, when the Latin American bishops were to hold their next general conference, would mark the half millennium of the first evangelization of the Americas. This anniversary, he added, would gain its full meaning with the commitment of the Church in this hemisphere to a new evangelization—"new in ardor, methods, and expression."[9]

A year and a half later, in a speech at the Olympic Stadium at Santo Domingo, the pope expanded on this theme.[10] The very day, October 12, 1984, he recalled, was the anniversary of the landing of Columbus at San Salvador, which initiated "the encounter between two worlds." The jubilee of 1992, he said, would be an occasion to recall the first evangelization of the Americas without triumphalism and without false modesty. That evangelization, he observed, had essentially marked the historical and cultural identity of Latin America. But today, in the face of secularization, corruption, and grinding poverty, the Church was called to redouble its efforts to lead the faithful to "the word of Christ and the founts of grace which are the sacraments." The new evangelization should generate hope in the future "civilization of love" which Paul VI had proclaimed.

Since 1984 John Paul II, in addressing audiences in North and South America, Asia, Africa, and Europe, has frequently referred to the need of a new evangelization. In several of his addresses since 1987 the pope has linked the new evangelization with the preparation for the jubilee celebration of the Incarnation in the year 2000.

In his apostolic exhortation on the laity *Christifideles laici* (December 30, 1988), he summarized many of his ideas regarding the new evangelization.[11] At a time when whole countries were falling into religious indifference, he declared, the laity had a special responsibility to demonstrate how Christian faith constitutes the only fully valid response to the problems and hopes that life poses to every person and society. Participating as they did in the prophetic mission of Christ, lay men and women should make their daily conduct a shining and convincing testimony to the gospel. He exhorted the laity to narrow the gap between faith and culture and to make use of new media of communication to proclaim the gospel that brings salvation.

The theme of the new evangelization is spelled out in greater detail in two major papal documents of 1990. In the first of these, a letter of June 29 to the religious of Latin America, the pope connects this effort with the novena of years that he had announced in 1983 to prepare for the anniversary of 1992.[12] Cordially inviting the religious of our day to emulate the generosity and commitment of the pioneers of evangelization, he called attention to the special needs of the present time. The new evangelization, he said, must deepen the faith of Christians, forge a new culture open to the gospel message, and promote the social transformation of the continent.

Then, at the end of 1990, John Paul II issued his encyclical on the Church's missionary activity, *Redemptoris missio*.[13] He distinguished more clearly than before between situations requiring pastoral care and others requiring evangelization. In some places, he said, the Church is adequately equipped with ecclesial structures and is able to devote itself to the pastoral care of the faithful, but in other regions the people are still in need of being evangelized. The situations of evangelization, he observed, are two. Primary evangelization is called for in regions where Christ and the gospel are not yet known. A second evangelization, or re-evangelization, is required in areas where large groups of Christians have lost a living sense of the faith and no longer consider themselves members of the Church.

In this encyclical the "new evangelization" seems to be identified especially with the re-evangelization of formerly Christian areas. But the compartmentalization is not rigid. When the pope speaks of the new audiences requiring first evangelization he mentions not only new geographical areas but also new cultural sectors such as the inner cities, migrants, refugees, young people, and the "new humanity" whose formation depends greatly on the mass media of communication (37).

Meaning of the "New Evangelization"

Drawing on scattered statements in different documents one may attempt a synoptic overview of what the pope seems to have in mind by the "new evangelization."[14] It is new, in part, because it is occasioned by the forthcoming commemoration of Christopher Columbus and, eight years later, the jubilee of the Incarnation. Grateful for the achievements of the past, the new evangelization must avoid denigrating the work of the early missionaries or judging them by the behavioral standards of our own day. No matter how well others did for their own age, the new evangelization cannot be a mere return to the missionary tactics of a former era. The persuasive heralding of the gospel message today requires a new quality of evangelization and methods attuned to the sensibility of our times. This adaptation is clearly implied in the idea of "new evangelization."

John Paul II sees the new evangelization as having a deeply theological motivation. It rests on a recognition that the living Christ is, through the Holy Spirit, the chief agent. To be effective bearers of the gospel, ministers of the Church must have a close personal relationship to the Lord. "Missionary dynamism," according to John Paul II, "is not born of the will of those who decide to become propagators of their faith. It is born of the Spirit, who moves the Church to expand, and it progresses through faith in God's love."[15] The new evangelization, he says, "is not a matter of merely passing on doctrine but rather of a personal and profound meeting with the Savior."[16] Although the name of Jesus Christ must be explicitly proclaimed (*RMis* 44), evangelization can never be a matter of words alone. "The witness of a Christian life is the first and irreplaceable form of mission" (*RMis* 42). Before we can pass on the gospel to others, it must first have permeated our own lives. "It is important to recall that evangelization involves *conversion,* that is, interior change."[17] It must emanate from a deep experience of God.

Animated by Christ and the Holy Spirit, the new evangelization is for that very reason a work of the Church. It "is the witness which the Son of Man bears to himself, perpetuated in the mission of the Church," which is sent by Christ to evangelize.[18] Looking on the Church as the corporate evangelizing subject, John Paul II insists that the effort must be borne by the entire membership, clerical, religious, and lay. Members of the Church act not as isolated individuals but in communion with the whole Church (at Puebla; also *RMis* 45) and in subordination to the bishops and the Holy See.

As a task of the universal Church, evangelization is also the primary responsibility of each local church, under its own diocesan bishop. Parish priests must see themselves as charged with the evangelization of fellow citizens who do not yet belong to the flock of Christ (*RMis* 67). Basic ecclesial communities can be important centers of evangelization, provided that they live in harmony with the Church (*RMis* 51). The family, as a kind of "domestic church," can be a powerful instrument of evangelization (*CL* 62). Since the family is the primary cell of the Christian community, it follows that families should evangelize families.[19]

Our times offer special challenges and special opportunities. Because of current demographic trends, the non-Christian population of the world in becoming proportionally greater every year. Yet, as the Catholic Church has explicitly recognized, seeds of the Word and rays of divine truth are present in the nonbiblical religious traditions (*RMis* 55). In the Day of Prayer at Assisi (October 27, 1986) and on other occasions, John Paul II has sought to bring the religions into a more cordial and cooperative relationship. He repeatedly insists that in proclamation and dialogue Christians should respect the freedom of their hearers (*RMis* 8, 39). Dialogue, however, should not limit or impede evangelization; rather, it should be seen as a component in the Church's evangelizing mission (*RMis* 55). The Christian in dialogue will have no reason for minimizing the conviction that all grace and salvation come from God through Jesus Christ (ibid.).

John Paul II frequently refers to disunity among Christians as an obstacle to evangelization. Christ prayed that his disciples might be one in order that the world might believe (Jn 17:21; *RMis* 1). The effort to bring the gospel to all nations can serve as "a motivation and stimulus for a renewed commitment to ecumenism" (*RMis* 50). The real but imperfect communion already existing among Christians permits a significant degree of common witness and collaboration in social and religious matters.

Among the other challenges of our time, the pope mentions the spread of secularism, religious indifference, and atheism (*CL* 34). In some countries there is a scarcity of qualified ministers; in others, efforts at evangelization are hampered by legislation that forbids the free profession of faith. Additional difficulties arise from the prevalence of political ideologies and from a culture of violence, drugs, and pornography. In many cities the teeming masses experience degrading poverty and paralyzing anonymity (*RMis* 37). The faithful are influenced by systems of communication that glorify the affluent life, instilling hedonism and consumerism. This new cultural world constitutes the kind of challenge that Paul encountered when he addressed the Athenians at the Areopagus (*RMis* 37).

The challenges themselves, according to the pope, may be seen as opportunities. While on the one hand people seem to be sinking more deeply into materialism and despair, we are witnessing, on the other hand, an anxious search for meaning, the craving for an inner life, and a desire to experience the presence of God in prayer (*RMis* 38). Evangelization must cultivate the seeds of the Word wherever they are present and interpret them as manifestations of an imperative need for salvation in Jesus Christ. In answer to people's anxious questioning and unsatisfied hopes, "the Church has an immense spiritual patrimony to offer mankind, a heritage in Christ, who called himself 'the way, the truth, and the life' (Jn 14:6)" (*RMis* 38). Evangelization, says the pope, "is the primary service which the Church can render to every individual and to all humanity in the modern world" (*RMis* 2).

Within the immense field of evangelization the evangelization of culture occupies a position of special preeminence. Faith cannot take root, express itself, and grow unless it incarnates itself in cultural forms (*CT* 53). In every culture, the pope remarks, there are seeds of the Word that tend to bear fruit in harmony with the gospel. Whoever seeks to evangelize must be able to understand the mentality and attitude of the modern world, to illuminate them from the perspective of the gospel, and purify and elevate the sound elements in the light of Christian revelation (*CL* 44). The missionaries of the past, the pope reminds us, did much to raise the level of the arts, including dance, music, and the theater. They rightly saw this as falling within their evangelizing mission.

John Paul II consistently teaches that Catholic social doctrine, because it is rooted in the revealed concept of the human, is a valid means of evangelization (*CA* 54). "Teaching and spreading her social doctrine are part of the Church's evangelizing mission" (*SRS* 41). Authentic human development must be grounded in an ever-deeper evangelization (*RMis* 58). By exposing the roots of unjust political and economic systems, evangelization goes to the very heart of social imbalances. It includes a dynamic commitment to the common good of society and to the ways of peace and justice. Just as some missionaries of former centuries raised their voices prophetically against the violation of the rights of indigenous peoples, so those who evangelize in our own day, by insisting on human dignity and integral development (*CA* 55), help to build a new civilization of love (*RMis* 51).

John Paul II is quite aware of the problems inherent in the modern means of communication and of the incapacity of mass media to take the place of direct encounter between persons. But notwithstanding their limitations, the new media may be responsibly used in the service of truth, solidarity, and peace, and may thereby contribute to evangelization.[20] "The communications media," he says, "have a wonderful power to bring the people of the world together. . . . The power of the communications media is undoubtedly very great, and it depends on us to guarantee that they will always be instruments at the service of truth, justice, and moral decency."[21] Because of its rapid development and deep formative influence, the world of the media requires the attention of the Church (*CL* 44). The gospel and its values must be made more present in the world of public communication, which may be seen as a new frontier for the evangelizing mission of the Church (*CL* 44). To integrate the Christian message into the new culture created by the mass media is a highly complex task, involving new languages, new techniques, and a new psychology (*RMis* 37).

Significance of the Evangelical Turn

In my judgment the evangelical turn in the ecclesial vision of Popes Paul VI and John Paul II is one of the most surprising and important developments in the Catholic Church since Vatican II. This development, as I have indicated, did not take place without a degree of preparation in Vatican II and preconciliar kerygmatic theology. But Paul VI went beyond the Council in identifying evangelization with the total mission of the Church. John Paul II, with his unique familiarity with world Catholicism, assigned the highest priority to evangelization in the mission of the Church.

While both popes notably broadened the concept of evangelization, they have retained the main emphasis of the earlier kerygmatic concept. For them, as for the kerygmatic theologians, the heart and center of evangelization is the proclamation of God's saving love as shown forth in Jesus Christ. Where the name of Jesus is not spoken, there can be no evangelization in the true sense (*EN* 22, 27; *RMis* 44). But it is not enough to speak the name. Christian initiation is incomplete without catechesis, which is a moment in the whole process of evangelization (*CT* 18). Evangelization must take account of the full implications of the gospel for individual and social existence.

All of this constitutes a remarkable shift in the Catholic tradition. For centuries evangelization had been a poor stepchild. Even when the term was used, evangelization was treated as a secondary matter, the special vocation of a few priests and religious. And even these specialists were more concerned with gaining new adherents for the Church than with proclaiming the good news of Jesus Christ. Today we seem to be witnessing the birth of a new Catholicism that, without loss of its institutional, sacramental, and social dimensions, is authentically evangelical.

Will the shift toward the evangelical model meet with general acceptance and successful implementation? In many parts of the Church the response has been clearly positive. Already in April 1974 the Federation of Asian Bishops' Conferences, preparing for the Synod of Bishops of 1974, issued a ringing declaration on "Evangelization in Modern Day Asia."[22] The Latin American Bishops at Medellín (1968) and Puebla (1979) gave a clear priority to evangelization. Their Fourth General Conference at Santo Domingo in 1992 will have as its theme "New Evangelization, Human Advancement, and Christian Culture."[23]

In 1986 an international organization known as Evangelization 2000 was founded with a headquarters in Rome, having as its principal purpose to promote a Decade of Evangelization that will end on December 25, 2000. This organization has already sponsored worldwide retreats for thousands of priests in Rome in 1984 and 1990. It is establishing networks of schools of evangelization and prayer groups to promote the success of the evangelization program. In our own country the National Conference of Catholic Bishops, which has long possessed a Committee on the Missions, has set up a Committee on Evangelization. Originally formed as an ad hoc committee in response to Paul VI's *Evangelii nuntiandi*, it has since been made a standing committee. Another ad hoc committee has been formed to make preparations for the Observance of the Fifth Centenary of the Evangelization of the Americas. In 1986 the U.S. bishops published a pastoral statement on World Mission, "To the Ends of the Earth,"[24] and on November 15, 1990, they approved a pastoral letter, "Heritage and Hope," looking forward to the anniversary of 1992.[25] A national plan for evangelization is being formed.[26] The bishops of the United States have responded to statements on evangelization issued by

Hispanic-American Catholics[27] and by Black Catholics.[28] In 1989 the episcopal conference of Texas issued an important pastoral letter urging parishes to establish evangelization committees and to become welcoming
communities celebrating vital and inspiring Sunday liturgies.[29]

Quite evidently the new evangelization will encounter inertia and resistance. As I mentioned already, the Catholic Church, especially in modern
times, has been principally oriented toward the pastoral care of its own
members. American Catholics are wary of evangelization for a variety of
reasons. They see it as the chosen trademark of revivalist and fundamentalist sects, some of them virulently anti-Catholic. They distrust the bibli-
cism, the individualism, the emotionalism, and the aggressive proselytism
of certain Protestant evangelistic preachers. Many are repelled by recent
revelations about the financial dealings and private lives of several prominent televangelists. In addition, Vatican II put many Catholics on guard
against anything smacking of triumphalism. Attempting to be modest and
self-critical, they often fail to proclaim their faith with confidence. Some
have been going through a process of doubt and reappraisal, and are
groping for ways of making better sense of their own heritage. Influenced
by the conviction that the assent of faith must be a free and personal
response to grace, and by American tradition that religion is a purely
private matter, they do not wish to bring pressure on anyone to undergo
a deep conversion of mind and heart.

Importance of the New Evangelization

Notwithstanding all these difficulties, I submit that the popes of our time
have correctly identified God's call to the Church in our day and have hit
on an effective remedy for the Church's present ills. The Church has
become too introverted. If Catholics today are sometimes weak in their
faith, this is partly because of their reluctance to share it. Unless the gospel
message were a truth to be communicated to others, it would not be of
great value for believers themselves. Once we grasp the universal validity
of the message, and its significance for the whole of human life, we gain
a new appreciation of the privilege of being its bearers and a new eagerness
to share it. As John Paul II asserts, "Faith is strengthened when it is given
to others" (*RMis* 2).

Evangelization, by concentrating on the basic Christian message, helps
us to see what is supremely worthwhile in our religion. If we believe

simply on the authority of the Church, without caring what the contents are, we can hardly be enthusiastic about our faith. But if we focus on the God of Jesus Christ, as disclosed in the gospel, our faith becomes a loving assent to an extraordinary piece of good news, intended by God for all the world. It is a message that we have no right to monopolize, to keep to ourselves (*RMis* 11; cf. 44).

Catholic spirituality at its best has always promoted a deep personal relationship with Christ. In evangelizing we are required to raise our eyes to him and to transcend excessive ecclesiocentrism. The Church is of crucial importance but is not self-enclosed. It is a means of drawing the whole world into union with God through Jesus Christ.

Too many Catholics of our day seem never to have encountered Christ. They know a certain amount about him from the teaching of the Church, but they lack direct personal familiarity. The hearing of the gospel, personal prayer, and the reception of the sacraments should establish and deepen that saving relationship. When Catholics regard religious worship as a mere matter of duty or routine, they become an easy prey for sectarian preachers who, notwithstanding their faulty understanding of the Christian message, give witness to a joyful encounter with the Lord.

The evangelical turn in Catholicism can make Catholics less vulnerable to the sects. It also has considerable ecumenical possibilities. One of the most vigorous branches of Protestantism in the United States today is Evangelicalism, the faith of many conservative Christians, especially in the Southern states. Until recently conservative Evangelicals have not been greatly interested in dialogue or collaboration with Catholics. Some, indeed, are anti-Catholic, partly because they have had so little contact with Catholicism. Yet there is increasing recognition that Catholics and conservative Evangelicals share many things in common, including a reverence for the canonical Scriptures and adherence to the central doctrines of the Trinity, the Incarnation, the atoning death and bodily resurrection of Jesus. In the realm of moral teaching, conservative Evangelicals, like Catholics, tend to be opposed to abortion and to defend traditional family values.

A number of authors have begun to call for a new ecumenism between Roman Catholics and evangelical Protestants.[30] Kenneth Craycraft, in a recent article, writes:

> The new ecumenism can be successful because of the peculiar qualities that each tradition brings with it. Catholics have an ancient and rich moral

vocabulary; it formed the great philosophical and theological traditions of the (pre-modern) West. The institutional memory and current organization of Catholicism make it effective at organizing and implementing its agenda. Evangelicals bring a sense of urgency and fervor to the project. They are converts and children of converts, with all the energetic zeal that that entails. Their emphasis on active personal discipleship and commitment to Sacred Scripture make evangelicals the yeast in the dough. Even committed Catholics have become complacent in recent years. Evangelicals will call us to a more energetic expression of our faith.[31]

In the dialogue here envisaged, Protestant Evangelicals can help Catholics overcome their excessive preoccupation with inner-Church issues, while Catholics can help Protestants overcome their own imbalances. Many of them have focused too narrowly on God's word in Scripture, and some have fallen into fundamentalistic literalism. Catholics can help Evangelicals to achieve a deeper grounding in tradition, a richer sacramental life, a more lively sense of worldwide community, and a keener appreciation of sociopolitical responsibility. These values, which are praised in the recent writings of certain Evangelicals, are prominent in the evangelization programs of Paul VI and John Paul II.

In recent years several authors have written about "the Catholic moment" in the life of our nation. This moment is often described in terms of the Church's potential contribution to a religiously informed public philosophy. Without denying the importance of this project, I would recall that the Catholic moment was originally, and rightly, described as one "in which the Roman Catholic Church in the world can and should be the lead church in proclaiming and exemplifying the Gospel."[32] The first and highest priority is for the Church to proclaim the good news concerning Jesus Christ as a joyful message to all the world. Only if the Church is faithful to its evangelical mission can it hope to make its distinctive contribution in the social, political, and cultural spheres.

NOTES

1. The Catholic kerygmatic movement began in Innsbruck with Joseph A. Jungmann and others. It then spread to other countries where it was taken up by writers such as Paul Hitz, André Rétif, Pierre André Liégé, and Domenico Grasso.

2. See, for example, Alfonso M. Nebreda, *Kerygma in Crisis?* (Chicago: Loyola University Press, 1965).

3. Paul VI, apostolic exhortation *Evangelii nuntiandi* (Washington, D.C.: USCC, 1975). Numbers in parentheses refer to paragraphs.

4. *Third General Conference of Latin American Bishops, Puebla: Conclusions.* Washington, D.C.: NCCB, 1979. Numbers in parentheses refer to paragraphs in this edition.

5. Ibid., 1–15; printed also in *Origins* 8 (February 8, 1979): 529–38.

6. Ibid., iii.

7. John Paul II, letter to Cardinal Casaroli establishing the Pontifical Council for Culture (May 20, 1982), quoted from *L'Osservatore Romano* (Ital. ed.), May 21–22, 1982, 3. Already earlier, in his apostolic exhortation *Catechesi tradendae* (October 16, 1979), John Paul II had spoken of the need for the gospel to "take flesh" in various cultures. See no. 53; text in *Origins* 9 (November 8, 1979): 329–48, at 342.

8. John Paul II, "The Task of the Latin American Bishop," *Origins* 12 (March 24, 1983): 659–62.

9. Ibid., 661.

10. John Paul II, "Building a New Latin America," *Origins* 14 (November 1, 1984): 305–10. Numbers in parentheses refer to pages in this edition.

11. John Paul II, apostolic exhortation *Christifideles laici, Origins* 18 (February 9, 1989): 561–95. Numbers in parentheses refer to paragraphs.

12. John Paul II, "Toward the Fifth Centenary of New World Evangelization," *Origins* 20 (September 6, 1990): 208–16.

13. John Paul II, encyclical *Redemptoris misso, Origins* 20 (January 31, 1991): 541–68. Numbers in parentheses refer to paragraphs.

14. In the remainder of this chapter, apostolic exhortations (*Catechesi tradendae, Christifideles laici*) and encyclicals (*Sollicitudo rei socialis, Centesimus annus, Redemptoris missio*) will be cited by the initials of the Latin title followed by paragraph number.

15. John Paul II, address of February 12, 1988, to Italian bishops on Liturgical Course, *L'Osservatore Romano* (Eng. ed.), March 14, 1988, 5; cf. *RMis* 21–30.

16. John Paul II, "Commissioning of Families of the Neo-Catechumenal Way," January 3, 1991, *L'Osservatore Romano* (Eng. ed.), January 14, 1991, 12.

17. John Paul II, "Address to Bishops of Malawi on Their *Ad Limina* Visit," August 23, 1988, *L'Osservatore Romano* (Eng. ed.), September 5, 1988, 3.

18. John Paul II, "Address to the Bishops of Brazil on Their *Ad Limina* Visit to Rome," February 24, 1990, *L'Osservatore Romano* (Eng. ed.), March 26, 1990, 8–9.

19. John Paul II, "Commissioning of Families of the Neo-Catechumenal Way," 12.

20. John Paul II, "Letter to Meeting of African Bishops," June 9, 1990, *L'Osservatore Romano* (Eng. ed.), August 6, 1990, 8.

21. John Paul II, "Message to Plenary Assembly of Pontifical Commission for Social Communications," March 3, 1988, *L'Osservatore Romano* (Eng. ed.), March 14, 1988, 9.

22. Federation of Asian Bishops' Conference, *For All the Peoples of Asia,* vol. 1: Texts and Documents (Manila: IMC Publications, 1984), 25–38.

23. Consejo Episcopal Latinoamericano (CELAM), *Documento de Consulta: Neuva Evangelización, Promoción Humana, Cultura Cristiana* (Bogota, Colombia: CELAM, 1991).

24. U. S. Bishops, "To the Ends of the Earth," *Origins* 16 (December 4, 1986): 457–66.

25. U. S. Bishops, "Heritage and Hope," *Origins* 20 (December 6, 1990): 413–26.

26. Archbishop Daniel Pilarczyk, "A New Orientation Toward Evangelization," *Origins* 20 (October 11, 1990): 295. A draft of a national plan for evangelization was circulated under the title "A Time to Share: Shaping a Catholic Evangelizing People" (draft of February 24, 1991). The final text, approved by the U. S. Bishops' Conference, was published with the title "Go and Make Disciples," *Origins* 22 (December 3, 1992): 423–32.

27. *U. S. National Pastoral Plan for Hispanic Ministry* (Washington, D.C.: USCC, 1987) and U.S. Bishops' Response to this in *Origins* 17 (December 10, 1987): 449–63.

28. National Conference of Catholic Bishops, *Here I Am, Send Me: A Conference Response to the Evangelization of American Catholics and the National Black Catholic Pastoral Plan* (Washington, D.C.: USCC, 1989) and U.S. Bishops' Response to this in *Origins* 19 (December 28, 1989): 485–92.

29. Catholic Bishops of Texas, "A Pastoral Letter on Evangelization," *Origins* 18 (April 27, 1989): 777–84.

30. I myself alluded to this desideratum in my article "Ecumenism Without Illusions: A Catholic Perspective," *First Things* 4 (June–July 1990): 20–25.

31. Kenneth R. Craycraft, "Our Kind of Ecumenism: Why Catholics Need to Be More Evangelical and Vice Versa," *Crisis* 9 (October 1991): 30–33, at 32.

32. Richard John Neuhaus, *The Catholic Moment: The Paradox of the Church in the Postmodern World* (San Francisco: Harper & Row, 1987), 283.

8

Historical Method and the Reality of Christ

April 2, 1992

The Problem of Faith and History

After a period of relative quiescence the quest of the historical Jesus has again become a center of controversy. Two major contributions to the theme—John P. Meier's *A Marginal Jew*[1] and John Dominic Crossan's *The Historical Jesus*[2]—appeared just before Christmas 1991 and were widely reviewed. They have provoked criticisms and counter criticisms, focusing primarily on issues of method.

The quest of the historical Jesus is not an idle pastime. It began in the eighteenth century as a fierce attack on the Christ of faith. Throughout the nineteenth century its aim was to establish another Christ to replace the Christ of dogma. In the words of Albert Schweitzer, who wrote the classic history of the early quest, "The dogma had first to be shattered before men could once more go out in quest of the historical Jesus, before they could even grasp the thought of his existence."[3] The assault on orthodox belief has not died out. Many historians of the present day share the same animus.

Can believers be indifferent to the historical quest? Can they keep their faith intact while letting historians do what they will with the Jesus of flesh and blood? Can they let go of the historical grounds that have heretofore sustained Christians in their belief? These questions raise difficult and fundamental issues about what faith is, what history is, and how the two are related.

For purposes of this paper faith will be understood as a firm adherence to a total vision of reality in the light of God's revealing word. For Christians that word comes to us preeminently in Christ, as he is known through the canonical Scriptures and the teaching of the Church. Faith involves a free, reasonable assent made possible by the grace of God, which enables us to discern and confidently embrace God's revealing word.

THE CONCEPT OF HISTORY

The concept of history is complex and controverted. In a very broad sense it includes everything we know, or think we know, about the human past, whether based on faith, on vague general impressions, or on methodical investigation.

In a narrower sense history is knowledge derived by means of a recognized method devised to provide reliable access to the human past. The method involves a kind of detective work by which we critically use the available sources, including documents that testify to past events. Applied to Christian origins, historical method will seek to ferret out the earliest and most reliable reports about Jesus and from them reconstruct the sayings and deeds that may most plausibly be attributed to Jesus and his circle.

There are no rules that automatically determine what accounts are to be accepted as accurate. Historians generally rely on rules of thumb.[4] For instance, they prefer accounts that can be traced to early witnesses and those that are attested by several independent sources. They are also inclined to credit reports that present Jesus as saying and doing what the Jews of his day would have avoided and assertions that would be embarrassing to the early Church. This principle of discontinuity (as it is often called) does not presuppose that Jesus was never in agreement with the Jews of his day or that his character and doctrine were generally out of phase with the teaching of the early Church, but simply that it is more difficult to account for dissimilar statements as originating from sources other than Jesus himself.

To give more precision to their method, some historians make assumptions of a philosophical character. According to a positivist view that was widely accepted fifty or a hundred years ago, history is a science analogous to physics or chemistry. It proceeds on the assumption that the world is a closed system in which causes and effects are connected by strict necessity. History, in that view, leaves no place for the unique, the exceptional, and especially not for events brought about by God's direct activity. On positivist grounds many historians wrote off the Gospels as unreliable, insofar as they portrayed Jesus as a utterly unique figure, conscious of a special relationship to God, and working miracles by divine power.

This positivist view, I shall maintain, is not convincing. The historian cannot antecedently rule out the possibility that something unique and unparalleled might happen, or that God might bring about exceptional events by an exercise of divine power. If positivist rules were adopted, history and faith would be on a collision course from the beginning.

Does the possibility of miraculous or supernatural events introduce a surd and thereby destroy the intelligibility of history? This might be the case if God frequently interposed his action without any plan or reason. In the view of theology, however, God respects the order of created causality that he himself has established. If he intervenes, he does so rarely and according to a rationale that has its own intelligibility. Where serious grounds exist for suspecting that God has acted in a direct, supernatural way, historians cannot dismiss the evidence in the name of historical integrity. They are invited to look higher and to enter into dialogue with theologians. Such dialogue is necessary for the sake of history itself. The theological intelligibility of the alleged event should enter into the assessment of the credibility of the reports.

After these abstract considerations regarding faith and history, I should like to survey the main positions that have been taken in the quest of the historical Jesus. I shall describe four basic approaches, the last of which I personally find the most satisfactory.

FIRST APPROACH: HISTORY AGAINST FAITH

According to the first position, history is antithetical to faith. The quest of the historical Jesus, as I have said, arose from hostility to dogma. In the works of Hermann Samuel Reimarus, David Friedrich Strauss, Ernest Renan, and others, efforts were made to substitute a purely human Jesus of history for the Christ of faith and dogma. This effort still goes on in our day, as may be seen from the works of John Allegro, Rudolf Augstein, Morton Smith, and Thomas Sheehan. Another partisan of this struggle, Paul Hollenbach, asserts that the Jesus of history is to be sought "in order to overthrow, not simply correct, [what José Porfirio Miranda calls] 'the mistake called Christianity.'" The mistake, according to Hollenbach, was the "divinization of Jesus as Son of David, Christ, Son of God, Second Person in the Trinity, etc."[5]

This historical procedure is of course unacceptable to Christian believers. They reply that antidogmatic historians are dogmatic in their own way, since they antecedently rule out the unique and the transcendent. Their approach ruptures the continuity between Jesus and the community of his followers. It does violence to the sources by expunging sayings and deeds of Jesus that are attested by what, according to the standard criteria, must be regarded as early and reliable traditions. Having reduced Jesus to the stature of a common prophet or wonder worker, this approach has difficulty in accounting for the extreme reactions of his followers and adversaries and for the rapid emergence of Christianity as a distinct religious faith.

Crossan's recent book *The Historical Jesus* in some ways resembles the first approach, just described. It portrays Jesus as a "peasant Jewish Cynic," whose conception of the kingdom of God involved "a religious and economic egalitarianism that negated alike and at once the hierarchical and patronal normalcies of Jewish religion and Roman power" (421–22). Crossan describes Jesus as a magician bent on subverting the existing social structures. He denies the historicity of the Last Supper, including the institution of the Eucharist. He likewise rejects the stories about the discovery of the empty tomb. The earliest accounts, he believes, saw no need for resurrection appearances between the departure of Jesus and his now-imminent return in glory. But Crossan does not portray himself as opposing the Christ of dogma. In fact, he defends the assertion that Jesus was wholly God and wholly man. "I find, therefore, no contradiction between the historical Jesus and the defined Christ, no betrayal whatsoever in the move from Jesus to Christ." (424). With his somewhat paradoxical and apparently selective appropriation of the Church's dogma, Crossan is able to affirm the identity between the historical Jesus and the Christ of faith.

SECOND APPROACH: SEPARATION BETWEEN HISTORY AND FAITH

The second major position may be called separationist. It maintains that history and faith, if each keeps within its legitimate sphere, can neither confirm nor contradict each other. History deals with empirical facts of the human past that are accessible to any rational person who uses historical method. Faith, on the other hand, deals with transcendent realities that are known only by revelation, freely accepted by religious believers thanks to the grace of God. The Jesus who lived and died in Palestine belongs to history; the living, risen Christ belongs to faith. This, roughly speaking, was the position of the dialectical theologians between the first and second world wars, particularly Rudolf Bultmann and Paul Tillich.

To judge from the first volume of his book *A Marginal Jew*, John P. Meier is not far removed from this second position. Because his views are subject to clarification and modification in future volumes, one can only speak tentatively at this point. I am also unsure about whether his method reflects his personal preferences or his desire to reach out to a wider audience, including non-Christians. In any case he keeps the Christ of faith well insulated from historical scrutiny, so that as a historian he can be content to let the chips fall where they may. Agreeing with Bultmann and his school that "the Jesus of history is not and cannot be the object of Christian faith," he writes:

> In the historical-critical framework, the "real" has been defined—and has to be defined—in terms of what exists within this world of time and space, what can be experienced in principle by any observer, and what can be reasonably deduced or inferred from such experience. Faith and Christian theology, however, affirm ultimate realities beyond what is merely empirical or provable by reason: e.g., the triune God and the risen Jesus. (197)

A little later Meier writes: "In the realm of faith and theology the 'real Jesus,' the only Jesus existing here and now, is this risen Lord, to whom access is given only in faith" (198).

Meier admits that there must be some continuity between the Jesus of history and the Christ of faith (5), inasmuch as the risen Jesus was previously the man from Nazareth. But he leaves it unclear, at least to this reader, whether any particular assertions about the earthly career of Jesus are required by faith. His discussion of the virginal conception of Jesus and of the resurrection may be used as examples.

Although he points out in a footnote that some theologians such as Rahner and Kasper are more conservative, he gives greater prominence to authors who call the virginal conception a *theologoumenon* (220)—a term he interprets as generally meaning "a theological narrative that does not represent a historical event."[6] As a believer Meier presumably accepts the virginal conception, but as a historian he cannot take account of supernatural explanations. As he limits himself to the human and the empirical, he can give only a weak response to the charge that Jesus was Mary's illegitimate child.

On the ground that the resurrection is knowable only by faith, Meier contends that it falls beyond the scope of a historical study of Jesus (13). Others maintain, more correctly I believe, that even if the resurrection in its full reality transcends the grasp of history, it has a historical aspect and that historical research can help to establish the fact that Jesus did rise from the dead. If the resurrection was something that happened to Jesus, and not simply to the community, its occurrence would seem to be pertinent to the history of Jesus. The fact of the resurrection casts a whole new light on the previous career of Jesus and gives credibility to sayings and deeds that might otherwise be written off as legend.

Meier repeatedly reminds his readers that he is not denying faith and revelation, only putting them in brackets. To judge from early reviews, non-Christians may find that Meier's attitude toward Jesus is not as neutral as he declares it to be. Christian believers, on the other hand, will wonder whether Meier the believer would disagree with Meier the historian. What would he say about the career of Jesus if he took his faith out of brackets? Perhaps in some other work Meier will find an opportunity to say how his account of the history of Jesus would differ if he were to avail himself of faith.

This second position has some plausibility because as Christians we do assent to transcendent realities not knowable apart from faith in God's word. History by itself cannot establish that Jesus is reigning in heavenly glory or that he makes himself present in the Eucharist. But, as I suppose Meier himself would admit, no total separation between history and faith is feasible. Most Catholic Christians consider themselves committed as believers to profess various facts about the earthly Jesus. While no official list is available, a good case can be made for including items such as the virginal conception of Jesus, his consciousness of his own divinity, his miraculous and prophetic powers, his redemptive intent, his institution of the Eucharist, his crucifixion, his empty tomb, and his bodily resurrection. If facts such as these were disproved, Christian faith would be seriously affected.

Recognizing the importance of these matters for faith, the Church has considered herself obliged to defend the historical value of the Gospels. Vatican Council II, following up on several earlier pronouncements, taught that the Gospels, "whose historical character the Church unhesitatingly asserts, faithfully hand on what Jesus the Son of God, while living among men, really did and taught" (*DV* 19). The second position, which severs the links between faith and history, fails to account for the Church's concern for the historicity of the Gospels.

THIRD APPROACH: HISTORY AS GROUND OF FAITH

According to the third major position, history is the ground of faith. That is to say, historical investigation establishes rational foundations for the commitment of Christian faith. This position has been developed in at least three different forms.

The first form is exemplified by many apologists of the early twentieth century, including Hilarin Felder and Louis Claude Fillion. Taking up the challenge of the rationalists, they argued that the Gospels, viewed as strictly historical sources, could provide conclusive proofs that Jesus claimed to be, and in fact was, the only-begotten Son of God.[7]

These authors used a rather naive approach, ignoring what most scholars of our own day hold about the authorship, date, and literary form of the Gospels. As a result the work of these apologists is no longer convincing. More recent apologists, such as Joachim Jeremias, take a much more sophisticated approach to the Gospels and therefore make more modest claims. Jeremias argues persuasively that Jesus was conscious of having a relationship of singular intimacy with God as his Father.[8] But it is hard to say that his arguments give more than a high probability that could be upset by further research. Few Christians would want their faith to depend on scholarly hypotheses such as these.

The second form of the third position is the "new quest of the historical Jesus," instituted in the late 1950s. Several former students of

Bultmann, rebelling against his divorce between faith and history, made use of a kind of existential history and tried to recreate an experience of encounter with Jesus on the basis of the earliest Gospel traditions. The works of Günther Bornkamm, Heinz Zahrnt, and James M. Robinson, representative of this school, may still be read with profit.

These works succeed, in my opinion, in achieving an impressive picture of Jesus based on the texts that have good claims to historical reliability. The members of this school, however, limit their quest to Jesus as he presented himself in his public life. They do not incorporate the further light given to the community by the events of Easter and Pentecost. Their work, like that of Jeremias, must be regarded as a helpful beginning that can put the reader on the road toward eventually accepting the Christ of faith.

The third form of the third position is represented by Wolfhart Pannenberg. For him history is the only mode of access to the reality of the past; faith gives no information in addition to history. But he defines history in a very comprehensive sense, so that it is capable of discerning the action of God. Pannenberg finds that the event of Jesus Christ, when interpreted in its own historical context, must be seen as the work of God himself, ushering in the final age of the world. Because the resurrection of Jesus is a historical fact, says Pannenberg, historical reasoning can exhibit Jesus as the self-revelation of God.[9]

Pannenberg avoids the simplistic arguments of earlier apologists. He takes a highly critical approach to the Gospels and does not admit the historicity of the virginal conception. But he does affirm the historicity of the empty tomb and at least of some post-resurrection appearances. Thus he arrives at a more complete Christology than is obtainable by the existential history of the "new quest."

Some difficulties may nevertheless be raised. Pannenberg's comprehensive concept of history is so broad that it deprives history of its character as a special discipline. But even in this inclusive sense, history does not seem to terminate in a firm intellectual commitment, higher than the fluctuating judgments of probability. Many theologians, among whom I count myself, would say that the historical arguments for the divinity of Jesus will not provide the full assurance of faith except for those who submit to the attraction and illumination of divine grace. With this reservation, however, I find great value in Pannenberg's argumentation.

Fourth Approach: The Gospels
as Interpreted History

I turn, therefore, to the fourth major position, the one that most appeals to me. I hold that Christian faith does not normally arise from, or rest on, a critical examination of the New Testament evidence concerning the Jesus of history. Rather it comes from God's revealing word as conveyed by the testimony of the Church. But because the word of God tells us something about past events, faith cannot be insulated from history in the broad sense of the term.

The Gospels are not merely or primarily works of history. Above all else they are Gospels—that is to say, proclamations of the good news of God's saving action in Jesus Christ. They are religious testimonies, composed for the sake of arousing and strengthening the life of faith. Richly charged with theological interpretation, they give us much deeper insight into the real meaning of Jesus than stenographic reports about him could ever do.

Composed as they were with a kerygmatic and pastoral concern, the Gospels should not be judged as though they were intended to be merely factual reports. The believer cannot say a priori that every Gospel narrative is an exact account of the event. The story of Jesus has been reworked in the light of the Church's Easter faith and then further adapted to meet the needs of the particular communities for which our four Gospels were written. According to the 1964 Instruction of the Biblical Commission, modern scholarship makes it evident that "the doctrine and life of Jesus were not simply reported for the sole purpose of being remembered, but were 'preached' so as to offer the Church a basis of faith and morals." The biblical interpreter, says the instruction, must seek to explain why the different evangelists narrated the life and words of Jesus in different ways.[10]

If they had been intended as simply historical works, the Gospels could be judged deficient. They do not satisfy our curiosity about many points. For example, they give us no description of Jesus and no exact chronology of his life. They recast many of his sayings, rearrange them into continuous discourses, combine distinct events into a single story, and take other liberties that would be unacceptable in academic history.

It is therefore legitimate and possible to probe behind the Gospels and try to reconstruct a more accurate and detailed account of the career of

Jesus. For Christian believers, the intention of the quest will not be to detract from the teaching of the New Testament but rather to provide additional data and thereby give a better understanding both of Christ and of the Gospels.

The Christian believer will use many of the same procedures as the neutral or hostile historiographer. Catholic and Protestant scholars, without prejudice to their faith, make use of textual criticism, source criticism, form criticism, redaction criticism, literary criticism, and historical criticism. It is essential to obtain reliable texts, to identify their literary genre, and to single out the more primitive strata of material. The properly historical phase comes with the movement from the texts, considered as data, to the words and deeds to which they refer. Applying criteria such as early attestation, multiple attestation, and discontinuity from late Judaism and from early Christianity, the historian can make more or less probable judgments about the reliability of the accounts.

It must be recognized, however, that judgments of historicity depend in great part on presumptions. Even those who try to bracket their faith have to use some presumptions about the kinds of reports that are to be viewed as credible. Because of differing presuppositions, some historians will admit, and others will discount, the antecedent possibility of revelation and miracles. In the area of religion, these presuppositions make all the difference. Believers who want to recover the full truth about Jesus will wish to take advantage of the light that faith can supply. They will not assume, even for purposes of the argument, that Jesus was less than faith declares him to be. To adopt such artificial restrictions would seriously prejudice the results. As John Henry Newman wrote in his critique of the apologetics of William Paley,

> Rules of court are dictated by what is expedient on the whole and in the long run; but they run the risk of being unjust to the claims of particular cases. Why am I to begin with taking up a position not my own, and unclothing my mind of that large outfit of existing thoughts, principles, likings, desires, and hopes, which make me what I am.[11]

Christians, convinced that Jesus was an utterly singular person, the incarnate Son of God, will be prepared to credit testimony that God acted in him in a totally unprecedented way. Faith is an advantage because it alerts us to the particular strand of history in which God has acted decisively for our salvation. But faith does not eliminate the need for scholarly inquiry. Certain kerygmatic and theological ingredients have to be filtered out by the critic who wishes to reconstruct what was actually said and done by Jesus in his earthly career.

LIMITS AND VALUES OF HISTORY

Historical method, when applied to the Gospel materials, has not yet led to a satisfactory consensus. Most historians can agree about a few general features of the public ministry of Jesus and the fact of his execution by the Roman authorities. But the different perspectives on the relationship between history and faith will lead to radically different views on matters of doctrinal significance. Even historians who share the same faith disagree about many details, such as the time and place at which Jesus was born, the duration of his public ministry, his messianic or divine claims, his intent to establish a Church, the dates of his Last Supper and of the crucifixion. Different historians will provide different theories and argue for them as best they can.

Of what use, then, is this historical investigation, conducted in the light of faith? Four main values occur to me.

1. On many points qualified historians will be able to supplement the information that could be gathered without reliance on their technical skills. They can give us probable answers to many questions that are not settled, one way or the other, by faith and theology. For example, they may have informed opinions about whether the Matthean or the Lukan form of the Beatitudes or the Lord's Prayer is closer to the actual words of Jesus, and about whether the Last Supper was celebrated as a Paschal meal. History may be able to clarify Jesus's attitudes on social and political questions such as war and revolution, the rights of women and the poor. On these and many other debatable questions, historical investigation provides probable answers that are of interest.

2. By identifying certain elements in the Gospel as historically factual, the historian can on some points confirm the faith of believers. Solid arguments can be made for holding that Jesus understood himself as bringing in the final age of salvation, that he chose apostles to share in his ministry during and after his own life, that he placed Peter at the head of the apostles, that he understood himself as having a singular intimacy with his heavenly Father, that he regarded his own death as redemptive,

and that he trusted that the Father would raise him from the dead. The figure of Jesus reconstructed by technical history, incomplete and tentative though it be, can be helpful to people who are inquiring into the credibility of the Christian religion.

3. Critical study of the Gospels enables us to distinguish more clearly between the competences of faith and history. In some cases historical investigation stands in tension with the teaching of the Church. For example, some serious scholars, including Catholics, think that the strictly historical evidence does not favor the virginal conception of Jesus or the perpetual virginity of Mary. Even if these scholars are correct, the difficulties that they raise can be taken in stride. For Catholics and, I suspect, most other Christians, faith does not rest on historical research but on the word of God authoritatively proclaimed by Scripture and tradition. As Newman said, no doctrine of the Church can be rigorously proved by history. In some cases the historical evidence may seem to point away from the Catholic doctrines. "In all cases," Newman concluded, "there is a margin left for faith in the word of the Church. He who believes the dogmas of the Church only because he has reasoned them out of History, is scarcely a Catholic."[12]

4. Historical study of the New Testament, finally, may contribute to the better understanding of faith and assist in the development of Christian doctrine. According to Vatican II, the work of exegetes is one of the means through which the judgment of the Church comes to maturity (*DV* 12). An instance of this may be the case of Jesus's knowledge and self-consciousness. Theologians of earlier centuries often spoke of Jesus' infused knowledge in such a way as to suggest that he did not need to learn from other people, from books, or from experience. Modern biblical scholarship has helped to nuance this view and has enabled us to make the psychology of Jesus more intelligible.[13]

Thoughtful Christians in our day are anxious to take advantage of modern historical research. Many look to Catholic biblical scholars to show how new findings in this area cohere with Catholic faith and teaching. But their expectations are disappointed when exegetes pursue their scientific investigations without regard for faith and theology.[14] Has the gap between theology and biblical scholarship become so wide that each must be pursued without reference to the other? I am confident that faith and intelligence, dogma and history, can and must be integrated. Historical scholarship, if it erects itself into a purely positive discipline independent of philosophy and faith, can only widen the gap. But, conducted in dialogue with philosophy and theology, the historical quest can cast added light on the reality of Christ.

Notes

1. John P. Meier, *A Marginal Jew: Rethinking the Historical Jesus*, vol. 1 (New York: Doubleday, 1991).

2. John Dominic Crossan, *The Historical Jesus: The Life of a Mediterranean Jewish Peasant* (San Francisco: HarperSanFrancisco, 1991).

3. Albert Schweitzer, *The Quest of the Historical Jesus* (New York: Macmillan, 1961), 3.

4. The criteria are discussed by Meier, *A Marginal Jew*, 168–84, and Crossan, *The Historical Jesus*, xxxi–xxxiv. In his footnotes Meier cites a large body of literature on the subject. The works of Norman Perrin and Harvey K. McArthur have been very influential.

5. "The Historical Jesus Question in North America Today," *Biblical Theology Bulletin* 19 (1989): 11–22, at 19 and 20.

6. Meier, *A Marginal Jew*, 237, note 41; cf. 244–45, note 76.

7. In my *Apologetics and the Biblical Christ* (Westminster, Md.: Newman, 1963), 6–10, I have given a fuller description of this "historicist" form of apologetics, with quotations from the works of Felder and Fillion.

8. See Joachim Jeremias, *New Testament Theology 1: The Proclamation of Jesus* (New York: Scribner's, 1971), 61–68.

9. The best single introduction to Pannenberg's thought on the historical Jesus is probably his *Jesus God and Man* (Philadelphia: Westminster, 1968).

10. "Instruction on the Historical Truth of the Gospels," nos. 9–10; text in Joseph A. Fitzmyer, *A Christological Catechism: New Testament Answers* (New York: Paulist, 1982), 131–40, at 135–37.

11. Newman, *Grammar of Assent*, chap. 10, sec. 2, no. 3.

12. "Letter to the Duke of Norfolk," in *Newman and Gladstone: The Vatican Decrees*, ed. Alvan Ryan (Notre Dame, Ind.: University of Notre Dame, 1962), 177.

13. See Ben F. Meyer, *The Aims of Jesus* (London: SCM, 1979), 110.

14. Some will be disappointed that the article "Jesus" in the *New Jerome Biblical Commentary* (Englewood Cliffs, N.J.: Prentice-Hall, 1990), 1316–28, is written from a perspective that prescinds from faith. (I assume that the author, John P. Meier, was carrying out his mandate from the editors.) The deficiency is partly offset by several later articles on "New Testament Thought" that take up New Testament Christology, miracles, and the resurrection of Jesus. But one misses an article along the lines of Prosper Grech's "Jesus Christ in History and Kerygma" in *The New Catholic Commentary on Holy Scripture*, ed. Reginald G. Fuller (rev. ed.; London: Nelson, 1975), 822–37.

9

Religion and the
Transformation of Politics

October 6, 1992

In an election year more often than at other times questions are raised
about the part that religion plays, or ought to play, in politics. Should
the Church attempt to influence the political outlook of its members
and that of the larger society? Should the leadership of the Church endorse certain legislative proposals, political platforms, parties, or candidates as deserving of support by the faithful? Should faithful Christians
look to the Church for guidance on political matters? Do Catholics in
public life in fact take positions that reflect their religious allegiance?

The separation between Church and State does not require a negative
reply to all these questions. Although religion and politics are distinct,
they are not separable. Political judgments are inevitably permeated with
moral and religious assumptions. Christian faith, without itself solving
political questions, has an undeniable impact on the believer's approach
to social and political life.

The influence of the Church on the political order takes place, I believe, at three distinct levels: that of particular policy issues, that of Catholic social teaching, and that of personal religion. Taking these three areas
in order, I shall consider the role of the Church with regard to each.

POLICY ISSUES

Jesus was repeatedly asked questions designed to make him take a stand
on the burning issues of the day, especially his attitudes toward the

Roman occupation government. From the Gospel accounts it would seem that he consistently refused to give direct answers to such questions. Although he had a great deal to say about how political and economic power should be used, he is not reported as proposing either violent or peaceful overthrow of the existing order. Instead of advocating social or political revolution, as some contemporary movements were doing, he drew the attention of his hearers to the urgency of spiritual reform. The same may be said of the twelve apostles, at least from what we know of their conduct after the Resurrection. They, together with Paul and other associates, concentrated on the religious message of the gospel and showed little or no interest in political institutions and processes.

While opposing emperor-worship on religious grounds, the Church remained generally aloof from political questions until the fourth century, when Christianity became the official religion of the Empire. Thereafter politics and religion came to be intermeshed. Making a close identification between citizenship and religious orthodoxy, the emperors made use of the Church to help solidify the unity of the Empire.

In the Middle Ages the Church gained a certain supremacy over the emperors, at least in Western Europe. The popes were often regarded as having jurisdiction over civil rulers in temporal matters. Later theologians explained that the temporal power of the pope was only indirect in the sense that it could not be exercised except for religious purposes. Popes could indeed depose rulers and change laws, but only in crisis situations, when the good of souls was at stake.

In modern times all theories of the temporal power of the ecclesiastical hierarchy have been practically abandoned. Catholics generally concede that the Church has no temporal jurisdiction, whether direct or indirect, except in the city-state of the Vatican. Churchmen cannot influence the political order except by their moral authority. Their practical judgments become effective only when mediated through appeals to reason and conscience.

This renunciation of temporal power has not meant a retreat of the Church from the public square. The Catholic Church in this country, through the various committees, exercises an unremitting surveillance over legislative and governmental issues in which a moral or religious component is perceived. The Conference issues regular statements and frequently provides testimony for congressional hearings. Since 1976 the Administrative Board of the U.S. Catholic Conference has issued every four years, in preparation for the November elections, a list of major issues on which the bishops have a clear position.[1]

The whole body of bishops occasionally issues pastoral letters on subjects of political concern. It published in 1983 "The Challenge of Peace" and in 1986 "Economic Justice for All." These letters, while not neglecting broader principles, contain rather specific applications and thus enter into technical realms such as counterforce targeting of military objectives, the production of particular weapons (the MX and Pershing II), the minimum-wage law, progressive taxation, and affirmative action. An even broader range of issues is covered in the quadrennial statements on political responsibility.

The bishops claim to be speaking as pastors, not as experts on military affairs, economics, or whatever. But when they make detailed applications of the kind I have mentioned, this distinction is hard to maintain. Recognizing the importance of secular input, the bishops conduct hearings to learn the views of experts and rely on specialists to draft their documents. Thus they implicitly acknowledge the inseparability of their conclusions from the facts and theories they accept from their consultants. They make choices among views that are held by sincere and intelligent Catholics.

When the American bishops published their pastoral letters on peace and economic justice, Catholics of a different political orientation formed committees and composed so-called lay pastoral letters expressing their own points of view. These lay pastorals do not appear to violate any principles of Catholic faith and morals. They are concrete evidence that commitment to Christ and the Church is compatible with a broad range of political options.

Because the specific applications cannot be vindicated from Scripture or tradition, it is generally wise for the bishops to avoid lending their authority to one position or another. When they intervene in controversial questions of a secular character they stir up opposition to themselves from within the Church and thereby undermine their own authority to teach and govern. The Synod of Bishops in 1971 made the following wise recommendation: "It does not belong to the Church, insofar as she is a religious and hierarchical community, to offer concrete solutions in the social, economic, and political spheres for justice in the world."[2]

In holding that it is generally best for the bishops to leave the specific policy issues up to lay experts, I am not implying that these issues are unimportant. Catholic lawmakers, judges, and public officials should make every effort to devise concrete programs compatible with faith and morals. In times of crisis it may also be necessary, for the prevention of greater evils, for the bishops to summon the faithful to take a united stand. Ordinarily, however, it is probably better for the bishops to allow these questions to be resolved through the inner workings of the political process. Care should be taken not to give the impression that the Church is a pressure group harassing office holders and candidates for office and seeking to control their political conduct by threatening them with ecclesiastical penalties. If this impression is given, the Church loses in public respect more than it gains by influencing particular decisions.

CATHOLIC SOCIAL TEACHING

Issue-oriented statements, however correct and persuasive they may be, fail to meet what many analysts regard as the major crisis of our day. Two visions of the American political experiment are struggling for supremacy. Some social commentators say that our nation today finds itself caught in a war between two cultures.[3] One culture, the more conservative, holds that law and policy must be in conformity with a transcendent, God-given order of justice and morality, and that the cultivation of public virtue is a condition of our survival as a free nation. The other culture, sometimes called progressivist, rejects the idea that we are bound as a nation to any permanent truths and moral principles. In the estimation of this second group the principles on which the nation stands can be indefinitely revised according to the prevailing assumptions of contemporary society. Progressivists commonly look on law as an instrument of individual and collective self-interest.

This culture war cannot be won by tactical battles about particular issues—even important issues such as the legalization of divorce, abortion, and euthanasia. For the policy statements of the bishops to be plausible and, in the long run, fruitful, they must be backed up by a coherent social and political philosophy.

A generation ago John Courtney Murray stated the case for such a philosophy with all necessary clarity in his masterly book *We Hold These Truths*.[4] The American experiment in ordered liberty, he held, rests on a public philosophy to which we are as a nation committed by our founding documents and by a long tradition of official interpretation. This public philosophy, Father Murray explained, is ultimately rooted in the sacredness of the human person. Every individual is endowed with a personal dignity that commands the respect of society in all its laws and institutions. The American public philosophy, moreover, implies the fundamental equality of all human beings and the solidarity of all in pursuit of the common good. In such a philosophy, Murray showed, freedom is protected; government has a limited role and is based on the consent of the governed. The State, as the juridical form of society, is not to be equated with the society as a whole. It is only one of the many institutions, both natural and freely constructed, by which people are joined in society. Law must be ordered toward justice, which provides it with its basis and goal. Law is a force for orderly change as well as for social stability. It serves not only to regulate action but also to educate the public conscience on matters of public morality.[5]

Murray believed that this political philosophy was inscribed in the founding documents and the central traditions of our nation. In *We Hold These Truths* he asserts that the Declaration of Independence, in its appeal to self-evident propositions, affirms an order of truth beyond politics, one that imparts to politics its fundamental human meaning. The Declaration, in contrast to the Jacobin laicist tradition of continental Europe, asserted the sovereignty of God over nations as well as over individual men and women: "The first article of the American political faith is that the political community, as a form of free and ordered life, looks to the sovereignty of God as to the first principle of its organization."[6]

Murray goes on to quote several presidents from John Adams to Eisenhower as supporting this view. In a proclamation of May 30, 1863, Lincoln declared that "it is the duty of nations as well as of men to own their dependence upon the overruling power of God, to confess their sins and trespasses in humble sorrow, yet with assured hope that genuine repentance will lead to mercy and pardon."[7]

In calling for national days of prayer, the presidents have been confident of being in accord with the First Amendment to the Constitution. The Supreme Court as late as 1952 asserted: "We are a religious people whose institutions presuppose a Supreme Being." The same principle, Murray maintains, had been formally espoused by the Supreme Court in 1815, 1892, and 1931. Thus the current opinion that religion is a purely private matter is a clear dissent from the political tradition of the United

States. That tradition, according to Murray, approves itself to the Catholic intelligence because its ethical and political principles stem from the ancient Christian tradition of natural law. The Catholic community still speaks in the ethical and political idiom familiar to the founders of the American Republic.[8]

Murray saw very clearly that his vision of the American ideal of a free society was being challenged. Contemporary relativism and pragmatism were undermining what had been the American consensus. When a political philosophy such as his own is presented, he observed, people very often respond on the level of emotion:

> Usually, the outcry is raised: But this is orthodoxy! Thus the great word of anathema is hurled. The limits of tolerance have been reached. We will tolerate all kinds of ideas, however pernicious; but we will not tolerate the idea of an orthodoxy. That is, we refuse to say, as a people: there are truths, and we hold them, and these are the truths.[9]

The crisis that Murray described is even more acute today because of the "culture wars" to which I have already alluded. It is here precisely that the Catholic Church may be able to make a major contribution. As several wise analysts have observed, this could be the Catholic moment in the history of our nation provided that Catholics have the confidence to draw on their resources and to speak out energetically.[10] Thanks to a long series of thinkers such as Augustine, Aquinas, Suárez, de Lugo, von Ketteler, Heinrich Pesch, Nell-Breuning, Maritain, and Murray himself, the Church has developed over the centuries a highly sophisticated body of thought about social and political principles. Since Leo XIII, some elements of this tradition have been incorporated into official Catholic teaching through papal encyclicals. Vatican II, in its Pastoral Constitution on the Church in the Modern World and its Declaration on Religious Freedom, helped to solidify this tradition.

The Catholic tradition of political thought has consistently opposed the revolution inaugurated by Machiavelli and continued in various forms by Hobbes, Locke, Rousseau, Kant, Marx, and Nietzsche. Criticizing this revolutionary tradition, which looks to human self-interest and the will to power rather than divine law and moral rectitude, Leo Strauss has said:

> Anyone who wishes to judge impartially of the legitimacy or the prospects of the great design of modern man to erect the City of Man on what

appear to him to be the ruins of the City of God must familiarize himself with the teachings, and especially the political teachings, of the Catholic Church, which is certainly the most powerful antagonist of that modern design.[11]

Pope John Paul II, speaking out of this Catholic tradition, called attention to its harmony with the American political experiment. At his meeting with President Reagan on September 10, 1987, he recalled the bicentennial of the U.S. Constitution, which was then being celebrated. He spoke of the American tradition of freedom as having been from the beginning directed to the formation of a well-ordered society, the preservation of human dignity, and the safeguarding of human rights. In language reminiscent of Murray, he continued:

> The only true freedom, the only freedom that can truly satisfy, is the freedom to do what we ought as human beings created by God according to his plan. It is the freedom to live the truth of what we are and who we are before God, the truth of our identity as children of God, as brothers and sisters in a common humanity. That is why Jesus Christ linked truth and freedom together, stating solemnly: "You will know the truth, and the truth will set you free" (Jn 8:32).[12]

The pope, as a former professor of philosophy with two doctoral degrees, was well equipped to speak convincingly about these principles. The social teaching of the Church has consistently been formulated through the active cooperation of Church leaders and university professors. The Catholic Church in America today has in its many universities a valuable resource for continuing this cooperation. In their departments of theology, philosophy, political science, economics, and sociology, these institutions may be expected to speak out of the Catholic tradition and to articulate the Catholic vision for our time and situation. They can transmit the heritage to new generations of students and can enter into dialogue with other points of view. In his apostolic constitution on Catholic universities (*Ex corde Ecclesiae*, 1990), the present pope has underlined the responsibilities of the university for research in the sacred sciences, for passing on the Catholic tradition, and for entering into dialogue with contemporary cultures.

The American political heritage, according to Murray, is threatened not only by hostile, ideologies but also by a new barbarism, in which reason is cast aside.

> Society becomes barbarian when men are huddled together under the rule of force or fear; when economic interests assume the primacy over higher values; when material standards of mass and quantity crush out values of quality and excellence; when technology assumes an autonomous existence and embarks on a course of unlimited self-exploitation . . . and when men come under the sway of the instinctual, the impulsive, the compulsive.[13]

In a year of heated campaign rhetoric this admonition against barbarism takes on fresh relevance. Such debate, as Murray recognized, is always in danger of sinking into passion and prejudice, appealing to the lowest human instincts. The only passion admissible in public discourse, according to Murray, is the passion for justice. The will to justice, he remarked, leads to clear understanding and is the ground of civic amity and peace. It is a task of Catholic intellectuals and universities to be a leaven, helping to raise the tone of public political argument toward that "cool and dry" quality that Murray regarded as essential.[14]

The social teaching of the Church is closely connected, but not identical, with its activity on the level of public policy, discussed in the first section of this paper. Social teaching is not directed in the first instance to legislation and policy issues but rather to education. It is designed to inculcate a proper perspective on the good society, the role of government, and the pursuit of pleasure, wealth, honor, and power.[15] If a choice is to be made as to where to place the emphasis, I would opt for education because it opens up the possibility of a lasting change for the better. Lobbying and pressure tactics, on the other hand, leave the basic situation unchanged. In the long run more good is done by changing people's vision and ideals than by the adoption of good laws and administrative decisions. If a consensus exists in favor of a healthy society, the implementation will almost take care of itself.

Let us assume, for instance, that by strong pressures it were possible for prolife organizations to obtain legislation that would criminalize all abortions throughout the entire nation. The victory could be a Pyrrhic one unless public opinion were dramatically changed. In all probability the police and the courts would not enforce the law, or the forbidden practice would be driven underground. Laws that run against the consensus of the people will generally be ineffective.

PERSONAL RELIGION

For the successful conduct of politics it is not enough to devise and teach a sound political philosophy. It is necessary to foster the qualities required for a people to engage in responsible self-government.

There has been a long-standing debate about whether moral virtue is needed for the success of the state. The tradition of political thought stemming from Machiavelli and Hobbes holds that it is sufficient for the power of the state to prevent vicious people from harming one another. Kant in his essay on Eternal Peace argued that mechanisms could be devised that would make intelligent persons collaborate for the good of society in spite of their selfish propensities. "The problem of establishing a state," he declared, "is solvable even for a people of devils, if only they have intelligence, though this may sound harsh."[16]

The classical tradition, stemming from Plato and Aristotle, held the contrary view. "The best regime," it held, "is the order most conducive to virtue."[17] The state exists for the sake of the good society. A nation of dissolute liars, even if it could hold together, would not be a good society, and thus would not fulfill the proper purpose of the State.

Augustine handed on this classical tradition in Christianized form to the West. In *The City of God* he wrote:

> When a man does not serve God, what justice can we ascribe to him, since in this case his soul cannot exercise a just control over the body, nor his reason over his vices? And if there is no justice in such an individual, certainly there can be none in the community of such persons.[18]

The Congregation for the Doctrine of the Faith, in its second Instruction on Liberation Theology (1986) aligned itself with this classical and Augustinian tradition. The Church, it declared, "considers that the first thing to be done is to appeal to the spiritual and moral capacities of the individual and to the permanent need for inner conversion, if one is to achieve the economic and social changes that will truly be at the service of man."[19] It went on to say:

Structures established for people's good are of themselves incapable of securing and guaranteeing that good. The corruption which in certain countries affects the leaders and the State bureaucracy, and which destroys all
honest social life, is a proof of this. Moral integrity is a necessary condition
for the health of society.[20]

A major task confronting the State is therefore that of fostering the personal virtues needed for the good society. In the United States we have
recently seen a growing realization that ethics and values need to be recovered. Increasing reliance is placed on legislation and judicial processes
for preventing social evils such as child abuse, sexual harassment, racial
discrimination, robbery, rape, and embezzlement. Litigation continues to
increase, but selfishness and hatred, violence and injustice are not overcome. In the words of Glenn Tinder, "Human beings in their passion for
justice have not devised institutions that they cannot in their pride and
selfishness outwit."[21]

Aleksandr Solzhenitsyn in his commencement address at Harvard in
1978 pointed out the fallacy. He said:

> A society with no other scale but the legal one is also less [than] worthy of
> man. . . . The letter of the law is too cold and formal to have a beneficial
> influence on society. Whenever the tissue of life is woven of legalistic rela-
> tionships, this creates an atmosphere of spiritual mediocrity that paralyzes
> man's noblest impulses.[22]

Among the virtues needed for society, an important place must be given
to friendship, mercy, and forgiveness, without which the endless passion
for revenge and retribution cannot be quelled. These qualities, since they
are rooted in human hearts, cannot be legislated by the government. Calling attention to this fact in his encyclical on mercy, *Dives in misericordia*,
John Paul II mentioned the role of the Church: "It is impossible to establish this bond [of mutual friendship] between people if they wish to regulate their mutual relationship solely according to justice. . . . The Church
must consider it one of her principal duties—at every stage of history and
especially in our modern age—to proclaim and introduce into life the
mystery of mercy, supremely revealed in Jesus Christ."[23]

Morality and religion, therefore, are inextricably intertwined. Virtuous
conduct is sustained by belief in a God to whom we are accountable in
all our actions. The moral life, as Plato and Kant recognized, can hardly

be sustained without the conviction that we live in a moral universe in which virtue and happiness are linked, at least in the life to come. Moral education, therefore, cannot be effectively accomplished except by persons who profess belief in a transcendent order. In America today, State-controlled schools, prohibited from professing any religious faith, are in a quandary about how to transmit the values and beliefs required to sustain the American experiment in ordered liberty.[24]

The academic teaching of morality and religion, of course, is not sufficient. Beliefs and values are transmitted by living example and by involvement in a community of faith. To undergo personal conversion to Christ, people must hear the proclamation of the gospel; they must respond in faith; they must pray, worship, and receive the sacraments.

The Church, I submit, can make its best contribution to the political order by being herself—by being the community of faith and worship that it was from its earliest days. Where faith is strong, Christians will be honest, loving, merciful, and respectful of the rights of others. They will have a sense of solidarity reaching out to the whole human family. They will recognize their own fragility and their need of God. To quote Tinder again: "The Christian sense of the depth and stubbornness of evil in human beings, along with the faith that the universe under the impulse of grace is moving toward radical re-creation, gives a distinctive cast to the Christian conception of political action and social progress."[25]

Because Christians hope in the promise of God's final Kingdom, already anticipated in the resurrection of Christ, they can have courage and realism amid the vicissitudes of life. Keeping their gaze fixed on the definitive outcome, believers can experience worldly success without complacency and pride; they are likewise able to encounter opposition, even defeat, without succumbing to the despair that lies at the root of so many human tragedies.

The Church, in its doctrinal heritage and sacraments, has unique resources for raising its members above the sordid quest for pleasure, wealth, and power, and for restraining the drives of hedonism, ambition, and pride that everywhere threaten civil peace and order. Among sincere practicing Christians, God's grace can work wonders, as we know from the examples of saints who have heroically sacrificed themselves for the sake of others.

In summary, then, we may conclude that the political order is not self-sufficient. It cannot succeed without a morally good society, and morality cannot be firmly established in the absence of religious faith. Faith helps to give a clear moral vision; it gives new motives for the practice of virtue and, if sincerely practiced, it leads its adherents into a transforming communion with God. The Christian religion is therefore conducive to what Pope Paul VI called "a civilization of love."

The Church, even without directly intervening in the political process, can make a major contribution to the political order by shaping the ideas and habits of the persons who constitute the society, making them morally and spiritually capable of responsible self-government. Those who govern the State will be well advised to esteem religion not only for its intrinsic values but also because it can promote the good society, which is the goal of the State as well.

NOTES

1. These statements on "Political Responsibility" may be found in *Origins* 5 (February 26, 1976): 565, 567–70; 9 (November 15, 1979): 349, 351–55; 13 (April 12, 1984): 732–36; 17 (November 5, 1987): 369, 371–75; 21 (October 24, 1991) 313, 315–23, and each four years thereafter. The Administrative Board of the U. S. Catholic Conference of Bishops was succeeded in this role by the Administrative Committee of the U. S. Conference of Catholic Bishops.

2. Synod of Bishops, "Justice in the World," 37, *Catholic Mind* 70 (March 1972): 52–64, at 58. Vatican II likewise called for a clear distinction between what the faithful do in their own name as citizens and what they do in the Church's name in union with the hierarchical leadership. See *Gaudium et spes*, 76.

3. James Davison Hunter, *Culture Wars: The Struggle to Define America* (New York: Basic Books, 1991).

4. John Courtney Murray, *We Hold These Truths* (New York: Sheed & Ward, 1960).

5. Ibid., 81.

6. Ibid., 28.

7. Ibid., 29.

8. Ibid., 43.

9. Ibid., 85.

10. The foundational book on this subject is Richard John Neuhaus, *The Catholic Moment* (San Francisco: Harper & Row, 1987).

11. Leo Strauss, *What Is Political Philosophy?* (Westport, Conn.: Greenwood Press, 1959), 281.

12. John Paul II, comments at meeting with Ronald Reagam, *Origins* 17 (September 24, 1987): 238–39, at 238.

13. Murray, *We Hold These Truths*, 13–14.

14. Ibid., 8.

15. J. Brian Benestad, *The Pursuit of a Just Social Order* (Washington, D.C.: Ethics and Public Policy Center, 1982), 124.

16. Immanuel Kant, "Eternal Peace" in *The Philosophy of Kant*, ed. Carl J. Friedrich (New York: Modern Library, 1949), 453.

17. Leo Strauss, *Political Philosophy: Six Essays* (Indianapolis: Bobbs-Merrill, 1975), 85.

18. Augustine, *The City of God*, book 19, chap. 21, trans. Marcus Dods (New York: Modern Library, 1950), 700.

19. Congregation for the Doctrine of the Faith, "Instruction on Christian Freedom and Liberation," no. 75, *Origins* 15 (April 17, 1986): 713–28, at 724.

20. Ibid.

21. Glenn Tinder, "Can We Be Good Without God?" *Atlantic Monthly* 246 (December 1989): 69–85, at 83.

22. In *Solzhenitsyn at Harvard*, ed. Ronald Berman (Washington, D.C.: Ethics and Public Policy Center, 1980), 7–8; cf. J. Francis Stafford, pastoral letter *Virtue and the American Republic* (privately printed, 1989), 5.

23. *Dives in misericordia*, no. 14, *Origins* 10 (December 11, 1980): 414.

24. See Richard John Neuhaus, *America Against Itself: Moral Vision and the Public Order* (Notre Dame, Ind.: University of Notre Dame Press, 1992), 46.

25. Tinder, "Can We Be Good Without God?" 84.

10

The Church as Communion

March 31, 1993

I gratefully dedicate this essay to the memory of Father John Meyendorff, one of the outstanding ecumenists of our time. Four years ago, on March 16, 1989, he responded to my spring McGinley lecture, and in so doing made very impressively the point that in spite of our differences, and perhaps partly because of them, we Roman Catholics and Orthodox need each other. I have greatly profited from reading some of Father Meyendorff's observations relating to the theme of the present lecture, the Church as communion. In an important paper that I heard him deliver at Louvain in 1971, he raised the question: "What is the *koinonia* and the 'unity' of the Church?" He promptly replied: "Obviously and primarily a unity of man *with God*, and only secondarily a unity of men with each other."[1] I wish that Father Meyendorff were here to respond to the present lecture, but since he cannot be, I cannot think of a better stand-in than Father Thomas Hopko, who has taken his place as dean of St. Vladimir's Theological Seminary.

COMMUNION ECCLESIOLOGY

There is broad agreement today that the Church is a communion (*koinonia, communio*). The Extraordinary Synod of Bishops, which was convened at Rome in 1985 to reflect on the significance of Vatican II, asserted in its Final Report: "The ecclesiology of communion is the central and fundamental idea in the Council's documents."[2] The Congregation for the Doctrine of the Faith, in a letter of May 28, 1992, added that the concept of communion "is very suitable for expressing the core of the mystery of the Church and can certainly be a key for the renewal of Catholic ecclesiology."[3]

The category of communion is ecumenically fruitful since it is widely accepted not only among Roman Catholics but also among Orthodox, Anglicans, and Lutherans.[4] The World Council of Churches, especially in its Faith and Order Commission, has favored this theme. The Working Document of the Fifth World Conference on Faith and Order, which is to meet at Santiago de Compostela, Spain, in August 1993, is entitled "Towards *Koinonia* in Faith, Life, and Witness."

In some ways this gravitation to the concept of communion is surprising, as the Church is never called a communion in Scripture, nor is it so called in the documents of any ecumenical council of the Catholic Church, including Vatican II. That council spoke of the Church as a sacrament of unity, as the Body of Christ, as Bride, and especially as People of God. It described communion as one of the bonds that unites the members of the Church to one another and to Christ the head.[5] Most of the commentaries took "People of God" to be the dominant idea of the council's ecclesiology. The Synod of 1985 seems to have made a deliberate effort to oust "People of God" from its position of primacy. Many of the bishops at the Synod, together with Cardinal Ratzinger, objected that that concept had been abused in a political and populist sense, thus tending to divide the Church into contesting classes and parties. Some theologians of a Marxist tendency proposed a "people's church" in opposition to the "hierarchical church." The Synod preferred the concept of communion because it was not amenable to sociological reduction and seemed conducive to internal unity and peace.

As a mere term, *communion* does not say a great deal. It is an abstract word, generally signifying a relation of fellowship, even intimacy. In Christian usage, the term has come to be used primarily in the context of Holy Communion, the reception of the Body and Blood of Christ. Not only through the Eucharist but through its other sacraments and ministrations, the Church puts its members in communion with God and with one another. To affirm that the members are in this kind of relationship, however, is not the same as to call the Church itself, substantively, a communion. The Congregation for the Doctrine of the Faith, acknowledging the vagueness of the term, has insisted that communion, to be a designation of the Church, needs to be integrated with the great images used in Scripture and tradition, such as People of God, Body of Christ, and sacrament.[6]

HISTORICAL FOUNDATIONS

The modern concept of the Church as communion is heavily indebted to the historical development of the first few centuries. The Church then existed not in the form of a single overarching society but rather in the form of local churches under their bishops. The faithful belonged to the Church insofar as they were admitted to communion by their own bishops. Travelers who were in good standing in their local church were commonly provided with letters of communion from their bishops that would entitle them to hospitality and admission to the sacraments in other dioceses. The bishops recognized other bishops as being in communion with themselves and with the universal Church. Certain serious offenses such as schism and heresy were seen as excluding their perpetrators from the Catholic communion.

In effect, then, the Church was a vast network of local churches under bishops who mutually recognized one another. The body of churches that were in communion could be called, in a certain sense, a communion. The communion was visible; it was established by the actions of the bishops issuing the appropriate letters and documents and was sealed by their liturgical actions, such as eucharistic concelebration and admission to the sacraments. To partake of the sacrament from a bishop was to enter into communion not only with the Lord but also with the bishop and with all who received the sacraments from him.

In theory all bishops had the power to enter into communion with, or break off communion with, one another. But, for reasons of prudence, they usually saw to it that they acted in concert with the more venerable metropolitan sees, especially those that could trace their foundation to apostles. The Church of Rome, by reason of its historical links with Peter and Paul, who had been martyred there, and perhaps also by reason of the political prestige of the city, its wealth, and its strategic importance as a center of communications, gradually came to be recognized as having a universal primacy. To be a Catholic meant, at least for many Christians, to be in communion with Rome. In situations of controversy authors such as Ambrose, Jerome, and Augustine made it clear that they chose to be in communion with the Church of Rome.

DECLINE AND REVIVAL

The communion concept of the Church declined in the second millennium. In the West, all the churches became subject to the jurisdiction of Rome. In the East, Constantinople was clearly the dominant church, after the other patriarchal churches (Alexandria, Antioch, and Jerusalem) had lapsed into schism or insignificance. At least in the West, the vertical lines of authority from Rome to the bishops replaced the horizontal lines of communion among bishops and among churches.[7]

The decline of communion theology in the West was accelerated by several factors. One of these was the revival of Roman law, which formalized the concepts of legislative and judicial power in the Church. The bishops of the local churches were seen as being under the supreme jurisdiction of the pope. The power of excommunication was for practical purposes in the hands of the pope, because to be in communion with the Church meant, in effect, to be in communion with Rome. The pope came to be viewed as supreme and universal bishop—the bishop of the Catholic Church.

Another factor was Scholastic theology, which, under the influence of Augustine, interiorized and spiritualized the concept of communion. For the great theologians of the thirteenth century, communion was the final spiritual effect of the devout reception of the sacraments. Communion, in this view, was an interior grace-given relationship of the individual with God. Sacraments such as baptism and the Eucharist were no longer seen as bringing one into communion with the local church and its bishop but rather into a universal, undivided communion of grace. All who were living in the grace of God were members of the body of Christ, a body now conceived as being mystical and invisible. Although the medieval concept of the Church included visible structures, communion was considered to be primarily interior. The seeds were being planted for the doctrine of the invisible Church, which flowered in some of the Protestant Reformers.

Reacting against the Reformers, the theologians of the Counter-Reformation gave greater emphasis to the institution, considered in juridical terms. They depicted the Church as a centralized body in which all the members, including bishops, were subjects of the pope as vicar of Christ. The local church came to be seen almost as an administrative unit under the pope, who wielded the fullness of power. Even ecumenical councils could not restrict the authority of the pope, since it was his prerogative to summon councils and to approve their decrees under pain of invalidity.

On the eve of Vatican II a number of authors, dissatisfied with the prevailing institutionalism, sought to revitalize the Church by a return to patristic models. This process led to a vision of the Church as an interpersonal communion, in which the ecclesial significance of the sacraments took on new meaning. The local church celebrating the Eucharist under the presidency of its bishop came to be seen as the paradigmatic realization of the Church. The bishops were regarded as representative heads of particular churches, receiving their basic powers directly from Christ himself through the sacrament of ordination. The bishops, as pastors of particular churches, were held to constitute a college, in which all the members were co-responsible for the supreme direction of the universal Church.[8]

VATICAN II

This revived communion theology had a major impact on Vatican II (1962–65). The doctrine of the Church as a communion of local churches contributed to a revitalization of the particular church and its liturgy. The Constitution on the Liturgy declared that "the Church reveals herself most clearly when a full complement of God's holy people, united in prayer and in a common liturgical service (especially the Eucharist), exercise a thorough and active participation at the very altar where the bishop presides in the company of his priests and other assistants" (*SC* 41). This principle was repeated in the Constitution on the Church to emphasize the theological importance of the particular church (*LG* 26) and in the Decree on the Bishops' Pastoral Office to bring out the dignity of the diocesan bishop (*CD* 11). The bishops, linked to one another in hierarchical communion, could make the supreme authority of the Church present in a given locality. Since they were fellow bishops with the bishop of Rome, they could not be regarded as mere delegates of the pope (*LG* 27). The pope was depicted not as an absolute monarch but as a moderator "presiding over the assembly of charity" (*LG* 13).

The council fathers were convinced that this communion-centered vision could be successfully integrated with the teaching of Vatican I about the universal primacy of the pope as successor of Peter. The papacy, they maintained, was needed both to protect legitimate diversity and to prevent diversity from impairing unity. Using communion theology to correct the excessive centralism and clericalism of recent centuries, the council encouraged different local and regional churches to take on their own distinctive character within the Catholic fellowship. "Through the common sharing of gifts and through the common effort to attain fullness in unity," said the Constitution on the Church, "the whole and each of the parts receive increase" (*LG* 13). And again: "The variety of local churches with one common aspiration is particularly splendid evidence of the catholicity of the undivided Church" (*LG* 23). Since Vatican II the bishops' conferences have developed in the various nations and continents, giving the Catholic Church an inner diversity that it previously lacked. The vernacular in the liturgy is only one element of this adaptation.

The idea of communion was also used at Vatican II to revitalize the theology of the laity. Laypeople, according to the council, are not just docile subjects executing the orders of the hierarchy. Through baptism and confirmation each individual has an active share in the threefold office of Christ as prophet, priest, and king (*LG* 31; *AA* 3) All Christians participate actively in the life and mission of the Church. Anointed by the Holy Spirit, they have a supernatural sense of the faith, equipping them to recognize what doctrines are in accordance with, or opposed to, the new life given in Christ (*LG* 12; cf. 25).

As is evident from what I have said, Vatican II blended earlier forms of communion ecclesiology with elements from the Scholastic and juridical heritage of the past few centuries. The council proposed an original synthesis that did not fully satisfy theologians exclusively committed to certain interpretations. Content to lay down the basic doctrinal principles, the council did not attempt to settle debated theological questions.

Two Tendencies

The debates at the council and in the subsequent literature have made it clear that within the broad category of Vatican II ecclesiology there are at least two major tendencies—a personalist approach that builds on early patristic models and a mystical approach that owes more to medieval

Augustinianism. These approaches do not lend themselves to easy labeling. Some authors contrast them as "ascending" and "descending" ecclesiologies, ecclesiologies "from below" and "from above." The approach that starts from the local community may in a certain sense be called particularist; the other, which starts from the global community, may be called universalist. Acknowledging the limited value of all these labels, I shall here speak of the universalist and particularist tendencies.

While few if any theologians conform perfectly to type, Leonardo Boff may be taken as a particularist within the communion genre. Henri de Lubac and Joseph Ratzinger, in his recent work, might be called moderate universalists and Jean-Marie Tillard, a moderate particularist. Most theologians combine some elements of each approach. My present concern is not with labeling individuals but with sketching two tendencies, both of which appeal to Vatican II, even though they focus on different phrases and texts from the council documents.

The two theologies differ in their very interpretation of the term *communio*. The universalists are inclined to understand it as meaning participation in the divine life, achieved through the objective means of grace, notably the sacraments. In this view the Christian's communion is (as we have heard from Meyendorff) in the first instance with God, and secondarily with all who share in the same divine life. Contemporary particularists, under the influence of modern personalism, commonly understand the term "communion" as directly signifying a fellowship of love and intimacy. This local community, in which the members know one another and interact, orients its members toward communion with God and with all other human beings, without restriction.

The two points of view have consequences all along the line, beginning with baptism. Does the sacrament of baptism incorporate a person into the local church, the universal Church, or both? Baptism is celebrated in a particular community, into which the candidate is received, but at the same time it makes that candidate a member of the universal Church. In my estimation the universal membership is more fundamental, since many of the baptized have no stable relationship to a particular parish or diocese and are nevertheless entitled to receive the sacraments wherever they go.

Similar questions arise concerning the Eucharist. Granted that the particular church has the power to offer the Eucharist, it may be asked whether that power makes the particular church self-sufficient or whether, on the contrary, the Eucharist is precisely what excludes all self-sufficiency on the part of the particular church.[9] In the particularist approach, the Eucharist appears as the sacrament that builds the individual congregation, bringing about fellowship among all who partake at the same altar. Universalists make the point that the Eucharist is essentially ordered toward the whole Church, in the name of which the sacrifice is offered. The celebrant mentions by name the bishops of other churches, and especially the pope. Holy Communion, say the universalists, unites the communicant first of all with God and, as a result, with all other Christians who are living in the grace of God.

The two approaches differ in their understanding of church organization. The particularists tend to see the universal Church as arising from particular churches that freely enter into fellowship. They defend what one of them calls "an ecclesiology of the universal church that begins with the local church (an ecclesiology 'from below')."[10] Each local church, they sometimes declare, has all the essentials required to constitute a church. Applying the principle of subsidiarity to the Church, they regard the machinery of universal government as a "subsidiary" structure to take care of exceptional cases that the local churches are not capable of handling on their own.

The universalists hold that Christ founded the Church on Peter and the apostles as a universal society and that it subsequently came to be divided into particular regional churches. The responsibilities of the universal leadership, they would say, are constitutive of the Church herself and not simply subsidiary. Unless a particular church is visibly joined to the universal body, its own integrity as a church is deficient. On this last point the universalists would seem to have Vatican II in their favor. The Church, it teaches, "organized in this world as a society, subsists in the Catholic Church, governed by the successor of Peter and the bishops in communion with him" (*LG* 8). Outside this structure there is no perfect unity, no full incorporation into the one Church of Christ (*LG* 14; *UR* 3).

How is the local church formed? According to universalists it is constituted from above, as the apostolic heritage of faith, sacraments, and ministry, perpetuated in the universal Church, is made available to new groups. The particularist view tends to see groups as being spontaneously formed, under the impulse of the Holy Spirit, and as constituting themselves, even to the extent of appointing their own official leadership. Some speak of the basic ecclesial community as the locus where "ecclesiogenesis" oc-curs.[11] The universal Church, from the particularist perspective, is formed through the mutual recognition and fellowship of churches that were originally local. A mediating position holds that the Church was from the beginning both universal and particular, since it always consisted of particular churches that belonged to a universal communion.

On the respective priorities between the particular and the universal Church, each party can find passages in Vatican II that, taken in isolation, seem to support its point of view. The particularists can quote from the Constitution on the Church (*LG* 23) the assertion that that "the one and only Catholic church" exists "in and from" the particular churches.[12] The universalists, however, call attention to the previous clause, in which the particular churches are declared to be formed according to the pattern of the universal Church,[13] which, according to the Decree on the Ministry of Bishops, is present and operative in them (*CD* 11). The particularists are on solid ground when they argue that the Holy Spirit can inspire ecclesial initiatives that are not directly dependent on the hierarchy of the great Church. But the universalists would seem to be correct in insisting that the Church was originally founded as a single society and only gradu-ally came to be articulated as a plurality of particular churches. The uni-versal Church is not, as some particularists allege, an abstraction; it is a concretely existing whole apart from which particular churches have no rightful existence.

The two tendencies within contemporary Catholicism both accept the episcopal form of government, but for different reasons: the universalists, because by the will and intention of Christ the identity of the Church is maintained by the apostolic succession of bishops; the particularists, be-cause episcopacy has decisive traditional, ecumenical, and practical war-rants. The two groups, moreover, understand the episcopate somewhat differently. The universalists hold that the episcopate is collegial by its very nature: by sacramental ordination the new bishop is received by other bishops into the body corporately charged with the supreme direction of the universal Church. It is very fitting, universalists assert, for bishops to be appointed as pastors of dioceses, but members of the hierarchy who receive no such appointment, they add, can still be bishops in the true sense of the term. For the particularists, on the contrary, a bishop is primarily the pastor of a diocese, and only for that reason is he entitled to have a voice in the episcopal college. In principle, then, the college should be made up of the responsible heads of particular churches. The universal-ist view of the episcopacy, I believe, has better support from Vatican II (*LG* 21–22), but the particularist view has stronger roots in history.

In both its expressions, Catholic communion theology accepts the pri-macy of the pope. The universalists look on the pope as the successor of Peter and as visible head of the whole flock of Christ. For them it is a secondary matter that he is bishop of Rome. Some even speculate that the primacy could be transferred from Rome to another see.

The particularist view holds that the primacy belongs in the first in-stance not to the pope but rather to the local church of Rome. In their view, the pope never acts as pope except when he acts as bishop of Rome. As a bishop he is a kind of elder brother, a senior colleague, but not more than a bishop. Whatever primacy he enjoys comes from the fact that his church, that of Rome, is heir to a preeminent apostolic heritage.[14] This opinion has excellent support in ancient Christian writers but is more difficult to reconcile with the two Vatican councils, both of which empha-size the status of the pope as Peter's successor.

Neither group favors a monolithic Church. Both accept diversity, but they have different attitudes toward it. The universalists see unity as the given and diversity as a matter of accommodation, inasmuch as it may be necessary for the Church to adapt itself to various cultures. Particularist theologians look on diversity as original and on unity as a subsequent achievement. Unity, according to them, is to be required only in necessary matters. As far as possible, they would say, diversity should be allowed.

ECUMENICAL CONSIDERATIONS

Ecumenism, finally, is differently understood in the two perspectives.[15] For the universalists it is a matter of reconstituting the unity of Christians by inducing all to accept the fullness of the apostolic heritage, indefectibly present in the Roman Catholic communion. They quote from Vatican II's Decree on Ecumenism that unity "subsists in the Catholic Church as something she can never lose" (*UR* 4). Following this line of thought, the Congregation for the Doctrine of the Faith last year called on the other churches to undergo a "new conversion to the Lord" so that they might "recognize the continuity of the primacy of Peter in his successors, the bishops of Rome."[16] This view puts special burdens on churches that are not Roman Catholic to acquire elements of the Christian patrimony that are still lacking to them.

No Catholic theologian will deny the desirability that all Christians should come to accept the Petrine office as exercised by the bishop of Rome. But surely the Congregation for the Doctrine of the Faith had no intention of reducing ecumenism to this one objective. The Catholic Church recognizes that the Petrine office is only one of many bonds constitutive of communion. Scripture and tradition call attention to many others, including the word of God, faith, baptism, the Eucharist, prayer, hospitality, and service toward the poor. All these elements, moreover, must be seen as instruments in the hands of the Holy Spirit, who bestows the grace of fellowship with God. Churches that from a Catholic perspective lack certain elements of the apostolic heritage may still possess many bonds of communion and may live in deep fellowship with the Father, the Son, and the Holy Spirit. The Roman Catholic Church, while retaining the full institutional heritage, may be deficient in its actual fidelity to the gospel. It may fall short of other communities in its life of faith, of prayer, and of practical charity.

The goal of ecumenism, as proposed by Vatican II and reaffirmed by the Synod of 1985, is to build on the incomplete communion that now exists among Christian churches and to progress, with God's grace, toward full communion. This vision of ecumenism is particularly pertinent to the relations between Rome and the Eastern churches, which Rome recognizes as possessing "true sacraments and especially, through apostolic succession, the priesthood and the Eucharist, whereby they are still linked with us in closest intimacy" (*UR* 15). The traditions of the Eastern churches are such that, in the words of the Decree on Ecumenism, "it is not surprising . . . if from time to time one tradition has come nearer than the other to a full appreciation of certain aspects of a revealed mystery, or has expressed them to better advantage" (*UR* 17). The authentic theological, spiritual, and liturgical traditions of the Eastern churches, according to the same Decree, "promote the right ordering of life and, indeed, pave the way to the full contemplation of Christian truth" (*UR* 17).

These quotations from Vatican II represent an ecumenism that avoids the extremes of universalism and particularism. Communion by its very nature should mean a union of parties that retain their distinct identities with a view to enriching one another. In the universal Church there must be bonds that are universal and bonds that are regional and local. The whole is suitably compared to a chorus of many voices. Some universal authority is needed to prevent chaos and confusion, but a measure of autonomy is desirable to avert monolithic uniformity. Through diverse but concordant liturgies, spiritualities, and systems of law and doctrine, the Church can best reflect the inexhaustible mystery of the triune God, who invites us to share in his life in ways that lie always open to deeper exploration.

NOTES

1. "The Unity of the Church and the Unity of Mankind," reprinted in John Meyendorff, *Living Tradition: Orthodox Witness in the Contemporary World* (Crestwood, N.Y.: St. Vladimir's Seminary Press, 1978), 129–48, at 135.

2. "The Final Report," II C 1, *Origins* 15 (December 19, 1985): 444–50, at 448.

3. "Some Aspects of the Church Understood as Communion," §1, *Origins* 22 (June 25, 1992): 108–12, at 108.

4. See Avery Dulles, "Communion," *Dictionary of the Ecumenical Movement* (Geneva: World Council of Churches; and Grand Rapids, Mich.: Eerdmans, 1991), 206–9.

5. See *Lumen gentium,* 14; cf. *Gaudium et spes,* 32, and many other texts.

6. "Some Aspects," §1, p. 108.

7. The decay of the "communion" concept of the Church in the Middle Ages has been traced by many authors. The classic essay on the subject is still Yves Congar, "De la communion des églises à une ecclésiologie de l'Église universelle," in *L'Épiscopat et l'Église universelle* (Paris: Cerf: 1962), 227–60. A recent treatment may be found in Medard Kehl, *Die Kirche: Eine katholische Ekklesiologie* (Würzburg: Echter Verlag, 1992), esp. 346–54.

8. This type of ecclesiology, which owes a great deal to the historical research of Henri de Lubac and Yves Congar, is exemplified in the volume *L'Épiscopat et l'Église universelle,* cited above, and in a follow-up volume, *La collégialité épiscopale* (Paris: Cerf, 1965). Both these volumes grew out of conferences at Chevetogne in Belgium at which Congar was a leading figure.

9. The latter alternative is asserted by the Congregation for the Doctrine of the Faith in "Some Aspects," §11, p. 110.

10. Joseph Komonchak, "The Church Universal as the Communion of Local Churches," in *Where Does the Church Stand?* ed. Giuseppe Alberigo and Gustavo Gutiérrez, Concilium 146 (Edinburgh: T. & T. Clark, 1981), 30–35, at 31.

11. According to Leonardo Boff, the term *ecclesiogenesis* was coined at the First Inter-Church Meeting of the Basic Communities of Brazil at Vitória, Brazil, in 1975. See his *Ecclesiogenesis: The Base Communities Reinvent the Church* (Maryknoll, N.Y.:

Orbis, 1986), 34–35. According to him, "The hierarchy has the sacramental function of organizing and serving a reality that it has not created but discovered, and within which it finds itself," (26).

12. "In quibus et ex quibus una et unica ecclesia catholica exsistit," *LG*, 23.

13. "Ad imaginem ecclesiae universalis formatis," *LG*, 23; cf. *CD*, 11, which speaks of the particular church, "in qua vere inest et operatur una sancta catholica et apostolica Christi ecclesia."

14. This general perspective is illustrated by Jean-Marie R. Tillard, *The Bishop of Rome* (Wilmington, Del.: Michael Glazier, 1986). See also the same author's *Church of Churches* (Collegeville, Minn.: Liturgical Press, 1992), 284–307.

15. "Some Aspects," §18, p. 111.

16. Several authors of great authority have recently presented Catholic ecumenism in the light of the ecclesiology of communion; for example, Johannes Willebrands, "Vatican II's Ecclesiology of Communion," *Origins* 17 (May 28, 1987): 27–33; Pierre Duprey, "A Catholic Perspective on Ecclesial Communion," in *Christian Authority: Essays in Honour of Henry Chadwick*, ed. G. R. Evans (Oxford: Clarendon, 1988), 7–19.

11

The Prophetic Humanism
of John Paul II

September 28, 1993

For some time I have been asking myself whether there is a single theme or rubric under which it might be possible to summarize the message of the pontificate of John Paul II. I have thought about the pope's concern for the inner unity of the Catholic Church, for the new evangelization, for the dialogue between faith and culture, and for the reconstruction of the economic order. All these themes are clearly important to John Paul II, but no one of them permeates his teaching as a whole. In seeking a more comprehensive topic I have hit on the idea of prophetic humanism.

In the case of this pope, like any other pope, it is difficult to ascertain which of his statements are actually composed by himself and which are simply accepted by him after having been drafted by others. I have no inside information to help me in this discernment. My method will be to rely principally on books and articles that he published under the name of Karol Wojtyla before he became pope, and then to take documents from his papacy that closely resemble these in style and in substance. Several of his encyclicals are so personal in tone that it seems safe to attribute them to the pope himself, even though he presumably had assistance in the final process of editing. Most of his major documents are amply furnished with footnotes that the pope himself would scarcely have had time to compose, but the substance of the text presumably reflects the pope's own thinking.

THE CONCEPT OF PROPHETIC HUMANISM

The concept of prophetic humanism requires some explanation. Any humanism must be a system of thought centered on the human person. The pope himself generally uses the term "man," which, at least in Latin, has no reference to gender. In quoting or paraphrasing his statements I shall sometimes use the English word "man" to mean an individual member of the human race. Near synonyms such as "person" are not always satisfactory, given the pope's understanding of personalization as a gradual process.[1] Persons, moreover, may be divine, angelic, and demonic as well as human.

Humanism, moreover, implies a high esteem for the human as having intrinsic value. As we shall see, the defense of the dignity of the human person and the promotion of human rights stand at the very center of the pope's program.

This program may be called prophetic for several reasons. A prophet is someone who speaks out of a strong conviction and with a sense of vocation. The pope evidently sees himself and the Church as divinely commissioned to be advocates of authentic humanity. The prophet speaks with a certain sense of urgency. Wojtyla, even when he writes as a philosopher, is never the detached academic. He is conscious of speaking to a world that is in the throes of a crisis—a crisis of dehumanization. Like most prophets, he senses that he is faced with enormous opposition and that his is perhaps a lonely voice. He is not afraid to confront others in his struggle to salvage human dignity.

Yet the pope is no pessimist. He is convinced that in the face of human needs God has provided an answer in Christ, who came that we might have life to the full. He sees the gospel as a message of hope, love, and truth not for Christians or Catholics alone but for every human being.[2] The Church, he believes, has an essential contribution to make to the task of making the world more human.[3] He repeatedly quotes from Vatican II the statement that the Church is called to be a sign and safeguard of the transcendence of the human person.[4]

The central and unifying task of the Church, for John Paul II, is to rediscover and promote the inviolable dignity of every human person.[5] "Man," as he puts it, "is the way for the Church." He explains that this means "man in the full truth of his existence, of his personal being and also of his community and social being."[6] The Church's mission must therefore be carried out with a view to humanity, and for that very reason with a view to God. Following Christ, who is both God and man, the Church must link anthropocentism and theocentrism in a deep and organic way.[7]

HUMAN DIGNITY

My first point will be to consider the pope's understanding of what it means to be human. Especially in his major philosophical work, *The Acting Person* (1969, revised 1977, English translation, 1979), he develops an original anthropology that owes something to classical Thomism and something to modern personalist phenomenology, especially as represented by Max Scheler (1874–1928). He is also conscious of points of contact with the philosophy of action of Maurice Blondel (1861–1949). In place of the Cartesian "cogito," which begins with the thinking subject, John Paul prefers to begin with action. "I act, therefore I am" might fairly characterize his starting point. Through action, he maintains, one can come to know the real character of the human being as a free, creative, responsible subject.[8] By my free actions, he asserts, I make myself what I am.[9]

Although John Paul's focus is initially on man as subject, his analysis brings out the necessary correlation with the object. As free and intelligent beings we are called to make decisions, and for these decisions to be meaningful they must conform to the truth. The root of human dignity consists in the capacity to transcend mere self-interest and embrace what is objectively true and good. One element in this objective order is the existence of other human beings with the same essential dignity as my own. With an explicit reference to Kant, Wojtyla declares that human beings must always be treated as ends, never as mere means.[10] He frequently quotes from Vatican II the statement that alone among all creatures on earth, man exists for his own sake.[11]

For Wojtyla the ethical dimension is determinative for the value of all human action. When I act according to truth I fulfill the deepest dynamism of my being and become good. When I do not act according to the truth I do not fulfill myself and I become bad. In his philosophical works Wojtyla does not explain very clearly how a person intuits the truth. As George Williams remarks, he "fails to provide the reader with what the conditions are for coming to the truth."[12] Williams hints that the operative ethics behind Wojtyla's proposal come from Christian revelation and Catholic tradition. In this I suspect that he is correct.

Speaking prophetically, the pope formulates his doctrine of freedom in opposition to a merely negative concept according to which freedom would consist in not being coerced or not being obligated by law. Already at Vatican II Bishop Wojtyla pleaded successfully for amendments to the Declaration on Religious Freedom to specify that freedom is not a mere entitlement to do whatever one pleases.[13] During his first visit as pope to the United States in 1979, he warned that the concept of freedom should not be used as a pretext for moral anarchy, as though it could justify conduct that violates the moral order.[14] Freedom, he insisted, is not an end in itself.[15] It is a capacity to fulfill one's deepest aspirations by choosing the true and the good. In this connection the pope likes to quote the saying of Jesus, "The truth shall make you free" (Jn 8:32).[16] When freedom is rightly understood, moral norms do not appear as a limitation. Truth is the guide to meaningful action, action in accordance with conscience.

We can, of course, disobey the voice of conscience and act against the truth as we perceive it. Violations of conscience do not bring about self-fulfillment; they result in anti-values and frustration.[17] The very ability to commit sin testifies in favor of the dignity of the person. Because we have the capacity freely to embrace the good, we also have the power to reject it. "To erase the notion of sin," says the pope, "would be to impoverish man in a fundamental part of his experience of his humanity."[18] The loss of the sense of sin, which seems to be an affliction of our time, is evidence of the failure to see man as a responsible moral subject oriented toward truth and goodness.

Thus far we have been looking at human dignity from a philosophical point of view, without reference to revelation, which confirms and enhances human dignity. As a theologian John Paul II draws initially on the creation narratives of Genesis. Man, he holds, was created to the image and likeness of God and destined to have dominion over the rest of creation (Gen 1:26–28).[19] But the full meaning of human life cannot be grasped except in the light of Christ, who, in revealing God, reveals humanity to itself.[20] There is no more impressive evidence for the value that God sets on the human than God's gift of his own Son as the price of our redemption.²¹ Every human being is intended by God to be redeemed and to come through Christ to final self-realization.

Some philosophers, influenced by Feuerbach and his school, have contended that God must be eliminated in order for man to attain his full stature. The present pope, like Henri de Lubac, argues just the contrary. The world must be reminded, he says, that while men and women can organize the world without God, *without* God it will always in the last analysis be organized *against humanity*.²² In denying the transcendent source and goal of our being, we would deprive man of the source of his true dignity. Without God as creator there would be no inviolable human rights. Without Christ as savior human hope would no longer extend to everlasting union with the divine. In this connection John Paul II quotes from Augustine the famous sentence, "You have made us for yourself, O Lord, and our hearts cannot find rest until they rest in you."²⁴

HUMAN EXISTENCE AS COMMUNAL

Against excessive individualism John Paul II insists that human existence is essentially communal. He writes: "Man's resemblance to God finds its basis, as it were, in the mystery of the most holy Trinity. Man resembles God not only because of the spiritual nature of his immortal soul but also by reason of his social nature, if by this we understand that he 'cannot fully realize himself except in an act of pure self-giving.' "²⁵ The pope then goes on to explain that human beings are intended to exist not only side by side, but in mutuality, for the sake of one another. The Latin term *communio* indicates the reciprocal giving and receiving that goes on within this relationship.

Human community is realized on many different levels from the family to the State and the international community. Vatican II, in its Pastoral Constitution on the Church in the Modern World, dealt with the family, culture, the economy, and the political community in four successive chapters. On each of these levels conscience obliges us to transcend the narrow limits of our own self-enhancement and to contribute to the good of others. In a small unit such as the family the members act primarily for the individual good of one another, but in larger groups the primary objective is the well-being of the group as such. As distinct from the "I–thou" community, the "we" society comprises a group who exist and act together for the sake, primarily, of the common good.²⁶

The Family

The family, according to John Paul II, is the basic cell of society and for that reason the primary locus of humanization.[27] The pope's doctrine of the family, adumbrated in his early work *Love and Responsibility* (1960),[28] is amplified in several documents from his papacy. He sees the family in a state of crisis, especially because of the reigning consumerist mentality that leads to false concepts concerning freedom and sexual fulfillment.[29] He draws on the traditional Catholic teaching regarding conjugal morality, divorce, and remarriage in order to protect the family as a stable community of generous love. Sexuality, he asserts, is realized in a truly human way only if it is an integral part of the loving communion by which a man and a woman commit themselves to one another until death.[30] The sexual relationship between married persons should always promote human dignity. The unitive meaning of marriage cannot be separated from the procreative. The deliberate exclusion of procreation, according to the pope, is detrimental to the unitive relationship between the couple.

Although Christian preachers have often proclaimed that wives should be subject to their husbands, John Paul II goes to some pains to point out that domination by the husband is a sign and effect of original sin. In the Christian order there should be an equality of mutual service between wives and husbands.[31] In this connection the pope sets forth a doctrine of women's rights based on the complementarity and communion between male and female.

The Order of Culture

Culture has been a major concern of John Paul II from his early days, when he developed his talents for music, poetry, and drama. Between 1977 and 1980 he published several important papers on the philosophy of culture. In 1982, when establishing the Pontifical Council for Culture, he wrote: "Since the beginning of my pontificate I have considered the Church's dialogue with the cultures of our time to be a vital area, one in which the destiny of the world at the end of the twentieth century is at stake."[32]

The pope's theory of culture is thoroughly humanistic: "Man lives a really human life thanks to a culture."[33] Man is the subject of culture, its object, and its term. Culture is *of* man, since no other being has culture; it is *from* man, since man creates it; and it is *for* man, since its prime purpose is human advancement.[34] Everyone lives according to some culture, which determines the mode of one's existence. Culture, as a human achievement, involves our capacity for self-creation, which in turn radiates into the world of products.[35] Culture is a materialization of the human spirit and at the same time a spiritualization of matter.[36] It thus serves to render our world more human.

We should not imagine that every culture, just because it is a culture, is above criticism. John Paul speaks of a dialogue between faith and culture. Like everything human, culture needs to be healed, ennobled, and perfected through Christ and the gospel.[37] Because culture is a human creation, it is also marked by sin. The Church must prophetically oppose what the pope, at his visit to Denver in August 1993, called "the culture of death."[38] On another occasion he said: "More than ever, in fact, man is seriously threatened by *anti-culture* which reveals itself, among other ways, in growing violence, murderous confrontations, exploitation of instincts and selfish interests."[39] In technologically advanced societies, people tend to value everything in terms of production and consumption, so that man is reduced to an epiphenomenon.[40] Authentic culture, on the contrary, resists the reduction of man to the status of an object. "It signifies the march towards a world where man can achieve his humanity in the transcendence proper to him, which calls him to truth, good, and beauty."[41]

One aspect of the contemporary crisis of culture is the crisis in education. To an alarming degree education has become focused on having rather than being. All too often it turns people into instruments of the economic or political system. In the alienated society, education is in danger of becoming a form of manipulation.[42]

The term "alienation," which the pope borrows from Marxist literature, is central to his social philosophy. For him it is the opposite of participation. In the good society all the members contribute to the common good and share in its benefits. Alienation arises when the society does not serve the dynamism of its own members, but unfolds at their expense, so that they, or some of them, feel cut off. The neighbor becomes the stranger, even the enemy.

THE ECONOMIC ORDER

The dynamics of participation and alienation, which are the key to John Paul II's theory of culture and education, are also central to his economic analysis. While he does not purport to give lessons in economics, he insists that any sound economy must accept the primacy of the human person and the common good as guiding principles. His teaching on this subject is set forth in three important encyclicals.

In the first of these, *Laborem exercens* (1981), he concentrates on the theological meaning of work, as a fulfillment of the biblical mandate to subdue the earth (Gen 1:28). He protests against systems in which man is treated as an instrument of production rather than as the effective subject of work.[43] By transforming nature, says the pope, man can achieve greater fulfillment as a human being.[44] All too often labor is regarded as a mere means to the production of capital and property, to the detriment of workers themselves. As a champion of human dignity, the Church has a duty to speak out in defense of the rights of labor.

In his second encyclical on economics, *Sollicitudo rei socialis* (1987), John Paul II recognizes personal economic initiative as a fundamental human right, stemming from the image of the Creator in every human being.[45] Does not the denial of the right to take initiatives in economic matters, he asks, "impoverish the human person as much as, or more than, the deprivation of material goods?"[46] Drawing, no doubt, on his experience behind the Iron Curtain, he castigates systems in which citizens are reduced to passivity, dependence, and submission to the bureaucratic apparatus.[47] He likewise criticizes consumerist societies in which things take priority over persons. "To 'have' objects and goods," he writes, "does not in itself perfect the human subject unless it contributes to the maturing and enrichment of that subject's 'being,' that is to say, unless it contributes to the realization of the human vocation as such."[48]

In *Centesimus annus* (1991), his third social encyclical, John Paul II returns to many of the same themes. He points out that while the natural fruitfulness of the earth was once the primary source of wealth, today the principal resource is rather the initiative and skill of human persons. He defends private property, profit, and the free market against the socialist alternatives. At the same time he cautions against consumerism, "in which people are ensnared in a web of false and superficial gratifications rather than being helped to experience their personhood in an authentic and concrete way."⁴⁹ He speaks at some length of the alienation that can arise in capitalist as well as in socialist societies.

From the beginning of his pontificate the present pope has shown a constant concern for the environment. Unlike some preservationists, he bases this concern less on the inherent goodness of nature than on what is genuinely good for humanity. In his first encyclical, *Redemptor hominis* (1979), he noted that the power of humanity to subdue the earth seems to be turning against humanity itself. Many seem to see no other meaning in the natural environment than its immediate use and consumption. Such exploitation, however, instead of making our life on earth more human, carries with it the threat of an "environmental holocaust."⁵⁰ At the root of our senseless destruction of the natural environment, he observes, lies a prevalent anthropological error, further described in *Centesimus annus*. We are often driven by a desire to possess things rather than respect their God-given purpose. We lack the disinterested attitude, born of wonder, that would enable us to find in nature the message of the invisible God. We also violate our obligations toward future generations.⁵¹

The Political Order

The thinking of John Paul II about politics and the State is closely intertwined with his reflections about culture and economics. Emphasizing the human dimension, he consistently speaks of the personalist values of participation, dialogue, and solidarity. The common good, he maintains, is threatened on the one hand by selfish individualism and on the other hand by totalitarian systems that trample on the rights of the individual person.⁵² No single group may be allowed to impose itself by power on the whole of society. The enormous increase of social awareness in our day requires that the citizens be allowed to participate in the political life of the community.⁵³ The pope accordingly praises the democratic system "inasmuch as it ensures the participation of citizens in making political choices, guarantees to the governed the possibility both of electing and of holding accountable those who govern them and of replacing them through peaceful means when appropriate."⁵⁴ Yet even his endorsement of democracy contains a warning against certain popular misunderstandings. Too often our contemporaries assume that agnosticism and skeptical relativism are the philosophy and basic attitude that best correspond to democratic forms of political life. John Paul II replies that on the contrary a democracy without objective values and ethical responsibility can easily turn into open or thinly disguised totalitarianism.[55] The rights of the human person must be acknowledged as inviolable.

The pope has repeatedly praised the Universal Declaration of Human Rights that was adopted by the United Nations in 1948. In his address to the United Nations in 1979, he enumerated, among the human rights that are universally recognized, "the right to life, liberty, and security of person; the right to food, clothing, housing, sufficient health care, rest and leisure; the right to freedom of expression, education and culture; the right to freedom of thought, conscience, and religion." This list (too long to be repeated here) ended with the "right to political participation and the right to participate in the free choice of the political system of the people to which one belongs."[56] In speaking of human rights the pope frequently alludes to the evils of abortion and euthanasia, which he regards as scandalous violations of human dignity.[57]

All these declarations of human rights are abstract. The pope clearly recognizes that philosophical and theological principles cannot be automatically translated into positive law or judicial practice. The talents of statesmen and jurists are needed to determine the extent to which a given right, for example, the right to education or free expression, can be implemented in a given situation.

THE CHURCH

Thus far, we have been speaking of essentially natural societies, whose existence does not rest on the gospel and on faith. In dealing with them, John Paul II speaks primarily as a philosopher. As a theologian and teacher of the People of God, he extends his theory of personal action, participation, and community into the order of revealed truth, where it becomes the basis of an ecclesiology.

John Paul II's ecclesiology is not a simple corollary of his general doctrine of society. The Church has a unique status and mission. In a memorable phrase he calls it "the social subject of responsibility for divine truth."[58] The gospel, he reminds us, does not spring spontaneously from any cultural soil. It always has to be transmitted by apostolic dialogue, because it comes to the Church through the apostles.[59] The message is that of Christ, who declared, "The word that you hear is not mine but is from the Father who sent me" (Jn 14:24).[60]

The idea of the gospel as a word coming down from above might appear to conflict with the view that the human vocation is to active self-realization. John Paul II is aware of this difficulty, and he replies that God's redeeming action in Christ comes to meet the deepest longings of the human heart for truth, freedom, life, and community. The gift of divine adoption enables us to fulfill our deepest identity in a surpassing manner.[61] The Church as communion is the locus of this personal and communal participation in the divine. It reflects and shares in the trinitarian communion of the divine persons among themselves.[62]

Thanks to the presence of the Holy Spirit in the hearts and minds of the faithful, the People of God experience a unique awareness of their divine adoption[63]: "The Christian bears witness to Christ not 'from outside' but on the basis of participation."[64] The entire People of God shares in the threefold office of Christ as prophet, priest, and king.[65] Each individual member is called to share in the life-giving mystery of redemption, to make a perfect gift of self and thereby to achieve definitive self-realization.[66] For it is always in giving that one finds one's true self.[67]

The members of the Church share in the threefold office of Christ in differentiated ways. All the ministries, whether hierarchical or charismatic, serve to build up the one community in unity.[68] The Holy Spirit gives the Church a corporate "sense of the faithful" to discern the meaning of God's word. This "supernatural sense of the faith," however, is not a matter of majority opinion. It is a consensus achieved through the collaboration of the various orders in the Church. In this process "pastors must promote the sense of the faith in all the faithful, examine and authoritatively judge the genuineness of its expressions, and educate the faithful in an ever more mature evangelical discernment."[69]

The special role of the hierarchy within the Church is reiterated by John Paul II. Instituted by Christ, the episcopal order, together with the pope as successor of Peter, has an irreplaceable responsibility for assuring the unity of the Church in the truth of the gospel.[70] Like charismatic gifts, hierarchical office is essentially a service toward the community. Its whole task is to build up the community of the People of God.[71] The pope warns against a laicism that denies the proper role of the hierarchy. The contrary error is clericalism, which arises either when the clergy usurp the competence of the laity or when the laity shirk their responsibilities and foist them on the clergy.[72]

In his Christology and ecclesiology, John Paul II frequently appeals to the category of prophetic testimony. Jesus Christ, he says, is the great prophet, the one who proclaims divine truth. The Church and all her members are called to share in his prophetic mission. The transmission of the sacred heritage of saving truth can be an extremely demanding task. When asked to preach a retreat to the papal curia, Cardinal Wojtyla chose as his title *Sign of Contradiction*. After describing the burdensome vocation of ancient prophets such as Jeremiah, he went on to say that the Church and the pope himself are often called to be signs of contradiction in our day. Secular society exerts heavy pressures on the Church and its hierarchy to relax moral norms and permit unbridled self-indulgence. The cardinal's answer was typically firm:

> In recent years there has been a striking increase in contradiction, whether one thinks of the organized opposition mounted by the anti-Gospel lobby or of the opposition that springs up in apparently christian and "humanistic" circles linked with certain christian traditions. One has only to recall the contestation of the Encyclical *Humanae vitae*, or that provoked by the latest Declaration by the Sacred Congregation for the Doctrine of the Faith, *Personae humanae*. These examples are enough to bring home the fact that we are in the front line in a lively battle for the dignity of man. . . . It is the task of the Church, of the Holy See, of all pastors to fight on the side of man, often against men themselves![73]

In an important speech on Catholic universities, John Paul II made a special appeal to them to be a "critical and prophetic voice" in confronting the increasingly secularized society of our day. It would be a mistake, he says, for such universities to attenuate or disguise their Catholic character. They must take full cognizance of their responsibility to affirm a truth that does not flatter but is absolutely necessary "to safeguard the dignity of the human person."[74] In the end, therefore, authentic humanism is compelled, for the sake of its own integrity, to become prophetic. Conscious that the dignity of the person rests both on freedom of conscience and on a transcendent order of truth most perfectly revealed in Christ, the faithful Christian must protest against dehumanizing forces, whether collectivistic or individualistic, whether absolutistic or relativistic. The testimony of the Church, like that of Christ, must be against the world for the world. By courageously taking up this task, John Paul II has made himself, in my estimation, the leading prophet of authentic humanism in the world today.

NOTES

1. See George Hunston Williams, *The Mind of John Paul II* (New York: Seabury, 1981), 207; also Robert F. Harvanek, "The Philosophical Foundations of the Thought of John Paul II," in *The Thought of Pope John Paul II*, ed. John M. McDermott (Rome: Pontificia Università Gregoriana, 1993), 9.

2. John Paul II, Address to the United Nations General Assembly, §§5–6, *Origins* 9 (October 11, 1979): 257–66, at 259–60.

3. *"Be Not Afraid!" André Frossard in Conversation with Pope John Paul II* (Toronto: The Bodley Head, 1984), 192.

4. Vatican II, *Gaudium et spes*, 76; quoted in Karol Wojtyla, *The Acting Person* (Dordrecht, Holland: D. Reidel, 1979), 302–3, note 9; idem, *Sources of Renewal: The Implementation of Vatican II* (San Francisco: Harper & Row, 1980), 36; John Paul II, encyclical *Redemptor hominis*, 13 (Washington, D.C.: U.S. Catholic Conference, 1979), at 41; idem, encyclical *Centesimus annus*, 55, *Origins* 21 (May 16, 1991): 1–24, at 21.

5. John Paul II, apostolic exhortation *Christifideles laici*, 37, *Origins* 18 (February 9, 1989): 561–95, at 578–79.

6. *Redemptor hominis*, 14.

7. John Paul II, encyclical *Dives in misericordia*, 51, *Origins* 10 (December 11, 1980): 401–16, at 403.

8. *The Acting Person*, 26–27; 303, note 12.

9. Ibid., 69–70; also Karol Wojtyla, "The Person: Subject and Community," *Review of Metaphysics* 33 (1979): 273–308, at 277.

10. *The Acting Person*, 309, note 40; *Christifideles laici*, 37.

11. Vatican II, *Gaudium et spes*, 24; cf. *Redemptor hominis*, 13; *Centesimus annus*, 53; also Karol Wojtyla, *Person and Community: Selected Essays* (New York: Peter Lang, 1993), 267; John Paul II, apostolic letter *Mulieris dignitatem*, 7, *Origins* 18 (October 6, 1998): 271–83, at 267.

12. Williams, *Mind of John Paul II*, 206.

13. Ibid., 176–77.

14. John Paul II, Homily at Logan Circle, Philadelphia, §6, *Origins* 9 (October 25, 1979): 308–10, at 309.

15. Ibid., §4, p. 309.

16. *Redemptor hominis*, 12.

17. Wojtyla, *Person and Community*, 286–87.

18. *"Be Not Afraid,"* 80.

19. Cf. *Redemptor hominis*, 9 and 15.

20. Vatican II, *Gaudium et spes*, 22, cited in *Redemptor hominis*, 8 and 10.

21. *Redemptor hominis*, 20.

22. John Paul II, "On the Catholic Universities," *The Pope Speaks* 34 (1989): 261–72, at 266. Cf. Henri de Lubac, *The Drama of Atheist Humanism* (Cleveland: World, 1963), ix.

23. John Paul II, *Centesimus annus*, 13; cf. de Lubac, *Drama*, 32.

24. Augustine, *Confessions*, 1.1; quoted in *Redemptor hominis*, 18; Address to Catholic Institute, Paris, *Origins* 10 (June 12, 1980): 52–58, at 54; Address at University of Vilnius, §4, *Origins* 23 (September 16, 1993): 235–37, at 236.

25. *Sources of Renewal*, 61, quoting Vatican II, *Gaudium et spes*, §24. See also John Paul II, *Original Unity of Man and Woman* (Boston: St. Paul Editions, 1981), 132; *Mulieris Dignitatem*, §7, p. 267.

26. Wojtyla, "The Person," 298.

27. *Christifideles laici*, 40.

28. John Paul II, *Love and Responsibility*, English translation of rev. (1980) ed. (New York: Farrar, Straus and Giroux, 1981).

29. Apostolic exhortation *Familiaris consortio*, 6 and 32, *Origins* 11 (December 24, 1981): 437–68, at 440 and 448.

30. *Familiaris consortio*, 11; John Paul II, *Original Unity of Man and Woman*, 80–84 et passim.

31. *Mulieris dignitatem*, §10, pp. 268–69.

32. Letter to Cardinal Agostino Casaroli, *L'Osservatore Romano*, (Eng. ed.), June 28, 1982, 19.

33. John Paul II, "The World As an Environment for Humanity," address to UNESCO, Paris, §6, *Origins* 10 (June 12, 1980): 58–64, at 60.

34. John Paul II, "Meeting with University Professors at Coimbra," §3, *L'Osservatore Romano*, (Eng. ed.), July 5, 1982, 6.

35. Wojtyla, *Person and Community*, 269.

36. John Paul II, "The World As an Environment for Humanity," §8, p. 60.

37. Vatican II, *Lumen gentium*, 17, quoted by John Paul II in encyclical *Redemptoris missio*, 54, *Origins* 20 (January 31, 1991): 541–68, at 557.

38. John Paul II, Homily at Denver, August 15, 1993, §3, *Origins* 23 (August 26, 1993): 177–80, at 179.

39. John Paul II, Address to Pontifical Council for Culture, January 16, 1984, §8; in *The Church and Culture since Vatican II*, ed. Joseph Gremillion (Notre Dame, Ind.: University of Notre Dame Press, 1985), 207–9, at 209.

40. Wojtyla, *Person and Community*, 272.

41. *"Be Not Afraid,"* 212.

42. John Paul II, "The World as an Environment for Humanity," §13, p. 61–62.

43. John Paul II, encyclical *Laborem Exercens*, 7, *Origins* 11 (September 24, 1981): 225–44, at 230.

44. Ibid., 9.

45. Encyclical *Sollicitudo rei socialis*, 15, *Origins* 17 (March 3, 1988): 641–60, at 646.

46. Ibid.

47. Ibid.

48. Ibid., 28.

49. *Centesimus annus*, 41.

50. Address at Vilnius University, §7, p. 237; *Redemptor hominis*, 15.

51. *Centesimus annus*, 37.

52. Wojtyla, *The Acting Person*, 271–95.

53. *Redemptor hominis*, 17.

54. *Centesimus annus*, 46.

55. Ibid.; cf. Address at Vilnius University, §3, p. 246.

56. John Paul II, "The World as an Environment for Humanity," §13, p. 262; cf. *Centesimus annus*, 47.

57. John Paul II, "The World as an Environment for Humanity," §21, p. 265; *Centesimus annus*, 47.

58. *Redemptor hominis*, 19.

59. Apostolic exhortation *Catechesi tradendae*, 553, *Origins* 9 (November 8, 1979): 329–48, at 342.

60. *Redemptor hominis*, 19.

61. Ibid., 18.

62. Wojtyla, *Sources of Renewal*, 138.

63. Ibid., 112.

64. Ibid., 219.

65. Ibid., 220; cf. *Christifideles laici*, 14, at 567.

66. Wojtyla, *Sources of Renewal*, 191; cf. 120.

67. Ibid., 121.

68. Ibid., 374.

69. *Familiaris consortio*, 5.

70. *Sources of Renewal*, 146–54.

71. Ibid., 374.

72. Ibid., 386.

73. Karol Wojtyla, *Sign of Contradiction* (New York: Seabury/Crossroad, 1979), 124.

74. John Paul II, "On the Catholic Universities," 266; cf. apostolic constitution *Ex corde Ecclesiae*, 32, *Origins* 20 (October 4, 1990): 265–76, at 271.

12

The Challenge of the Catechism

October 20, 1994

The Cultural Context

The *Catechism of the Catholic Church* is the boldest challenge yet offered to the cultural relativism that currently threatens to erode the contents of Catholic faith. According to a widely prevalent view, religious truth consists in an ineffable encounter with the transcendent. This encounter may be expressed in symbols and metaphors, but it cannot be communicated by propositional language, since it utterly surpasses the reach of human concepts. All statements about revelation, moreover, are said to be so culturally conditioned that they cannot be transferred from one age or one cultural region to another. Every theological affirmation that comes to us from the past must be examined with suspicion because it was formulated in a situation differing markedly from our own. Each constituency must experience the revelation of God anew and find language and other symbolic forms appropriate to itself.

Mystical empiricism of this type inevitably devaluates specific beliefs. It makes light of the efforts of previous generations to formulate the faith in creedal and dogmatic assertions. In this perspective, the traditional view that a dogma is a divinely revealed truth is no longer taken seriously. The struggle to maintain doctrinal consensus in the universal Church is viewed as a threat to the creativity of local churches.

This sophisticated relativism, widespread though it be among intellectuals, has had only limited impact on the mass of the Catholic faithful and is firmly rejected by the hierarchical leadership of the Church. Pope John Paul II and Cardinal Joseph Ratzinger, who are the intellectual equals of any other religious thinkers of our day, have consistently opposed this trend. In their view divine revelation can be formulated, at least in part, in irrevocably and universally true creedal and dogmatic propositions. Recognizing the need to defend the doctrinal patrimony of the Church from present-day skepticism and relativism, many leaders of the Church became convinced that the time had come for a new universal catechism.

THE BACKGROUND

The last officially authorized catechism for the universal Church had been the Roman Catechism produced in 1566, just after the Council of Trent. The intention of Vatican I (1869–70) to commission a brief catechism was never brought to a definitive vote, because the council was interrupted by war and indefinitely prorogued. At Vatican II (1962–65), some of the fathers, including Cardinal Alfredo Ottaviani and Archbishop Marcel Lefebvre, argued in favor of a compendium of all Catholic doctrine, but the council contented itself with prescribing a "general catechetical directory," which was duly issued in 1971.

The publication of *De Nieuwe Katechismus* by the Dutch bishops in 1966 raised serious questions. Some maintained that the best response to the ambiguities and omissions detected in that volume would be a new catechism for the universal Church, but many believed that the time was not ripe for such a project. The Holy See in 1968 therefore issued only a set of amendments to be incorporated into the Dutch catechism.

At the Synod of Bishops in 1974, dedicated to the theme of evangelization, the Polish language group, including Cardinal Karol Wojtyla, spoke in favor of a universal catechism, but the proposal was not accepted at that time. At the 1977 assembly of the Synod, on "catechesis in our time," a number of bishops proposed a catechism that would be normative for the universal Church, but there was no unanimity regarding the nature or desirability of such a work. The Synod therefore made no recommendation on the subject.

The call for a universal catechism received much greater support at the Extraordinary Synod of 1985. Celebrating the twentieth anniversary of the close of Vatican II, bishops from all over the world were summoned to consider the interpretation and impact of the council. In their preparatory reports for this Synod, several of the episcopal conferences had already called for a universal catechism. At the assembly itself, the bishops noted a regrettable tendency to play off the pastoral against the doctrinal import of the council and to overlook the continuity between the teaching of the council and previous authoritative statements. In recommending a universal catechism Cardinal Bernard Law, archbishop of Boston, directly challenged the thesis that the current need was for greater decentralization. He asserted:

> I propose a Commission of Cardinals to prepare a draft of a Conciliar Catechism to be promulgated by the Holy Father after consulting the bishops of the world. In a shrinking world—a global village—national catechisms will not fill the current need for a clear articulation of the Church's faith.[1]

This proposal was then taken up by several other Synod fathers, including an archbishop from Burundi, the Latin patriarch of Jerusalem, the archbishop of Dakar, and the Cardinal Prefect of the Congregation of the Clergy, Silvio Oddi. After favorable reception in many of the language groups (*circuli minores*), the proposal found its way into the final report of the Synod, which declared:

> There is a strong general desire that a catechism or compendium of all Catholic doctrine be drawn up, as regards both faith and morals, in order to serve as a point of reference for catechisms and compendiums prepared in different regions. The presentation of doctrine must be biblical and liturgical, offering sound doctrine while being at the same time adapted to the life of Christians today.[2]

In his closing address of December 7, 1985, the pope indicated his satisfaction with this suggestion.

EARLY REACTIONS

Not surprisingly, reformist theologians considered the project ill advised. In an article published in the international review *Concilium* in 1989, Herbert Vorgrimler, a distinguished disciple of Karl Rahner, pointed out the tensions involved in the mandate. He particularly attacked the assumption that there can be something like a *fixed, unchangeable "deposit" of teaching of faith and morals* which "in itself" has never been affected by history and may not be affected by transmission in the processes of inculturation. It is easy to see why this idea is very seductive, since it guarantees firm ground under the feet, in the heads and in the mouths of preachers and teachers in any conceivable situation in which the Church may find itself. However, it is more problematic than is realized or admitted, because it conceives of this "deposit" on the model of Platonic ideas, and does not allow for essential features of Christianity such as the *history of dogma* and its understanding.[3]

After raising a number of further questions about the desirability and possibility of the new catechism, Vorgrimler concluded, "If the work is started with a serious programme . . . it is clear that it will not be completed either in this pontificate or in the next."[4]

Two years later, *Concilium* followed up Vorgrimler's article on the catechism with a whole volume, which enlarged upon the previous criticisms.[5] In their introduction to the volume, the editors, Johann-Baptist Metz and Edward Schillebeeckx, expressed agreement with those who reject "the notion of a deposit of faith transcending history and culture and notionally precedent to all inculturation" (5). David Tracy, in his essay for this volume, wrote: "The hope for an adequate 'world catechism' seems, at best, illusory" (28). He predicted that the catechism would be an example of "unwelcome and unacknowledged Eurocentrism in a polycentric world church" (36). In another contribution, Metz himself, echoing Vorgrimler's complaints, warned against "official centralism as a defensive protection for unity" and against the illusion of a "fixed and unchangeable 'deposit' of doctrinal teaching" subsisting in some Platonic world of ideas (82).

Other contributors to the same volume objected that the catechism was unnecessary. According to Hermann Häring, the Decalogue, the Lord's Prayer, the sacraments, and the creed are sufficient as binding elements safeguarding the common faith. "If these elements are interpreted on the basis of the experience of Jesus and applied to present-day experience, and if they are constantly being understood afresh, they are more than enough for unity and peace" (72). Still later in the volume, another contributor, Emilio Alberich, warned that the universal catechism could be an obstacle to the successful inculturation of the faith. With some understatement, he remarked that "experts and researchers in catechetics have not received the proposal of a universal catechism with much enthusiasm" (94).

Notwithstanding the opposition, preparations went ahead. On June 10, 1986, the pope assigned the task to an international commission of twelve cardinals and archbishops, with Joseph Ratzinger as president. This committee was assisted by an editorial committee of seven bishops, one each from Spain, Italy, France, England, the United States, Chile, and Argentina, and by a Maronite priest working in Lebanon, who was an expert on Eastern theology. Christoph Schönborn, O.P. [now cardinal-archbishop of Vienna], was appointed editorial secretary.

The editorial committee, acting on instructions from the papal commission, drew up an outline that was reviewed by the commission in May 1987.[6] With the collaboration of many theologians, an "advance draft" of the entire work was completed in December 1987 and was considered by the commission in May 1988. A second draft was prepared for discussion by the commission in February 1989. In November 1989 a "revised draft" or "provisional text" was sent out to all the bishops' conferences in the world for comments and criticisms by the bishops. About 1,000 replies were received, containing some 24,000 suggested changes. While requesting many improvements, the great majority of the bishops were satisfied with the revised draft as the basis for a definitive text.

A number of theologians gained access to the provisional text of 1989 and voiced their criticisms, predictably negative. Nicholas Lash, writing for the London *Tablet*, recommended that the draft be rejected, even as a basis for discussion. He added that the Synod of Bishops, at a future meeting, should reconsider the advisability of the whole project.[7] Richard McBrien, with great assurance, told the *Philadelphia Inquirer*, "The project should be abandoned."[8] Thomas J. Reese spoke for many progressive theologians when he wrote, in his introduction to a volume of essays on the provisional text:

> In my opinion the document needs to be totally rewritten. It cannot be saved by amendments that only tinker with the text. If this were a draft submitted to an ecumenical council, it would deserve an overwhelming *"non placet"* from the bishops. It is questionable whether a universal catechism is needed at all and whether the papal commission can write one that fulfills the criteria of being faithful to Vatican II or useful for the Church.[9]

REVISION AND PROMULGATION

Following the desires of the large majority of the bishops, the commission decided to amend the existing text, taking the criticisms into account. In the revision much greater attention was paid to the hierarchy of truths, so that the reader would never lose sight of the central mystery of faith—the triune God who calls us to communion with himself. The biblical citations were carefully reviewed by Scripture scholars to make sure that they were appropriate. It was decided to abandon any effort to describe specific non-Christian religions, such as Islam, Hinduism, and Buddhism. Greater emphasis was placed on the positive relations between Christianity and Judaism and on ecumenical relations with other Christian churches and communities. A new section was introduced on states of life within the Church: hierarchy, laity, and consecrated life. Greater emphasis was placed on the vocation of all the baptized to holiness. In the revision of the treatise on Christian conduct, the commandments were more clearly presented as developments of the twofold precept of love of God and neighbor. The links between observance of the law and the practice of evangelical perfection were clarified. Greater attention was paid to the social doctrine of the Church. The epilogue on the Lord's Prayer was expanded into a full-scale treatment of Christian prayer. Vast improvements were made in the style and presentation, so that the choppy first version was turned into a polished text that, for the most part, is pleasing to read.[10]

The final text was approved by the commission and submitted to the pope on February 14, 1992. The pope gave his approval on June 25, 1992, and in an apostolic constitution of October 11, 1992, significantly entitled *Fidei depositum*, declared the catechism to be "a valid and legitimate instrument for ecclesial communion and a sure norm for the teaching of the faith." Reflecting on the process by which the Catechism was produced, Cardinal Ratzinger has written:

> It is still a sort of wonder to me that a readable, for the most part intrinsically unified and, in my opinion, beautiful book arose out of such a complex editorial process. The constant growth of unanimity among such different minds as were represented in the editorial committee and in the commission was for me, and for all those who took part in the project, a magnificent experience in which we often believed that we felt a higher hand guiding us.[11]

The published text, in many languages, has been a remarkable commercial success. A document initially directed to bishops, and only through them, to religious educators and others (12), the Catechism has proved to be unexpectedly popular with lay readers. More than a million copies were sold in France; more than two million are in print in the United States. Some people are speaking of the "phenomenon" of the Catechism: it evidently responds to a deep hunger in the people of God for the bread of solid doctrine.

MERITS OF THE CATECHISM

In spite of some opinions to the contrary, the Catechism does respond to a felt need. Although Paul VI could in some sense rightly say that Vatican II was the great catechism of our time,[12] the council did not organize its teaching in a systematic way. Besides, it left many important doctrines untreated. After the council, therefore, questions were raised as to whether the teaching of previous popes and councils on these untouched issues were still in force. Had they been quietly abrogated by the council's silence?

The Catechism sets forth the whole body of Catholic teaching in an organic manner. It is a serene, comprehensive presentation of the authoritative teaching of Scripture and Catholic tradition, systematically distributed in four parts dealing respectively with the creed, the sacraments, Christian conduct, and prayer. These parts are broken down into familiar divisions: the twelve articles of the creed, the seven sacraments, the ten commandments, and the seven petitions of the Our Father. The Catechism as a whole is a magnificent panorama, breathtaking in its scope. Where else could one find between two covers a digest of full teaching of the Church, down through the ages, about almost any conceivable point from the dogma of the Trinity to the morality of gambling? As a catechism should, the book concentrates on doctrine, set forth in a clear and orderly manner. Yet the presentation is free from the subtle and technical distinctions characteristic of Scholasticism. Closely packed with information, it is unencumbered by professional jargon and therefore accessible to a wide public.

While preeminently concerned with truth, the book is no mere head trip. It speaks to the heart, eliciting prayer and devotion. Although the creed skips from the birth of Jesus to his passion and death, the Catechism contains a section on the mysteries of the life of Jesus (512–50), in which the inner mystery of his incarnate existence radiates with captivating power. Devotion to Mary, which permeates the entire Catechism, is treated most explicitly in the article on the communion of saints (963–75). Many other doctrinal sections, such as the presentation of the symbols of the Holy Spirit (694–701), invite the reader to meditation. The authors have drawn liberally on liturgical texts and have incorporated moving passages from the ancient fathers and medieval and modern saints and mystics. In these selections care has been taken to draw from Eastern as well as Western sources. The voices of women as well as men are heard.

Beauty, Truth, and Goodness

An unexpected bonus is the aesthetic quality of the product. The book as a whole is admirably proportioned, so that it rises like a vast basilica over the ground that it covers. It maintains a clear focus: the mystery of the eternal Father who blesses the world by sending the Son and the Holy Spirit. Each of the four major parts is introduced by a color-plated reproduction of an ancient fresco, sculpture, or miniature. The text dwells on the capacity of beauty to evoke the sense of the divine. Following the Book of Wisdom, it remarks on the beauty of the world as evidence that the Creator is supremely beautiful:

> Even before revealing himself to man in words of truth, God reveals himself to him through the universal language of creation, the work of his Word, of his wisdom: the order and harmony of the cosmos—which both the child and the scientist discover—"from the greatness and beauty of created things comes a corresponding perception of their Creator," "for the author of beauty created them" (2500; cf. Wis 13:3,5).

The Catechism can therefore quote St. Augustine issuing the challenge:

> Question the beauty of the earth, question the beauty of the sea, question the beauty of the air distending and diffusing itself, question the beauty of the sky . . . question all these realities. All respond: "See, we are beautiful." Their beauty is a profession [*confessio*]. These beauties are subject to change. Who made them if not the Beautiful One [*Pulcher*] who is not subject to change?" (32, quoting Augustine, *Sermo* 241,2)

In keeping with this approach, the Catechism calls attention to the beauty and love visible in Christ, who "reflects the glory of God" (2501, quoting Heb 1:3). Great importance is attached to the symbolism in the mysteries of the life of Jesus and to the symbolic forms under which the Holy Spirit has been made known to us. In expounding the ingredients of sacramental worship, the Catechism brings out the communicative power of signs and symbols taken from nature, from human culture, and from sacred history, including especially the actions and career of Jesus. The symbolism of baptism, for instance, is powerfully conveyed by the following passage from St. Gregory of Nazianzus:

> Baptism is God's most beautiful and magnificent gift. . . . It is called *gift* because it is conferred on those who bring nothing of their own; *grace* since it is given even to the guilty; *Baptism* because sin is buried in the water; *anointing* for it is priestly and royal as are those who are anointed; *enlightenment* because it radiates light; *clothing* since it veils our shame; *bath* because it washes, and *seal* as it is our guard and the sign of God's Lordship. (1216)

In the treatment of liturgical song, the Catechism quotes an eloquent passage from Augustine on the tears of devotion with which as a neophyte he heard the hymnody in the Catholic Church (1157). St. John Damascene is invoked as a witness to the way in which the beauty of holy images can assist Christian prayer and contemplation (1162). The treatment of the eighth commandment ("You shall not bear false witness"), after dealing at some length with truth in communications, ends rather surprisingly but gratifyingly with a plea for the promotion of sacred art in the Church (2502–3).

Readers of the Catechism are introduced to God not only as the source of all beauty but also as the absolute and immutable reality from whom all truth and goodness flow forth. Truth, we are reminded, is beautiful in itself; it carries with it the joy and splendor of spiritual beauty (2500). As sovereign truth, God alone fully satisfies the mind's quest for explanation and meaning. Being truth itself, God cannot deceive. In giving us intelligence and a capacity for truth, he orders us to himself. The added light of revelation, far from impeding the human quest for understanding, assists the mind to escape from its own darkness.

Goodness, which ranks with beauty and truth as the third transcendental, is the attractiveness and beneficence of being. As the fullness of being,

God is supremely lovable and supremely loving. Creation is attributed to the generosity of divine love, which wills to share its own goodness. Human beings are primary recipients of God's blessings. Fashioned in the image and likeness of God, they are called to participate forever in the divine life. On this point the Catechism recalls the words of St. Catherine of Siena:

> What made you establish man in so great a dignity? With unimaginable love you have looked upon your creatures within yourself! You have fallen in love with them; for by love you created them, and by love you have given them a being capable of tasting your eternal Goodness. (356, quoting Catherine of Siena, *Dialogue* 4, 13 "On Divine Providence"; translation modified)

From this vision of reality, it evidently follows that the supreme calling of every human being is to love God in return and to live according to the law of love. All the commandments of God and of the Church are traced back to the twofold precept of love, which Jesus himself quoted from the Jewish Torah. The core of Christian morality is the new law of the gospel, infused into human hearts by the Holy Spirit. Christ is in his own person the way of perfection (1952). The beatitudes, which stand at the beginning of this section of the Catechism, are said to "depict the countenance of Jesus Christ and portray his charity" (1717). They point forward to the blessedness so aptly described by Augustine: "There we shall rest and see, we shall see and love, we shall love and praise. Behold what will be at the end without end. For what other end do we have, if not to reach the kingdom which has no end?" (1720, quoting Augustine, *De civ. Dei* 22, 30)

A remarkable feature of the Catechism is the extent to which the treatment of the Church, the sacraments, morality, and prayer are permeated by references to Christ and the Holy Spirit. The entire Christian life is presented as a response to the gift and call of God—a response made possible by faith and the sacraments. The commandments do not appear as external impositions but as consequences that flow connaturally from membership in the people of the New Covenant (2062). In the New Covenant, "prayer is *Christian* insofar as it is communion with Christ and extends throughout the Church, which is his Body" (2565). The Lord's Prayer is characterized, in Tertullian's admirable phrase, as "the summary of the whole gospel" (2761).

In giving these glimpses of the new Catechism, I hope to have shown that it is not the kind of work that would be expected to spring from the heads of arid bureaucrats, anxious to defend their own authority. The authors have faithfully carried out their mandate to produce a work that is biblical and liturgical in tone rather than legalistic or Scholastic. As Ratzinger righly claims, the Catechism is not ecclesiocentric; it is centered on God, who freely and lovingly turns to us by sending us his Son to be our brother and his Holy Spirit to dwell in our hearts. Having this focus, it manifests and evokes heartfelt praise, which at times rises almost to the pitch of ecstasy. It is a book to be read in small sections and savored in a leisurely way.

THE FOURFOLD CHALLENGE

In referring to the "challenge" of the Catechism, as I do in my title, I do not mean to suggest that it is a contentious piece of work. On the contrary, it is calm and irenic. By gathering up the doctrinal patrimony of Catholic Christianity, the Catechism does not add to the burden of belief; it leaves the individual doctrines with the same authority they had before the Catechism was written.[13] The Catechism refrains from polemics; it does not refute or condemn adversaries, nor is it defensive in tone. It contains only a few apologetical sections, and these, printed in small type, are evidently intended to help the reader understand the Church's positions rather than to convince the unbeliever.

For all that, the Catechism does issue some real challenges. By confidently setting forth what the Church has taught down through the centuries, the Catechism by implication takes on modern scholars who have criticized the inherited patrimony on the basis of new methodologies in exegesis, historical research, and epistemology. The challenges may be seen as directed against four very popular tendencies: positivist exegesis, historicist dogmatics, revisionist speculation, and experience-based catechetics. The challenges, of course, are mutual, since the Catechism is challenged by those it challenges.

USE OF SCRIPTURE

With regard to exegesis, some would have liked the Catechism to analyze the biblical texts in their own context, without reference to the doctrinal tradition. The Catechism takes a different path. Following Vatican II, it affirms that Scripture should be read as an inspired document, in the framework of the Church's faith. The effort to read Scripture by a positivistic use of historical-critical tools, while it may be useful up to a point, can lead to impasses, such as the dichotomy between the Jesus of history and the Christ of faith.

This doctrinal approach is not rejected by all biblical experts. A distinguished Old Testament scholar, Joseph Jensen, O.S.B., concedes that the Catechism's approach might strike some readers, accustomed to the historical-critical method, as uncritical. But he rejects the charge on several grounds. The Catechism is entitled to speak from the perspective of Christian faith, which it intends to affirm. Its emphasis on the typological meanings of the Old Testament, moreover, accords well with the use of the Old Testament in the New. Furthermore, modern developments in hermeneutics suggest that the Catechism is on target. A classic text, even one that is not divinely inspired, contains depths of meaning that escape the original author and appear only in the light of later reflection.[14]

A New Testament scholar, Luke Timothy Johnson, is equally affirming. After remarking that the Catechism almost totally bypasses critical biblical scholarship, he registers no regrets, "for truth to tell, the contributions of critical biblical scholarship either to real history or to authentic theology have not up to now been particularly impressive and have certainly not had the character of transmitting faith to succeeding generations."[15]

The Catechism does not deny, but on the contrary affirms, the value of textual and historical criticism. Its authors were quite aware that the literal meaning of many key texts from Scripture is debated among exegetes of different schools. Since the Church generally refrains from taking official positions on matters of technical exegesis, such as dating, authorship, and literary dependence, the Catechism leaves scholars free to take their own positions. Biblical experts were nevertheless consulted to make sure that the assertions are not based on faulty readings or indefensible interpretations.

The Catechism makes no claim that the biblical texts it cites are proofs of the Church doctrine. Rather, they are seen as indications pointing toward what the Church, with the assistance of the Holy Spirit, has come to see in the course of centuries. Often enough the biblical grounding consists in the convergence of many texts, no one of which is decisive in itself.

HISTORY AND HISTORICISM

Professional historians of dogma have a concern similar to that of technical exegetes. Some of them are unhappy that the Catechism, while quoting from ancient documents, has failed to indicate the context in which these pronouncements were made.[16] But a catechism, by its very nature, must expound Church teaching in a systematic, rather than a historical, order. In so doing, it brings together statements that have been made in different situations and different periods of history. Occasionally, where the stages of development are especially important, the Catechism supplies concise historical expositions in small type. But this historical information is not allowed to interfere with the primary task of the Catechism, which is to set forth the resultant doctrines rather than to trace the process of their formation. The Catechism does not purport to do the work of a course in historical theology.

By gathering up statements from different ages, the Catechism implicitly teaches that the truths of Christian faith are not time-bound. The questions addressed by past popes and councils are still with us: Does God involve himself in human history? Is Jesus the eternal Son of the eternal Father? Did he rise in body from the dead? Generally speaking, the answers given to these and other questions in the creeds and dogmas of the Church are still intelligible to us—more so, frequently, than the speculations of contemporary theologians, who insist on the necessity of novel formulations.

While her teaching can be differently expressed in different ages, the Church cannot disavow her apostolic foundations and her doctrinal commitments. The revelation, permanently given in Christ, has been authoritatively mediated by Scripture and tradition. The concept of a "deposit of faith," so irksome to the progressivist mentality, is authentically biblical and Christian. Christianity would dissolve itself if it allowed its revealed content, handed down in tradition, to be replaced by contemporary theories.

THEOLOGICAL SPECULATION

Some systematic theologians, reviewing the Catechism, have expressed their disappointment that it does not endorse speculative positions that they personally espouse. Here again, the question to be asked is whether these positions belong in a catechism. Do they represent the received doctrine of the Church? As Schönborn remarks with reference to the descent of Christ into hell, "New interpretations, such as that of a Hans Urs von Balthasar (the contemplation of Holy Saturday), however profound and helpful they may be, have not yet experienced that reception which would justify their inclusion in the Catechism."[17]

The doctrine of original sin caused particular difficulty, and was studied at length by a special commission. In the past fifty years, numerous theologians have proposed ways of updating the traditional teaching, which relied heavily on contestable interpretations of the creation narratives in Genesis and of Paul's letter to the Romans. Like many modern theologians, the Catechism interprets original sin in a Christological framework as the "reverse side" of redemption (389), but, unlike some, it adheres for the most part to the Augustinian positions that have long been dominant in the West and were reaffirmed by Paul VI in a speech of 1966.[18] As Schönborn says in this connection, "It cannot be the task of the Catechism to represent novel theories which do not belong to the assured patrimony of the faith."[19] A close reading of the Catechism shows that the authors were aware of the figurative language of the biblical accounts and do not impose a literalist understanding of the Genesis stories about Adam and Eve. It remains the task of religious educators and theologians to show how certain traditional formulations, repeated in the Catechism, may be subject to reinterpretation in the light of modern science and exegesis.

PEDAGOGICAL CONCERNS

Religious educators, in assessing the Catechism, articulate two major concerns. First, some of them feel that a universal catechism by its very nature inhibits the freedom of local churches to adapt the presentation of the faith to the needs of their own region.[20] Conscious of this objection, the Catechism explicitly declares that the methods and presentation of doctrine must be adjusted according to the "culture, age, spiritual maturity, and social and ecclesial condition" of different audiences. This adaptation is to be made by particular catechisms and teachers of religion, using the present catechism only as a point of reference (24). In promulgating the Catechism, John Paul II cautioned that it was not intended to replace approved local catechisms "which take into account various situations and cultures, while carefully preserving the unity of faith and fidelity to Catholic doctrine."[21] Cardinal Ratzinger was even more specific:

> Making the content of catechesis more intelligible, while respecting the organic and hierarchical character of Christian truths; deepening and broadening the themes only sketched; expressing them in a language more fitted to the times and more close to the integral richness of the faith; proclaiming the assertions of faith in a way that is more faithful and more attentive to the exigencies, the expectations, and the problematics of those being addressed: these are only some of the tasks that await those who undertake the work of catechetical proclamation, in their indispensable work of inculturating the faith in general and the *Catechism of the Catholic Church* in particular.[22]

Faithful adherence to Catholic doctrine has always been a high priority, but is especially urgent in our day, when new ideas that originate in any locality travel with the speed of light across the face of the globe. The bishops at the Synod assembly of 1985, though they came from all parts of the world, did not clamor for greater regional autonomy. On the contrary, they regarded a unified compendium of Catholic doctrine as a necessary help for maintaining the unity of the Church's faith in the "global village," which the world is now becoming.

The second point raised by many religious educators is that experience, rather than established doctrine, should provide the starting point.[23] The commission responsible for the Catechism carefully considered the possibility of beginning with a description of contemporary human experience, but it eventually decided that this point of departure would be too arbitrary, depending on the angle of vision selected. Contemporary experience, they concluded, is too various and ephemeral to offer a solid platform that would apply today and tomorrow, in New York and Madagascar, Bangladesh and Moscow. The decision was accordingly made to keep the focus on the Church's patrimony of faith. Nevertheless, the Catechism does begin inductively with a description of how the search for God arises out of common human experience. The method is not a pure deductive intellectualism.[24]

Nothing in the Catechism prevents the religious educator from seeking points of insertion for Christian doctrine in the actual experience of men and women today. But the Catechism constitutes a challenge to any method that would reduce faith to personal experience. No analysis of contemporary experience can by itself disclose the contents of Christian faith, such as the Trinity, the Incarnation, and the Resurrection, which are known only from revelation. Cardinal Ratzinger rightly finds fault with a kind of "theological empiricism" in which present-day experience is allowed to block the dynamism of the original sources. Speaking of certain European catechetical programs, he remarks that they emphasize experience and method to the detriment of faith and content. Such instruction, he observes, has proved itself incapable of arousing interest.[25] The word of God must be allowed to shine forth again as a power of salvation. The truths of revelation must be presented in their organic unity, apart from which they can seem meaningless.

A prominent American religious educator, Francis D. Kelly, speaks in similar terms. He characterizes the new Catechism as "a clarion call for catechesis to refocus clearly on the objective mystery of faith, on its doctrinal, moral, and ascetical content, as the most solid and fruitful foundation for building the faith community."[26] Catechists, he goes on to say, "need to recapture this sense of mission and confidence if they are going to be effective in our culture."[27]

The Christian faith does not need to be made interesting by sophisticated pedagogical techniques. If allowed to present itself in all its splendor and depth, it seizes the hearts of all who have ears to listen. Although the *Catechism of the Catholic Church* is not a perfect book, the symphony of faith does echo through its pages. To be carried away by that symphony, we have only to drop our resistances, allow the book deliver its message, and let it change our points of view.

THE CATECHISM should not be seen as a burden or a fetter. It does not purport to give the final, definitive word on all the questions it treats. Indeed, it explicitly encourages exegetes, theologians, and religious educators to go beyond it in exercising the skills of their respective disciplines. But it reminds them to take cognizance of the great heritage that the Church transmits to us. As a reliable compendium of Catholic doctrine, the Catechism brings together the wisdom of the centuries in an appealing synthesis. By virtue of its consistency, beauty, and spiritual power, it offers a veritable feast of faith.

NOTES

1. *L'Osservatore Romano* (Eng. ed.), July 7, 1986, 3. This text is a summary of Cardinal Law's oral intervention.

2. Final Report IIB(a)4. On the basis of the Latin text, I have departed slightly from the translation in *Origins* 15 (December 19, 1985): 444–50, at 448.

3. Herbert Vorgrimler, "The Adventure of a New 'World Catechism,'" in *Orthodoxy and Heterodoxy*, ed. J.-B. Metz and E. Schillebeeckx, Concilium 192 (Edinburgh: T. & T. Clark, 1987), 103–9. Italics in original.

4. Ibid., 109.

5. World Catechism or Inculturation? ed. J.-B. Metz and E. Schillebeeckx, Concilium 204 (Edinburgh: T. & T. Clark, 1989).

6. For a more detailed account of the process, see the "Update on the Universal Catechism" given by Cardinal Joseph Ratzinger to the Synod of Bishops on October 25, 1990, and published in *Origins* 20 (November 8, 1990): 356–59.

7. Nicholas Lash, "Concerning the Catechism," *Tablet* 244 (March 24, 1990): 404–6.

8. Quoted in Michael J. Schaffer, "Vatican Document is a Draft of Division," *Philadelphia Inquirer*, March 25, 1990. Cf. Thomas J. Reese, introduction to *The Universal Catechism Reader* (San Francisco: HarperSanFrancisco, 1990), 11.

9. Reese, ibid.

10. Many of the revisions mentioned in this paragraph are listed by Ratzinger in his "Update on the Universal Catechism."

11. In Joseph Cardinal Ratzinger and Christoph Schönborn, *Introduction to the Catechism of the Catholic Church* (San Francisco: Ignatius, 1994), 25.

12. Cited in the prologue to the *Catechism of the Catholic Church* (Vatican City: Libreria Editrice Vaticana, 1994), §10, p. 9.

13. "The individual doctrines that the Catechism affirms have no other authority than that which they already possess," writes Joseph Cardinal Ratzinger in "The *Catechism of the Catholic Church* and the Optimism of the Redeemed," *Communio: International Catholic Review* 20 (1993): 469–84, at 479.

14. Joseph Jensen, O.S.B., "Beyond the Literal Sense: The Interpretation of Scripture in the *Catechism of the Catholic Church*," *The Living Light* 29 (Summer 1993): 50–60.

15. Luke Timothy Johnson, in "The Catechism: Four Responses," *Commonweal* 120 (May 7, 1993): 14–18, at 17.

16. For example, René Marlé makes the criticism, "A certain number of medieval texts [cited by the Catechism] will remain hard to understand for nonspecialist readers, unable to restore them to their historical and cultural context and hence to ascertain what such propositions can contain of permanent value for faith." See his "Un Catéchisme de l'Église Catholique," *Nouvelle revue théologique* 377 (December 1992): 689–95, at 695.

17. Schönborn in *Introduction to the Catechism*, 75.

18. The text of Paul VI's allocution of July 11, 1966, is conveniently accessible in *The Companion to the Catechism of the Catholic Church* (San Franciso: Ignatius, 1994), 114–17.

19. Ibid., 71.

20. We have already noted this concern among the *Concilium* theologians. Emilio Alberich, a Spanish professor of catechetics, warns, "A genuine and legitimate inculturation of the faith will be impossible if the future universal catechism sets out to establish one, unique language of faith, with the exception of the traditional patrimony of the sources, or attempts to create doctrinal formulae which have to be learned by rote." See his "Is the Universal Catechism an Obstacle or a Catalyst in the Process of Inculturation?" *World Catechism or Inculturation?* 88–97, at 96.

21. John Paul II, apostolic constitution *Fidei depositum*, reprinted in the *Catechism of the Catholic Church*, 1–6, at 6.

22. Joseph Cardinal Ratzinger, "Catechismo e inculturazione," *Il Regno—Documenti* 37 (November 1, 1992): 588; quoted by Joseph A. Komonchak, "The Authority of the Catechism," in Berard L. Marthaler, ed., *Introducing the Catechism of the Catholic Church* (New York: Paulist, 1994), 18–31, at 27.

23. "Recently, C. Ellis Nelson, head of Union Theological Seminary's Religious Education Department, visited Catholic catechetical centers throughout Europe. On his return to this country he wrote a paper which pointed out that nearly everywhere he went, the stress was on experience centered learning" (Gabriel Moran, *Design for Religion* [New York: Herder and Herder, 1970], 24). The same could be said of religious education in much of the United States today.

24. On the alternatives between the inductive and deductive approaches see Ratzinger in *Introduction to the Catechism*, 20–22.

25. Ratzinger in *Introduction to the Catechism*, 14. See also Joseph Cardinal Ratzinger, "Sources and Transmission of the Faith," *Communio: International Catholic Review* 10 (1983): 17–34, at 19 and 22–23.

26. Francis D. Kelly, "The Catechism in Context," *The Living Light* 29 (Summer 1993): 29–38, at 34.

27. Ibid., 36.

13

Crucified for Our Sake

Love, Violence, and Sacrifice

April 10, 1995

When I was a college student, I took a course on the painting of the North Italian Renaissance. At one point the professor showed us a slide projection of an immense canvas of the crucifixion by Tintoretto. Pointing to it he declared, "This is the greatest painting ever made of the greatest event in the history of the world." These words made a deep impression upon me, and the more I ponder them the more convinced I become that the cross of Christ constitutes the very center of world history.[1]

Each year in Holy Week we are invited to enter into this central mystery, which is simultaneously the climax of two histories—the history of human sin and that of divine mercy. On Good Friday we shall be adoring the cross and singing some of the great liturgical hymns, such as the *Vexilla Regis* and the *Pange Lingua*. Toward the end of this second hymn comes the following stanza:

> Tree, which solely wast found worthy
> the world's great Victim to sustain
> Harbor from the raging tempest!
> Ark, that saved the world again!
> Tree, with sacred blood anointed
> of the Lamb for sinners slain.[2]

This hymn, like many of the ceremonies of Holy Week, directs our gaze to Jesus as the Paschal victim, the Lamb sacrificed to redeem the sins of the world by his most precious blood.

SACRIFICE UNDER SCRUTINY

The sacrificial interpretation of the death of Jesus is questioned in some recent literature. Karl Rahner, perhaps the most influential Catholic theologian of our century, speaks in measured terms. The general idea of sacrifice in the history of religions, he declares, is difficult to defend, and the concept of expiatory sacrifice, although present in some "late" New Testament soteriology, offers little help today toward understanding the salvific significance of the death of Jesus.[3]

The most sustained attack on the notion of sacrifice has been mounted by the Catholic anthropologist René Girard in a series of books.[4] He traced the concept of sacrifice to a type of mythical thinking found in the rituals and literature of many cultures. Driven by a deep psychological mechanism, people tend to overcome their rivalries and mutual hostilities by turning their aggression on an innocent party, who becomes a kind of scapegoat. Girard referred in this connection to the ceremony in Leviticus in which the Jews loaded their sins on a goat and sent it out into the desert, handing it over to an evil spirit, while at the same time killing another goat and offering its blood to the Lord for the sins of the people (Lev 16:5–10). Rituals of this nature have given support to the idea of sacred violence, of peace mysteriously achieved through the slaying of an innocent victim.

Jesus, Girard maintained, did not interpret his own death as a sacrifice, although it has been so interpreted in much Christian theology. "I also believe," he wrote, "that the sacrificial interpretation of the Passion and the Redemption cannot legitimately be extrapolated from the text of the New Testament—though an exception must perhaps be made in the case of the Epistle to the Hebrews."[5] Under the influence of this distorted theology, Girard believed, Christians have often sought to achieve peace or purity by acts of sacred violence. He mentioned in this connection the recurrent violence in Christian history, exemplified by pogroms, the burning of heretics, witch trials, crusades, and other religious wars.

I speak of these positions of Girard in the past tense because he has recently changed his position. In an interview published in 1993, he declared that in dismissing Hebrews in his *Things Hidden Since the Foundation of the World*, "I was completely wrong." Although the notion of sacrifice in primitive form is unacceptable, he now believes that "there should be a valid use of it" in Christian theology.[6] But Girard's earlier opposition to the idea of sacrifice continues to exert considerable influence.[7]

The secularization of violence since the Enlightenment has not diminished the problem. According to Girard, violence in our day is all the more threatening because people have ceased to believe that the destruction of the victim is truly redemptive. He predicts that as humanity vainly attempts to reinstate the scapegoat mechanism without the accompanying religious faith, violence will become more terrible than ever. Events such as the Nazi holocaust and the massacres in Cambodia and Rwanda seem to substantiate this premonition. These "sacrificial crises," as Girard calls them, arise when primitive passions, no longer endowed with religious meaning, overwhelm the cultural institutions designed to restrain them.[8]

The United States is by no means immune to the irrational and destructive uses of force. We have a long tradition of riots and posses, lynchings and gang warfare. Random shootings, Mafia-style executions, serial murders, police brutality, rapes, child abuse, and spousal abuse crowd our daily headlines. The prison population continues to swell but the prison system itself is a factory of violent crime. Capital punishment is often seen as a form of revenge against the criminal. A new approach to the problem of violence is clearly needed. Can the cross of Christ suggest such an avenue of approach?

The death of Jesus can be treated simply as one more chapter in the bloody chronicle of violence. Many recent studies, dealing with the crucifixion on the sociological and psychological level, present it as a hostile reaction by religious and political powers who felt threatened by the teaching of Jesus. In this way, the death of Jesus is reduced to a tragic event, like the death of many prophets and heroes, but the unique religious significance is missed. Because these sociopolitical approaches do not get to the heart of the drama—the unfolding of the relationship between the Father and the Son—they fail to show a way out of the cycle of violence. Is the sacrificial interpretation, enshrined in the liturgy of Holy Week, a misreading of the Passion or the very heart of its revealed meaning?

BIBLICAL DATA

As Rahner and Girard acknowledge, the testimony of Sacred Scripture is fundamental. Unlike these authors, I am convinced that the idea of sacrifice is found not only in a few "late" New Testament texts such as the

Letter to the Hebrews but in nearly all the New Testament accounts of the death of Jesus.[9] Already in the Synoptic Gospels Jesus describes himself as one sent to give his life as a ransom for many (Mk 10:45; Mt 20:28). With an unmistakable allusion to the blood of the covenant that Moses sprinkled on the people (Ex 24:6–8), Jesus speaks of the Eucharist as his covenant blood, poured out for the many (Mk 14:24; Mt 26:28). In the Garden of Gethsemane he submits reverently to the Father, who does not will to remove the chalice from him (Mk 14:36; Mt 26:39; Lk 22:42). The story of the Passion unfolds against the background of the Jewish Passover feast.

In the Gospel of John, the sacrificial motif becomes more explicit. In the first chapter John the Baptist introduces Jesus as the Lamb of God who takes away the sin of the world (Jn 1:29)—a passage reminiscent of the Passover lamb, whose blood saved the Israelites from the avenging angel in Egypt (Ex 12:1–11), and the lamb described in Isaiah as being led to the slaughter as a sin offering (Is 53:7, 10). In chapter 6, John quotes Jesus as speaking of his body as the bread that he will offer up, in dying, for the life of the world (Jn 6:51). In the tenth chapter Jesus speaks of himself as the Good Shepherd who, in obedience to the Father's command, lays down his life for the sheep, and is loved by the Father for so doing (Jn 10:11, 17–18).

Paul, making an explicit comparison between Jesus and the Passover lamb, writes: "Christ, our paschal lamb, has been sacrificed" (1 Cor 5:7). In his letter to the Romans, Paul teaches that God has set Jesus forth as an expiatory sacrifice, accomplished by his blood (Rom 3:25). Elsewhere Paul depicts Jesus as having humbled himself and become obedient to the Father to the point of death (Phil 2:8). In the Pauline letter to the Ephesians, Christ is said to have given himself up for us, as "a fragrant offering and sacrifice to God" (Eph 5:2).

The sacrificial interpretation of the death of Jesus is found once again in the letters of John, in which Jesus is said to have expiated the sins of the whole world (1 Jn 2:2; 4:10). In the book of Revelation, the twenty-four elders fall down before the Lamb, and sing to him a new song of praise for having by his blood ransomed a vast multitude "from every tribe and tongue and people and nation" (Rev. 5:9).

In clearly sacrificial language, Peter's first letter speaks of our redemption "with the precious blood of Christ, like that of a lamb without blemish or spot" (1 Pt 1:19). The priesthood of Jesus and the perfection of his sacrifice are the central theme of the letter to the Hebrews. We are cleansed from sin, the author declares, by the blood of Christ, who through the eternal Spirit offered himself without blemish to God (Heb 9:14). The blood of Christ, shed on the Cross, accomplishes what the Jews sought in vain to accomplish through the blood of bulls and goats (Heb 10:4). The voluntary self-offering of Jesus is thus interpreted as a liturgy of obedience manifesting the unity between the Father and the Son in the eternal Spirit.

Many of the Church fathers, notably Augustine, described the death of Jesus as a perfect act of worship, the summation of all the sacrifices that had previously been offered.[10] The Council of Ephesus in 431 defined under anathema that Jesus offered himself as a sacrifice not for his own benefit but for ours (can. 10; DS 261). The Council of Trent taught that the bloody sacrifice of the Cross fulfilled and perfected the sacrifices of the Old Law and secured eternal redemption for the people.[11]

The Second Vatican Council, in texts too numerous to list here, repeats many of the standard affirmations of Scripture and earlier councils. It states, for instance, that Christ offered himself up as a spotless victim on the altar of the cross[12] and that he "gave himself as a victim to sanctify humankind."[13]

After Vatican II, Paul VI, in his *Credo of the People of God* (1968), wrote, "We believe that our Lord Jesus Christ by the sacrifice of the Cross redeemed us from original sin and all personal sin."[14] The recent *Catechism of the Catholic Church* speaks of the death of Jesus as the Paschal sacrifice and as the sacrifice of the New Covenant—the sacrifice that completes and surpasses all other sacrifices.[15]

WHOSE SACRIFICE?

In view of the massive consensus of the New Testament authors, the theologians, and magisterial documents, it seems clear that the sacrificial concept of the death of Jesus belongs to the enduring heritage of Christian faith. But that concept must be rightly understood. The objections raised by the critics can help us to refine the notion of sacrifice.

Opponents of the sacrificial interpretation often put the question, who sacrificed Jesus? Three possible answers must be considered: the Father, the Son, and the human opponents of Jesus. It is unthinkable, say the questioners, that God the Father would have put his own Son to death, because such an action would be brutal and unjust. But Jesus could not have sacrificed himself, or he would have been guilty of the sin of suicide. If, finally, the enemies of Jesus performed the sacrifice by condemning him to death and crucifying him, Christianity must be accused of sanctifying unjust violence. Since the sacrifice could not have been offered by any of the possible agents, the sacrificial interpretation must be abandoned. So runs the objection.

There is nothing new about this objection. It was familiar to the classical theologians and was answered by Thomas Aquinas, among others. To some extent the questions are answered by recalling the very meaning of "sacrifice." In Christian theology it refers to the sacred action by which a creature freely acknowledges the supreme dominion of God by offering some created good in order to express subjection to God, to please and honor him, and to obtain God's favor or to enter into deeper union with him. Since sacrifice is by its very definition offered to God by a creature, it is evident, in the first place, that the Father is not the one offering but the one to whom the offering is made. Second, the definition rules out the idea that the executioners of Christ were the ones doing the offering, for they performed not a holy deed but a heinous crime. Their activity, as St. Thomas puts it, was more a malefaction than a sacrifice ("*magis fuit maleficium quam sacrificium*").[16]

It remains, therefore, that Christ was the offerer. He made the offering as man, in submission to his heavenly Father. His suffering and death, freely endured, fulfilled the notion of a sacrifice. As the Letter to the Ephesians expresses it, "Christ loved us and gave himself up for us, a fragrant offering and sacrifice to God" (Eph 5:2). Theologians add that it was the most perfect of all sacrifices because the gift offered, the sacred humanity of our Lord, was most perfect, because the offerer, the God-man, was most perfect, and because the offering was made with the most perfect love.

ROLE OF THE FATHER

The role of the Father with reference to the sacrifice has been variously understood on the basis of several biblical texts. Paul exclaims that God "did not spare his own Son but gave him up for us all" (Rom 8:32).

Isaiah, in passages often applied to Christ, writes concerning the Suffering Servant: "We esteemed him stricken, smitten by God, and afflicted. . . . The Lord has laid on him the iniquities of us all" (Is 53:4–10). These passages have led to some rather disturbing interpretations. Martin Luther, for example, maintained that although Jesus was sinless, he was punished by God, who laid on him all the guilt of sinful humanity.[17] Calvin likewise declares: "The guilt that held us liable for punishment has been transferred to the head of the Son of God."[18] Karl Barth, standing within this tradition, writes of Jesus: "He stands before the Father at Golgotha burdened with all the actual sin and guilt of man and of each individual man, and is treated in accordance with the deserts of man as the transgressor of the divine command."[19] Still more recently, Jürgen Moltmann speaks of the crucified Jesus being rejected and abandoned by his Father.[20] Some Catholic preachers such as Bourdaloue and Bossuet have eloquently discoursed on the way in which God vented his anger upon his innocent Son.[21]

This punitive view of the crucifixion must, I believe, be rejected. It is false to imagine that the Father treats the Son with anger or chastises the innocent in place of the guilty. It would have been a wicked and cruel act, says Thomas Aquinas, for God to hand over an innocent man to torment and death against his will, but God did not do this. Instead, by the infusion of charity, God inspired Christ with the will to suffer for us.[22]

While Jesus went freely and lovingly to his death, he did so because the Father so commanded. The New Testament authors are unanimous on this point. According to the Synoptic Gospels, Jesus in the Garden undergoes an agony before he submits to what he recognizes as the Father's will (Mk 14:36 par). In the Gospel of John, Jesus freely and voluntarily fulfills the command to drink the cup that the Father has given him (Jn 10:18; 14:31; 18:11). Paul in his Letter to the Romans remarks on how the obedience of Christ became a source of righteousness for the many (Rom 5:19), and in the Letter to the Philippians he holds up the example of Jesus, who became obedient even unto death on the cross (Phil 2:8). The Letter to the Hebrews tells us that Jesus, Son though he was, learned obedience through the things that he suffered (Heb 5:8).

We cannot deny, therefore, that the Father commanded Jesus to go to his cruel death. Thus the problem of the Father's complicity remains. Even if the Father did not physically sacrifice his Son, he would seem to have made himself morally responsible by commanding the Son to offer his life. What loving father could issue such a command? In her criticism of Moltmann's theology of the cross, Dorothee Sölle remarks that that author, fascinated by God's brutality, falls into a kind of theological sadism.[23] Another author expresses dissatisfaction with atonement theories that seem to justify "cosmic child abuse."[24]

Perhaps an analogy will help us to deal with this difficulty. Let us imagine a human father whose son is a brilliant military leader. At a time when the nation is being unjustly attacked, and when all citizens are being summoned to arms, this father, though deeply attached to his son, might encourage the son to go to the front. When the fighting grows fierce, he might even refrain from sending a helicopter to rescue his son, realizing that that his son's escape would demoralize the army and occasion a national defeat. If he knew that news of the son's heroic death would arouse the nation to resist the aggression, the father might, despite his filial affection, encourage his son to die. If he were in a position to do so, the father might even command his son to remain at his post in the face of inevitable death.

In the case of the Passion, God did not command anyone to put Jesus to death but he certainly willed that Jesus should endure the suffering that evil men were to inflict upon him, rather than renounce his mission of preaching the gospel. When Jesus was arrested and condemned, God could have worked a miracle to deliver him. But, seeing the great good that would result from the death of Jesus, God did not bring him down from the cross. This was not because he lacked affection for his son, but because the suffering and death of Jesus were capable of bringing about the redemption of the world. Pondering this mystery, Paul marvels at God's redemptive love for sinners, which prevents God from sparing his own Son.

We must also remember that the cross is only the negative phase of the Paschal mystery by which Jesus enters into the fullness of glory through his resurrection from the dead. The Son's obedience would be rewarded by his exaltation to the right hand of the Father. By allowing the Passion to unfold, God taught us that suffering and death are not the ultimate evil, and that even the most cruel death can be a point of entry into eternal blessedness.

Besides being a physical evil from Jesus' side, the death of Jesus was a moral evil on the part of those who brought it about. God did not will or condone the moral evil, any more than he wills or condones any sin. In granting us freedom, God allows us to commit sin, the kind of act by which he is most offended. Objectively speaking, the death of Jesus may be called the greatest of all sins, though the subjective responsibility of individuals of course depends upon the measure of freedom and knowledge with which they acted.

Some have raised the question whether God could not have redeemed us in some other way—for example, by simply decreeing that all sin was forgiven. So far as the human mind can see, this could have been possible for God—but we cannot say that it would be better. The actual plan of redemption through the bloody sacrifice of the cross in many ways surpasses a mere decree of forgiveness. It better teaches us the destructiveness and gravity of sin; it shows forth more dramatically the depth of God's love for us. It also provides us with an inspiring example, so that we may follow in Christ's footsteps (1 Pt 2:21). And finally, it gives consolation to all who have to endure abandonment or unjust suffering. They can be sustained by the realization that the Son of God, sinless though he was, endured even greater spiritual and physical pain than theirs, and was heard for his reverence (Heb 5:7).

Much has been written about Jesus' cry of abandonment from the cross. In words that may well be historically accurate, Matthew and Mark depict Jesus as crying out, in the words of the Psalmist, "My God, my God, why have you forsaken me?" (Mt 27:46, Mk 15:34; cf. Ps 22).[25] Since Jesus is quoting a Psalm, it is dangerous to use these words as a basis for probing into Jesus' psychological state of mind or for a theological determination of the relations between the Father and the Son. Moltmann, again, is the theologian who has gone the furthest in this direction. He speaks of this cry of abandonment as revealing the enmity between the Father and the Son, who is rejected by the Father and who suffers the torments of hell.[26] Thomas Aquinas is much more prudent when he explains that Jesus was abandoned by the Father in the sense that the Father did not rescue him from his distress.[27]

In any case, there is no evidence that Jesus despaired, as some have conjectured. Still less are we entitled to say that he suffered the pains of hell, since hell is the condition of hardened sinners who have neither hope nor love. The accounts of the death of Jesus in the Gospels of Luke and John make it clear that he continues to trust in his Father, confident that he will soon be in paradise (Lk (Declaring that his mission is accomplished (Jn 19:30), he lovingly surrenders his spirit into the Father's hands (Lk 23:46). Even the twenty-second Psalm, if one reads beyond the first verse, is an expression of deep hope and confidence. Beginning as a lament, it turns into a song of thanksgiving to the God who saves from death.

> I will tell of your name to my brethren;
> in the midst of the congregation I will praise you . . .
> All the ends of the earth shall remember and turn to the Lord . . .

As Walter Kasper points out, "According to the practice of the time, saying the opening verse of a psalm implied the whole psalm."[28]

"For Our Sake"

Sacrifice, as we have seen, is by its very nature offered to God. But it is also offered on someone's behalf. The Council of Ephesus, in the anathema to which I have already referred, declared that Jesus offered the sacrifice not for himself but for others—that is to say, for us men and women. This important truth is also taught in the creed of Constantinople, from which I have taken the title of this lecture, "He was crucified for our sake." In the Synoptic Gospels this directedness to others is made explicit in the words "for many" (ἀντὶ πολλῶν) found in several of the sayings of Jesus. He declared that he was giving his life as a ransom for many (Mk 10:45), and that in the Eucharist his body and blood were given and poured out for many (Mt 26:28; Mk 14:24). Paul records Jesus' words at the Eucharist as "for you" (ὑπὲρ ὑμῶν) 1 Cor 11:24).

The statement that Christ suffered "for us" can be understood as meaning not only that he suffered on our behalf but that he did so in our place. In Evangelical Protestant circles it is common to speak of "substitutionary atonement," but this expression, in my opinion, can be misleading. Christ may indeed be said to suffer in our place in the sense that guilty humanity deserved to undergo the suffering that was undeservedly inflicted upon him, the sinless one. But the term "substitution" suggests that he did only what could have been done by those for whom he substituted. That is manifestly untrue. If you and I had been crucified in place of Jesus, the world would not have been redeemed.

I find it helpful to distinguish between a substitute and a representative. Substitution occurs when one thing simply takes the place of another, like a worn-out tire on a car. In the case of substitution, the replacement itself can be replaced at any time. Human beings as persons are not substitutable, but they are representable.[29] Those being represented are not strictly replaced; they retain their personal identity and responsibility. In his sufferings Christ lovingly identified himself with everyone in need of redemption and willed to experience the pain and sorrow that sinners deserved to suffer. Without replacing fallen humanity, he became its representative before God, pleading with the Father for our forgiveness.

Following the New Testament, theologians have called the cross a sacrifice of expiation. Christ is said to have atoned for all sins, satisfied for all guilt, and paid the price for the redemption of all. These expressions are correct, but, like the idea of sacrifice itself, they must be carefully explained. The blood of Christ is not an object offered to God in repayment for an offense, as in many religions the blood of animals was thought to placate the divine anger. The Christian idea of redemption discloses on one hand that sinful humanity is incapable of redeeming itself, and on the other hand that God is not a tyrant whose anger needs to be appeased or whose honor needs to be vindicated by human sacrifices. The order is reversed. The movement of redemption does not go from sinful humanity to a vengeful God, but from a merciful God to his needy creatures. As Paul writes to the Corinthians, "God was in Christ, reconciling the world to himself" (2 Cor 5:19). In his sacrifice, Christ offers himself, as the Letter to the Hebrews puts it, "through the eternal Spirit" (Heb 9:14). In his obedient submission to the movement of the Holy Spirit, Christ carried out the Father's redemptive plan. The blood of Jesus is his very self, lovingly offered on our behalf. He expiates for sin in the sense that his self-offering is more pleasing to God than all sins are displeasing to him.[30]

SACRIFICE—WITH A DIFFERENCE

In the light of all that has been said thus far we may return to the questions of Rahner and Girard, with which I began. On many points they are quite correct. With Rahner we may agree that the general conception of sacrifice in the history of religions is not serviceable in theology. Still less is Christ's redemptive action reducible to the kind of sacred violence often implied by the concept of expiatory sacrifice.

Girard's analysis of the scapegoat mechanism is extremely helpful for understanding aspects of the gospel story that were not sufficiently attended to in classical theology. Drawing on his abundant knowledge of the psychoanalytic literature, Girard is able to show how the Roman and Jewish authorities entered into an alliance against Jesus, diverting their mutual hostility by concentrating on a common victim. Thus Luke can write, "Herod and Pilate became friends with each other that very day, for before this they had been at enmity with each other" (Lk 23:12). According to the Gospel accounts, groups viewed as representing the people were also clamoring for Jesus' execution.[31]

The innocence of the victim is acknowledged by the cynical saying attributed to Caiaphas in the Gospel of John: "It is expedient for you that one man should die for the people, and that the whole nation should not perish" (Jn 11:50). John notes that on the supernatural plane, this prediction was transcendently fulfilled: Jesus died for the salvation of all the scattered children of God. But on the human plane, Caiaphas's scheme proved illusory, as sacred violence always does. The Romans were to destroy the holy city of Jerusalem a generation later.

For Girard, the nonviolent character of Jesus' response constitutes a new and definitive revelation of God. In his earlier writings, he made a sharp distinction between religions that espouse sacred violence and the religion of Jesus, which transcends the mechanisms of violence and in so doing exposes the deceptive character of those mechanisms. Defining sacrifice as he did in terms of violent destruction, he proposed a nonsacrificial interpretation of the cross. Girard's critics, however, say that his definition of sacrifice was too narrow. It did not do justice to the full range of pagan religion, in which sacrifice has other aspects, such as praise, homage, and gratitude toward God. More importantly, Girard's definition of sacrifice fell far short of the Christian understanding which, as we have seen, pervades the New Testament. As noted above, Girard himself has come to recognize this and has corrected his earlier position.

The Christian idea of sacrifice as a Spirit-inspired movement of obedience to the redemptive plan of God differs radically from the pagan concept that a vengeful God can be placated by the destruction of material things, including the death of innocent human beings. In terms of sound theology, the brutal action of Jesus' executioners was an unholy act, far removed from authentic sacrifice. The sacrifice consisted not in the infliction of a painful death but on the contrary, in violence lovingly and obediently endured in homage to God. The sinful character of the world into which Christ came made it in some sense necessary for his redemptive action to be accomplished in a painful way, through suffering and death.

The unrestricted love of God, present and active in Jesus, enabled the sacrifice of the cross to benefit all members of the divided human family, thus achieving in a transcendent way what the sacred violence was supposed to achieve. Paul speaks of the wall of hostility between Jew and Gentile as having been broken down in the flesh of Jesus, and of the peace effected by the reconciling power of his blood (Eph 2:11–17).

In his meekness, Jesus forges an alternative to the path of violence. He refuses to return evil for evil. Allowing his enemies to unload their hostility upon him, he lovingly prays for their forgiveness. Using ideas borrowed from Girard, the theologian Raymund Schwager can say quite truly, "What no human imagination could have dreamed has actually happened: the law of revenge became the law of redeeming love. The curse was repaid with blessing. The conspiracy of hatred was answered with an outpouring of love."[32]

PURIFICATION THROUGH WORSHIP

The liturgy of Holy Week, focused though it be on the bloody sacrifice, does not reinforce sentiments of anger and violence. On the contrary, it leads to repentance for hostile acts and sentiments. Through contemplation of the crucified Christ, our hearts are purged of jealousy and resentment. As a sacred victim, Jesus effects the reconciliation that other sacrifices were powerless to achieve. Far more than the bronze serpent raised by Moses in the desert, the cross of Jesus brings spiritual healing. Looking upon him whom our sins have pierced, we can experience a profound inner conversion.

Jesus is not just an isolated individual who died some two thousand years ago. Raised to eternal glory, he lives and works today. He is the second Adam, the progenitor of a new redeemed humanity. He is the head of the Church, which is his body. And we who are baptized in his name, who profess the creed with our lips, are living members of that body. Christ is not a mere substitute, doing in our place what we fail to do. Nor is he a mere example, inspiring us to imitate him. If we are members of his body, he lives in us, breathes his Spirit into us, and inclines us from within. If we do not resist the inner leading of the Spirit, we will be taken up into the sacrificial movement of his life, thankfully accepting what he has done for us. In so doing we can be lifted out of the spiral of violence in which our world seems to be engulfed. We become part of a new community, with a mission to regenerate the whole world. Borne by the Spirit of Christ, we can rise above the mechanisms of violence that have been so brilliantly analyzed by Girard and his followers. We may be obliged, with Jesus, to bear some of the bitter fruits of sin, including abuse, hostility, and persecution. Sharing in his cross, we can pray and intercede, as he did, for our broken world, and thus contribute in some measure to the final triumph of nonviolence, which goes by the name of the reign of God.

Notes

1. "The legacy of the crucifixion narrative," according to Gil Bailie, is "the world's wellspring of moral and religious truth and its ultimate guarantor of intellectual clarity." See his *Violence Unveiled: Humanity at the Crossroads* (New York: Crossroad, 1995), 275–76.

2. The Latin original is more powerful that the English. It reads:

> *Sola digna tu fuisti*
> *Ferre saecli pretium*
> *Atque portum praeparare*
> *Nauta mundo naufrago*
> *Quem sacer cruor perunxit*
> *Fusus Agni corporis.*

3. Karl Rahner, *Foundations of Christian Faith* (New York: Crossroad, 1982), 282–83.

4. René Girard, *Violence and the Sacred* (Baltimore, Md.: Johns Hopkins University Press, 1977); *The Scapegoat* (Baltimore, Md.: John Hopkins University Press, 1982); *Things Hidden Since the Foundation of the World* (Stanford, Calif.: Stanford University Press, 1987).

5. Girard, *Things Hidden*, 224.

6. Girard, interview with Rebecca Adams in *Religion and Literature* 252 (1993): 9–33, at 28–29.

7. Robert Daly, in his foreword to Raymund Schwager's *Must There Be Scapegoats? Violence and Redemption in the Bible* (San Francisco: Harper & Row, 1987), states that Girard's theory has "prepared the way for a quantum leap in our understanding of the biblical writings" (v). Robert G. Hamerton-Kelly, in his *Sacred Violence: Paul's Hermeneutic of the Cross* (Minneapolis: Fortress, 1992), maintains that Girard has made it possible for us to see the pivotal importance of the cross in Paul and to accept Luther's theology of the Cross. In a sequel, *The Gospel and the Sacred Poetics of Violence in Mark* (Minneapolis: Fortress, 1994), Hamerton-Kelly applies Girard's theory of mimetic violence or scapegoating to Mark. Gil Bailie in his *Violence Unveiled: Humanity at the Crossroads* applies Girard's hermeneutics of sacred violence to a variety of contemporary social crises.

8. Bailie, *Violence Unveiled*, 262.

9. See Albert Vanhoye, "Sacerdoce du Christ et culte chrétien selon l'Épître aux Hébreux," *Christus* 28 (1981): 216–30. See also Robert North, "Violence and the Bible: The Girard Connection," *Catholic Biblical Quarterly* 47 (1985): 1–27, especially 18–21.

10. Augustine, *Enchiridion ad Laurentium de fide, spe, caritate*, 10:13; 13:41, PL 40:248–49 and 253.

11. Council of Trent, session 22, chapter 1; Denzinger-Schönmetzer, *Enchiridion symbolorum*, 1739–40.

12. Vatican II, *Unitatis redintegratio*, 2.

13. Vatican II, *Presbyterorum ordinis*, 13.

14. *The Christian Faith in the Doctrinal Documents of the Catholic Church*, ed. J. Neuner and J. Dupuis, 6th ed. (Staten Island, N.Y.: Alba House, 1995), 25.

15. *Catechism of the Catholic Church* (Vatican City: Libreria Editrice Vaticana, 1994), 613–14.

16. Thomas Aquinas, *Summa theologiae*, part III, qu. 48, art. 3, ad 3.

17. Martin Luther, *Commentary on Galatians* (1535), chap. 3, verse 13: "Whatever sins I, you, and all of us have committed or may commit in the future, they are as much Christ's own as if He Himself had committed them. . . . If Christ Himself is made guilty of all the sins we have committed, then we are absolved from all sins, not through ourselves but through Him" (LW 26:278, 280).

18. John Calvin, *Institutes of the Christian Religion*, II.16.5; LCC ed., I:509–10.

19. Karl Barth, *Church Dogmatics* (Edinburgh: T. & T. Clark, 1957), II/2, p. 758.

20. Jürgen Moltmann, *The Crucified God* (New York: Harper & Row, 1974), 145–53. Similar language is used by Hans Urs von Balthasar, who speaks of a separation (*Trennung*) between the Father and the Son, but who goes on to speak of a unity of love between them effected by the Holy Spirit. See his *Theodramatik* IV, *Das Endspiel* (Einsiedeln: Johannes Verlag, 1983), 236–37.

21. See the quotations given in Bernard Sesboüé, *Jésus-Christ: L'unique Médiateur: Essai sur la rédemption et le salut* (Paris: Desclée, 1988), 71–73.

22. Thomas Aquinas, *Summa theologiae*, part III, qu. 47, art. 3, ad 1 and ad 2.

23. Dorothee Sölle, *Suffering* (Philadelphia: Fortress, 1975), 27–28.

24. Rita Nakashima Brock, *Journeys by Heart: A Christology of Erotic Power* (New York: Crossroad, 1988), 56; cf. Elizabeth Johnson, "Jesus and Salvation," *Proceedings of the Catholic Theological Society of America* 49 (1994): 1–18, at 15.

25. The arguments for and against historicity are summarized by Raymond E. Brown in his *The Death of the Messiah* (New York: Doubleday, 1994), 2:1083–85.

26. Moltmann, *The Crucified God*, 145–53; *The Trinity and the Kingdom* (San Francisco: Harper & Row, 1981), 80–83.

27. Thomas Aquinas, *Summa theologiae*, part III, qu. 47, art. 3c.

28. Walter Kasper, *Jesus the Christ* (New York: Paulist, 1976), 118. For a survey of interpretations see Gérard Rossé, *The Cry of Jesus on the Cross* (New York: Paulist, 1987).

29. Dorothee Sölle, *Stellvertretung* (Stuttgart: Kreuz Verlag, 1966); English translation, *Christ the Representative* (London: SCM, 1967). In German, the terms *Ersatz* and *Stellvertretung* correspond to the terms "substitution" and "representation" in English.

30. For the ideas in this paragraph I am partly indebted to Joseph Ratzinger, *Introduction to Christianity* (New York: Seabury/Crossroad, 1969), 214.

31. "By the time of his trial and passion Jesus had succeeded in uniting an improbable, indeed unprecedented, coalition against him: the Roman authorities, the Sadducees, the Pharisees, even Herod Antipas. And in destroying him, this unnatural combination appears to have acted with a great measure of popular support. What conclusions can be drawn from this?" Paul Johnson, *A History of Christianity* (New York: Macmillan, 1976), 29. In a work influenced by Girard, Raymund Schwager gives a careful analysis of the attitudes of the Pharisees, the Sadducees, the Zealots, and probably the Essenes. He remarks that the historical question of the participation of the people will probably never be answered with certitude. See his *Must There Be Scapegoats?* 183–87.

32. Schwager, *Must There Be Scapegoats?* 214.

14

John Paul II and the Advent of the New Millennium

November 16, 1995

ANNIVERSARIES IN SALVATION HISTORY

The Church celebrates different aspects of her relationship to God by recalling different events in the history of salvation. Every Sunday, for example, is a little Easter, a remembrance of the resurrection, and every Friday a recollection of the Passion. On a larger scale, the liturgical year is arranged so as to provide occasions to ponder various phases of God's redemptive work, such as the birth of Christ, his suffering and death, his resurrection and ascension. Two weeks from now we shall be entering the season of Advent, in which we seek to dispose ourselves to receive more abundantly the graces connected with the Nativity, which we await at Christmastide, and also to prepare ourselves to meet the Lord as judge and savior at the end of time. Advent is a season of self-examination, hope, expectation, and intense prayer. If our preparation is successful, each Christmas can be for us a new Bethlehem.

Beyond the rhythms of the liturgical year, the Church designates holy years to commemorate major anniversaries of great events concerning our redemption. The bimillennium of the birth of Christ, which is now less than five years away, will be a particularly solemn jubilee. Because the birth of Christ was itself an outward event, the celebration of the jubilee, according to the present pope, should be outwardly manifested (*TMA* 16).

When John Paul II was elected pope, his friend and mentor, Cardinal Stefan Wyszynski of Warsaw, told him, "If the Lord has called you, you must lead the Church into the third millennium."[1] The pope has taken this mandate to heart. His first encyclical, published early in 1979, began with a statement that the Church is already in a season of Advent, preparing for the great jubilee of the year 2000 (*RH* 1). More recently, he has spoken of the preparations for this celebration as "a hermeneutical key for my pontificate" (*TMA* 23; cf. *EA* 18).

In his writings on the subject, John Paul II situates the coming jubilee within the framework of an imposing theology of history. The Christian faith, he points out, is eminently historical. Time has a beginning, a middle, and an end, and is at all points related to the eternity of God. St. Paul speaks of the coming of Christ as the fullness of time (Gal 4:4), because at that moment eternity actually enters time, and God becomes an actor on the stage of human history (*TMA* 9). Christ, the Lord of time, to whom all ages belong, plunges into the midst of time, and becomes, in the words of Vatican II, "the focal point and goal of all human history" (*GS* 10, quoted in *TMA* 59). Because Christ remains present through his Spirit, especially in the Church, all of us since Pentecost live in what Scripture calls the last days, the final hour (Acts 2:17; Heb 1:2; 1 Jn 2:18; quotations in *TMA* 10; cf. *D&V* 61). It is theologically correct to make a sharp distinction between the periods before and since the coming of Christ, B.C. and A.D.

This does not mean, however, that the end of history is imminent. The Holy Father is very careful to avoid the excesses of millenarianism.[2] Before the year 1000 a few preachers appear to have predicted that the reign of the Antichrist was about to begin, though there is no evidence of the widespread terror depicted by certain anticlerical French historians. Aware that we live today in a highly charged atmosphere in which the flames of mass hysteria can easily be ignited by fanciful speculations, the pope provides no basis for either utopian prognostications or dire apocalyptic premonitions. Instead he calls upon the faithful to prepare soberly for "that new springtime of Christian life which will be revealed if Christians are docile to the action of the Holy Spirit" (*TMA* 18). "As the second millennium after Christ's coming draws to an end," he declares, "an overall view of the human race shows that this mission [entrusted by Christ to the Church] is still only beginning and that we must commit ourselves wholeheartedly to its service" (*RMis* 1).

The pope evidently looks upon the Blessed Virgin Mary as the primary patroness of this new Advent. During the Marian Year of 1986–1987, celebrating the 2000th anniversary of Mary's birth, he issued an encyclical, *Redemptoris Mater*. He described Mary as the "morning star" (*Stella matutina*), whose appearance, like the dawn, announces the proximity of Christ, the "Sun of Justice" (*Sol Justitiae*), before he rises visibly over the horizon (*RMat* 3). Throughout the years from 1986 to the end of the century Mary's presence upon earth is to be gratefully recalled. Just as the Blessed Virgin carried the Christ Child in her womb before his birth, so the present millennium, in its final years, bears within itself the seeds of the millennium now waiting to be born.

Already in 1983, John Paul II called upon Mary to inspire in the Church the same sentiments with which she awaited the birth of the Lord in the lowliness of our human nature (*APD* 9). Every Christian is invited to look forward to this great jubilee with the deep faith, humility, and confidence in God that characterized the Virgin Mother in her days of expectancy.

Occasionally, but less frequently, John Paul II speaks in this connection of John the Baptist, who can also be considered a patron saint for Advent. By giving his life in witness to truth and justice, John became "the forerunner of the Messiah by the manner of his death" (*VS* 91; cf. Roman Missal for August 29 and Mk 6:17–29). While the Church does not imitate the sternness of this holy prophet, it seeks, as he did, to move all who practice injustice to repentance and conversion (*TMA* 19). Christians now hear a fresh summons to prepare the way of the Lord, pointing anew to Jesus as "the One who was to come" (cf. Lk 7:20), "the Lamb of God who takes away the sins of the world" (Jn 1:29, quoted in *TMA* 19).

THE MEANING OF JUBLIEES

I have already referred to the coming anniversary as a jubilee. We are all familiar with the custom of silver, golden, and diamond jubilee anniversaries of weddings and ordinations. These are times of gratitude for the favors of past years, occasions for rededication and renewal of trust.

John Paul II points out that the custom of jubilees is a very ancient one, going back to Old Testament times. According to the law of Moses, as we find it in the books of Exodus, Leviticus, and Deuteronomy, every seventh year was dedicated in a special way to God, and every fiftieth year was a major jubilee celebration. During sabbatical and jubilee years the earth was to be left fallow, slaves were to be liberated, and debts forgiven (*TMA* 12).

The prescriptions for the jubilee year represented hopes and ideals rather than actual facts, but they were valid insofar as they foreshadowed the new era of Christ the Redeemer (*TMA* 13). According to Luke's Gospel, Jesus began his public ministry at Nazareth by announcing the fulfillment in his person of the prescriptions of the jubilee as set forth in Isaiah: "The Spirit of the Lord is upon me, because he has anointed me to preach good news to the poor. He has sent me to proclaim release to the captives and recovering of sight to the blind, to set at liberty those who are oppressed, to proclaim the acceptable year of the Lord" (Lk 4:18–19).

This quotation from Isaiah, which Jesus applies to himself, suggests appropriate ways of celebrating the coming jubilee. The year 2000 should be seen as a season of the Lord's favor, in which the presence of the Holy Spirit will be more deeply experienced, impelling Christians to preach the gospel with new power, giving hope of liberation to the marginalized and the oppressed. According to John Paul II, the great jubilee of the year 2000 "contains a message of liberation by the power of the Spirit, who alone can help individuals and communities to free themselves from the old and new determinisms, by guiding them with the 'law of the Spirit, which gives life in Christ Jesus,' thereby discovering and accomplishing the full measure of man's true freedom" (*D&V* 60). The relief of poverty, the liberation of captives, and the forgiveness of debts are means whereby the basic equality of all human beings is asserted, and whereby the rich are reminded that the earth and its fullness belong, in the final analysis, to God (cf. Ps 24:1). In the Catholic tradition jubilee years are times when the Church shows particular indulgence in granting the remission of sins and of the punishments due to them (*TMA* 14).

Evangelization as a Priority

In the vision of Pope John Paul, "the Second Vatican Council was a providential event whereby the Church began the more immediate preparation for the jubilee of the second millennium" (*TMA* 18). From the point of view of the history of salvation, he writes, that council may be viewed as "the cornerstone of the present century which is now rapidly approaching the third millennium" (*EA* 2). The best preparation for the new millennium, consequently, will be "a renewed commitment to apply, as faithfully as possible, the teachings of Vatican II to the life of every individual and of the whole Church" (*TMA* 20). That council is "the great beginning—the Advent as it were—of the journey leading us to the threshold of the third millennium" (*UUS* 100). The great themes of the council, such as evangelization, religious freedom, ecumenism, interreligious dialogue, and openness to the world have set the agenda for our time.

The program of evangelization for the final part of the century is set forth in the encyclical *Redemptoris missio*, which builds upon Paul VI's magnificent apostolic exhortation, *Evangelii nuntiandi*, issued in 1975, just twenty years ago. John Paul's encyclical begins with the stirring words: "The mission of Christ the redeemer, which is entrusted to the Church, is still very far from completion. . . . It is the Spirit who impels us to proclaim the great works of God: 'For if I preach the gospel, that gives no ground for boasting. For necessity is laid upon me. Woe to me if I do not preach the gospel' (1 Cor 9:16)." All four Gospels, as well as the Acts of the Apostles, make it clear that the Church received from Christ the mission to preach the gospel to all nations, to the whole world, to every creature (*RMis* 22–23). On the eve of the year 2000 the Church must prepare to render an account of its fidelity to this essential charge.

The pope remarks on a variety of factors that make the missionary task especially urgent in our time. New challenges and new opportunities are present. The number of people who do not know Christ and who do not belong to the Church has almost doubled since the close of Vatican II (*RMis* 3). The traditionally Christian nations of the West are in need of reevangelization, since they have witnessed a dramatic decline of faith, connected in some ways with false concepts of freedom and with a relativistic view of truth. Many people have lost the sense of God and are drawn into a kind of hedonism that renders them almost impervious to the message of the gospel (see *EV* 22–23). In some parts of the world secular governments, seeking to protect a national or regional religion, erect barriers against Christian proclamation.

Notwithstanding these grave obstacles, the pope finds grounds to hope for a new springtime of evangelization. Under the dehumanizing pressures of technology and consumerism, many are hungering for spiritual nourishment. New opportunities for proclamation are offered by the rapidity of travel and the abundance of new media of communication. Certain gospel ideals and values, such as human dignity, peace, solidarity, and freedom, have become part of the patrimony of the whole world (*RMis* 3, 86). The year 1989 witnessed the collapse of some oppressive regimes that were blocking the spread of the gospel. Thus the pope can say: "God is opening before the Church the horizons of a humanity more fully prepared for the sowing of the gospel. I sense that the moment has come to commit all of the Church's energies to a new evangelization and to the mission *ad gentes*. No believer in Christ, no institution of the Church can avoid this supreme duty: to proclaim Christ to all peoples" (*RMis* 3).

Ecumenism and Interreligious Dialogue

Another priority of the Second Vatican Council was ecumenism. As the new millennium approaches, the Church must interrogate itself on its fidelity to this mandate. Jesus at the Last Supper prayed for his disciples "that they may all be one . . . so that the world may believe that thou hast sent me" (Jn 17:21). What account can Christian leaders give to their Master if they have allowed the sign of unity to be defaced by conflict and division? The task of evangelization, so urgent in these closing years of the present century, is gravely impeded by the mutual divisions among Christians (*RMis* 36, 50). In the words of Vatican II: "This discord openly contradicts the will of Christ, provides a stumbling block to the world, and inflicts damage on the most holy cause of proclaiming the good news to every creature" (*UR* 1). Reflecting on this text, John Paul II asks, "When non-believers meet missionaries who do not agree among themselves, even though they all appeal to Christ, will they be in a position to receive the true message?" (*UUS* 98).

The great jubilee of the year 2000 calls for major celebrations on the part of all Christians, whether Catholic, Protestant, or Orthodox. It would be a scandal if the different churches and Christian communities were unable to come together with a greater show of unity than they have displayed in recent centuries. Glancing over the history of the past, John Paul II notes that the millennium that is about to end is the period in which most of the great separations between Christians have occurred

(*D&V* 62). The final years of the second millennium, he says, demand "the promotion of fitting ecumenical initiatives so that we can celebrate the Great Jubilee, if not completely united, at least much closer to overcoming the divisions of the second millennium" (*TMA* 34).

This ecumenical emphasis, always prominent in the teaching of John Paul II, has been intensified in the past year with his apostolic letter *Orientale lumen*, written to the Catholic Church on relations with the East (May 2, 1995) and with his encyclical letter *Ut unum sint* (May 25, 1995). In the first of these documents he pleads with a holy impatience for the day when the churches of the East and West may come together at the Lord's table, confessing the one faith in mutual harmony. He expresses the hope that the arrival of the third millennium may be an occasion for the discovery that these two major branches of Christianity have been walking in close company, perhaps even without knowing it (*OL* 28).

The recent encyclical on ecumenism strikes a note of optimism, expressing the pope's intense desire that the year 2000 may see a significant advance along the path to unity, thus fulfilling the call made with such impassioned commitment by the Second Vatican Council (*UUS* 1). The encyclical contains a detailed exposition of the various means to unity, including theological dialogues and the reception of their results by the respective churches. Mention is also made of the importance of practical cooperation among the churches and the crucial necessity of prayer for unity, since full communion can only be a gift of the Holy Spirit. The new millennium, says the pope, "will be an exceptional occasion, in view of which she [the Church] asks the Lord to increase the unity of all Christians until they reach full communion" (*UUS* 3).

Human Solidarity

John Paul II does not restrict the significance of the coming millennium to the religious sphere. In his view, it has a salutary potential for the entire human race, even in secular relationships. The popes of the present century, he observes, have accepted their responsibility to defend the values of peace of justice and the principles of international order. Evangelization, if it is to be complete and integral, calls for the safeguarding of human dignity and human rights (*TMA* 22).

The jubilee, as understood by John Paul II, has secular and social implications that appear prominently in Jesus' proclamation of his mission, as already quoted from Luke's Gospel. "Commitment to justice and peace," says the pope, "is a necessary condition for the preparation and celebration of the jubilee" (*TMA* 51). Reflecting on the Old Testament prescriptions regarding debts, he asks whether the jubilee might not be an appropriate time for "reducing substantially, if not canceling outright, the international debt which seriously threatens the future of many nations" (ibid.).

To illustrate how John Paul II weaves together the religious and the secular aspects of the coming jubilee, it may suffice to recall his address to the United Nations on October 5, 1995. He there commented on the global acceleration of the quest for freedom as one of the outstanding phenomena of our time. The moral dynamics of this universal quest clearly appeared during the nonviolent revolutions of 1989. These uprisings were provoked by the sense of personal dignity that had been ignored and violated by totalitarian regimes. But, as we have learned in the past few years, freedom calls for discipline. To prevent liberty from deteriorating into license or being abused by the arrogance of power, it is necessary to develop a shared awareness of universal human rights and the sense of belonging, as it were, to a "family of nations." The politics of nations, said the pope, can never ignore the transcendent, spiritual dimension of human existence without detriment to the cause of freedom.

In the conclusion of his United Nations address the pope called attention to the role of the Church in sustaining faith, hope, and love in an age when people are tempted to cynicism, despair, and violence. The antidote to the fear that darkens human existence, he said, must be a common effort to build a civilization of love, founded on the universal values of peace, solidarity, justice, and freedom. "Thus, as we approach the 2000th anniversary of the birth of Christ, the Church asks only to be able to propose respectfully this message of salvation and to be able to promote, in charity and service, the solidarity of the entire human family" (UN 17). On the ground that each and every person has been created in the 'image and likeness' of God, the pope went on to maintain that human beings have within them a capacity for wisdom and virtue and are able, with the help of God's grace, "to build in the next century a civilization worthy of the human person, a true culture of freedom. . . . In doing so, we shall see that the tears of this century have prepared the ground of a new springtime of the human spirit" (UN 18).

In his book *Crossing the Threshold of Hope*, John Paul II eloquently explains the role of faith in overcoming the paralyzing effects of fear. Christ alone, he asserts, can give the assurance of God's love that is needed by those who struggle to regenerate contemporary society. "At the end of the second millennium, we need, perhaps more than ever, the words of the Risen Christ: 'Be not afraid!' " (221).

REPENTANCE AND CONVERSION

Echoing the message of John the Baptist, Advent preachers commonly call for a serious examination of conscience, repentance, and conversion. The joy of any jubilee, according to John Paul II, must be based on the forgiveness of sins, penance, and reconciliation (*TMA* 32). Conscious of the sinfulness of her members, the Church does not tire of doing penance. As she presents herself anew to the Lord, she must ask herself how much of Christ's message has been heard and implemented in life (*Letter to Women*, 3).

In the spirit of John the Baptist John Paul II summons the whole Church to a collective examination of conscience regarding the mistakes and sins of the past millennium. At the head of the list of sins to be reckoned, he mentions offenses against ecclesial communion. While repenting the misdeeds that have divided Christians from one another, the Church should with great insistence invoke the Holy Spirit for the grace of unity (*TMA* 34).

As a second sin requiring corporate penance and conversion, John Paul II mentions the acquiescence given to intolerance and even to violence used in the service of truth (*TMA* 35). He does not indicate in detail what he has in mind, but one can easily imagine that he is thinking of events such as the Crusades, the wars of religion, and the excesses of the Inquisition. He might also have in mind the Church's compromises with the slavery system and with persecutions of the Jews. Vatican II, in his judgment, has made it clear that the freedom of conscience demands the renunciation of any undue pressure to obtain acceptance of religious truth (*RMis* 7 and 39).

It will be recalled that in 1979 John Paul II ordered a reexamination of the case of Galileo. After more than a decade of study the papal commission reported its finding that Galileo's judges, erroneously believing that the Copernican theory conflicted with revealed truth, wrongfully forbade Galileo to teach the theory. The pope, in October 1992, delivered an address to the Pontifical Academy of Sciences on the lessons to be derived from the Galileo case. He emphasized the need to distinguish between the proper spheres of theology and science and the responsibility of theologians to keep themselves regularly informed of scientific advances.[3]

Under the rubric of past mistakes calling for correction, it is of great interest to note the statements in the pope's *Letter to Women* on the eve of the Fourth World Conference on Women at Beijing last September. For many centuries, he observed, the dignity of women had been unacknowledged; they had been relegated to the margins of society and even reduced to servitude. This situation was contrary to the teaching and example of Jesus, who always honored the dignity of women. Because such patterns of behavior have been so heavily ingrained in the cultural heritage, it is difficult to assign culpability, but the pope was prepared to say, "If objective blame, especially in particular historical contexts, has belonged to not just a few members of the Church, for this I am truly sorry" (*Letter to Women*, 3). He expressed the wish that, as the Church moves into the new millennium, this regret might be transformed into a new commitment to recognize what he called "the feminine genius" (ibid., 11).

As is evident from these examples, John Paul II does not wish the Church's examination of conscience to be confined to the past. "On the threshold of the new millennium Christians need to place themselves humbly before the Lord and examine themselves on the responsibility which they too have for the evils of our day" (*TMA* 36). Among the shadows of our age the pope singles out religious indifference, the loss of the sense of the transcendent, ethical relativism, and the crisis of obedience vis-à-vis the Church's teaching authority (*TMA* 36). He exhorts Catholics to examine themselves on the fidelity with which they have received the teaching of Vatican II regarding the primacy of the word of God, the value of the liturgy, the ecclesiology of communion, and openness to dialogue with the world without sacrifice of their courage in witnessing to the truth. In another context the pope declares that the European nations are today obliged to make a serious examination of conscience with regard to the threat of exaggerated nationalism (*TMA* 27).

STAGES OF PREPARATION

In conclusion, I would like to say something about the concrete planning for the coming jubilee year. A schedule has been drawn up on the basis of extensive consultation, including a special consistory of cardinals that met in June 1994. For the period until the end of 1996 John Paul II proposes a phase of remote preparation given to inculcating awareness of the situation and instilling the required attitudes, such as hope, prayerfulness, and sorrow for the sins and mistakes of the past. During this period, or shortly thereafter, the pope expects there to be continental synods for the Americas, Asia, and perhaps Oceania, following along the general lines of the synods already held for Europe and Africa (*TMA* 38).

The synod for the Americas would concentrate on the new evangelization and on issues of justice, especially with regard to international economic relations. The synod for Asia would deal principally with the challenges to evangelization offered by the encounter with local cultures and with world religions such as Buddhism and Hinduism. The synod for Oceania, the pope indicates, could contribute to the dialogue between Christianity and the aboriginal monotheistic religions found in that part of the world.

John Paul II lays great stress on the importance of regional churches and their own celebrations of jubilees recalling their distinctive histories. Christian history, as he sees it, may be compared to a single river into which many tributaries pour their waters so as to give joy to the city of God (cf. Ps 46:4).

The years from 1997 to 1999, constituting the period of proximate preparation, have each their own theme. The general movement of the triennium will be from Christ, through the Holy Spirit, to God the Father, but each year will also have a Marian dimension. The year 1997 is to be one of faith, in which Christians will seek to renew their appreciation of baptism and their relationship to Christ the Son of God. Mary, the Mother of Jesus, will be invoked as a model of faith (*TMA* 40–43). In 1998, attention will shift to the sanctifying presence of the Holy Spirit, the sacrament of confirmation, and the theological virtue of hope. Notice will be taken of the signs of hope present in the world of our day and of the Virgin Mary, the Spouse of the Holy Spirit, as an exemplar of Christian hope (*TMA* 44–48). Finally, the year 1999 will focus on God the Father. It will be the occasion for a more intense celebration of the sacrament of penance, for the practice of charity, and for the building of a civilization of love. Praise will be directed to Mary, the beloved daughter of the Father, under the aspects of her holiness and her love for God and neighbor (*TMA* 49–54).

The climactic year, of course, will be the bimillennium itself. The plan is for the celebration to be conducted simultaneously in the Holy Land, in Rome, and in local churches throughout the world (*TMA* 55). John Paul II hopes for an ecumenical meeting of all Christians, planned in cooperation with representatives of other Christian traditions, with invitations extended to other religious bodies who might wish to acknowledge the joy shared by the disciples of Christ. The pope speaks of his own intense desire to visit Jerusalem and the Holy Land. "It would be very significant," he writes, "if in the year 2000 it were possible to visit the places on the road taken by the people of God of the Old Covenant, starting from the places associated with Abraham and Moses" (*TMA* 24). He notes the symbolic potential of places such as Bethlehem, Jerusalem, Mount Sinai, and Damascus for furthering dialogue with Jews and Muslims (*TMA* 53).

PROSPECTS FOR THE JUBILEE

It is too early to judge the impact of this elaborate plan of John Paul II, but it would seem that the first reactions have been positive. Committees have been formed in Rome to consider the historical, theological, and pastoral dimensions of the program. In many dioceses and councils of churches, plans are being laid for local and regional celebrations. The first soundings seem to indicate that other Christian bodies will gladly cooperate with the Catholic Church to give a positive ecumenical tone to the celebrations that might otherwise occur in competitive and antagonistic ways.

The coming jubilee is surely an occasion for joy and gratitude, but it presents dangers that should not be overlooked. If celebrated without recognition of the need for repentance and renewal, the festivals could take on a triumphalistic tone that would embarrass Christians and repel adherents of other faiths. If the ecumenical and interreligious dimensions were neglected, the jubilee could lead to tensions and rivalries among religions and especially among Christian bodies. If exclusively ritual in its focus, the bimillennium could be dismissed as empty pageantry by those concerned with the future of humanity on earth.

Great credit is due to the Holy See and to the present pope for the care they have taken to avoid these risks. They have called for penance as a preparation for the celebration, thus precluding undue complacency. Looking beyond the Catholic community, they have made provision for the participation of all Christian groups in ecumenical services. The sensitivities of the Jewish community and of other religious bodies are likewise respected. The emphasis given to peace, solidarity, human rights, and economic justice should provide assurance that the focus will not be too narrowly devotional.

More difficult than the preparation of the plan, of course, will be its execution. Total success is not to be expected, since many will fail to hear and heed the call. Yet in many quarters I seem to sense an attitude of eager expectancy. A jubilee of such magnitude presents rare opportunities, critically important for the future of faith and civilization. In contrast to the first millennium, when faith in Christ was confined to a small area of the globe, Christianity is now a worldwide phenomenon having a vital impact on all sectors of human existence. As the largest branch of Christianity, the Catholic Church has special responsibilities for leadership in the coming jubilee. By their manifest devotion to the Incarnate Lord, Catholics can bear witness to the enduring power of the Word made flesh. By their spirit of ecumenism and their openness to dialogue, they can help to bring all communions and all faiths into friendship and cooperation. By their efforts on behalf of justice in the world, they can help to build a society of freedom, solidarity, and peace. To the extent that each of us carries out these imperatives, the year 2000 may mark a new phase in that special presence of the Lord which began in the cave at Bethlehem. Even this side of the end of history, the Advent prayer of Christians, "Come, Lord Jesus," may yet be answered in striking and surprising ways.

NOTES

1. Quoted in a news report for Catholic News Service by John Thavis, *Origins* 24 (November 24, 1994): 404.

2. 2. See Bernard McGinn, *Visions of the End: Apocalyptic Traditions in the Middle Ages* (New York: Columbia University Press, 1979), 88–90; see also Hillel Schwartz, "Millenarianism: An Overview," *Encyclopedia of Religion* 9:521–32.

3. 3. For the pope's address and Cardinal Poupard's report of the commission, see *Origins* 22 (November 12, 1992): 369–75.

15

___

Priesthood and Gender

April 10, 1996

The most controversial statement that has come from the Holy See during the pontificate of John Paul II concerns the priestly ordination of women. On Pentecost Sunday, 1994, Pope John Paul II issued a brief letter, *Ordinatio sacerdotalis*, which concluded with the words, "In order that all doubt may be removed regarding a matter which pertains to the Church's divine constitution itself, in virtue of my ministry of confirming the brethren (cf. Lk 22:32) I declare that the Church has no authority whatsoever to confer priestly ordination on women and that this judgment is to be definitively held by all the Church's faithful."[1]

THE CONVERGENT ARGUMENT

On October 28, 1995, the Congregation of the Doctrine of the Faith, in a document approved by the pope, responded to a question put to it about whether the teaching of *Ordinatio sacerdotalis* was to be understood as belonging to the deposit of the faith. After replying in the affirmative, the Congregation added that the doctrine, founded on the written word of God, had been constantly held in the tradition of the Church, and has been infallibly set forth by the ordinary and universal magisterium. In his apostolic letter, therefore, the pope was not *making* the teaching infallible but *confirming* a teaching that was already infallible for the reasons stated.

Ordinatio sacerdotalis is the culmination of a long series of documents issued under Paul VI and John Paul II since 1975. In these documents the case against women's ordination is made under four principal headings: Bible, tradition, theological reasoning, and magisterial authority. These components are not to be taken in isolation but in convergence, since none of them is an independent authority. According to Vatican II, "Sacred tradition, sacred Scripture, and the teaching authority of the Church, in accord with God's most wise design, are so linked and joined together that one cannot stand without the others, and that all together, each in its own way under the action of the one Holy Spirit contribute effectively to the salvation of souls" (*DV* 10).

The biblical component in the argument is twofold: first, that Christ did not call women to the apostolic ministry, since he selected only men as members of the Twelve; and second, that the apostles themselves, faithful to the practice of Christ, chose only men for priestly offices, those of bishop, presbyter, and their equivalents.

The argument from tradition is that the Catholic bishops have always observed the norm of conferring sacred orders only on men, whereas sects that ordained women to the priesthood, or permitted them to perform priestly functions, were denounced as heretical. The fathers of the early centuries and the theologians of the Middle Ages regarded the question as settled.[2] Since the sixteenth century Catholic theologians have regularly characterized the Church's practice as grounded in divine law and have judged the opposed position as heretical or at least verging on heresy.[3]

The theological reasoning is to the effect that the ministerial priest shares in a representative way in the office of Christ as Bridegroom of the Church, and must therefore be, like Christ, of the male sex. A woman could not suitably represent Christ in this particular capacity.

The teaching of the magisterium, as the fourth component, has likewise been constant. In the early centuries many bishops and a few popes spoke to the question, and over the past twenty years or more, explicit statements from the Holy See have made it clear that the hierarchical magisterium is unwavering in holding that the ministerial priesthood cannot be exercised by women.

Impressive though this convergent argument is, it has not dispelled all doubt. Since about 1970 a number of voices have been raised, even in the Catholic Church, favoring the admission of women to priestly orders. Although many of the faithful have been convinced by the official pronouncements of recent years, others have responded negatively. The critics include theologians of acknowledged professional competence. The objections they have raised to the standard arguments cannot be written off as merely flippant. The Congregation for the Doctrine of the Faith has itself acknowledged, in another context, that the difficulties raised against magisterial teaching can sometimes "contribute to real doctrinal progress and provide a stimulus to the magisterium to propose the teaching of the Church in greater depth and with a clearer presentation of the arguments."[4] With this thought in mind, I shall here explore ten of the principal objections that are commonly raised.

THE PRACTICE OF CHRIST

With regard to the practice of Christ, a double objection is raised: first, that Jesus did not ordain *anyone* to the priesthood, and secondly, that there is no evidence that he intended his decision to call only men as members of the Twelve to be binding on all future generations.

To the first part of this objection it must be answered that according to Catholic teaching, Christ did confer the ministerial priesthood on his apostles. Although the exact moment when he did so is not important for our present question, it may be recalled that according to the Council of Trent he bestowed priestly powers on the Twelve at the Last Supper when he commissioned them to celebrate the Eucharist.[5] This assertion of the Council of Trent, which represents a reading of Scripture in light of Catholic tradition, still remains the authoritative teaching of the Church, as can be seen from many documents issued in recent years. In the Roman Missal of Paul VI (1970), the chrism Mass of Holy Thursday commemorates the institution of the priesthood at the Last Supper. John Paul II, in his letter to bishops on Holy Thursday, 1980, *Dominicae cenae*, asserts that the priesthood came into being together with the Eucharist at the Last Supper.[6]

The question whether Christ's choice of a male priesthood is permanently normative for the Church raises issues about the very nature of sacraments. The Congregation for the Doctrine of the Faith makes the point that sacraments "are principally meant to link the person of every period to the supreme event of the history of salvation."[7] The present case is similar to that of the institution of the Eucharist, in which Christ's choice of bread and wine, although it may not have been the only possibility open to him, is viewed as establishing the elements to be used in celebrating Mass. In ordaining priests, as in celebrating the Eucharist, the Church is conscious of doing what Christ did and of having no power to alter this. The claim of abiding force for Christ's own practice, supported as it is by the biblical data, is powerfully confirmed by the other three arguments—from tradition, theological reasoning, and magisterial teaching—which are still to be considered in this lecture.

Practice of the Early Church

The evidence concerning the practice of the apostolic Church has also been contested. Many today call attention to the 1975 study of the Pontifical Biblical Commission which, it is sometimes alleged, found no difficulty against the ordination of women. Even if the Biblical Commission had so concluded, the objection would have little force, since this Commission is not an organ of the magisterium, but a purely advisory body. In fact, however, the report of the Commission clearly stated that Christ chose only men for apostolic leadership and that the first communities, as we know them from the Acts and the Pauline letters, "were always directed by men exercising the apostolic power. . . . The masculine character of the hierarchical order which has structured the Church since its beginning thus seems attested in an undeniable way." The Commission added, however, that according to the majority of the members "it does not seem that the New Testament by itself alone will permit us to settle in a clear way and once and for all the problem of the possible accession of women to the presbyterate."[8] This conclusion is fair enough. The recent documents do not claim that the question can be definitively settled by Scripture alone, but only that the New Testament supports the tradition of the Church. All the biblical evidence we have about priestly office in the primitive Church tends to confirm its exclusively masculine character.[9]

The Argument from Tradition

Challenging the argument from tradition, some authors maintain that the question of women's ordination is a new one for the Church and that more time is needed for dialogue and reflection before the magisterium can properly decide the matter. As a matter of fact, however, the question is almost as old as Christianity itself. In the early centuries heretical sects, including Gnostics, Montanists, Priscillianists, and Collyridians, introduced a female priesthood in various parts of the Christian world, but their initiatives were rejected by Catholic bishops and theologians such as Irenaeus, Epiphanius, John Chrysostom, and Pope Gelasius I.[10]

The question arose again in the Middle Ages because of the practices of the Cathari and the Waldensians. Once again the Catholic authorities denied that the pastoral office or priesthood could be conferred on women. The great theologians of high Scholasticism, including Bonaventure, Thomas Aquinas, Duns Scotus, and Durandus, were unanimous in holding that the Church had no power to ordain women.[11] In this opinion they were joined by an outstanding medieval feminist, Hildegard of Bingen, who was adamant in opposing a feminine priesthood.[12] The issue of priesthood for women was again raised in Germany after the First World War, but leaders of the Catholic feminist movement themselves rejected the idea. Edith Stein, among others, considered carefully whether women could be priests, but on the basis of her study concluded in the negative.[13]

Admittedly, the question has taken on new urgency since World War II, at which time many mainline Protestant and Anglican churches began ordaining women to pastoral office, including the episcopate. Partly for this reason a flurry of new studies began to appear in the early to middle 1970s. Pope Paul VI spoke frequently to the question. In an address of April 1975, occasioned by the International Women's Year sponsored by the United Nations, he insisted that while the role of women should be vigorously promoted, the Church had no power to change the behavior of Christ and his call to women, which did not include apostleship or ordained ministry.[14] In a letter to the Archbishop of Canterbury of November 30, 1975, Paul VI stated very clearly that the Catholic Church "holds that it is not admissible to ordain women to the priesthood, for very fundamental reasons." He added: "These reasons include: the example recorded in the sacred scriptures of Christ choosing his apostles only from among men; the constant practice of the Church, which has imitated Christ in choosing only men; and her living teaching authority, which has consistently held that the exclusion of women from the priesthood is in accordance with God's plan for his Church."[15]

The most complete official study of our question remains to this day the Declaration of the Congregation of the Doctrine of the Faith, *Inter insigniores*, issued with the approval of Paul VI over the signature of

Cardinal Franjo Šeper on October 15, 1976, the feast of St. Teresa of Avila. This document proposed the various arguments I have mentioned and concluded that the practice of the Church, based as it is on Christ's example, conforms to God's plan for his Church.

Before issuing the brief declaration mentioned at the opening of this paper, John Paul II treated the question at greater length in several important documents, such as his apostolic exhortation on the laity *Christifideles laici* and his apostolic letter on women, *Mulieris dignitatem* (both issued in 1988). On the precise question of ordination he has strongly reaffirmed the positions of Paul VI, who stood in solidarity with the immemorial tradition of the Church. These considerations should make it evident that we are not dealing with a new and unprecedented question.

SOCIOCULTURAL CONDITIONING?

In some quarters, however, it is still objected that the tradition of the Church, and likewise the practice of Christ and the apostles, have been socially and culturally conditioned. Some argue that women were in a position of social inferiority and were therefore not considered eligible for anything resembling priestly office. But the evidence does not support this objection. Whatever the social inferiority of women may or may not have been, priestesses were common in pagan religions throughout the Greco-Roman world. They were a familiar institution among the Babylonians and the Assyrians, the Egyptians and the Greeks. If Christ followed the practice of the Jews in this regard, that practice was itself shaped by divine revelation and stood in contrast with that practice of the surrounding peoples, such as the Canaanites. Nor was the practice of Judaism by itself determinative for Christ. Where his mission required, he showed an astonishing independence from Jewish customs.

Notwithstanding their exclusion from priestly office, women played a prominent part in salvation history, both in the Old Testament and in the New. Figures such as Deborah and Esther were celebrated in the Hebrew Scriptures, as were the Blessed Virgin Mary, Elizabeth, Anna, Mary Magdalen, Martha, and other holy women in the Gospels. In the Acts and the letters of Paul, mention is made of many women who were prominent in the early Church. Some, such as the daughters of Philip the Evangelist, were prophetesses. But no women were members of the

Twelve, nor, it would seem, were they bishops or presbyters.[16] In excluding women from these offices but not from other ministries, the Church
was presumably guided by its understanding of the will of Christ in establishing the apostolic office.

Christians should exercise great care in invoking arguments from social
conditioning. Such arguments can easily be used to evacuate the contents
of revelation and call into question almost any moral teaching, including
the Ten Commandments. While conceding the existence of certain socially conditioned customs, Christians are convinced that the Jews of old
and the Christians under the guidance of Christ and the Holy Spirit were
able to discern God's will concerning the fundamental relations between
the sexes, including institutions such as monogamous heterosexual marriage. As we shall see, the divine order regarding marital relations is intimately bound up with the symbolism surrounding priesthood.

FAULTY BIOLOGY?

Yet another objection arises because of the state of biological science in
the early centuries. The Church's tradition regarding priesthood is held
to have been shaped by the opinion of Aristotle and other ancient authors
that women were genetically inferior. This opinion, now recognized as
false, was occasionally alluded to by theologians in their discussion of
women's position in the Church. Thomas Aquinas accepted Aristotle's
faulty biology, but when he comes to an explicit consideration of the
reasons why women cannot be ordained, he does not argue that women
are weaker in mind or in body. In fact, he acknowledges that some women
have greater spiritual and intellectual qualities than men. He remarks that
they can be rulers in civil society, that they can receive the charism of
prophecy, and they can serve as religious superiors and abbesses in the
Church. But he holds that a woman cannot be an apt subject for receiving
the sacrament of orders for symbolic reasons, namely the lack of natural
resemblance between them and what holy orders must signify.[17]

In medieval Catholicism, Mary was generally regarded as the greatest
of all the saints, but this eminence did not qualify her for ordination. In
the words of Pope Innocent III, "Although the Blessed Virgin Mary was
of higher dignity and excellence than all the Apostles, it was to them, not
her, that the Lord entrusted the keys of the Kingdom of heaven."[18]

The Iconic Argument

With respect to the theological reasoning, the Congregation for the Doctrine of the Faith and the popes have appealed to the "iconic" argument to suggest reasons why Christ chose to reserve the priesthood to men. The argument is that the ministerial priest has to represent Christ, especially in the Eucharist, which is the sacrament that preeminently "expresses the redemptive act of Christ, the Bridegroom, toward the Church."[19] The words of institution are no mere narrative about the past; they are performative speech-acts whereby Christ himself, through the priest, accomplishes the sacramental sacrifice. The shift to the present tense and the first person singular are therefore essential. Uttering the words, "This is my body . . . this is my blood," the priest puts on the very person of Christ. In order for him to be identified with Christ as Bridegroom, it is fitting for the priest to be of the male sex. This argument is much used in Eastern Orthodox theology and has been prominent in the West at least since the times of Hildegard and Bonaventure.

To this it is sometimes objected that representation, according to the biblical concept, is simply an authorization to speak in the name of another and that the messenger need not bear a natural resemblance to the person represented. The objection would hold if the priest were simply a messenger, passing on a verbal report, but in fact the priest is a symbolic figure, who serves as both a sign and an instrument in performing the very action of Christ as Bridegroom. This symbolic argument does not prove that Christ could not have called women to the priesthood, but it helps us to see that his decision in the matter was not arbitrary. In order for Christ himself to be the Bridegroom of the Church, as God had been Bridegroom of Israel, he had to be a man. For similar reasons it was highly suitable that those who were called to put on the person of Christ in sacramental actions such as presiding at the Lord's Supper should also be of the male sex.

Unjust Discrimination?

An additional line of attack on the rationale for the existing order is that it is an injustice toward women to exclude them as a class. Some compare this exclusion to racial discrimination, which has at times been practiced even in the Church. But the Church cannot be guilty of discrimination in this matter, because it is unconditionally bound to follow what it understands to be Christ's will in the matter. In providing for distinct roles for men and women in the Church, Christ did not violate the order of justice any more than God was unjust in giving women alone the power to bear children.

The ministerial priesthood is not a mark of personal superiority but a humble service to be used for the sake of the whole people of God. Although they cannot exercise this particular calling, women are not excluded from the full benefits of the redemption and from other forms of ministry. They can rise to the highest degree of sanctity, as is clear in the case of Mary. As religious superiors they can govern large communities. They can exercise the charisms of prophecy, knowledge, and wisdom; they can be teachers, spiritual directors, and the like. Two woman saints, Catherine of Siena and Teresa of Avila have been designated as doctors of the Church. In the Church as in civil society, the role of women has been rapidly advancing in recent years. John Paul II has branded the marginalization of women as an evil, due in part to cultural conditioning, and has repeatedly called for the elimination of all discrimination against women in the Church and in society.[20] He does not condone injustice toward women.

ECUMENICAL CONSIDERATIONS

Some object that the reservation of ordination to men in the Catholic Church is unecumenical, since it puts a barrier between Catholics and most other Christians, at least in the Western world. The recent popes have been acutely conscious of this obstacle, as attested by the pleas of Paul VI to Archbishop Coggan[21] and of John Paul II to Archbishop Runcie[22] not to authorize female ordinations in the Church of England. But ecumenism must surely include the churches of the East, which do not ordain women, as well as conservative Protestant groups, which adhere strictly to the biblical practice. The ecumenical argument therefore cuts both ways. If the Catholic Church were to ordain women, a new barrier would be created between it and the ancient churches of the East. The Orthodox would be convinced that Rome had capitulated to the liberal Protestant view of ministry. Besides, it must be said that authentic ecumenism does not permit the churches to depart from the order prescribed by Christ in their effort to promote external unity. As Cardinal Ratzinger points out, one of the fundamental issues between the Catholic Church and those sprung from the Reformation has always been "what priesthood is, whether a sacrament or ultimately a service to be regulated in its ordering by the community itself."[23]

IS THE TEACHING DEFINITIVE?

Regarding the argument from magisterial teaching, some maintain that in spite of the recent emphatic statements of John Paul II and Cardinal Ratzinger, the question remains an open one for Catholics. To this it must be answered that the highest doctrinal authorities in the Church, the pope and the prefect of the Congregation for the Doctrine of the Faith, have made it clear that in their judgment the question is irrevocably settled. As I have mentioned, the pope, invoking his authority as successor of Peter, declared that the Church has no authority whatsoever to confer priestly ordination on women and that this judgment is to be definitively held by all the faithful. The term "definitively held," as used the documents of Vatican II and in several official statements of the Congregation for the Doctrine of the Faith, is reserved to the kind of assent to be given to infallible teaching.[24] Any doubt about the equivalence of the two terms is removed by the response of the Congregation for the Doctrine of the Faith, which explained the pope's term "definitively held" as implying infallibility.

A final objection, somewhat technical in character, has to do with Cardinal Ratzinger's appeal to the ordinary and universal magisterium as the basis for infallibility. According to Vatican II, the college of bishops is not infallible in its day-to-day teaching except when the bishops unanimously hold that the faithful are obliged to give definitive assent to a particular doctrine. Has this unanimity been established in the present case? So far as appears, the bishops have not been polled by questionnaires such as those circulated by Popes Pius IX and Pius XII respectively preceding their definitions of the dogmas of the Immaculate Conception and the Assumption.

In answer, we may say, first of all, that the consensus of the present-day episcopate is not adduced as the sole ground for infallibility in the present case. The certainty and irreversibility derive from the biblical, traditional, and theological data in combination with the consensus of the contemporary magisterium. Regarding this last component, we must recognize that the Holy See has taken soundings and is better positioned to know the mind of the worldwide episcopate than are the theologians who have raised critical questions. Finally, it should be noted that the teaching of the pope is a decisive ingredient in the universal and ordinary magisterium. Speaking for the episcopal college as its head, the successor of Peter can solidify the consensus by his own authoritative interpretation of it, somewhat as Peter gave conceptual and verbal solidity to the faith of the Twelve when he spoke for them in his confession at Caesarea Philippi.

Whether the decision of *Ordinatio sacerdotalis* is to be accepted on a motive of faith can still be legitimately discussed. The pope and the cardinal have not called for an act of divine or theological faith but simply for a firm assent. But inasmuch as this assent is to be given to a teaching contained in the deposit of faith, it seems hardly distinguishable from an act of faith. The *de fide* status of the doctrine, however, has not been so clearly taught that one may accuse those who fail to accept it of heresy. As yet no canonical penalties have been applied against dissenters, but if they "pertinaciously reject" the teaching, they would no doubt make themselves liable to a "just penalty" by virtue of canon law (can. 1371, §1). If one compares the grounds for this teaching with the evidence given for Catholic doctrines such as the Immaculate Conception, the Assumption, and papal infallibility, the biblical and traditional basis for the nonordination of women would seem to be firmer. This doctrine is solidly grounded in Scripture. From the earliest centuries it has been in peaceful possession throughout Catholic Christianity; it has been constantly observed in the practice of the Church, confirmed by canon law and by the virtually unanimous agreement of the Fathers and Doctors who have dealt with the question.

Whether one accepts the recent pronouncements of the Holy See on this question depends in great measure on the extent to which one trusts the authoritative teaching office. It is my judgment that in matters such as this, where plausible arguments can be made for contrary views, it is imperative to have a doctrinal authority capable of settling the matter. According to the First and Second Vatican Councils, Christ equipped the Church with a Petrine office precisely in order to prevent the People of God or the episcopate from falling into discord, especially on matters affecting the validity of sacraments.

The decision of certain Anglican churches to admit women to the priesthood functioned as a catalyst, giving new urgency to the question within Roman Catholicism. Many Catholics and non-Catholics were beginning to ask whether the Catholic Church might not follow suit. If the magisterium had remained silent, some bishop might have ventured to ordain a woman, claiming that the ordination was valid by divine law, as occurred in the Episcopal Church some twenty-five years ago. The issue had to be clarified, and no one but the pope, speaking in communion with the college of bishops, was in a position to speak with full authority.

Some Catholics are of the opinion that the authorities should not have spoken until a consensus emerged through free discussion in the Church. The evidence does not, however, suggest that a longer period of unfettered debate would have brought about a consensus or furthered the interests of truth. Public opinion in the Church can easily be swayed by secular trends and ideologies that are alien to the authentic Catholic heritage. As in matters of sexual ethics, so in the question of gender and priesthood, the contemporary climate of opinion is predominantly hostile to the biblical and Catholic heritage. If the Church were to yield to the pressures of public opinion and political correctness, it would betray its mission and forfeit its capacity to speak prophetically to the world. Continuing to uphold the revelation given to it in Christ and the Scriptures, as handed down in sacred tradition, the Church must be prepared to risk unpopularity and to become, if necessary, a "sign of contradiction."

THE RISE OF FEMINISM

I do not mean to suggest that the Church should embark on a course of antifeminism. The recent popes, beginning with John XXIII, have reckoned the emancipation of women as one of the "signs of the times" through which God continues to speak to the Church today.[25] But the signs of the times are to be discerned, according to Vatican II, in the light of the gospel, as interpreted by the living Church.[26]

In the course of history, new and valid insights into social realities have frequently spawned radical movements that would subvert the values of Christian civilization. For example, the doctrine of human rights that surfaced in the eighteenth century gave rise to excesses such as the Jacobinism of the French Revolution. Such excesses, however, do not negate the truths that lie at the basis of the movements themselves. In the American Constitution and its Bill of Rights, we have a moderate assertion of human rights that can be reconciled with the Christian heritage.

The present-day movement for an alteration of Church teaching on women's ordination is not necessarily a sign of radical feminism, since some radical feminists reject the whole idea of ordained priesthood, while others maintain that a church of women can ordain its own priests without regard for official doctrine. Moderate feminism, avoiding such extremes, can be a healthy and promising movement in the Church. It can promote the dignity and status of women in fidelity to the Catholic tradition, with due regard to Scripture and due respect for the living magisterium, which speaks with the authority of Christ. In faith we may be confident that such a course will be the most fruitful in enabling both men and women to realize their highest potentialities.

Legitimate questions can still be raised. Because the biblical and historical evidence is complex and at some points obscure, doubts can arise about the meaning and force of certain texts from Scripture and the Church Fathers. The "iconic" or "symbolic" argument, in the forms hitherto proposed, may be in need of refinement in order to increase its persuasive force. As for the teaching of the magisterium, it remains to be clarified whether the doctrine is to be believed by an act of divine and Catholic faith. It would be desirable if further information were offered regarding the thinking of the bishops throughout the world and the binding character that they attribute to the doctrine. While the equal dignity of men and women is clearly established in official teaching, it remains to be shown how the true worth and talents of women can be adequately respected and utilized if women are not eligible for priestly and episcopal orders. The question whether women can be ordained to the diaconate requires further exploration. Further study may be needed to determine whether women can hold jurisdiction, and if so, under what conditions. In my opinion, a calm and open discussion of issues such as these is not only legitimate but, if conducted without acrimony, could clarify and advance the doctrine of the Church.

CONCLUSIONS

The conclusions of this lecture can be summarized in four brief statements:

In view of the force of the convergent argument and the authority of the papal office, Catholics can and should give the full assent that the pope has called for.

Because the official teaching runs against the prevailing climate of opinion and because plausible objections have been widely publicized, it is inevitable that a significant number of Catholics, in a country such as our own, will fail to assent.

Those who disagree with the approved teaching, while they are entitled to propose their difficulties, should refrain from treating the question as doctrinally undecided and should abstain from strident advocacy. Pressures for doctrinal change at this point would be futile and even detrimental, since they would provoke countermeasures on the part of Church authorities. The net result would be to divide the Church against herself.

The pastoral leadership of the Church, recognizing the complexity of the theological issues and the inevitability of dissenting views, should be patient with Catholics who feel unable to accept the approved position. While assuring the integrity of Catholic doctrine, the bishops should show understanding for dissenters who exhibit good will and avoid disruptive behavior. Such pastoral consideration, however, should not be taken as a license to contest or call into doubt the tradition of the Church, confirmed as it is by recent pronouncements of exceptional weight.

Notes

1. John Paul II, "*Ordinatio sacerdotalis*: apostolic letter on Ordination of Women," *Origins* 24 (June 9, 1994): 49–52; quotation from 51.

2. See Emmanuel Doronzo, *Tractatus dogmaticus de ordine* 3 (Milwaukee: Bruce, 1962), 406–16; Haye van der Meer, *Women Priests in the Catholic Church?* (Philadelphia: Temple University Press, 1973), 46–99; Manfred Hauke, *Women in the Priesthood?* (San Francisco: Ignatius, 1986), 404–68. For more recent discussion, see Sara Butler, *The Catholic Priesthood and Women* (Chicago: Hillenbrand Books, 2007).

3. The period since the Reformation has not been extensively studied, but some indications are given in Ludwig Ott, *Handbuch der Dogmengeschichte* vol. 4, part 5, *Das Weihesakrament* (Freiburg: Herder, 1969), 165–66. See also Hauke, *Women in the Priesthood?* 468.

4. Congregation for the Doctrine of the Faith, "*Donum veritatis*: Instruction on the Ecclesial Vocation of the Theologian," §30, *Origins* 20 (July 5, 1990): 117–26, at 123.

5. Council of Trent, Sess. XXII, decree on the sacrifice of the Mass, can. 2 (DS 1752); Sess. XXIII, doctrine on the sacrament of order, chap. 1 (DS 1764).

6. John Paul II, apostolic letter *"Dominicae cenae*: Mystery and Worship of the Holy Eucharist," 2, *Origins* 9 (March 27, 1980): 653–66, at 655. Cf. *CCC*, 611.

7. Congregation for the Doctrine of the Faith, *"Inter insigniores*: On the Admission of Women to the Ministerial Priesthood," §4, *Origins* 6 (February 3, 1977): 519–24, at 521. Cardinal Ratzinger emphatically makes the same point in his commentary on *Ordinatio sacerdotalis*, "Grenzen kirchlicher Vollmacht," *Internationale katholische Zeitshrift: Communio* 23 (1994): 337–45, esp. 340–41.

8. Pontifical Biblical Commission, "Can Women Be Priests?" *Origins* 6 (July 1, 1976): 92–96; quotations from 95 and 96. According to an editor's note, the members at the Plenary Session of the Commission voted 12–5 that biblical grounds alone are not enough to preclude the possibility of ordaining women.

9. In recent exegetical literature, some scholars argue that a woman named Junia is listed among the apostles in Romans 16:7. According to the RSV, the text reads: "Greet Andronicus and Junias, my kinsmen and my fellow prisoners; they are men of note among the apostles, and they were in Christ before me." Although the best Greek manuscripts give the name Junias in masculine form, it is possible to follow a minority reading, in which case Andronicus and Junia would probably be a husband-and-wife team. It is debatable whether they are being named as apostles or simply designated as enjoying a high reputation among the apostles. If they are themselves named as "apostles," the term "apostle" is here being used not in the sense of those who had seen the Lord and been officially commissioned as witnesses of the gospel, but in a broad sense of the term as itinerant missionaries. See Francis Martin, *The Feminist Question* (Grand Rapids, Mich.: Eerdmans, 1994), 100, and Manfred Hauke, "*Ordinatio Sacerdotalis*: das päpstliche Schreiben zum Frauenpriestertum im Spiegel der Diskussion," *Forum katholische Theologie* 11 (1995): 270–98, at 287–88.

10. The letter of Pope Gelasius does not deal directly with the ordination of women, but in the reasons it gives for rejecting the service of women at the altar it implicitly teaches that women cannot be priests. See van der Meer, *Women Priests*, 93; Hauke, *Women in the Priesthood?* 423.

11. See Hauke, *Women in the Priesthood?* 445–68; Joseph A. Wahl, "The Exclusion of Woman from Holy Orders," S.T.D. dissertation abstract (Washington, D.C.: Catholic University of America, 1959), 45–58.

12. See Augustine Thompson, "Hildegard of Bingen on Gender and the Priesthood," *Church History* 63 (1994): 349–64.

13. Edith Stein, *Collected Works*, vol. 2, *Essays on Women* (Washington, D.C.: ICS Studies, 1987), esp. 82–85. The historical context is well explained in Hilda C. Graef, *The Scholar and the Cross: The Life and Work of Edith Stein* (Westminster, Md.: Newman, 1955).

14. Paul VI, "Women—Disciples and Co-Workers," *Origins* 4 (May 1, 1975): 718–19.

15. Paul VI, Letter to Archbishop Donald Coggan, November 30, 1975; *Origins* 6 (August 12, 1976): 131.

16. Nor, would it seem, are women to be numbered among the *proistamenoi* (1 Th 5:12) and *hegoumenoi* (Heb 13:7, 24). See Martin, *Feminist Question*, 111.

17. Thomas Aquinas, *Summa theol.*, *Suppl.* 39.1.

18. Innocent III, Letter of December 11, 1210 to the Bishops of Palencia and Burgos, included in *Corpus Iuris, Decret.* Lib. 5, Tit. 38, *De Paenit.*, ch. 10; ed. A. Friedberg (Leipzig: Tauchnitz, 1881), vol. 2, col. 886–87; quoted in *Inter Insigniores*, note 11.

19. John Paul II, apostolic letter "*Mulieris dignitatem*: On the Dignity and Vocation of Women," 26; *Origins* 18 (October 6, 1988): 261–83, at 279.

20. See especially his "Letter to Women" written in preparation for the United Nations World Conference on Women in September 1995; text in *Origins* 25 (July 27, 1995): 137–43. A year and a half after this lecture was given, he made Thérèse of Lisieux third female Doctor of the Church.

21. See note 14.

22. Text in *Origins* 19 (June 8, 1989): 64.

23. Ratzinger, "Grenzen kirchlicher Vollmacht," 344–45.

24. *Lumen gentium* 25; Profession of Faith, *Origins* 18 (March 16, 1989): 661, 663, at 663); CDF Instruction, *Donum veritatis*, §16, p. 121.

25. John XXIII, encyclical *Pacem in terris*, 41; text in *The Gospel of Peace and Justice*, ed. Joseph Gremillion (Maryknoll, N.Y.: Orbis, 1976), 209–10.

26. Vatican II, *Gaudium et spes*, 4.

16

The Travails of Dialogue

November 19, 1996

THE DIALOGIC TURN

Before the Second Vatican Council, the Catholic Church was polemically arrayed against other groups, including the non-Christian religions, non-Catholic Christianity, and the modern world. John XXIII deserves the credit for having seen that this posture was interfering with the mission of the Church. Following his lead, Vatican II renounced anathematization and espoused dialogue. The new stance of the Church was expressed during the council by Paul VI's first encyclical, *Ecclesiam suam* (1964).[1] God, he maintained, initiated a dialogue of salvation by turning to the world in love, making himself accessible through revelation, and appealing for the free response of faith. Imitating God's action in Christ, the Church must address the world in the spirit of dialogue. It should clearly proclaim the message of salvation as revealed truth, but should do so humbly, in a spirit of trust and respect for the sensitivities of the hearers. Such a Church would listen before speaking and would be alert to discover the elements of truth in the opinions of others.

Paul VI in this encyclical spoke of three concentric circles of dialogue with those outside the Church—the world, the monotheistic religions, and the other Christian communities. Then, in a closing section, he spoke of the possibilities of dialogue within the Catholic Church itself—a dialogue predicated on the supposition that the members of the Church are bound by the word of God and are obedient to the authorities instituted by Christ. By setting evangelization within the context of dialogue, while continuing to insist on authority and submission, Paul VI made an important though cautious advance.

Pope John XXIII had founded the Secretariat for Promoting Christian Unity in 1960. Paul VI, implementing his own vision of the three concentric circles that surrounded the Church of Rome, set up additional secretariats for Dialogue with Non-Christian Religions and with Non-Believers. The three secretariats corresponded to the documents of Vatican II on Ecumenism, on Non-Christian Religions, and on the Church in the Modern World.

John Paul II was an enthusiastic participant at the Second Vatican Council, and in his book *Sources of Renewal* he sought to explain for the people of his diocese of Krakow the importance of dialogue within the Church and with the three great sectors of humanity that lie beyond the visible limits of the Church.[2] The concept of dialogue appeals to this pope because of his personalist orientation in philosophy. He pays tribute to philosophers of dialogue, such as Martin Buber and Emmanuel Lévinas, for having enriched human self-understanding.[3] In his philosophical work *The Acting Person,* the future pope maintained that the principle of dialogue is very aptly suited to the structure of human communities insofar as it strengthens human solidarity and promotes constructive communal life.[4]

As pope, John Paul II has continued to emphasize this theme in his great apostolic exhortations. In *Reconciliatio et paenitentia* (1984) he speaks of the importance of "permanent and renewed dialogue within the Catholic Church herself" and of the need to listen to others with respect, to refrain from all hasty judgments, and to subordinate personal opinions to matters of faith.[5] In his encyclical on ecumenism, *Ut unum sint* (1995), he speaks at length of dialogue as a means for examining the disagreements that hinder full communion among Christians. Love for the truth, he says, is essential to dialogue, but it must be accompanied by charity toward one's partners in dialogue and humility with regard to the truth that comes to light, attitudes especially needed when the dialogue seems to call for a revision of one's own previous assertions and attitudes.[6] In his encyclical on the Church's missionary activity, *Redemptoris missio* (1990), the pope calls for dialogue with the followers of other religions, but he emphasizes that this does not take the place of missionary proclamation, which always remains necessary. Through dialogue, he says, the Church seeks to discover seeds of the Word and rays of truth in other religions. Dialogue also leads the Church to examine her own identity more deeply and to improve the quality of her own witness.[7]

The strong approval given to dialogue by the recent popes puts the Catholic Church unequivocally on record as favoring this style of encounter. But dialogue, as the Church understands it, makes heavy demands that are not always respected. The term is often used carelessly, deceptively, and abusively to mean something else than what the Church understands by dialogue.

POSTCONCILIAR EXPECTATIONS

In the middle 1960s, there was a great surge of enthusiasm for dialogue. Books were published with titles such as *The Miracle of Dialogue* (Reuel Howe) and *From Anathema to Dialogue* (Roger Garaudy). By treating others as partners rather than adversaries, dialogue, it was thought, could overcome inveterate divisions and generate shared insights surpassing the capacities of any single contributor.[8]

In the decade following Vatican II, dialogue became almost a substitute for authority. Ecclesiastical superiors were expected to enter into dialogue with their subjects, so that decisions could be reached by consensus. Religious education was pursued not with a view to indoctrination but for the sake of eliciting insights through dialogue. Here at Fordham, I recall, an experimental college known as Ben-Salem was inaugurated, in which all decisions regarding curriculum and lifestyle were to be reached by consensus rather than by authority. But the project was unrealistic. Since unanimity could almost never be achieved, the decision-making process was paralyzed, and the college soon collapsed.

In the area of Church doctrine, dialogue became the new watchword. An instance was the debate about contraception. Without waiting for the papal commission to complete its study, theologians proposed their own solutions. By the time that the papal decision was promulgated, in the summer of 1968, multitudes of Catholics had already made up their minds. Parties had been formed which resisted the implementation of the Roman decision and sought to neutralize or even reverse it. The widespread dissent resulting from the discussion made it evident that dialogue, pursued without due regard for the solidity of Catholic tradition and the authority of the pastoral magisterium, could have negative effects.

Recent Proposals and Reactions

In recent months, two much-discussed proposals coming from members of the American hierarchy have again raised new questions about dialogue within the Church. On June 29, 1996, the retired archbishop of San Francisco, John R. Quinn, speaking at Campion Hall, Oxford University, pointedly asked whether the Holy See had engaged in appropriate dialogue before making decisions regarding a great variety of matters, including contraception, general absolution, the appointment of bishops, the approval of the Catechism of the Catholic Church, clerical celibacy, and the ordination of women. Although the archbishop did not say that he disagreed with any of the decisions he mentioned, he expressed his regret that the decisions had been made with insufficient prior discussion. He called for extensive inner reforms within the Catholic Church to give more autonomy to local churches and thereby, as he thought, facilitate ecumenical relations with other Christian groups.[9]

Hard on the heels of the Quinn address came the publication on August 12 of a statement drawn up by the National Pastoral Life Center in New York and released by the late Cardinal Joseph Bernardin of Chicago. Bearing the ominous title "Called to be Catholic: Church in a Time of Peril," this statement lamented the atmosphere of suspicion and acrimony in the Church today and called for a renewed spirit of civility, dialogue, and broad consultation.[10] Candid discussion, it stated, is inhibited by the imposition of a narrow party line. More room needs to be given for legitimate discussion and diversity. A new "common ground" needs to be forged among all who are willing to affirm "basic truths" and pursue the remaining disagreements in a spirit of dialogue. Such dialogue, the authors maintained, could be a welcome alternative to mutual accusations of infidelity and a present remedy for polarization.

The statements coming from Quinn and Bernardin have been catalysts for arousing a fascinating dialogue about dialogue among members of the American hierarchy. Cardinal John O'Connor of New York issued a lengthy response to Quinn. He pointed out that in fact curia officials, as well as the pope, have carried out long and wide consultations with bishops before reaching decisions on many of the issues mentioned by Archbishop Quinn. He asked how issues such as clerical celibacy, the ordination of women, and general absolution could have been more extensively discussed than they were without arousing false expectations.[11]

Cardinal Bernardin's statement was quickly answered by four cardinals, who published independent critiques. Cardinal Bernard Law of Boston focused on the concept of dialogue. His words are worth quoting:

> The fundamental flaw in this document is its appeal for "dialogue" as a path to "common ground."
>
> The Church already has "common ground." It is found in sacred Scripture and tradition, and it is mediated to us through the authoritative and binding teaching of the magisterium. The disconnect that is so often found today between that Catholic common ground and [the] faith and practice of some Catholics is alarming.
>
> Dialogue as applied to this pastoral crisis must be clearly understood, however. Dissent from revealed truth or the authoritative teaching of the Church cannot be "dialogued" away. Truth and dissent from truth are not equal partners in ecclesial dialogue. Dialogue as a pastoral effort to assist in a fuller appropriation of the truth is laudable. Dialogue as a way to mediate between the truth and dissent is mutual deception.[12]

Cardinal Adam Maida of Detroit made a similar point. "This statement," he said, "may create some confusion since it seems to suggest that Catholic teachings are open to dialogue and debate. . . . Dialogue is a helpful tool and step in a larger process, but of itself it cannot solve religious differences. Genuine dialogue among Catholics can happen only when we begin with the Scripture and Church teachings and keep our minds and hearts open to conversion. We build up the body of Christ most effectively as we pray together, asking to have the ability to hear the Holy Spirit speaking in our leaders."[13]

Cardinal James Hickey of Washington spoke in much the same terms. While agreeing that rifts in the Church needed to be healed, he maintained that the proposal to do so through dialogue was ill-advised. The statement of the National Pastoral Life Center, he said, obscures the true common ground which is found in Scripture and tradition and comprehensively expressed in the Catechism of the Catholic Church.[14]

Finally, Cardinal Anthony Bevilacqua of Philadelphia stated his opinion that a polite debate about divergent views regarding Catholic teaching would not adequately address the problem or heal the differences. The imperative need is for renewed confidence in Jesus Christ, who never ceases to strengthen us through the teaching and sacraments of the Catholic Church.[15]

The reaction to the Bernardin statement was not uniformly negative. Cardinal Roger Mahony of Los Angeles allowed his name to be associated with the statement, and several bishops commented favorably. On October 11, Bishop Anthony Pilla, without making any mention of the Quinn or Bernardin proposals, urged greater use of dialogue as a path to Catholic unity. "Lack of willingness and ability to enter into dialogue," he declared, "is a greater long-term threat to unity than are disagreements and dissenting voices."[16]

Cardinal Bernardin himself took cognizance of the criticisms in a statement released by him on August 29. With regard to dialogue, he conceded that the very idea has sometimes been cheapened by those who turn it into a tool of single-minded advocacy. He also granted that dialogue is not in every case or at every moment the universal solution to all conflicts. While acknowledging the limits of dialogue, he insisted that at the present time there is critical need for greater dialogue within the Church as a way of moving beyond polarization.[17] In an address of October 24, Cardinal Bernardin declared once again that dialogue does not imply compromise. His "common ground," he observed, was not intended to propose some lowest common denominator but to aim at the fullest possible internalization of the truth.[18] Did he mean to suggest that renewed dialogue would be likely to bring about a deeper appropriation of Church teaching? If so, it may be for others to show that this prospect is realistic.

The reactions in the Catholic Press were mixed. On the whole both the Quinn and the Bernardin statements were hailed by the liberal press and adversely criticized by the more conservative organs, though some liberal commentators found the membership of the Bernardin committee too conservative for their taste. In a careful analysis of the Quinn and Bernardin statements and of the hierarchical responses to them, Bishop Kenneth E. Untener pointed out that the responses to the papers ascribed positions to the authors that the authors had not actually taken. In particular, he objected that "the negative interpretation of dialogue read into the Cardinal Bernardin paper by those who criticized it does not reflect a high standard of discussion."[19]

RIVAL CONCEPTS OF DIALOGUE

My own reflection on the situation is that the difficulty with the statements, especially that of Cardinal Bernardin, is not so much with they actually said as with what they seemed to imply, and would be understood as implying in the current atmosphere. Their statements on dialogue were inevitably interpreted in light of prevailing conceptions of dialogue in use among contemporary theoreticians, rather than in the context of the classical concepts used by Plato and Augustine and the personalist concepts proposed by the popes.[20] I should like to illustrate this with regard to dialogue theory in comparative religion and democratic political theory.

Dialogue among the religions, according to many prominent experts, could be far more successful if all would agree that the divisive doctrines were classified as fallible human efforts to probe the depths of the divine. Paul Knitter, for instance, holds that it is disastrous for dialogue to insist on the finality and superiority of God's revelation in Christ.[21] Another expert, John Hick, in an article on "The Non-Absoluteness of Christianity," argues that the modern dialogic setting precludes any a priori assumption that Christianity is superior to other faiths.[22]

In the context of this relativistic pluralism, the word "dialogue" takes on a new meaning. The supposition is that in dialogue you are not trying to urge your own position, but to reach an accommodation in which both parties can live in peace. Cardinal Ratzinger in a recent address analyzes the concept of dialogue that is operative in the religious pluralism of thinkers such as Hick and Knitter. In their theology, he remarks,

> the notion of dialogue—which has maintained a position of significant importance in the Platonic and Christian tradition—changes its meaning and becomes both the quintessence of the relativist creed and the antithesis of conversion and the mission. In the relativist meaning, to dialogue means to put one's own position, i.e., one's faith, on the same level as the convictions of others without recognizing in principle more truth in it than that which is attributed to the opinion of the others. Only if I suppose in principle that the other can be as right, or more right than I, can an authentic dialogue take place.
>
> According to this concept, dialogue must be an exchange between positions which have fundamentally the same rank and therefore are mutually relative. Only in this way will maximum cooperation and integration between the different religions be achieved. The relativist dissolution of Christology, and even more of ecclesiology, thus becomes a central commandment of religion. To return to Hick's thinking, faith in the divinity of one concrete person, as he tells us, leads to fanaticism and particularism, to the disassociation between faith and love, and it is precisely this which must be overcome.[23]

A second series of problems arises within the context of recent American political theory. In the new liberalism a sharp line is drawn between the public and the private. All belief systems, in this framework, are relegated to the private sphere, so that no public authority may adjudicate questions of truth. Political philosophers such as John Rawls, Richard Rorty, and Bruce Ackerman, following in the traces of Immanuel Kant, have made a strict separation between the good and the right. People have rights, it is said, but the rights are purely procedural. In this context, dialogue is recommended, but those who enter the dialogue must abandon any effort to urge their own conception of the good or the true. In civil dialogue, the question of truth does not arise, since all substantive moral and religious commitments have been removed from the public agenda.

Michael J. Sandel has summarized the principles of this new political philosophy in his recent book, *Democracy's Discontent*.[24] He characterizes the dominant public philosophy as that of the "procedural republic." In this framework we are required to bracket our moral and religious obligations when we enter the public realm. Questions of justice and rights must be decided without affirming one conception of the good over others. One cannot publicly discuss whether an unborn child has human, personal life, because this is viewed as a metaphysical or religious question. The woman's "right to choose" is allowed to prevail, as it were, by default. The purpose of the legislature and the judiciary is to make it possible for people to live together in community, to establish a modus vivendi. Rules of society are compromise formulas by which the members agree to live while continuing to differ in their private opinions.

Authors such as Sandel maintain, convincingly I believe, that the procedural republic does not offer adequate foundations for a healthy self-governing society. It creates a moral void. Political association sinks to the level of a mere coalition in which the members are not inspired by any shared vision of the good. But my intention in this paper is not to settle the political question. I am concerned with the fallout from this political philosophy in the religious realm. Christians are being drawn to regard questions of truth and morality as essentially private ones, to be settled by each individual in the intimacy of one's own conscience.

As Andrew Greeley and others have shown, large numbers of Americans today are "communal Catholics" who adhere to the Church as the home in which they were nurtured and the place to which they are bound by ties of family and friendship, but who do not accept the teaching authority of popes and councils, especially in matters of morality.[25] They turn to the Church for its ritual and sacramental ministry, but they do not expect it to instruct them on questions of truth and moral goodness. Communal Catholics follow their own judgment in many matters of dogma and moral conduct. Presuming that no one can be bound in conscience to accept official teaching, they regard dissent as a right. In a privatized Church, as in the "procedural republic," no scope is allowed for public adjudication of questions of truth and morality. These attitudes, however, undermine the very essence of Catholic Christianity, which authoritatively proclaims a religion founded on divine revelation and intended for all humankind. The Church has a public faith that is not subject to debate.

Because of the inroads of privatization, the call for greater dialogue among Catholics on points such as contraception or ordination of women is seen as a readiness to settle for something less than the full doctrine of the Church and to reach a pragmatic modus vivendi among Catholics who continue to disagree about substantive issues. This would lend support for the view, already widespread, that Catholics are free to hold opinions contrary to the official teaching of the Church, at least if they adhere to "basic truths." Even if Archbishop Quinn and Cardinal Bernardin did not wish to legitimize dissent, their statements could easily be interpreted as favoring the view that the teaching of the Church is not binding in conscience. The support given to these statements by individuals and groups who are known to diverge from current teaching confirmed this suspicion. The impression was given that some "common ground" other than the official doctrine of the Church was being proposed in an effort to reach out to alienated Catholics.

AMBIGUITIES OF DIALOGUE

It is time to draw some conclusions. First of all, it should be said that dialogue, properly understood, is an excellent thing, whether carried on within the Church or between the different Christian churches or different religions. But it needs to be kept in mind that authentic dialogue is premised on truth and is directed to an increment of truth. Where the conditions are not met, true dialogue cannot occur. For example, if one of the parties is not interested in a serious search for consensus in the truth but only in gaining public recognition or in extorting concessions, dialogue would be a deception. Paul VI in *Ecclesiam suam* remarked that atheistic Communism was perverting discussion by using it not to seek and express truth but to serve predetermined utilitarian ends; and this strategy, he said, "puts an end to dialogue" (§107). Cardinal Ratzinger, recalling the student uprisings of 1968, declared that he then learned the lesson that there are times when dialogue would become a lie and would amount to collaboration with terrorism.[26] To turn to a more classical example, Jesus evidently judged that on certain occasions excoriation rather than dialogue should be directed at the Pharisees. And when brought to trial before Herod, Jesus responded not with dialogue but with silence. In our day, groups that call for dialogue in order to confront the Church with inexorable demands must be met with a firm refusal.

In a number of the ecumenical dialogues carried on in recent years, the question of truth has in fact been focal. Important and unexpected convergences have in some cases been achieved. But, like anything human, ecumenical dialogue has its limits. If the aim is to bring the churches into closer harmony, the members of the dialogue teams will have to accept a certain discipline. They must adhere to the traditions of their respective communities and have a realistic sense of how far these communities can go without betraying their authentic heritage. If the dialogue produces ambiguous statements or agreements that will be repudiated by the communities, it could do positive harm to the ecumenical cause.

Dialogue is not a panacea. It does not automatically lead to full consensus. In all honesty, dialogue teams will sometimes have to declare that they cannot overcome certain hard-core differences on which the partner churches cannot both be right. Theologians do not have the authority to change the doctrines of their churches, and it is unfair to expect them to arrive at full agreement unless the churches are prepared to change their respective doctrines.

Interreligious dialogue can also be very productive if conducted without abandonment of principles and without false irenicism, according to the principles set forth in the encyclical *Redemptoris missio*. But the dialogue among the great religions has been recently plagued by a relativistic pluralism. If methodological rules are laid down that require the parties to renounce or conceal the points on which they disagree, dialogue can become inhibitive and impoverishing. The fault lies not with dialogue itself but with theorists who seek to evade the rigorous demands of dialogue.

Referring to interreligious relations, the Holy See published in 1991 an important document on "Dialogue and Proclamation." Dialogue, it declared, "does not mean that the partners should lay aside their respective religious convictions. The opposite is true. The sincerity of interreligious dialogue requires that each enter into it with the integrity of his or her own faith. . . . Interreligious dialogue and proclamation, though not on the same level, are both authentic elements of the Church's evangelizing mission. . . . They are intimately related. . . . True interreligious dialogue on the part of the Christian supposes the desire to make Jesus Christ better known, recognized and loved."[27]

As for dialogue within the Church, it is always in order if the purpose is to understand its teaching better, to present it more persuasively, and to implement it in a pastorally effective way. But the conditions laid down by Paul VI must be kept in mind. He made it clear that obedience to ecclesiastical authority, rather than independence and criticism, must prevail (*Ecclesiam suam* §§118–19). The conditions for intraecclesial dialogue are not easy to realize today, in a society such as our own. Open discussion may be counterproductive if its purpose is to prolong debate on issues that are ripe for decision or to legitimize positions that the teaching authorities have decisively rejected. Far from achieving consensus, such dialogue would serve to build up mutually opposed constituencies and thus further polarize the Church. Under present conditions, any proposal for dialogue within the Church must be very carefully formulated if it is not to expand the zone of disagreement within the Church. An imprudent yielding to pleas for tolerance and diversity could easily weaken the Church as a community of faith and witness.

Polarization is not normally the result of clear and confident teaching of the Church's heritage of faith. It is more likely to arise when the true teaching is obscured by the indulgence of contrary opinions. The hierarchical magisterium must be vigilant to prevent and correct error in matters of doctrine. Pastoral authorities who are fully conscious of their responsibilities will not use dialogue as a subterfuge for shirking the onerous tasks of their office. They will rise to the challenge of Paul's admonition to Timothy to "convince, rebuke, and exhort," and to be "unfailing in patience and in teaching" (2 Tim 3:2). Authentic dialogue, even at its best, has limits. It cannot appropriately replace every other form of communication. Evangelization, as Paul VI and John Paul II have insisted, is a permanent priority of the Church. Dialogue, to be sure, has a legitimate place in all missionary witness, creedal confession, dogmatic teaching, and catechetical instruction, but these proclamatory modes of discourse are not reducible to dialogue pure and simple. A paramount internal need for the Church today is the faithful transmission of the Catholic patrimony as embodied in works such as the Catechism of the Catholic Church. Christian proclamation, even when conducted within a context of dialogue, presupposes that there is a divine revelation, embodying the truth that leads to eternal life. All revelation, in the Christian understanding, comes from the divine Word, which is one and eternal. When Christians engage in dialogue, they do so with the hope of making that one Word better known. In a sense, therefore, Christianity is mono-logic. Authentic dialogue would be futile unless it helped us to hear the one divine Word. "This is my beloved Son; listen to him" (Mk 9:8).

Notes

1. Paul VI, encyclical *Ecclesiam suam: The Paths of the Church* (New York: Paulist, 1963). Part III bears the title "Dialogue."

2. Karol Wojtyla/John Paul II, *Sources of Renewal: The Implementation of Vatican II* (San Francisco: Harper & Row, 1979), esp. 26–34.

3. John Paul II, *Crossing the Threshold of Hope* (New York: Knopf, 1994), 35–36.

4. John Paul II, *The Acting Person* (Boston: D. Reidel, 1979), 287.

5. John Paul II, apostolic exhortation "Reconciliation and Penance," 25; *Origins* 14 (December 20, 1984): 432–52, at 446.

6. John Paul II, encyclical *Ut unum sint* 36 (Vatican City: Liberia editrice Vaticana, 1995), 42.

7. John Paul II, encyclical *Redemptoris missio* 55–56 (Boston: St. Paul Books and Media, 1991), 72–74.

8. See Reuel L. Howe, *The Miracle of Dialogue* (New York: Seabury, 1963), 79.

9. John R. Quinn, "Considering the Papacy," *Origins* 26 (July 18, 1996): 119–27.

10. "Called to be Catholic: Church in a Time of Peril," *Origins* 26 (August 29, 1996): 165–70.

11. John Cardinal O'Connor, "Reflections on Church Governance," *Origins* 26 (August 29, 1996): 171–75. Other comments by Bishop James McHugh and Archbishop Rembert Weakland follow in the same issue of *Origins*.

12. Bernard Cardinal Law, "Response to 'Called to be Catholic,'" *Origins* 26 (August 29, 1996): 170–71, at 170.

13. Adam Cardinal Maida, "Reaction to the Catholic Common Ground Project," *Origins* 26 (September 12, 1996): 200–201, at 200.

14. James Cardinal Hickey, "Reaction to the Catholic Common Ground Project," *Origins* 26 (September 12, 1996): 202–3.

15. Anthony Cardinal Bevilacqua, "Reaction to the Catholic Common Ground Project," *Origins* 26 (September 12, 1996): 197, 199, at 199.

16. Bishop Anthony M. Pilla, "Virtues for the Journey to the Year 2000," *Origins* 26 (October 24, 1996): 295–98.

17. Joseph Cardinal Bernardin, "Questions and Answers: The Common Ground Project," *Origins* 26 (September 12, 1996): 204–6, at 205.

18. Joseph Cardinal Bernardin address, "Faithful and Hopeful," October 24, 1996, *Origins* 26 (November 14, 1996): 353–58.

19. Kenneth E. Untener, "How Bishops Talk," *America* 175 (October 19, 1996): 9–15, at 12.

20. On the classical concept of dialogue see Joseph Ratzinger, *The Nature and Mission of Theology* (San Francisco: Ignatius, 1993), 34.

21. Paul Knitter, "World Religions and the Finality of Christ: A Critique of Hans Küng's *On Being a Christian*," *Horizons* 5 (1978): 151–64.

22. John Hick, "The Non-Absoluteness of Christianity," in *The Myth of Christian Uniqueness*, ed. John Hick and Paul F. Knitter (Maryknoll, N.Y.: Orbis, 1987), 16–36, at 23.

23. Joseph Ratzinger, "Relativism: The Central Problem for Faith Today," *Origins* 26 (October 31, 1996): 309–17, at 312.

24. Michael J. Sandel, *Democracy's Discontent* (Cambridge, Mass.: Belknap, 1996).

25. Father Greeley says of the communal Catholic that, while being at ease with Catholicism, "he does not care much what the church as an institution says or does not say, does or does not do." Andrew M. Greeley, *The Communal Catholic: A Personal Manifesto* (New York: Seabury/Crossroad, 1976), 9.

26. See E. J. Dionne Jr., "The Pope's Guardian of Orthodoxy," *New York Times Magazine*, 24 November 1985, 58.

27. Pontifical Council for Interreligious Dialogue, "Dialogue and Proclamation," §§48 and 77, *Origins* 21 (July 4, 1991): 121–35, at 129–30 and 133.

17

The Ignatian Tradition and Contemporary Theology

April 10, 1997

I n this academic year we commemorate the 150th anniversary of the arrival of the Jesuits at Fordham in 1846. Father Joseph A. O'Hare and Dr. John W. Healey have suggested the topic and the title of this lecture, and I have gratefully accepted their suggestions. I shall not be speaking about the Jesuits of Fordham, but at the end of the talk you will probably have your own opinions as to whether they are true to what I am calling the Ignatian tradition.

SAINT IGNATIUS AS SPIRITUAL MASTER

Where would contemporary theology be except for the works of Pierre Teilhard de Chardin, Henri de Lubac, Karl Rahner, Bernard Lonergan, Hans Urs von Balthasar, and John Courtney Murray? These great giants of the mind unquestionably belong to the advance guard of the Second Vatican Council and, except for Teilhard, who had died in 1955, were among the leading interpreters of the council's work. And if one asks what these men had in common, the obvious reply is that all of them were deeply formed by the *Spiritual Exercises* and by the teaching of Saint Ignatius of Loyola, whom they took as their spiritual guide. Teilhard de Chardin, Rahner, de Lubac, and Balthasar, upon whose achievements I shall focus my remarks, give clear manifestations of this intellectual genealogy.

De Lubac, in a short book on Teilhard de Chardin, notes that his *The Divine Milieu* is permeated by Ignatian motifs such as passionate love of Jesus Christ, ardent longing for Christ's Kingdom, and boldness in conceiving grand designs to serve him.[1] Balthasar, in a volume on de Lubac, remarks on the centrality of the Church in that author's theological vision and comments:

> One could show that this center—a pure passageway for pure transmission of the gift—is also the center of the Ignatian spirit. Henri de Lubac lives so intimately in and from this spirit that he diffidently refrains from quoting the holy founder of the Society of Jesus among the thousands who throng his footnotes.[2]

Even this statement is not strong enough. As we shall see, de Lubac in *The Splendor of the Church* refers to various passages in the *Spiritual Exercises* and to the Ignatian "Letter on Obedience."

Speaking of himself, Balthasar likewise gladly confesses his indebtedness as a theologian to Saint Ignatius, whose *Spiritual Exercises* he translated into German. Referring to his experiences as a student at Lyons, he says, "Almost all of us were formed by the *Spiritual Exercises*, the great school of christocentric contemplation, of attention to the pure and personal word contained in the gospel, of lifelong commitment to the attempt at following."[3] The *Spiritual Exercises*, he writes, provide "the charismatic kernel of a theology of revelation that could offer the unsurpassed answer to all the problems of our age that terrify Christians."[4]

As for Karl Rahner, he declared in an interview at the age of seventy-five, "In comparison with other philosophy and theology that influenced me, Ignatian spirituality was indeed more significant and important. . . . I think that the spirituality of Ignatius himself, which one learned through the practice of prayer and religious formation, was more significant for me than all the learned philosophy and theology inside and outside the order."[5]

These expressions of appreciation on the part of twentieth-century theologians are in some ways surprising since Ignatius, though he was a great spiritual leader, scarcely comes up for mention in histories of Catholic theology. He aspired to no theological originality. For the training of Jesuit students he recommended the doctrine of Thomas Aquinas.[6] Instead of calling for innovation, he directed that Jesuit professors should adhere to the safest and most approved opinions, avoiding books and authors that were suspect.[7]

What inspires the creativity of modern systematic theologians is not primarily the theological views of Ignatius but rather his mysticism. Modern authors speak frequently of this as an incarnational mysticism, a sacramental mysticism, and an ecclesial mysticism. They mention Ignatius's mysticism of service, of reverential love, of the Cross, and of discernment.[8] Whereas other mystics may find communion with God by withdrawing from activity in the world, the contrary is true of Ignatius. He seeks union with God primarily by dwelling within the mysteries through which God makes himself present in our world—especially the mysteries of the incarnate life of the eternal Son. It is a mysticism of action, whereby we unite ourselves with the mission of Christ in the Church.

I should like to comment on four themes from the *Spiritual Exercises* that have particularly inspired twentieth-century theologians: seeking God in all things, the immediacy of the soul to God, obedience to the hierarchical Church and, lastly, the call to glorify Christ the King by free and loving self-surrender into his hands. I shall illustrate each of these themes—the cosmic, the theistic, the ecclesial, and the Christological—from the writings of one of the theologians already mentioned.

Finding God in All Things

In the *Constitutions of the Society of Jesus*, Saint Ignatius prescribes that Jesuits "should often be exhorted to seek God our Lord in all things."[9] In the "First Principle and Foundation," at the opening of the *Exercises*, he teaches that sickness and health, poverty and riches, dishonor and honor, a short life and a long life, can all serve as means to that union with God that makes for our eternal salvation (*Sp. Ex.* 23). In the "Examination of Conscience" he writes that those advanced in the spiritual life constantly contemplate God our Lord "in every creature by His essence, power, and presence" (*Sp. Ex.* 39). In the "Contemplation to Obtain Divine Love," at the end of the *Exercises*, Ignatius reflects on how God dwells in all creatures and especially in human beings, who are created "in the likeness and image of the Divine Majesty" (*Sp. Ex.* 235). Indeed, says Ignatius, God works and labors not only in human persons but also in the elements, the plants, and the animals (*Sp. Ex.* 236; cf. 39). From this and similar passages it seems evident that God can be found in all things.

Saint Ignatius's close disciple, the Mallorcan Jerome Nadal, contended that Ignatius was endowed with a special grace "to see and contemplate in all things, actions, and conversations the presence of God and the love of spiritual things, to remain a contemplative even in the midst of action."[10] Nadal believed that to be a contemplative in action and to find God in all things were graces or charisms especially proper to the Society of Jesus.[11]

Among modern Jesuit authors, none has extolled the sense of the divine omnipresence more eloquently than Pierre Teilhard de Chardin in his classic work *The Divine Milieu*. This work was written, according to the author, with the intention of instructing the reader "how to see God everywhere, to see Him in all that is most hidden, most solid and most ultimate in the world."[12] The divine milieu, Teilhard declares, "discloses itself to us as a modification of the deep being of things"—a modification that does not alter the perceptible phenomena, but renders them translucent and diaphanous, so that they become epiphanies of the divine.[13]

In successive chapters, Teilhard explains how to find God in the positive experiences of successful activity and in the negative experiences of failure and diminishment. The cross, he maintains, enables sickness and death to be paths to victory. His is a mystical spirituality that involves detachment from all creatures for the sake of union with the divine. As he wrote in a private letter of October 22, 1925, "After all, only one thing matters, surely, 'to see' God wherever one looks." The Protestant pastor Georges Crespy observes quite correctly: "It is not difficult to recognize the Ignatian inspiration of the *Milieu Divin*."[14]

For Teilhard, the realization of God's universal presence was not simply an ascetical principle for his own interior life. It was the inspiration of his lifelong quest to build a bridge between Christian faith and contemporary science. Having meditated deeply on the Kingdom of Christ, as set forth in the *Spiritual Exercises*, Teilhard was filled with ardent longing to set all things on fire with the love of Christ.[15] Aflame with this missionary zeal, he saw the worlds of science beckoning to him as the new territory to be evangelized. In 1926, referring to a recent lecture by a Harvard professor on the dawn of thought in the evolution of species, he wrote in a letter:

However farfetched the notion might appear at first, I realized in the end that, *hic et nunc*, Christ was not irrelevant to the problems that interest

Professor Parker; it only needed a few intermediate steps to allow a transition from his positivist psychology to a certain spiritual outlook. This realization cheered me up. Ah, there lie the Indies that draw me more strongly than those of St. Francis Xavier.[16]

Just as the early Jesuit missionaries sought to adopt all that was sound in the cultures of India and China, so Teilhard sought to utilize the new findings of science as points of access to faith in Christian revelation. In his enthusiasm he identified Christ as the Omega point toward which all the energies of religion and science were converging. This hypothesis certainly went far beyond anything that Saint Ignatius would have imagined, but it may be in part an outgrowth of the Ignatian vision of Christ in glory as the "eternal Lord of all things" (*Sp. Ex.* 98); it recalls the universalistic horizons of the meditations on the Kingdom of Christ, the Incarnation, and the Two Standards.

Whatever the weaknesses of the Teilhardian synthesis, it should not be dismissed as a kind of secularism. He explicitly warned against this error: "The sensual mysticisms and certain neo-pelagianisms (such as Americanism)," he wrote, "have fallen into the error of seeking divine love and the divine Kingdom on the same level as human affections and human progress."[17] The Christ into whom all things must be gathered was for him none other than the historical Jesus, who had been crucified under Pontius Pilate. When he spoke of the convergence of all religions, he added that they must converge on the Christian axis, "the other creeds finding in faith in Christ the proper expression of what they have been seeking as they grope their way towards the divine."[18] In *How I See* he presented the Catholic Church as "the central axis of the universal convergence and exact point at which blazes out the meeting of the Universe and the Omega Point."[19] Repudiating every kind of vague syncretism, he insisted that Christianity is the phylum through which the evolution of the religions must pass in order to achieve its goal. From Rome, in 1948, he wrote, "It is here in Rome that we find the Christic pole of the earth; through Rome, I mean, runs the ascending axis of hominization."[20] As we shall see, this ecclesial and Roman spirituality is also thoroughly Ignatian.

IMMEDIACY TO GOD

A second theme from the *Spiritual Exercises* is that of the immediacy of the soul to God. In the "Annotations for the Director" in the introduction to the *Exercises*, Saint Ignatius admonishes the director to refrain from urging the retreatant to choose the more perfect way of life. "It is more suitable and much better," he says, "that the Creator and Lord in person communicate himself to the devout soul in quest of the divine will, and that He inflame it with love of Himself." The director should therefore "permit the Creator to deal directly with the creature, and the creature directly with its Creator and Lord" (*Sp. Ex.* 15). In choosing a way of life, Ignatius later declares, the individual should turn with great diligence to prayer in the presence of God our Lord (*Sp. Ex.* 183) and assess whether the inclination one feels toward a given choice descends purely from above, that is, from the love of God (*Sp. Ex.* 184). It is possible for God to act directly on the soul, giving spiritual joy and consolation that are not humanly prepared for by any preceding perception or knowledge on the part of the creature (*Sp. Ex.* 329–30). Since God alone can act in this manner, such consolation can be a sure sign of God's will (*Sp. Ex.* 336).

Among modern theologians who have built on this Ignatian theme, none is more explicit than Karl Rahner. On the ground that God can draw the soul suddenly and entirely to himself, Rahner argues that it is possible for the human mind to have an experience of God, as he immediately bestows himself in grace. Rahner rereads St. Ignatius, just as he rereads Thomas Aquinas, in light of a transcendental philosophy that has its roots in the work of the Belgian Jesuit Joseph Maréchal. The basic idea of this philosophy is that the human spirit, while it knows objects in the world through sense experience, is oriented beyond all objects to a nonobjectifiable divine mystery. The entire enterprise of theology, he maintains, must be sustained and energized "by a previous unthematic, transcendental relatedness of our whole intellectuality to the incomprehensible infinite."[21] "The meaning of all explicit knowledge of God in religion and in metaphysics is intelligible," he says, "only when all the words we use there point to the unthematic experience of our orientation toward the ineffable mystery."[22] All conceptual statements about God, for Rahner, live off the nonobjective experience of transcendence as such.[23]

This nonobjective transcendental knowledge of God may be seen as the keystone of Rahner's whole theology. As Francis Fiorenza has noted, it forms the background of many of Rahner's characteristic theses: God's presence to man in grace and revelation, the "supernatural existential," the anonymous Christian, the ontological and psychological unity of

Christ, the limitations of Christ's human knowledge, the historicity of dogma, the nonobjective factor in the development of dogma, and many other points.[24]

Rahner recasts the theology of the sacraments on the ground that they do not mediate grace in a reified way but bring about and express an experience of grace that consists in a direct contact between the soul and God.[25] He cautions against the trap of imagining that God should be identified with any one "categorially" mediated religious presence, such as the Bible or the sacraments.[26] After all, Rahner might say, there is no such thing as bottled grace!

On the ground that every individual is in immediate contact with God through grace, Rahner develops an original theory of the relationship between the charismatic and the institutional elements in the Church. The charisms, or gifts of the Holy Spirit, he holds, are in principle prior to the institution. The charismatic element, in fact, is "the true pith and essence of the Church," the point where the lordship of Christ is most directly and potently exercised. The external structures of the Church, in his system, are seen as subordinate to the self-actualization of the transcendental subject, achieved by grace.[27] Office holders in the Church are obliged not to stifle the Holy Spirit but to recognize and foster the free movements of the Spirit in the Church.[28]

Holding that the articulation of dogma always falls short of the reality to which it refers, Rahner pleads for a high level of tolerance for doctrinal diversity in the Church.[29] He favors a pluriform Church with structures that are adaptable to local and transitory needs.[30] The institutional forms, for him, are radically subordinate to the nonthematic experience of grace. The student of the *Spiritual Exercises* is reminded in this connection of the way in which Ignatius instructs the director to adapt the meditations to the age, education, and talents of those making the Exercises. Retreatants are encouraged to adopt whatever posture best enables them to pray. For Ignatius, external forms and practices were always secondary to spiritual fruits.

On the ground that the human spirit is always and everywhere open to God's gracious self-communication, Rahner draws a further consequence. All persons, he contends, have some experience of the immediate presence of the divine, and have the possibility of living by God's grace, even if they have failed to arrive at explicit belief in God or in Christ. Even those who have never heard the proclamation of the gospel may be, in Rahner's famous phrase, "anonymous Christians." We have a right to hope for the salvation of all.

Rahner combines his conviction that God is found in transcendental experience with the characteristically Ignatian tenet of God's presence in all things. While insisting on the primacy of the inner experience of God in the depths of consciousness, Rahner holds that this experience is actualized through encounters with inner-worldly realities. The transcendental is not the remote; it continually mediates itself through particular historical experiences. In an early essay on "Ignatian Mysticism of Joy in the World" Rahner celebrates the distinctively Jesuit affirmation of the world and its values, the disposition to accept the achievements of culture, to esteem humanism, and to adapt to the demands of varying situations.[31] Once we have found the God of the life beyond, he concludes, we are able to immerse ourselves in the work required of us in our world today. Since God is active at all times and places, he argues, there is no need to flee to the desert or return to the past to find him. Like Teilhard, therefore, Rahner interprets Ignatius as having laid the foundations of a lay theology that discovers God's presence in worldly realities.

Rahner, again like Teilhard, accepts the Ignatian theology of the cross. He insists that God is to be found not only in the positive but also in the negative experiences of life, including failure, renunciation, sickness, poverty, and death. Just as the passion and death were central to Christ's redeeming work, so privation and self-denial can be paths to the ultimate renunciation that each of us will have to undergo in death. God is greater than either our successes or our failures. He, the *Deus semper maior*, is our only lasting hope.[32]

ECCLESIAL OBEDIENCE

Saint Ignatius of Loyola, while recognizing the immediacy of the individual soul to God, strongly emphasizes the mediation of the Church. He repeatedly speaks of the Church as the Mother of believers and the Bride of Christ (*Sp. Ex.* 353). "In Christ our Lord, the Bridegroom, and in his Spouse the Church," he asserts, "only one Spirit holds sway" (*Sp. Ex.* 365). Ignatius in the *Exercises* speaks of serving Christ in the Church militant and on two occasions refers to it as "the hierarchical Church" (*Sp. Ex.* 170, 353), a term apparently original with Ignatius.[33] One manuscript of the *Exercises* used by Saint Ignatius himself adds that the hierarchical Church is "Roman" (*Sp. Ex.* 353). Ignatius takes it for granted that no one could be called by the Holy Spirit to do anything forbidden by the hierarchical Church (*Sp. Ex.* 170). This ecclesial mysticism is recaptured in the theology of the French Jesuit Henri de Lubac as well as in that of his friend and disciple, Hans Urs von Balthasar.

De Lubac, like Rahner, was strongly influenced by Maréchal's view that the human spirit is constituted by a dynamic drive to transcend all finite objects in quest of that which is greater than everything conceivable.[34] The dynamism of the human spirit toward the vision of God, he believed, surpasses all the affirmations and denials of both positive and negative theology.[35] A ceaseless inquietude of the soul toward God drives the whole process forward.[36] Primordial knowledge comes to itself in reflexive concepts, but these concepts are never final; they are always subject to criticism and correction.[37]

Conscious though he is of this inner drive, de Lubac does not fall into religious individualism. Picking up the Ignatian designations of the Church as Bride of Christ and as Mother of all Christ's faithful, he affirms that a "mystical identity" exists between Christ and the Church. He repudiates every tendency to introduce an opposition between the mystical and the visible, between spirit and authority, or between charism and hierarchy.[38] Although the Church has an invisible dimension, it is essentially visible and hierarchical. "Without the hierarchy which is her point of organization, her organizer and her guide," he declares, there could be no talk of the Church at all.[39]

In a celebrated passage of *The Splendor of the Church*, de Lubac paints a glowing portrait of the loyal Christian, one who seeks to be what Origen termed a "true ecclesiastic." Like Saint Ignatius, such as person will always be concerned to think with and in the Church,[40] cultivating the sense of Catholic solidarity, and accepting the teaching of the magisterium as a binding norm.[41] The ecclesiastical person, according to de Lubac, will not only be obedient but will also love obedience as a way of dying to self in order to be filled with the truth that God pours into our minds.[42] De Lubac discountenances negative criticism and complaint. "Today," he writes, "when the Church is in the dock, misunderstood, jeered at for her very existence and even her sanctity itself, Catholics should be wary lest what they want to say simply to serve her better be turned into account against her."[43] A certain delicacy will prompt them to refrain from public criticism. In these assertions de Lubac echoes the teaching of Saint Ignatius in his "Rules for Thinking with the Church."

THE CALL OF THE KING

A final theme in the *Spiritual Exercises* that has inspired modern disciples of Saint Ignatius is the call of Christ in the meditation on the Kingdom. All persons with good judgment, Ignatius maintains, will offer themselves entirely to labor with Christ in order to share in his victory (*Sp. Ex.* 96). But those who wish to distinguish themselves in service will wish to imitate Christ in bearing all wrongs, and suffering abuse and poverty, in order to give greater proof of their love (*Sp. Ex.* 97–98). The drama of the following of Christ through his sufferings to ultimate victory is central to the entire theological project of Hans Urs von Balthasar.

Balthasar's theology of revelation is centered about the self-manifestation of the divine majesty, a theme he himself connects with the Ignatian motto, *ad maiorem Dei gloriam.*[44] The glory of God, he holds, overwhelms and captivates all who perceive it. The culminating manifestation of God's glory is Jesus, the crucified and risen one. Jesus glorifies God by the faithful execution of his mission, which is the prolongation in time of his own origin from the Father.[45]

The perfection of human beings cannot be measured by abstract ethical rules but only by their response to the call that Christ addresses to them. That call is always to share in the lot and mission of the Lord. The Church incorporates its members into Christ, first of all through baptism into his death. Christians achieve the freedom of children of God by renouncing their self-will, putting on the mind of Christ. In Balthasar's ecclesiology, therefore, obedience is central and constitutive. To be Church is to be, like Mary, the "handmaid of the Lord." The Church's task, like hers, is to hear the word and do it.[46]

In developing his theology of obedience, Balthasar draws extensively on the *Spiritual Exercises* of Saint Ignatius, and especially on the "Rules for the Election" and the "Rules for Thinking with the Church." Christian perfection, he has learned from Ignatius, consists in a faithful and loving response to God's call.[47] The love of Christ, in his view, requires not only the observance of the commandments but the following of the evangelical counsels, which are nothing but the form of Christ's redeeming love.[48]

Balthasar's large volume *The Christian State of Life* is an extended commentary on the Call of Christ described in the Ignatian meditation on the Kingdom. The vocation to the consecrated life, in the view of Balthasar, is a fundamental feature of the Church. Since Jesus called the Twelve to poverty, chastity, and obedience during his public ministry, the state of the evangelical counsels existed even before the priestly state. By renouncing every desire of their own, Christians are best able to share in the absolute freedom that is in God. The prayer of Saint Ignatius, "Take, Lord, and Receive," magnificently expresses the sacrifice of personal freedom for the sake of living by the divine will alone.[49]

The following of the Crucified Lord takes on concrete form in the hierarchical Church, which retains its Christological form thanks to the authority of office holders over other members of the Church. If this opposition between hierarchy and faithful were dissolved, he writes, "all that would remain would only be a formless mush of ethical instructions."[50] Like de Lubac, therefore, Balthasar holds that office and charism belong together. From one point of view, office may be seen as a special charism for coordinating other charisms and bringing them into the unity of the Church as a whole.[51]

Recognizing the centrality of the office of Peter, Balthasar wrote a thick volume against what he describes as the "venomous" and "irrational" anti-Roman feeling that has been spreading among Catholics since Vatican II. Within the Christological mystery, he asserts, the Jesuit ideal of combining personal maturity with loving submission to ecclesial authority does not involve the absurdity that some have found in it.[52] In its vow of special obedience to the pope, the Society of Jesus as a body practices the disponibility or universal availability that lies at the heart of the Ignatian ideal of "indifference."[53]

SYNTHESIS OF OPPOSITES

These reflections on four Ignatian themes as found in four twentieth-century Catholic theologians suggest authentic and apostolically fruitful ways of thinking about God, Christ, Church, and world. In a longer presentation many other themes and authors could profitably be studied. One might wish to survey the missionary theology of Pierre Charles and Jean Daniélou, the ecumenism of Augustin Bea, the theology of conversion of Bernard Lonergan, and the views of John Courtney Murray on religious freedom. In all these authors, it would be possible to trace Ignatian motifs based on the *Spiritual Exercises*. Reference should also be made to theological disciples of Ignatius who are teaching and writing today. Considerations of time, and the limitations of my own knowledge, prevent me from exploring these interesting questions in this essay.

Ignatian principles, as I have tried to indicate, can lead to a variety of theological systems. In the *Spiritual Exercises* themselves there seems to be an inbuilt tension between immediacy and mediation, between personal freedom and obedience, between universalism and ecclesiocentrism, between horizontal openness to the world and reverence for the sacred and the divine. Some theologians such as Teilhard de Chardin and Rahner put greater emphasis on immediacy to God, personal freedom, and universalism, whereas others like de Lubac and Balthasar, especially in their later work, insist more on ecclesial mediation, sacramentality, and obedience. The "Rules for the Discernment of Spirits" seem to point in one direction, the "Rules for Thinking with the Church" in the other. But because both emphases are valid, and are held together in the *Exercises*, they must be harmoniously reconciled in theology.

The Ignatian charism, as I understand it, consists in the ability to combine the two tendencies without detriment to either. A purely mechanical obedience without regard for the movements of the Spirit and a purely individualistic reliance on the Spirit without regard for ecclesiastical authority would be equally foreign to the heritage we have been exploring. For Ignatius it was axiomatic that Christians are called to achieve authentic freedom by surrendering their limited freedom into the hands of God. The theologian who is most prayerfully open to the impulses of the Spirit is best able to enter into the mind of the Church and by this means to interpret the Christian faith in fullest conformity with the intentions of the Lord himself.

NOTES

1. Henri de Lubac, *Teilhard de Chardin: The Man and His Meaning* (New York: Mentor Omega Books, 1965), 113–14.

2. Hans Urs von Balthasar, *The Theology of Henri de Lubac: An Overview* (San Francisco: Ignatius, 1991), 118–19.

3. Hans Urs von Balthasar, *My Work in Retrospect* (San Francisco: Ignatius, 1993), 51.

4. Ibid., 21.

5. Karl Rahner, interview by Leo J. O'Donovan in *America* 140 (March 10, 1979): 177–80 at 178; reprinted in *Karl Rahner in Dialogue*, ed. Harvey D. Egan (New York: Crossroad, 1986), 190.

6. *Constitutions of the Society of Jesus* (St. Louis: Institute of Jesuit Sources, 1996), §464.

7. Ibid., §§358, 464.

8. For these and other appellations see Harvey D. Egan, *Ignatius Loyola the Mystic* (Wilmington, Del.: Michael Glazier, 1987).

9. *Constitutions* §288.

10. Joseph de Guibert, *The Jesuits: Their Spiritual Doctrine and Practice* (Chicago: Loyola University Press, 1964), 45.

11. With reference to "finding God in all things" Nadal writes, "We believe that what we have recognized here as a privilege given to Father Ignatius has also been granted to the whole Society; and we are confident that the grace of that prayer has been prepared in the Society for all of us, and is indeed something connected with our vocation," *Mon. Nadal*, IV, 652. See Josef Stierli, "Ignatian Prayer: Seeking God in All Things," in *Ignatius of Loyola: His Personality and Spiritual Heritage, 1556–1956*, by Friedrich Wulf and others (St. Louis: Institute of Jesuit Sources, 1977), 135–63, at 143.

12. Pierre Teilhard de Chardin, *The Divine Milieu* (New York: Harper & Bros., 1960), 15.

13. Ibid., 110.

14. Henri de Lubac, *The Religion of Teilhard de Chardin* (New York: Desclee, 1967), 282.

15. De Lubac, ibid., pp. 225 and 362, quotes from letters in which Teilhard prays for the grace to will nothing except to set the world on fire. De Lubac notes that this desire echoes the communion antiphon of the Mass of Saint Ignatius, "I came to cast fire on the earth, and would that it were already kindled!"

16. Pierre Teilhard de Chardin, *Letters from a Traveller* (New York: Collins, 1962), 127–28.

17. Teilhard de Chardin, *Divine Milieu*, 86 n. 1.

18. De Lubac, *Teilhard de Chardin: The Man and His Meaning*, 177.

19. Ibid., 179.

20. Christopher Mooney, *Teilhard de Chardin and the Mystery of Christ* (New York: Harper & Row, 1966), 159.

21. Karl Rahner, *The Priesthood* (New York: Herder and Herder, 1973), 6; cf. *Karl Rahner: Theologian of the Graced Search for Meaning*, ed. Geffrey B. Kelly, introduction, 36.

22. Karl Rahner, *Foundations of Christian Faith* (New York: Crossroad, 1982), 53.

23. Rahner, "The Concept of Mystery in Catholic Theology," *Theological Investigations* 4 (Baltimore: Helicon, 1966), 36–73, at 49–50.

24. Francis Schüssler Fiorenza, introduction to Karl Rahner, *Spirit in the World* (New York: Herder and Herder, 1968), xliv.

25. Rahner, "Thoughts about the Sacraments in General," in Kelly, *Karl Rahner*, 288.

26. Kelly, "Introduction," 58.

27. Karl Rahner, "Observations on the Factor of the Charismatic in the Church," *Theological Investigations* 12 (New York: Seabury/Crossroad, 1974), 81–97, at 83.

28. Karl Rahner, "Do Not Stifle the Spirit," *Theological Investigations* 7 (New York: Herder and Herder, 1971), 72–87.

29. Kelly, "Introduction," 23.

30. Ibid., 26–27.

31. Karl Rahner, "The Ignatian Mysticism of Joy in the World," (1937), *Theological Investigations* 3 (Baltimore: Helicon, 1967), 277–93.

32. Cf. Avery Dulles, "The Spiritual Theology of Karl Rahner," in *Jesuit Spirit in a Time of Change*, ed. Raymond A. Schroth (Westminster, Md.: Newman, 1968), 23–41, at 41.

33. See Yves Congar, *L'Église de S. Augustin à l'époque moderne* (Paris: Cerf, 1970), 369.

34. Henri de Lubac, *The Discovery of God* (Chicago: Regnery, 1967), 90–91.

35. Balthasar, *Henri de Lubac*, 12.

36. Ibid., 96.

37. Ibid., 94.

38. Henri de Lubac, *The Splendor of the Church* (San Francisco: Ignatius, 1986), 91.

39. Ibid., 88.

40. Ibid., 249.

41. Ibid., 244–45.

42. Ibid., 258, 265.

43. Ibid., 287.

44. Balthasar, *My Work*, 82.

45. Hans Urs von Balthasar, "The Priest of the New Covenant," *Spirit and Institution: Explorations in Theology* IV (San Francisco: Ignatius, 1995), 353–81, at 356.

46. Balthasar, "Christology and Ecclesial Obedience," ibid., 139–67, at 147–48.

47. Balthasar, *My Work*, 20.

48. Ibid., 51.

49. Hans Urs von Balthasar, *The Christian State of Life* (San Francisco: Ignatius, 1983), 400.

50. Balthasar, "Priest of the New Covenant," 377.

51. Balthasar, "Christology and Ecclesial Obedience," *Explorations in Theology* IV, 157; cf. idem, "Charis and Charisma," *Explorations in Theology* II (San Francisco: Ignatius, 1991), 301–14, at 313–14.

52. Hans Urs von Balthasar, *The Office of Peter and the Structure of the Church* (San Francisco: Ignatius, 1986), 50–51.

53. Balthasar, "Christology and Ecclesial Obedience," 164. See in this connection Balthasar's explanation of Ignatian "indifference" as involving "availability for everything the Spirit will send and dispose" in his "Preliminary Remarks on the Discernment of Spirits," *Explorations in Theology* IV, 337–52, at 342.

18

Mary at the Dawn of the New Millennium

November 19, 1997

For John Paul II, Mary is the primary patroness of the advent of the new millennium. As the mother of Christ she is preeminently an advent figure—the morning star announcing the rising of the Sun of Righteousness. Like the moon at the dawn of a new day, she is wholly bathed in the glory of the sun that is to come after her. Her beauty is a reflection of his.

The glories of Mary have only gradually been discovered by the Church in the course of nearly two thousand years of study and contemplation. The basic lines of Catholic Mariology are by now beyond dispute, enshrined as they are in the Scriptures, in the liturgy, in prayer, poetry, song, and art, in the writings of saints and theologians, and in the teaching of popes and councils. Mary holds a secure place as the greatest of the saints, conceived and born without original sin and free from actual sin at any point in her life. Full of grace, she is exemplary in her faith, hope, love of God, and generous concern for others. Having virginally conceived the Son of God in her womb, she remained a virgin throughout life. At the end of her earthly sojourn she was taken up body and soul into heaven, where she continues to exercise her spiritual motherhood and to intercede for the needs of her children on earth. This body of teaching, constructed laboriously over long centuries, belongs inalienably to the patrimony of the Church and can scarcely be contested from within the Catholic tradition. It goes without saying that John Paul II accepts this heritage without question.

WOJTYLA'S MARIOLOGY

These convictions have not come to the present pope only as a result of being installed in his office. He has been a devoted son of Mary ever since early youth, when he worshiped at her shrines in the neighborhood of his native Wodowice. During the Nazi occupation of Poland, as a chaplet leader in a "living rosary," he joined in prayers to Mary for peace and liberation. He also studied the works of Saint Louis Grignion de Montfort, from whom he takes his motto as pope, *totus tuus* ("I am wholly yours"), referring to the Blessed Virgin.

It would be a mistake to think of Karol Wojtyla's attachment to Mary as the fruit of sentimentality. He emphatically denies that Marian teaching is a devotional supplement to a system of doctrine that would be complete without her. On the contrary, he holds, she occupies an indispensable place in the whole plan of salvation. "The mystery of Mary," writes the pope, "is a revealed truth which imposes itself on the intellect of believers and requires of those in the Church who have the task of studying and teaching a method of doctrinal reflection no less rigorous than that used in all theology" (*ORE*, 10 January 1996)[1].

As a bishop at Vatican II, Wojtyla made several important interventions regarding Mary. He favored the inclusion of Mariology within the Constitution on the Church, but he pleaded for a different location of the text, so that, instead of being a final chapter, it would immediately follow chapter 1 on the Mystery of the Church. Mary, he declared, having built up Christ's physical body as Mother, continues this role in the Mystical Body.[2] Since she is Mother of Christ and of Christians, she ought to be considered early in the document, he said, rather than relegated to a kind of appendix at the end.[3]

"For practical reasons," however, the Doctrinal Commission judged it necessary at that stage to keep the section on Mary at the end of the Constitution on the Church—a decision that unfortunately made it possible for some commentators to say that Vatican II had demoted the status of Mary. The Commission also rejected several proposals to designate

Mary formally as Mother of the Church, and even to make that term the title of the chapter. But it did declare that "the Catholic Church, taught by the Holy Spirit, honors her with the affection of filial piety as a most loving mother" (*LG* 53). To the great satisfaction of Archbishop Wojtyla, Paul VI at the end of the third session, on November 21, 1964, explicitly proclaimed Mary to be Mother of the Church (see RH 22; *RMat* 47).

The Mariology of John Paul II appears in concentrated form in his encyclical *Redemptoris mater* (1987) and more diffusely in a series of seventy Wednesday audience catecheses on Mary delivered between September 6, 1995, and November 12, 1997. In general his teaching may be called pastoral rather than speculatively theological. The pope is more concerned with communicating the faith of the Church and fostering authentic piety than with proposing new theories. But rather frequently one comes across phrases and statements that reflect personal insights of his own.

The key term that unifies the pope's Mariology, as I see it, is that of motherhood. Mary is the mother of the Redeemer, mother of divine grace, mother of the Church. The Council of Ephesus in the fifth century established the foundational dogma of Mariology, that Mary is Mother of God, *theotokos* (literally, "God-bearer"). The pope calls attention to the ecumenical value of this dogma (*RMat* 30–32): it is accepted by practically all Christians, and has given rise to beautiful hymns, especially in the Byzantine liturgy, which in turn inspired the salutation in the great Anglican hymn, "Ye Watchers and Ye Holy Ones":

> O higher than the cherubim,
> More glorious than the seraphim,
> Lead their praises, Alleluia!
> Thou bearer of th'eternal Word,
> Most gracious, magnify the Lord, Alleluia!

With his great interest in the theme of redemption, John Paul II frequently calls attention to Mary's involvement in the saving mission of her Son, beginning with the Annunciation, when she consented to the plan of the Incarnation and received the signal grace of divine Motherhood. As the virgin mother, she conceived through faith and obedience to the divine Word that came to her from on high (*RMat* 13).

Like Christ's own redemptive mission, Mary's role in salvation history was not exempt from sorrow. In many texts John Paul II recalls how, at the presentation of the infant Christ in the Temple, Simeon prophesied that Mary's soul would be pierced by a sword. This prophecy was to be fulfilled on Calvary, where Mary's compassion perfectly mirrored the passion of her Son, whose sufferings reverberated in her heart (*ORE*, 9 April 1997).

After the death of Jesus, according to the pope, Mary's motherly office assumes a new form. In saying to the Beloved Disciple, "Behold your mother," Jesus places the apostles under her maternal care (Jn 19:25–27). In the days following the Ascension we find Mary in the company of the apostles prayerfully and confidently waiting for the Holy Spirit, who had already overshadowed her at the Annunciation, to descend upon the Church. There is a mysterious correspondence, therefore, in Mary's maternal relationships to Jesus and to the Church. By her unceasing intercession she cooperates with maternal love in the spiritual birth and development of the sons and daughters of the Church (*RMat* 44). "Choosing her as Mother of all humanity," writes the pope, "the heavenly Father wanted to reveal the maternal dimension of his divine tenderness and care for men and women of every age" (*ORE*, 22 October 1997).

NEW MARIAN DOGMAS?

As the present millennium draws to a close, certain groups of Catholics are pressing for new dogmatic definitions officially conferring upon Mary the titles "coredemptrix," "mediatrix of all graces," and "advocate of the people of God."[4] A Dutch mystic, Ida Peerdeman, who died in 1995, predicted that John Paul II would proclaim this threefold title of Mary as the "final dogma." A group calling itself Vox Populi Mariae Mediatrici, based in the United States and headed by Mark Miravalle, a lay professor of theology at Steubenville, has been gathering signers, including many cardinals and bishops, calling for this triple definition. According to *Newsweek* for August 25, 1997, the pope has received 4,340,429 signatures from 157 countries requesting him to make this dogmatic proclamation. Miravalle is quoted as claiming that the date of the proclamation has actually been set: May 31, 1998, a day when the feast of Pentecost coincides with the former feast of Mary Mediatrix of All Graces.

There is nothing unusual about campaigns to confer more exalted titles on Mary. The dogmas of the Immaculate Conception and the Assumption were preceded by floods of petitions. After World War I the Belgian

Cardinal Désiré Mercier took the leadership in a drive for a dogmatic definition that Mary was universal mediatrix of grace. Pius XI appointed three commissions to study this question, but no further action was taken. Many bishops, however, obtained permission for the Mass and Office of Our Lady Mediatrix of All Graces to be celebrated in their dioceses. In 1950 the first International Mariological Congress, meeting in Rome, asked for a dogmatic proclamation of Mary's universal mediation. But Pius XII did not implement this request. In fact he replaced the feast of Mary Mediatrix with that of the Queenship of Mary in 1954.

In order to assess the acceptability of the three proposed titles it will be helpful to glance as their past usage in Catholic theology and magisterial teaching.[5]

THE PROPOSED TITLES

Of the three proposed titles, "advocate" is least burdened with difficulties. It was used in the patristic age by Irenaeus and John Damascene, and in the Middle Ages by Bernard and many others. In the *Salve Regina* we implore Mary as "most gracious Advocate" to turn her eyes of mercy toward us. The fact that the title "advocate" is applied to Holy Spirit in the Fourth Gospel (Jn 14:16, 26; 15:26; 16:7) and to Christ in the First Letter of John (1 Jn 2:1) can hardly constitute an objection, since Mary's advocacy, as that of a created person, takes place on a different level. If she is not our advocate, what could her intercession mean? To deny her this title would be in effect to reject the whole doctrine of the intercession of the saints.

The title "mediatrix" is likewise very ancient. It goes back to the fifth century (Basil of Seleucia) and was in common usage by the eighth century (Andrew of Crete, Germanus of Constantinople, and John Damascene). Medieval saints such as Bernard of Clairvaux, Bonaventure, and Bernardine of Siena frequently use the title. In modern times it was further popularized by Saints Louis Grignion de Montfort and Alfonsus Liguori.

The designation of Mary as "mediatrix" is a commonplace in papal documents. Leo XIII in 1896 said of her, "No single individual can even be imagined who has ever contributed or ever will contribute so much toward reconciling man with God. . . . She is therefore truly His [Christ's]

Mother and for this reason a worthy and acceptable 'Mediatrix to the Mediator'" (*PTM* §194). Pius X in 1904 said that by reason of the union she had with Jesus she is "the most powerful Mediatrix and advocate of the whole world with her Divine Son" (*PTM* §233). Benedict XV in 1915 in an address to the Consistory of Cardinals declared, "The faith of her believers and her children's love consider her not only God's Mother, but also the Mediatrix with God" (*PTM* §261). Pius XI in 1928 declared that Christ willed "to make His Mother the advocate for sinners and the dispenser and mediatrix of His grace" (*PTM* §287; cf. §323). Pius XII in 1940, without actually using the term "mediatrix," urged faithful Christians to have recourse to Mary since, as Bernard had taught, "It is the Will of God that we obtain all favors through Mary" (*PTM* §356).

In preparation for Vatican II, and in response to many petitions, the Doctrinal Commission in 1962 proposed a schema formally declaring that Mary was mediatrix, but several eminent cardinals, including Augustin Bea, Paul Emile Léger, and Bernard Alfrink, argued that the title was not yet sufficiently clarified in theology to warrant a conciliar pronouncement and that a formal declaration would be ecumenically counterproductive. In the final text, therefore, the council contented itself with the very moderate statement that because of her motherly care, Mary is invoked in the Church by titles such as "advocate" and "mediatrix" (*LG* 62).

In his sixty-fourth catechesis on Mary (September 24, 1997) John Paul II affirms that Mary is indeed mediatrix inasmuch as she "presents our desires and petitions to Christ, and transmits the divine gifts to us, interceding continually on our behalf" (*ORE*, 1 October 1997). In his encyclical on Mary, the pope characterizes Mary's mediation as maternal; it is motherhood in the order of grace (*RMat* 21, 38). It is intercessory in nature, since it reaches out toward the Son and has a universal embrace corresponding to his saving will for all humanity (*RMat* 40). From these statements we may conclude that Mary's mediation, according to John Paul II, extends in some way to all the gifts of grace.

The difficulty is often raised that to speak of Mary in these terms derogates from the unique mediatorship of Jesus Christ, which is formally affirmed in Scripture (1 Tim 2:5). Mary's mediation might even seem to interfere with an immediate union between the Christian and the Lord. In replying to this difficulty, the pope repeats the teaching of Vatican II that "all the saving influences of the Blessed Virgin . . . originate from the divine pleasure; they flow forth from the superabundance of the merits of

Christ, rest on his mediation, depend entirely upon it, and draw all their power from it. In no way do they impede the immediate union of the faithful with Christ. Rather, they foster this union" (*LG* 60; cf. *RMat* 38). Mary's mediation, according to the council, "takes nothing away from the dignity and power of Christ the one mediator, and adds nothing to it" (*LG* 62; cf. *ORE*, 8 October 1997). If these principles are kept in mind, the doctrinal objections to the title "mediatrix" lose much of their force.

As for the title "coredemptrix," it has a more checkered history. Having first appeared in theology toward the end of the fourteenth century, it becomes prominent in papal teaching in the first half of this century. Benedict XV in 1918 went so far as to assert that Mary "with Christ redeemed mankind" (*PTM* §267). Pius XI, addressing a group of pilgrims in 1933, declared, "From the nature of His work the Redeemer ought to have associated His Mother with His work. For this reason we invoke her under the title of Coredemptrix. She gave us the Savior, she accompanied him in the work of Redemption as far as the Cross itself, sharing with Him the sorrows of the agony and of the death in which Jesus consummated the Redemption of mankind" (*PTM* §326). Again in 1935, he addressed Mary in prayer, "Mother most faithful and most merciful, who as coredemptrix and partaker of thy dear Son's sorrows didst assist Him as He offered the sacrifice of our Redemption on the altar of the Cross" (*PTM* §334). But Pius XII studiously avoided the term. Instead he spoke of Mary as the loving Mother, "inseparably joined with Christ in accomplishing the work of man's redemption" (*PTM* §778). Paul VI and Vatican II made no mention of Mary as coredemptrix. The very term seemed to contradict the common teaching that although there are many mediators of intercession there is but one mediator of redemption, Jesus Christ.[6] All Catholics agree that Christ was the sufficient cause of our redemption. The question concerns the manner in which he associated his mother with himself in this action.

In line with previous popes, John Paul II holds that Mary cooperated with Christ at every stage from his coming into the world to his death upon the cross, where her soul was pierced with grief as his heart was pierced with a lance. Although the pope does not speak of Mary as "coredemptrix" in any of his encyclicals or other major documents, he did use the term in occasional speeches, at least until 1985.[7] For example, in an address at the Marian shrine of Guayaquil, Ecuador, on January 31, 1985, he declared, "As she was in a special way close to the Cross of her Son, she also had to have a privileged experience of his Resurrection. In fact, Mary's role as coredemptrix did not cease with the glorification of her Son" (*ORE*, 11 March 1985).

In the few cases where the present pope has used the term "coredemptrix," it seems to be a concise way of referring to Mary's intimate association with her Son in his redemptive action. This interpretation is borne out by his Wednesday audience catechesis of April 9, 1996:

> Moreover, when the Apostle Paul says, "For we are God's fellow workers" (1 Cor 3:9), he maintains the real possibility for man to co-operate with God. The collaboration of believers, which obviously excludes any equality with him, is expressed in the proclamation of the Gospel and in their personal contribution to its taking root in human hearts.
>
> However, applied to Mary, the term "co-operator" acquires a specific meaning. The collaboration of Christians in salvation takes place after the Calvary event, whose fruits they endeavor to spread by prayer and sacrifice. Mary, instead, co-operated during the event itself and in the role of mother; thus her co-operation embraces the whole of Christ's saving work. She alone was associated in this way with the redemptive sacrifice that merited the salvation of all mankind. In union with Christ and in submission to him, she collaborated in obtaining the grace of salvation for all humanity. (*ORE*, 16 April 1996)

Whether he is speaking of Mary's mediation or of her role in redemption, the pope always makes it clear that he is referring to her participation in Christ's own action, which is by itself incomparable and sufficient. The doctrine of Mary as coredemptrix cannot mean that she stands on the same level with Christ or makes up for any deficiency in his redemptive action. But since Christ's mediation does not exclude the cooperation of subordinate mediators, so, it would seem, he could freely associate others with his redemptive action without ceasing to be the full and sufficient cause. If this point is clearly understood, it is acceptable to speak of Mary as having been in some way conjoined with Christ in his redemptive work, and in that qualified sense as "coredemptrix."

WILL THE TITLES BE DEFINED?

As things now stand, however, I think it unlikely that the pope will dogmatically proclaim any or all of the three proposed titles, especially the title of coredemptrix. My first reason for thinking so is the pope's complete loyalty to the intentions of Vatican II, which was cautious in its use of Marian titles and made no reference to "coredemptrix." Following the council, John Paul II has thus far been careful to avoid both maximalism and minimalism and to refrain from personally deciding issues that are still open to theological debate (*ORE*, 10 January 1996). Like John XXIII and Paul VI before him, he has until now abstained from making any ex cathedra pronouncements and attaching anathemas to his teaching. Although he recognizes his power as pope to speak authoritatively to the universal episcopate, he evidently prefers to teach collegially, and without canonical censures, expressing what he perceives as being the consensus of the episcopal college.

Second, it must be noted that these dogmas would provoke considerable confusion among Catholics and great ecumenical dismay, especially in Protestant and Anglican circles. Some might think that Mary was being exalted to become a fourth person in the godhead[8] or at least that the unique mediatorship of Christ or the sufficiency of his redemptive act was being obscured. Even the Orthodox, who might agree with the substance of the proclamation, would be opposed to the manner of its issuance if it came from the pope speaking ex cathedra. The pope, who places ecumenism high on his agenda, would surely take account of these sentiments.[9]

Third, the exact content of the proposed dogmas is still unclear. Mary's mediation or advocacy could be understood, or misunderstood, as implying that she can make God change his plans or that she is more merciful than her Son. It raises the question whether all prayers must be channeled through Mary in order to be heard by God. If she is coredemptrix, does that mean that she cooperates directly and immediately in the redemptive action of Christ, offering him up on the cross, or only indirectly and remotely—for example, by becoming mother of the Redeemer and consenting to his sacrificial death? What, if anything, does her cooperation add that would not be present without it? Mariologists have debated points like this with great subtlety, without however reaching any full agreement. These unsettled points suggest that any dogmatic definition might be premature.

Fourth, the community of Mariological scholars seems to be opposed. At Czestochowa in Poland in August 1996, a commission of fifteen Catholic theologians from the Pontifical International Marian Academy, chosen for their specific competence in this area, together with three officers of the Society and five non-Catholic theologians, unanimously recommended against any dogmatic definition of the Marian titles of mediatrix, coredemptrix, and advocate. Their reason was partly ecumenical, but more substantively that the titles are ambiguous and lend themselves to misunderstanding. Using similar arguments, an International Mariological Symposium, meeting at Rome on October 7–9, 1997, registered overwhelming opposition to the proposed papal definitions and especially to that of coredemptrix.

Finally, we have a statement of the papal press secretary, Joaquin Navarro-Valls on August 18, 1997, declaring that no proclamation of any new Marian dogmas is at present planned or under study by the pope or any Vatican commission. It is "crystal clear"—he is quoted as saying—that the pope will not solemnly define any of these three titles as dogmas.[10]

If the pope wishes to honor Mary in some special way at the approach of the new millennium, he would have other possibilities than to proclaim new dogmas. He could, for example, declare that these beliefs are worthy of credence, or he could establish some new liturgical feast honoring Mary by one or another of these titles. Due recognition of Mary in the celebration of the great jubilee does not, however, necessitate any doctrinal or liturgical innovations.

THEMES FOR 1997–1999

In his apostolic letter *The Coming of the Third Millennium*, John Paul II makes a number of concrete suggestions with implications for Marian practice and devotion. He relates the last three years of the current millennium to the three divine persons and the three theological virtues. 1997, he declares, is a time to concentrate on faith with special reference to Jesus Christ as the divine Son. Then 1998 would be a time for emphasizing the Holy Spirit and the virtue of hope. And 1999 is to be an occasion for turning to God the Father and for special emphasis on the virtue of charity.

Each of these three years, according to the pope, has a Marian dimension. She is the virginal mother of the Son, the immaculate spouse of the Holy Spirit, and the fairest daughter of the Father. She is also exemplary in her faith, hope, and charity.

In the year 1997, therefore, we have been urged to contemplate Mary's journey of faith in relation to the incarnate Son. At the Annunciation, she responded in faith to the angel's message that she was chosen to become the mother of the Redeemer. In uttering her *fiat* she entered the history of the world's salvation through the obedience of faith (*D&V* 51; cf. *RMat* 13). At the Visitation she was praised by Elizabeth with the words: "Blessed is she who believed that there would be a fulfillment of what was spoken to her from the Lord" (Lk 1:45; *RMat* 8).

Mary's faith was to be severely tested by the flight into Egypt, the loss of the child Jesus in the Temple, his rejection at Nazareth, and especially his crucifixion at Golgotha, which the pope describes as "perhaps the deepest *kenosis* of faith in human history" (*RMat* 18). But her faith continually grew as she pondered the meaning of the words addressed to her. Her obedient submission in faith was, in the expression of Irenaeus, the act that untied the knot of Eve's disobedience, thus enabling humanity to rise again to communion with God. Mary's faith is perpetuated in the Church as it makes its own pilgrimage of faith (*RMat* 28).

By pondering Mary's faith in Christ in 1997 Christians will have disposed themselves for meditation on the Holy Spirit and on hope, the themes proposed for 1998. Mary's faith, itself a gift of the Holy Spirit, enabled her to conceive her Son by the power of that same Spirit (*D&V* 51). Her faith flowered in an ardent and unfailing hope. Just as Abraham hoped against hope that he would become the father of many nations (Rom 4:18), so Mary trusted against all appearances that the Lord would place her Son upon the throne of David, where he would reign in unending glory (Lk 1:32–33; *RMat* 13–15). The hope of the whole people of ancient Israel came to its culmination in Mary, who in her Magnificat praised God's fidelity to the promises he had made to Abraham and to his posterity forever (Lk 1:55; *RMat* 35). She is thus a radiant model for all who entrust themselves to God's promises. The image of the Virgin praying with the apostles in the Cenacle, says John Paul II, can become a sign of hope for all who call upon the Holy Spirit to deepen their union with God (cf. *RMat* 33).

Finally, as the most highly favored daughter of the Father, Mary may be viewed as the supreme model of love toward God and neighbor—the theme proposed for 1999. Out of affection for her cousin Elizabeth, she hastens into the hill country to assist her and share with her the good news of the Annunciation (*RMat* 12). In the Magnificat, she expresses her joy of spirit in God her Savior, who has looked upon her lowliness and done great things for her (*RMat* 35–36). In the same hymn she expresses solidarity with Yahweh's beloved poor, thus anticipating the Church's preferential option for the poor (*RMat* 37). At Cana she manifests her active charity by helping to relieve the embarrassment of her hosts, thus occasioning the miracle by which Christ first displayed his messianic power over nature (*RMat* 21). Mary's love for God is brought to its deepest fulfillment in heaven, where she continues to intercede lovingly for her children on earth. This she will continue to do until all things are subjected to the Father, so that God will become all in all (*RMat* 41).

The Church follows in the paths marked out for her by Mary. Like her the Church believes, accepting with fidelity the word of God (*RMat* 43). It preserves the faith by keeping and pondering in its heart all that God speaks to it (*RMat* 43). Sustained by the Holy Spirit amid the afflictions and hardships of the world, the Church unceasingly looks forward in hope to the promise of future glory. In imitation of Mary, the fair daughter of Zion, the Church continually praises the Father's mercies and imitates his love for men and women of every nation, the righteous and the unrighteous. The Church's prayers for the needs of the whole world blend with Mary's petitions before the throne of God.

Besides being an icon of the whole Church, Mary is in a particular way a model for women. The contrasting vocations of virginity and motherhood meet and coexist in her (*MD* 17). The single, the married, and the widowed can all look to her for inspiration. In Mary women can find an exemplar of "the loftiest sentiments of which the human heart is capable: the self-offering totality of love; the strength that is capable of bearing the greatest sorrows; limitless fidelity and tireless devotion to work; the ability to combine penetrating intuition with words of support and encouragement" (*RMat* 46; cf. *ORE*, 31 January 1996).

MEANING OF THE JUBILEE

The Mariology of John Paul II is closely interwoven with his theology of time. Mary could receive the fullness of grace because the fullness of time had arrived (Gal 4:4; *TMA* 1, 9). This fullness, says the pope, "marks the moment when, with the entrance of the eternal into time, time itself is redeemed" (*RMat* 1).

Jubilee years are more than sentimental recollections of the past. They are woven into the texture of salvation history. Christ began his public ministry by proclaiming the arrival of the great jubilee, the year of the Lord's favor predicted by the prophet Isaiah (Lk 4:16–30; cf. Is 61:1–2; *TMA* 11). We continue to live in this era of redemption, this jubilee season of grace and liberation. Just as the Scripture was fulfilled in the hearing of those gathered in the synagogue of Nazareth, so it is fulfilled anew in our hearing, if we will only listen. Every jubilee celebration of the Church recalls and reactivates the arrival of the fullness of time.

Like the Incarnation itself, the coming jubilee has a Marian as well as a Christological dimension. The child does not enter the world apart from Mary his blessed mother, the *theotokos*. In her pilgrimage of faith, hope, and love she blazes the trail on which the Church is to follow. She continues to go before the people of God (*RMat* 6, 25, 28), coming to the help of her clients who seek to rise above their sins and misery (*RMat* 51–52). Just as before the coming of Christ she was the "morning star" (*stella matutina*), so she remains, for us who are still on the journey of faith, the "star of the sea" (*stella maris*) guiding us through the dark journey toward the moment when faith will be transformed into the everlasting vision in which we look upon God our Savior "face to face" (*RMat* 6).

Notes

1. The letters *ORE* in parentheses refer *L'Osservatore Romano*, English edition. The abbreviation *PTM* in this chapter refers to *Papal Teachings on Our Lady* (Boston: Daughters of St. Paul, 1961).

2. Written intervention of September 1964, in AS III/2, 178–79.

3. Joint submission with the other bishops of Poland, about Sept. 1964, AS II/3, 856–57.

4. For news reports see Tim Unsworth, "Pope May Declare Mary 'Coredemptrix,'" *National Catholic Reporter*, 18 July 1997, 11–12; Kenneth L. Woodward, "Hail, Mary," *Newsweek*, August 25, 1997, 49–55.

5. See C. O. Vollert and J. B. Carol, "Mary, Blessed Virgin, II (in Theology)," *New Catholic Encyclopedia* 9:347–64; also Michael J. O'Carroll, *Theotokos: A Theological Encyclopedia of the Blessed Virgin Mary* (Wilmington, Del.: Michael Glazier, 1983), s.v. "Advocate," 5–6; "Mediation," 238–45; "Intercession, Mary's," 186–89; and "Redemption, Mary's Part in the," 305–9.

6. See *Confutatio* drawn up against the Augsburg Confession, quoted in *The One Mediator, The Saints, and Mary*, ed. H. George Anderson et al, (Augsburg: Minneapolis, 1992), 29, 342.

7. The only case since 1985 known to me is in a meditation on the Angelus given on October 6, 1991, commemorating the sixth centenary of the canonization of

St. Bridget of Sweden. Here the pope mentions that Bridget invoked Mary under various titles including that of "Coredemptrix." See *ORE*, 14 October 1991: 4.

8. Referring to the current drive for dogmatization, Kenneth Woodward writes, "In place of the Holy Trinity, it would appear, there would be a kind of Holy Quartet, with Mary playing the multiple roles of daughter of the Father, mother of the Son and spouse of the Holy Spirit," "Hail Mary," 49.

9. See John Paul's encyclical *Ut unum sint* §79 on the importance of ecumenical dialogue about the Virgin Mary.

10. "The pope will not solemnly proclaim Mary 'Coredemptrix' (Co-redeemer), 'Mediatrix' (Mediator), and 'Advocate,' Navarro-Valls said. 'This is crystal clear'"— CNS news dispatch of August 18, 1997; cf. *Catholic New York*, 21 August 1997.

19

Should the Church Repent?

April 15, 1998

I n his apostolic letter "On the Coming of the Third Millennium," dated November 10, 1994, Pope John Paul II said that while the great jubilee of the year 2000 is to be a time of joyful celebration, the joy should be based on forgiveness and reconciliation. It is therefore appropriate that the Church should prepare herself by recalling the sinfulness of her children. The Church, he said, cannot cross the threshold of the new millennium without encouraging them to repent and purify themselves of past errors and instances of infidelity, inconsistency, and slowness to act. He went on to speak of sins against Christian unity and of intolerance and violence in the service of truth. Turning to failures of our day, he asked Catholics to consider how much they had allowed themselves to be infected by the prevailing climate of secularism and relativism, thus contributing to the current crisis of obedience in the Church. He also called for an appraisal of the reception and implementation of the Second Vatican Council.[1]

JOHN PAUL'S PROPOSALS FOR REPENTANCE

The pope gathered up his thoughts on the theme most comprehensively in an unsigned twenty-three-page memorandum sent to the cardinals in the spring of 1994, in preparation for the consistory that met later in that year. This memorandum—which may well have been written by the pope himself[2]—was never published, but it was studied by all the cardinals and has been summarized and quoted in various places. It proposed "an attentive examination of the history of the second millennium in order to acknowledge the errors committed by its members and, in a certain sense, in the name of the Church."[3] "The Church," it says, "should be aware with ever greater clarity of how much the faithful have proven to be unfaithful throughout the centuries, sinning against Christ and his Gospel."[4]

The idea of acknowledging the faults of members of the Church, and especially of persons acting in the name of the Church, has been with John Paul II ever since his election to the papacy in the fall of 1978. Early in his pontificate he established a committee to reassess the condemnation of Galileo. This committee in 1984 reported its findings to the effect that Galileo's judges committed an "objective error" in rejecting a theory that later proved to be sound.[5] The memorandum of 1994, after alluding to this retraction, went on to speak of other cases in which the autonomy of the sciences might have been infringed. In addition, it declared, violence and undue pressure have been inflicted in the service of faith by the Inquisition, by religious wars, and by disregard of the rights of the human person.[6] In his opening address at the consistory John Paul II expressed his intention in the following strong words:

> With the approach of this Great Jubilee the Church needs a *metanoia*, that is, a discernment of the historical faults and failures of her members in responding to the demands of the gospel. Only the courageous admission of the faults and omissions of which Christians are judged to be guilty in some degree, and also the generous intention to make amends, with God's help, can provide an efficacious initiative for the new evangelization and make the path to unity easier.[7]

As a result of the pope's initiative, an immense program for the coming jubilee has been put in place. The first international meeting of the Central Committee for the Great Jubilee was held at the Vatican on February 15–16, 1996, with 107 delegates from national conferences of bishops and Catholic Eastern churches, and six additional delegates from sister churches.[8] Of the eight commissions for the jubilee, the one most directly concerned with the theme of repentance and conversion is the historico-theological commission, which has two sections, the historical and the theological. The historical section has opted to concentrate for the present on anti-Semitism and the Inquisition, leaving other questions for later study.

The historical section has already convened an international symposium on "The Roots of Anti-Judaism in the Christian Milieu," which met at the Gregorian University last fall. The purpose of this symposium was not to make a final declaration but to study the facts and present them to the pope. A month earlier, the Gregorian University had hosted an international symposium on the theological aftermath of Auschwitz. Shortly after these two symposia, on March 16, 1998, the Holy See's Commission on Religious Relations with the Jews released its document, "We Remember: A Reflection on the Shoah." This document expressed deep sorrow and repentance for the sins and failures of Christians during that terrible crisis.[9]

A similar symposium is planned on the theme of the Inquisition, or more correctly, the Inquisitions. The committee will have to face the delicate problem of evaluating the morality of judicial procedures that measured up, it would seem, to the standards of their day but failed to protect the rights of the accused and the freedom of consciences according to the standards of our own time. It will also have to consider the extent to which the Church was responsible for each Inquisition.

In a third phase, the Church's official self-examination will focus on the reception of Vatican II, especially the major thrust of its four great constitutions. Many other themes, besides, could figure in the Church's examination of conscience. An Italian journalist published in 1997 a book collecting no less than ninety-four statements of John Paul II expressing sorrow or repentance for corporate sins in which Catholics and other Christians have been implicated.[10] In addition to the two themes just mentioned, this book deals in other chapters with topics as diverse as the Crusades, dictatorships, divisions among Christians, discrimination against women, religious and secular wars, coercion of consciences, colonial oppression, black and Indian slavery, the Mafia, the genocide in Rwanda, and resistance to new scientific discoveries (Galileo, Darwin, and others). The pope's statements on these points are quite diverse in character, as might be expected because of differences in the Church's relationship to each of these issues. It would be too much to say that in each case the pope has pronounced a *mea culpa* on behalf of the Church.

Among the steps to be taken the pope generally proposes one or more of the following: beseeching God's forgiveness, asking forgiveness from others who have been injured, extending forgiveness to them for any harm they may have inflicted on Catholics, a firm purpose of amendment regarding the future, and what the pope calls the "purification" or "healing" of memories, which would be hoped for as the result of all the preceding.

The pope's proposals for repentance raise some very difficult theological questions that are being debated by experts all over the world. At the consistory of 1994, many cardinals are said to have expressed misgivings. Shortly after the consistory, Cardinal Giacomo Biffi, archbishop of Bologna, detailed his reservations in a book, *Christus Hodie*, published in 1995. In the United States, Professor Mary Ann Glendon of Harvard Law School has voiced some reservations, and in England the journalist-historian Paul Johnson has expressed his dismay that the pope is taking part in what Johnson describes as the charade of bogus apologies. On the basis of these and other comments I should like to discuss under seven headings some common objections and some possible replies.

THE HOLINESS OF THE CHURCH

The Church, some contend, cannot repent, for it is always holy. According to Cardinal Biffi, the Church, considered in the very truth of its being, has no sins, because it is Christ's Mystical Body. We belong to the "total Christ" insofar as we are holy, not insofar as we lack holiness. Our sins are, so to speak, "ontologically extraecclesial," since they place us in opposition to the very nature of the Church.[11]

The distinction between the Church as holy and its members as sinful has a long and venerable history. Biffi is able to quote from St. Ambrose the sentence, "The Church is wounded not in itself but in us" (*Non in se sed in nobis Ecclesia vulneratur*).[12] Pius XII in his encyclical on the Mystical Body of Christ maintained that the Church is holy in her sacraments, her deposit of faith, her divinely given constitution, and the gifts and graces by which the Holy Spirit continues to work in her. "It cannot be laid to her charge," he concluded, "if some members fall weak or wounded."[13] The Second Vatican Council, following Pius XII, carefully avoided speaking of the Church itself as sinful or as committing sins. The great ecclesiologist Charles Journet, in an article on the ecclesiology of Vatican II, pointed out that while from a purely empirical point of view the Church may appear to be sinful, the eye of faith is able to discern that the Church in its theological reality as Body of Christ is sinless, albeit not without sinners.[14]

Some theologians respond to Cardinal Biffi's position by contesting the distinction he is making. Joseph Komonchak, for example, contends that the distinction implies that the Church as sacrament of Christ is some vague transcendent reality, far off in the empyrean.[15] But this charge is unfair, since Journet and Biffi are talking about the Church here on earth. They prefer to define it in terms of its formal principles and in terms of what its members are at their best and are called to become. But the Church may also be described more concretely and empirically as it appears in history, with its admixture of good and evil, saints and sinners. Although these two perspectives on the Church are different, neither can be called wrong.

Theologians of both groups can acknowledge that while sin is present in the Church, the Church is not related in the same way to holiness and sin. She exists most perfectly in Mary and the saints, who live according to the inner law of her being and exemplify her true nature. They are most receptive to the Church's faith and sacraments, and to the guidance of the Holy Spirit, who has been poured forth upon her. Members of the Church who fall into sin and error are less intimately united with the Church. Serious sin, indeed, erects a barrier between the sinner and the Church and may even in some cases result in excommunication. By obtaining absolution from their sins, the members become reconciled and reunited not only with God but also with the Church.

John Paul II's proposal does not require the attribution of sin to the Church. He seems, indeed, to concede what Cardinal Biffi asserts about the holiness of the Church. In the documents we are considering, he takes pains to avoid saying that the Church itself has sinned. Although he has at least once spoken of the Church as "holy and sinful,"[16] the pope's normal practice is to attribute sin more precisely to the "members" or "children" of the Church. In addressing the symposium at the Gregorian University on the roots of anti-Judaism in November 1997, he spoke of prejudices and erroneous views in the "Christian world" and explicitly declared that he was not ascribing them to the Church as such.[17]

Even so, however, sin exists within the Church. Affected as they are by the secular culture of their day and by the weight of their own fallen humanity, the members resist the truth and goodness that the Church by her nature tends to instill in them. Whether they be popes, bishops, priests, religious, or laity, they can be unfaithful not only individually but also corporately, and even sometimes when claiming to act in the name of the Church. The Church is injured and contaminated by their conduct. Vatican II could therefore declare that the Church, "embracing sinners in her bosom, is at the same time holy and always in need of being purified, and incessantly pursues the path of penance and renewal" (*LG* 8). She does collective penance in seasons such as Lent. A corporate examination of conscience is therefore very much in order.

COLLECTIVE GUILT

A second objection is that contrition on the part of the Church involves the concept of collective guilt, which is theoretically questionable and practically dangerous. According to the general teaching of Catholic theologians, sin in the proper sense of the word is always the choice of an individual, personal will, and therefore cannot be imputed to the Church or any other collective subject.[18] In the words of John Paul II, "There is nothing so personal and untransferable in each individual as merit for virtue or responsibility for sin."[19]

The concept of collective guilt has been responsible for great evils in history, such as blaming the Jews as a people for the crucifixion of Jesus. Vatican II, attempting to overcome this misunderstanding, declared that the sufferings of Jesus could not be charged against all the Jews living at that time, still less against the Jews of today.[20] Ed Koch, onetime mayor of New York, in a newspaper column, recently wrote, "Blaming Christians for the Holocaust would be as unjustified as holding Jews accountable for the death of Jesus. Individuals were responsible in both situations."[21] Thus it must be asked: is the pope reintroducing the unfortunate concept of collective guilt?

As a first approach to an answer, we may perhaps turn to the Bible. In certain texts God is apparently portrayed as punishing the whole people for the sins of a few. A Jewish author, in a current journal article, writes: "God views the People Israel as an eternal community, not just as disconnected individuals. We are all responsible for all. . . . Maybe to emphasize our interconnectedness, the Lord does not practice precision bombing."[22] In the later books of the Old Testament, however, the prophets insist that the Israelites of their day are not being punished for sins they did not themselves commit. Jeremiah declares: "Each one shall die for his own sin" (Jer 31:30). Ezekiel says still more explicitly: "The son shall not suffer for the iniquity of the father, nor the father suffer for the iniquity of the son; the righteousness of the righteous shall be upon himself, and the wickedness of the wicked shall be upon himself" (Ezek 18:20).

In our eagerness to avoid the concept of collective guilt, we should be on guard against exaggerated individualism. Every sin has social ramifications. It lowers the moral level of the society to which the sinner belongs. In so doing it contributes to structural evils that afflict society at every level: families, neighborhoods, and nations. These "social sins," as John Paul II teaches, are the result of the accumulation of many personal sins.[23] We are all inclined to accept, support, and even exploit the structural evils of the society to which we belong. To a greater or lesser degree we are implicated in the materialism, consumerism, and prejudices of our culture and in its violent and discriminatory tendencies. Sins such as anti-Semitism and racism have been more than merely individual aberrations.

Evils committed by Christians, especially if they are frequent or habitual and are done in the name of the Church, are very damaging to the Church's mission. In its Pastoral Constitution on the Church in the Modern World, Vatican II notes that believers, "to the extent that they neglect their own training in the faith, or teach erroneous doctrine, or are deficient in their religious, moral, or social life . . . must be said to conceal, rather than reveal, the authentic features of God and religion" (*GS* 19). The Decree on Ecumenism says that as a result of the failure of Catholics to live by the revealed truth and the sacraments, "the radiance of the Church's face shines less brightly in the eyes of our separated brethren and of the world at large, and the growth of God's kingdom is retarded" (*UR* 4).

To regret the past and to ask pardon is not necessarily to judge oneself guilty. It implies only that we stand in some kind of solidarity with those who have done wrong. Thus parents can ask forgiveness for the misbehavior of their children, or children for that of their parents, and even be ashamed of it, without feeling culpable for that misconduct.

In the case of the Church we must recognize not only our moral solidarity with other members but also what may be called mystical solidarity. As fellow members of the one Body of Christ, we are bound together in a single organic whole. We benefit from one another's merits and suffer from one another's faults.[24] As Paul writes in First Corinthians: "If one member suffers, all suffer together; if one member is honored, all rejoice together. Now you are the body of Christ and individually members of it" (1 Cor 12:26–27). More than any merely social or political group, the Church retains her identity through time. Richard John Neuhaus has eloquently written: "In the Church, the dead are not dead; in Christ we live in communion with all who are in Christ—past, present, and future. We are implicated in the weakness of sinners as, happily, we are implicated in the holiness of the saints."[25]

JUDGING THE PAST

Penitence for offenses committed long ago involves a further difficulty. We are in no position to judge the culpability of persons who lived in past centuries and in cultures foreign to our own. In the words of Paul Johnson, "There is something repellent, as well as profoundly unhistorical, about judging the past by the standards and prejudices of another age."[26] When we attempt such judgments, he says, we place ourselves in a position of moral superiority, and thus our expression of repentance is really a disguised manifestation of pride.

In responding to this difficulty we may follow the general line taken by the papal theologian Georges Cottier, O.P. It is true, he says, that we cannot judge the subjective guilt of our predecessors centuries ago. But without pretending that we are morally superior, we can judge that they made certain mistakes. Their moral failures may have been extenuated or excused by their good faith. Nevertheless it is still proper for us, their successors, to express sorrow for the objective wrongness of what they did. Without judging the subjective guilt of our forebears we can say that some of their actions were objectively wrong and deserve to be disavowed.[27]

APOLOGIZING FOR THE FAULTS OF OTHERS

Regardless of whether the evil actions were committed in our own or in another culture, say the objectors, it is artificial and insincere to apologize for the misdeeds of other persons. Paul Johnson, in the article already referred to, says that the modern fashion of public breast-beating has not one iota of genuine sincerity in it. These "bogus apologies" in his judgement are "disguised attempts to gain moral kudos at the expense" of others. Regrettably, he remarks, even the pope seems to be taking part in this charade.

Such apologies are very much in vogue among the politicians of our day. Mayor Giuliani of New York has recently apologized to the Jewish community of Crown Heights for the failure of the city administration under Mayor Dinkins to have prevented the riots in 1991, and some blacks are asking him to apologize for the injuries they suffered in the same incident. President Clinton has come close to apologizing for the involvement of Americans in the slave trade. To whom are such apologies due? How far back in time should one go? Should the mayor of Milan, asks Cardinal Biffi, make amends for the misdeeds of the Sforzas in the fifteenth century? Or should the Spaniards apologize to the English for the Great Armada, to use one of Johnson's examples?

In reply, it must be said in the first place that apologies to other people are not the true intent of the pope's proposal. Declarations of repentance are quite another matter, since repentance is directed primarily to God, from whom forgiveness must ultimately come. Repentance would seem to be singularly appropriate for the Church as a people uniquely called to holiness. Commenting on the "Declaration of Repentance" issued last fall by a group of French bishops, Jean Duchesne observes that, because of misleading stories in the press, the Declaration was "interpreted as a purely human business, where God virtually need not have been mentioned, [with the result] that the fundamentally religious and spiritual substance has too often been overlooked."[28]

When we repent for corporate misdeeds, we acknowledge that we are not morally superior but are in some way implicated. Jesus indicated that the Pharisees of his day were guilty of the same faults as those who persecuted the prophets (Mt 23:29–33). In a similar way, we would do well to acknowledge that we are tempted to adopt the ecclesiastical narrowness and pride that have afflicted some Christians in the past. Unless we explicitly disavow such attitudes, we can hardly avoid succumbing to them.

By concentrating on religious repentance, it is possible to circumvent the complex problems involved in apologies. The farther we go back in time, the more questionable apologies become. If the Inquisition violated the human rights of certain defendants, repentance may be in order even though we cannot identify any living person who could receive our apology or grant forgiveness. But if the offended parties still exist, there is nothing to prevent the Church from apologizing to them, making amends, and asking their forgiveness.

THE RISK OF SCANDAL

Cardinal Biffi and others further object that in calling for ecclesiastical penance, the faithful, especially those who are young or less educated, will be scandalized and confused. They might draw the conclusion that the Church is not holy and is not a reliable guide.

In reply, it should be mentioned in the first place that the pope is not proposing confessions of doctrinal error, but only confessions of failure to act according to the Church's standards of belief and conduct. The proposal does not call into question the holiness of the Church or the reliability of her message. But the Church has always admitted that her members, whether ordained or lay, commit sins and practical blunders. Every Christian, even though he be a priest, a bishop, or a pope, daily says the prayer, "Forgive us our sins as we forgive those who sin against us."

While some Catholics are perhaps scandalized by admissions of fault, others are scandalized rather by the refusal to admit such faults. They reproach their fellow Christians for what they see as their constant tendency to justify everything that has been done by their coreligionists, especially by persons purporting to act in the name of the Church. The repentance proposed by the pope can perhaps remove this source of scandal.

EXPLOITATION BY HOSTILE CRITICS

Still others object that admissions of fault on the part of the Church would play into the hands of the Church's enemies. At the consistory of 1994 some bishops from Eastern Europe are said to have remonstrated that the proposed declarations of contrition would support the charges made by atheistic Communism to the effect the Church has consistently impeded human progress. Mary Ann Glendon warns of the danger that "sincere expressions of regret" on the part of Catholics may be "opportunistically exploited by persons or groups who are only too eager to help the Church rend her garments and to heap more ashes on the heads of Catholics." "Let us be vigilant," she writes, "to prevent [our public acts of repentance] from being hijacked or exploited."[29]

Thus far, in the statements dealing with matters such as the Galileo case and the Holocaust, Church officials have been careful to guard against exaggerations. In the case of the Holy See's statement on the Holocaust, some were dissatisfied because it did not condemn the alleged failure of Pius XII to speak out with sufficient clarity on the subject. For some critics of the Church, as Professor Glendon says, "no apology will ever be enough until Catholics apologize themselves into nonexistence."[30]

Our aim cannot be to appease the implacable foes of the Church, who will complain no matter what is done. But the fear that others will take advantage of our repentance should not deter us from doing what is morally required of us. While hostile critics will be dissatisfied, many persons of good will be appreciative.

BENEFITS TO BE EXPECTED

Finally it is asked, what purposes would be achieved by such acts of repentance? Since there is no way of undoing the past, would it not be better to let bygones be bygones rather than dredge up painful memories? From a study of the documents, I believe it is possible to distinguish a variety of benefits.

First, there is the purely religious goal of conversion and reconciliation with God. There can be no holiness without conversion and no conversion without acknowledgment of an unworthy and sinful past. In becoming aware that we belong to a community that has frequently failed its divine Lord, and in so doing failed other human groups, we are delivered from unwholesome pride. Relieved of the compulsion to defend the whole record of the past, we are less inclined to make scapegoats out of others. Freed from unrealistic perfectionism, we can turn humbly to God with the realization that his forgiving love is the only true source of our security.

In the second place, corporate penance has an ecumenical goal. Since the faults of Catholics have unquestionably contributed to Christian divisions, repentance may facilitate the path to reunion. In his encyclical on ecumenism, John Paul II speaks of the need to overcome our clannish exclusiveness, our reluctance to forgive, our pride, our presumptuous disdain, and our unevangelical proclivity to condemn the other side.[31] By repentance and mutual forgiveness Christians of different ecclesial bodies can heal the smoldering resentments that derive from actions committed centuries ago, such as the mutual condemnations of Rome and Constantinople, the sack of Constantinople, the martyrdoms of the Reformation period, and the massacre of St. Bartholomew's Day.

Thirdly, the proposed action would assist the new evangelization for which John Paul II has repeatedly called. Evangelization is not a matter of self-promotion on the part of the Church's members. Far from seeking to persuade the world of their own perfection, Christians acknowledge that they are at best unprofitable servants. Like Paul, they proclaim not themselves but Christ and him crucified, to the glory of God most high. If any of us are inclined to boast, let us imitate Paul by boasting of our weakness so that the power of Christ may dwell in us (cf. 2 Cor 12:9). We do not ask others to join a flawless community but to enter into a vast company of sinners who find redemption and forgiveness in Christ. He, the treasure of the Church and the light of the world, deigns to speak and act in us and to incorporate us, unworthy though we be, in his body here below, his holy Church.

As the Church purifies herself from sin and the effects of sin, she grows into deeper union with her divine Lord and advances toward her heavenly goal, where Christ and the saints now dwell in glory. By putting off the encumbrances of worldly attachments, the Church makes herself ever more transparent to the Lord, who lives in her so that she may live in him. The kingdom of God, already present in mystery, is obscured by tepidity and infidelity but is made powerfully present by penance and renewal. The program of contrition and reconciliation initiated by John Paul II is therefore charged with hope and promise. Faithfully carried out, it could usher in a new springtime of Christian life.

NOTES

1. John Paul II, *On the Coming of the Third Millennium*: apostolic letter "*Tertio Millennio Adveniente*" 33–36 (Washington, D.C.: United States Catholic Conference, 1994), pp. 42–48.

2. Luigi Accattoli, in his *When a Pope Asks Forgiveness* (New York: Alba House, 1998), 58, gives strong reasons for holding that the author of the memorandum is indeed the pope himself.

3. Quoted ibid., 57.

4. Ibid.

5. See the quotation from Cardinal Paul Poupard, president of the Pontifical Council for Culture, *Origins* 19 (October 26, 1989): 340.

6. Quoted in *When a Pope Asks Forgiveness*, 57.

7. Ibid., 58.

8. Ibid., 71.

9. Commission for Religious Relations with the Jews, "We Remember: A Reflection on the Shoah," *Origins* 27 (March 26, 1998): 669–75; cf. Avery Dulles, "The Church and the Shoah," *America* 178 (April 4, 1998): 3–4.

10. *When a Pope Asks Forgiveness*, xv.

11. According to the English translation of Accattoli's book, Cardinal Biffi said that the sins of Christians are "in their essence are outside the Church" (64). Joseph A. Komonchak, however, translates Biffi's term as "ontologically extra-ecclesial." See his "Preparing for the New Millennium," *Logos: A Journal of Catholic Thought and Culture* 1 (Summer 1997): 34–55, at 46.

12. Ambrose, *De virginitate* 8:48. In his commentary on Luke, Ambrose spoke of the Church as *casta meretrix* (chaste prostitute). Cardinal Biffi, in his *Casta Meretrix: Saggio sull'ecclesiologia di Ambrogio* (Euntes docete 41; Casale Monferrato: Piemme, 1996), shows that this phase cannot properly be used to prove that the Church is "*simul justa et peccatrix*," as Hans Küng, for example, suggests in *The Church* (New York: Sheed & Ward, 1967), 328.

13. Pius XII, *The Mystical Body of Christ*: encyclical "*Mystici Corporis*," 66; *The Papal Encyclicals 1939–1958*, ed. Claudia Carlen (Wilmington: N. C.: McGrath, 1981), 50. The official text, without numbered paragraphs, appears in *Acta apostolicae sedis* 35 (1943): 193–248, at 225.

14. Charles Journet, "Le caractère théandrique de l'Église," *L'Église de Vatican II*, Unam Sanctam 51b (Paris: Cerf, 1967), 299–311, especially 310–11. Journet here refers to his own longer discussion of the "sinless Church not without sinners" in *L'Église du Verbe incarné* (Paris: Cerf, 1962), 2:1,115–28.

15. Komonchak, "Preparing for the New Millennium," 50.

16. John Paul II, at a prayer vigil at Fatima on May 12, 1982, referred to "the Church, living, holy, and sinful"; *L'Osservatore Romano*, 31 May 1982. See Komonchak, "Preparing for the New Millennium," 54 n. 10.

17. John Paul II, "The Roots of Anti-Judaism," *Origins* 27 (November 13, 1997): 365–67, at 365.

18. Francis A. Sullivan, in his *The Church We Believe In* (New York: Paulist, 1988), remarks at 82, "Although persons entrusted with leadership in the church, even at the highest levels, can be guilty of grave sin in their personal lives and even when

they are acting in the name of the church, it is not correct to say that in such a case the church commits sin. The commission of sin is always the choice of a personal free will."

19. John Paul II, apostolic exhortation *Reconciliatio et Paenitentia* §16 (Boston: St. Paul Books and Media, n.d), 36.

20. Vatican II, Declaration on Non-Christian Religions, *Nostra aetate*, 4.

21. Ed Koch, "Vatican Apology Is a Gesture Jews Should Accept," New York *Daily News*, 27 March 1998, 53.

22. David Klinghoffer, "Anti-Semitism Without Anti-Semites," *First Things* 82 (April 1998): 10–13, at 12.

23. John Paul II, *Reconciliatio et paenitentia* §16, 39.

24. The Vatican Commission in "We Remember," §5, declared: "As members of the Church we are linked to the sins as well as the merits of all her children," 674.

25. Richard John Neuhaus, "Apologies on the Cheap," *First Things* 82 (April 1998), 63–64, at 64.

26. Paul Johnson, "And Another Thing," *Spectator*, 8 November 1997, 8.

27. "Although good faith excuses, this does not mean that any behavior which we disapprove of today could have been objectively correct in its time," Georges Cottier, O.P., "La Chiesa davanti alla Conversione," in *Tertio Millennio Adveniente: Testo e Commento Teologico-Pastorale* (Cinisello Balsamo: San Paolo, 1996); quoted in *When a Pope Asks Forgiveness*, 70.

28. Jean Duchesne, "Letter from Paris," *First Things* 80 (February 1998): 12–14, at 12.

29. Mary Ann Glendon, "Contrition in the Age of Spin Control," *First Things* 77 (November 1997): 10–12, at 12.

30. Ibid.

31. John Paul II, encyclical *Ut Unum Sint*, §15.

20

Human Rights

The United Nations and Papal Teaching

November 18, 1998

THE UNIVERSAL DECLARATION

On December 10 of this year, the world will be celebrating the fiftieth anniversary of the Universal Declaration of Human Rights, which was adopted with unanimous approval by the United Nations General Assembly in 1948.[1] The cornerstone of the Declaration was article 3, proclaiming the right to life, liberty, and security of the person. Articles 4–21 went on to specify other civil and political rights. Articles 22–27 dealt with a series of economic, social, and cultural rights. All these rights were laid down as "a common standard of achievement for all peoples and all nations."

The Universal Declaration was only the first part of a prospective International Bill of Human Rights. It was followed in 1966 by two important covenants: The International Covenant on Economic, Social, and Cultural Rights and the International Covenant on Civil and Political Rights. In 1993 the UN-sponsored World Conference on Human Rights adopted the Vienna Declaration and Programme of Action. These instruments agree in affirming that "all human rights derive from the dignity and worth inherent in the human person" (to repeat the language of the Vienna Declaration). The rights and freedoms set forth in the international covenants are to be implemented in the measure possible, but are subject to limitations as needed to protect national security, public order, public health or morals, and the rights and freedoms of other persons.[2]

The remarkable consensus reflected in these documents was the product of generations of political thought in which the medieval natural law tradition was filtered through modern democratic theory and enhanced by the personalist philosophy that flourished in the years following World War II. The atrocities of dictatorships such as Hitler's gave strong motivation to spell out binding norms that would limit the naked power of the State.

CATHOLIC TEACHING ON HUMAN RIGHTS

The Catholic Church in the twentieth century has developed its own body of teaching on human rights. The groundwork was laid by the encyclicals of Leo XIII on the rights of labor and those of Pius XI on the economy and on the oppressive regimes of his day (Communism, Fascism, and National Socialism). During the Second World War, Pius XII, looking forward to a new world order, called for a recognition of the rights that flowed from the dignity of the person both as created in the image of God and as called to participate by grace in God's eternal blessedness. In his Christmas Radio Address of 1942, Pius XII proposed a list of basic personal rights, including the rights to life, to religious freedom, to family life, to work, to choose a vocation, and to make proper use of material goods.[3]

After World War II, Catholics such as Jacques Maritain cooperated in the writing of the Universal Declaration. The future Pope John XXIII, in his capacity as nuncio at Paris and permanent observer at UNESCO, interested himself in the work of the Commission on Human Rights.[4] Thus it is not surprising that later, in his encyclical *Pacem in terris* (1962), he spoke approvingly of the UN Declaration, calling it "an act of the highest importance" and "an important step forward on the path toward the juridico-political organization of the world community" (*PT* 143, 144). In the same encyclical, John XXIII set forth a comprehensive and detailed charter of human rights based on natural law. With numerous quotations from Pius XII, Pope John emphasized freedom of conscience, freedom of assembly, freedom of migration and the right to take part in public affairs—all of which had appeared in the Universal Declaration. He also pointed out that these rights involve correlative duties, which are likewise enjoined by natural law.

Vatican II, especially in its Pastoral Constitution on the Church in the Modern World, took up the teaching of John XXIII and amplified it in the light of divine revelation. Only in Christ, it insisted, can the dignity of the human person be rightly understood (*GS* 22). The human person, standing above the rest of visible creation, has inviolable rights and duties. Among these the council listed "everything necessary for living a life truly human, such as food, clothing, and shelter; the right to choose a state of life freely and to found a family, the right to education, to employment, to a good reputation, to respect, to appropriate information, to activity in accord with the upright norm of one's own conscience, to protection of privacy and to rightful freedom in matters religious too" (*GS* 26). In the following section (*GS* 27) the council set forth an extensive list of violations of human rights, including abortion, euthanasia, slavery, and other social evils.

In his encyclical *Populorum progressio* (1967) and in his apostolic letter *Octogesima adveniens* (1971), Paul VI attempted to apply Catholic social teaching to new problems such as industrialization, urbanization, the migration of peoples, and discrimination. He welcomed the progress that had been made in incorporating human rights into international agreements, but noted the persistence of actual discrimination and exploitation (*OA* 23). He called for a true humanism that opens itself to the Absolute, thereby giving human life its true meaning (*PP* 42).

John Paul II on Human Rights

Of all the popes in history, none has given so much emphasis to human rights as John Paul II. While continuing to affirm their basis in natural law as known to reason, he proclaims that Christ and the gospel constitute the true and adequate foundation of human rights. All peoples, he says, are called to open themselves to the Christian message, in which alone the meaning of human existence becomes clear.

John Paul II frequently speaks of the Universal Declaration of Human Rights. In his first encyclical, *Redemptor hominis* (1979), he described it as a "magnificent effort" to establish the objective and inviolable rights of persons, including the freedom of religion (*RH* 17). Again in his United Nations address of October 2, 1979, he spoke of the Universal Declaration as "a milestone on the long and difficult path of the human race" (§7). He particularly warned against the Declaration being subjugated to political interests and the thirst for power. In his UN address of October 5, 1995, he called the Universal Declaration "one of the highest expressions of the human conscience of our time" (§2). And in his message for World Peace Day, January 1, 1998, he took note of the fiftieth anniversary of the Declaration and warned that it "must be observed integrally both in its spirit and letter" (§2).

On various occasions, the pope has proposed lists of rights that are, as he says, universally recognized. At the UN in 1979 he began, as does the Universal Declaration, with the rights to life, liberty, and security of person. He went on to include most of the commonly recognized political, civil, social, and economic rights. These rights, according to the pope, always concern the full realization of the human person (§13). Violation of such rights, in his view, is "a form of warfare against humanity" (§16).

The problem of human rights was crucial to the thinking of John Paul II long before he became pope. As he mentioned in one of his speeches at Vatican II (September 28, 1965), his experience in Poland taught him that the dialogue with Marxism can most fruitfully begin with anthropology and specifically with the dignity of the human person. He developed his Thomistic brand of personalism in his early books *Love and Responsibility* and *The Acting Person*. In each of these books he emphasizes the self-constitution of the person through free and responsible activity.

In expounding the philosophical foundation of human rights John Paul II insists that they do not derive from positive law, either human or divine, but are inscribed in the very nature of reality. From the prohibitions in the "second tablet" of the Ten Commandments we might get the impression that our obligations to other human beings are simply imposed by divine decree. But John Paul II points out that these commandments are simply the reverse side of the positive commandment to love our neighbor. He quotes from the *Catechism of the Catholic Church*: "The Ten Commandments are part of God's Revelation. At the same time, they teach us the true humanity of man. They bring to light the essential duties, and therefore, indirectly, the fundamental rights inherent in the nature of the human person" (*CCC* 2070; cf. *Veritatis splendor* 13). When we are commanded not to murder, commit adultery, steal, bear false witness, and the like, these negative rules, according to the pope, "express with particular force the ever urgent need to protect human life, the communion of persons in marriage, private property, truthfulness and people's good name" (*VS* 13).

In his philosophy of the person, John Paul II sets forth the ontological foundation of human rights. A person, he teaches, is an individual of a rational nature with an inner spiritual life. Because persons are intelligent and free, they exist with a certain independence. No one else can decide for me what I will do and intend.[5]

From the fact that we are thinking subjects capable of making decisions on our own, it follows that we must be allowed to determine our own activity. Even God, who could overrule our freedom, allows each of us to decide whether to seek him or to reject him. Freedom, of course, brings obligations with it. I am bound in conscience to adhere to what I find to be truly good and reject what I am able to discern as evil.

Among the primary obligations of conscience, John Paul II reckons responsibility toward fellow human beings. All human persons, since they are endowed with the same rational nature, are fundamentally equal. It is immoral to turn persons into slaves or otherwise exploit them, though of course they may be required to contribute by their labor to the common good. The common good is a goal shared by all members of the society, whether that society be a family, a voluntary association, or a political unit. Since it redounds to the advantage of each member, the common good is not a limitation on human rights but an enhancement. It gives the members of the community greater opportunities to achieve their personal self-realization and solidifies their mutual union.

The first and most fundamental right of the human being, according to John Paul II, is to be respected as a person. By the natural law we are bound to will the good of others, and in that sense to love them. No matter how evil others may be, I can have no right to hate them, or to will them to suffer harm. In *Love and Responsibility* Wojtyla sets forth what he calls the personalistic principle, namely that the only suitable attitude toward a person is love.[6] If we love a person, he holds, we will be just to that person.[7] Negatively stated, the principle implies that a person may not be treated simply as an object of pleasure or convenience.[8]

Particular rights flow in various ways from the value of the person. Justice, unlike love, goes out not directly to the person but to things, such as food, shelter, and reputation.[9] Declarations of human rights set forth the immunities and entitlements that normally flow from the condition of being human, but of course their implementation varies according to particular circumstances. In legislative and policy decisions public authorities are required to heed the demands of the natural law and never to violate "the fundamental and inalienable rights of the human person" (*VS* 97).

In the light of Christian revelation, John Paul II solidifies and expands the basis for human rights. Their obligatory character, he points out, arises because the natural law is not a mere accident of nature but reflects the eternal law of God, from whom all moral obligations derive. Only God, the supreme good, constitutes the unshakable foundation and essential condition of morality (*VS* 99).

The transcendent dignity of the human person derives most fundamentally from being created as a visible image of the invisible God. More than this, we are "redeemed by the blood of Christ, and made holy by the presence of the Holy Spirit" (*VS* 10). Our human dignity is fully revealed in Christ, whose sacrifice eloquently expresses how precious we are in the eyes of the Creator. Tarnished by sin, our dignity is definitively restored through the cross and shown forth in the resurrection (cf. *RH* 10).

SPECIFIC RIGHTS

Certain particular human rights come to the fore in the teaching of John Paul II. Among them first place should no doubt be accorded to the right to life, which is the principal theme of his long encyclical, *Evangelium vitae* (1995). Here he teaches that because human life has a sacred and inviolable character, it is gravely immoral to destroy innocent human life. He then applies this general principle with special emphasis to two cases: abortion and euthanasia, both of which he brands as heinous crimes. In his discussion of abortion he warns against experimentation on embryos, and in treating of euthanasia he rejects the legitimacy of suicide and physician-assisted suicide. He admits that in self-defense it may sometimes be necessary to kill aggressors and he concedes, very reluctantly, that capital punishment may sometimes be required to protect society against criminals.

In his apostolic exhortation on the family, *Familiaris consortio* (1981), John Paul II eloquently defends what he calls the "inviolable rights of the family" as "the basic cell of society" (*FC* 46). Summarizing the recommendations of the Synod of Bishops the previous year, he calls for a charter of family rights (ibid.). The Holy See did in fact draw up such a charter, and released it in November 1983. In its long list of rights it included the right to marry, to have children, to educate children in accordance with one's moral and religious convictions, and to choose schools for them.[10]

In his encyclical on labor, *Laborem exercens* (1981), the pope takes up the right to work in the framework of human rights as a whole. Adopting a personalist approach, he rejects the treatment of workers as mere means of production and insists that work should, as far as possible, benefit the workers themselves. He defends the importance of trade unions, provided that they behave responsibly rather than as mere power blocs promoting particular interests. Among the rights of working people, he mentions adequate leisure, health care, and insurance against accidents and old age.

On many occasions John Paul II has called for the application of human rights to international relations. For example, in his 1979 speech at the United Nations he traced the scourge of war to the denial of human rights, which, he said, "destroys the organic unity of the social order and then affects the whole system of international relations" (§11). Only through safeguarding the full rights of every human being, he said, can peace be ensured at its very roots (§19).

In his second social encyclical, *Sollicitudo rei socialis* (1987), John Paul II spoke of human rights in connection with international social and economic development. He protested against the tendency to look only to the material aspects of development rather than to personal rights in their full range (*SRS* 33). More attention, he said, should be given to cultural, political, and simply human rights, including religious freedom, the right to share in the building of society, and freedom to take initiatives in economic matters (*SRS* 15).

In his third social encyclical, *Centesimus annus* (1991), written to celebrate the hundredth anniversary of Leo XIII's *Rerum novarum*, John Paul II praises the way in which documents such as the Universal Declaration of Human Rights shifted the center of the social question to the international level, but he expresses disappointment at the failure of the UN to establish, thus far, effective means for the resolution of international conflicts (*CA* 21). Welcoming the resurgence of democratic regimes in formerly Communist parts of Europe, he proposes once again a list of basic human rights similar to those he had enumerated in his first UN address (*CA* 47). On several occasions the pope has called for international juridical structures that effectively safeguard the fundamental rights of individuals and communities.[11]

VOICES OPPOSED TO HUMAN RIGHTS

The Universal Declaration has been enormously influential. In the words of Professor Henry Steiner of Harvard Law School, "No other document has so caught the historical moment, achieved the same moral and rhetorical force, or exerted so much influence on the [human rights] movement as a whole."[12] The principles of the Declaration have been built into many international treaties and into new constitutions of states in Africa, Asia, Latin America, and Europe. Its influence was crucial in the peaceful elimination of apartheid in South Africa.

The success, however, is far from complete. Repression, slavery, torture, and even genocide still go on in many parts of the world. These evils cannot be overcome without a deeper commitment and a broader consensus than now exist. The philosophical foundations of human rights are increasingly called into question. Several pervasive objections call for special consideration.

Some historical scholars dismiss the human rights movement as the product of Enlightenment individualism. Alasdair MacIntyre, for example, denies that human rights have any basis in Hebrew thought or in classical or medieval philosophy, let alone in Arabic or Asiatic culture. The truth, he says, is plain: "There are no such rights, and belief in them is one with belief in witches and unicorns."[13]

While we may concede that the idea of human rights did not explicitly surface until modern times, the concept of human dignity, from which such rights follow, is very ancient. As philosophers such as Jacques Maritain have argued, the medieval natural law tradition implicitly contains the idea of human rights.[14] On the other hand, the tradition stemming from Thomas Hobbes and John Locke undermines the very concept of human rights. John Courtney Murray correctly stated:

> The individualism of Locke's law of nature results in a complete evacuation of the notion of the "rights" of man. It is quite evident that Locke's state of nature reveals no *ordo juris*, and no rights in any recognizably moral

sense. There is simply a pattern of power relationships—the absolute lord-ship of one individual balanced against the equally absolute lordship of others. Significantly, Locke uses the word "power" more frequently than the word "right" in describing the state of nature.[15]

The Catholic doctrine of human rights, therefore, is not based on Lockean empiricism or individualism. It has a more ancient and distin-guished pedigree.

A second line of objection comes from relativism and pragmatism. In 1997, the head of the Chinese government, Jiang Zemin, argued that since all is relative in the world of politics, there is no way of judging whether it is better to protect or punish dissidents.[16] The American philosopher Richard Rorty, while expressing a predilection for what he calls "our Eu-rocentric human rights culture," dismisses what he calls "human rights foundationalism."[17] Fraternity, he says, is a sentiment that can be induced by education but not a belief that can be supported by a theory. In his pragmatist philosophy there is no way of ascertaining whether belief in human rights is any more valid than the doctrine of Nietzsche, who looked on universal human rights as a device enabling the weak and de-generate to protect themselves against the strong, whose domination over the weak is the goal of human history. Rorty furnishes no grounds for asserting the objective superiority of the "Eurocentric human rights cul-ture" over racist cultures that would deny human rights to certain classes of persons, such as blacks in pre–Civil War America or Jews in Nazi Germany. Although he favors the protection of the weak and the op-pressed, the "human rights culture" in his system appears to be nothing more than a culturally conditioned prejudice. Relativism and pragmatism represent regressions from the Universal Declaration and subsequent cov-enants, which insist that human rights are objective since they rest on the inherent dignity of the human person.

Thinkers of a third school reject the idea of human rights on the ground that they rest upon a rigid moralism that interferes with the at-tainment of limited human objectives.[18] Flexibility and compromise, they contend, are often needed for success in social, political, and international relations.

This objection might be valid if all rights were absolutized. But the idea of human rights allows for great variety in its practical applications. While genuine rights must always be respected, the requirement of affirmative action varies greatly from case to case. Thus, it is always necessary to abstain from killing innocent persons, but the positive obligation of individuals and organizations to defend and promote life depends on many contingent factors.

The Universal Declaration should be seen as an organic whole, in which different rights receive different emphasis. The Preamble referred to certain rights as "fundamental" insofar as they can never be gainsaid without violating the dignity of the human person. It implied that the rights to life, liberty, and security of person, listed first, enjoyed a certain primacy over the others. According to Mary Ann Glendon's interpretation, the foundation is the dignity of the human person.[19]

The International Theological Commission, in a statement composed in 1983, recognized a certain hierarchy of rights, including three major divisions. On the highest level are the right to life, the fundamental equality of persons, and their right to freedom of conscience and religion. On the second level are civil, political, economic, social, and cultural rights flowing from the fundamental rights just mentioned. These rights have to be implemented in limited degrees according to the possibilities of actual situations. On the third and lowest level are rights that, without being strictly obligatory, are desirable for human progress. This last category refers to ideals rather than imperative demands.[20]

Some authors, using similar distinctions, maintain that social, economic, and cultural rights should be designated as desirable social goals rather than as rights in the strict sense. The statement of the Ramsey Colloquium "On Human Rights" reproaches the Universal Declaration for creating confusion by conflating civil and political rights with those that are economic and social. The socioeconomic and cultural rights, it maintains, are not enforceable by law and should be described as "duties in solidarity" rather than rights.[21]

Beyond doubt, we should be conscious of the different levels of human rights and of their different political and legal consequences. But we should not be overrestrictive. While it would be too much to make a right out of every social goal, it would be an exaggeration to hold that the only true rights are immunities from harm and to deny all positive entitlements. The child is truly entitled to parental care; the worker is has a positive right to a just wage. This does not necessarily mean that the power of the State should be invoked. According to the principle of subsidiarity, well established in the tradition of Catholic political thought, higher governmental agencies should not take over functions that private agencies or local governments are competent to perform. But if the lower agencies fail to do their duty, it may be necessary for national and international agencies to step in.

We should also be cautious, I suggest, in speaking of human rights as absolute or inalienable. Every right is absolute in the sense that no one may violate it so long as the right is really present. But most rights, including the "basic" rights to life, liberty, and personal security, can be limited by emergency situations or forfeited by misconduct. In times of peril, policemen, firemen, and soldiers, among others, are required to take risks that infringe on their personal security. Criminals sometimes lose their rights to liberty and even to life. But even when condemned to imprisonment or death, they retain their human dignity, which entitles even the worst offenders to be treated with respect and not wantonly abused.

Critics of a fourth school protest against rights claims in the name of a hermeneutics deriving from the great masters of suspicion, Marx, Nietzsche, and Freud.[22] The language of human rights, they allege, is simply a mask for individual or collective self-interest. This objection is often made by supporters of Marxist regimes when countering accusations from the First World that they violate human rights.

The objection undoubtedly identifies a real temptation, but it should not be pressed to the point of cynicism. We all suffer from a tendency to notice deficiencies in the conduct of others while overlooking our own failures. Any particular group, whether it be a labor union, a nation, or a coalition, runs the risk that it will use rights-language unilaterally to justify itself and to place unreasonable burdens on others. The articulation of human rights may help to expose and overcome this tendency. If rights are not to be mere self-assertion, they must be grounded in principle and be accompanied by acknowledgement of correlative duties. It is necessary to take a standpoint above individual and collective self-interest. Nongovernmental human rights organizations may be in a position to adopt a critical posture toward all nations. The Catholic Church, with its commitment to the gospel and its long history of social and political thought, is in a particularly good position to rise above ideology and self-interest.

Perhaps the most dangerous threat is a fifth one, coming from human rights advocates whose legal thinking is positivistic. In the tradition of "social contract" thought that derives from Thomas Hobbes, some assert that human rights stem from a kind of mutual nonaggression pact. All rights, therefore, arise from social enactment.[23] If this theory were correct, no one's rights would be inalienable, since the terms of the pact depend on the discretion of the signers. Human rights, moreover, would not be universal, since some people could be excluded from the contract. There would be no moral obligation to enter into a social contract with persons who were severely handicapped or otherwise unable to contribute to the general good.[24]

Positivism is widespread in contemporary ethical thinking. Values are commonly treated as expressions of merely personal preferences.[25] The danger is that individuals and nations might be induced to sign and abide by conventions that would be indefinitely open to revision. In the proposed International Criminal Court, nations might be coerced into accepting specious rights contrary to the natural law. By a final absurdity, wrongful acts would be treated as rights.[26]

This positivistic doctrine of human rights is directly opposed to the spirit and letter of the Universal Declaration, which states in its preamble, "These rights derive from the inherent dignity of the human person." Human rights, if they are to stand up against tyrannical infringements, must be seen as prepolitical. Once rights are viewed as the product of political arrangements, they cease to be sacred and inviolable.

THE TRANSCENDENT GROUND OF RIGHTS

A final question is whether the concept of inviolable rights demands a religious basis. Prominent philosophers as diverse as John Finnis and Ronald Dworkin propose purely secular arguments to show that the intrinsic value and sacredness of human life can be vindicated without any reference to God.[27] John Rawls thinks it possible to argue for human rights without any philosophical conception of the human person.[28] The Universal Declaration makes no reference to God, and many of its signers were atheists or agnostics. We may therefore agree that one may have a relatively high doctrine of human rights without appeal to a metaphysical or theological basis.

What may be questioned is whether a solid and coherent theory of rights can be developed without reference to a transcendent source. Pope John Paul II memorably indicates the necessity of such a grounding:

If there is no transcendent truth, in obedience to which man achieves his full identity, then there is no sure principle for guaranteeing just relations between people. . . . Thus, the root of modern totalitarianism is to be found in the denial of the transcendent dignity of the human person who, as the visible image of the invisible God, is therefore by his very nature the subject of rights which no one may violate—no individual, group, class, nation, or state. Not even a majority of a social body may violate these rights. (*CA* 44)

The sacred rights of every human being are greatly strengthened by recognition of their basis in divine law. Without reference to this transcendent source, human rights are vague and fragile.[29] Vaclav Havel, president of the Czech Republic, summed up the matter cogently when receiving the Philadelphia Liberty Medal at Independence Hall in Philadelphia on July 4, 1994: "The Declaration of Independence, adopted 218 years ago in this building, states that the Creator gave man the right to liberty. It seems man can realize that liberty only if he does not forget the One who endowed him with it."[30]

IMPORTANCE OF THE ANNIVERSARY

The fiftieth anniversary of the Universal Declaration of Human Rights is indeed a major milestone. The Declaration was composed at a propitious moment in history when humanistic personalism was giving new life to the centuries-old tradition of natural law and natural rights. Since its adoption it has been widely acclaimed as setting "a common standard of achievement" for peoples and nations.

Without a sound basis in philosophical anthropology, the human-rights tradition can easily be dismissed or perverted. Because it is no longer deemed self-evident that all men and women share a common nature and are endowed with inherent dignity and freedom, the inviolable rights of the person are at risk. This jubilee celebration should therefore be coupled with a fresh resolve to defend and promote the idea of human rights embodied in the Declaration.

NOTES

1. While there were forty-eight votes in favor and no dissenting votes, eight nations, including the Soviet bloc, Saudi Arabia, and South Africa, abstained. See

"Universal Declaration of Human Rights (1948)," *First Things* 82 (April 1998): 28–30, at 28.

2. *The United Nations and Human Rights* (New York: United Nations, 1978), 29.

3. *The Major Addresses of Pope Pius XII*, 2: *Christmas Messages*, ed. Vincent A. Yzermans (St. Paul, Minn.: North Central, 1961), 60–61.

4. See John S. Nurser, *For All Peoples and All Nations: The Ecumenical Church and Human Rights* (Washington, D. C.: Georgetown University Press, 2005), 24 n. 45; 165.

5. Karol Wojtyla (Pope John Paul II), *Love and Responsibility* (New York: Farrar, Straus, Giroux, 1981), 21–24.

6. Ibid., 41.

7. Ibid., 42.

8. John Paul II, *Crossing the Threshold of Hope* (New York: Knopf, 1994), 201.

9. John Paul II, *Love and Responsibility*, 42.

10. Holy See, "Charter of the Rights of the Family," *Origins* 13 (December 15, 1983): 461–64.

11. Several statements of John Paul II on the place of human rights in international law are quoted in the statement of Archbishop Renato R. Martino as head of the papal delegation at the conference in Rome on the formation of an International Criminal Court. See the Vatican Press release of June 16, 1998.

12. Henry J. Steiner, "Securing Human Rights," *Harvard Magazine* 101 (October 1998): 45–46, 94–95, at 45.

13. Alasdair MacIntyre, *After Virtue: A Study in Moral Theory*, 2nd ed. (Notre Dame, Ind.: University of Notre Dame, 1984), 69. Ernest Fortin, in his many essays on medieval and modern political theory, agrees that the modern notion of human rights is irreducibly different from traditional natural law thinking. See his *Classical Christianity and the Political Order* (volume 2 of his Collected Essays; Lanham, Md.: Rowman & Littlefield, 1996), especially chapters 11, 12 and 13.

14. Jacques Maritain argues in *The Rights of Man and Natural Law* (New York: Charles Scribner's Sons, 1943) that "the dignity of the person means nothing if it does not signify that by virtue of the natural law, the human person has the right to be respected, is the subject of rights, possesses rights" (p. 65).

15. John Courtney Murray, *We Hold These Truths: Catholic Reflections on the American Proposition* (New York: Sheed & Ward, 1960), 307.

16. This example in mentioned by Elliott Abrams in his "Reflections on the Universal Declaration of Human Rights," *First Things* 82 (April 1998): 25–27, at 26.

17. Richard Rorty, "Human Rights, Rationality, and Sentimentality," in *On Human Rights: The Oxford Amnesty Lectures, 1993*, ed. Stephen Shute and Susan Hurley (New York: Basic Books, 1993), 111–34.

18. J. Bryan Hehir explains this position in his "Human Rights and U.S. Foreign Policy: A Perspective from Theological Ethics," in *The Moral Imperatives of Human*

Rights: A World Survey, ed. Kenneth W. Thompson (Washington, D.C.: University Press of America, 1980), 1–23, at 1–2.

19. Mary Ann Glendon, "Reflections on the UDHR," *First Things* 82 (April 1998): 23–25; idem, "Knowing the Universal Declaration of Human Rights," *Notre Dame Law Review* 73 (May 1998): 101–25.

20. "Propositions on the Dignity and Rights of the Human Person," in *International Theological Commission: Texts and Documents*, ed. Michael Sharkey (San Francisco: Ignatius, 1989), 251–66, esp. 252–53.

21. "On Human Rights," *First Things* 82 (April 1998): 18–22, at 21.

22. For an exposition of this position see Hehir, "Human Rights and U.S. Foreign Policy," 3. He mentions that this line of criticism appears in many Third World commentaries on U.S. foreign policy.

23. For a nuanced argument to this effect, see David Gauthier, "Between Hobbes and Rawls," in the volume *Rationality, Justice, and Social Contract* edited by him and Robert Sugden (Ann Arbor, Mich.: University of Michigan Press, 1993), 24–39.

24. This criticism is made by Robert Sugden, "The Contractarian Enterprise," in *Rationality, Justice and the Social Contract*, 1–23, at 5. Michael J. Perry, *The Idea of Human Rights: Four Inquiries* (New York: Oxford, 1998), observes that "Gauthier's self-regarding argument does not aim to justify anything close to the range of rights established in international law—in the International Bill of Human Rights, for example" (32).

25. Michael Schooyans convincingly makes this point in his unpublished lecture, "Natural Law and Human Rights: The Person, the Family, and the State." This lecture was sponsored by the Catholic Family and Human Rights Institute and given at the United Nations headquarters in New York on May 27, 1998.

26. The problem is illustrated by present controversies about rights to contraception, same-sex marriage, abortion, and assisted suicide.

27. Ronald M. Dworkin, *Life's Dominion: An Argument about Abortion, Euthanasia, and Individual Freedom* (New York: Knopf, 1993); John Finnis, *Natural Law and Natural Rights* (New York: Oxford University Press, 1980). For a critique of Dworkin, see Perry, *The Idea of Human Rights*, 25–29. On Finnis, see the review by Ernest Fortin in his *Collected Essays*, 2:243–64.

28. John Rawls, "The Law of Peoples," in *On Human Rights*, 41–82, especially 68–71. See also his *A Theory of Justice* (Cambridge, Mass.: Belknap, 1971).

29. Michael J. Perry, "Is the Idea of Human Rights Ineliminably Religious?" chapter 1 of his *The Idea of Human Rights*.

30. Vaclav Havel, "The New Measure of Man," reported in *New York Times*, 8 July 1994, at A27.

21

Can Philosophy Be Christian?

The New State of the Question

April 7, 1999

THE PROBLEM

The possibility of a Christian philosophy was fiercely debated in the late 1920s and the early 1930s, especially in France, where several distinguished historians of philosophy, including Émile Bréhier, vigorously denied that there had been, or could be, any such thing.[1] It was, Bréhier said, as absurd as a Christian mathematics or a Christian physics.[2] Genuine philosophy, in his opinion, had been suffocated by Christian dogma in the Middle Ages, and did not reemerge until the seventeenth century, when Descartes picked up about where the Greeks had left off.

The Catholic medievalist Étienne Gilson led the counterattack. He opened his Gifford Lectures, *The Spirit of Mediaeval Philosophy*, with two chapters devoted respectively to the problem and the notion of Christian philosophy, which he defined as "every philosophy which, although keeping the two orders formally distinct, nevertheless considers the Christian revelation as an indispensable auxiliary to reason."[3] In a series of books and articles published over the next few decades Gilson demonstrated the vibrancy of medieval philosophy. He convincingly argued that the biblical concepts of God, creation, history, and the human person had made a decisive impact on the whole history of modern philosophy.[4]

In our own time, at least here in the United States, there seems to be a rather general recognition that Christians have a distinctive approach to

---

philosophy. We have had since 1926 an American Catholic Philosophical Association, which now has some 1,200 members, but there was nothing equivalent for Protestants until 1979, when William P. Alston, Alvin Plantinga, and several of their friends established the Society of Christian Philosophers. Today, twenty years later, it counts more than a thousand members, and enrolls a rapidly growing number of younger scholars. It is thoroughly ecumenical in its constituency.[5]

These initiatives, however, are scarcely typical of the university world, which finds the concept of Christian philosophy paradoxical, even nonsensical. Some philosophers simply rule out any consideration of revelation as lying beyond the purview of their discipline. Emotivists in the tradition of Alfred Ayer still dismiss religion as noncognitive. A host of agnostics, pragmatists, relativists, and deconstructionists, while differing among themselves, form a common front in opposition to revelation as a font of abiding truth.

Pope John Paul II, in his 1998 encyclical *Fides et ratio*, shows himself acutely aware of the present intellectual climate. With his customary courage, he dares to challenge current trends in both philosophy and theology and in so doing posits the question of Christian philosophy in a new form. From the very beginning of the encyclical, John Paul II reminds his readers that philosophy, in its etymological sense, means the love of wisdom (3).[6] Philosophy, therefore, is a human search for truth about ultimate questions (73); it is a journey awakened by wonder springing from contemplation of creation (4).

In a stricter sense, the pope maintains, philosophy is a rigorous mode of thought; it elaborates a systematic body of knowledge in which the elements are held together in organic unity by logical coherence (4). Ideally, the system should comprehend reality in all its dimensions, but the pope acknowledges that no one system achieves this ideal. Because of the limits of the human mind and the particularities of human cultures, every philosophical system is partial and incomplete. For this reason philosophical inquiry holds the primacy over philosophical systems (4).

Philosophy, according to the pope, operates within the order of natural reason (9), using its own methods (49), which differ from those of theology. Although philosophers disagree among themselves about the methods of their discipline, they appear to be unanimous in holding that philosophy does not derive its proofs from the word of God, received in faith.

Theology, by contrast, is "a reflective and scientific elaboration of the understanding of God's word in the light of faith" (64). According to John Paul II, the starting point of theology is always the word of God given in history and accepted in faith (73). By "faith" he means a free and personal decision to acknowledge the truth of what is revealed "because it is God himself who is the guarantor of that truth" (13). The chief purpose of theology is to provide an understanding of revelation and of the content of faith (93). The heart of theological inquiry is the mystery of the triune God, which becomes accessible to faith through the Incarnation of the Son and the descent of the Spirit of truth upon the Church (93).

THREE CLASSICAL POSITIONS

Christian philosophers have reached no agreement about how philosophy is related to faith. The classical positions fall into three main types.

According to the first school of thought, there is a Christian philosophy, and in fact the only true and adequate philosophy is Christian. In the early centuries of the Christian era, apologists such as Justin and Clement maintained that Christianity is the true philosophy (38), but they seem to have been using the term "philosophy" in a broad sense as equivalent to human wisdom. In the Middle Ages, Saint Anselm made a sharper distinction between faith and reason. Having accepted the existence of God and the fact of the Incarnation on authority in faith, he tried to demonstrate these truths by "necessary reasons" that would compel the assent of Jews and pagans who did not credit the authority of Christian Scripture. He apparently considered that he had succeeded in this endeavor.[7] Much later, rationalist philosophers such as Hegel contended that the mysteries of the Trinity and the Incarnation, initially accepted by faith, could be demonstrated by pure reason, at which point faith would no longer be needed in order to affirm them as true.

Hegel and his school, being rationalists, were convinced that reason is superior to faith. They integrated theology with philosophy by letting it be swallowed up by philosophy. But it is also possible to integrate the two disciplines to the advantage of theology. In the nineteenth century the traditionalists, denying the autonomy of reason, held that all true philosophy was based on divine revelation, accepted in faith. In our own century

Gilson came to the conclusion that in reasoning about God and things necessary to salvation "no one can pretend to reach truth unless he relies upon revelation to safeguard him against error."[8] The remarkable advances achieved by philosophy in the Middle Ages, he contends, were due to the guidance and enrichment it received from revelation.

While this view tends to merge the objects of philosophy and theology, it usually preserves a difference of method since theology proceeds by way of authority whereas philosophy relies on evidence and intrinsic reasoning. Christian philosophy, as Gilson came to use the term, meant "the use the Christian makes of philosophical reason when, in either of these two disciplines [philosophy and theology], he associates religious faith and philosophical reflection."[9] According to Gerald McCool, Gilson understood Christian philosophy as the philosophical moment in Catholic theology.[10] While retaining a formal distinction between the two disciplines, he argued that the Christian should not try to develop a philosophy independent of theology.[11]

The second classical position is the direct contrary of the first. Instead of saying that philosophy must be Christian, the neo-Thomists of the Louvain school, following in the footsteps of Cardinal Désiré Mercier, hold that philosophy must proceed rigorously by its own methods, without allowing itself to be influenced by faith. Fernand Van Steenberghen, representing this school, insisted that philosophy must be open on an equal basis to believers and nonbelievers. Christian philosophers, he contended, should not allow themselves to be isolated in a ghetto, as would occur if Gilson's positions prevailed.

While concurring with the rationalists that there could be no specifically Christian philosophy, the Louvain neo-Thomists rejected Bréhier's negative assessment of medieval philosophy. The faculties of philosophy in the medieval universities, they maintained, achieved significant advances in the strictly philosophical field, without allowing faith or theology to interfere with their autonomy. The same can be done by the believer today.[12]

As Christian believers, Mercier and Van Steenberghen of course accepted revelation. They also insisted that it was possible to reflect on revelation in a scientific way. But such reflection, they maintained, was by definition theology, since it was done in the light of faith.

The two classical positions thus far described stand at opposite ends of the spectrum. The first school maintains that philosophy ought to be

Christian, since it requires the positive influence of faith; the second school denies the possibility of Christian philosophy on the ground that philosophy must be a self-contained product of autonomous reason.

Between these two contrasting positions there are several mediating positions, which make up my third category. Jacques Maritain, differing only slightly from Gilson, argued that human reason, although limited in range, can achieve significant insights about ultimate questions without the help of revelation. Revelation attests to many naturally knowable truths such as the existence of God, the spirituality of the rational soul, and the dependence of the whole world on God's creative action. In dealing with truths that can in principle be known both by revelation and by reason, Christian philosophers may allow faith to indicate where the truth lies, but as philosophers they are obliged to establish their conclusions by independent reasoning. Maritain concludes with a typically Scholastic distinction: philosophy can be Christian in the order of exercise, but not in the order of specification.[13] Christian philosophy is philosophy itself conducted by a thinker who profits from revelation.[14]

A second mediating position is that usually identified with the name of Maurice Blondel. He held that neo-Thomists such as Van Steenberghen and Maritain treated philosophy too much as though it were a self-contained system, in which revelation could appear as a mere intruder. The whole supernatural order could then be written off by nonbelievers as an unnecessary superstructure over and above a self-sufficient world of reason and experience. As an alternative to this extrinsicism, Blondel contended that philosophy, when it operates without any reference to faith, becomes aware of its own limits. It can discover within the human person an inner dynamism toward a goal that nature cannot reach and toward a truth that reason cannot discover. Blondel rejected the idea of a philosophy that would be Christian in the sense of being based on revelation, but he held that all sound philosophy, holding fast to its own principles, would lead to the threshold of revealed truth. It could thus be Christian in spirit and in orientation.[15]

Henri de Lubac, developing a third mediating position, agreed with Gilson on the necessity for philosophy to be informed by Christian revelation in order for it to learn the most important truths of the natural order. Blondel, in his view, spoke too much as though the philosopher could begin in a void without regard for tradition and culture. But in agreement with Blondel, de Lubac held that philosophy is affected by the natural desire for the supernatural; it is naturally Christian and is oriented toward revelation as its own completion. The positions of Gilson and Blondel thus correct and complete each other.[16]

PHILOSOPHY PRIOR TO FAITH

Building on these classical positions, John Paul II in *Fides et ratio* distinguishes three states or stances of philosophy in relation to faith. He speaks of a philosophy prior to faith, a philosophy positively influenced by faith, and a philosophy that functions within theology to achieve some understanding of faith.

In describing the first state of philosophy, John Paul II accepts the thesis of Van Steenberghen and Maritain that there can be authentic philosophy outside of faith. Arguing rigorously from rational criteria, one can attain conclusions that are true and certain (75). In affirming this position, the pope would seem to be on solid ground. Plato and Aristotle, while lacking the guidance of Jewish and Christian revelation, rank among the greatest philosophers of all time. They ably refuted sophistic errors such as materialism, relativism, and hedonistic pragmatism. They showed the capacity of reason to discern the intelligible features of the real order. They laid a solid groundwork for the metaphysical principles of contradiction, sufficient reason, and causality.

John Paul II, however, does not settle for a closed system of rational knowledge. With Blondel and de Lubac, he is keenly aware that an autonomous philosophy cannot be self-sufficient. The journey of philosophy, he holds, cannot be completed without faith. Just as faith seeks understanding, so, conversely, understanding seeks faith (16–23). Philosophy, in perceiving its own limits, can serve as a preparation for the gospel.

This basically Augustinian position has roots that long antedate Blondel. Even before the Christian era, Plato recognized pressing questions that the philosopher could not answer without the help of a divine revelation, which he himself did not claim to have received. In Plato's *Phaedo*, Simmias confesses to Socrates the difficulty of attaining certitude about the fate of the soul after death. The wise man, he says, should take the best and most irrefragable of human theories and let them serve as a raft upon which to sail through life "not without risk, as I admit, if he cannot find some word of God which will more surely and safely carry him."[17]

The insufficiency of reason was expressed in another way by Immanuel Kant, who claimed that, in showing reason's incompetence to attain speculative certitude about questions concerning God, freedom, and immortality, he was making room for faith. Kant may have excessively minimized the scope of theoretical reason, and his conception of faith may have fallen short of Christian orthodoxy, but we may concur with his thesis that by recognizing the limits of reason we can better appreciate the need for faith.

Schooled in post-Kantian personalist phenomenology, John Paul II is deeply sensitive to the subjective component in human knowledge. Philosophy, as he sees it, is not so much a set of conclusions as a mode of inquiry (76). As I have said, it is first of all a process of exploration and only secondarily a matter of systematization (4).

Philosophy, in this Augustinian perspective, is not a dispassionate clinical inquiry; it has to be pursued with trust, commitment, and creative imagination. Again and again in his encyclical, John Paul II adverts to the unquenchable thirst for truth that God has implanted in the human heart (opening sentence and 29). Modern philosophy, he observes, has the great merit of focusing attention on the human spirit and its yearning to understand (5). Human knowledge, he says, is a journey that allows no rest (18, 33). In the footsteps of Anselm, the pope asserts that "the intellect must seek what it loves: the more it loves, the more it desires to know" (42). The philosopher should be driven by a passion for ultimate truth, a passion that faith can intensify (56).

The philosopher, considered in the order of actual existence, is no stranger to belief. Anyone who begins to philosophize does so as a member of a community that has received a body of beliefs and values transmitted from the past. Only after such views have been unreflectively assimilated does the philosopher bring critical inquiry to bear (31). The tools of critical reason have themselves been forged and refined in the philosophical tradition.

Even when embarking on the quest for new insights, reason is sustained by a certain primordial faith. The discoverer begins by assuming that the thirst for truth, so ineradicably rooted in the human heart, is not vain and useless. The sense that there is an answer waiting to be found sustains the confidence and perseverance needed to conduct the search (29). At this point in his encyclical the pope speaks in terms reminiscent of the great philosopher of science, Michael Polanyi.

John Paul II, as I understand him, would agree with Blondel that the human spirit has an inbuilt restlessness toward the divine, an inner exigency for a supernatural message of salvation. But he would probably add, as de Lubac and Karl Rahner do, that philosophy would not be able to articulate the concept of the supernatural without help from revelation. When practiced in a Christian culture, philosophy receives its concept of the supernatural from the believing community.[18]

The passage from autonomous philosophy to faith does not take place without a conversion. John Paul II is sensitive to the perspectives of Christian existentialism, typified by Søren Kierkegaard and Fyodor Dostoyevsky. The word of the cross, he acknowledges, seems to crush and contradict the philosopher's ideal of wisdom. The wisdom of the cross challenges every philosophy (23).[19] But truth cannot be incompatible with truth. "At the summit of its searching reason acknowledges that it cannot do without what faith presents" (42). In the final analysis, truth proves to be one. Christ, who calls himself the truth, brings the quest of philosophy to a surpassing fulfillment (34).

PHILOSOPHY AIDED BY FAITH

Our consideration of the insufficiency of autonomous reason brings us to the second state of philosophy, which arises after revelation has occurred and been accepted in faith. John Paul II agrees with those who hold that Christian revelation can make a valid contribution to philosophy, as may be seen from the examples of outstanding thinkers such as Thomas Aquinas. With Gilson and Maritain, he teaches there is such a thing as Christian philosophy. The term, he says, serves "to indicate a Christian way of philosophizing, a philosophical speculation conceived in dynamic union with faith" (76). It includes important developments of philosophical thinking that would not have happened without the stimulus of the word of God (76).

The term "Christian philosophy" should not be restricted to the Middle Ages. John Paul II, as I understand him, would find the term appropriate to describe the philosophical writings of the Cappadocian Fathers, Augustine, and other patristic authors, not to mention the Christian thinkers of modern times. Philosophers such as Locke, Leibniz, Malebranche, and others would be unintelligible without reference to their Christian faith.

While John Paul II accepts the term "Christian philosophy," he warns against certain misunderstandings. The term, he explains, does not mean that the Church has an official philosophy. It might have been thought a century ago that Thomism was the Church's one philosophy, but the present pope avoids taking that position. At the time of Leo XIII, he declares, it seemed that "renewed insistence upon the thought of the Angelic Doctor" was "the best way to recover the practice of a philosophy consonant with the demands of faith" (57). While encouraging recourse to the wisdom of Aquinas, John Paul II allows for a plurality of systems. Acceptable systems of philosophy, he believes, must share the metaphysical realism of St. Thomas, including his position on the natural knowability of the existence of God (53). The Angelic Doctor is an authentic model for all who seek the truth and who wish to profit from revelation without sacrificing the just autonomy of reason (78). He evinced an exemplary passion in the search for objective truth (44) and exhibited admirable courage by tackling new problems and entering into dialogue with the Arab and Jewish thought of his time (43).[20]

Among the great medieval philosophers, John Paul II singles out the "great triad" of Anselm, Bonaventure, and Thomas Aquinas (74). He has words of praise for John Henry Newman, Antonio Rosmini, Vladimir Soloviev, and Vladimir Lossky (74), all of whom philosophized in the light of their Christian faith without being classifiable as Thomists. Although he does not mention Blondel and Max Scheler by name, he finds merit in the philosophy of immanence and phenomenology (59). While discountenancing an unprincipled syncretism, he is prepared to learn from alien philosophical movements, even those which he finds dangerous and debilitating. "The currents of thought which claim to be postmodern," he writes, "merit appropriate attention." But they should not be allowed to destroy all certitude and inculcate a total absence of meaning (91).

In his reflections on Christian philosophy, John Paul II distinguishes between two kinds of benefit that faith confers upon it. The first is an influence on the thinking subject. Faith purifies philosophical reason in a twofold way. On the one hand, it cures philosophy of the pride to which it has at times been subject and with which it was reproached by Paul, Pascal, and Kierkegaard, among others. On the other hand, faith inspires philosophy with courage to tackle certain difficult questions, such as the problem of evil and suffering, that might seem insoluble except for the light cast on them by revelation (76).

The second influence of faith upon philosophy is objective. Revelation, as already mentioned, assists reason to discover certain truths that are in principle accessible to reason but might never be found in fact without revelation. John Paul II places in this category the ideas of creation as the action of a free and personal God; sin as an offense against God; the dignity, freedom, and equality of human persons; and the meaning of history as event (76).

The pope at one point speaks of reason and faith being interior to each other (17). The relationship between them, he says, is circular (73). Philosophy, by offering its specific skills, contributes to the better under-standing of revelation. Revelation can assist philosophy by stirring it to explore unsuspected paths and by warning it against false trails.

Because of the intimate connection between philosophy and faith, the ecclesiastical magisterium, in its ministry to faith, cannot ignore philoso-phy. It has a right and a duty to encourage promising initiatives and to warn against aberrations incompatible with the Church's faith. This discernment should not be seen as an intrusion but as a service to right reason and to the philosopher's quest for truth (50–51).

Philosophy Within Faith

Thus far we have been speaking of philosophy as an independent branch of study, standing apart from theology, even though influenced by it. Before concluding, we must consider philosophy in its third state, in which it functions within theology, which takes its departure from revela-tion received in faith. Revelation goes beyond reason in the sense that it contains many truths that philosophy cannot discover. These truths are strict mysteries, but they are not conundrums.

Revelation, since it comes from the divine Logos, is inherently intelligi-ble (66). With the help of philosophy, the theologian can achieve a lim-ited but nevertheless very fruitful understanding of mysteries of faith. Speculative theology makes use of philosophy in its reflection on revealed truths such as the processions of the Trinity, the union of the two natures in the person of Jesus Christ, and the concepts of guilt and atonement that lie at the basis of moral theology (66).

In connection with dogmatic theology, John Paul II states that the hallowed term *ancilla theologiae* has a legitimate meaning even though it is subject to misunderstanding. The service rendered by philosophy, he says, is not a matter of servile submission to commands given by theology as a higher discipline. Rather, the term means that philosophy, while holding fast to its own principles, can be fruitfully used within theology (77). This utilization in no way impairs the proper autonomy of philosophy, for, if philosophy were denatured, it could not perform its distinctive service. One of the benefits of sound philosophy is to show that the truth of dogmatic formulas is not tied to any particular time or culture, as some have imagined (95–96). Truth is universal by its very nature (27).

To amplify somewhat the pope's teaching on dogmatic theology, it may be helpful to recall several points of traditional teaching from Thomas Aquinas and the First Vatican Council. Although reason cannot prove the existence or even the possibility of strict mysteries such as the Trinity and the Incarnation, it can expose the errors of those who attempt to demonstrate their impossibility.[21] Philosophical reason, furthermore, can show the analogies between the orders of nature and grace; it can exhibit the internal coherence of the whole supernatural order as revealed by Christianity, casting light on each revealed truth by manifesting its harmony with other revealed truths and with the goals of human existence.[22] Meditation on the data of revelation can show, finally, that the truths of faith fulfill those aspirations of the human heart which, as Blondel showed, cannot be satisfied by anything within the order of nature.

THE NEW STATE OF THE QUESTION

In terms of the debates of the 1930s, John Paul II's positions differ from those of all the principal contestants. To the basic question whether there is such a thing as Christian philosophy he answers, against Bréhier and Van Steenberghen, that there is. Against Blondel, he holds that such philosophy is Christian in its substance and content, not simply in its orientation. Against Gilson, he holds that there can be a valid philosophy that is not influenced by revelation, and that the Christian philosopher need not be a theologian. And finally, against Maritain he contends that Christian philosophy can be practiced in a variety of styles and is not necessarily

Thomistic. On the whole, the pope's positions coincide most closely with those of de Lubac, who sought to mediate between Blondel and Gilson.

Even if John Paul II had done nothing more than to sort out what is and is not acceptable in the earlier positions, his encyclical would be sufficient to establish a new state of the question. But he also takes a positive step forward. In the encyclical and in several of his unofficial writings before and after he became pope, he expresses his view that personalist anthropology must stand at the center of Christian philosophy today. The philosophy of consciousness, developed according to phenomenological method, can throw new light on the subjectivity of the person, which stands at the basis of culture, civilization, and politics.[23] Biblical revelation has taught Christian philosophers such as Gabriel Marcel and Jewish philosophers such as Martin Buber and Emmanuel Lévinas that the whole of human existence is a coexistence in dialogue, and that the primary dialogue partner is the God of our faith.[24]

Personalist phenomenology, practiced according to the principles of the Lublin school of Thomism, can contribute to a much needed renewal of metaphysics (83).[25] The forms of metaphysics that were still flourishing in the 1930s are languishing today. The battle is no longer between Cartesian rationalists, German idealists, and Catholic neo-Scholastics. Many contemporary philosophers, proclaiming the "end of metaphysics" (55), are embracing agnosticism, relativism, and consequentialist pragmatism, or devoting their energies to purely formal questions concerning language and hermeneutics (5, 47, 81–82). Theology, for its part, all too often evades the challenge of truth. Falling into fideism or sheer positivism, many theologians limit themselves to sociological, linguistic, and historical studies of the Bible and Church teaching (48, 55, 61, 94). Both disciplines are therefore in need of conversion. They must alike regain their sapiential dimension.

The encyclical is a pressing appeal for faith and philosophy to "recover their profound unity which allows them to stand in harmony with their nature without compromising their mutual autonomy" (48). Once the distinction of goals and methods is in place, the intimate association between the two disciplines can be restored. Understood no longer as closed systems but as inquiries aimed at ultimate truth, they can be seen not as rivals or enemies, but as allies. The old debates about the turf belonging to each discipline and about their respective preeminence need not greatly trouble us today. The current need is for dialogue and mutual support.

Faith and reason, as described by John Paul II, are united like the two natures of Christ, which coexisted without confusion or alteration in a single person. Christian wisdom, similarly, involves a synthesis of theology and philosophy, each supporting and benefiting the other. The pope also uses an analogy from Mariology. Just as Mary, without impairment to her virginity, became fruitful by offering herself to the Word of God, so philosophy, he says, can become more fruitful by offering itself to the service of revealed truth (108).

Integral Christian wisdom, which sometimes goes by the name of philosophy or theology, draws on the full resources of reason and revelation alike. It is exemplified by the intellectual projects of Augustine, Bonaventure, and Thomas Aquinas, who sought to achieve a universal wisdom by synthesizing the totality of knowledge under the auspices of faith.

Vatican II taught that "faith throws a new light on everything," thus making it possible for the believer to reflect not simply on the word of God but on the whole of life from the perspective of the word of God (*GS* 11). In particular, the mystery of the human person takes on new meaning in the light of Christ, who is the key, the focal point, and the goal of all human history (*GS* 10).

Fides et ratio begins with the statement that faith and reason are the two wings on which the human spirit soars to the contemplation of truth. The entire encyclical is an inspiring summons to the pursuit of a wisdom in which theology and philosophy are harmoniously integrated to the advantage of both and the detriment of neither.

The program set forth in the encyclical is radical and bold, especially in view of the troubled climate of the academic world today. Philosophers and theologians who wish to implement the pope's vision must resolutely struggle against mighty odds. But a measure of success is attainable, especially in universities that stand within the Christian and Catholic tradition. A revitalized Christian philosophy could reinvigorate our nation and our culture. This revitalization is also a key element in John Paul II's strategy for the new evangelization. By reestablishing the harmony between faith and reason, it can help to prepare for the new springtime of faith that is envisaged as Christianity enters upon its third millennium.

NOTES

1. A good introduction to the debate may be found in Maurice Nédoncelle, *Is There a Christian Philosophy?* (New York: Hawthorn Books, 1960), esp. 85–99.

2. Émile Bréhier, "Y a-t-il une philosophie chrétienne?" *Revue de métaphysique et de morale* 38 (1931): 133–62, at 162.

3. Étienne Gilson, *The Spirit of Mediaeval Philosophy* (New York: Scribner's, 1940), 37.

4. See, in particular, Gilson's interventions in the debate, "La notion de philosophie chrétienne," *Bulletin de la Société française de philosophie* 31 (April–June 1931): 37–93. Gilson's final position is well indicated in his book *The Philosopher and Theology* (New York: Random House, 1962).

5. Richard John Neuhaus, "The Public Square," *First Things* 90 (February 1999): 68–80, at 79. See also *Faith and Philosophy: Journal of the Society of Christian Philosophers* 15 (April 1998) for reflections on the twentieth anniversary of the society.

6. Numbers in parentheses in the text refer to paragraphs of the encyclical.

7. Anselm, *Cur Deus homo?* 2:22. For similar statements see his *Proslogion*, 4, and the Appendix to his *Monologion*, "On Behalf of the Fool," 8.

8. Gilson, *The Philosopher and Theology*, 188.

9. Ibid., 198.

10. Gerald A. McCool, "How Can There Be Such a Thing as Christian Philosophy?" in *Philosophical Knowledge*, ed. John B. Brough et al. 54 (1980): 126–34, at 132.

11. John F. Wippel, "The Possibility of a Christian Philosophy: A Thomistic Perspective," *Faith and Philosophy* 1 (1984): 272–90, at 278.

12. Fernand Van Steenberghen, "Philosophie et christianisme," in his *Études philosophiques* (Quebec: Éditions du Préambule, 1985), 11–57. In his section of the book he reprints, among other pieces, his intervention at the second day of the *Journée d'études de la Société thomiste* on the notion of "Christian philosophy" (1933).

13. Jacques Maritain, *An Essay on Christian Philosophy* (New York: Philosophical Library, 1955), 11.

14. Ibid., 30.

15. Maurice Blondel, "La philosophie chrétienne existe-t-elle comme philosophie?" *Bulletin de la Société française de Philosophie* 31 (1931): 86–92. See also his *Le problème de la philosophie catholique* (Paris: Bloud & Gay, 1932), 127–77.

16. Henri de Lubac, "On Christian Philosophy," *Communio* 19 (1992): 478–506.

17. Plato, *Phaedo*, 85c–d, *The Dialogues of Plato*, trans. B. Jowett (New York: Random House, 1937), 1:470.

18. De Lubac, "On Christian Philosophy," 488; Karl Rahner, *Foundations of Christian Faith* (New York: Crossroad, 1982), 24–25, 126. On Rahner, see further William V. Dych, "Philosophy and Philosophizing in Theology," in *Continuity and Plurality in Catholic Theology: Essays in Honor of Gerald A. McCool, S.J.*, ed. Anthony J. Cernera (Fairfield, Conn.: Sacred Heart University Press, 1998), 13–34, at 20.

19. The contrast between Christian wisdom and rationalist wisdom, brilliantly expressed by existentialist thinkers such as Kierkegaard, is recalled by Augusto Del Noce in his article "Thomism and the Critique of Rationalism: Gilson and Shestov," *Communio* 25 (1998): 732–45.

20. Romanus Cessario, "Thomas Aquinas: A Doctor for the Ages," *First Things* 91 (March 1999): 27–32, especially at 32.

21. Thomas Aquinas, *Summa contra Gentiles*, Book I, chap. 9.

22. Vatican I, Constitution on Catholic Faith, *Dei Filius*, chap. 4 (DS 3016).

23. Karol Wojtyla, "The Task of Christian Philosophy Today," in *The Human Person*, ed. G. F. McLean, *Proceedings of the American Catholic Philosophical Association* 53 (1979): 3–4.

24. John Paul II, *Crossing the Threshold of Hope* (New York: Knopf, 1994), 36–37.

25. Ibid. In *FR* 83 the pope explains that by metaphysics he does not mean any particular school of thought, such as Hegelianism, but the conviction that true and certain knowledge is not restricted to the realm of the empirical.

22

Justification Today

A New Ecumenical Breakthrough

October 26, 1999

One of the central themes of the New Testament, if not the central theme, is the way to obtain salvation. To be on the right road is, in New Testament terminology, to be justified. The corollary is that unless we are justified, we are unrighteous and are on the road to final perdition. In other words, justification, as a right relationship with God, is a matter of eternal life or death. If it is not important, nothing is.

THE HISTORICAL BACKGROUND

According to Christian faith, justification is a gift of God, who grants it through his Son and the Holy Spirit. Fifteen hundred years of intense reflection left us with a number of specific questions. Four seem to me to be crucial: (1) Is justification the action of God alone, or do we who receive it cooperate by our response to God's offer of grace? (2) Does God, when he justifies us, simply impute to us the merits of Christ or does he transform us and make us intrinsically righteous? (3) Do we receive justification by faith alone or only by a faith enlivened by love and fruitful in good works? (4) Is the reward of heavenly life a free gift of God to believers or do they merit it by their faithfulness and good works?

In the sixteenth century, Martin Luther came up with answers to all these questions based primarily on his study of Paul. He affirmed, first, that justification, as God's act, is independent of all human cooperation. Justification, secondly, consists in the favor of God, who freely imputes to us the merits of Christ. It is not a matter of inner renewal. Justification, in the third place, is received by faith alone, independently of any good works or obedience to God's law. And finally, eternal life is a sheer gift; it is not merited by good behavior.

At the Diet of Augsburg in 1530, the Emperor Charles V ordered the Lutheran party to explain its position. They did so in the Augsburg Confession, composed by Philip Melanchthon at the behest of Luther. A group of theologians assembled by the emperor studied that Confession and faulted it at several points, especially for its teaching on merit.

After several colloquies had unsuccessfully attempted to reconcile the Catholic and Lutheran positions, the Council of Trent in 1547 set forth the official Catholic doctrine in its Decree on Justification. The council taught that although justification is an unmerited gift, it needs to be freely accepted, so that human cooperation is involved. It taught, second, that justification consists in an inner renewal brought about by divine grace; third, that justification does not take place by faith without hope, charity, and good works; and finally, that the justified, by performing good works, merit the reward of eternal life. For the next four hundred years the two churches went their separate ways. The divisions were hardened by polemical tracts. But in the ecumenical climate of the present century, as represented by Vatican II, both sides have striven to appreciate what is authentically Christian in the other's positions and to achieve the greatest possible degree of consensus. Bilateral dialogues dealing with justification have been conducted on the international level and in several countries.

In 1983, the United States Lutheran-Catholic Dialogue published an important statement that highlighted twelve important points of agreement.[1] The sixty-page statement concluded with a Common Declaration setting forth what it called "a fundamental consensus on the gospel." According to this declaration, justification is an undeserved gift granted through Jesus Christ and received in faith, whereby we pass from sin to freedom and fellowship with God in the Holy Spirit.[2] At the end of its statement, the Dialogue asked the respective churches to study this consensus and make appropriate decisions for the purpose of confessing the faith in unison.[3] It also stated that in view of the convergences achieved, the remaining theological differences about the doctrine of justification, though serious, need not be considered church-dividing.[4]

The American dialogue had important repercussions. An ecumenical group of Protestant and Catholic theologians in Germany in 1985 undertook a study of the condemnations issued by each church in the sixteenth century.[5] Concluding that none of these condemnations held against the partner church today, this study proposed that the churches make binding pronouncements to the effect that those condemnations should no longer be cited as if they still held against the other church. The canons on justification in the Council of Trent and in the Lutheran Book of Concord figured prominently in this study.

From 1986 to 1993, the Lutheran-Roman Catholic International Commission conducted its own study of the problem of justification and in its final statement, *Church and Justification*, supported the conclusions of the North American dialogue and applied them to ecclesiology.[6] Thus the road seemed clear for the churches to take some official action signifying their acceptance of the results of the dialogues.

THE JOINT DECLARATION

The Joint Declaration was drafted in 1994 by a small committee of church officials and ecumenical professionals appointed by the Holy See and the Lutheran World Federation. Their mandate was to summarize the results of the dialogues and pave the way for a public act of solidarity and reconciliation.

The Lutheran World Federation submitted the draft to 124 Lutheran member churches and obtained responses from three-quarters of them. Of those eighty-nine responses, eighty were favorable, five opposed, and four mixed. In the light of the official reactions and private theological critiques,[7] the text was revised to produce the final version of 1997.[8] On June 16, 1998, the governing council of the Lutheran World Federation in Geneva, Switzerland, unanimously approved the Joint Declaration.

The Roman authorities were not bound to conduct any formal consultation, but informal reactions were obtained. Because the Holy See had been heavily involved in the composition, its acceptance was taken for granted. But to the surprise of many observers, the Council for Promoting Christian Unity on June 25, 1998 released an "Official Response" expressing a number of severe criticisms and apparently calling into question the consensus expressed by the Joint Declaration.[9]

After a flurry of conferences, the parties drew up an "Official Common Statement," an "Annex," and a "Note on the Annex" that addressed some of the Roman questions and got the process back on track.[10] The official signing ceremony is scheduled to be held in Augsburg on Sunday, October 31, 1999, the date that Lutherans annually observe as Reformation Day. Cardinal Edward Cassidy, president of the Pontifical Council for the Unity of Christians, and Bishop Walter Kasper, secretary of the same council, will sign for the Catholic Church. Bishop Christian Krause, president of the Lutheran World Federation, and Ishmael Noko, general secretary, will sign for the Lutherans. The event will be a historic one because the disagreements on the doctrine of justification are generally regarded as the principal cause of the division between Protestants and Catholics in the sixteenth century.

The heart of the Joint Declaration is surely paragraph 15, and more particularly the sentence: "Together we confess: By grace alone, in faith in Christ's saving work and not because of any merit on our part, we are accepted by God and receive the Holy Spirit, who renews our hearts while equipping and calling us to good works." This consensus does not go beyond the clear conclusions of the dialogues. While it is in perfect accord both with the Augsburg Confession and with the Decree on Justification of the Council of Trent, it dispels some false stereotypes inherited from the past. Lutherans have often accused Catholics of holding that justification is a human achievement rather than a divine gift received in faith, while Catholics have accused Lutherans of holding that justification by faith does not involve inner renewal or require good works. By mentioning both faith and works, both acceptance by God and the gift of the Holy Spirit, this sentence strikes an even-handed balance calculated to satisfy both sides.

If the Joint Declaration had stopped at this point, it would have been a breakthrough of sorts because the two churches have never in the past jointly expressed their shared convictions about justification. But the Declaration goes further. In the following paragraphs it addresses an assortment of subordinate questions that have proved divisive. First of all comes a general question of method: Does the doctrine of justification hold a privileged position as the criterion by which all other Christian doctrines are to be judged, or is it to be viewed as one doctrine among many? Then the Joint Declaration takes up seven more specific issues. To simplify somewhat the language of the Declaration, one could list these issues as questions:

1. Do the justified cooperate in the preparation for, and reception of, justification?
2. Is justification a divine decree of forgiveness or interior renewal?
3. Is justification received by faith alone or by faith together with hope and charity, which bring one into communion with God?
4. Does concupiscence, that is to say, our innate tendency to be self-indulgent, make us sinners, even when we do not give in to it?
5. Is God's law given only in order to accuse sinners of their failures, bringing them to repentance, or also to provide them with a rule of life that they can and must observe?
6. Does faith include an assurance that one will in fact attain final salvation?
7. Are the heavenly blessings for which we hope rewards that we also merit, or are they to be understood exclusively as undeserved gifts from God?

Each of these seven points, like the preliminary question about criteria, is treated in three phases: a brief formulation of the consensus, a Lutheran perspective, and a Catholic perspective. Lutherans and Catholics are not expected to accept each other's perspectives, but only to acknowledge that these perspectives are tolerable, in the sense that they escape the condemnations pronounced by each church in the sixteenth century. But even this, as we shall see, is a bold statement, difficult to defend.

THE OFFICIAL CATHOLIC RESPONSE

The delicacy of the matter is illustrated by the Official Response of the Catholic Church to the Joint Declaration issued in June 1998. It is divided into two parts. The first is an acceptance of the remarkable convergence already achieved. The second part calls for theological clarification of some unresolved issues.

In this second section the Official Response is rather blunt, but the seriousness of the matter calls for more than diplomacy. For example, it asks about the doctrinal authority of the Lutheran World Federation and the synods or ecclesial bodies it consulted. Can they speak decisively for the Lutheran community? The Response also calls attention to some lacunae in the Joint Declaration, such as its lack of attention to the sacrament of penance, in which justification is restored to those who have lost it. In addition, it contests the Lutheran view that the doctrine of justification is the supreme touchstone of right doctrine. It asserts, on the contrary, that the doctrine of justification must be integrated into the "rule of faith," which is centered on the triune God, the Incarnation, the Church, and the sacraments. Most importantly for our present purposes, the Catholic Response raises the question whether the Lutheran positions as explained in the Joint Declaration really escape the anathemas of the Council of Trent. Without repeating the exact words of the Official Response, I can indicate some of the objections it poses regarding the first, second, fourth, and seventh of the issues I have mentioned in my summary of the Joint Declaration.

Regarding the first issue, human cooperation in the preparation for and reception of justification, the Council of Trent taught under anathema that the recipients of justification cooperate freely in their own justification and do not receive it purely passively as if they were puppets (can. 4, DS 1554). The Joint Declaration contends, on the contrary, that human beings possess "no freedom in relation of salvation" (§19) and that "God's gift of grace in justification remains independent of human cooperation" (§24). It reports Lutherans as holding that we are merely passive in receiving grace and make no contribution to our own justification, even while conceding that we are "fully involved personally in [our] faith" (§21). These statements are intelligible only if one understands justification as a divine action, prior to any human act of faith or love. The Catholic Response quite understandably asks whether the Joint Declaration on this point can be harmonized with Trent, which, as we shall see, teaches a very different doctrine of justification.

The second issue goes right to the heart of the matter and is considered by the Official Response the most serious obstacle to agreement. Does justification consist in an imputation of Christ's righteousness, as Lutherans generally hold, or in an interior renewal and sanctification, as the Council of Trent taught? The Lutherans distinguish between justification and sanctification, making the first prior to the second, whereas for Trent justification and sanctification are two sides of the same coin. The Joint

Declaration seeks to achieve consensus by treating justification and sanctification as two distinct but inseparable aspects of God's saving action. The process involves both the forgiveness of sin and the divine self-gift. Lutherans, who emphasize the element of forgiveness, do not deny renewal, but they insist that God's justifying action is not dependent on the transformative effects of his grace. Catholics, who emphasize interior renewal through the reception of God's gift, do not wish to deny that God's saving initiative precedes our response and is independent of it.

Does this explanation succeed in bridging the gap between the two positions? The answer depends on what kind of renewal is understood to be involved in justification. Are we really made righteous through being interiorly renewed, as the Council of Trent insisted (can. 10, DS 1560), or is our righteousness a nonimputation of sin or an imputation of the "alien righteousness" of Christ, as Lutherans have commonly said? So far as I can see, the Lutheran position in the Joint Declaration favors the theory of alien righteousness that was rejected at Trent. This reading of the Lutheran position is confirmed by the handling of the fourth issue, that of concupiscence—a technical term signifying the disorderly desires and spiritual weakness that afflict our fallen human nature. Lutherans hold that the justified person remains a sinner because "concupiscence" is not removed by baptism. In their view the justified person is, as the phrase goes, *simul justus et peccator*. Catholics, by contrast, hold that concupiscence is not sin, and that justification removes all that can properly be called sin. The Council of Trent taught that justification effectively makes us righteous and condemned the view that our justification is only an imputation of Christ's righteousness (DS 1560–61). It also condemned under anathema the view that concupiscence is sin (DS 1515). When the Lutherans say that concupiscence makes people sinners, they seem to imply that it makes us guilty before God and needs to be forgiven or at least covered over by the merits of Christ. This was and is contrary to Catholic teaching.

Still another issue flagged by the Official Catholic Response was that of merit, the seventh on my list. The Joint Declaration states quite correctly the position of both our churches, namely that nothing preceding justification merits justification. In that sense justification is a totally free gift of God. But Lutherans and Catholics have disagreed about whether one can, after justification, merit the increase of grace and the reward of eternal life. Trent clearly says yes.[11] Lutherans have denied this. The Joint Declaration attempts the following compromise:

> When Catholics affirm the "meritorious" character of good works, they wish to say that, according to the biblical witness, a reward in heaven is promised to these works. Their intention is to emphasize the responsibility of persons for their actions, not to contest the character of those works as gifts or far less to deny that justification always remains the unmerited gift of grace. (38)

This statement seems to fall short of what Catholics believe and what Trent teaches under anathema. The fact that a reward is promised does not make it merited, since one can promise to bestow rewards that are undeserved. In the Catholic view, justification makes us capable of meriting in a true sense. Yet eternal life is also a gift because our capacity to merit is God's gift, which is itself unmerited.

Many other objections could be raised against the claim of the Joint Declaration that the condemnations of the sixteenth century no longer apply to the partner churches, even on the particular issues it took up. On the third issue in my list, whether we are justified by faith alone, it is very difficult to make out a consensus since the Lutheran position is based on the assumption that faith is the means whereby we are clothed with the merits of Christ, in whom we believe. They reject justification as interior renewal because in their view such renewal is always imperfect and presupposes justification. Here again, no agreement has been reached.

Because of the serious criticisms made in the Official Response, many assumed that the Joint Declaration was as good as dead. But the Holy See, almost unaccountably, continued to insist on its readiness to sign. How could they agree to sign a document that they found so defective?

The Annex appended to the Official Common Statement of 1999 purports to give further clarifications, but I personally do not find it helpful. It simply piles up more quotations from Scripture and from the sixteenth-century documents that were presumably familiar to the authors of the Catholic response.

To explain the attitude of the Holy See, it seems important to say something about ecumenical method as currently understood in the Catholic Church. Vatican II, which is normative, lays down the basic principles. It states that the separated churches can acknowledge each other as truly Christian and as being in a state of real though imperfect communion (*UR* 3). Dialogues between experts from different churches and ecclesial communities should be undertaken with a view to restoring full communion (*UR* 4). The deposit of faith has been handed down in different ways in different places and cultures (*UR* 14). The deposit of faith is one thing, and theological formulation quite another (*GS* 62). Varying theological formulations must often be considered complementary rather than conflicting. "It is hardly surprising, then, if sometimes one tradition has come nearer than the other to an apt appreciation of certain aspects of a revealed mystery, and has expressed them more lucidly" (*UR* 17).

John Paul II in his encyclical on ecumenism reaffirms these principles and insists that theological dialogue must take account of the ways of thinking and historical experiences of the other party (*UUS* 36). Assertions that reflect different ways of looking at the same reality, he says, should not be treated as though they were mutually contradictory (*UUS* 38).

According to an older theological model ecumenism would aspire to take the statements of the Lutheran Book of Concord and those of the Catholic councils one by one, examine them atomistically, and fit them into a single internally coherent system. What seems to be surfacing is a willingness to acknowledge that we have here two systems that have to be taken holistically. Both take their departure from the Scriptures, the creeds, and early tradition. But they filter the data through different thought-forms.

DIFFERENT THOUGHT-FORMS

The Catholic thought-form, as expressed at Trent, is Scholastic, and heavily indebted to Greek metaphysics. The Lutheran thought-form is more existential, personalistic, or, as some prefer to say, relational.[12]

The Scholastics adopt a contemplative point of view, seeking explanation. Luther and his followers, adopting a confessional posture, seek to address God and give an account of themselves before God. In that framework all the terms take on a different hue. For a Lutheran to say that we are merely passive in receiving justification, that we are justified by faith alone, that justification is an imputation of the righteousness of Christ, that the justified continue to be sinners, that concupiscence is sin, that God's law accuses us of our guilt, and that eternal life is never merited—all these statements are possible and necessary in the Lutheran system. These statements find strong resonances in the Catholic literature of proclamation and spirituality.

In the dialogues of the past fifty years, Catholics and Lutherans have come to respect one another as Christian believers. We find that in spite of our different thought-forms we can say many things—the most important things—in common. And precisely because of our different perspectives we can learn from one another. Lutherans can teach Catholics that we must be in some sense passive in submitting to God's word, that we must always acknowledge ourselves as sinners, that God's law never ceases to accuse us, that we must throw ourselves on God's mercy, and that we depend on the perfect righteousness of Christ, without being able to make it completely our own. For all these reasons it now seems appropriate to measure the Lutheran theses against some standard other than the decrees of Trent, valid though those decrees are in Catholic dogmatic teaching.

The Official Catholic Response, in its concluding section, calls for deeper reflection on the biblical foundation in light of a joint effort on the part of Lutherans and Catholics to forge a language that can make the doctrine of justification more meaningful to men and women of our day. In face of a world that is so alien to the gospel, our churches are called to unite their forces in restoring missionary and evangelistic power to the gospel message of God's powerful mercy.

These considerations, I think, are behind the eagerness of the Catholic Church, at the very highest level, to sign the Joint Declaration, even while recognizing that theologians have not yet been able to establish how, or to what extent, certain Lutheran positions can be reconciled with official Catholic teaching. It is not enough to say that we have different frameworks of discourse. It is necessary to establish that Lutheran proclamation and Catholic speculation are both legitimate derivatives of the same gospel, and therefore compatible. Performative language cannot be unrelated to informative; the law of prayer must harmonize with the law of belief. The Joint Declaration, helpful though it be, has not overcome all difficulties. More theological work is still needed.

SIGNIFICANCE OF THE ACCORD

The Declaration differs from documents of the Catholic magisterium that are drafted and promulgated by persons in full communion with the Church of Rome. The Roman Response indicates that theological misgivings can legitimately be expressed from the Catholic side, and the same will presumably be true among Lutherans. But notwithstanding all the theological reservations on both sides, the signing of the Declaration with the "blessing" of John Paul II can be a powerful symbolic event. It says clearly to a world that hovers on the brink of unbelief that the two churches that split Western Christendom on the issue of justification nearly five centuries ago are still united on truths of the highest import. They can confess together that we are sinful members of a sinful race, that God offers us the gift of justification, that this offer comes through Christ, our only Savior, that it is received in faith, that the Holy Spirit is conferred upon those who believe, and that, having been inwardly renewed, they are called and equipped to excel in deeds of love. In view of this shared heritage of faith, we are confident that our doctrinal formulations, currently expressed in different idioms, can in the end be reconciled. Our readiness to declare the nonapplicability of the sixteenth-century condemnations on justification is based on this conviction.

NOTES

1. *Justification by Faith: Lutherans and Catholics in Dialogue VII*, ed. H. George Anderson, T. Austin Murphy, and Joseph A. Burgess (Minneapolis: Augsburg, 1985), §156, p. 71.

2. Ibid., §161, pp. 73–74.

3. Ibid., §165, p. 74.

4. Ibid., §154, p. 70.

5. *The Condemnations of the Reformation Era: Do They Still Divide?* ed. Karl Lehmann and Wolfhart Pannenberg (Minneapolis: Fortress, 1990).

6. Lutheran-Roman Catholic Joint Commission, *Church and Justification* (Geneva: Lutheran World Federation, 1994), esp. 13–17.

7. For a sampling of theological reactions see *Dialog*, Spring and Summer issues of volume 36 (1997) and *Pro Ecclesia* 7 (Fall 1998) and 8 (Spring 1999). My own critical comments in "On Lifting the Condemnations" in *Dialog* 35 (Summer 1996): 219–20, are based on the draft text of 1994. Many of them no longer apply to the revised Joint Declaration of 1997.

8. Lutheran-Catholic Dialogue, "Joint Declaration on the Doctrine of Justification," *Origins* 28 (July 16, 1998): 120–27.

9. Doctrinal Congregation and Unity Council, "Official Catholic Response to Joint Declaration," *Origins* 28 (July 16, 1998): 130–32. With special emphasis on one point, that of *simul iustus et peccator*, this response stated that the divergences "must . . . be overcome before we can affirm, as is done generically in No. 41, that these points no longer incur the condemnations of the Council of Trent" (§5, p. 131). For commentary, see Richard John Neuhaus, "The Public Square: Setback in Rome," *First Things* 86 (October 1998): 80–82.

10. The "Official Common Statement" and the "Annex" are printed together in *Origins* 29 (June 24, 1999): 87–88. The "Note on the Annex with Reference to the Questions Raised in the Catholic Response" follows on p. 89.

11. Cf. Trent, DS 1545–46, 1582.

12. On the subject of thought-forms, see Otto H. Pesch, "Existential and Sapiential Theology: The Theological Confrontation between Luther and Thomas Aquinas," in *Catholic Scholars Dialogue with Luther*, ed. Jared Wicks (Chicago: Loyola University Press, 1970), 61–81. In this helpful essay Pesch takes up many of our questions here: the assurance of salvation, cooperation, the Lutheran *simul*, and salvation by faith alone.

23

The Papacy for a Global Church

March 22, 2000

U ntil the late nineteenth century, the Catholic Church was predominantly geared to traditional societies that were stable and agrarian. To be a Catholic, in most cases, meant to be the heir of longstanding traditions that had been handed down from generation to generation in local communities. As a result of urbanization, which was intensified by the Industrial Revolution, all of this began to change. In increasing numbers, Catholics flocked to the cities and became involved in industries and professions. With better means of travel, they began to migrate to new countries where the Catholic faith had not as yet taken root. The Catholic Church came to need institutional structures that would guarantee its stability and unity in a changing and diversified world.

Vatican I and Vatican II

The popes, about the time that they lost the Papal States, awakened to their planetary responsibilities and in so doing made the papacy a more potent symbol of unity and continuity for Catholics all over the world. The decrees of the First Vatican Council (1869–70), followed by the Code of Canon Law of 1917, gave the pope practically unlimited authority over the development of doctrine and ecclesiastical legislation throughout the world. The pope came to be recognized, more than ever before, as the vicar of Christ. Through its diplomatic corps, the Holy See was morally present in a multitude of nations, overseeing the affairs of the Church and interacting with secular governments. By means of nuncios and apostolic delegates, Rome controlled the appointment of bishops everywhere.

The progressive centering of the Church on Rome was sometimes resented at the periphery. Historically minded theologians cherished the memory of a remote past when local and regional churches enjoyed a large measure of autonomy, managed their own affairs, and dealt with Rome only as a court of final appeal. Already in the mid-nineteenth century, Newman wrote nostalgically of the Middle Ages, when, as he put it, "a question was first debated in a University, then in one University against another, or by one order of Friars against another;—and then perhaps it came before a theological faculty; then it went to the Metropolitan; and so, by various stages and through many examinations and judgments, it came before the Holy See. But now," Newman complained, "all courts are superseded because the bishops refer every case immediately to Rome, which makes a prompt decision, often on grounds of expediency."[1]

The Protestant Prince Otto von Bismarck, the chancellor of the new German Empire, interpreted Vatican I as having made the pope in effect the bishop of every diocese in the world. The German bishops formulated a vigorous denial, which was approved on two occasions by Pius IX. The bishops remained true pastors of their flocks and were not demoted to being pawns of the pope.

At the Second Vatican Council (1962–65), bishops from Western Europe (France, Belgium, Holland, and Germany), together with their theological advisers, were intent on removing every semblance of justification for Bismarck's critique. They spearheaded a program of reform that sought to restore the dignity and rights of individual bishops and give real though limited autonomy to regional churches. This program was welcomed by the missionary bishops of Asia and Africa, who were anxious to insert the Catholic faith more deeply into the lives of believers who were strangers to the cultures of Italy and Western Europe. Romanization and Europeanization were regarded as obstacles to the necessary adaptation and inculturation.

Vatican II, however, did not undo the accomplishments of Vatican I. While giving new powers to the bishops and the local churches, it kept intact the prerogatives of the papacy, as previously defined. It even amplified papal supremacy by the attention it devoted to the pope's ordinary teaching power.

Among the achievements of Vatican II we may note, first of all, the stimulus it gave to inculturation. The council clearly taught that the expression and practice of the faith in different regions should be adapted to the natural gifts, traditions, and customs of the people, always keeping in mind the dangers of syncretism and separatism.

Connected with this diversified catholicity was a second principle: the retrieval of the local or regional church as having its own pastoral and theological integrity. With several textual references to the second-century apologist Ignatius of Antioch, the Constitution on the Liturgy declared, "The Church reveals herself most clearly when a full complement of God's people, united in prayer and in a common liturgical service (especially the Eucharist), exercise a thorough and active participation at the very altar where the bishop presides in the company of his priests and other assistants" (*SC* 41; cf. *LG* 28). Particular churches, therefore, were not mere branch offices of the universal Church but churches in their own right.

Third, Vatican II upgraded the episcopate. Rejecting the opinion of some authors that the bishop was simply a priest with higher responsibilities, it taught that every bishop receives by episcopal ordination the fullness of the ministerial priesthood. In this connection the council formulated, fourthly, the doctrine of collegiality. It taught that all bishops who are in communion with Rome are members of the supreme directorate of the entire Church. According to Vatican II, the college of the apostles with and under Peter perpetuates itself as the college of bishops with and under the pope.

To implement the four principles just stated, Vatican II made several structural changes. First, it called for the internationalization of the Roman Curia, which up to then had been almost exclusively Italian. Second, it erected a system of episcopal conferences, one for each major nation or territory in the world. Each conference had its own president, elected by the conference according to its own statutes. Third, the council, together with Pope Paul VI, established the Synod of Bishops, a new and unprecedented institution. It is a body of bishops that meets periodically in Rome to discuss matters of concern to the universal Church, thus keeping the pope in vital contact with representatives of churches from afar.

PAUL VI'S NEW STYLE

Pope Paul VI clearly understood the achievements of Vatican II and sought to renew the papal office in the context of the global Church. He firmly internationalized the Roman Curia. Under his regime the episcopal conferences and the Synod of Bishops found their identity. Following a suggestion of the Synod of Bishops, he established an international theological commission. Departing from the tradition that the pope should always remain in Rome—a tradition that John XXIII had slightly breached by traveling to Assisi and Loreto—Paul VI made trips to the Holy Land, India, The United States, Portugal, Turkey, Colombia, Switzerland, Uganda, and the Far East. In the course of these travels he visited the World Council of Churches in Geneva, the headquarters of the United Nations in New York, and the Conference of Latin American Episcopates at Medellín. He had highly symbolic meetings with leaders of other churches. While engaging in missionary evangelization, he also promoted friendly dialogues with the great religions. Thus the papacy under Paul VI was no longer focused on Italy or Europe, but turned outward to the universal Church and indeed to the whole world.

JOHN PAUL II AND THE GLOBAL CHURCH

John Paul II is likewise a pope of Vatican II. As a young bishop, Karol Wojtyla participated in all four sessions of the council; he enthusiastically supported its teaching and applied it assiduously in his Archdiocese of Krakow. After the council he was elected to attend the first meeting of the Synod of Bishops (1967). Before becoming pope he attended the Synod meetings of 1969, 1971, 1974, and 1977. At the meeting of 1969 he manifested his theological understanding of, and support for, the doctrine of collegiality. From 1971 on he served as an elected member of the permanent council of the Synod—a standing committee that prepares the agenda for future meetings.

The election of Cardinal Wojtyla to be the first non-Italian pope since the sixteenth century dramatically underlined the international character of the contemporary papacy. Like Paul VI, John Paul II sees himself more as a pastor and evangelizer than as a administrator. He has made about a hundred trips outside of Italy in the twenty-two years of his pontificate thus far. He has twice addressed the General Assembly of the United Nations in New York, and has spoken at UNESCO in Paris. Many of his trips have been designed primarily to promote dialogue with other Christian churches, for example in Scandinavia, Romania, and Georgia. Other journeys, such as those to Morocco, Egypt, and Israel, have been occasions for interreligious manifestations. In the name of social justice he has forcefully denounced oppressive regimes and promoted participatory forms of government as more consonant with the dignity and freedom of the human person. The success of the bloodless revolutions in Central and Eastern Europe in 1989 has been attributed in great part to his moral influence. Although he sedulously abstains from partisan politics, no pope since the Middle Ages—or perhaps in all time—has been such a major actor on the world stage.

New Institutions of Unity

As might be expected from his previous experience with the Synod of Bishops, John Paul has continued to rely heavily on that institution throughout his papacy. Like Paul VI, he has held regular sessions of the full assembly of the Synod of Bishops approximately every three years. In addition, he called an extraordinary meeting in 1985 to celebrate the twentieth anniversary of the conclusion of Vatican II. He has convoked special sessions of the Synod for the bishops of Holland, Ukraine, and Lebanon in addition to a number of continental synods, such as the five assemblies leading up to the Great Jubilee—for Africa, America, Asia, Oceania, and Europe.

Like Paul VI before him, John Paul II works closely with the national and regional conferences of bishops. They often propose names of persons recommended for appointment to sensitive positions in Rome; they elect representatives for the Synod of Bishops; and they prepare responses to the drafts of many important Roman documents. When he travels to a foreign country, the pope regularly makes a speech to the conference of bishops and sometimes enters into dialogue with its members, as he did in Los Angeles in 1987. Like earlier popes, he meets regularly in Rome with individual bishops and groups of bishops, who come every five years to discuss with him the developments, opportunities, and problems in their part of the world.

An original feature of the present pontificate is the use that John Paul II has made of the College of Cardinals, which had long been a merely honorary group except for its statutory function of electing a new pope. On five occasions between 1979 and 1994, John Paul II has gathered the cardinals in a special consistory to seek out their ideas and to obtain their cooperation in important matters, such as the preparations for the present jubilee year. The College of Cardinals is not in competition with the college of bishops, but it serves as a smaller group within the total college that can be summoned more expeditiously, more conveniently, and more economically. For similar reasons, the pope sometimes holds meetings of archbishops and meetings of heads of episcopal conferences. All of these types of session manifest his desire to govern the Church in a collegial way, taking account of the wisdom and sensitivities of bishops throughout the world.

JOHN PAUL II ON INCULTURATION

On the issue of inculturation, the present pope is strongly affirmative. Since the beginning of his pontificate, he has consistently urged the importance of incarnating the faith in the many cultures of the world. In 1982 he set up a new Pontifical Council for Culture. In 1985 he wrote an important encyclical on Cyril and Methodius, the apostles of the Slavs, naming them as patron saints of all Europe and praising them for having composed a Slavic liturgy, which was approved in Rome. On trips to Latin America, Asia, and Africa he regularly speaks on the importance of adapting the life and liturgy of the Church to the traditions and cultures of these regions.

Conscious of his mission to maintain the entire flock of Christ in unity, John Paul II sees to it that inculturation is conducted with great care. Cultures are not morally and religiously neutral. They reflect and promote definite sets of values. For this reason every culture must be diligently appraised in the light of Christ and the gospel. No human culture is perfectly attuned to the gospel. Cultures, consequently, have to be evangelized. They must be transformed in order to be hospitable to, and supportive of, authentic Christianity.

Cultures can, in addition, be self-enclosed and divisive. John Paul II warns, therefore, that while cultivating the sound values of their people,

324 | *Church and Society*

cultures must be open to dialogue with one another. The various cultural expressions of Christianity must be in mutual harmony. Christians of different cultural regions must be able to recognize one another as fellow members of the same body, sharing the same apostolic heritage. If these conditions are met, the plurality of cultures in the Church can be a positive asset. It can bring the riches of the nations to Christ the Lord, to whom they were given as an inheritance (Ps 2:8; cf. *LG* 13).

ECUMENICAL OUTREACH

Just as Jesus said, "I have other sheep that are not of this fold" (Jn 10:16), John Paul II feels a keen pastoral responsibility toward non-Roman Catholic Christians. In his encyclical on ecumenism, *Ut unum sint*, he invited the leaders and theologians of non-Roman Catholic churches to suggest ways in which he as pope could facilitate the road to Christian unity. Some of the early responses coming from other churches seemed to say that the very existence of a primacy as it had been defined at Vatican I and Vatican II is ecumenically unacceptable. But more recently the Anglican/ Roman Catholic International Commission indicated a remarkable openness on the part of Anglicans to the idea of a universal papal primacy.[2] Individual Protestant theologians such as Wolfhart Pannenberg[3] have seen the desirability of having a pope for all Christians.[4]

A number of Catholic theologians have taken the pope's appeal as an occasion for expressing their own views on how the papal office might advantageously be restructured. Not surprisingly, the suggestions have come principally from authors who are discontent with recent developments. Essentially, their complaint is that the papacy has become too active and powerful. Wishing to give greater autonomy to the bishops and the local churches, they frequently invoke the principle of subsidiarity.

THE PRINCIPLE OF SUBSIDIARITY

The principle of subsidiarity comes from Catholic social thought. John Paul II in his encyclical *Centesimus annus* gives a very concise explanation of this principle: "A community of a higher order should not interfere in the internal life of a community of a lower order, depriving the latter of its functions, but rather should support it in case of need and help to coordinate its activity with the activities of the rest of society, always with a view to the common good" (*CA* 48). This principle was first articulated in relation to secular governments, which are established from below. Beginning with the family, people find it necessary to form successively larger communities in order to obtain benefits that cannot be assured by the smaller or lower units. But the highest authorities, such as the sovereign state, should not do what the family or smaller voluntary societies can do. The state is thus an auxiliary, a *subsidium*, which supplements public and private agencies such as municipalities, schools, businesses, churches, and clubs.

It is debated to what extent, or exactly how, subsidiarity applies to the Church. Unlike the state, the Church was established, so to speak, from above, by God's action in Christ, who gave special powers to Peter and the Twelve. The Church began to pulse with life when the Holy Spirit descended upon the Church as a whole at Pentecost. Only subsequently, as the faith spread to Antioch, Rome, Alexandria, and other cities, was it necessary to set up local authorities in charge of particular churches. The particular churches were, as Vatican II puts it, "fashioned after the model of the universal Church," which is therefore in some sense prior to them, even though it also depends on them (*LG* 23). They can be called churches inasmuch as "the Church of Christ is truly present in all legitimate local congregations" (*LG* 26).

Because the principle of subsidiarity has been formulated with reference to secular societies, its applicability to the Church is debatable. Whatever the outcome of that debate, it must be conceded that merely local problems should, if possible, be handled locally. In today's world, however, local questions often have ramifications for the universal Church, thus requiring the involvement of higher authority.

PATRISTIC MODELS

In their zeal for local freedom and autonomy, some authors have called for a return to patristic and medieval models. In the ancient Church the bishops of the apostolic sees of Jerusalem, Antioch, and Alexandria were considered to have special authority in the Eastern portion of the Church, as Rome did in the West. But before resurrecting the patriarchal model, one should keep in mind that the difficulties to which it led. The patriarchates quarreled among themselves, with Antioch and Alexandria seeking to eject each other from the Catholic communion. Later Constantinople, and still later Moscow, claimed patriarchal status, but were hostile to each other. The Orthodox Church today is plagued by rivalries among the autocephalous national churches of Eastern Europe.

Even in the West, which was blessed by having only one apostolic patriarchate, nationalism has been a major obstacle to unity. It contributed to the loss of Germany, Scandinavia, England, and Scotland to the Catholic Church, while France, Austria, Spain, and Portugal sometimes teetered on the brink of schism. The resurgence of Roman authority in the nineteenth century was a signal benefit. It enabled Catholics of different nations to maintain a lively sense of solidarity even through the two world wars of the twentieth century.

In our electronic age, when information travels with the speed of light, global authority is more important than ever. Rome cannot sit back inertly while doctrinal issues are debated on the local level, as might have been done when communications were slow and transportation was difficult. Today, Rome is drawn in as soon as a controversy arises. The Holy See is asked to pronounce on one side or the other of the dispute.

There is no question of going back to the pre–Vatican II arrangement. The council was surely right in calling for inculturation and for a renewed emphasis on the local church as a center of pastoral life and worship. The time was ripe for the internationalization of the Roman Curia, which has been thoroughly accomplished since Vatican II. Thanks to the episcopal conferences and the Synod of Bishops, bishops from all over the world now assist the pope in the government of the universal Church. The pope is morally obliged to make use of these mechanisms. He also does well to call smaller and briefer meetings of heads of episcopal conferences, archbishops, and cardinals.

The process of growth at the extremities places more burdens than ever on the Roman center. It is not a question of choosing between centralization and decentralization. Decentralization could be disruptive unless the centrifugal forces were balanced by equal and opposite centripetal tendencies. In the words of Vatican II, the chair of Peter "presides over the whole assembly of charity and protects legitimate differences, while at the same time it sees that such differences do not hinder unity but rather contribute to it" (*LG* 13).

In the light of these principles, I should like to comment on some proposals for reform that have frequently surfaced in recent theological literature. Five recurrent suggestions seem to merit special mention.

Proposals for Reform

First of all, there is the issue of the nomination of bishops. Since the mid-nineteenth century, the selection of bishops by secular princes and by cathedral chapters has all but vanished. No Catholic wants to go back to the old system in which civil governments practically chose most of the bishops. Under the present system the papal nuncio or delegate has major responsibility for gathering names from his personal knowledge and in consultation with appropriate persons. The appointments are then discussed in the Congregation of Bishops, which includes bishops from different regions, who make their own suggestions. The pope receives all the recommendations and makes the final choice.

Many reform-minded theologians would like a more open and juridical process in which names are submitted by the local church, filtered through the national or regional conference of bishops, and eventually proposed to Rome for approval or disapproval. Since the process of appointment is always subject to improvement, suggestions of this kind should not be rejected out of hand. But the proposals I have seen are not free from weaknesses. By erecting representative committees, they would promote factionalism and political power struggles within local churches. By considering only names that are surfaced within the diocese, they would also create a risk of excessive inbreeding. A church with a deviant tendency would perpetuate its own eccentricity rather than have it corrected. Besides, the process of filtering the names through a succession of committees could hardly be confidential. In the end, Rome would be under pressure to choose the names proposed or to explain why it was not doing so. But there might be reasons of a confidential nature militating against an appointment that could not be made public without injury to the candidate's reputation. Besides, the current process allows consideration of a larger pool of possibilities than would be familiar to any diocesan committee. Although mistakes are occasionally made, the existing procedure, in my opinion, has given us a generally excellent body of bishops who can be trusted to serve as faithful pastors of their flocks. They compare favorably, I believe, with the elected bishops of other churches.

A second issue has to do with the powers of the Synod of Bishops. As presently constituted, it consists primarily of bishops elected by their respective episcopal conferences, which are represented according to their relative size. It meets about once every three years for relatively brief sessions not more than a month in length. The bishops could hardly afford to be absent from their sees for longer or more frequent periods. The Synod is not a legislative body but a forum for the bishops to express their views on the theme of the meeting and foster consensus among them. The Synod assemblies often make useful suggestions to the pope and the Curia. The apostolic exhortations that issue from these assemblies have demonstrated the value of the Synodal process.

There are voices in the Church that would like to see the Synod transformed into a body that could make laws and issue binding doctrinal pronouncements. Given the ad hoc composition of the assemblies, and the relatively brief time of the meetings, I am inclined to disagree. I doubt that the Catholic faithful would wish to be bound by the decrees of such an assembly. The pope can, of course, give the Synod power to decide some issue by majority vote, but he has thus far preferred to seek recommendations from the Synod and let the Roman congregations follow up with the necessary action. The assembly of 1985, for example, made four major recommendations: the early completion of the Code of Canon Law for Eastern Catholic churches, the preparation of a universal catechism or compendium of Catholic doctrine, a study of the nature and authority of episcopal conferences, and a study of the applicability of the principle of subsidiarity to the internal life of the Church. In his closing speech at the Synod the pope accepted the first three suggestions, all of which have been carried out in subsequent years. As for the principle of subsidiarity, it seems well to allow the question to mature in theological literature before the magisterium makes a formal pronouncement.

A third issue under discussion is the role of the episcopal conferences, such as, in this country, the National Conference of Catholic Bishops. As constituted by Vatican II, they are primarily consultative in nature. They permit the bishops of a nation or region to benefit from one another's wisdom and coordinate their policies as they govern their own dioceses. The conferences do not normally make binding legislation, but they can do so on occasion either by unanimous vote or by a two-thirds majority together with a formal approval (*recognitio*) from Rome.

In the summer of 1998, the pope published a letter in which he clarified the nature and doctrinal authority of episcopal conferences, as the Synod assembly of 1985 had requested. He ruled that the conferences could not teach obligatory doctrine without a two-thirds majority followed by Roman recognition. Some critics contend that this ruling showed excessive distrust of the conferences. But Vatican II did not establish the conferences as doctrinal or legislative organs. How could the Catholic people in the United States be bound by a vote of their bishops to profess some belief that was not taught throughout the Church? Do the diocesan bishops and the Catholic people really want to be bound by the majority vote of their bishops' conference—especially if it be a small conference that might have less than a dozen members?

A fourth point under discussion is the power of the Roman Curia. The pope cannot effectively govern the universal Church without a kind of cabinet consisting of the Roman congregations, tribunals, and councils. The heads of these organs are normally bishops, and in the case of congregations, cardinals. Diocesan bishops often complain that Rome is interfering too much in the affairs of the local churches. But Rome rarely intervenes on its own initiative. It is usually responding to complaints from the local church against some questionable proceeding.

A couple of examples may be helpful. In 1993 Rome intervened to quash a rather free and inaccurate English translation of the *Catechism of the Catholic Church*, which was about to be published over the protests of the authors of the *Catechism* and other experts. An international consultation was held in Rome, as a result of which the translation was held up and revised.

A recent issue that has attracted some attention is the October 26, 1999, decision of the Congregation for Divine Worship and Sacraments to review English translations of the liturgy composed by the International Committee for English in the Liturgy (ICEL), a rather cumbersome joint commission with members appointed by eleven conferences of bishops. For some years now, the texts produced by this body according to its own philosophy of translation have met with mounting criticism from bishops and groups of the faithful, but the commission, being international, is not under the authority of any bishops' conference. The United States bishops found themselves in the anomalous position of not being able to control the texts of their own liturgical books. The new regulations have the advantage of giving the bishops' conferences an agency to which they can

330 | *Church and Society*

appeal for correcting what they perceive as deficiencies in the ICEL texts. In this as in many other cases the authority of Rome functions to protect local churches from questionable exercises of power by national or international agencies while at the same time safeguarding the integrity of the Roman rite.

In doctrinal matters, Rome's policy has generally been to encourage the diocesan bishops and the bishops' conferences to take greater responsibility for overseeing the orthodoxy of what is preached and taught in their respective areas. But the bishops usually rely upon Rome to assure themselves that they are teaching in communion with the universal Church, since doctrines are by their very nature universal. The Congregation for the Doctrine of the Faith cannot avoid being drawn into discussions where questions of orthodoxy are raised.

A fifth and final question has to do with papal teaching authority. The present pope has several times made conclusive doctrinal determinations on controversial questions without any formal vote by the college of bishops. In these cases he has used his own authority as universal primate to "confirm the brethren" (cf. Lk 22:32), authoritatively gathering up the general consensus of bishops, past and present. Even if a few bishops disagree, the voice of the pope together with a solid majority of other bishops suffices for a moral consensus and makes it unnecessary to conduct a poll or call for a vote. Such cumbersome processes could easily prevent a timely and effective response to critical situations.

DIALECTIC OF CENTRALIZATION AND DIVERSITY

Since Vatican II, the principal drama within the Catholic Church has been the dialectical tension between centralizing and decentralizing tendencies. The decentralizers tend to see themselves as progressives, and to depict their adversaries as restorationists, but the opposite case can equally well be made. Those who want to reinstate the conditions of the patristic or medieval Church tend to be nostalgic and anachronistic.

In the end, the question should not be posed as an either/or. Precisely because of the increased activity of particular churches and conferences, Rome is required to exercise greater vigilance than ever, lest the unity of the Church be jeopardized. The global character of the Catholic Church today, together with the rapidity of modern communications, makes ineluctable new demands on the papal office.

It would be beyond my power to predict what the shape the papacy will take on fifty or a hundred years hence, but I venture to say that it will never go back to the status that it had in the early centuries. The developments that have taken place with and since the two Vatican councils can scarcely be reversed. The global Church, in a world of rapid communications, demands a primatial office that holds all local and regional churches in dialogue and reaches out to the whole world with the truth and love of Christ. John Paul II has discharged this mission in a highly creative way.

NOTES

1. Letter to William Monsell, January 13, 1863, in *The Letters and Diaries of John Henry Newman* (London: Thomas Nelson, 1961), 20:391. Again in his *Apologia*, Newman speaks glowingly of the Middle Ages, when a local teacher might hazard a proposition, which would smolder for some time until it would come before a bishop or professor, to be discussed in theological faculty. Rome would not speak, Newman concludes, until the question had been ventilated and turned over on every side. In the *Apologia* Newman does not explicitly state his worries about precipitate decisions from Rome. On the contrary, he emphasizes the moderate use that the popes had commonly made of their power. See John Henry Newman, *Apologia Pro Vita Sua* (Garden City, N.Y.: Doubleday Image, 1956), 340–41.

2. Anglican-Roman Catholic Dialogue, "The Gift of Authority," *Origins* 29 (May 27, 1999): 17–29.

3. Wolfhart Pannenberg, "Die lutherische Tradition und die Frage eines Petrusdienstes an der Einheit der Christen," in *Il Primato del Successore di Pietro: Atti del simposio teologico* (Vatican City: Libreria Editrice Vaticana, 1998), 472–75.

4. In this connection reference should be made to the interesting volume of essays, *A Pope for All Christians? An Inquiry into the Role of Peter in the Modern Church*, ed. Peter J. McCord (New York: Paulist, 1976), with contributions by distinguished theologians representing the Lutheran, Roman Catholic, Baptist, Reformed, Orthodox, Methodist, and Anglican perspectives.

24

The Death Penalty

A Right-to-Life Issue?

October 17, 2000

Among the major nations of the Western world, the United States is singular in still having the death penalty.[1] After a five-year moratorium, from 1972 to 1977, capital punishment was reinstated in U.S. courts. Objections to the practice have come from many quarters, including the American bishops, who have consistently opposed the death penalty. The National Conference of Catholic Bishops in 1980 published a predominantly negative statement on capital punishment, approved by a majority vote of those present though not by the required two-thirds majority.[2] Pope John Paul II has at various times expressed his opposition to the practice, as have other Catholic leaders in Europe.

Some Catholics, going beyond the bishops and the pope, maintain that the death penalty, like abortion and euthanasia, is a violation of the right to life and an unauthorized usurpation by human beings of God's sole lordship over life and death. Did not the Declaration of Independence, they ask, describe the right to life as "unalienable"?

While sociological and legal questions inevitably impinge upon any such reflection, I am here addressing the subject as a theologian. At this level the question has to be answered primarily in terms of revelation, as it comes to us through Scripture and tradition, interpreted with the guidance of the ecclesiastical magisterium. Any authentic Christian judgment must be informed by this teaching.

BIBLICAL DATA

In the Old Testament the Mosaic Law specifies no less than thirty-six capital offenses calling for execution by stoning, burning, decapitation, or strangulation. Included in the list are idolatry, magic, blasphemy, violation of the Sabbath, murder, adultery, bestiality, pederasty, and incest. The death penalty was considered especially fitting as a punishment for murder, since in his covenant with Noah, God had laid down the principle, "Whoever sheds the blood of man, by man shall his blood be shed, for God made man in his own image" (Gen 9:6).[3] In many cases God is portrayed as deservedly punishing culprits with death, as happened to Korah, Dathan, and Abiram (Num 16). In other cases individuals such as Elijah, Daniel, and Mordecai are God's agents in bringing a just death upon guilty persons.

In the New Testament the right of the State to put criminals to death seems to be taken for granted. Jesus himself refrains from using violence. He rebukes his disciples for wishing to call down fire from heaven to punish the Samaritans for their lack of hospitality (Lk 9:55). Later he admonishes Peter to put his sword in the scabbard rather than resist arrest (Mt 26:52 par.). At no point, however, does Jesus deny that the State has authority to exact capital punishment. In his debates with the Pharisees, Jesus cites with approval the apparently harsh commandment, "He who speaks evil of father or mother, let him surely die" (Mt 15:4; Mk 7:10, referring to Ex 21:17; cf. Lev 20:9). When Pilate calls attention to his authority to crucify him, Jesus points out that Pilate's power comes to him from above—that is to say, from God (Jn 19:11). Jesus commends the good thief on the cross next to him, who has admitted that he and his fellow thief are receiving the due reward of their deeds (Lk 23:41).

The early Christian community evidently had nothing against the death penalty. It approved of the divine punishment meted out to Ananias and Sapphira when they are rebuked by Peter for their fraudulent action (Acts 5:1–11). The Letter to the Hebrews makes an argument from the fact that "a man who has violated the law of Moses dies without mercy at the testimony of two or three witnesses" (Heb 10:28). Paul repeatedly refers to the connection between sin and death.[4] He writes to the Romans, with an apparent reference to the death penalty, that the magistrate who holds authority "does not bear the sword in vain; for he is the servant of God to execute his wrath on the wrongdoer" (Rom 13:4). No passage in the New Testament disapproves of the death penalty.

CATHOLIC TRADITION

Turning to Christian tradition, we may note that the Fathers and Doctors of the Church are virtually unanimous in their support for capital punishment, even though some of them such as St. Ambrose exhort members of the clergy not to pronounce capital sentences or serve as executioners. To answer the objection that the fifth commandment forbids killing, St. Augustine writes in *The City of God*:

> The same divine law which forbids the killing of a human being allows certain exceptions, as when God authorizes killing by a general law or when he gives an explicit commission to an individual for a limited time. Since the agent of authority is but a sword in the hand, and is not responsible for the killing, it is in no way contrary to the commandment, 'Thou shalt not kill' to wage war at God's bidding, or for the representatives of the State's authority to put criminals to death, according to law or the rule of rational justice.[5]

In the Middle Ages a number of canonists teach that ecclesiastical courts should refrain from the death penalty and that civil courts should impose it only for major crimes. But leading canonists and theologians uphold the right of civil courts to pronounce the death penalty for very grave offenses such as murder and treason. Thomas Aquinas and Duns Scotus invoke the authority of Scripture and patristic tradition, and give arguments from reason.

Giving magisterial authority to the death penalty, Pope Innocent III required disciples of Peter Waldo seeking reconciliation with the Church to accept the proposition, "The secular power can, without mortal sin, exercise judgment of blood, provided that it punishes with justice, not out of hatred, with prudence, not precipitation" (DS 795).

In the high Middle Ages and early modern times, the Holy See authorized the Inquisition to turn over heretics to the secular arm for execution. In the Papal States the death penalty was imposed for a variety of offenses. The Roman Catechism, issued in 1566, three years after the end of the

Council of Trent, taught that the power of life and death had been entrusted by God to civil authorities and that the use of this power, far from involving the crime of murder, is an act of paramount obedience to the fifth commandment.[6]

In modern times, Doctors of the Church such as Robert Bellarmine and Alphonsus Liguori held that certain criminals should be punished by death. Venerable authorities such as Francisco de Vitoria, Thomas More, and Francisco Suárez agreed. John Henry Newman, in a letter to a friend, maintained that the magistrate had the right to bear the sword, and that the Church should sanction its use, in the sense that Moses, Joshua, and Samuel used it against abominable crimes.[7]

Throughout the first half of the twentieth century the consensus of Catholic theologians in favor of capital punishment in extreme cases remained solid, as may be seen from approved textbooks and encyclopedia articles of the day. The Vatican City State from 1929 until 1969 had a penal code that included the death penalty for anyone who might attempt to assassinate the pope. Pope Pius XII in an important allocution to medical experts declared that it was reserved to the public power to deprive the condemned of the benefit of life in expiation of their crimes.[8]

Summarizing the verdict of Scripture and tradition, we can glean some settled points of doctrine. It is agreed that crime deserves punishment in this life and not only in the next. In addition, it is agreed that the State has authority to administer appropriate punishment to those judged guilty of crimes and that this punishment may, in serious cases, include the sentence of death.

THE ABOLITIONIST POSITION

As I said in my opening remarks, there are some who believe that because the right to life is sacred and inviolable, the death penalty is always wrong. The respected Italian Franciscan Gino Concetti, writing in *L'Osservatore Romano* in 1977, made the following powerful statement:

> In light of the word of God, and thus of faith, life—all human life—is sacred and untouchable. No matter how heinous the crimes . . . [the criminal] does not lose his fundamental right to life, for it is primordial, inviolable, and inalienable, and thus comes under the power of no one whatsoever.

If this right and its attributes are so absolute, it is because of the image which, at creation, God impressed on human nature itself. No force, no violence, no passion can erase or destroy it. By virtue of this divine image, man is a person endowed with dignity and rights.[9]

To warrant this radical revision—one might almost say reversal—of the Catholic tradition, Father Concetti and others explain that the Church from biblical times until our own day has failed to perceive the true significance of the image of God in man, which implies that even the terrestrial life of each individual person is sacred and inviolable. In past centuries, it is alleged, Jews and Christians failed to think through the consequences of this revealed doctrine. They were caught up in a barbaric culture of violence and in an absolutist theory of political power, both handed down from the ancient world. But in our day, a new recognition of the dignity and inalienable rights of the human person has dawned. Those who recognize the signs of the times will move beyond the out-moded doctrines that the State has a divinely delegated power to kill and that criminals forfeit their fundamental human rights. The teaching on capital punishment must today undergo a dramatic development corresponding to these new insights.

This abolitionist position has a tempting simplicity, but is not really new. It has been held by sectarian Christians at least since the Middle Ages. Many pacifist groups, such as the Waldensians, the Quakers, the Hutterites, and the Mennonites have shared this point of view. But, like pacifism itself, this absolutist interpretation of the right to life found no echo at the time among Catholic theologians, who accepted the death penalty as consonant with Scripture, tradition, and the natural law.[10]

The mounting opposition to the death penalty in Europe since the Enlightenment has gone hand in hand with a decline of faith in eternal life. In the nineteenth century the most consistent supporters of capital punishment were the Christian churches, and its most consistent opponents were groups hostile to the churches.[11] When death came to be understood as the ultimate evil rather than as a stage on the way to eternal life, utilitarian philosophers such as Jeremy Bentham found it easy to dismiss capital punishment as "useless annihilation."

Many governments in Europe and elsewhere have eliminated the death penalty in the twentieth century, often against the protests of religious believers. While this change may be viewed as moral progress, it is probably due, in part, to the evaporation of the sense of sin, guilt, and retributive justice, all of which are essential to biblical religion and Catholic faith. The abolition of the death penalty in formerly Christian countries may owe more to secular humanism than to deeper penetration into the gospel.

CRITIQUE OF ABOLITIONISM

Arguments from the progress of ethical consciousness have been used to promote a number of alleged human rights that the Catholic Church consistently rejects in the name of Scripture and tradition. The magisterium appeals to these sacred authorities as grounds for repudiating divorce, abortion, homosexual relations, and the ordination of women to the priesthood. If the Church feels herself bound by Scripture and tradition in these other areas, it seems inconsistent for Catholics to proclaim a "moral revolution" on the issue of capital punishment.

The Catholic magisterium does not, and never has, advocated unqualified abolition of the death penalty. I know of no official statement from popes or bishops, whether in the past or in the present, that denies the right of the State to execute offenders at least in certain extreme cases. The American bishops, in their majority statement on capital punishment, conceded that "Catholic teaching has accepted the principle that the state has the right to take the life of a person guilty of an extremely serious crime."[12] Cardinal Bernardin, in his famous speech on the "Consistent Ethic of Life" here at Fordham in 1983, stated his concurrence with the "classical position" that the State has the right to inflict capital punishment.[13]

Although Cardinal Bernardin advocated what he called a "consistent ethic of life," he made it clear that capital punishment should not be equated with the crimes of abortion, euthanasia, and suicide. Pope John Paul II spoke for the whole Catholic tradition when he proclaimed, in *Evangelium vitae*, that "the direct and voluntary killing of an innocent human being is always gravely immoral" (*EV* 57). But he wisely included in that statement the word "innocent." He has never said that every criminal has a right to live, nor has he denied that the State has the right in some cases to execute the guilty.

Catholic authorities justify the right of the State to inflict capital punishment on the ground that the State does not act on its own authority but as the agent of God, who is supreme lord of life and death.[14] In so holding, they can properly appeal to Scripture. Paul, in the passage from Romans already quoted, holds that the ruler is God's minister in executing God's wrath against the evildoer (Rom 13:4). In the First Letter of Peter, Christians are admonished to be subject to emperors and governors, who have been sent by God to punish those who do wrong (1 Pt 2:13). Jesus, as already noted, apparently recognized that Pilate's authority over his life came from God (Jn 19:11).

Pius XII, in a further clarification of the standard argument, holds that when the State, acting by its ministerial power, uses the death penalty, it does not exercise dominion over human life but only recognizes that the criminal, by a kind of moral suicide, has deprived himself of the right to life. In the pope's words, "Even when there is question of the execution of a condemned man, the State does not dispose of the individual's right to life. In this case it is reserved to the public power to deprive the condemned person of the enjoyment of life in expiation of his crime when, by his crime, he has already dispossessed himself of his right to life."[15]

In answer to the question in the title of my lecture, therefore, I conclude that the death penalty is not in itself a violation of the right to life. The real question for Catholics is to determine the circumstances under which that penalty ought to be applied. That penalty is appropriate, I contend, when it is necessary to achieve the purposes of punishment and when it does not have disproportionate evil effects. I say "necessary" because I am of the opinion that killing should be avoided if the purposes of punishment can be obtained by bloodless means.

Purposes of Punishment

The purposes of criminal punishment are rather unanimously delineated in the Catholic tradition. Punishment is held to have a variety of ends that may conveniently be reduced to the following four:

1. Rehabilitation. Insofar as possible, the penalty should strive to heal the offender, with the aim of bringing him to repentance, moral reform, and readmission to normal civil life.

2. Defense against the criminal. As the custodian of peace and good order, the government should protect society by preventing the malefactor from committing additional crimes. Incarceration is a common means of such restraint.

3. Deterrence. It is desirable for punishment to have the effect of dissuading others from committing similar crimes. This requires that the punishment be recognized as unpleasant and even harsh.

4. Retribution. Punishment should strive to redress the right order, which has been violated by the crime. The offender should be required to pay a price for the offense committed. If possible, also, the victims of the crime should be compensated for the wrong they have suffered.

Granted that punishment has these four aims, we may now inquire whether the death penalty is the apt or necessary means to attain them.

1. Rehabilitation. Capital punishment does not reintegrate the criminal into society; rather, it cuts off any possible rehabilitation. The sentence of death, however, can and sometimes does move the condemned person to repentance and conversion. There is a large body of Christian literature on the value of prayers and pastoral ministry for convicts on death row or on the scaffold. In cases where the criminal seems incapable of being reintegrated into human society, the death penalty may be a way of achieving the criminal's reconciliation with God.[16]

2. Defense against the criminal. Capital punishment is obviously an effective way of preventing the wrongdoer from committing future crimes and protecting society from him. Whether execution is necessary is another question. The very fact that a criminal is alive may constitute a threat that he might attack fellow prisoners or prison guards or might be released or escape and do further harm. But, as John Paul II remarks in *Evangelium vitae* (*EV* 56), modern improvements in the penal system have made it extremely rare for execution to be the only effective means of defending society against the criminal.

3. Deterrence. Executions, especially where they are painful, humiliating, and public, may create a sense of horror that would prevent others from being tempted to commit similar crimes. But the Fathers of the Church censured spectacles of violence such as those conducted at the Roman Coliseum. Vatican II's Pastoral Constitution on the Church in the Modern World explicitly disapproved of mutilation and torture as

offensive to human dignity (*GS* 27). In our day death is usually administered in private by relatively painless means, such as injections of drugs,
and to that extent it may be less effective as a deterrent. Sociological
evidence on the deterrent effect of the death penalty as currently practiced
is ambiguous, conflicting, and far from probative.

4. Retribution. In principle, guilt calls for punishment. The graver the
offense, the more severe the punishment ought to be. In Holy Scripture,
as we have seen, death is regarded as the appropriate punishment for
serious transgressions. Thomas Aquinas held that sin calls for the deprivation of some good, such as, in serious cases, the good of temporal or even
eternal life. By consenting to the punishment of death, the wrongdoer is
placed in a position to expiate his evil deeds and escape punishment in
the next life. After noting this, St. Thomas adds that even if the malefactor
is not repentant, he is benefited by being prevented from committing
more sins.[17]

Retribution by the State has its limits because the State, unlike God,
enjoys neither omniscience nor omnipotence. According to Christian
faith, God "will render to every man according to his works" at the final
judgment (Rom 2:6; cf. Mt 16:27). Retribution by the State can only be
a symbolic anticipation of God's perfect justice.

For the symbolism to be effective, the society must believe in the existence of a transcendent order of justice, which the State has an obligation
to protect. This has been true in the past, but in our day the State is
generally viewed simply as an instrument of the will of the governed. In
this modern perspective, the death penalty expresses not the divine judgment on objective evil but rather the collective anger of the group. The
retributive goal of punishment is too easily misconstrued as a self-assertive
act of vengeance.[18]

The death penalty, we may conclude, has different values in relation
to each of the four ends of punishment. It does not rehabilitate the criminal but may be an occasion for bringing about salutary repentance. It is
an effective but rarely necessary means of defending society against the
criminal. Whether it serves to deter others from similar crimes is a disputed question, difficult to settle. Its retributive value is impaired by lack
of clarity about the role of the State. In general, then, capital punishment
has some limited value but its necessity is open to doubt.

HARM ATTRIBUTED TO THE DEATH PENALTY

There is more to be said. Thoughtful writers have contended that the death penalty, besides being unnecessary and often futile, can also be positively harmful. Four serious objections are commonly mentioned in the literature.

1. There is a possibility that the convict may be innocent. John Stuart Mill, in his well-known defense of capital punishment, considers this to be the most serious objection. In responding, he cautions that the death penalty should not be imposed except in cases where the accused is tried by a trustworthy court and found guilty beyond all shadow of doubt.[19]

It is common knowledge that even when trials are conducted, biased or kangaroo courts can often render unjust convictions. Even in the United States, where serious efforts are made to achieve just verdicts, errors occur, although many of them are corrected by appellate courts. Poorly educated and penniless defendants often lack the means to procure competent legal counsel; witnesses can be suborned or can make honest mistakes about the facts of the case or the identities of persons; evidence can be fabricated or suppressed, and juries can be prejudiced or incompetent. Some death-row convicts have been exonerated by newly available DNA evidence. Columbia Law School has recently published a devastating report on the percentage of reversible errors in capital sentences from 1973 to 1995.[20] Since it is altogether likely that some innocent persons have been executed, this first objection is a serious one.

2. The death penalty often has the effect of whetting an inordinate appetite for revenge rather than satisfying an authentic zeal for justice. The execution is not seen as a divine judgment but rather as an expression of hatred for the criminal. By giving in to a perverse spirit of vindictiveness or a morbid attraction to the gruesome, the courts contribute to the degradation of the culture, replicating the worst features of the Roman Empire in its period of decline.

3. Capital punishment cheapens the value of life. By giving the impression that human beings sometimes have the right to kill, it fosters a casual attitude toward evils such as abortion, suicide, and euthanasia. This was a major point in Cardinal Bernardin's speeches and articles on what he called a "consistent ethic of life." Although this argument may have some validity, its force should not be exaggerated. Many people who are

strongly pro-life on issues such as abortion support the death penalty, insisting that there is no inconsistency, since the innocent and the guilty do not have the same rights.[21]

4. Some hold that the death penalty is incompatible with the teaching of Jesus on forgiveness. This argument is complex at best, since the quoted sayings of Jesus have reference to forgiveness on the part of individual persons who have suffered injury. It is indeed praiseworthy for victims of crime to forgive their debtors, but such personal pardon does not absolve offenders from their obligations in justice. John Paul II points out that "reparation for evil and scandal, compensation for injury, and satisfaction for insult are conditions for forgiveness."[22]

The relationship of the State to the criminal is not the same as that of a victim to an assailant. Governors and judges are responsible for maintaining a just public order. Their primary obligation is toward justice, but under certain conditions they may exercise clemency. In a careful discussion of this matter Pius XII concluded that the State ought not to issue pardons except when it is morally certain that the ends of punishment have been achieved.[23] Under these conditions, requirements of public policy may warrant a partial or full remission of punishment. If clemency were granted to all convicts, the nation's prisons would be instantly emptied, but society would not be well served.

In practice, then, a delicate balance between justice and mercy must be maintained. The State's primary responsibility is for justice, although it may at times temper justice with mercy. The Church rather represents the mercy of God. Showing forth the divine forgiveness that comes from Jesus Christ, the Church is deliberately indulgent toward offenders, but it too must on occasion impose penalties. The Code of Canon Law contains an entire book devoted to crime and punishment. It would be clearly inappropriate for the Church, as a spiritual society, to execute criminals, but the State is a different type of society. It cannot be expected to act as a Church. In a predominantly Christian society, however, the State may be expected to lean toward mercy provided that it does not thereby violate the demands of justice.

It is sometimes asked whether a judge or executioner can impose or carry out the death penalty with love. It seems to me quite obvious that such officeholders can carry out their duty without hatred for the criminal, but rather with love, respect, and compassion. In enforcing the law, they may take comfort in believing that death is not the final evil; they may pray and hope that the convict will attain eternal life with God.

The four objections are therefore of different weight. The first of them, dealing with miscarriages of justice, is relatively strong; the second and third, dealing with vindictiveness and with the consistent ethic of life, have some probable force. The fourth objection, dealing with forgiveness, is relatively weak. But taken together, the four may suffice to tip the scale against the use of the death penalty in a given society.

The Catholic magisterium in recent years has become increasingly vocal in opposing the practice of capital punishment. Pope John Paul II in *Evangelium vitae* declared that "as a result of steady improvements in the organization of the penal system," cases in which the execution of the offender would be absolutely necessary "are very rare, if not practically non-existent" (*EV* 56). Again at St. Louis in January 1999 the pope appealed for a consensus to end the death penalty on the ground that it was "both cruel and unnecessary."[24] The bishops of many countries have spoken to the same effect.

The American bishops, for their part, had already declared in their majority statement of 1980 that "in the conditions of contemporary American society, the legitimate purposes of punishment do not justify the imposition of the death penalty."[25] Since that time they have repeatedly intervened to ask for clemency in particular cases. Like the pope, the bishops do not rule out capital punishment altogether, but they say that it is not justifiable as practiced in the United States today.

In coming to this prudential conclusion, the magisterium is not changing the doctrine of the Church. The doctrine remains what it has been: that the State, in principle, has the right to impose the death penalty on persons convicted of very serious crimes. But the classical tradition held that the State should not exercise this right when the evil effects outweigh the good effects.[26] Thus the principle still leaves open the question whether and when the death penalty ought to be applied. The pope and the bishops, using their prudential judgment, have concluded that in contemporary society, at least in countries like our own, the death penalty ought not to be invoked because, on balance, it does more harm than good. I personally support this position as a responsible prudential judgment in the current situation.

CONCLUDING SUMMARY

In a brief compass I have touched on numerous and complex problems. To indicate what I have tried to establish, I should like to propose, as a final summary, ten theses that encapsulate the Church's doctrine, as I understand it.

1. The purpose of punishment in secular courts is fourfold: the rehabilitation of the criminal, the protection of society from the criminal, the deterrence of other potential criminals, and retributive justice.

2. Just retribution, which seeks to establish the right order of things, should not be confused with vindictiveness, which is reprehensible.

3. Punishment may and should be administered with respect and love for the person punished.

4. The person who does evil may deserve death. According to the biblical accounts, God sometimes administers the penalty himself and sometimes directs others to do so.

5. Individuals and private groups may not take it upon themselves to inflict death as a penalty.

6. The State has the right, in principle, to inflict capital punishment in cases where there is no doubt about the gravity of the offense and the guilt of the accused.

7. The death penalty should not be imposed if the purposes of punishment can be equally well or better achieved by bloodless means, such as imprisonment.

8. The sentence of death may be improper if it has serious negative effects on society, such as miscarriages of justice, the increase of vindictiveness, or disrespect for the value of innocent human life.

9. Persons who specially represent the Church, such as clergy and religious, in view of their specific vocation, should abstain from pronouncing or executing the sentence of death.

10. Catholics, in seeking to form their judgment as to whether the death penalty is to be supported as a general policy, or in a given situation, should be attentive to the guidance of the pope and the bishops. Current Church teaching should be understood, as I have

sought to understand it, in continuity with Scripture and tradition.

NOTES

1. As of December 18, 1999, Amnesty International's website lists 106 nations as "total abolitionist in law or practice." Included in this category are Australia, Austria, Belgium, Canada, Czech Republic, France, Germany, Greece, Hungary, Ireland, Italy, the Netherlands, Poland, Portugal, Romania, the Slovak Republic, Spain, Sweden, Switzerland, the United Kingdom, and the Vatican City State. Among the ninety "retentionist" countries are Afghanistan, Algeria, Chile, China, Cuba, Ethiopia, India, Indonesia, Iran, Iraq, Japan, Kenya, Libya, Nigeria, North Korea, Pakistan, Philippines, Russian Federation, South Korea, Taiwan, Tanzania, Uganda, Ukraine, United States of America, Viet Nam, and Zimbabwe. Some other countries are listed as "abolitionist for ordinary crimes only" (e.g., Argentina, Brazil, Israel, Mexico, Peru), and still others as "abolitionist de facto" (e.g., Sri Lanka, Turkey).

2. United States bishops, "Statement on Capital Punishment," *Origins* 10 (November 27, 1980): 373–77. The statement was adopted by a vote of 145 to 31, with 41 bishops abstaining, the highest number of abstentions ever recorded. According to the rules of the conference, the statement should not have been adopted, since a two-thirds majority of the conference was lacking. But no bishop arose to make the point of order. See Thomas J. Reese, "Conflict and Consensus in the NCCB/USCC," in *Episcopal Conferences: Historical, Canonical, and Theological Studies*, ed. Thomas J. Reese (Washington, D.C.: Georgetown University Press, 1989), 114–15; also idem, *A Flock of Shepherds The National Conference of Catholic Bishops* (Kansas City, Mo.: Sheed & Ward, 1992), 149–50. Since this lecture was delivered, the U. S. Conference of Catholic Bishops has adopted another statement, "A Culture of Life and the Penalty of Death," *Origins* 35 (November 24, 2005): 394–99.

3. Some commentators maintain that Gen 9:6 is simply a popular proverb and is not being approved. But there are many similar texts that impose the death penalty for murder; for example, Ex 21:12; Lev 24:17; Num 35:16–20.

4. When he lays down the principle, "The wages of sin is death" (Rom 6:23), Paul may have in mind the death of the soul but he probably means to refer to physical death as well. See Rom 1:32 and similar texts.

5. Augustine, *The City of God*, book 1, chapter 21 (Garden City, N.Y.: Doubleday Image, 1958), 57.

6. For further details on the history see James J. Megivern, *The Death Penalty: An Historical and Theological Survey* (New York: Paulist, 1997). He treats the Roman Catechism on 166–74.

7. John Henry Newman, Letter to John Rickards Mozley of April 4, 1875; *Letters and Diaries* (Oxford: Oxford University Press, 1961–84), 27:263–67, at 264.

8. Pius XII, speech to the First International Congress on Histopathology of Nervous Systems, September 13, 1952; AAS 44 (1952): 779–89, at 787. English translation, "The Moral Limits of Medical Research," in *The Major Addresses of Pope Pius XII*, vol. 1, ed. Vincent A. Yzermans (St. Paul: North Central, 1961), 225–43, at 232–33.

9. Gino Concetti, O.F.M., "Può ancora ritenersi legitima la pena di morte," *L'Osservatore Romano*, 23 January 1977, 2; French trans., "La peine de mort peut-elle encore être considérée comme légitime?" *Documentation Catholique* 74 (1977): 187–88.

10. An opponent of capital punishment in 1867 lamented that "the abolitionist reform of the death penalty has not yet found a single representative among the Catholic clergy." Édouard Thamiry, who quotes this opinion in 1929, was able to find one exception by his time—the Abbé Charles-Pélage Le Noir, who foresaw a coming apocalyptic age in which no one would be punished by death. See É. Thamiry, "Mort (peine de)," *Dictionnaire de Théologie Catholique* 10:2500–2508, at 2501.

11. This is the judgment of Richard J. Evans in his *Rituals of Retribution: Capital Punishment in Germany 1600–1987* (New York: Oxford University Press, 1996), 901, quoted by Megivern, *Death Penalty*, 213.

12. U.S. Bishops, "Statement on Capital Punishment," 374.

13. Cardinal Joseph Bernardin, "A Consistent Ethic of Life: An American-Catholic Dialogue," *Origins* 13 (December 29, 1983): 491–94, at 492. The text may also be found in Joseph Cardinal Bernardin and others, *Consistent Ethic of Life* (Kansas City, Mo.: Sheed & Ward, 1988), 1–11, at 6.

14. Augustine has been quoted earlier. Thomas Aquinas frequently quotes Rom 13:4 to show that the magistrate pronouncing the death penalty is acting by divine mandate. See his *Summa contra Gentiles*, book 3, chapter 146, and his *Catechetical Instructions*, on the Fifth Commandment.

15. Pius XII, "Moral Limits of Medical Research," AAS 44 (1952): 787. For the sake of closer conformity to the French original, I have slightly modified the translation in *The Major Addresses of Pope Pius XII*, 1:232–33. Pius XII sets forth his doctrine of crime and punishment at greater length in several other addresses in this volume, especially those on "International Penal Law" (*Major Addresses*, 1:258–69) and on "Crime and Punishment" (*Major Addresses*, 1:306–28).

16. This point is briefly but powerfully made by Romano Amerio in his chapter on the Death Penalty in *Iota Unum: A Study of Changes in the Catholic Church in the XXth Century* (Kansas City, Mo.: Sarto House, 1996), 429–38, at 434–35.

17. Thomas Aquinas, *Summa theologiae*, part II/II, qu. 25, art. 6, ad 2.

18. Steven A. Long, "*Evangelium vitae*, St. Thomas Aquinas, and the Death Penalty," *The Thomist* 63 (1999): 511–52, esp. 548.

19. John Stuart Mill, "Speech in Favor of Capital Punishment" delivered in Parliament on April 21, 1869. In the text as given by website on http://ethics.acusd.edu, Mill declares: "There is one argument against capital punishment, even in

extreme cases, which I cannot deny to have weight—on which my hon. Friend justly laid great stress, and which never can be entirely got rid of. It is this—that if by an error of justice an innocent person is put to death, the mistake can never be corrected; all compensation, all reparation for the wrong is impossible." Mill answers that in the British courts of his day the rules of evidence are such as to provide security against unjust conviction; juries and judges follow the maxim, "It is better that ten guilty should escape than that one innocent person should suffer."

20. The report *A Broken System: Error Rates in Capital Cases 1973–1995* is available on www.law.columbia.edu/news/Press Releases.

21. For some statistics dealing primarily with Catholics, see James R. Kelly and Christopher Kudlac, "Pro-Life, Anti-Death Penalty?" *America* 182 (April 1, 2000): 6–8.

22. John Paul II, encyclical *Dives in misericordia* (1980), 14.

23. Pius XII, "Crime and Punishment" address prepared for the Italian Association of Catholic Jurists, released on February 5, 1955. Text in *Major Addresses* 2:306–28, at 326.

24. Pope John Paul II, Homily in the Trans World Dome, St. Louis, January 27, 1999; *Origins* 28 (February 11, 1999): 599–601, at 601.

25. "Statement on Capital Punishment," 375.

26. Thomas Aquinas, referring to the authority of Augustine, wrote, "If, through the infliction of punishment, more or greater sins follow, then the infliction of the punishment is not included under justice." *Summa theologiae*, part II/II, qu. 43, art. 7, ad 1.

25

Religious Freedom— a Developing Doctrine

March 21, 2001

A ccording to John Henry Newman, whose two hundredth birth-day we celebrated exactly a month ago, Christianity came into the world as a single idea, but time was necessary for believers to perceive its multiple aspects and spell out their meaning. The Christian idea has gradually taken possession of minds and hearts in such a way that its significance is more precisely grasped as the centuries pass.[1] For this reason the doctrine of the faith undergoes a process of development through time. The Second Vatican Council, endorsing the insights of Newman, devoted an important paragraph of its Constitution on Divine Revelation to the Church's growth in understanding the tradition handed down from the apostles (*DV* 8).

One of the most striking developments in twentieth-century Catholicism is the doctrine of religious freedom set forth by the Second Vatican Council. The Declaration on Religious Freedom, known by its Latin title *Dignitatis humanae*, took up two very sensitive questions, the one dealing with the right of individual persons and groups to religious freedom; the other, with the duties of the State toward religion. Regarding the first point, the council taught that all human persons have by nature an inherent right to be free in seeking religious truth, in living and worshiping according to their religious convictions, and in bearing witness to their beliefs without hindrance from any human power. This principle was theologically grounded in the fact that God, respecting the dignity of the human person, invites a voluntary and uncoerced adherence to religious truth. The act of faith, being free by its very nature, cannot be compelled.

Regarding the second point, the council taught that the State has an obligation to protect the inviolable rights of all citizens, including that of religious freedom (*DH 6*). It did not teach that the State was obliged to give legal privileges to Christianity or Catholicism, although it did not rule out such arrangements. It did deny that civil government had the authority to command or prohibit religious acts (*DH 3*).

If *Dignitatis* is compared with earlier Catholic official teaching, it represents an undeniable, even a dramatic, shift. The question must therefore be asked: Was the Declaration a homogeneous development within the Catholic tradition, or was it a repudiation of previous Church doctrine? Although the question could be put much more broadly, the controversy has centered chiefly on the teachings of three popes: Gregory XVI (1831–46), Pius IX (1846–78), and Leo XIII (1878–1903). I shall accordingly take these three popes as the point of comparison or contrast.

The question is of some importance. At the council itself some conservative bishops, including Marcel Lefebvre, held that *Dignitatis* was contrary to established Catholic teaching and could not be adopted without violence to the Catholic faith. When the Declaration was approved by an overwhelming majority of the council fathers (2308 to 70) notwithstanding his protests, Lefebvre founded a traditionalist movement that ended in schism from Rome.[2]

The case for reversal is defended at the other end of the spectrum by theological revisionists who applaud *Dignitatis*. Vatican II's repudiation of earlier Catholic teaching on religious freedom, they argue, makes it likely that other Catholic doctrines, such as that of Paul VI on contraception, may someday be overturned.[3]

Thus Archbishop Lefebvre and the revisionists, for very different reasons, agreed that *Dignitatis* was a reversal of earlier Catholic teaching. Their thesis, however, receives no support from the document itself, which declares explicitly that it "leaves intact the traditional Catholic teaching on the moral obligation of individuals and societies toward the true religion and the one Church of Christ" (*DH 1*). It also claims to be speaking in harmony with the tradition and doctrine of the Church and to be developing the doctrine of recent popes on the inviolable rights of the human person and on the constitutional order of society (ibid.).

During the council, Bishop Émile De Smedt of Bruges, as the official spokesman (*relator*) for the commission that composed the document, defended its compatibility with earlier Catholic teaching.[4] A series of other cardinals and bishops, including Archbishop Gabriel-Marie Garrone of Toulouse[5] and Archbishop Lawrence Shehan of Baltimore,[6] spoke in support of De Smedt's position. During and after the council theologians such as Roger Aubert[7] and John Courtney Murray,[8] followed by a host of others, defended the council's claim that *Dignitatis* is a harmonious adaptation, not a correction, of previous Catholic teaching. In Murray's own words, the Declaration represented "an authentic development of doctrine in the sense of Vincent of Lerins, 'an authentic progress, not a change, of the faith.'"[9]

As Newman himself intimated, doctrine of a social or political character does not follow exactly the same course of development as pure dogma.[10] It is not simply spun out of the original deposit of faith but emerges with a certain irregularity according to the vicissitudes of history. Pope John Paul II explains that the social teaching of the magisterium is under continual revision insofar as the unchanging principles of the gospel need to be upheld in varying social situations. The fundamental principles are constant, but the judgments and adaptations are ever new.[11] A measure of discontinuity may therefore be expected in successive responses to novel situations. Such discontinuity, however, does not require reversals unless the Church at an earlier time ruled out precisely the development that was to occur under changed circumstances.

In order to perceive the consistency we have to understand the teaching of the nineteenth-century popes in relation to the social, cultural, and political circumstances of their day. Gregory XVI and Pius IX were speaking within the relatively narrow horizon of Catholic Europe and Latin America, where traditional religion was under attack from militant secularist liberalism, represented by the Jacobinism of the French Revolution and the Italian laicism typified by Count Cavour. Gregory XVI in his encyclical *Mirari vos* (1832) condemned the extreme liberalism of Félicité de Lamennais, which would allow all kinds of unfounded, libelous, and subversive opinions to be circulated without any legal restrictions. In this context he characterized as "insanity" (*deliramentum*) the view "according to which freedom of conscience must be asserted and vindicated for everyone whatsoever" (*DS* 2730). Pius IX in his encyclical *Quanta cura* (1864) repeated this condemnation (§3).

The Syllabus of Errors is a favorite source for those who wish to demonstrate an about-face of Catholic teaching on freedom of religion and on Church–State relationships. It was not a part of the encyclical *Quanta cura* but an unsigned appendix to it, containing a catalogue of previously condemned errors. According to John Henry Newman the Syllabus has no more doctrinal authority in itself than an index or table of contents taken apart from the book to which it refers.[12] While Newman may have minimized the authority, he was right at least to the extent that the propositions must be interpreted in relation to the original documents from which they are excerpted.[13]

Some of the propositions of the Syllabus of Errors, taken at face value, do sound contrary to Vatican II. Regarding personal conscience, Proposition 15 rejects the view that "each individual is free to embrace and profess the religion that he judges true by the light of reason." *Dignitatis*, however, teaches that "every man has the duty, and therefore the right, to seek truth in matters of religion, in order that he may with prudence form for himself right and true judgments of conscience, with the use of suitable means" (*DH* 3). Was the Syllabus, then, condemning what would later be approved by Vatican II? Before answering we must inquire what Pius IX meant by the freedom of the individual to follow the light of reason. Proposition 3 of the Syllabus gives the needed clue. It denies that "human reason without any relation at all to God, is the sole judge of true and false, good and evil, is a law unto itself, and is sufficient by its natural powers to procure the welfare of individuals and peoples." *Dignitatis*, in harmony with the Syllabus, states that "the highest norm for human life is the divine law—eternal, objective, and universal—whereby God orders, directs, and governs the entire universe" (*DH* 3). In a later paragraph *Dignitatis* declares that the Church is, by the will of Christ, the authoritative teacher of truth, that all disciples are obliged to accept and defend revealed truth, and that all men and women are invited, according to the measure of grace given to them, to accept and profess the faith (*DH* 14). Vatican II, therefore, is far from teaching that unaided human reason, without reference to God, is the supreme criterion of truth.

Several propositions from the Syllabus speak of Church–State relationships in ways that seem problematic today. Proposition 55 condemns the view that "the Church must be separated from the State, and the State from the Church." But this proposition is taken from Pius IX's allocution *Acerbissimum vobiscum* of 1852 dealing with the persecution of the Church in New Granada (modern Colombia). At that time and place the State, under pretext of separating itself from the Church, imposed a ruthless secularization, denying all public recognition and legal rights to religious organizations. It confiscated all seminaries, reduced marriage to a purely civil contract, suppressed religious schools, and claimed the right to appoint all bishops and pastors. Quite obviously *Dignitatis* does not accept that so-called "separation," which really amounts to the State's control of the entire social order. *Dignitatis*, in fact, sets forth a long list of freedoms that the Catholic Church claims for herself (*DH* 4). At no point, moreover, does it use the ambiguous expression "separation of Church and State."

Proposition 77 of the Syllabus rejects the view that "in our age it is no longer suitable for the Catholic religion to be considered the sole religion of the State, excluding all other religions." This statement does not imply that the Catholic Church should always and everywhere be the religion of the State. It simply asserts that in the mid-nineteenth century the acceptance of Catholicism as the sole established religion could in some places be suitable—a position that Vatican II does not deny. The council allows that even today it may be desirable in some places for the State to give special recognition to some one religion, but it adds that if this is done "the right of all citizens and religious communities to religious freedom must at the same time be recognized and upheld" (*DH* 6).

Pius IX's immediate successor, Leo XIII, set forth the Catholic teaching on freedom in an important encyclical, *Libertas praestantissimum* (1888). True freedom, he maintained, is a capacity to do not only what we wish but what we ought. The so-called "modern freedoms" of worship, speech, and conscience, he warned, could become destructive unless carefully defined. Liberty of worship might be taken to mean an entitlement to choose any religion or none according to one's fancy. Liberty of speech could be interpreted as a right to make groundless, deceptive, or slanderous statements. Liberty of conscience could seem to imply a license to disobey God and persons who speak with divine authority. Leo's condemnation of false freedoms, even though it targeted errors prevalent a century ago, retains its validity and relevance today.

Dignitatis went beyond Leo XIII in affirming that people in error have certain human rights. In particular, they have the right not to be interfered with by the State in acting according to their religious convictions, unless in so doing they disturb what the council calls the "just public order" (*DH* 2, 3). A significant number of bishops expressed anxiety that *Dignitatis* would affirm the right to hold or disseminate error, thereby reversing the previous teaching of many popes. In his final *relatio* of November 19, 1965, Bishop De Smedt sought to quiet these fears. He sharply denied that the text he was presenting affirmed any right to error.[14] Confirming De Smedt's position, the *Catechism of the Catholic Church* asserts: "The right to religious liberty is neither a moral license to adhere to error, nor a supposed right to error, but rather a natural right of the human person to civil liberty, i.e., immunity, within just limits, from external constraint in religious matters by political authorities" (2108).[15]

Regarding the relations of Church and State, Leo XIII maintained that, while the two have different functions, they must act in harmony. In his 1885 encyclical *Immortale Dei,* for instance, he teaches that society as such and the government through which it acts have a duty to recognize and support the true religion. Rulers as well as subjects "are bound absolutely to worship God in that way which he has shown to be his will" (§6). Later Leo states that "it is not lawful for the State, any more than for the individual, either to disregard all religious duties or to hold in equal favor all kinds of religion" (§35). In most of his social teaching he presupposes a regime in which the civil government exercises quasi-paternal authority in caring for the religious well-being of the citizens.

Dignitatis is more reserved in describing the religious responsibilities of the State. It teaches that, on the negative side, the State must avoid all coercion, unless religious freedom is being misused to violate the rights of other citizens, to disturb the public peace, or to undermine public morality—three provisos that the council reiterates and summarizes under the heading of "public order" (*DH* 7). Positively, according to the Declaration, the State must "recognize and promote the religious life of its citizens" (*DH* 3), for it is clear, according to *Dignitatis*, that "society will itself benefit from the fruits of justice and peace that result from people's fidelity to God and his holy will" (*DH* 6).

These religious responsibilities are in line with what Leo XIII designated as the "care of religion."[16] Vatican II did not adopt the liberal concept of the religiously or morally neutral State—one that concerns itself only with civil peace and material prosperity.

Many bishops at Vatican II feared that the council would deny the duty of the civil government toward the one true religion as affirmed by a whole series of popes. *Dignitatis* stated explicitly that the one true religion subsists in the Catholic Church and that it accepted "the traditional Catholic teaching on the moral obligation of individuals and societies toward the true religion and toward the one Church of Christ" (*DH* 1). The question was raised whether this meant that the obligation rested on the citizens, as distinct from the State. On this issue, as on the supposed right to profess error, Bishop De Smedt in his final *relatio* gave a decisive answer. He explained that the text, as revised, did not overlook or deny but clearly recalled Leo XIII's teaching on the duties of the public authority (*potestatis publicae*) toward the true religion.[17] These words may be taken as an official commentary on the text—indeed, the only official commentary we have on this particular point. We may therefore conclude that *Dignitatis* does not negate earlier Catholic teaching on the duties of the State toward the true faith.

Speaking to a worldwide community in a period of rapid flux, Vatican II wisely refrained from trying to specify exactly what kind of help the Church ought to expect from the State. That question must be variously answered according to the constitution of the State, the religious makeup of the population, and the traditions of the society. No one formula could be suitable for all countries today, though any legitimate arrangement must, as I have said, respect the rights of all citizens.

The main difference between the doctrine of the nineteenth-century popes and that of *Dignitatis* is in the means that each envisages. Pius IX and Leo XIII, writing in an age when paternalistic monarchies were still normal in most Catholic countries, evidently preferred to see the Catholic Church in a legally privileged position. Vatican II, speaking within a more democratic and religiously pluralistic situation, placed greater reliance on indirect support. If the State would simply establish conditions under which the Church could carry on its mission unimpeded, it would do more for the Church than many Christian princes had done in the past. On the final day of the council, December 8, 1965, Pope Paul VI addressed to temporal rulers the question "What does the Church ask of you today?" And he answered: "She tells you in one of the major documents of this council. She asks of you only liberty, the liberty to believe and to preach her faith, the freedom to love her God and serve him, the freedom to live and to bring to men her message of life."[18]

For a correct interpretation of the shift between the nineteenth-century popes and Vatican II, it is necessary to take account of the intervening history. In the nineteenth century the principal threat to faith came from anticlerical liberalism, inspired by the slogans of the French Revolution. In the twentieth century, Christian faith was confronted by oppressive atheistic regimes, such as Soviet Communism and German National Socialism. Beginning with Pius XI, the popes vigorously upheld the rights of the human person against totalitarian systems of government. Pius XII in his wartime messages and John XXIII in his social encyclicals became stalwart champions of universal human rights. *Dignitatis* could therefore claim that, by amplifying the doctrine of religious freedom on the basis of the dignity of the human person, it was developing the teaching of the more recent popes without contradicting previous Catholic tradition.

Besides the transformation of the political climate, a number of other factors contributed to the adjustments we have noted. Catholic theology in the nineteenth century was dominated by Scholastic ontological categories, but in the twentieth it was profoundly influenced by personalist phenomenology, which brought with it a keener appreciation of human dignity and freedom. Then again, the twentieth century saw the rise of the ecumenical movement, which made the churches more ready to see one another as allies in a common struggle against secularism and irreligion. The Declaration on Religious Freedom, initially drafted by the Secretariat for Promoting Christian Unity, was seen as a help for overcoming tensions among religious groups.

IN THE TITLE FOR THIS LECTURE I describe religious freedom as "a developing doctrine." The purpose of the present participle is to suggest that the development did not end with Vatican II. In the forty years since the council the process has continued, especially by way of clarification and application. Pope John Paul II, who enthusiastically welcomed and promoted religious freedom at the council, has been a leader in bringing its doctrine forward.

The present pope's first and most important contribution has been to set the teaching of *Dignitatis* in the framework of a comprehensive theory of human freedom based on classical theology and contemporary personalist insights. Using *Dignitatis* in combination with *Gaudium et spes*, the Pastoral Constitution on the Church in the Modern World, he has insisted that freedom cannot be adequately defined in purely negative terms, as a mere immunity from coercion. More fundamentally, freedom is a power of self-determination whereby the human person actively tends toward, embraces, and adheres to what is perceived as true and good. In this process conscience is a valuable instrument, but is not the ultimate norm. It does not tell us what is right or wrong unless it is properly informed. Conscience itself therefore summons us to seek the true good and to make use of whatever authoritative guidance is available.[19]

A second contribution of John Paul II is his move beyond individualism. A partial or hasty reading of *Dignitatis* might give the impression that its real concern is to protect the individual person from oppression by social authorities. The present pope has given greater attention to the right of religious groups, including the Church, to enjoy religious freedom. The religious needs of individuals, he points out, are not protected unless freedom is accorded to institutions that serve religion.[20] While pressing this claim against Marxist governments in Eastern Europe, China, and Cuba, he has also made a powerful plea for the freedom of Christian churches to carry on their religious ministries in Islamic regions.

Building on the accomplishments of *Dignitatis*, John Paul II has, in the third place, identified and repudiated an error that he calls "integralism"—namely the confusion between what belongs to Caesar and what belongs only to God. Religious integralism, as he defines it, fails to distinguish between the spheres of competence of faith and civil life. Integralists have sometimes excluded from the civil community all who do not profess the established religion. This was notably the case when the axiom *Cuius regio eius religio* (The religion of the people is that of their ruler) was in place. With an apparent reference to some non-European countries, the Pope noted that this confusion of competences still obtains in certain parts of the world.[21]

Going beyond Vatican II, John Paul II has, in the fourth place, recognized the necessity of repentance for the errors of the past. Especially at the time of the Reformation, Protestant and Catholic rulers often cruelly exiled, imprisoned, or executed those of their subjects who did not adhere to the religion favored by the State. Christians of many different ecclesial traditions have frequently persecuted Jews, Gypsies, and other minorities. Vatican II was aware of this violence, but touched on it very lightly in a subordinate clause, as though it were a minor and rare aberration (*DH* 12). John Paul II, in the name of all Catholics, asks forgiveness for the wrongs inflicted by their predecessors, and at the same time pledges the Church's forgiveness for all that Catholics have suffered in persecutions directed against them.[22] This plea for mutual forgiveness was a key element in the program for the Great Jubilee of the Year 2000.[23]

Finally, Pope John Paul II has elucidated the difference between mere tolerance and reconciliation. In the civil sphere, it may be necessary to tolerate certain unacceptable practices because the effort to suppress them would bring about greater evils. But mere tolerance is static; it cannot serve as a principle of growth. In interreligious dialogue and in ecumenism, therefore, efforts should be to move toward unity in the fullness of truth. This endeavor is germane to the quest for freedom, since we have the word of Jesus: "The truth will make you free" (Jn 8:32). To settle for doctrinal compromises or a simple agreement to disagree would be a disservice to freedom itself.

THE PROBLEM OF RELIGIOUS FREEDOM is still a burning issue in the world of our day. In some regions atheistic governments are actively harassing or persecuting all religious believers. Elsewhere Christians and others are being oppressed by governments seeking to impose religious unity by force. The gospel of religious freedom still needs to be effectively proclaimed in various regions of Indonesia, India, the Near East, and Northern Africa. In the former Soviet Union the Orthodox Church is faced by quandaries not unlike those faced by Western European and Latin American Catholics on the eve of Vatican II.

In countries like the United States, the churches enjoy a blessed degree of freedom to carry out their mission. The greatest threat to religion, in my estimation, is the kind of secularism that would exclude religion from the public forum and treat churches as purely private institutions that have no rightful influence on legislation, public policy, and other dimensions of our common life. When churches speak out on issues such as abortion, euthanasia, marriage, and divorce, they are accused of transgressing the barrier between Church and State. Even the courts often interpret the nonestablishment provision of the First Amendment so as to prevent any public role for religion, thereby inhibiting the free exercise of religion. Legal, fiscal, and regulatory pressures render it difficult for Catholic charitable and educational institutions to maintain their distinctive identity. In the name of free exercise, religious communities should have the means they need to act according to their principles and to transmit their faith to new generations. They are also entitled to argue for laws and public policies that are in conformity with what they regard as sound reason and the law of God. The State has no right to coerce religious believers to perform acts that violate the moral norms of their communities.

While suitable public recognition should be given to the major religions within the body politic, the question of direct government assistance is much more complex. The difficulty is illustrated by divergent reactions of committed believers to President Bush's recent proposal to give public funding to faith-based initiatives of a social and charitable character. Some complain that if they do not receive State aid they will be inhibited in their free exercise of religion, while others fear that the embrace of governmental aid, with the regulation that would attend such aid, might suffocate the freedom that the churches now enjoy. These disagreements about matters of policy belong to the prudential, not the doctrinal, order. They can exist among persons who fully accept the current Catholic teaching on religious freedom.

OVER THE PAST FIFTY YEARS we have seen a strong and welcome development of the doctrine of religious freedom. Articulating the principles of the gospel in new situations, the Church has found a new voice. She speaks with a fresh awareness of the freedom that God wills for all human beings and with a deeper realization of the limited competence of civil governments. As the Church adapts her social teaching to changing political and social circumstances, she comes to a sharper perception of certain aspects and consequences of the gospel. The teaching of the nineteenth-century popes was not erroneous, but was limited by the political and social horizons of the time. In the words of *Dignitatis*, Vatican II brought forth from the Church's treasury "new things in harmony with those that are old" (*DH* 1). This process of development must continue as the Church faces the new problems and opportunities that arise in successive generations.

NOTES

1. John Henry Newman, *An Essay on the Development of Christian Doctrine* (1878 ed.), 29–30.

2. See Michael Davies, *Apologia Pro Marcel Lefebvre,* part 1, *1905–1976* (Dickinson, Tex.: Angelus Press, 1979), especially xiv, 425–41.

3. The writings of Daniel C. Maguire, Charles E. Curran, and Richard A. McCormick represent this point of view. J. Robert Dionne in his *The Papacy and the Church* (New York: Philosophical Library, 1987), 125–94, gives a detailed scholarly argument for the reversalist position.

4. Émile De Smedt's *relatio* of November 18, 1963, is in Vatican II, *Acta synodalia* II/5: 485–95.

5. *AS* III/2:533–35.

6. *AS* IVF/1:396–97.

7. Roger Aubert, "La liberté religieuse du Syllabus de 1864 à nos jours," in *Essais sur la liberté religieuse* (Paris: A. Fayard, 1965), 17–18.

8. John Courtney Murray, "Vers une intelligence du développement de la doctrine de l'Eglise sur la liberté religieuse," in La *Liberté religieuse: Déclaration "Dignitatis humanae personae"* (Paris: Ed. du Cerf, 1967), 111–47.

9. Ibid., 138.

10. Newman, *Essay on Development*, 42–45. I say "intimated" because at this point Newman is discussing the development of political institutions, not precisely the development of sociopolitical teaching.

11. John Paul II, encyclical *Sollicitudo rei socialis*, 3.

12. John Henry Newman, *Letter* to *the Duke of Norfolk* (1875), chapter 7 in *Newman and Gladstone: The Vatican Decrees*, ed. Alvin Ryan (Notre Dame, Ind.: University of Notre Dame, 1962), 73–228, at pp. 150–66.

13. Each of the Propositions in the *Syllabus of Errors* is discussed in relation to the original documents to which it refers in Lucien Choupin, *Valeur des Décisions Doctrinales et Disciplinaires du Saint-Siège*, 2nd ed. (Paris: Beauchesne, 1913), 185–413.

14. Émile De Smedt, *relatio* of November 19, 1965: "Nowhere is it affirmed—nor could it be rightly affirmed, as is evident—that there is a right to propagate error," *AS* IV/6:725.

15. Brian W. Harrison in his valuable *Religious Liberty and Contraception* (Melbourne, Australia: John XXIII Fellowship Co-op, 1988) speaks in this connection not of a *ius faciendi* but of a *ius exigendi*—a right to be left alone by other human beings (129).

16. See Enrique Torres Rojas, *La Libertad Religiosa en Leo XIII y en el Concilio Vaticano II* (Vitoria, Spain: Editorial ESET, 1968), 46–74, especially 62–63.

17. De Smedt, final *relatio, AS* IV/6:719.

18. Message to Rulers," spoken by Cardinal Achille Lienart of Lille and others, in *The Documents of Vatican II*, ed. Walter M. Abbott, S.J. (New York: America Press, 1966), 729.

19. John Paul II writes at some length about the role of conscience in the encyclical *Veritatis splendor* (1993), §§54–64.

20. John Paul II, U.N. address, October 2, 1979, §20.

21. John Paul II, "The United Europe of Tomorrow," Strasbourg, October 11, 1988, §10, *Origins* 18 (October 27, 1988): 330–32, at 332.

22. Several statements to this effect are excerpted in Luigi Accattoli, *When a Pope Asks Forgiveness* (Staten Island, N.Y.: Alba House, 1998): 145–55.

23. John Paul II, apostolic letter *Tertio Millennio Adveniente* §35. See also his text for the penitential service for the First Sunday of Lent, March 12, 2000, *Origins* 29 (March 23, 2000): 645–48.

26

Christ Among the Religions

November 7, 2001

The relations between the various religions of the world have often been hostile, and in many places they remain so today. When we pick up the daily newspaper, we can hardly avoid reading about conflicts between Jews and Muslims, between Muslims and Hindus, between Hindus and Sikhs, or between Sunnis and Shiites. All of these faiths have at one time or another clashed with Christianity, which, for its part, has contributed more than its share to interreligious tension and warfare. Christians have persecuted Jews and have fought holy wars against Muslims. Within Christianity there have been internecine wars, especially between Protestants and Catholics, but sometimes also with Eastern Orthodox. Struggles of this kind continue to rage in Northern Ireland, for example, although it would be unfair to describe the Catholic Church as a belligerent in that conflict since its authorities have disapproved of violence on either side.

The present armed intervention in Afghanistan is sometimes described as a religious war. This interpretation is on the whole false, but it contains a grain of truth. From the American standpoint, there is nothing we are less interested in than a war against Islam. Our own nation is hospitable to Muslims, who constitute nearly three million of its inhabitants. They enjoy full freedom of worship throughout North America and Western Europe. A new crusade would gain no support from any major power in the West and would certainly not receive the blessing of Christian religious authorities. Our quarrel with Osama bin Laden has to do only with his politics of violence, which may not be in accord with the tenets of authentic Islam.

From the Arab side, religion is part of the picture, but Muslim extremists such as bin Laden seem to be working for ends that are cultural, political, ethnic, and economic rather than exclusively religious. They resent the power of the United States and its allies, which they perceive as arrogant and brutal. Even more fundamentally, they are repelled by what they perceive as the culture of the West. Their quarrel is not primarily with Christianity as a religion but much more with what they regard as the loss of religion in the West: its excessive individualism, its licentious practice of freedom, its materialism, its pleasure-loving consumerism. They see this hedonistic culture as a threat since it exercises a strong seductive power over many young people in the traditionally Islamic societies of Asia, Africa, and other continents.

If this analysis is correct, globalization might be seen as an underlying cause of the conflict in Afghanistan. Modern means of travel and communication bring together cultures that have developed in relative autonomy in different regions of the earth. The encounter produces a kind of culture shock, especially in nations that have not gone through the gradual process of industrialization and modernization that occurred two centuries ago in the West.

Christians of North America and Western Europe have by now grown accustomed to rubbing shoulders with Jews, Muslims, Hindus, Buddhists, and members of practically every other religion that can be named. Where immigration is taking place on a large scale, and modern means of communication are generally available, no religion is any longer in a position to claim exclusive domination of a region and shelter its faithful from contact with other faiths. Like it or not, most of us are destined to live in a religiously mixed society that includes people of many faiths and of no faith at all.

For this reason we have to discuss the ways in which different religions can relate to each other. I should like in this lecture to propose a typology consisting of four possible models: coercion, convergence, pluralism, and tolerance.

COERCION

The first model, coercion, predominated throughout the greater part of human history. In most periods of history, political authorities have wanted to enforce unity of religion within their respective jurisdictions and to compel the populations of subject peoples to adopt the religion of the conqueror. The Roman Empire for a while accepted religious pluralism, but the emperors soon began to insist that divine honors be paid to themselves. They consequently came to persecute religions such as Christianity, which refused such worship. When the Roman Empire adopted Christianity as its official religion, the emperors began to enforce Christian orthodoxy and persecute all other religions, including dissident forms of Christianity. The pattern of a single religion for a single State remained normative until early modern times, even after the Reformation. The terrible wars and persecutions of the sixteenth and seventeenth centuries were largely brought about by the assumption that every State must have only one religion, that of its ruler (*cuius regio eius religio*).

In this situation, wars between States frequently became, under another aspect, wars between religions. The Crusades vividly illustrate this fact. Although the Europeans are usually depicted as the aggressors, much of the military action was in fact defensive. The Turks conquered Syria, North Africa, and large portions of European soil, including Portugal, Spain, southern France, and parts of Italy and Switzerland in the West as well as the Balkans, present-day Yugoslavia, and Hungary in the East. The advance of the Turks meant, of course, the extension of Islam as a religion, and their retreat, more often than not, meant the Christianization of the territories they had lost, as can be seen from fifteenth-century Spain, which expelled all Jews and Muslims who did not convert to Christianity.

In the present situation of the "global village," this coercion model is difficult to maintain. As a result of the bloody "wars of religion," Europe and the United States learned the lesson that the cost is too great. From the perspective of Christian theology, it is indefensible to try to convert people by the sword. Protestants and Catholics have alike learned that adherence to the faith must be a free and uncoerced act. Past efforts to force conversions have served to discredit religion and have contributed to the spread of indifferentism and irreligion.

True, there are still rulers in the world who seek to enforce uniformity of faith. They are troublesome neighbors and threats to global peace. From a Christian point of view, their coercive policies must be disapproved. In time, I suspect, they will come to recognize that their policies are mistaken. For, as I have said, modern means of travel and communication make it very difficult to prevent the growth of different religious communities in every region of the globe. Although authoritarian governments may resist the penetration of other faiths, as they are doing in some Muslim, Hindu, and Buddhist regions today, the barriers will ultimately be pierced and crumble. Sooner or later, populations that have been compelled to adopt the religion of their rulers will demand freedom to make conscientious choices and testify to their sincerely held convictions.

In spite of setbacks, the tide of history has been running in favor of religious freedom. The Soviet Union was not able to enforce its atheist ideology beyond the span of seventy years. Religious coercion survives only in nations that have come late to modernity. It is promoted by extremists who sense that desperate measures are needed to save their theocratic vision of the State.

CONVERGENCE

The second model for relating the religions to one another is one of convergence. On the ground that the religious impulse is essentially the same in all peoples some scholars contend that the religions agree in essentials and that their differences are superficial. In the 1970s John Hick, among others, contended that the religions could agree on the basis of theocentrism, recognizing their differences about the means of salvation as culturally relative.[1] But theocentrism is not a satisfactory platform for dialogue with the many religions that are polytheistic, pantheistic, or atheistic. Even faiths that are clearly theistic, such as Judaism, Islam, and Christianity, are unwilling to surrender their convictions regarding the way to God, whether it be the law of Moses, the Koran, or Jesus Christ.

A number of scholars, abandoning the theocentric idea of religious convergence, have recently turned to what they call the "soteriocentric" model.[2] All religions, they maintain, agree that the purpose of religion is to give salvation or liberation, which they understand in different ways, perhaps because of the variety of cultures. By dialogue about liberation, it is presumed, they could overcome their mutual divisions.

The basic premise of these convergence theories is that all religions, at least in their differentiating features, are human constructions—faltering attempts to articulate the holy and transcendent mystery by which human existence is encompassed. This theory, however, runs counter to the official teaching and historic identity of the religions, and meets with resistance on the part of religiously minded people, who contend that their specific faith is true, even that it is divinely revealed. Christians hold that central doctrines of their own faith, such as the Trinity and the Incarnation, belong to revelation and cannot be sacrificed for the sake of achieving some putative reconciliation. Orthodox Jews adhere passionately to the law of Moses and to rabbinic tradition. Muslims, for their part, regard the Koran as the final revelation of God and look to Muhammad as the greatest and last of the prophets. Soteriology is a point of division, because the religions vehemently disagree about the way to salvation. Soteriocentrism, therefore, is no more promising than theocentrism as a remedy for disunion.

Pluralism

The third model of religious encounter is that of pluralism. By this I mean not simply the fact of religious plurality, but the view that it is a blessing. The contention is that each religion reflects certain aspects of the divine. All are partially true but need to be supplemented and counterbalanced by the elements of truth found in the others. The coexistence of all overcomes the errors and limitations of each taken alone. As the fourth-century rhetorician Symmachus maintained in his debate with Saint Ambrose, "It is impossible that so great a mystery should be approached by one road only."[3]

This approach has a certain appeal for relativists, who maintain that the human mind cannot attain objective truth, and that religion is an expression of merely subjective feelings. But it will not appeal to orthodox believers, who hold that the doctrines of their religion are objectively and universally true. Christianity stands or falls by the claim that there really are three persons in God and that the second of them, the eternal Son, became incarnate in Jesus Christ. Christians gladly admit that there are elements of truth and goodness in other religions, but they continue to insist that God's revelation in Christ is intended to be transmitted to all peoples. Committed Jews and Muslims likewise regard their religions as divinely revealed and reject any attempt to put all religions on the same level.

This negative response does not of course mean that members of different religions have nothing to learn from one another. Christianity has developed over the centuries by entering into contact with a great variety of philosophies and religions, which have enabled Christians to find implications in their own faith that they would not otherwise have recognized. Christianity grows like an organism that takes in food from the environment in which it finds itself and assimilates that food into itself. It does not admit the validity of doctrines and practices that run counter to its own self-understanding. As we shall soon be seeing, dialogue can increase the mutual respect of the different religions, but experience gives no ground for supposing that it leads to the conclusion that all religions are equally good and true. On points where they contradict one another, at least one of them must be wrong.

Tolerance

We turn, then, to the fourth option, which I call tolerance. Tolerance is not the same thing as approval. We tolerate things that we find less than acceptable because we find ourselves unable to suppress them or because the suppression would be too burdensome or morally evil. In the eighteenth century, the principle of toleration—as expressed, for example, in John Locke's famous *Letter Concerning Tolerance*—came to be generally accepted in many countries of Western Europe. That principle was fundamental to the American experiment in ordered freedom. From the beginning we had in this nation a great variety of Christian denominations that regarded one another as mistaken. The American political settlement did not require them to approve of each other's doctrines and practices, but it did insist that they avoid any effort to coerce the members of other denominations to agree with them. In the course of time, the religious scene has become increasingly diverse. It contains many more varieties of Christianity than were originally present. In addition, the nation has welcomed to its shores multitudes of Jews, Muslims, Buddhists, and Hindus. With rare exceptions, all of these religious groups live peaceably together, not interfering with each other's teaching, life, and worship. The American experiment has worked well enough to offer a possible model for the global international community that is currently experiencing its birth pangs.

THE FOUR MODELS AND VATICAN II

Although the term "tolerance" has not been not extensively used in Catholic official teaching during the past fifty years, this fourth model, in my opinion, is the one that best coheres with the doctrine of the magisterium. Pius XII in an important address of 1953 stated that in the world community then coming into being, the Catholic Church would not expect to have a privileged position or to be recognized as the established religion. It would ask only that the various religions be allowed full freedom to teach their own beliefs and practice their own faith.[4] Vatican II in its Declarations on Non-Christian Religions and on Religious Freedom endorsed this model as suitable for individual nation-states.

Vatican II explicitly renounces the use of any kind of coercion, whether physical or moral, in order to bring others into the Catholic fold. It taught that the religious freedom of all citizens and religious communities should be recognized and upheld, even in commonwealths that give special recognition to some one religion (*DH* 6). For the peace of civil society and the integrity of the religions themselves it is essential to cultivate an atmosphere of mutual tolerance and respect.

Vatican II has sometimes been misunderstood as though it had adopted the pluralist model, renouncing the exclusive claims of Christianity.[5] But in point of fact, the council insisted on the unique truth of the Catholic faith and on the duty of all persons to seek the true religion and embrace it when found (*DH* 1).

Vatican II proclaimed a very high Christology. It taught that God had established Christ as the source of salvation for the whole world (*LG* 17) and that he is "the goal of human history, the focal point of the longings of history and civilization, the center of the human race, the joy of every human heart, and the answer to all its longings" (*GS* 45). The council quoted Paul to the effect that God's intention is "to reestablish all things in Christ, both those in the heavens and those on the earth" (*GS* 45, quoting Eph 1:10).

As a consequence of its high Christology Vatican II took great care to insist on the unique mediatorship of Christ and to emphasize the abiding importance of missionary activity. Acknowledging Christ as the redeemer of the world, the council called on Christians to disseminate the gospel as broadly as possible. To be ignorant of the gospel or to deny it would be to overlook or reject God's greatest gift to humankind. The Church by its intrinsic dynamism tends to expand and to take in members from every race and nation. The Decree on the Church's Missionary Activity holds since all human beings have sinned and fallen short of the glory of God, "all have need of Christ as model, master, liberator, savior, and giver of life" (*AG* 8).

As for the non-Christian religions, the council taught that they often contain "seeds of the word" and "rays of that divine truth which enlightens all men," but it did not teach that these religions were revealed, or that they were paths to salvation, or that they were to be acceptable alternatives to Christianity. Judaism, of course, holds a special position among the non-Christian religions, since the faith of Israel is the foundation on which Christianity rests (cf. *NA* 4). The Hebrew Bible is a permanently valid and inspired record of God's revelation to his elect People before the coming of Christ (*DV* 14).

The council is far from teaching that the other religions are free from error. It declares that "rather often people, deceived by the Evil One, have become caught up in futile reasoning and have exchanged the truth of God for a lie, serving the creature rather than the Creator (cf. Rom 1: 21, 25). Consequently, to promote the glory of God and procure the salvation of all such persons, and mindful of the command of the Lord, 'preach the gospel to every creature' (Mk 16:16), the Church painstakingly fosters her missionary work" (*LG* 16).

Evangelization, according to the Decree on Missionary Activity, frees the rites and cultures of the nations "from all taint of evil, and restores [them] to Christ as their source, who overthrows the devil's domain and wards off the manifold malice of evil-doing" (*AG* 9). These sentences imply that the other religions are by no means adequate substitutes for Christianity. The implication is that they may in some respects hinder the salvation of their own adherents. To that extent the council's attitude toward them is one of qualified approval and toleration.

The charge is sometimes made that absolute convictions, such as the claims made for Jesus Christ by the Scriptures and the councils, give rise to oppression and violence. I believe that the contrary is true. The leaders in the antislavery movement of the nineteenth century and the civil rights movement of the twentieth century, as well as the great champions of nonviolence, have been, more often than not, men and women of strong religious conviction.

Persons who recognize no moral absolutes lack any solid grounds for defending human rights and human dignity. Anyone who is unsure whether the taking of innocent human life is unconditionally forbidden will be able to make only a weak case against genocide and against the massive slaughter of innocents that occurs in abortion clinics all over the world. It is possible, of course, that a few opponents of abortion may misguidedly murder those who commit abortions, but these killings are rare; they also violate Catholic ethical principles, which forbid individuals to take the law into their own hands.

Christians are tolerant of other religions not in spite of but in part because of their certainty about revelation. Revelation assures them that God made human beings in his own image as free and responsible subjects. It also teaches that faith is by its very nature a free act. Vatican II's Declaration on Religious Freedom makes it clear that Christians must respect the right and duty of all persons to seek the truth in matters of religion and to adhere to it when found. Believers must be allowed to profess and practice their religion, provided in so doing they do not disturb the requirements of just public order.

Strategies for Coexistence

The posture of tolerance and qualified approval, if it is reciprocated, opens the way for a variety of strategies that may lead to peaceful and friendly coexistence. First I should like to mention the avenue of knowledge. The different religious groups will normally experience a healthy impulse to get to know one another by encountering them in actual life and by obtaining accurate information about them through study and reading. In a religiously diverse society, people should be educated not only in their own faith but also, to some degree, in the faiths of others with whom they will have to interact. All should be on guard against caricatures based on prejudice or ignorance.

Second, the groups can engage in certain joint programs based on a common recognition of basic moral values. Opportunities arise for people of different faiths to work together for objectives such as the defense of the family, the rights of migrants and refugees, the relief of poverty and hunger, the prevention and cure of disease, the promotion of civil and international peace, and the care of the environment. Religious groups, because of their authority over the consciences of the faithful, can give powerful motivation for humanitarian reform.

Third, the groups can bear common witness regarding the religious and moral convictions that they share in common. Most religions agree on the importance of prayer and worship. They encourage the pursuit of holiness and speak out against socially harmful vices such as anger, theft, dishonesty, sexual promiscuity, and drunkenness. In a society that is threatened by selfishness and hedonism, the harmonious voices of religious leaders can greatly help to raise the tone of public morality.

On occasion, the different groups can unite for interfaith services of prayer and worship. This fourth expression of qualified approval occurred very dramatically in the days of prayer for peace sponsored by Pope John Paul II in 1986 and 1993. Many interfaith meetings for prayer and silent reflection have been held in New York and other cities since the terrible events of September 11, 2001.

Still another critical need, frequently noted by Pope John Paul II, is the healing of memories. Religion, since it relies heavily on tradition, perpetuates the past experiences of the faith-community, including its moments of glory, suffering, and humiliation. Injuries that were inflicted generations or centuries ago continue to rankle and breed hostility. Unless the sources of resentment are honestly faced, they poison the atmosphere, so that men and women living today are unjustly blamed for the real or imagined misdeeds of their ancestors. If friendship is to be restored, the communities should disavow the conduct attributed to their predecessors. They may fittingly apologize for what their forebears may have done and extend forgiveness for the wrongs their own communities have suffered. John Paul II has courageously followed this procedure in his dealings with other Christian churches, with Jews, and with Muslims. Expressions of repentance and forgiveness constitute a fifth category of interreligious action.

Since the Second Vatican Council, the Catholic Church has placed strong emphasis on a sixth program, namely, theological dialogue. Paul VI set up a special secretariat, which continues to exist as the Pontifical Council for Interreligious Dialogue.[6] In dialogues of this type the parties explain their beliefs to one another, explore ways in which they can live amicably together, enrich themselves from one another's insights, and seek to narrow the disagreements by finding convergences. Dialogues of this type have proved extremely useful for improving relations among different Christian communions. They likewise hold great promise for interfaith relations.

Valuable though it be, dialogue is not a panacea. It cannot be expected to overcome all disagreements. After shared insights have been achieved and convergences established, the parties will normally come to recognize that full unity cannot be achieved by dialogue alone. The religions may be firmly committed to contradictory positions, which they could not abandon without sacrificing their identity. Although Christians will undoubtedly hope that their partners in the dialogue will come to recognize Christ as Savior of the world, any such result lies beyond the expectations and horizons of dialogue itself. Dialogue is intended to achieve agreements that the parties can achieve within the framework of their declared religious commitments.

It is sometimes said that dialogue is a sign of weakness, since it implies uncertainty about the adequacy of one's own positions. In my opinion, dialogue is rather a sign of strength. It takes considerable self-confidence to listen patiently while others tell you why they think you are wrong. Groups that have not reflected deeply on the grounds of their beliefs quite understandably shy away from a dialogue for which they are not prepared.

If dialogue is misused, it can do positive harm. One error would be to make it a platform for proselytization, with the aim of converting the dialogue partner to one's own faith. This would be a distortion of the purpose of dialogue, which differs from missionary proclamation. The opposite error would be to conceal or renounce the convictions of the group to which one belongs, thus raising false expectations. Quite obviously, dialogue teams are not authorized to change the doctrines of their religious communities.

Rightly pursued, however, dialogue is one of the most auspicious paths for the growing encounter of the great religions. It does not have to start with the most sensitive and disputed issues. The parties will generally do better to begin with topics on which there is promise of achieving a significant measure of consensus. Paul VI, in his encyclical *Ecclesiam suam* , suggested that common ideals such as religious freedom, human brotherhood, sound culture, social welfare, and civil order might be taken as themes of interreligious conversation (*colloqium*).[7] It might also be possible to conduct dialogues on some properly religious themes, such as the value of prayer and the nature of mystical experience, which seems to occur in similar ways in different religious traditions.[8] One could imagine very fruitful dialogues about suffering and happiness, life and death, speech and silence. The most important result of such encounters would be for the participants to get to know and respect one another. Friendship among qualified representatives of different religions could help to overcome some of the accumulated hostility and to restore trust.

In the opening years of the third millennium, interreligious dialogue is not a luxury. Together with the other five strategies I have recommended, it may be required to prevent disastrous collisions between major religious groups. In the present crisis, the religions have a great opportunity to overcome hostility and violence among peoples and to promote mutual esteem and cordial cooperation. But the stakes are high. If the various religious communities refuse to adopt programs of tolerance and to engage in respectful dialogue, there is a serious danger of relapsing into mutual recrimination and hatred. Religion may once again be abused, as has so often happened in the past, to justify conflict and bloodshed. As John Paul II said with reference to the events of September 11, "We must not let what has happened lead to a deepening of divisions. Religion must never be used a reason for conflict."[9] Religious believers must take the lead in building a world in which all peoples can live together in peace and brotherhood.

NOTES

1. John Hick, *God and the Universe of Faiths* (New York: St. Martin's, 1973); *God has Many Names* (London: Macmillan, 1980). A good account of Hick's position is available in Paul F. Knitter, *No Other Name?* (Maryknoll, N.Y.: Orbis, 1985), 146–52.

2. This version is expounded in Paul F. Knitter, "Toward a Liberation Theology of Religions," in *The Myth of Christian Uniqueness: Toward a Pluralistic Theology of Religions*, ed. John Hick and Paul F. Knitter (Maryknoll, N.Y.: Orbis, 1987), 178–200.

3. See Arnold Toynbee, *Christianity Among the Religions of the World* (New York: Scribner's, 1957), 112.

4. Pius XII, Allocution *Ci riesce*, AAS 45 (1953): 794–802, esp. 797.

5. In the summer of 2000, the Congregation for the Doctrine of the Faith responded to this misunderstanding of Vatican II in the Declaration *Dominus Iesus: The Unicity and Salvific Universality of Jesus Christ and the Church.*

6. Cardinal Francis Arinze, the president of the Pontifical Council for Interreligious Dialogue, has published a small but valuable volume, *Meeting Other Believers:*

The Risks and Rewards of Interreligious Dialogue (Huntington, Ind.: Our Sunday Visitor, 1997).

7. Paul VI, encyclical *Ecclesiam suam* (1964), 112.

8. Authors such as Bede Griffiths and Thomas Merton have described how the experience of mystical prayer can be a bond of union among members of different religious communities.

9. Words of Pope John Paul II in Kazakhstan, September 23, 2001; text in " 'Into Central Asia,' " *Inside the Vatican* 9 (October 2001): 18.

27

When to Forgive

April 10, 2002

I n his contribution to a recent volume on forgiveness, Martin Marty hazards the opinion that if there were a single word that expressed the very heart of the Christian message, it might well be "forgiveness." Christians, he says, are called to experience both forgiveness from God and forgiveness among fellow human beings inspired by that divine forgiveness. Marty goes on to observe that forgiveness is not an exclusively Christian concept. It figures prominently in many other religions and, indeed, functions beyond every religious context.[1]

Pope John Paul II has made forgiveness one of the pillars of his program for the Church and the world. In an encyclical of 1980 on Divine Mercy, he wrote, "The Church rightly considers it her duty to guard the authenticity of forgiveness, both in life and behavior and in educational and pastoral work. She protects it simply by guarding its source, which is the mystery of the mercy of God himself as revealed in Jesus Christ."[2] In his pastoral care for the Church, this pope has spared no effort to revivify the sacrament of penance and reconciliation as the ordinary means by which sin is forgiven in the Church. Forgiveness is also a cornerstone of his strategy for ecumenism and interreligious relations. During the Great Jubilee of 2000 he pleaded with some success for the forgiveness of international debts. Finally, he regards forgiveness as a necessary means for achieving and preserving civil peace within and between nations.

The supreme instance of forgiveness, for Christians, is the redemption. Sin has alienated the whole human race from God. We are worthy of condemnation. But in Jesus Christ God shows forth his mercy; he forgives our debts to him. This act of forgiveness, like all such acts, is costly. The

Cross of Christ teaches us that God does not forgive unexpiated sin. Forgiveness does not mean pretending that evil does not exist or forgetting it, but remembering it, facing its full malice, regretting it, and atoning for it.

THE MEANING OF FORGIVENESS

While regularly praising forgiveness, Christians are generally confused about its meaning and application. In the title of this lecture I ask: when to forgive. The question, in its full extension, might be rephrased by asking who should forgive, who should be forgiven, and under what circumstances. The answer has to be somewhat complex because of the variety of concepts contained under the rubric of forgiveness. The dictionaries generally recognize two dimensions. Forgiveness, they tell us, means the renunciation both of resentment and of claims to requital. Each of the two terms, "resentment" and "requital," calls for distinctions.

The necessary distinctions were lucidly set forth by the Anglican Bishop Joseph Butler in his sermons on resentment and forgiveness delivered early in the eighteenth century.[3] In my analysis I shall be guided in part by his. The first term, "resentment," applies to three kinds of emotional reaction in the presence of evil: impulsive anger, deliberate malice, and moral indignation.

The sudden passion of anger is, so to speak, morally neutral. God has implanted in human nature an instinct to react adversely to threats of harm or destruction. Since this impulse is spontaneous and beneficial for self-preservation and self-defense, it is not evil in itself. But it is dangerous because, unless controlled, it is capable of turning into hatred.

The second form of resentment, deliberate malice, is morally wrong. Christ in the Gospel requires us to overcome the temptation to return evil for evil. He exhorts us to love our enemies and pray for those who persecute us (Mt 5:44). He gave an example of love of enemies in praying to his Father to forgive those who were crucifying him (Lk 23:34). Forgiveness, in the sense of renouncing hatred and overcoming personal anger, is a Christian imperative.

Resentment, in the third place, can be morally good. We ought to be indignant when we witness unjust and cruel behavior. Although Jesus was never malicious toward his enemies, he displayed righteous anger toward the Pharisees because they were distorting God's law and misleading their followers. He also showed indignation when he overturned the tables of the money changers in the Temple and drove out the merchants with a whip. By his example he made it clear that his disciples are not always obliged to forgive. As we shall see, there are conditions for forgiveness.

In addition to the forswearing of resentment, forgiveness has a second aspect, the renunciation of requital. This aspect concerns not the sentiments of the forgiver but the behavior expected of the other party. The renunciation takes either of two forms. In its first form it means the remission, in whole or in part, of a claim to reparations for an injustice or to payment of a debt. Although borrowing is not a sin, Jesus in the Gospels frequently uses it as an analogy for guilt, which is a kind of debt toward God. He says that unless we treat our debtors generously, God will not forgive our debts, our sins.

The Gospel precepts and parables have to be correctly understood. Just as God has a right to demand reparation for past sin, so creditors, likewise, have a right to insist on full payment if the debtor is in a position to pay. There is no general obligation to forgive debts. But when the debtor is in difficulty, and truly wants to pay, the creditor ought to show mercy by granting a delay, a reduction of the amount, or outright cancellation. The same is true of reparation or compensation for harm that is not financial, such as insult or bodily injury. We may, and sometimes should, give up the claim to personal compensation. Love for the other party may oblige us to do so.

In its second form, the forgoing of requital may be the act of an authority mitigating or canceling due punishment. Parents, while exercising authority over their children, should always be available to them with tender love and compassion. They must be disposed to forgive, but not to dispense with repentance. When punishment is exacted, it should be administered as an act of love, so that the children, making amends for their misdeeds, may learn to behave better in the future.

The State, which is responsible for public order, is obliged to punish criminals for the sake of redressing offenses against the common good, rehabilitating the criminal, and protecting society against new violence. The pardoning of criminals, therefore, is the exception, not the rule. Normally it presupposes that the purposes of punishment have already been fulfilled and that clemency will bring tangible social benefits. In relatively rare cases, heads of State grant pardon and amnesty because it would simply be too expensive, divisive, or impractical to administer due punishment.

When public authority fails to act, people are sometimes tempted to take the law into their own hands and inflict what they regard as due punishment. This system of vigilante justice has often led to grave social disorders. It is not a proper substitute for the rule of law.

On the basis of this analysis we may distinguish at least four types of forgiveness. As a matter of sentiment it can mean either the suspension of personal animosity or of moral indignation toward others; as a matter of conduct, it can mean release either from indebtedness or from punishment. General statements about forgiveness must take account of all these dimensions. If forgiveness were simply the opposite of malice or vengefulness, the theory would be relatively simple. Since these attitudes are always forbidden, forgiveness would always be required. But the problem is more complex. It involves questions about when to renounce moral indignation, forceful resistance, the exaction of just compensation, and the imposition of just penalties.

The Giver and the Recipient of Forgiveness

With these concepts of forgiveness in mind we may now turn to the central questions: who may forgive, who may be forgiven, and under what conditions?

In most cases, the party who forgives is the one who has suffered injury or to whom a debt is due. In cases where the injured party is deceased or unable to act, another party, such as a family member, may represent the victim or creditor whether in foreswearing resentment or in remitting a debt. Where an offense is made against public order, the bearers of public office are the proper persons to impose or remit a just penalty. For the time being, I transmit the question of forgiveness between groups, because I intend to treat it later.

The recipient of forgiveness is the person who has committed an offense or incurred a debt. Forgiveness for injuries can extend beyond the perpetrator to those who encouraged or culpably failed to prevent them. Relatives or compatriots are likely to share the moral attitudes of the offenders, imitating and defending their conduct. The Old Testament vividly expresses the idea of solidarity in guilt when it speaks of the iniquities of the fathers being visited on the children (Ex 20:5, etc.).

No one has a strict right to forgiveness. The prospect of easy or auto-matic forgiveness could in fact give aid and comfort to aggressors and thus promote injustice. Well-ordered love may require that aggressors be resisted and punished rather than appeased. In particular cases, to be sure, a seemingly uncalled-for act of forgiveness, as a dramatic demonstration of love, may anticipate and bring about the adversary's conversion. But apart from these exceptions, forgiveness ordinarily presupposes certain conditions in the person being forgiven.

CONDITIONS OF FORGIVENESS

The usual conditions of forgiveness are three: that the person receiving it be sorry for any wrong committed, be resolved to desist from continuing or repeating the evil action, and be prepared to make satisfaction, as far as possible. To be disposed for forgiveness one need not expect to avoid future misdeeds, but one must be resolved to take effective measures to prevent such acts. A habitual sex offender, for example, ought not to receive absolution without intending to avoid situations in which the recurrence of such sins is likely.

These conditions would seem to be required even by God, so far as we can judge from Scripture. When Israel experiences God's wrath in the Old Testament, she stands in fear of divine punishment. The people con-fess their sins, beg for mercy, do penance, and resolve to keep God's law in the future. By these means they seek to dispose themselves for God's forgiveness, should he be pleased to grant it.

It is sometimes thought that these conditions were swept away by the great revelation of God's mercy in the New Testament. If so, Christianity could be a source of danger to morality and justice. W. H. Auden, in his Christmas Oratorio, *For the Time Being*, places this objection on the lips of the tyrant Herod. After the visit of the Magi, Herod voices the fear:

> Justice will be replaced by Pity as the cardinal human virtue, and all
> fear of retribution will vanish. Every corner-boy will congratulate himself:
> 'I'm such a sinner that God had to come down in person to save me. I
> must be a devil of a fellow.' Every crook will argue: 'I like committing
> crime. God likes forgiving them. Really the world is admirably arranged.'[4]

The idea that Christianity enthrones forgiveness in place of justice and teaches universal forgiveness is a gross misunderstanding. Jesus, like John the Baptist, in fact warns his hearers to take measures to escape the punishment they deserve. They must pray for pardon, as we regularly do in the Lord's Prayer. But prayer is only one of several prerequisites. Even while insisting on the imperative to forgive, Jesus mentions admonition and repentance: "If your brother sins, rebuke him, and if he repents, forgive him, and if he sins against you seven times in the day, and turns to you seven times, and says, 'I repent,' you must forgive him" (Lk 17:3–4). In his parables Jesus alludes to reparation as well as repentance. In the parable of the Prodigal Son, for instance, the younger son resolves to tell his father: "I have sinned against heaven and before you; I am no longer worthy to be called your son; treat me as one of your hired servants" (Lk 15:19). Again, in the parable of the unforgiving servant, the servant pleads with his master: "Lord, have patience with me, and I will pay you everything" (Mt 18:26).

The story of Zaccheus in Luke's Gospel provides the present pope with material for a very timely instruction on the sacrament of penance in his Holy Thursday letter to priests this year.[5] Zaccheus is moved to exclaim: "Lord, the half of my goods I give to the poor; and if I have defrauded anyone of anything, I restore it fourfold." At that Jesus replies: "Today salvation has come to this house" (Lk 19:8–9). Zaccheus does not receive forgiveness until he has resolved to compensate those he had defrauded and to be generous toward the poor.

Jesus frequently mentions one additional condition: that persons who seek forgiveness from God must forgive those who trespass against them, as we say in the Lord's Prayer. "If you do not forgive men their trespasses," says Jesus, "neither will your Father forgive your trespasses" (Mt 6:15; cf. 18:35, etc.).

Neither in the Old Testament nor in the New, therefore, is it taught that forgiveness takes the place of justice, or that God always forgives sins, or that we ought to forgive everyone all the time. Pope John Paul II insists on these objective requirements. "In no passage of the Gospel message," he writes, "does forgiveness, or mercy as its source, mean indulgence toward evil, toward scandals, toward injury or insult. In any case, reparation for evil and scandal, compensation for injury, and satisfaction for insult are conditions for forgiveness."[6]

An objection can be raised from the New Testament itself against the doctrine of forgiveness here proposed. In a passage mentioned above, Jesus is reported as pleading from the Cross for his executioners: "Father, forgive them, for they know not what they do" (Lk 23:34). Although this verse is lacking in many good and diverse ancient authorities, we may concede, with most modern editors, that it is authentic.[7] Since Jesus here speaks of forgiveness, we must assume that he is judging his executioners to be guilty, even though partly excusable. Yet he makes no reference to remorse or reparation as prerequisites. Is it significant that, instead of directly forgiving his enemies, he appeals to the Father to do so? Jesus may well be supposing that the process of forgiveness that he is initiating will not become complete until the malefactors have been brought to repentance. If so, the text poses no difficulty against the theory of forgiveness for which I am arguing.

The Church has received from Christ the mission to forgive sins in his name. After his resurrection he tells the Apostles: "If you forgive the sins of any, they are forgiven" (Jn 20:23). In his final appearance to the Eleven, as recounted by Luke, he sends them forth with the commission "that repentance and forgiveness of sins should be preached in his name to all nations" (Lk 24:47). They are not to proclaim forgiveness to the unrepentant, but are to call their hearers to repentance with a view to the remission of sins.

The Church has taken this commission seriously. She understands the forgiveness of sins to be a sacred rite, a sacrament, an encounter with the living Christ, who uses the Church as an instrument of reconciliation. As conditions for the worthy reception of the sacrament by the baptized, the Church specifies these four: sorrow for past sin, integral confession, a firm purpose of amendment, and willingness to make satisfaction. Satisfaction, in the case of injustice toward others, includes restitution. These conditions seem to me to be in perfect accord with the teaching of Jesus as we know it from the Gospels.

THE COST AND BENEFITS OF FORGIVENESS

Before taking up the social and political aspects of forgiveness, we should consider, even though briefly, the burdens and benefits. Forgiveness is obviously burdensome to the person who forgives, because it involves a renunciation of feelings of resentment, warranted or unwarranted, and of claims to compensation, which is, or is thought to be, due. It is by no means easy to give up feelings of hostility toward those who have offended us, or to exact less by way of satisfaction than we are entitled to receive.

Forgiveness can also be burdensome to those who receive it. They may find it humiliating to acknowledge their indebtedness, to accept pardon from their former enemies, and to be dispensed from the ordinary requirements of just behavior. Perhaps they do not want to enjoy benefits they did not earn. In *Paradise Lost*, Satan positively resists reconciliation. Acknowledging that he has been defeated in battle, he still clings to his hostile passions; "th'unconquerable will and study of revenge, immortal hate, and courage never to submit or yield."[8] Such dispositions, harbored in the soul, arm it against accepting pardon, even though it be tendered.

The burdens of forgiveness, however, are generally outweighed by its benefits. The recipient is liberated from the hostility of the person offended and from a burden of debt or punishment. According to the type of forgiveness in question, the enemy is restored to friendship, the guilty to innocence, the debtor to solvency, and the prisoner to freedom.

What is less obvious, but no less real, is the benefit accruing to the person who forgives. As Shakespeare profoundly observed in Portia's famous speech, mercy brings blessings upon "him that gives and him that takes."[9] The giver is blessed by being relieved of the anger that rankles in the heart and of preoccupation with obtaining redress. These benefits, however, are elusive because, as I have said, forgiveness is difficult. An outward profession of forgiveness without sincere good will accomplishes nothing for the person who bestows it. Likewise unavailing is the repression of angry feelings. Driven underground, resentment asserts itself in depression and in psychosomatic illnesses such as ulcers.

Jesus in the Gospels calls for "forgiveness from your heart" (Mt 18:35). To achieve genuine good will toward those who have hurt us demands great spiritual strength, inner freedom, and in some cases, religious faith. To be able to say in all sincerity to the repentant murderer of a loved one, "I forgive you," would be almost impossible without religious motivation. But Christians, believing as they do that God sacrificed his own Son to forgive them, sometimes find the strength to say, "I forgive you because I am a Christian."

In addition to the proximate benefits just mentioned, forgiveness may lead to reconciliation. Where grievances exist on both sides, reconciliation presupposes mutual offerings of pardon mutually accepted. Once reconciled, enemies become friends and fellow members of a new and larger community.

St. Paul sums up the whole mission of Christ under the heading of reconciliation. Through Christ, he says, God "reconciled us to himself and gave us the ministry of reconciliation" (2 Cor 5:18). Christ died, he says, in order to reconcile the world to God, "making peace by the blood of his cross" (Col 1:20). Through Christ people who have been divided by enmity receive the possibility of being joined in friendship. In asserting this, Paul is thinking especially of the endemic hostility between Jews and Gentiles (Eph 2:14–16).

SOCIAL AND POLITICAL FORGIVENESS

These reflections of Paul raise what will be the final question to be discussed in this lecture. What are the social and political implications of the Christian doctrine of forgiveness? Without prejudice to other religions, which may be able to find motivations for forgiveness in their own traditions, I am convinced that Christianity, put into practice, provides extraordinarily valuable medicine for the conflicts that plague the world today. Clans, nations, and ethnic or religious groups are often separated by a deep-seated collective animosity that defies merely juridical, political, or military solutions. Vendettas go on from generation to generation, erupting in ever new acts of violence. Recent outbursts of terrorism are glaring evidence of this disease.

A modern secular Jewish philosopher, Hannah Arendt, recognizes the essential role of forgiveness in enabling societies to overcome the heritage of past injustices. "The possible redemption from the predicament of irreversibility—of being unable to undo what one has done though one did not, and could not, have known what he was doing—is the faculty of forgiving." She goes on to say, "The discoverer of the role of forgiveness in the realm of human affairs was Jesus of Nazareth. The fact that he made this discovery in a religious context and articulated it in religious language is no reason to take it any less seriously in a strictly secular sense."[10]

Pope John Paul II is deeply convinced that societies as well as individuals stand in need of forgiveness:

Families, groups, societies, states, and the international community itself need forgiveness in order to renew ties that have been sundered, go beyond sterile situations of mutual condemnation and overcome the temptation to discriminate against others without appeal. The ability to forgive lies at the very basis of the idea of a future society marked by justice and solidarity.[11]

In his message for the World Day of Peace, January 1, 2002, Pope John Paul emphatically declares that there can be no peace without justice, and no justice without forgiveness.[12] A politics of forgiveness is both a moral imperative and a practical necessity.

Acts of aggression by one State or alliance against another may be considered as offenses calling for resentment and retribution. The first duty of civil authority is to defend the rights of its own citizens, if necessary by a just war. While the enemy is engaged in hostile action, forgiveness is scarcely possible except in the sense that hatred and vengefulness should be renounced. Once the war is ended, the alternatives of punishment and forgiveness present themselves. After the First World War, the Allied Powers insisted on inserting a "war guilt clause" in the Treaty of Versailles, placing full responsibility for the devastation on the defeated powers. Inordinate reparations were imposed on Germany, creating financial chaos and planting the seeds of another war. After the Second World War, wiser policies prevailed. Germans who were deemed personally guilty of serious crimes were tried at Nuremberg, and in some cases severely punished, but the German people as a whole were treated generously.

The Japanese Peace Treaty was likewise inspired by a politics of forgiveness. John Foster Dulles, who negotiated the treaty on behalf of the United States, characterized it as "a treaty of reconciliation." Although it did not entirely omit reparations, it imposed no permanent disabilities or limitations of sovereignty. Dulles was conscious of the religious dimensions of the settlement. Speaking of the Peace Conference of 1951, he declared, "All the delegates at San Francisco who accepted a religious view of the world, whether Christian, Buddhist, or Moslem, found inspiration from the fact that the treaty invoked the principle of moral law."[13] But to demonstrate that the treaty could also be justified on pragmatic grounds, Ambassador Dulles quoted Plato to the effect that wars will never cease so long as the victors execute vengeance on the vanquished.[14] Adhering to Plato's counsel, he insisted on terms that would favor Japan as well as the Allied Powers. This decision has led to a half century of friendship and cooperation.

Special problems arise when forgiveness is sought for injustices committed and suffered by persons no longer living. Is anyone now in a position to offer or demand apologies or compensation? This question arises, for example, in connection with slavery in the United States. In Europe the memories of the Holocaust are still fresh. Orthodox Christians remember the sack of Constantinople in 1204 almost as if they had been there. Irish Protestants and Catholics have vivid but mutually contrasting memories of the Battle of the Boyne in 1690 and the Easter Rising of 1916. These memories continue to kindle hatred and strife. For any real resolution, forgiveness is required. But who is in a position to ask or bestow forgiveness for actions when the victims and perpetrators are dead?

Fyodor Dostoevsky wrestled with the dilemma of vicarious forgiveness in *The Brothers Karamazov*. Speaking of the atrocious murder of a child by an angry landowner, Ivan Karamazov tells his brother Alyosha:

> I don't want the mother to embrace the oppressor who threw her son to the dogs! She dare not forgive him! Let her forgive him for herself, if she will, let her forgive the torturer for the immeasurable suffering of her mother's heart. But the suffering of her tortured child she has no right to forgive; she dare not forgive the torturer even if the child were to forgive him.

Ivan then draws the conclusion: "I would rather remain with my un-avenged suffering and unsatisfied indignation, *even if I were wrong.*"[15]

At issue is the question whether there is sufficient solidarity and moral continuity in the respective groups for the living to make or receive apologies and reparations for bygone offenses. Dostoevsky's Ivan, with his radical individualism, gives a negative answer. But Pope John Paul II boldly pursues an opposite course. He evidently considers that, as chief pastor of the Catholic Church today, he is in a position to seek forgiveness for the religious intolerance and violence inflicted long ago by Catholics on Orthodox Christians, Protestants, Jews, and others. He has several times expressed regrets to these groups, and has likewise extended to them the forgiveness of the Catholic Church for what it has suffered at their hands.

It can be debated whether the concept of forgiveness is strictly applicable to such cases. Even if the whole Church in previous centuries were judged to have incurred some kind of collective guilt, it would still have to be shown that that guilt has been inherited by the Church today. Is the pope in a position to take responsibility for what some Frankish Crusaders did in the thirteenth century or what some bigoted churchmen did in Czechoslovakia in the fifteenth or sixteenth century? Perhaps not, but even so, the pope's apologies have positive symbolic value. Minimally, they show that Catholics of today do not share the religious intolerance of their forebears or approve of their violent acts.

Such apologies, as implicit requests for forgiveness, are steps along the path to reconciliation. For reconciliation to be attained, the party to whom the apology is directed must accept it, extend forgiveness, and in some cases must make its own apologies. If each party feels that it has been offended by the other, reciprocal apologies are required to eradicate the seeds of conflict. Only then can the parties enter into a community of love.

HEALING OF MEMORIES

In this connection it may be helpful to reflect on what Pope John Paul II and others call the healing of memories.[16] By this I understand the need not to draw a veil over past conflicts but to face them with perfect honesty, in the hope that each group will listen sympathetically to the stories of the other, overcome misunderstandings and exaggerations, recognize its own misdeeds, and begin to forge a common fund of shared memories.

Scott Appleby, in his recent book *The Ambivalence of the Sacred*, explains how religious groups in Northern Ireland and in South Africa have been able to transcend sectarian memories and achieve a measure of shared consciousness.[17] Something similar, I believe, has happened in the United States with regard to the Civil War. Partly because of Abraham Lincoln's posture of forgiveness, so memorably expressed in his Second Inaugural, Yankees have found ways to revere the skill and valor of Confederate soldiers, and vice versa.

In the case of South Africa, when apartheid came to an end, a bloodbath was averted by an unusual process of reconciliation. The government established a so-called Truth and Reconciliation Commission that gave amnesties very liberally to former officials of the oppressive National Party and, I believe, to some revolutionaries who had committed atrocities. Such amnesties were given only on condition that the recipients would make a full public disclosure of the crimes they had committed. Because the TRC did not require remorse, apologies, and reparations as conditions for escaping prosecution, it has sometimes been accused of offering "cheap grace." However that may be, the TRC successfully warded off violence and effected a remarkable measure of reconciliation. The new government achieved the goal of preventing the endless cycle of reprisals.[18]

Both in Northern Ireland and in South Africa the prevalent Christian ethos has greatly assisted the relatively successful (though still incomplete) process of reconciliation. Reconciliation may be more difficult to achieve among groups that do not share the Christian faith. It will be for them to judge whether they can find resources for a politics of forgiveness in their own religious or secular traditions. Without some such an ethos, it almost inevitable that the present politics of violence will continue and even intensify.

The spirit of forgiveness, I would contend, is essential for the preservation of human community, whether in the home, the neighborhood, the nation, or the world. It is no less necessary for disposing individual persons to receive forgiveness from God. The conferral of forgiveness presupposes certain conditions to have been fulfilled. By itself, therefore, forgiveness will not solve all personal and social problems, but these problems cannot be solved without the spirit of forgiveness. The strongest motive for that spirit is the realization of our own great need of forgiveness and of the extremes to which God has gone in order to bring us the forgiveness we need.

NOTES

1. Martin E. Marty, "The Ethos of Christian Forgiveness," in *Dimensions of Forgiveness: Psychological Research and Theological Perspectives*, ed. Everett L. Worthington Jr. (Philadelphia: Templeton Foundation Press, 1998), 9–28, at 11.

2. John Paul II, encyclical *Dives in misericordia*, 14.

3. *Fifteen Sermons*, vol. 2 of *The Works of Joseph Butler* (Oxford: Clarendon, 1896). Sermon 8 is "Upon Resentment" and Sermon 9 "Upon the Forgiveness of Injuries."

4. W. H. Auden, *Collected Poems* (New York: Random House, 1976), 304; quoted by Marty, "The Ethos," 13.

5. John Paul II, "Ministers of Mercy: The Sacrament of Reconciliation," *Origins* 31 (April 4, 2002): 704–8.

6. John Paul II, encyclical *Dives in misericordia*, 14.

7. Most modern versions include the verse, but some, such as the New American Bible, print it in brackets.

8. John Milton, *Paradise Lost*, book 1, line 105.

9. William Shakespeare, *The Merchant of Venice*, Act IV, scene 1.

10. Hannah Arendt, *The Human Condition: A Study of the Central Conditions Facing Modern Man* (Garden City, N.Y.: Doubleday Anchor, 1959), 237, 238.

11. John Paul II, "World Day of Peace Message," §9; *Origins* 31 (December 20, 2001): 461–66 at 465.

12. Ibid., §15, p. 466.

13. Quoted in Mark Toulouse, *The Transformation of John Foster Dulles* (Macon, Ga.: Mercer University Press, 1985), 239.

14. "Japan's Future: An Interview with John Foster Dulles," *Newsweek*, 10 September 1951, 31–35; quotation from Plato at 31. The reference is to Letter VII, secs. 336–37.

15. Quoted in Donald W. Shriver, Jr., *An Ethic for Enemies: Forgiveness in Politics* (New York: Oxford University Press, 1995), 64.

16. The term "purification of memory" appeared in John Paul II, *Incarnationis mysterium*, the Bull of Indiction for the Holy Year 2000, §11, *Origins* 28 (December 10, 1998): 446–53, at 450. The theological implications are explored in the document of the International Theological Commission, "Memory and Reconciliation," *Origins* 29 (March 16, 2000): 625–44. Cardinal Francis Arinze speaks of "healing historical memories" in the context of interfaith dialogue in his *Meeting Other Believers* (Huntington, Ind.: Our Sunday Visitor Publishing Division, 1998), 98–99.

17. R. Scott Appleby, *The Ambivalence of the Sacred: Religion, Violence, and Reconciliation* (Lanham, Md.: Rowman & Littlefield, 2000), chapter 5, 167–204.

18. The granting of amnesties in Guatemala in 1996 has proved much less successful. In the absence of an effective system of justice, human-rights abuses there continue to be perpetrated with impunity, except for the action of vigilante groups that take the law into their own hands.

28

The Population of Hell

November 20, 2002

Sometimes the complaint is heard that no one preaches about hell any longer. The subject of hell, if not attractive, is at least fascinating, as any reader of Dante's *Inferno* or Milton's *Paradise Lost* can testify. Since our time this evening is too short for a full exploration, I shall limit the scope of my inquiry to the question of numbers: how many of us may be expected to go there?

NEW TESTAMENT TEACHINGS

As we know from the Gospels, Jesus spoke many times about hell. Throughout his preaching, he holds forth two, and only two, final possibilities for human existence: the one being everlasting happiness in the presence of God, the other everlasting torment in the absence of God. He describes the fate of the damned under a great variety of metaphors: everlasting fire, outer darkness, tormenting thirst, a gnawing worm, and weeping and gnashing of teeth.

In the parable of the sheep and the goats, Jesus indicates that some will be condemned. The Son of man says to the goats: "Depart from me, you cursed, into the eternal fire prepared for the devil and his angels" (Mt 25:41). In the Gospel of John, which says comparatively little about hell, Jesus is quoted as saying: "The hour is coming when all who are in the tombs will hear [the Father's] voice and come forth, those who have done good to the resurrection of life, and those who have done evil, to the resurrection of judgment" (Jn 5:28–29).

The apostles, understandably concerned, ask, "Lord, will those who are saved be few?" Without directly answering their question Jesus replies, "Strive to enter by the narrow door; for many, I tell you, will seek to enter and not be able" (Lk 13:23–24). In the parallel passage from Matthew, Jesus says: "Enter by the narrow gate, for the gate is wide and the way is easy that leads to destruction, and those who enter by it are many. For the gate is narrow and the way is hard that leads to life, and those who find it are few" (Mt 7:13–14). In a parable immediately following this exchange, Jesus speaks of those who try to come to the marriage feast but are told, "Depart from me, all you workers of iniquity. There you will weep and gnash your teeth" (Lk 13:27–28). In another parable, that of the wedding guest who is cast out for not wearing the proper attire, Jesus declares, "Many are called, but few are chosen" (Mt 22:14). Taken in their obvious meaning, passages such as these give the impression that there is a hell, and that many go there—more, in fact, than are saved.

The New Testament does not tell us in so many words that any particular person is in hell. But several statements about Judas can hardly be interpreted otherwise. Jesus says that he has kept all those whom the Father has given him except the son of perdition (Jn 17:12). At another point Jesus calls Judas a devil (Jn 6:70), and yet again says of him, "It would be better for that man if he had never been born" (Mt 26:24; Mk 14:21). If Judas were among the saved, these statements could hardly be true. Many saints and Doctors of the Church, including Saint Augustine and Saint Thomas Aquinas, have taken it as a revealed truth that Judas was reprobated.[1] Some of the Fathers place the name of Nero in the same select company, but they do not give long lists of names, as Dante would do.

References to punishment after death in the remainder of the New Testament simply confirm the teaching of the Gospels. In the Book of Acts, Paul says that those ordained to eternal life have believed his preaching, whereas those who disbelieved it have judged themselves unworthy of eternal life (Acts 13:46–48). Peter's first letter puts the question this way: "If the righteous man is scarcely to be saved, where will the impious and sinner appear?" (1 Pt 4:18). The Book of Revelation teaches that there is a fiery pit where Satan and those who follow him will be tormented forever. It states at one point, "As for the cowardly, the faithless, the polluted, as for murderers, fornicators, sorcerers, idolaters, and all liars, their lot shall be the lake that burns with fire and brimstone, which is the second death" (Rev 21:8).

The testimony of Paul is complex. In his first letter to the Thessalonians, he speaks of the coming divine judgment, in which Jesus will inflict vengeance "upon those who do not know God and upon those who do not obey the gospel of our Lord Jesus. They shall suffer the punishment of eternal destruction and exclusion from the presence of the Lord" (1 Th 1:9–10). In his letter to the Romans, Paul says that the impenitent Jews are storing up wrath for themselves on the day of judgment (Rom 2:5). In writing to the Corinthians he distinguishes between those who are being saved by the gospel and those who are perishing because of their failure to accept it (1 Cor 1:18). In a variety of texts he gives lists of sins that will exclude people from the kingdom of God (1 Cor 6:9–10; Gal 5:19–21; Eph 5:3–6). And he tells the Philippians: "Work out your salvation in fear and trembling" (Phil 2:12).

Some passages in the letters of Paul lend themselves to a more optimistic interpretation, but they can hardly be used to prove that salvation is universal. In Romans 8:19–21, Paul predicts that "creation itself will be set free from its bondage of decay and obtain the glorious liberty of the children of God" but the text seems to have reference to the world of nature; it does not say that all human beings will achieve the glorious liberty in question. In 1 Corinthians 15:28, Paul speaks of all things being ultimately subjected to Christ, but he does not imply that subjection means salvation. He presumably means that the demonic powers will ultimately be defeated. In Philippians 2:9–10, he predicts that eventually every knee will bow to Christ and every tongue confess him. But this need not mean a confession that proceeds from love. In the Gospels the devils proclaim that Jesus is the Holy One of God, but they are not saved by recognizing the fact.

Equally unavailing, in my opinion, are appeals to passages that say that God's plan is to reconcile all things in Christ (Eph 1:10; Col 1:19–20). Although this is surely God's intent, he does not override the freedom that enables men and women to resist his holy will. The same may be said of the statement that God "desires all men to be saved and come to the knowledge of the truth" (1 Tim 2:4). Paul is apparently seeking to stimulate the apostolic zeal of missionaries who will bring the saving truth of Christ to all who do not yet believe. The absolute necessity of faith for salvation is a constant theme in the writings of Paul. I see no reason, then, for ranking Paul among the universalists.

THE CATHOLIC TRADITION

The constant teaching of the Church supports the idea that there are two classes: the saved and the damned. Three general councils of the Church (Lyons I, 1245; Lyons II, 1274; and Florence, 1439) and Pope Benedict XII in his bull *Benedictus Deus*, issued in 1336, have taught that everyone who dies in a state of mortal sin goes immediately to suffer the punishments of hell. The eternity of damnation is likewise taught with emphasis by several general councils, including Lateran IV (1215) and Lyons I (1245), and by the Catechism of the Catholic Church (*CCC* 1022, 1035). Several local councils in the Middle Ages, without apparently intending to define the point, state in passing that some have actually died in a state of sin and been punished by eternal damnation.[2]

The relative numbers of the elect and the damned are not treated in any Church documents, but they have been a subject of discussion among theologians. Among the Greek Fathers, Irenaeus, Basil, and Cyril of Jerusalem are typical in interpreting passages such as Matthew 22:14 as meaning that the majority will be consigned to hell. St. John Chrysostom, an outstanding doctor of the Eastern tradition, was particularly pessimistic: "Among thousands of people there are not a hundred who will arrive at their salvation, and I am not even certain of that number, so much perversity is there among the young and so much negligence among the old."[3]

Augustine may be taken as representative of the Western Fathers. In his controversy with the Donatist Cresconius, Augustine draws upon Matthew and the Book of Revelation to prove that the number of the elect is large, but he grants that their number is exceeded by that of the lost.[4] In Book 21 of *The City of God* he rebuts first the idea that all human beings are saved; then that all the baptized are saved, then that all baptized Catholics are saved, and finally that all baptized Catholics who persevere in the faith are saved. He seems to limit salvation to baptized believers who refrain from serious sin or who, after sinning, repent and are reconciled with God.

The great Scholastics of the Middle Ages are not more sanguine. Thomas Aquinas, who may stand as the leading representative, teaches clearly in the *Summa theologiae* that God reprobates some persons.[5] A little later he declares that only God knows the number of the elect.[6] But Thomas gives reasons for thinking that their number is relatively small. Since our human nature is fallen, and since eternal blessedness is a gift far beyond the powers and merits of every created nature, it is to be expected that most human beings fall short of achieving that goal.[7]

The leading theologians of the baroque period follow suit. Francisco Suárez, in his treatise on predestination, puts the question squarely: How many are saved? Relying on the Gospel of Matthew, Saint John Chrysostom, Saint Augustine, and Pope Saint Gregory, he proposes the following estimation. If the question is asked about all men living between the creation and the end of the world, the number of the reprobate certainly exceeds that of the elect. This is to be expected because God was not rightly known before the coming of Christ, and even since that time many remain in darkness. If the term "Christian" is taken to include heretics, schismatics, and baptized apostates, it would still appear that most are damned. But if the question is put about those who die in the Catholic Church, Suárez submits his opinion that the majority are saved, since many die before they can sin mortally, and many others are fortified by the sacraments.[8]

Suárez is relatively optimistic in comparison with other Catholic theologians of his day, not to mention Protestants, of whom I do not intend to speak tonight. Peter Canisius and Robert Bellarmine were convinced that most of the human race are lost.

Several studies published by Catholics early in the twentieth century concluded that there was a virtual consensus among the Fathers of the Church and the Catholic theologians of later ages to the effect that the majority of humankind go to eternal punishment in hell. But even if this consensus be granted, it is not binding, because the theologians did not claim that their opinion was revealed, or that to take the opposite view was heretical. Nor is the opinion that most people attain salvation contradicted by authoritative Church teaching.[9]

Mention should here be made of a minority opinion among some of the Greek Fathers.[10] Clement of Alexandria, Origen, Gregory Nazianzen, and Gregory of Nyssa sometimes speak as though in the end all will be saved. Origen, the most prominent representative of this view, is generally reported as teaching that at the end of time, the damned, now repentant and purified, will take part in the universal restoration of all things (*apoka-tastasis*). In 563, three centuries after Origen's death, a local council of Constantinople convened by the Emperor Justinian condemned his views on this and several other topics (DS 411). Even in his lifetime, however, Origen claimed that his adversaries had misunderstood or misrepresented him. A number of distinguished scholars down through the centuries have defended his orthodoxy on the fate of the damned.[11] The doctrine of the eternity of hell has been firmly in place at least since the seventh century and is not subject to debate in the Catholic Church.

Twentieth-Century Speculations

About the middle of the twentieth century, there seems to be a break in the tradition. Since then a number of influential theologians have favored the view that all human beings may or do eventually attain salvation. Some examples may be illustrative.[12]

In a "reverie" circulated among friends but not published until after his death, the philosopher Jacques Maritain included what he called a "conjectural essay" on eschatology, in which he conjectures that the damned, although eternally in hell, may be able at some point to escape from pain. In response to the prayers of the saints, he imagines, God may miraculously convert their wills, so that from hating him they come to love him. After being pardoned, they will then be delivered from the pain of sense and placed in a kind of limbo. They will still be technically in hell, since they will lack the beatific vision, but they will enjoy a kind of natural felicity, like that of infants who die without baptism. At the end, he speculates, even Satan will be converted, and the fiery inferno, while it continues to exist, will be have no spirits to afflict.[13] This, as Maritain acknowledged, is a bold conjecture, since it has no support in Scripture or tradition and contradicts the usual understanding of texts such as the parable of the Last Judgment scene of Matthew. But the theory has the advantage of showing how the Blood of Christ might obtain mercy for all spiritual creatures, even those eternally in hell.

Karl Rahner, another representative of the more liberal trend, holds for the possibility that no one ever goes to hell. We have no clear revelation, he says, to the effect that some are actually lost. The discourses of Jesus on the subject appear to be admonitory rather than predictive. Their aim is to persuade his hearers to pursue the better and safer path by alerting them to the danger of eternal perdition. While allowing for the real possibility of eternal damnation, says Rahner, we must simultaneously maintain "the truth of the omnipotence of the universal salvific will of God, the redemption of all by Christ, the duty of men to hope for salvation."[14] Rahner therefore believes that universal salvation is a possibility.

The most sophisticated theological argument against the conviction that some human beings in fact go to hell has been proposed by Hans Urs von Balthasar in his book *Dare We Hope "That All Men Be Saved?"* He rejects the ideas that hell will be emptied at the end of time and that the damned souls and demons will be reconciled with God. He also avoids asserting as a fact that everyone will be saved.[15] But he does say that we have a right and even a duty to hope for the salvation of all, because it is not impossible that even the worst sinners may be moved by God's grace to repent before they die. He concedes, however, that the opposite is also possible. Since we are able to resist the grace of God, none of us is safe. We must therefore leave the question speculatively open, thinking primarily of the danger in which we ourselves stand.

At one point in his book Balthasar incorporates a long quotation from Edith Stein, now Saint Teresa Benedicta of the Cross, who defends a position very like Balthasar's. Since God's all-merciful love, she says, descends upon everyone, it is probable that this love produces transforming effects in their lives. To the extent that people open themselves to that love, they enter into the realm of redemption. On this ground Stein finds it possible to hope that God's omnipotent love finds ways of, so to speak, outwitting human resistance.[16] Balthasar says that he agrees with her.

This position of Balthasar seems to me to be orthodox. It does not contradict any ecumenical councils or definitions of the faith. It can be reconciled with everything in Scripture, at least if the statements of Jesus on hell are taken as minatory rather than predictive. Balthasar's position, moreover, does not undermine a healthy fear of being lost. But the position is at least adventurous. It runs against the obvious interpretation of the words of Jesus in the New Testament and against the dominant theological opinion down through the centuries, which maintains that some, and in fact very many, are lost.

The conviction of earlier theologians that relatively few are saved rests, I suspect, partly on the assumption that faith in Christ, baptism, and adherence to the Church are necessary conditions for salvation. The first two of these conditions are clearly set forth in the New Testament, and the third has been taught by many saints, councils, popes, and theologians. But these conditions can be interpreted more broadly than one might suspect. In recent centuries it has become common to speak of implicit faith, baptism "by desire," and membership in the "soul" of the Church, or membership *in voto* ("by desire"). Vatican II declares that all people, even those who have never heard of Christ, receive enough grace to make their salvation possible.

The Church continues to insist that explicit faith, reception of the sacraments, and obedience to the Church are ordinary means to salvation. Pius IX in the Syllabus of Errors (1864) accordingly condemned the proposition: "We should at least have good hopes for the eternal salvation of those who are in no way in the true Church of Christ" (DS 2917). Pius XII in his encyclical on the Mystical Body of Christ (1943) taught that even those who are united to the Church by bonds of implicit desire—a state that can by no means be taken for granted—still lack many precious means that are available in the Church and therefore "cannot be sure of their salvation" (DS 3821). Vatican II said that anyone who knows that the Catholic Church was made necessary by Christ and refuses to enter her cannot be saved (LG 14). If we accept these teachings, we will find it unlikely that everyone fulfills the conditions for salvation.

Pope John Paul II in his *Crossing the Threshold of Hope*, mentions the theory of Balthasar. After putting the question whether a loving God can allow any human being to be condemned to eternal torment, he replies, "And yet the words of Christ are unequivocal. In Matthew's Gospel He speaks clearly of those who will go to eternal punishment (cf. Mt 25:46)." As justification for this assessment the Pope puts the rhetorical question: Can God, who is ultimate justice, tolerate terrible crimes and let them go unpunished? Final punishment would seem to be necessary to reestablish the moral equilibrium in the complex history of humanity.[17]

In a General Audience talk of July 28, 1999, the pope gave a moderate restatement of his position:

Christian faith teaches that, in the risk of saying "yes" or "no" that marks creaturely freedom, some have already said no. They are the spiritual creatures who rebelled against God's love and are called demons (cf. Fourth Lateran Council, DS 800–801). What happened to them is a warning to us human beings: it is a continuous call to avoid the tragedy to which sin leads and to model our lives on that of Jesus, which unfolds under the sign of "yes" to God.

Damnation remains a possibility, but we are not granted to know without special divine revelation which human beings are effectively involved in it. The thought of hell—and even less the improper use of biblical images—must not create neurosis or anxiety, but is a necessary and healthy warning to freedom within the proclamation that the risen Jesus has conquered Satan, giving us the Spirit of God, who makes us cry "Abba, Father!" (Rom 8:15; Gal 4:6).[18]

CURRENT CONTROVERSIES

A number of theologians have adversely criticized Baltasar's position. In a supplement to his book, Balthasar himself reports that one reviewer accused him of supporting "the salvation optimism that is rampant today and is both thoughtless and a temptation to thoughtlessness."[19] At an international videoconference organized by the Holy See's Congregation for the Clergy last November, Jean Galot, with an apparent reference to Balthasar, said that the hypothesis of hell as a mere possibility "removes all effectiveness from the warnings issued by Jesus, repeatedly expressed in the Gospels."[20] At the same conference, Father Michael F. Hull of New York contended that Balthasar's theory is "tantamount to a rejection of the doctrine of hell and a denial of man's free will."[21] In this country Father Regis Scanlon, O.F.M. Cap., accused von Balthasar of being a Hegelian relativist who "smuggles into the heart of the Catholic a serious doubt about the truth of the Catholic faith."[22] Scanlon himself takes it to be Catholic teaching that some persons, at least Judas, are in fact eternally lost. This article set off a sharp controversy between two Catholic editors, Richard John Neuhaus and Dale Vree.

Neuhaus fired the opening salvo in the June/July 2000 issue of *First Things*. Defending von Balthasar against Scanlon, he cited the passages from the pope's *Crossing the Threshold of Hope* mentioned above and referred also to his own book, *Death on a Friday Afternoon*, in which he argued from several New Testament texts that although we cannot be certain, we may indeed hope and pray for the salvation of all.[23] Vree came back in the *New Oxford Review* for January 2001 with an article defending Regis Scanlon and rejecting Neuhaus's exegesis of the biblical texts that he had quoted. He also found a statement in Neuhaus's book that could be interpreted as implying that everyone will be saved.[24]

Neuhaus responded in *First Things* that Vree's attack was based on a misrepresentation. He had never taught the doctrine known as universalism, namely that all will be saved. He asserted only that we may hope that all will ultimately come to salvation. This probably should have been an end to the matter, but Vree in the May 2001 issue of *NOR* insisted that he had not misread Neuhaus's book and repeated his charges. In its July/August issue the *NOR* published a defense of Neuhaus by Janet Holl Madigan, which made serious charges against Vree and against the *NOR* itself. Vree responded in the same issue.

Then in the August/September issue of *First Things*, Neuhaus himself offered a clarification of what he intended to say in his book. He presented an excellent case for holding that we may hope and pray for the salvation for all. In an editorial in *NOR* for October 2001, Vree expressed moderate satisfaction with Neuhaus's clarification, but he still had objections to various statements that Neuhaus had not retracted.

Like Vree, I accept the substance of this final intervention of Neuhaus, but I find some obscurity in his argument. He says that certain Pauline texts (most of which I have cited above) "support" universal redemption. If we give priority to these passages, Neuhaus argues, we have to interpret the Gospel passages about damnation as "admonitory and cautionary, solemn warnings of a terrible possibility."[25]

Neuhaus does not say (and, I am sure, does not mean) that Paul in the passages he quotes actually teaches universal salvation. If so, Paul would be turning the Gospel warnings into empty threats, and would be taking a position contrary to the constant tradition of the Church. I can agree that these "optimistic" passages, taken in isolation, could be interpreted as expressing a confidence that all will be saved. But that interpretation is unacceptable even as an interpretation of Paul's mind, because it runs counter to other texts in which Paul evidently supposes that some are in fact lost. I have already quoted several of these texts. My conclusion would be that even if we give full value to the Pauline passages quoted by Neuhaus, the Gospel warnings could still be understood as predictions that some will be condemned.

Neuhaus at one point remarks that according to some theologians "perhaps the fate of Judas is that of total annihilation."[26] Since I understand that he does not personally accept this hypothesis, it can hardly advance his argument that hell may be empty. Although some Protestants teach annihilation, the hypothesis, as Vree points out, is incompatible with Catholic orthodoxy. The constant teaching of the magisterium has been that unrepentant sinners are sent to eternal punishment. Judas, therefore, must be in hell unless he repented and was saved.

It is unfair and incorrect to accuse either Balthasar or Neuhaus of teaching that no one goes to hell. They grant that it is probable that some or even many do go there, but they assert, on the ground that God is capable of bringing any sinner to repentance, that we have a right to hope and pray that all will be saved. The fact that something is highly improbable need not prevent us from hoping and praying that it will happen. According to the *Catechism of the Catholic Church*, "In hope, the Church prays for 'all men to be saved' (1 Tim 2:4)" (*CCC* 1821). At another point the Catechism declares: "The Church prays that no one should be lost" (*CCC* 1058).

FINAL ASSESSMENT

You might ask at this point whether there has been any shift in Catholic theology on the issue we are discussing. I think the answer is still yes, though the shift is not as dramatic as some imagine. The earlier pessimism was based on the unwarranted assumption that explicit Christian faith is absolutely necessary for salvation. This assumption has been corrected, particularly at Vatican II. There has also been a healthy reaction against the type of preaching that revels in depicting the sufferings of the damned in the most lurid possible light. An example would be the fictional sermon on hell that James Joyce recounts in his *Portrait of the Artist as a Young Man*. This kind of preaching fosters an image of God as an unloving and cruel tyrant, and in some cases leads to a complete denial of hell or even to atheism.

Today a kind of thoughtless optimism is the more prevalent error. Quite apart from what theologians teach, popular piety has become saccharine. Unable to grasp the rationale for eternal punishment, many Christians take it almost for granted that everyone, or practically everyone, must be saved. The Mass for the Dead has turned into a Mass of the Resurrection, which sometimes seems to celebrate not so much the resurrection of the Lord as the salvation of the deceased, without any reference to sin and punishment. More education is needed to convince people that they ought to fear God who, as Jesus taught, can punish soul and body together in hell (cf. Mt 10:28).

The search for numbers in the demography of hell is futile. God in his wisdom has seen fit not to disclose any statistics. Several sayings of Jesus in the Gospels give the impression that the majority are lost. Paul, without denying the likelihood that some sinners will be die without sufficient repentance, teaches that the grace of Christ is more powerful than sin: "Where sin increased, grace abounded all the more" (Rom 5:20). Passages such as these permit us to hope that very many, if not all, will be saved.

All told, it is good that God has left us without exact information. If we knew that virtually everybody would be damned, we would be tempted to despair. If we knew that all, or nearly all, are saved, we might become presumptuous. If we knew that some fixed percent, say fifty, would be saved, we would be caught in an unholy rivalry. We would rejoice in every sign that others were among the lost, since own chances of election would thereby be increased! Such a competitive spirit would hardly be compatible with the gospel.

We are forbidden to seek our own salvation in a selfish and egotistical way. We are keepers of our brothers and sisters. The more we work for their salvation, the more of God's favor we can expect for ourselves. Those of us who believe and make use of the means that God has provided for the forgiveness of sins and the reform of life have no reason to fear. We can be sure that Christ, who died on the Cross for us, will not fail to give us the grace we need. We know that in all things God works for the good of those who love him, and that if we persevere in that love, nothing whatever can separate us from Christ (cf. Rom 8:28–39). That is all the assurance we can have, and it should be enough.

NOTES

1. Augustine, *Tractates on the Gospel of John*, 107, ch. 17, nos. 9–13; Thomas Aquinas, *De Veritate*, I, qu. 6, art. 2.

2. Council of Quiercy, A.D. 853, DS 623; Council of Valence, A.D. 855, DS 630.

3. John Chystostom, homily 24 *in Act. Apostolorum*, PG 60:189, cf. A. Michel, "Élus (nombre des)," *DTC* 4: 2350–78, at 2365.

4. Augustine, *Contra Cresconium*, book 3, chap. 66, in *Oeuvres de S. Augustin* 31 (Paris: Desclée de Brouwer, 1968), 425.

5. Thomas Aquinas, *Summa theologiae*, part I, qu. 23, art. 3.

6. Ibid., art. 7 corp.

7. Ibid., ad 3.

8. Francisco Suárez, *De Deo Uno et Trino*, book 6, chap. 3, in his *Opera omnia*, 1:524–26.

9. The question of relative numbers of the saved and the lost is fully discussed by A. Michel, "Élus." Among those who hold that it is obligatory Catholic doctrine that the majority are damned he mentions Francis X. Godts, *De paucitate salvandorum* (third edition, Brussels: J. de Meester, 1899). Michel himself holds that the question may be freely debated.

10. John R. Sachs, "*Apocatastasis* in Patristic Theology," *Theological Studies* 54 (1993): 617–40.

11. See Hans Urs von Balthasar, *Dare We Hope "That All Men Be Saved?"* (San Francisco: Ignatius Press, 1988), 59–62; idem, "Origenes und die *Apokatastasis*," *Theologische Zeitschrift* 14 (1958): 174–90.

12. For a broader survey, including some authors I shall not mention, see John R. Sachs, "Current Eschatology: Universal Salvation and the Problem of Hell," *Theological Studies* 52 (1991): 227–54.

13. Jacques Maritain, "Beginning with a Reverie," in his *Untrammeled Approaches* (Notre Dame, Ind.: University of Notre Dame Press, 1997), 3–26.

14. Karl Rahner, "Hell," *The Concise Sacramentum Mundi* (New York: Seabury/Crossroad, 1975), 602–4, quotation from 603–4.

15. Balthasar, *Dare We Hope*, 163–70; Hans Urs von Balthasar, *Theo-Drama* (San Francisco: Ignatius, 1998), 5:290.

16. Edith Stein, *Welt und Person* (Freiburg: Herder, 1962), 158–59. Cf. Balthasar, *Dare We Hope*, 218–21.

17. John Paul II, *Crossing the Threshold of Hope* (New York: Knopf, 1994), 185, 186. In his apostolic exhortation *Reconciliatio et paenitentia*, the pope remarks on the present decline of the sense of sin and on the tendency to pass "from too much emphasis on the fear of eternal punishment to preaching a love of God that excludes any fear of punishment deserved by sin" (RP 18).

18. *Insegnamenti di Giovanni Paolo II* 22/2 (July–December 1999): 82, my translation. The English version of the same talk originally published in *L'Osservatore Romano* (Eng. ed.), August 4, 1997, 7, seems to endorse the Balthasar position. The crucial sentence reads: "Eternal damnation remains a possibility, but we are not granted without special divine revelation, the knowledge of whether or which human beings are effectively involved in it." But the 1999 disk on which *L'Osservatore Romano* published and Adobe Acrobat version of all its editions later changed the English text by deleting the words "whether or." In any case, the *Insegnamenti* text is the authoritative one.

19. Balthasar, "A Short Discourse on Hell," in the English translation of *Dare We Hope*, 163–254, quoting on 164 from the German periodical *Theologisches*, 1986, at 7255.

20. Jean Galot, S.J., "Eschatology from the Second Vatican Council to Our Days," Videoconference on Contemporary Eschatology on www.clerus.org.

21. Michael F. Hull, "Errors in Contemporary Eschatology," ibid.

22. Regis Scanlon, "The Inflated Reputation of Hans Urs von Balthasar," *New Oxford Review* 67 (March 2000): 17–24.

23. Richard John Neuhaus, *Death on a Friday Afternoon* (New York: Basic Books, 2000), 42–70.

24. Neuhaus conjectures that Christ from the Cross counted certain everyone as his own whether or not they entered the Catholic Church. The task of missionaries, then, is to let them know that they have been found (*Death on a Friday Afternoon*, 182). He does not say that everyone is saved. In a subsequent article he explains what he meant: "All are found, and therefore not lost. That some may chose not to accept the gift of being found is quite another matter"; Neuhaus, "Will All Be Saved?" *First Things* 115 (August/September 2001): 78.

25. Richard John Neuhaus, "Will All Be Saved?" 78.

26. Ibid., 79.

29

True and False Reform
in the Church

April 23, 2003

A Perennial Theme

The long experience of the Catholic Church has included many seasons of decline and renewal. Throughout the centuries, the Church has striven by preaching and exhortation to help individual Christians reform their lives. At various times reformers have arisen to make the consecrated life a more authentic school of perfection. One thinks in this connection of the Cistercians and Trappists as reformed branches of the Benedictine order, and of the Discalced Carmelites, who conducted a thoroughgoing reform of their order in sixteenth-century Spain. The universal Church likewise has undertaken major institutional reforms; for example, the Gregorian Reform of the eleventh century, which imposed stricter discipline on the clergy and secured the independence of the Church from secular control.

At many times in her history the Church has been threatened by false reforms that, if accepted, would have denatured her. Such reforms were attempted by the Encratites in the second century, the Donatists in the fourth century, the Waldensians in the twelfth, the Spiritual Franciscans in the thirteenth, Wycliffe in the fourteenth, and Jan Hus in the fifteenth.

The Conciliar movement in the fifteenth century brought forth some good fruits, but came to a bad end at the Council of Basel. Attempting to convert the Church into a kind of constitutional monarchy, it ran afoul of the Catholic doctrine of papal primacy.

By the beginning of the sixteenth century the necessity of a thoroughgoing reform was generally recognized. After the failure of the Fifth Lateran Council to achieve this objective, the whole Church teemed with reform movements, notably among Christian humanists such as Desiderius Erasmus, John Colet, and Lefèvre d' Étaples. Catholic cardinals such as Gaspar Contarini, James Sadoleto, Reginald Pole, and John Peter Caraffa proposed timely reforms some years before the Council of Trent.[1] Luther and his colleagues also took up the theme of reform, but in the name of correcting abuses they attacked essentials of the Catholic faith and became separated from the Church. The reform decrees of Trent targeted some of the real abuses and continued to bear excellent fruits long after the council. But in the next few centuries, the term "reform" became suspect among Catholics because it seemed to have a Protestant ring.

The First Vatican Council ran counter to certain reform movements of the nineteenth century. It successfully eliminated the remnants of Conciliarism and crushed ecclesiastical nationalism in the form of Gallicanism in France and its counterparts in several other nations. As a result, the papacy maintained uncontested control of the Catholic Church through the middle of the twentieth century.

During the decade after World War II, the Church in Europe, especially in France, experienced a revitalization thanks to a number of movements that may be grouped under the heading of "*ressourcement*." The Second Vatican Council was able to build effectively on the revival of biblical and patristic studies, the liturgical movement, kerygmatic theology, the catechetical renewal, the lay apostolate, the ecumenical movement, and the social apostolate. Aware of the negative connotations of terms like "reformation," Vatican II used such language very sparingly, but did not shrink from implementing some of the desiderata of Luther and the early Protestants.

Fearing that the term "reform" had too negative a connotation, the council spoke by preference of purification and renewal (*renovatio*). The Constitution on the Church, for example, declared, "The Church, embracing sinners in her bosom, is at the same time holy and always in need of being purified, and incessantly pursues the path of penance and renewal" (*LG* 8).

In one passage, Vatican II spoke explicitly though very guardedly of ecclesial reform. This passage, in the Decree on Ecumenism, touches not only on personal but also on institutional reform:

Christ summons the Church, as she goes her pilgrim way, to that continual reformation of which she is always in need insofar as she is an institution of men here on earth. Therefore, if the influence of events or of the times has led to deficiencies in conduct, in Church discipline, or even in the formulation of doctrine (which must be carefully distinguished from the deposit itself of faith), these should be appropriately rectified at the proper moment. (*UR* 6)

This passage is, as I have noted, very cautiously phrased. In stating that the Church is subject to reform to the extent that it is a human institution, it implies the presence of a divine element that is not subject to reform. It rules out any attempt to tamper with the deposit of faith.

Two Directions Since Vatican II

Since Vatican II reform movements have proliferated, but some of them have been ambiguous or misconceived. On the left we find initiatives that seek to make the Church more tolerant, more liberal, and more democratic. Some progressivist reformers aim to dissolve the Church's hierarchical structure and transform her into an egalitarian democracy. Bishops have now and again criticized or condemned liberalizing movements such as the "We Are Church" movement, which originated in Austria, and the "Call to Action" here in the United States.

Moderately to the right are orthodox but intransigent theologians who aspire to "reform the reforms" introduced in the wake of Vatican II. At the extreme right the Church is confronted by movements that seek to undo the work of the council itself, restoring what they venerate as Tridentine Catholicism. The Holy See has condemned the reactionary traditionalism of Archbishop Marcel Lefebvre. His breakaway church and a variety of so-called *Sedevacantist* movements are certainly schismatic if not openly heretical.[2]

The Meaning of Reform

In order to make a sound evaluation of reform movements, it will be helpful to unpack the concept of reform itself. To reform is to give new and better form to a preexistent reality, while preserving the essentials.

Unlike innovation, reform implies organic continuity; it does not add something foreign or extrinsic. Unlike revolution or transformation, reform respects and retains the substance that was previously there. Unlike development, it implies that something has gone wrong and needs to be corrected. The point of departure for reform is always an idea or institution that is affirmed but considered to have been imperfectly or defectively realized. The goal is to make persons or institutions more faithful to an ideal already accepted.

Reform may be either restorative or progressive. Restorative reform seeks to reactualize a better past or a past that is idealized. Progressive reform aims to move ahead toward an ideal or utopian future. Either style can run to excess. Restorative reform tends toward traditionalism; progressive reform, toward modernism. But neither direction can be ruled out. Sometimes the past needs to be repristinated; at other times, it may need to be transcended.

In any discussion of reform, two opposite errors are to be avoided. The first is to assume that because the Church is divinely instituted, it never needs to be reformed. This position is erroneous because it fails to attend to the human element. Since all the members of the Church, including the pope and the bishops, are limited in virtue and ability, they may fail to live up to the principles of the faith itself. When guilty of negligence, timidity, or misjudgment, they may need to be corrected, as Paul, for example, corrected Peter (Gal 2:11).

The second error would be to assail or undermine the essentials of Catholic Christianity. This would not be reform but dissolution. Paul rebuked the Galatians for turning to a different gospel (Gal 1:6). The Catholic Church is unconditionally bound to her Scriptures, her creeds, her dogmas, and her divinely instituted hierarchical office and sacramental worship. To propose that the Church should deny the divinity of Christ, or retract the dogma of papal infallibility, or convert herself into a religious democracy, as some have done in the name of reform, is to misunderstand both the nature of Catholicism and the nature of reform.[3]

At the outset, therefore, I wish to make it clear that anyone seeking to reform the Church must share the Church's faith and accept the essentials of her mission. The Church cannot take seriously the reforms advocated by those who deny that Christ was Son of God and Redeemer, who assert that the Scriptures teach error, or who hold that the Church should not require orthodoxy on the part of her own members. Proposals coming from a perspective alien to Christian faith should be treated with the utmost suspicion if not dismissed as unworthy of consideration.

The Church must be herself, and must not strive to become what nonbelievers might like her to be. Her first responsibility is to preserve intact the revelation and the means of grace that have been entrusted to her. Her second responsibility is to transmit the faith in its purity and make it operative in the lives of her members. Her third responsibility is to help persons who are not yet her members, and human society as a whole, to benefit from the redemptive work of Christ.

PRINCIPLES FOR VALID REFORM

More than a decade before Vatican II, the French Dominican Yves Congar wrote a book with the title *True and False Reform in the Church*.[4] The work was considered controversial in its day, but it has, I think, been vindicated as thoroughly orthodox. It is still in my opinion the most searching theological treatise on our subject. Drawing to some degree on Congar's fine exploratory work, I should like to suggest a few principles by which reform proposals in our day might be assessed.

1. According to Congar, "The great law of a Catholic reformism will be to begin with a return to the principles of Catholicism."[5] Vatican II, echoing his words, taught that "every renewal of the Church essentially consists in an increase of fidelity to her own calling" (*UR* 6).

Catholicism derives its principles from God by way of revelation. The most authoritative guidance comes from Holy Scripture understood in the light of apostolic tradition, inasmuch as this is the normative channel whereby revelation is transmitted. In his reform of the liturgy, Pius X issued a call to return to the sources ("*Revertimini ad fontes*"). Pius XII declared that speculation becomes sterile if it neglects to return continually to the sacred sources of Scripture and tradition, which contain inexhaustible treasures of truth.[6]

2. Any reform conducted in the Catholic spirit will respect the Church's styles of worship and pastoral life. It will be content to operate within the Church's spiritual and devotional heritage, with due regard for her Marian piety, her devotion to the saints, her high regard for the monastic life and the vows of religion, her penitential practices, and her eucharistic worship. A truly Catholic reform will not fanatically insist on

the abstract logic of an intellectual system but will take account of concrete possibilities of the situation, seeking to work within the framework of the given.

3. A genuinely Catholic reform will adhere to the fullness of Catholic doctrine, including not only the dogmatic definitions of popes and councils, but doctrines constantly and universally held as matters pertaining to the faith. In this connection cognizance will be taken of the distinction made by Vatican II between the deposit of faith and the formulations of doctrine.[7] Because human thought and language are inevitably affected by cultural and historical factors, it may be necessary from time to time to adjust the language in which the faith has been proclaimed.[8] Repeated in a new situation, the old formulations can often be misleading, as instanced by the examples of Baius and Jansenius in the seventeenth century. These scholars quoted Augustine to the letter but did not take account of the changed meaning of his words.

4. True reform will respect the divinely given structures of the Church, including the differences of states of life and vocations. Not all are equipped by training and office to pronounce on the compatibility of new theories and opinions with the Church's faith. These functions are, in fact, reserved to the hierarchical magisterium, though the advice of theologians and others will normally be sought.

5. A reform that is Catholic in spirit will seek to maintain communion with the whole body of the Church, and will avoid anything savoring of schism or factionalism. St. Paul speaks of anger, dissension, and party spirit as contrary to the Spirit of God (Gal 5:20). To be Catholic is precisely to see oneself as part of a larger whole, to be inserted in the Church universal.[9]

6. Reformers will have to exercise the virtue of patience, often accepting delays. Congar finds Luther especially lacking in this virtue.[10] But even Luther, stubborn and unyielding though he often was, cautioned his disciple Andreas Karlstadt on the importance of proceeding slowly, so as not to offend simple believers who were unprepared for changes that were objectively warranted.[11] Prudent reformers will recognize that they themselves stand under correction, and that their proposals, even if valid, may be premature. As Newman reminded his readers, there is such a thing as a good idea whose time has not yet come. Depending on the circumstances, Church authorities may wisely delay its acceptance until people's imaginations become accustomed to the innovation.[12]

7. As a negative criterion, I would suggest that a valid reform must not yield to the tendencies of our fallen nature, but must rather resist them. Under color of reform, we are sometimes tempted to promote what flatters our pride and feeds our self-interest, even though the gospel counsels humility and renunciation. Persons who have prestige, influence, and power usually want to retain and increase these; those who lack them want to acquire them. Both groups must undergo conversion.

8. For similar reasons we must be on guard against purported reforms that are aligned with the prevailing tendencies in secular society. One thinks in this connection of the enormous harm done in early modern times by nationalism in religion, a major factor contributing to the divisions of the Reformation era and to the enfeeblement of the Catholic Church during the Enlightenment. The liturgical and organizational reforms of Joseph II in Austria, the Civil Constitution on the Clergy enacted in France in 1790, the extreme liberalism of Félicité de Lamennais early in the nineteenth century, and the evolutionary religion of the Modernists at the dawn of the twentieth century—all these movements afford examples of initiatives perfectly attuned to spirit of their times but antithetical to the true character of Catholic Christianity.

In our day the prevailing climate of agnosticism, relativism, and subjectivism is frequently taken as having the kind of normative value that belongs by right to the word of God. We must energetically oppose reformers who contend that the Church must abandon her claims to absolute truth, must allow dissent from her own doctrines, and must be governed according to the principles of liberal democracy.[13] False reforms, I conclude, are those that fail to respect the imperatives of the gospel and the divinely given traditions and structures of the Church, or which impair ecclesial communion and tend rather toward schism. Would-be reformers often proclaim themselves to be prophets, but show their true colors by their lack of humility, their impatience, and their disregard for the Sacred Scripture and tradition.

It is often asserted that reformers ought to speak prophetically. This may well be true, provided that the nature of prophecy be correctly understood. Thomas Aquinas made an essential distinction between prophecy as it functioned in the Old Testament and as it functions within the Church. The ancient prophets, he says, were sent for two purposes: "to establish the faith and to rectify behavior." In our day, he adds, "the faith is already founded, because the things promised of old have been fulfilled in Christ. But prophecy which has as its goal to rectify behavior neither ceases nor will ever cease."[14] Prophetism since the time of Christ, as Congar reminds us, must always be inscribed within the framework of apostolicity. "Any prophetism that would, in one way or another, look for a revelation still open to substantial accretions or admit the possibility of changes in the apostolic revelation, is not true prophetism of the Church."[15] To give in to revolutionary impulses would impoverish the Church's divinely given legacy and impair her mission to the world.

INSTITUTIONAL REFORM?

Since the Second Vatican Council, ill-considered projects for institutional reform have become a consuming passion among certain intellectuals. Under the circumstances it is understandable that some excellent theologians react negatively to the very idea. Joseph Ratzinger makes an important point: "The reform that is needed at all times does not consist in constantly remodeling 'our' Church according to our taste, or in inventing her ourselves, but in ceaselessly clearing away our subsidiary constructions to let in the pure light that comes from above and that is also the dawning of pure freedom."[16] He goes on to observe that "the more administrative machinery we construct, be it the most modern, the less place there is for the Spirit, the less place there is for the Lord, and the less freedom there is."[17]

Henri de Lubac speaks in similar terms:

> *I do not believe that structural reforms*, about which there has been much debate for some years, *are ever the main part of a program that must aim at the only true renewal, spiritual renewal.* I even fear that the present-day inflation of such projects and discussions furnishes an all-too-convenient alibi to avoid it. The conciliar formula "*Ecclesia semper purificanda*" seems to me as to others "much superior to the '*Ecclesia semper reformanda*' which is used so extensively nearly everywhere." But *I do believe, on the other hand, that any disturbance, any change, or any relaxation of the essential structure of the Church would suffice to endanger all spiritual renewal.*[18]

De Lubac is not here denying the desirability of any and all institutional reforms, but only insisting we should not exaggerate their importance and that we always take care to leave intact the essential and abiding structures of the Church. He is surely correct in thinking that no social reorganization will be able to overcome the human tendency to sin and error. The most perfect structures, in the hands of incompetent or selfish administrators, will only make things worse. But where people are motivated by faith and generosity, even deficient structures will be tolerable.

CURRENT NEEDS FOR REFORM

No matter what is to be said about the proper balance between personal and institutional reform, it should be clear that the Church of our day has no cause for complacency. At least here in the United States, it stands in urgent need of far-reaching intellectual, spiritual, and moral regeneration. Some of the issues to be addressed, I submit, are the following:

Religious illiteracy has sunk to a new low. We urgently need an effective program of catechesis and religious education on all levels. The *Catechism of the Catholic Church* is only the first step in this revival, since the renewal it stands for cannot be implemented without the formation of a corps of trained catechists and the preparation of suitable materials for the religious education of different age-groups and constituencies.

Dissent is rampant, not only on secondary and reformable teachings but even on central doctrines of the faith. Catholics should be trained to have greater confidence in the magisterium, which enjoys a special assistance from the Holy Spirit. They should willingly conform their private judgment to its teaching, even when no dogmatic definition has been made.

The call for a new evangelization strongly issued by Paul VI and John Paul II has fallen, it would seem, on deaf ears. The majority of Catholics have little appreciation of their mission to spread the faith as a precious gift intended for all. In some cases they behave as if faith were an unwelcome burden. Members of fundamentalist sects, Mormons, and Pentecostals commonly exhibit a stronger missionary thrust than Catholics.

Liturgical laws are often flouted. The sacraments need to be celebrated with dignity and reverence. The Mass should be seen not simply as a communal meal celebrated by a local community but as the sacrifice of the universal Church performed in union with the whole body of bishops and the bishop of Rome as its head. As Pope John Paul II reminds us in his recent encyclical, Holy Communion cannot be worthily received except by persons who are in union with the Church and free from serious sin.[19]

Religious practice is falling off. Many fail to attend Mass on Sundays and holydays. The sacrament of Penance is neglected by the vast majority of Catholics. There is a serious dearth of vocations to the priesthood and the religious life.

The immoral behavior of Catholics, both lay and clergy, is a cause of scandal and defections. Under this heading I would include not only sexual abuse of minors, which has been so extensively publicized in recent years, but sex outside of marriage, abortion, divorce, alcoholism, the use and marketing of drugs, domestic violence, defamation, and financial scandals such as falsification of records and embezzlement. The morality of Catholics all too often sinks below the standards commonly observed by Protestants and unbelievers.

Self-evidently, these and similar reforms ought to be undertaken under the leadership of the bishops. Unfortunately, however, the prestige of the bishops is today at a new low. In some cases there is alienation between bishops and priests. Laity are in some places organizing against bishops and seeking to apply fiscal pressures and negative publicity as means to bring about what they see as reforms. This situation makes for new problems, likewise calling for reform. The Church cannot be made to function like a political community, with adversarial parties contending for supremacy.

Some of the alienation between different groups may result from mechanisms introduced in the wake of Vatican II. The council exalted the episcopacy to an unprecedented peak of power and responsibility. No normal individual is capable of being at once the chief teacher, the leading mystagogue, and the principal administrator for millions of Catholics, responsible for a huge array of parishes, schools, universities, hospitals, and charitable organizations. Bishops are also expected to be in constant consultation with pastoral councils and senates of priests. Within the diocese the bishop holds the fullness of legislative, judicial, and executive power.

In addition to their tasks within their respective dioceses, bishops are regularly engaged in the deliberations and decisions of the national episcopal conference to which they belong and in some cases have assignments from one or more of its multiple committees. A number of them are also involved in the government of the universal Church. They occasionally serve on congregations of the Holy See, and perhaps take part in assemblies of the Synods of Bishops. No wonder that there are failures in the handling of certain assignments of priests and other personnel.

According to the job description in the official directories, the bishop ought to be a man of high culture, firm in faith, solid in orthodoxy, a paragon of holiness, graciously winning in personality, able to assess the talents and weaknesses of others, skilled at managing large corporations and conducting fiscal policy, eloquent in the pulpit, fearless under criticism, indefatigable, and always self-possessed. Do we have in the United States a sufficient supply of priests with all these qualities? Many of the candidates being elevated to the episcopate, it would seem, are men of ordinary abilities, kind and hardworking, but incapable of measuring up to the almost superhuman responsibilities of the office. They run the risk of being morally, psychologically, and spiritually crushed under the burdens. As a prime structural problem, therefore, I would single out for special attention the episcopal office. What can be done to restore the priestly and pastoral ministry of bishops to its position of primacy?

In this context, the relationship between clergy and laity may be need some reconsideration. The distinction of roles, clearly spelled out by the Second Vatican Council, can be overstepped from both sides. Bishops, in their zeal to give explicit pastoral direction on every question and to control everything that goes on in their diocese, sometimes infringe on the proper competence of the laity, whose responsibility it is to apply the gospel to the circumstances of the marketplace, the professions, and political life. But the laity should understand that doctrinal teaching, pastoral governance, and liturgical leadership are tasks ordinarily reserved to persons in holy orders, especially the pope and bishops.

Within the Church herself, the laity have certain rights and responsibilities, as sharers by baptism in the threefold office of Christ, prophet, priest, and king. Their talents should be used for the benefit of the Church. Although the order of the Catholic Church cannot be congregational, members of the congregation can make a positive contribution, especially where their professional skills and experience are needed. There is every reason why the voice of the faithful should be heard, provided it does not come from an adversarial stance, as part of a scheme to seize power.

I submit, therefore, that a great deal of thought and probably some experimentation are needed to arrive at the correct via media between clericalism and laicism. Plenty of organs for collaboration now exist: plenary councils, diocesan synods, diocesan and parish councils, and committees. New structures would not seem to be necessary. Often more is accomplished by informal consultations than by official meetings.

For the sake of successful cooperation, the respective responsibilities of clergy and laity must be clearly demarcated. Whenever the functions are confused, misunderstandings, tensions, and conflict follow. Successful cooperation might help to reduce the excessive load of responsibility that now weighs upon bishops.

CONCLUSION

The idea of reform is as old as Christianity itself. Reform is by definition a good thing, and frequently is needed both on the personal and on the institutional level. But history teaches that reform can be misconceived and indiscreet. The only kind of reform that the Church should consider is one based on authentically Christian and Catholic principles. Holy Scripture and Catholic tradition give the necessary parameters. All who propose ecclesial reform should make it clear at the outset that they sincerely embrace these principles. Otherwise they should not be invited to participate in the process.

Where existing institutions prove clearly inadequate, institutional reform has a claim on our consideration. But it is less important and fruitful in the long run than personal reform, which requires purification of the heart from pride, sensuality, and lust for power. Where there is a humble and loving spirit, combined with firm faith and stringent self-discipline, institutional reform will be at once less urgent and easier to achieve.

NOTES

1. A select committee of cardinals submitted to Pope Paul III the *Consilium de Ecclesia emendanda* in 1538. A translation may be found in *Readings in Church History*, ed. Colman Barry (Westminster, Md.: Newman, 1967), 2:96–102.

2. On Catholic ultraconservative movements, see Michael W. Cuneo, *The Smoke of Satan: Conservative and Traditionalist Dissent in Contemporary American Catholicism* (New York: Oxford University Press, 1997).

3. James Carroll, *Constantine's Sword: The Church and the Jews* (Boston: Houghton Mifflin, 2003), especially Part VIII, "A Call for Vatican III," 547–604.

4. Yves Congar, *Vraie et fausse Réforme dans l'Église* (Paris: Cerf, 1950; rev. ed., 1968). I shall be referring to the 1968 edition.

5. Ibid., 308.

6. Pius XII, encyclical *Humani generis*, 31.

7. Vatican II, pastoral constitution *Gaudium et spes*, 62, citing the speech of Pope John XXIII at the opening of the Council. The same idea is reflected in the quotation from *UR* 6 given earlier.

8. This is acknowledged by the Congregation of the Doctrine of the Faith in its 1973 Declaration *Mysterium Ecclesiae*, §5.

9. Congar, *Vraie et fausse Réforme*, 241–76.

10. Ibid., 281.

11. Christopher M. Bellitto, *Renewing Christianity: A History of Church Reform from Day One to Vatican II* (New York: Paulist, 2001), 124–25.

12. John Henry Newman, preface to third edition of *The Via Media of the Anglican Church* (London: Longmans, Green, 1897), lv–lvi.

13. See James Carroll, "Enhancing Democracy: The Key to Religious Reform," an address to the Call to Action Conference of November 2, 2002, *National Catholic Reporter*, 15 November 2002, 3–5.

14. Thomas Aquinas, *In Matthaeum* ch. 11, *Opera omnia* 19 (Paris: Vivès, 1876), 397.

15. Congar, *Vraie et fausse Réforme*, 199–200.

16. Joseph Ratzinger, *Called to Communion: Understanding the Church Today* (San Francisco: Ignatius, 1996), 140.

17. Ibid., 146.

18. Henri de Lubac, *The Motherhood of the Church* (San Francisco: Ignatius, 1982), 33, italics his. The quotation is from Jean-Jacques von Allmen, "Remarques sur la constitution dogmatique *Lumen gentium*," *Irénikon* (1966): 40. De Lubac adds in a footnote that he does not reject, for all that, the second formula.

19. 19. John Paul II, encyclical *Ecclesia de Eucharistia*, 36–37; 44–45.

30

John Paul II and the Mystery of the Human Person

October 21, 2003

A s the literary output of Pope John Paul II has accumulated, expanding almost beyond the assimilative powers of any one reader, and as he celebrates the silver jubilee of his pontificate, I have been asking myself, as I am sure that many others have: What lies at the very heart of his message? Is there some one concept that could serve as a key to unlock what is distinctive to this pope as a thinker? My thesis will be: the mystery of the human person. As pope, he is of course bound to the whole dogmatic heritage of the Church, but he presents it in a distinctive way, with his own emphases, which are in line with his philosophical personalism.

YEARS AS PROFESSOR AND BISHOP

In his early years as a professor of ethics at the University of Lublin in Poland, Karol Wojtyla, the future Pope John Paul II, like other members of the philosophical faculty, identified himself as a Thomist. While enthusiastically affirming the teaching of Thomas Aquinas on most points, he took note of one weakness. St. Thomas paid too little attention to the human person as experienced from within. In a paper on "Thomistic Personalism" delivered in 1961 he declared,

> [W]hen it comes to analyzing consciousness and self-consciousness—there seems to be no place for it in St. Thomas' objectivistic view of reality. In

any case, that in which the person's subjectivity is most apparent is presented by St. Thomas in an exclusively—or almost exclusively—objective way. He shows us the particular faculties, both spiritual and sensory, thanks to which the whole of human consciousness and self-consciousness—the human personality in the psychological and moral sense—takes shape, but that is also where he stops. Thus St. Thomas gives us an excellent view of the objective existence and activity of the person, but it would be difficult to speak in his view of the lived experiences of the person.[1]

Wojtyla was satisfied that St. Thomas correctly situated the human person in terms of the general categories of being, as an individual subsisting in an intellectual nature. But he wished to enrich Thomas's doctrine of the person by reference to our experience of ourselves as unique ineffable subjects. Each person is an "I," an original source of free and responsible activity.

Wojtyla's experience as a young bishop at Vatican II confirmed and deepened his personalism. He was particularly involved in writing the Pastoral Constitution on the Church in the Modern World, *Gaudium et spes*, which speaks of "the exalted dignity proper to the human person" and of universal, inviolable human rights (*GS* 26). In another of John Paul's favorite passages, *Gaudium et spes* states that human beings are the only creatures that God wills for their own sake, and adds that they cannot rise to their full stature except through a disinterested gift of self (*GS* 24).

Bishop Wojtyla enthusiastically accepted the council's teaching that the human person is excentric rather than egocentric. Paradoxically, we cannot fulfill ourselves except through transcending ourselves and giving ourselves in love toward others. Sometimes John Paul II calls this the "law of the gift."[2] He thus provides an anthropological grounding for the paradoxical sayings of Jesus in the Gospels about how we can find true life by dying for his sake and unintentionally find spiritual death by clinging selfishly to life.

At Vatican II, Cardinal Wojtyla entered vigorously into the debates on religious freedom. The council opened its declaration on that subject with sentences that could almost have come from the pen of Bishop Wojtyla, had he been one of the authors: "A sense of the dignity of the human person has been impressing itself more and more deeply on the consciousness of contemporary man. And the demand is increasingly made that men should act of their own judgment, enjoying and making use of a responsible freedom, not driven by coercion but motivated by a sense of duty" (DH 1).

At the council and many times since, John Paul II has quoted from John 8:32: "You will know the truth, and the truth will make you free" (e.g., *RH* 12; *VS* 34 and 87). Throughout his pontificate he would never cease to be a firm champion of human freedom, including religious freedom. He is on principle opposed to physical and moral coercion as infringements of human dignity.

While glorying in freedom, the pope insists that it is not an end in itself but a means of personally adhering to the true good, as perceived by a judgment of conscience. "Authentic freedom," he writes, "is never freedom 'from' the truth but always freedom 'in' the truth" (*VS* 64). When freedom is abused, it diminishes itself, falling into chains. As he told the General Assembly of the United Nations in 1995, "Detached from the truth about the human person, freedom deteriorates into license in the lives of individuals, and in political life it becomes the caprice of the most powerful and the arrogance of power. Far from being a limitation upon freedom or a threat to it, reference to the truth about the human person—a truth universally knowable through the moral law written on the hearts of all—is, in fact, the guarantor of freedom's future."[3]

The pope is quite aware that this concept of freedom is not widely accepted and understood. "The essential bond between Truth, the Good, and Freedom has been largely lost sight of in present-day culture" (*VS* 84). Libertarianism erroneously severs the bonds between freedom and responsibility. Because freedom is inevitably linked with responsibility, we are accountable for the use we make of it.

In his continuing struggle against Marxism in Poland after Vatican II, Cardinal Wojtyla identified the doctrine of the person as the Achilles' heel of the Communist regime. He decided to base his opposition on that plank. In 1968 he wrote to his friend, the future Cardinal Henri de Lubac:

> I devote my very rare free moments to a work that is close to my heart and devoted to the metaphysical significance and the mystery of the PERSON. It seems to me that the debate today is being played on that level. The evil of our times consists in the first place in a kind of degradation, indeed in a pulverization, of the fundamental uniqueness of each human person. This evil is even much more of the metaphysical than of the moral order.

To this disintegration, planned at times by atheistic ideologies, we must oppose, rather than sterile polemics, a kind of "recapitulation" of the mystery of the person.[4]

As pope, John Paul II would continue to insist that the extraordinary brutality of the twentieth century was due to an unwillingness to recognize the inherent value of the human person, who is made in the image and likeness of God, who confers upon it inalienable rights that can neither be bestowed nor withdrawn by any human power. "The human person," he proclaims, "receives from God its essential dignity and with it the capacity to transcend every social order so as to move toward truth and goodness" (*CA* 38.1).

In *The Acting Person*, a work published shortly before he became pope, Cardinal Wojtyla expounded a theory of the person as a self-determining agent that realizes itself through free and responsible action. Activity is not something strictly other than the person: it is the person coming to expression and constituting itself. Persons, moreover, are essentially social and oriented to life in community. They achieve themselves as persons by interaction, giving to others and receiving from them in turn. To reconcile the good of the community with that of its individual members, Wojtyla proposes a theory of participation. All must contribute to the common good, which then redounds to the benefit of the individual members. This teaching on participation and the common good contains an implicit critique not only of Marxist collectivism but also of libertarian individualism and anarchist alienation.

THEMES OF THE PAPACY

Since becoming pope, John Paul II has used personalism as a lens through which to reinterpret much of the Catholic tradition. He unhesitatingly embraces all the dogmas of the Church, but expounds them with a personalist slant.

As a first example of this personalism, one might select the pope's conception of the Christian life itself. In his closing homily at the World Youth Day in August 2000, the pope told his hearers, "It is important to realize that among the many questions surfacing in your minds, the decisive ones are not about 'what.' The basic question is 'who': to whom am I to go? whom am I to follow? to whom should I entrust my life?"[5] In another message to youth he declared: "Christianity is not an opinion and does not consist of empty words. Christianity is Christ! It is a Person."[6]

In his encyclical on missionary activity, *Redemptoris missio*, John Paul speaks of the Kingdom in personalist terms. "The kingdom of God," he writes, "is not a concept, a doctrine, or a program subject to free interpretation, but it is before all else a *person* with the face and name of Jesus of Nazareth, the image of the invisible God" (*RMis* 18). The face of Jesus is for this pope almost a synonym for the person. His apostolic constitution on the Church in America begins with a stirring chapter "On the Encounter with the Living Christ." In his program for the third millennium, *Novo millennio ineunte*, he declares that the Church's task is to make the face of Christ shine in every historical period, a task that requires that we ourselves first contemplate his face (*NMI* 16). The ancient longing of the Psalmist to see the face of the Lord (Ps 27:8) is surpassingly fulfilled in Christian contemplation of the face of Jesus (*NMI* 23). The pope's apostolic letter on the Rosary speaks at length of contemplating Jesus, as it were, through the eyes of Mary.

Personalism permeates the ecclesiology of John Paul II. "The Church," he teaches, "wishes to serve this single end: that each person may be able to find Christ, in order that Christ may walk with each person the path of life" (*RH* 13:1). He goes on to describe the Church as "the community of disciples, each of whom in a different way—at times not very consciously and consistently—is following Christ. This shows also the deeply 'personal' aspect and dimension of this society" (*RH* 21). The pope often asserts that the ultimate reality and model of the Church is the divine communion of persons realized eternally in the Holy Trinity (*SR* 121).

In various documents, John Paul II exhorts us to find the face of Jesus not only in the Gospels but also in the sacraments. "The risen Jesus accompanies us on our way and enables us to recognize him, as the disciples of Emmaus did, 'in the breaking of the bread' (Lk 24:35)" (*NMI* 59). John Paul II's recent encyclical on the Eucharist has the same personalistic dimension. The Eucharist, he says, forms the Church because it brings the baptized into full communion and friendship with Christ. When we receive him devoutly in Holy Communion, he abides in us even as we abide in him (*EE* 22). The encyclical ends by recalling that the bread we receive is the Shepherd who feeds us. It quotes the eucharistic hymn of Thomas Aquinas. "*Bone pastor, panis vere*" ("Come, Good Shepherd, bread divine") (*EE* 62).

A profound personalism undergirds Pope John Paul's theology of ecumenism and interreligious relations. "If prayer is the soul of the ecumenical movement and of its yearning for unity," he writes in his encyclical on ecumenism, "it is the basis and support for everything the council defines as 'dialogue.' This definition is certainly not unrelated to today's personalist way of thinking. The capacity for dialogue is rooted in the nature of the person and his dignity. . . . Although the concept of 'dialogue' might appear to give priority to the cognitive dimension (*dia-logos*), all dialogue implies a global, existential dimension. It involves the human subject in his or her entirety; dialogue between communities involves in a particular way the subjectivity of each. . . . Dialogue is not simply an exchange of ideas. In some way it is always an 'exchange of gifts'" (*UUS* 28). A little later he asserts: "Dialogue does not extend exclusively to matters of doctrine but engages the whole person; it is also a dialogue of love" (*UUS* 47).

These statements on ecumenical dialogue apply analogously to interreligious dialogue. In his encyclical on missionary activity John Paul II teaches that dialogue is an essential part of the Church's evangelizing mission. Christian proclamation and dialogue are not opposed to each other but are inextricably interlinked (*RMis* 55).

The personalist theme shows up almost everywhere in the teaching of this pope. Think, for example, of his apostolic constitution on Catholic higher education. Because of its essential connection with Christ as the way, the truth, and the life, the Catholic university is imbued with a kind of universal humanism (*ECE* 4). It enables people to rise to the full measure of their humanity, created in the image of God and renewed in Christ and his Spirit (*ECE* 5). Quoting from an earlier speech of his, the pope adds:

> It is essential that we be convinced of the priority of the ethical over the technical, of the primacy of the person over things, of the superiority of the spirit over matter. The cause of the human person will only be served if knowledge is joined to conscience. Men and women of science will truly aid humanity only if they preserve 'the sense of the transcendence of the human person over the world and of God over the human person'" (*ECE* 18, quoting UNESCO address of 1980 and Vatican II, *GE* 10).

Personalism also penetrates the pope's teaching on social matters. In the first of his social encyclicals, *Laborem exercens*, he expounds a highly original theology of work, based on the relationship between the person and activity. Human beings, he asserts, are called to participate in God's own creative activity by productive labor. The pope censures economism as the error of "considering labor solely according to its economic purpose" (*LE* 13.3). Since the workers are persons, they are of more value than their products. Through their labor they should be able to transform nature, making it serve as a more fitting habitation for humankind, and at the same time perfect themselves as persons rather than suffer degradation. To the extent that labor is onerous and painful, this may be seen as a just penalty for human sin and may be spiritually fruitful when patiently accepted and united to the sufferings of Christ (*LE* 27).

Some commentators thought that *Laborem exercens* was anticapitalist and that it advocated a kind of socialism, not doctrinaire or ideological but moral.[7] But this interpretation cannot stand in view of the pope's other social encyclicals, which call for a free participatory society. His encyclical on economic development, *Sollicitudo rei socialis*, illustrates this position. Building on notions already sketched in *Laborem exercens*, the pope defines solidarity as a virtue, whereby people firmly commit themselves not to exploit others but to work for their good and even to "lose themselves" for the sake of others. The virtue of solidarity applies analogously to corporations and nations, which must responsibly contribute to the general good of society and of humanity as a whole (*SRS* 38–40).

The theme of development provides John Paul with an occasion to speak again of personal initiative and participation. "Development," he states, "demands above all a spirit of initiative on the part of the countries which need it. Each of them must act in accordance with its own responsibilities, not expecting everything from the more favored countries. . . . Each must discover and use to the best advantage its own area of freedom" (*SRS* 44). While opposing all kinds of exploitation of the poor and marginalized, the pope affirms the right of human initiative in undertaking new economic ventures.

The pope's experience of living under a Marxist regime in Poland turned him against the welfare state. The controlled economy, he maintains, "diminishes, or in practice absolutely destroys, the spirit of initiative, that is to say, the creative subjectivity of the person" (*SRS* 15.2).

The notion of creative subjectivity moves to center stage in John Paul II's third social encyclical, *Centesimus annus*. "The free market economy," it states, "is the most efficient instrument for utilizing resources and effectively responding to needs" (*CA* 34.1). At one point the pope pointedly asks whether formerly Communist nations seeking to rebuild their econo-mies should be advised to embrace capitalism. His answer is a carefully qualified yes. He is in favor of the business economy, the market econ-omy, the free economy, but he is convinced that the energies unleashed by the market need to be contained within a strong juridical framework and a public moral culture so that the economy is kept in service to the common good (*CA* 42).

Whereas his predecessors had tended to look on wealth as an accumula-tion of material possessions, John Paul II as a personalist adds a new factor. He points out that the primary source of wealth today is the human spirit with its fund of knowledge and its creative capacities (*CA* 32). Wealth, therefore, consists more in what we are than in what we have.

TENSIONS WITH PREVIOUS TRADITION

Much more could be said about the pope's personalism as illustrated, for example, in his concept of the priest as acting "in the person of Christ" in consecrating the host and chalice at the altar and in giving absolution in the sacrament of Penance, which he refers to as "the tribunal of mercy." But the examples already adduced should probably suffice to establish my thesis about the importance of the personalist perspective in the thought of John Paul II. But before concluding, I should like to reflect on several points at which this perspective stands in tension with previous Catholic tradition.

1. Natural theology. At least since the time of Thomas Aquinas, the Catholic tradition has insisted that the existence of the one personal God, creator and goal of all things, can be established by human reason on the basis of things seen. The standard arguments have been based on the principle of causality, contingency, the degrees of perfection, and the principle of finality. The present pope nowhere rejects these arguments, but he is curiously silent about them. Instead he takes his point of depar-ture from the longings of the human heart for personal communion with others and with the divine. For personalist philosophers such as Martin Buber and Emmanuel Lévinas, he writes, "the path passes not so much through being and existence [as in St. Thomas] as through people and their meeting each other" in co-existence and dialogue. We encounter God as the ultimate Thou (*CTH* 36). This approach is highly suggestive,

but the pope does not develop it in detail. And so we are left with questions such as these: Can a rigorous and convincing proof be erected on a personalist foundation? If so, is it to be preferred to the traditional ontological and cosmological arguments? Have these other arguments been exposed as deficient? I believe that the thought of John Paul II can be integrated with the tradition.

2. Natural law. When he writes on natural law, the present pope speaks more of the human person than of human nature. As Janet Smith points out, he wishes to integrate the natural law into his personalist framework, thus avoiding the charge of "biologism" sometimes directed against standard presentations.[8] "The true meaning of the natural law," says the pope, is that "it refers to man's proper and primordial nature, the 'nature of the human person,' which is *the person himself*" (*VS* 50.1).

The Oxford professor Oliver O'Donovan, objects that the pope seems overindebted to the idealist tradition, which "understands the rationality of the moral law as something grounded in the human mind."[9] But in his work as a professor, Karol Wojtyla anticipated this objection and sought to answer it. In an essay on "The Human Person and Natural Law," he firmly rejected the view of Kant and the idealists, who would allow reason to impose its own categories on reality. For Wojtyla reason discerns and affirms an objective order of reality and value that is prior to reason itself. The freedom of the human person is not to be understood as though it meant emancipation from all constraints.[10] Although the mind must conform to the real order, natural law as a moral obligation is not something merely mechanical or biological. It presupposes a subject with personal consciousness.

3. Contraception. The question of natural law comes up concretely in the pope's writings on contraception. Following Popes Pius XI and Pius XII, Paul VI in his encyclical *Humanae vitae* argued primarily from natural law, contending that contraception is intrinsically evil because the generative faculties are intrinsically ordered toward the raising up of life (*HV* 13). But the present pope, in his various writings on the subject, says nothing about the intrinsic ordering of the faculties. He speaks of sexual union as a tangible expression of love between a man and a woman who generously and unreservedly give themselves to each other. Contraception, he maintains, is "a falsification of the inner meaning of conjugal love," since it turns sexuality into a means of hedonistic satisfaction (*FC* 32.4). Paul VI in *Humanae vitae* had already spoken of conjugal love as a

reciprocal personal gift of self and had warned that the practice of contraception could easily lead to the lowering of the partners into mere instruments of selfish enjoyment (*HV* 8, 17).

Some authors contend that if Paul VI had more consistently followed the personalist rather than the legalist approach, his condemnation of contraception would have been more warmly received.[11] The question therefore arises: Does John Paul II intend to correct Paul VI by substituting a superior argument, or does he mean to leave intact all that Paul VI said about the ontological dimension of the moral law, adding only a further reflection on the subjective or psychological dimension?[12] I suspect that he intends to support the tradition, not to supersede it. But he wants to induce people to be open to life out of love, not just as a matter of submitting to law as a constraint.

4. The death penalty. In a McGinley lecture several years ago, I spoke at some length of the pope's views on the death penalty. Although he does not hold that the death penalty is intrinsically evil, his deep respect for human life inclines him to reject capital punishment in practice. He allows for it when there is no other way to defend society against the criminal, but he also holds that in advanced societies today there are alternatives more in accord with human dignity. When convicts on death row are about to be executed, the pope regularly sends messages to governors asking them to grant clemency.

Earlier official teaching, up through the pontificate of Pius XII, consistently supported capital punishment. Catholic moral theologians regularly quoted St. Paul to the effect that secular rulers do not bear the sword in vain; they are God's ministers or instruments in executing his wrath upon wrongdoers (Rom 13:4). Thus the authority of the state to put criminals to death does not conflict with the maxim that God alone is the master of life. But John Paul II, to the best of my knowledge, never quotes this text. Why not, I wonder. Does he believe that governments in the modern democratic society still rule with divine authority or that they enjoy only the authority given them by consensus of the governed? Can retributive punishment be a valid reason for the death penalty?

Some Catholics interpret John Paul II as opposing the mainstream Catholic tradition and therefore as perhaps teaching unsound doctrine.[13] Personally I am not convinced that he wishes to break with that tradition. In my earlier McGinley lecture I contended that his statements can be read in a way compatible with the tradition on the death penalty.[14]

5. Just war. Similar issues arise with respect to just war. John Paul II, while denying that he is a pacifist, deplores military action as a failure for humanity. In the encyclical *Centesimus annus* he called attention to the success of nonviolent resistance in bringing about the overthrow of Communism in Eastern Europe. He then pleaded eloquently for a world order in which the need for war would be eliminated. "Never again war," he writes, "which destroys the lives of innocent people, teaches how to kill, throws into upheaval even the lives of those who do the killing and leaves behind a trail of resentment and hatred. Just as the time has finally come when in individual states a system of private vendetta and reprisal has given way to the rule of law, so too a similar step forward is now urgently needed in the international community" (*CA* 52.1).

In his World Peace Day message of January 1, 2002, John Paul II declared that there is no peace without justice and no justice without forgiveness. Does he mean that the pursuit of justice and forgiveness ought to banish all thought of war? Some astute critics believe that the pope is preparing the way for a doctrinal development that would greatly restrict the conditions of a just war.[15] Is he discarding the just war tradition in favor of what George Weigel calls "a species of functional or *de facto* pacifism"?[16]

Personalism undoubtedly favors the use of persuasion rather than force. It makes for a reluctance to admit that negotiation can at a certain point become futile. But realism may sometimes require the use of military force. The pope has several times countenanced what is called "humanitarian intervention" to put an end to bloody massacres (e.g., in Ruanda, East Timor, and Bosnia). He made no objection to the American military action against Afghanistan in 2002. In essentials, I suspect, the classical just war doctrine is still intact, but new and difficult mediating principles are needed especially in cases where the belligerents are not sovereign states with professional troops but factions or terrorist organizations.

6. Social order. I have already commented on the social and economic teaching of the present Pope. Michael Novak sees this teaching, especially in *Centesimus annus*, as supplying the rationale needed for building a new order of society. The key concepts in this new synthesis, Novak finds, are those of the acting person, the right to personal economic initiative, the virtues associated with entrepreneurship, and human creativity grounded in the *imago Dei* implanted in every woman and man by the Creator himself.[17]

Not all commentators share Novak's enthusiasm. Father James Hug, for example, ruefully writes of *Centesimus annus*: "Some of the language suggests that U.S. neoconservatives helped to shape its content." He looks forward to the day when he and "the progressive segment of the Church justice community" will be able to have comparable input into papal social teaching.[18]

These varying reactions leave us with the question: Is the social teaching of the present pope a passing deviation or a permanent shift? I would hazard the opinion that his personalist slant will continue to enrich Catholic political and economic theory for the foreseeable future.

7. Kingship of Christ. In his talks and writings Pope John Paul II speaks frequently of Christ's threefold office as prophet, priest, and king. While he elaborates on the first two members of this triad, he has relatively less to say about Christ's kingly office. The Feast of Christ the King was instituted by Pius XI in 1925 to make it clear that Christ "holds all nations under his sway" (encyclical *Quas primas* 20).

"Nations," wrote Pius XI, "will be reminded by the annual celebration of this feast that not only individuals but also *rulers and princes are bound to give public honor and obedience to Christ*" (*QP* 32, italics supplied). John Paul II, by contrast, speaks of Christ's lordship as a triumph of humble submission and of his kingdom as a "kingdom of love and service."[19] He says relatively little about Christ as lawmaker and judge, perhaps because these themes fit less well into his personalist scheme.

Vatican II's Declaration on Religious Freedom, with its accent on the mutual independence of Church and State, has made it more difficult to speak with the boldness of Pius XI.[20] But we should not allow ourselves to forget that Christ, who lived humbly as a servant in our midst, has been crowned with glory and that he reigns as sovereign Lord at the right hand of the Father.

8. The Last Judgment. John Paul II of course accepts the article of the Creed that Christ "will come again to judge the living and the dead." But he quotes by preference from the Fourth Gospel that "God sent the Son into the world, not to condemn the world, but that the world might be saved through him" (Jn 3:17). "Only those who will have rejected the salvation offered by God in his boundless mercy," he writes, "will be condemned, because they will have condemned themselves."[21] A little later he adds that eternal punishment is not to be attributed to God's

initiative, because in his merciful love God can only desire the salvation of the human beings he has created.[22]

Damnation, according to the pope, means definitive separation from God "freely chosen by the human person and confirmed with death."[23] Paraphrasing the parable of the sheep and goats, he says that the Lord Jesus will come to "question" us when we appear before him.[24] But in the parable itself, the Son of Man actually sentences some to hell with the words: "Depart from me, you cursed, into the eternal fire that has been prepared for the devil and his angels" (Mt 25:41). The shift in imagery betrays the pope's reluctance to speak of Christ as judge.

9. Purgatory. The Catholic tradition has depicted purgatory as a place where the debt of temporal punishment for forgiven sins is paid. The classical proof text from Scripture (2 Macc 12:41–45) speaks of sacrifices being offered to atone for the sins of slain Jewish soldiers. The Second Council of Lyons taught that the souls in purgatory undergo cleansing punishments. Paul VI in 1967 reiterated the doctrine that even after sins have been remitted, a debt of expiation may remain to be paid in purgatory.[25] But John Paul II, in texts familiar to me, makes no mention of punishment or expiation in purgatory. Instead he speaks of it only as a state of "purification" or cleansing preparing the soul to enter into the fullness of eternal life.[26]

Here, as in the case of hell, we must ask, does the personalism of John Paul II incline him to neglect or minimize the penal aspects? If so, is he simply making a pastoral adaptation on the ground that purgatory can better be understood, or be more ecumenically acceptable, if no mention is made of the punitive dimension? Or is he introducing a new development in which God will no longer been seen as punishing? I am inclined to think that the connection between sin and punishment is so deeply ingrained in Scripture and tradition that it will never be eliminated from Catholic teaching.

CONCLUSION

Pope John Paul II is not a man of one idea. As I have said, he accepts the whole dogmatic heritage of the Church. In his philosophy he combines personalist phenomenology with a strong Thomistic metaphysics. He therefore has many resources with which to address the complex questions we have been considering.

Personalism has its clearest applications in the realm of privacy and one-to-one relations. It is crucial in individual self-realization and in marriage and family life—themes on which John Paul II has written luminously. More remarkably, he has found ways of extending personalism to deal with political and economic issues, drawing on his conceptions of human action, personal participation, and free initiative. Although personalism cannot be an adequate tool for handling the larger issues of law and order, war and peace, John Paul II has injected important new considerations into the fields of business, jurisprudence, political science, and international relations.

Theologically, likewise, the pope is a personalist. He writes movingly of the desire for God inscribed in the human heart. He dwells joyfully on the one-to-one relation between the individual believer and Jesus Christ, mediated through the Scriptures, the sacraments, and the Church. His concentration on God's amazing love and mercy is a welcome antidote to pessimistic preachers who have portrayed God as a demanding master and a rigorous judge. But, as John Paul would surely recognize, God's love cannot be played off against his justice. The pope knows well that the love of God cannot exist without his call to obedience to God's commandments and that persons who reject God's love must reckon with his justice.

John Paul II, however, shies away from threatening words. Fear, in his view, diminishes the scope of freedom and makes only a poor Christian. He holds up the more perfect motives of hope, trust, and love as grounds for joyful adherence to the Lord. Amid all the anger and turmoil of our times, John Paul II stands as a beacon of hope. With calm insistence he stands by the theme of his inaugural homily: "Do not be afraid. . . . Open wide the doors to Christ. He alone has the words of life, yes, of eternal life."[27]

NOTES

1. Karol Wojtyla, *Person and Community: Selected Essays* (New York: Peter Lang, 1993), 170–71. See also Wojtyla's critique of the Boethian definition of the person in his article "Subjectivity and the Irreducible in the Human Being," 209–17.

2. John Paul II, *Person and Community*, 194; cf. his *Sign of Contradiction* (New York: Seabury/Crossroad, 1979), 58.

3. John Paul II, address of October 5, 1995 to U.N. General Assembly, §12; *Origins* 25 (October 18, 1995): 293–99, at 297–98.

4. Henri de Lubac, *At the Service of the Church* (San Francisco: Ignatius, 1993), 171–72.

5. John Paul II, "Closing Homily at Tor Vergata," §3; *Origins* 30 (August 31, 2000): 184–86, at 185.

6. John Paul II, Message to Seventeenth World Youth Day as quoted in Stefano Alberto, "Real Presence, Not Pious Remembrance," *Traces* 5 (June 2003): 40.

7. Gregory Baum, *The Priority of Labor: A Commentary on "Laborem Exercens"* (New York: Paulist, 1982), 80–88.

8. Janet E. Smith, "Natural Law and Personalism in *Veritatis Splendor*," in *John Paul II and Moral Theology*, ed. Charles E. Curran and Richard A. McCormick (New York: Paulist, 1998), 67–85.

9. Oliver O'Donovan, "A Summons to Reality," in *Considering "Veritatis Splendor,"* ed. John Wilkins (Cleveland: Pilgrim Press, 1994), 41–45, at 44.

10. Karol Wojtyla, "The Human Person and Natural Law," *Person and Community*, 181–85.

11. See George Weigel, *Witness to Hope* (New York: HarperCollins, 1999), 206–10.

12. An affirmative answer to this question is suggested by John Paul II, *The Theology of the Body* (Boston: Pauline Books and Media, 1997), 386–90.

13. Antonin Scalia, "God's Justice and Ours," *First Things* 123 (May 2002), 17–21. See also the letters on this article in *First Things* 126 (October 2002): 8–16, and Justice Scalia's response, 16–18.

14. Avery Dulles, "Catholicism and Capital Punishment," *First Things* 112 (April 2001): 30–35. An exchange of letters followed in *First Things* 115 (September 2001): 7–16.

15. Drew Christiansen, "Hawks, Doves and Pope John Paul II," *America* 187 (August 12–19, 2002): 9–11.

16. George Weigel, "The Just War Tradition and the World After September 11," *Logos* 5 (Summer 2002): 13–44.

17. Michael Novak, *The Catholic Ethic and the Spirit of Capitalism* (New York: Free Press, 1993), 232.

18. Jim Hug, "*Centesimus Annus*: Rescuing the Challenge, Probing the Vision," *Center Focus*, (August 1991), 1ff; quoted by Novak, *Catholic Ethic*, 138.

19. John Paul II, Homily of November 21, 1999; *L'Osservatore Romano*, (Eng. ed.), November 24, 1999, 1, 3.

20. The ideas in this paragraph are set forth in far greater detail in the Ph.D. dissertation of Victor L. Austin, "A Christological Social Vision: The Uses of Christ in the Social Encyclicals of John Paul II" (Fordham University, 2002).

21. John Paul II, General Audience of July 7, 1999, in *The Trinity's Embrace: God's Saving Plan* (Boston: Pauline Books & Media, 2002), 225.

22. John Paul II, General Audience of July 28, 1999; ibid., 233.

23. Ibid.

24. John Paul II, encyclical *Sollicitudo rei socialis*, 13.

25. Paul VI, "Apostolic Constitution on the Revision of Indulgences," in *Vatican Council II: The Conciliar and Postconciliar Documents*, ed. Austin Flannery (Northport, N.Y.: Costello, 1975), 63–79, at 66.

26. John Paul II, *The Trinity's Embrace*, 234–37.

27. John Paul, II, "The Inaugural Homily," *Origins* 8 (November 2, 1978), 305–8, quotation from 307–8.

31

The Rebirth of Apologetics

March 2, 2004

THE TASK OF APOLOGETICS

For the Christian it is axiomatic that faith is a gift of God, a grace. Since the Council of Orange in the sixth century, the Church has consistently taught that even the first beginnings of faith depend on the working of the Holy Spirit.[1] But the councils of the Church assure us that even so, faith is not a blind leap into the dark but an act fully consonant with reason.[2]

Over the centuries, Christian theology has exerted itself to keep the proper balance. Faith, besides being a gracious gift of God, is also a free and responsible decision on the part of the believer. God's grace does not circumvent or suppress our native powers, but guides and elevates them so that they may act more perfectly. The believer has motives for believing that would not be present were it not for the light of grace. In his great encyclical *Faith and Reason*, Pope John Paul II repeatedly declares that faith, by sharpening the inner eye of the mind, enables reason to rise above itself and in no sense diminishes it.[3] Reinforcing reason, faith enables it to transcend its normal limits.[4]

Faith, therefore, is not a simple achievement of reason. It is the work of reason submitting to the word of God, which comes by way of revelation. God, as the infinite source of all that is or can be, lies immeasurably beyond all that we can infer from the created order. His inner self and intentions are known only to himself unless he chooses to reveal them. For our sakes he has revealed something of himself and his saving plans so that we may love and serve him better. God's great and unsurpassable

---

revelation of himself is his Son, his eternal Word, who has become flesh in Jesus Christ. The Christian clings to that living and incarnate Word, in whom salvation is to be found.

In this framework we may consider the task of apologetics, the rational defense of faith. Apologetics cannot and should not attempt to demonstrate the truth of the mysteries of faith, which, as I have said, lie beyond human investigation and are believed on the strength of God's word, more certain than any logical deduction. But in order to believe, we must find reasons for judging that what purports to be God's word really is his word. To spell out these reasons in a systematic way is the task of apologetics.

Jesus in his life on earth gave reasons for believing in him. He pointed to his wonderful deeds, which fulfilled the messianic prophecies of the Old Testament and were wrought by the power of God. Since the first Easter the Church has regarded Christ's loving self-abasement on the Cross, followed by his glorious resurrection, as the preeminent sign of his divine Sonship. For the past two thousand years, apologists have contended that for those willing to ponder the evidence, the reasons for believing are more than adequate. They give ample assurance that it would be unreasonable to withhold assent.

CHANGING FORMS OF APOLOGETICS

Apologetics has to meet the adversaries of the faith where they are in each successive generation.[5] In the first three centuries the literature was predominantly defensive: it sought to stave off persecution by convincing Roman officials that the Christians were good citizens who obeyed the laws and prayed for the emperor. In the next few centuries, apologetics turned more aggressively to refute philosophers who claimed that Stoicism and neo-Platonism could provide all that was needed for a blessed life. Then in the Middle Ages Christian apologists increasingly directed their attention to Jews and Muslims, arguing that Jesus fulfilled the messianic prophecies of the Hebrew Bible, whereas Muhammad did not.

In early modern times apologetics took on fresh philosophical opponents. On one hand, it sought to refute skeptics, who contended that reason could know nothing about God, the soul, and immortality; on the other hand, it responded to rationalists, who maintained that human reason could prove so much about these realities that no revelation was needed.

In the nineteenth century, Christian apologetics underwent still another shift. It responded to natural scientists and historical critics who attacked the reliability of the Bible on what they regarded as scientific and historical grounds. Apologists had to show that new discoveries concerning the antiquity of the universe and human origins did nothing to detract from God's role as Creator and that modern historical criticism did not invalidate the biblical record of God's revelatory deeds and words.

Toward the middle of the twentieth century apologetics, perhaps for the first time, acquired a bad name among Christians themselves. Thriving organizations such as the Catholic Evidence Guild and the Catholic Truth Society suddenly vanished from the scene. Apologetics courses, which had been a mainstay of religious instruction in colleges and seminaries, disappeared from the curriculum. In their place a new discipline known as fundamental theology emerged. Unlike apologetics, fundamental theology did not try to speak to unbelievers but contented itself with analyzing for the sake of believers how God brings human beings to assent to his word.

Recent Criticisms of Apologetics

Why did this sudden collapse occur? Four principal reasons may be offered.

The unpopularity of apologetics arose, first of all, from its own excesses. Among many Christian thinkers apologetics threatened to absorb almost the whole of theology. In some cases it tried to prove too much, claiming to demonstrate by cogent arguments not only the credibility but the truth of Christian revelation. Meeting the scientific historians on their own ground, the Swiss Capuchin Hilarin Felder maintained that the Gospels are "in their full extent and in the strictest sense of the word, historical authorities and scientific evidence."[6] Then, he concluded to his own satisfaction if not that of the reader, "Just as only that study of Christ which confesses the Messiahship and divinity of our Saviour can lay claim to the spirit of Christianity, so only can such a study claim to follow a scientific method. Every christological conception which regards Jesus as a mere man is, if historically considered, a fanciful monstrosity."[7] Apologetics fell under suspicion for promising more than it could deliver and for manipulating the evidence to support the desired conclusions. It did not always escape the vice that Paul Tillich labeled "sacred dishonesty."[8]

A second defect was the proneness of apologists to revise Christian doctrine to make it more acceptable to the secular mind. Liberal Protestant theologians, abandoning the effort to prove the divinity of Christ, settled for a diluted version of the faith in which Christ was no more than a sublime ethical teacher who inculcated the love of God and neighbor. These apologists ceased to defend supernatural occurrences such as the virginal conception of Jesus, his miraculous deeds, and his glorious resurrection. Reacting against this retreat from orthodoxy, the great Swiss Protestant Karl Barth judged that apologetics by its very nature leads to compromise with unbelief. Apologists, he charged, seeking to make the gospel credible, marched onto the field carrying a white flag, and ended by surrendering essentials of the faith.[9]

Barth's criticisms contain a salutary warning. Some Christian literature today pursues a kind of doctrinal minimalism. Seeking to show how little one needs to believe, such apologetics gives the impression that belief is a burden rather than a privilege. If faith is to be trimmed back to the furthest limits, as this approach recommends, the reader begins to wonder why anyone should be asked to carry the incubus of faith at all?

A third temptation is for apologists to emphasize human activity at the expense of grace. They sometimes write as though we could reason ourselves into believing. Reacting against this distortion, some Protestants went to the opposite extreme. On the ground that human nature is totally corrupted by the Fall, they contended that it could play no role at all in the approach to faith. Giving a new interpretation to the doctrine of justification by faith alone, they dismissed apologetics as an effort of sinful human beings to justify themselves without grace. This exaltation of blind faith frequently goes hand in hand with a strong predestinationism. Choosing whom he wants to save, God infuses faith in some and leaves the rest of the human race to sink into perdition. In this fideist framework apologetics would be quite pointless. But Catholics, at least, will not follow this route because the Church teaches that God offers his grace to all but coerces none to believe. Faith, as I have said, is a fully human act performed with the help of grace.

The unpopularity of apologetics does not stem exclusively from theological considerations such as the three already considered. Sociological factors are at work. In a pluralist society like our own, religious faith is felt to be divisive. To avoid conflict, Christians frequently take refuge in the excuse that people should be left free to make up their own mind about what to believe. After all, they say, no one can be argued into faith. Even to raise the question of truth in religion is considered impolite.

This withdrawal from controversy, though it seems to be kind and courteous, is insidious. Religion becomes marginalized to the degree that it no longer dares to raise its voice in public. Such privatization has debilitating consequences on the faith of believers themselves. If we do not consider that it is important for others to hear the Christian proclamation, we inevitably begin to question its importance for ourselves. The result is a massive loss of interest in religious teaching. The reluctance of believers to defend their faith has produced all too many fuzzy and listless Christians, who care very little about what is to be believed. Their half-hearted religion is far removed from that of the apostles and the martyrs. It is a degenerate offspring of authentic Christianity.

THE REVIVAL OF APOLOGETICS

Recognizing that faith is enfeebled if its rational grounds are denied, committed Christians are today returning to apologetics. The titles of recent books register the change of climate. Not long ago it was typical to find books with titles such as *The Bankruptcy of Apologetics* (Willard L. Sperry), *Unapologetic Theology* (William A. Placher), and *Humble Apologetics* (John G. Stackhouse, Jr.), but today there are some refreshing alternatives. In 1990 Paul Griffiths published his carefully reasoned *An Apology for Apologetics*, and in 2001 William A. Debski and Jan Wesley Richards edited a collection of essays, *Unapologetic Apologetics: Meeting the Challenges of Theological Studies*. These last two titles are indicative of the resurgence.

All over the United States, there are signs of a revival. Evangelical Protestants are taking the leadership. Apologists of the stature of Norman L. Geisler, William Lane Craig, and J. P. Moreland are publishing scholarly works on natural theology and Christian evidences. Unlike the liberal Protestants of an earlier vintage, these Evangelicals insist on orthodoxy; they uncompromisingly maintain the fundamental Christian doctrines of the Trinity, the Incarnation, the Atonement, and the bodily resurrection of Jesus. And their method succeeds. The churches that combine a concern for orthodoxy with vigorous apologetics are growing. Their seminaries attract large numbers of enthusiastic students.

A similar revival is occurring, albeit more slowly, in Catholic circles. Peter Kreeft, at Boston College, plies an apologetics not far removed from that of the Evangelicals mentioned above. Scott Hahn and several colleagues at the Franciscan University of Steubenville, Ohio, confidently proclaim that the Protestant Bible points to the truth of the Catholic faith. EWTN, the network founded by Mother Angelica, broadcasts very successful programs of popular apologetics. Karl Keating, who runs the institute called Catholic Answers in San Diego, has done much to stem the tide of Hispanics defecting to fundamentalist Protestant sects. There is also a renewal of interest in English Catholic converts of the last century, including G. K. Chesterton, Ronald Knox, and Arnold Lunn. Many recent converts are publishing their own stories of faith.

These efforts, to be sure, meet with some criticism from within the Catholic Church.[10] The authors are accused of holding a propositional view of revelation, of proof-texting, and of triumphalism. The accusations must be weighed. If they come from a mentality that minimizes the doctrinal component of the faith or shrinks from any kind of confrontation, the criticisms should probably be discounted. Apologetics has to be somewhat controversial; it should forthrightly defend the settled teaching of the Church.

FROM SCIENCE TO PERSONALISM

Contemporary apologetics uses a variety of methods. The "classical approach," which dates from early modern times, adheres to patterns familiar since the seventeenth century. First, it uses philosophy to prove the existence of God and the possibility of revelation; then it turns to historiography to vindicate the biblical record of sacred history and its culmination in Jesus Christ. This approach can be quite effective with readers who are adept in philosophy and who have some prior interest in Holy Scripture. But it must be practiced with discretion, lest it fall into a kind of rationalism.

In natural theology, care must be taken to build on the intuition of being that undergirds traditional metaphysics. If one tries to prove God's existence by the methods of empirical science or purely conceptual logic, the proofs do not stand up under rigorous examination.

In their handling of biblical evidences for revelation, some contemporary apologists, like their predecessors a century ago, seek to establish the historicity of the biblical miracles by objective historical method. I have no desire to fault the enterprise. Skeptical historians strive in vain to disprove the facts that Jesus claimed divinity for himself and rose corporeally from the dead. But the evidential approach cannot be expected to succeed with historians who practice their craft with agnostic or atheistic presuppositions. They will generally admit that Jesus existed and attracted some committed disciples through his preaching and wonderful deeds, but will protest that their method cannot say anything about the supernatural. They will give no serious consideration to the claims that Jesus was born of a virgin mother or that he left the tomb and ascended to heaven in his risen body. To overcome the objections raised by analytic philosophy and secular historiography, apologetics needs to shift its ground. It must find a method by which people can open their minds to ideas they would otherwise dismiss as untenable.

Here, as in many other matters, Pope John Paul II has given timely leadership. Personalism, he believes, is the best medicine for awakening the world from its metaphysical slumber.[11] He begins his arguments for the existence of God not by reflecting on the finitude, mutability, contingency and order of the universe, as was traditionally done, but on the aspirations of the human heart for communion with the divine. In his view, human beings are made for transcendent truth, and such truth turns out to be a person who says of himself, "I am the truth." The Church is a place in which human persons enter into communion with one another in Jesus Christ. The Pope thus presents an intersubjective or interpersonal version of Christianity that can be a very attractive alternative to readers who suffer from the anonymity of contemporary collectivism or the isolation of contemporary individualism.

In his program for the new evangelization, Pope John Paul II reminds his readers that the world today looks not so much for arguments as for witnesses, that is to say, for believers who will testify by word and deed to a Lord whom they have encountered in experiences of faith.[12] "Belief," according to the Pope, "is often humanly richer than mere evidence, because it involves an interpersonal relationship and brings into play not only a person's capacity to know but also the deeper capacity to entrust oneself to others, to enter into a relationship with them which is intimate and enduring."[13] This emphasis on personal trust, I believe, holds great promise for the renewal of apologetics.

EPISTEMOLOGY OF PERSONAL TESTIMONY

In recent centuries, apologetics has concentrated mainly on how we get to God. It has relied on quasi-scientific methods of inquiry that owe more to Descartes, Locke, and Spinoza than to the prayerful searching of an Augustine, an Anselm, a Pascal, or a Newman. In a revealed religion such as Christianity, the key question is how God comes to us and opens up a world of meaning not accessible to human investigative powers.

The answer, I suggest, is testimony. Revelation, as God's word, is a form of divine testimony. Faith is by its nature an acceptance of the word of God, the witness who can neither deceive nor be deceived. God's word comes to us through human witnesses: the prophets and apostles, the inspired authors of Holy Scripture, and the tradition of the Church, which faithfully passes on and interprets what it has received from Christ and the apostles. From its first beginnings Christianity has been propagated through the living testimony of believers. The apostles were conscious of imparting a message that came from God. The Book of Revelation records the testimony of John, "who bore witness to the word of God and to the testimony of Jesus Christ" (Rev 1:2). Paul writes of himself, "We are ambassadors for Christ, God making his appeal through us." He congratulates the Thessalonians for receiving his teaching "not as the word of men but as what it really is, the word of God" (1 Th 2:13). Believers today have to rely likewise on testimony.

Personal testimony calls for an epistemology quite distinct from the scientific, as commonly understood. The scientist treats the datum to be investigated as a passive object to be probed, mastered, and brought within the investigator's intellectual horizons. In scientific inquiry, interpretations proffered by others are not accepted on authority but are tested by critical probing. But when we proceed by testimony, the situation is very different. We undergo an interpersonal encounter, in which the witness plays an active role, making an impact upon us. Without compelling us to believe, the witness calls for a free assent that involves personal respect and trust. To reject the message is to withhold confidence in the witness. To accept it is a trusting submission to the witness's authority. To the extent that we believe, we renounce our autonomy and willingly depend on the judgment of others.

The methods of apologetics outlined above—natural theology and academic history—are primarily scientific. As philosophers or historians, we treat the data as something impersonal to be brought within the compass of our own world of thought. This method is useful for confirming certain doctrines and refuting certain errors, but it rarely leads to conversion. Since the passage from unbelief to Christian faith involves conversion to a radically new outlook, testimony plays an indispensable role. Through the words of his witnesses God can bring us to affirm what we could not have discovered for ourselves.

To demonstrate that belief in religious testimony can be warranted, apologetics is required. It must present criteria for credibility. Some of the criteria have already been worked out in other disciplines. Historians, journalists, and juries regularly rely on witnesses. To avoid mistakes they have to devise tests of reliability. They look for witnesses who are in a position to know and who have no motive for deceiving others. For factual details they prefer early sources, as close as possible to the events, and seek to find multiple independent witnesses.

Analogous criteria may be used in apologetics for evaluating religious testimony, such as that contained in Scripture. But the criteria used for academic history are not fully applicable. The biblical authors are not professional historians, concerned with reporting exactly what Jesus had said and done on this or that occasion. They are believers aiming to communicate the gospel and evoke faith in Christ the Savior. As we read at the conclusion of John's Gospel, "These words are written that you may believe that Jesus is the Son of God, and that believing you may have life in his name" (Jn 20:31).

Proposed Criteria

It is difficult to devise criteria for evaluating religious testimony, but some rules of thumb may be proposed. I suggest the following five: convergence, firmness, novelty, transformation, and illuminative power.[14]

In the first place, the New Testament testimony is early, multiple, and convergent. The Evangelists come from different communities and give different perspectives on the life of Christ, yet they agree on substantials. The New Testament contains many theologies but only one vision of Christ and the Christian life. All the accounts present Jesus as the Son who speaks and acts with sovereign majesty, who lays down his life for the redemption of the world and rises triumphant from the grave. They agree that he held forth a revolutionary ideal of human life, exalting poverty, humility, love of neighbor, and patience in suffering as the way to eternal salvation.

Second, the authors do not speak as inquirers trying to fathom the purposes of God by human speculation, but rather as witnesses to a truth that has come to them with the strength of a revelation. Accepting what they have been taught as the word of God, they proclaim it with unwavering assurance. The firmness of their conviction is an indication that God has spoken to them with proofs of power.

Third, the message they proclaim is one that they would not have accepted had it not been for a visitation from on high. As pious Jews they had held that Yahweh alone was God and that no human being could be divine. But now, after encountering Jesus, they pay him divine honors, call upon him as Lord and God, and worship him as the equal of the Father. Apart from revelation, what could have convinced them that a lowly Galilean carpenter was Lord of the universe?

Fourth, the apostles and their associates were transformed by the message they proclaimed. They did not take possession of it but were possessed by it. From timid disciples, anxiously bolting the doors of the Upper Room, they became apostles openly proclaiming their faith at the risk of imprisonment, scourging, and martyrdom. No external opposition could keep them from speaking of what they have seen and heard. Their extraordinary dynamism is evidence of God's transforming power.

Fifth, the qualities of the message are such as would befit a revelation. It provides clues to the riddles of suffering and death, which no human philosophy could unravel. It gives hope to those who, humanly speaking, have nothing to hope for; it offers means of forgiveness to sinners plunged in a morass of guilt. Overturning the barriers between nation and nation and the hostility between different races and ethnic groups, the gospel promotes a civilization of universal peace and love.

The content of the message is no less remarkable. It presents the image of Jesus, the incarnate Lord who speaks and acts with unprecedented

authority, confounding his enemies but showing mercy on repentant sinners and compassion on the weak and the outcast. Rejected by his own,
he willingly lays down his life. Praying for his executioners, he dies naked
and abandoned on the cross, only to be taken up into glory by the Father.
The story of Jesus, vivid in its details and majestic in its pattern, surpasses
human powers of invention. It is so captivating that some have taken it
as evidence of its own truth.

The figure of Jesus is even more impressive when seen in the perspectives of salvation history. He arrives on the scene at the conclusion of a
thousand years of prophetic literature that looked forward in hope to the
advent of a Redeemer. The faith aroused by Jesus has persisted for two
thousand years, winning adherents of vast numbers from every land and
nation. The Christian community continues to be a vital force in the
world. In spite of the human weakness of her members, the Church is a
sign, a sacrament filled with Christ's presence, an enduring witness to her
own divine origin.

How, then, does an apologetics of committed religious testimony compare with other methods, such as the classical approach through natural
theology and the evidential approach that appeals to scientific history?
Testimony, as I have explained it, has an interpersonal character. The
witness addresses us actively, placing us in the position of recipients who
must seek to understand. Personal address can surprise and challenge us,
furnish us with new categories, and thus dispose us for conversion. To the
extent that we open ourselves up to testimony, we learn to rely on trustworthy witnesses and submit to their authority. This fiducial attitude
prepares us for religious conversion as a personal submission to the divine
witness who speaks to us in Christ.

Bearing Witness to the Divine Witness

While I applaud the resurgence of apologetics that we have recently seen
in this country, I suggest it could benefit from the kind of personalism
that Pope John Paul II professes. I have for some years been advocating
an apologetics of religious testimony. It could capitalize on the personalist
categories with which Christian philosophers such as Gabriel Marcel have
familiarized us: testimony, invitation, response, engagement, fidelity, and
communion. These categories attune us to biblical thinking and especially
to the Gospels as documents of faith.

The apologetics of personal testimony is particularly suited to the genius of Catholicism. In the act of Catholic faith, reliance on testimony goes out indivisibly to Christ and to the Church through which he continues his mission in the world. Such testimony invites us not only to individual conversion but also to communion with the whole body of believers.

Recent popes have been calling the Catholic Church to a new evangelization. To evangelize, we must allow the testimony of God, of the apostles, and of the Church to speak through us. This we cannot do so with confidence and success unless we have assured ourselves that the testimony is credible and unless we are able to convince others that this is the case. Holy Scripture instructs us not to neglect apologetics. "Always be prepared," says the First Letter of Peter, "to give a defense (*apologian*) of the hope that is in you" (1 Pt 3:15). If we love Christ and cherish our faith, and if we wish to spread its saving influence, we will not shirk this important responsibility. The time is ripe, the need is urgent, for a rebirth of apologetics.

NOTES

1. Second Council of Orange, canon 5; Denzinger-Schönmetzer, *Enchiridion symbolorum*, 375.

2. First Vatican Council, *Dogmatic Constitution on the Catholic Faith*, chap. 3; DS 3009–10.

3. John Paul II, encyclical *Fides et Ratio*, 16, 43, and passim.

4. Ibid., 68.

5. On the history of the discipline see Avery Dulles, *A History of Apologetics* (1971; new edition, San Francisco: Ignatius, 2004).

6. Hilarin Felder, *Christ and the Critics*, trans. John L. Stoddard, 2 vols. (London: Burns Oates and Washbourne, 1924), 1:116.

7. Ibid., 2:442, 444.

8. Paul Tillich, *Systematic Theology*, 3 vols. (Chicago: University of Chicago, 1951–1963), 1:36.

9. Karl Barth, *Protestant Theology in the Nineteenth Century* (Valley Forge, Pa.: Judson Press, 1973), 442, 444.

10. For indications of this line of criticism, see Richard R. Gaillardetz, "Do We Need a New Apologetics?" *America* 190 (February 2, 2004): 26–33.

11. Avery Dulles, "John Paul II and the Mystery of the Human Person," above, 414–29.

12. John Paul II, encyclical *Redemptoris Missio*, 41–47.

13. John Paul II, encyclical *Faith and Reason*, 32.

14. These five criteria correspond to the ones given in Avery Dulles, *Apologetics and the Biblical Christ* (Westminster, Md.: Newman, 1963), 36–40.

32

A Eucharistic Church

The Vision of John Paul II

November 10, 2004

Karol Wojtyla has always had a deep eucharistic piety. Each year since becoming pope he has written a letter to priests for Holy Thursday. In 2003 he released his most recent encyclical, *Ecclesia de Eucharistia*, emphasizing the bonds between the Eucharist and the Church. Last spring he announced the beginning of a eucharistic year, which began a month ago, on October 7, and which will culminate in the Assembly of the Synod of Bishops on the Eucharist in October 2005. The theme for this assembly is to be "The Eucharist: Source and Summit of the Life and Mission of the Church." In view of these developments it might be appropriate to set forth the eucharistic ecclesiology of John Paul II. I shall develop the topic in my own fashion, always keeping in mind the teaching of the pope.

EUCHARISTIC ECCLESIOLOGY

A eucharistic ecclesiology does not mean that everything in the Church can be derived from the Eucharist. In the course of his encyclical the pope quotes without attribution the statement of Cardinal Henri de Lubac, "The Eucharist builds the Church and the Church makes the Eucharist."[1] The lines of causality therefore run in both directions. Neither is absolutely prior to the other, but each was instituted by Christ with a view to the other. Unless there were a Church, there would be no one to celebrate the Eucharist, but unless there were a Eucharist, the Church would lack the supreme source of her vitality.

The Church renews herself by continually returning to the sources of her own life. By immersing herself in the Eucharist she takes on the characteristics of that great mystery of faith. Because the greater assimilates the lesser, the usual law of eating is reversed. In this case, we do not transform our nourishment into ourselves, but we are transformed into it. In receiving Holy Communion we let Christ into our hearts to make them like his own (*LG* 26). The Catholic tradition applies to the Eucharist the famous passage from Augustine in which Christ is depicted as saying: "I am your food, but instead of my being changed into you, it is you who will be transformed into me."[2] This transformation means concretely that the ideas, attitudes, and sentiments of pastors and faithful are remolded in the likeness of those of Jesus Christ as he gives himself to us in loving obedience to his Father's command. In this way the Church becomes, as I put it in the title of this lecture, eucharistic.

One of the most original and interesting points in the encyclical is the observation that the Eucharist has the four attributes that we apply to the Church in the Nicene-Constantinopolitan Creed: one, holy, catholic, and apostolic (*EE* 26). Although the pope develops only the last of these attributes, apostolicity, I should like to consider how all four ecclesial marks may be found in the Eucharist, and how they help us to understand the sacrament better. It would be best, I think, to begin with the attribute of holiness, in the absence of which all the other attributes would be valueless.

HOLINESS

Holiness is not just moral rectitude, though it certainly includes this. As an attribute proper to God, holiness belongs to God's inner being. The Israelites of old were profoundly aware that God was the exemplar and source of all holiness. He dwells on high in unapproachable light, where he is served by countless hosts of angels and saints, who prostrate themselves before him in humble adoration.

For any creature to become holy, God must bring it into a union with himself. By adopting Israel, God made it a holy nation set apart and consecrated to his service. In the New Testament we learn that the all-holy God, by an almost incredible act of condescension, appears in the flesh. Jesus Christ, the Holy One of God, comes on a mission to save and sanctify the world.

Christ founded the Church as the People of God of the New Testament. The First Letter of Peter reminds its readers: "You are a chosen race, a royal priesthood, a holy nation, God's own people" (1 Pt 2:9). The Letter to the Ephesians depicts the Church as the fruit of Christ's loving sacrifice. "He loved the Church and gave himself up for her, that he might sanctify her, having cleansed her by the washing of water with the word, that he might present the Church to himself in splendor, without spot or wrinkle or any such thing, that she might be holy and without blemish" (Eph 5:25–27).

As we know from the Creed, the Church is always holy. She is holy in her divine head, Jesus Christ, to whom we sing in the Gloria, "You alone are holy." She is holy in the doctrines taught by the Lord and in the sacraments by which he remains present with his people. All the sacraments are holy and have power to sanctify, but the Eucharist is "most holy" because in it Christ himself is substantially present, performing his supreme redemptive act. Thomas Aquinas wrote, in a frequently quoted passage, that the Eucharist contains the entire spiritual wealth of the Church.[3]

Inasmuch as this august sacrament is quintessentially holy, it is to be approached with the greatest reverence. It is celebrated by priests who are consecrated by the sacrament of holy orders. In the rite of ordination, the ordaining prelate addresses to the new priest the following charge:

> Your ministry will perfect the spiritual sacrifice of the faithful by uniting it to Christ's sacrifice, the sacrifice that is offered sacramentally through your hands. Know what you are doing and imitate the mystery you celebrate. In the memorial of the Lord's death and resurrection, make every effort to die to sin and to walk in the new life of Christ.[4]

Whenever we join in celebrating the Eucharist, we may profitably recall how the Lord hastened to his Passion, with an almost impatient eagerness for its accomplishment (cf. Lk 12:50). Uniting themselves to him, priests and faithful die to sin and become alive to God. Crucifying the flesh with its sinful tendencies, they pray to be strengthened by Christ's passion, hidden within his wounds, and inebriated by his blood.

The holiness of the Eucharist demands that those who receive the sacrament be sanctified by baptism and be attuned to the mystery by faith.

Jesus symbolically washed the feet of the apostles to make them clean before he celebrated the Last Supper with them. The Church at all times bears in mind the warning of St. Paul: "Whoever eats of the bread or drinks of the cup unworthily is guilty of profaning the body and blood of the Lord" (1 Cor 11:27). Conversely, those who become Christ's members by feeding on his body take on new obligations. It would be a profanation, Paul tells us, for them to enter into sexual union with prostitutes (1 Cor 6:15–17).

One of the earliest liturgical prayers of the Church, *The Didache of the Twelve Apostles*, repeats the Lord's warning, "Do not give what is sacred to dogs," and then draws the application that those who are holy should come to the altar, while those who are not should repent.[5] In his encyclical, Pope John Paul reminds the faithful that they should not receive Communion if they have committed serious sin and have not been absolved in the sacrament of Penance (*EE* 36).

To be made holy by the Eucharist, it does not suffice for us to be physically present at Holy Mass or to receive Communion physically. We must participate personally by reverently hearing the Word of God and sharing in the mind of the Church as she worships. The congregation is called to join in the Church's self-offering, entering in spirit into Christ's own redemptive work (*LG* 11).

Eucharistic holiness is never merely individual; it is ecclesial. The more closely the faithful are conjoined to Christ, the more intimately are they united to one another in his body. The attribute of holiness therefore leads directly into that of unity.

UNITY

The Church is one for a variety of reasons. The Lord founded her with a single mission and a single system of government, under the visible headship of Peter and his successors. She is held together by her Scriptures, her creeds, and her sacraments, and by the Holy Spirit who is at work in the hearts and minds of the faithful.

The Holy Eucharist stands out as one of the most important instruments and signs of unity. Although Masses are celebrated in many different times and places, each alone and all together constitute one and the same sacrifice, that of Christ on the cross. As the Council of Trent taught, the victim is one and the same, but the manner of offering is different. The sacrifice that was first offered in a bloody manner is now offered in an unbloody manner, under the forms of bread and wine. Each Mass "re-presents" the sacrifice of Calvary, making it present once again. The Eucharist therefore possesses a mysterious unity that is not paralleled by anything else in history. By participating in the Eucharistic sacrifice and receiving Holy Communion, we are drawn into mystical fellowship with one another in Christ.

Paul says in First Corinthians that the Church is one body because her members partake of the one bread, which is Christ the Lord (1 Cor 10:17). The Church Fathers were keenly conscious of this unitive power. Many of them, including John Chrysostom, dwell on the symbolism of the bread and wine, which suggest how many things can be fused into unity, as many individuals are in the Church. The loaf is made up of many grains of wheat; the chalice is made up from the juice of many grapes.[6]

The Didache of the Twelve Apostles, written about the end of the first century, contains the petition, "As this piece [of bread] was scattered over the hills and then was brought together and made one, so let your Church be brought together from the ends of the earth into your Kingdom."[7] In the Third Eucharistic Prayer we ask that we who are nourished by Christ's body and blood may become one body, one spirit in him.

In the Middle Ages, when efforts were made to specify the distinctive grace of each of the seven sacraments, it was agreed that the sacramental grace proper to the Eucharist was the unity of the Mystical Body. Thomas Aquinas calls it the "sacrament of ecclesiastical unity"[8] and the "sacrament of the unity of the Mystical Body,"[9] He also quotes St. Augustine, who calls it "the sign of unity and the bond of charity."[10]

You might object, of course, that baptism has the same effect. By one Spirit, says Paul, we were all baptized into one body (1 Cor 12:13). There is, he says, one faith, one Lord, one baptism (Eph 4:5). But theologians tell us that baptism has these effects because it is intrinsically ordered to the Eucharist. Baptism effects a kind of initial incorporation into Christ, which is completed and perfected by the Eucharist, the sacrament of full initiation. The Eucharist presupposes baptism just as the ability to take nutrition presupposes a living organism. The Eucharist strengthens us to live up to the demands of our baptism.

For the Eucharist to function as a sacrament of unity, a measure of unity must already exist among those who partake of it. They must not only be baptized but must be one among themselves. They must have a will to be in unity and peace with the whole Church. If anyone were to receive this sacrament of unity while intending to remain apart from the body and its visible head, in a situation of heresy or schism, the meaning of the action would be contradicted by the contrary disposition. It would be wrong for anyone to say, "I don't want to belong to your community but I want to receive Communion with you." Nor could they properly say, "I don't accept your pastors and doctrines but I want to partake of your sacraments."

As the preeminent sacrament of unity, the Eucharist ordinarily presupposes that the participants are in full ecclesial communion with one another. Communion is normally reserved to Catholics but, as the pope notes toward the end of his encyclical, there are exceptional circumstances in which baptized Christians belonging to other communities may be admitted for the occasion to Holy Communion (*EE* 45).

CATHOLICITY

The question of unity leads directly to another. Unity among whom? Or among what? The mystery of the Eucharist helps us to answer these questions and in so doing points to the catholicity of the Church. In instituting the sacrament, the Lord had an absolutely universal vision, embracing all peoples of all times and, it would seem, the whole cosmos. He speaks of his blood poured out not only "for you" but also "for the many," in the sense of all. In this sense, the Eucharist is "catholic."

The Eucharist is offered in the first instance for members of the Church, but in the broader sense it is a prayer for all human beings living and dead, for whom Christ sanctifies himself. "If I be lifted up," he says, "I will draw everyone [or, according to some manuscripts, "all things"] to myself" (Jn 21:32). The Eucharist is an acceptable sacrifice that "brings salvation to the whole world," as we say in the Fourth Eucharistic Prayer. According to the prediction of the prophet Malachi, it is the spotless victim offered in every place among the nations, from East to West, from the rising of the sun to its setting (Mal 1:11).

The pope's recent encyclical speaks of the "cosmic" character of the Eucharist. The natural elements, transformed by human hands into bread and wine, are further transmuted into the glorified body and blood of

Christ. Celebrated on the altar of the world, the Eucharist unites heaven and earth. "It embraces all creation. The Son of God became man in order to restore all creation, in one supreme act of praise, to the One who made it from nothing" (*EE* 8).

In his own poetic style, the French Jesuit Teilhard de Chardin liked to meditate on the Eucharist as the first fruits of the new creation. In an essay called "The Monstrance" he describes how, kneeling in prayer, he had a sensation that the Host was beginning to grow until at last, through its mysterious expansion, "the whole world had become incandescent, had itself become like a single giant Host."[11] Although it would probably be incorrect to imagine that the universe will eventually be transubstantiated, Teilhard correctly identified the connection between the Eucharist and the final glorification of the cosmos.

The prayers of the liturgy remind us that the Eucharist is celebrated in union with the local bishop, the pope, and the Catholic Church throughout the world. More than this, it is celebrated in solidarity with the faithful departed as a prayer that they may find light, happiness, and peace. Vatican II's Constitution on the Liturgy speaks of the saints in glory. "In every Mass, we sing a hymn to God's glory with all the warriors of the heavenly army; venerating the memory of the saints, we hope for some part and fellowship with them; and we eagerly await the Savior, our Lord Jesus Christ, until he, our life, shall appear and we too will appear with him in glory" (*SC* 8).

The Church of the first centuries was acutely conscious of the Eucharist as a bond among churches.[12] In the diocese of Rome there was a practice of sending a fragment of the consecrated host from the bishop's church to outlying parish churches to signify the unity between the Eucharist celebrated by the presbyters and his own. When bishops came on visits, the local bishop would often invite them to concelebrate with him. The faithful of such churches received eucharistic hospitality as a sign of communion. The refusal to recognize a church led inevitably to a refusal to participate in its eucharistic celebrations or to let its members participate in one's own Eucharist.

The universalist understanding of catholicity was called into question half a century ago by a Russian Orthodox theologian then writing in Paris, Nicholas Afanassieff, an early exponent of "eucharistic ecclesiology."[13] His dominant idea was that the Church is fully realized in the local worshiping community, where the sacrament is celebrated. In every such community, he maintained, the Catholic Church is present in its totality. On this ground he concluded that there is no theological justification for ecclesiastical superstructures such as metropolitan and patriarchal sees, not to mention a papacy. The logic of his argument implied that the pastor of every parish is equal the bishop in authority.

Afanassieff did not deny that the Eucharist must be catholic, but he defined the catholicity of the Church in a qualitative sense as meaning her full reality. He was not interested in what is sometimes called horizontal or geographical catholicity—the communion among all members of Christ's Church and among particular churches. He attributed no theological significance to overarching structures of unity.

Afanassieff does not represent the consensus of Orthodox theologians. Several prominent Orthodox colleagues, including John Meyendorff and John Zizioulas, have corrected his view of catholicity.[14] Zizioulas insists that according to the will of Christ the Church is a communion not only in a given locality but throughout the world. The Eucharist by its nature expresses and solidifies communion among churches, all of which strengthen one another by their complementary gifts and mutual support. In other words, the unity of which I have spoken earlier in this lecture is not simply internal to any particular Church or eucharistic community; it binds all together into a harmonious reciprocity.

Several liberation theologians have resurrected Afanassieff's error. The Brazilian Leonardo Boff maintained that the Church is not constituted hierarchically from above; it "reinvents" itself from below, by the action of believers at the "base." Some European Catholics, following a similar logic, hold that any local community has from Christ, who is present in it, the power to constitute itself as a church and to produce its own Eucharist.[15] They sometimes argue that every local community has a right to the Eucharist, and from this they deduce the power of the congregation to designate one of its own members to preside at Mass.[16]

Against errors such as these Joseph Ratzinger has strongly reasserted the classical doctrine of the catholicity of the Eucharist. Because catholicity is an "inner dimension" of the Eucharist, no particular church can bestow upon itself the power to perform the Eucharistic sacrifice. The local community becomes a church only by being received into the universal Church, which is the body of Christ, who is one and indivisible (cf. 1 Cor 1:13).[17]

Many of these ideas are reaffirmed by the official teaching of the Congregation for the Doctrine of the Faith. As prefect of that Congregation, Cardinal Ratzinger in 1992 issued the important "Instruction on Some Aspects of the Church Understood as Communion." Ecclesial communion, he there taught, has its center in the Eucharist. Baptism is an initial incorporation into the body, which is built up and vivified through the Eucharist. The Instruction declares:

> The rediscovery of a eucharistic ecclesiology, though being of undoubted value, has however sometimes placed one-sided emphasis on the principle of the local church. It is claimed that where the Eucharist is celebrated the totality of the mystery of the Church would be made present in such a way as to render any other principle of unity or universality inessential.[18]

The Eucharistic Prayers of the Roman Missal make it clear that every legitimate Eucharist is celebrated in union with the diocesan bishop, the whole body of bishops, and the pope, for otherwise it would be deficient in catholicity. A Eucharist celebrated in separation from the college of bishops and the faithful of their churches would lack the attribute of catholicity.

Apostolicity

As may be seen from the last few sentences, the catholicity of the Eucharist is closely bound up with its fourth attribute, apostolicity. Our ears have grown accustomed to hearing the Church called apostolic, but the apostolicity of the Eucharist is a rather novel expression. The doctrine, however, derives from Christian antiquity, which recognized that the Eucharist could not be validly celebrated except by a priest ordained by a bishop who stood in the apostolic succession. In the early centuries, the ordinary celebrant of the Eucharist was the bishop, but he could invite members of the presbyteral college to celebrate with him or in his place, since they were by ordination sharers in the same priesthood as his.

Apostolicity expresses the fact that the Church, at the Eucharist as elsewhere, is a hierarchical community, under the supervision of leaders authorized and empowered to act in the name of Christ. Apostolicity also links each and all of the bishops historically with the Twelve as the source of their powers. Jesus at the Last Supper entrusted the Eucharist to the

Twelve who were his table companions, commanding them to do in commemoration of him what he was then doing. The Twelve were the original representative heads of the New Israel, and as the New Israel entered into the postapostolic age, their functions had to be transmitted to others. The rite of ordination signifies that priestly powers do not have a merely human origin but come only from the Lord through apostolic succession.

Explaining the apostolicity of the Eucharist, Pope John Paul II asserts that the ministry of a validly ordained priest links the Eucharist historically to the sacrifice of the Cross and to the Last Supper (29). Any eucharistic celebration requires as a condition of its validity the presidency of a bishop or a priest who acts in the person of Christ (32). There can be no such thing as a lay Eucharist or priestless Mass. Deacons and others may, under certain conditions, conduct a service of the Word, followed by a Communion service, but care should be taken to make it clear that this is not a Mass, a Eucharist, because the sacrifice cannot be offered without a priest. Those who preside at such services have a responsibility to create in the congregation a hunger for the Eucharist and to make them conscious of the importance of priestly vocations. The local community has a responsibility to foster vocations so that the people will not be left without the priceless gift of the Eucharist.

Because the Eucharist has its roots in what Jesus did at the Last Supper, it must be celebrated with the same elements. The church uses bread and wine, not rice and beer or any such substitute. Conceivably, Jesus could have used bitter herbs and milk, though they would not aptly have symbolized his body and blood. What counts, however, is what he did. The apostolicity of the Eucharist would seem to demand this degree of identity.

EUCHARISTIC RENEWAL

We enter upon this Eucharistic Year with a deep consciousness that the Church is in dire need of renewal. Although she remains irrevocably holy in her divine Head and in her apostolic heritage of faith, sacraments, and ministry, she is sinful in her members and in constant need of being purified. Many of the faithful are ignorant of her teachings; some few defiantly reject them. Even the clergy are not exempt from grave and scandalous sins, as we have learnt all too well in these recent years. The

Church can be renewed only by turning with ardent love to her eucharistic Lord, asking to be fed on the Bread of Angels and refreshed from the wellsprings of salvation.

Imperfect in holiness, the Church is likewise feeble in her unity. She suffers from tensions among national and ethnic groups and from ideological conflicts between different factions. At the Table of the Lord, all these differences can be taken up into a higher unity. The worshipers become like grains in a single loaf, drops in one chalice.

Catholicity is often a mere label that we use without any realization of what it involves. When we use the term to justify our particularism over and against others, our horizons are too narrow. The Eucharist can enable us to rise above this timid and inward-looking mentality. It will inflame us with Christ's loving desire to share our hope and joy with all the world. As the first fruits of the new creation, the Eucharist can make us look forward in hope to the new heavens and the new earth.

Apostolicity is also difficult to maintain. In spite of our faith, we run the risk of being cut off from the vine that gives true life. The prevalent secular and democratic culture tricks us into imagining that we can produce whatever we need for our salvation. But the Eucharist reminds us that grace and salvation come from on high and that they are channeled through Christ and the apostles. We must humbly receive redemption through disciples commissioned to speak and act in the person of Christ. The Church is most of all herself when she gathers in worship around her apostolic leaders, who maintain communion with one another and with their predecessors in the faith. Through the Eucharist celebrated in this way, Christ assembles his flock, one, holy, catholic, and apostolic.

NOTE

1. John Paul II, encyclical *Ecclesia de Eucharistia*, 26. Cf. Henri de Lubac, *The Splendor of the Church* (San Francisco: Ignatius, 1986), 134.

2. Augustine, *Confessions* 7, 10, 16; cf. Henri de Lubac, *Catholicism* (London: Burns, Oates and Washbourne, 1950), 44.

3. Thomas Aquinas, *Summa theologiae*, part III, qu. 65, art. 3 ad 1.

4. *The Rites of the Catholic Church*, 2 (New York: Pueblo, 1979), 63.

5. "The Teaching of the Twelve Apostles, Commonly Called the *Didache*," quoted from *Early Christian Fathers*, ed. Cyril C. Richardson (New York: Macmillan, 1970), pp. 161–79, at 9,5 and 10,6, pp. 175–76.

6. John Chrysostom, *Homilies on First Corinthians*, 24,2; PG 61:200. Cf. John Paul II, *Ecclesia de Eucharistia*, 23.

7. "The Teaching of the Twelve Apostles," 9,4, p. 176.

8. Thomas Aquinas, *Summa theologiae*, part III, qu. 73, art. 2, sed contra.

9. Ibid., part III, qu. 73, art. 3c.

10. Augustine, *In Joan. Evang.*, Tract 26, n. 17; cf. Thomas Aquinas, *Summa theologiae*, part III, qu. 73, ad 3; qu. 79, art. 1c.

11. Pierre Teilhard de Chardin, in *Hymn of the Universe* (New York: Harper & Row, 1960), 46–49.

12. Ludwig Hertling, *Communio: Church and Papacy in Early Christianity* (Chicago: Loyola University Press, 1972), 23–28.

13. Nicholas Afanassieff, "Una Sancta," *Irénikon* 36 (1963): 436–75, esp. 452–54. Cf. Paul McPartlan, *The Eucharist Makes the Church* (Edinburgh: T&T Clark, 1993), 98–120.

14. John Meyendorff, *Orthodoxy and Catholicity* (New York: Sheed & Ward, 1966), 157–60; John Zizioulas, *Being as Communion* (London: Longman, Darton and Todd, 1985), 23–25, 132–33, 155–58. Meyendorff, in his Foreword to this book, expresses his agreement with Zizioulas against Afanassieff.

15. Leonardo Boff, *Ecclesiogenesis: The Base Communities Reinvent the Church* (Maryknoll, N.Y.: Orbis, 1986), esp. 61–75.

16. Joseph Ratzinger, *Principles of Catholic Theology* (San Francisco: Ignatius, 1987), 285–87, particularly criticizes Joseph Blank and Edward Schillebeeckx for asserting the right of the community to appoint one of its own number to preside at the Eucharist.

17. Ibid., 293.

18. Congregation for the Doctrine of the Faith, "Some Aspects of the Church Understood as Communion (*Communionis notio*)," *Origins* 22 (June 25, 1992): 108–12, at 110.

33

How Real Is the Real Presence?

February 15, 2005

Last fall, at the beginning of this year of the Eucharist, I devoted my McGinley Lecture to the subject "The Eucharist and the Church." Because a number of the questions had to do with the real presence of Christ in this sacrament, I promised to take the real presence as the topic for my next lecture. There have been moments when I almost regretted the promise, because the subject is very profound and mysterious. It taxes the human mind to the utmost. In the end we have to exclaim that we have here an ineffable mystery, which only the mind of God can fully understand. Nevertheless, something should be said, because God has not revealed himself simply to mystify us. He wants us to imitate the Blessed Virgin, who pondered deeply the words spoken to her.

MEANING OF REAL PRESENCE

At the very outset it must be said that the Church believes the real presence as a matter of faith, simply because it is taught by Christ, as attested by Scripture and tradition. Jesus said clearly, "This is my body . . . this is my blood," and in controversy with the Jews he insisted that he was not just using metaphors. "My flesh is food indeed, and my blood is drink indeed. He who eats my flesh and drinks my blood abides in me, and I in him. As the living Father sent me, and I live because of the Father, so he who eats me will live because of me" (Jn 6:55–57). Many of the disciples found this a hard saying and parted from his company, but Jesus did not moderate his statements to win them back.

The Fathers and medieval doctors have confidently proclaimed the real presence century after century, notwithstanding all objections and misconceptions. Then in 1551 the Council of Trent gave a full exposition of the Catholic doctrine of the Eucharist in which the real presence receives special emphasis. Repeated by many popes and official documents since that time, the teaching of Trent remains today as normative as ever. The *Catechism of the Catholic Church* is content to quote it verbatim several times (*CCC* 1374, 1376–77).

In describing Christ's presence in this sacrament, the Council of Trent used three adverbs. He is contained in it, said the council, "truly, really, and substantially" (DS 1651). These three terms are the keys that open the door to Catholic teaching and exclude contrary views, which are to be rejected.[1]

In saying in the first place that Christ is *truly* contained under the Eucharistic species, the council repudiated the view that the sacrament is a mere sign or figure pointing away from itself to a body that is absent, perhaps somewhere in the heavens. This assertion is made against the eleventh-century monk Berengarius and some of his Protestant followers in the sixteenth century.

Second, the presence is *real*. That is to say, it is ontological and objective: ontological because it takes place in the order of being, not merely in the order of signs; objective because it does not depend on the thoughts or feelings of the minister or the communicants. The body and blood of Christ are present in the sacrament by reason of the promise of Christ and the power of the Holy Spirit, which are attached to the proper performance of the rite by a duly ordained minister. In so teaching, the Church rejects the view that faith is the instrument that brings about Christ's presence in the sacrament. According to Catholic teaching, faith does not make Christ present, but it gratefully acknowledges that presence and allows Holy Communion to bear fruit in holiness. To receive the sacrament without faith is improper, even sinful, but the lack of faith does not render the presence unreal.

Third, Trent tells us that Christ's presence in the sacrament is *substantial*. The word "substance" as here used is not a technical philosophical term, such as might be found in the philosophy of Aristotle. It was used in the early Middle Ages long before the works of Aristotle were current. "Substance" in commonsense usage denotes the basic reality of the thing—that is, what it is in itself. Derived from the Latin root *sub-stare*, it means what stands under the appearances, which can shift from one moment to the next while leaving the subject intact. Appearances can be deceptive. You might fail to recognize me when I put on a disguise or when I become seriously ill, but I do not cease to be the person I was; my substance is unchanged. There is nothing obscure, then, about the meaning of "substance" in this context.

Substance, meaning what a thing is in itself, may be contrasted not only with appearance but also with function, which has reference to action. Christ is present in a transitory way by his dynamic power and action in all the sacraments, but in the Eucharist is his presence inherent and abiding. For this reason, the Eucharist may be adored. It is the greatest of all sacraments. After the consecration the bread and wine have become, in a mysterious way, Christ himself. Vatican II quotes St. Thomas to the effect that this sacrament contains the entire spiritual wealth of the Church, for the Church has no other spiritual riches than Christ and what he communicates to her.[2]

The Council of Trent spoke also of the process by which this presence of Christ comes about. It stated that the bread and wine are totally changed; they cease to be what they were and become what they were not. The whole substance of the bread and wine becomes the body and blood of Christ, and, because Christ cannot be divided, they become also his soul and his divinity (DS 1640, 1642). The whole Christ is made present under each of the two forms.

The change that occurs in the consecration at Mass is sui generis. It does not fit into the categories of Aristotle, who believed that every substantial change involved a change in the appearances or what he called accidents. When I eat an apple, it loses its perceptible qualities as well as its substance as an apple. It becomes part of me. But in the consecration of bread and wine at Mass, the outward appearances remain unchanged. The Church has coined the term "transubstantiation," to designate the process by which the whole substance, and only the substance, is changed into the body and blood of Christ. A special word is needed to designate a process that is unique and unparalleled.

In teaching that the species are unchanged, the Church indicates that the physical and chemical properties remain those of bread and wine. Not only do they look and weigh the same; they retain the same nutritive value that they had before the consecration.[3] It would be futile to try to prove or disprove the real presence by physical experiments, because the presence of Christ is spiritual or sacramental, not physical in the sense of measurable.

Avoidance of Naïve Realism

To clarify the Church's teaching on the real presence, it will be helpful, I think, to contrast it with several erroneous positions. The presence of Christ may be understood either too carnally or too mystically, too grossly or too tenuously, too naively or too figuratively.

The naively realist error may be illustrated by the reaction of the Jews at Capharnaum who were shocked by the words of Jesus. They evidently thought that he was advocating cannibalism, which they rightly regarded as a horrible sin. Some Christians have understood the presence of Christ in the Eucharist in too materialistic a way, without sufficiently distinguishing between his natural and his sacramental presence. They sometimes imagine that he could suffer if the host were desecrated or that he could be lonely in the tabernacle. I read somewhere of a young schoolgirl who feared that if she ate ice cream after taking Holy Communion, Jesus would suffer from the cold.

In the early Middle Ages a number of theologians, following Paschasius Radbertus, maintained that Jesus in the Eucharist takes over the forms of bread and wine as his own proper appearances. Why could he not do so, they asked, since in the Resurrection he appeared as a pilgrim and a gardener not recognizable to his disciples? What we see when we look upon the host, and what we swallow in Holy Communion, they tell us, is the body and blood of Christ in a disguised form. Some held that by the consecration the elements lose the nutritive capacity that belonged to them as bread and wine.[4]

To avoid the implication that Christ in glory could suffer the indignity of being crushed by the teeth of communicants, some early medieval thinkers held that the body of Christ on the altar is not the same as the one in heaven. In fact, they spoke of the three bodies of Christ: his natural body, which is now in heaven; his sacramental body, which is in the Eucharist; and his ecclesial body, which is the Church.[5] This position has never been condemned by the Church, but it is no longer widely held, perhaps because, contrary to the mind of its advocates, it seems to suggest that the body in the Eucharist is not the one born of the Virgin Mary. If so, we could not sing to it: "*Ave verum corpus, natum de Maria Virgine.*"

St. Thomas Aquinas develops what we may call a mediating position. On the one hand, he avoids speaking of the Eucharist as a special body (sacramental or mystical), but on the other hand he asserts that the risen and glorified body of Christ has a different existence in heaven and in the sacrament. He contrasts Christ's existence in himself and his existence under the sacrament as two different states or modes of being. According to his natural mode of existence Christ is in heaven, and according to his eucharistic mode of existence, he is in the sacrament.[6] The body of Christ is truly present in the Eucharist, but not in the way bodies are in place. Its parts and dimensions cannot be measured against other bodies. His circumference is not that of the host.

In opposition to the naive realists, therefore, St. Thomas holds that when we look at the host we do not see the shape and colors that properly belong to the body of Christ, but those of the host itself. We are not in the same situation as the disciples before the Ascension, to whom Christ appeared in his own body. When we look at the host or chalice on the altar, the visible aspects or phenomena are still those of the bread and wine.

St. Thomas objects to himself that some have reported seeing the boy Jesus or his Most Precious Blood in a consecrated host. He replies that God is able to bring about a miraculous change in the host so that it could look like a boy or human blood, but that what appears in such a case could not be the qualities of Christ himself.[7]

Looking at the Host or the Precious Blood, we cannot say that the head is here and the feet are there. Christ's presence in this sacrament resembles that of the soul in the body. My soul is not partly in my head, partly in my heart, partly in my hands, but is entirely present in the whole and in every part. And so it is with Christ in the Eucharist. When a host is broken, each fragment contains Christ as fully as did the whole. A single drop of the Precious Blood contains as much of him as a whole chalice. As a helpful comparison St. Thomas uses the example of an image in a mirror. When the mirror is broken, each fragment can reflect the whole object, just as the entire mirror previously did.[8]

If the location and contours of the host are not those of Christ, the question arises: can we still say that Christ is carried about in procession or that he is placed in the tabernacle? Do we not eat his flesh and drink his blood? Yes, says St. Thomas, he is moved, eaten, and drunk, but not in his own proper dimensions. He is moved, eaten, and drunk in his eucharistic mode of existence, insofar as his presence coincides with the palpable properties or "accidents" of the bread and wine. He is not physically harmed by any violence done to the sacrament because its physical properties are not properly his.

Christ's presence in the Blessed Sacrament is therefore knowable only by the intellect, which accepts the word of God in faith.[9] The presence may be called sacramental because the appearances of the bread and wine indicate where Christ's body and blood are present. They are signs or sacraments of a reality that is present and operative in them.

The eucharistic presence, real though it be, does not cancel out the absence of which Jesus spoke when he took leave of his disciples at the Last Supper. The Eucharist is a memorial of Jesus' historical presence here on earth and a pledge of his return in glory, when we shall be able to see him as he is.

From what I have said, you can see that the presence of Christ in this sacrament is unique and mysterious. Spiritual guides warn us not to inquire too curiously, because our minds can easily become confused in speaking about such an exalted mystery. It is better simply to accept the words of Christ, of Scripture, of tradition, and of the Church's magisterium, which tell us what we need to know: Christ is really but invisibly present in this sacrament. His presence is such that the bread and wine after the consecration are truly, really, and substantially his body and blood, but according to a mode of existence that differs from his presence in heaven.

Reductionist Explanations

Let us turn now to the minimizing errors. The Council of Trent is sometimes attacked on the ground that it focused too narrowly on one of the ways Christ is present in the liturgy. According to Paul VI and the Second Vatican Council, these authors remind us, Christ is present in the liturgy in no less than five ways: in the congregation when it gathers for prayer; in the word of God when it is proclaimed; in the priests when they preside at the liturgy; in the sacraments when they are administered; and finally, in the Host and Chalice when they are offered at Mass.

The presence in the consecrated elements, these authors maintain, is only one of the five, and should not be taken as though it alone were real.

In fact, they say, it should be seen as subordinate to the presence in the Church, of which it is a sacramental sign. Did not Augustine and Thomas Aquinas teach that the purpose of the sacrament is to bring about the unity of the Church as Christ's mystical body? Some theologians therefore began to say that Christ's primary presence is in the gathered assembly.[10]

According to the teaching of the Church, the multiple presences of Christ are real and important, but the presence in the Eucharist surpasses all the others. Some fifteen years before Vatican II, Pope Pius XII called attention to four of the ways in which Christ is present in the liturgy. But he was careful to point out that these presences are not all on the same level. The divine Founder of the Church, he wrote, "is present . . . above all under the eucharistic species."[11]

Paul VI, in his encyclical of 1965, gave a similar listing, adding to Pius XII's list a fifth: Christ's presence in the proclamation of the word.[12] But he left no doubt about which presence is primary. After noting the manifold presences of Christ, he declared: "There is another way, and indeed most remarkable, in which Christ is present in His Church in the sacrament of the Eucharist, which is therefore among the rest of the sacraments 'the more pleasing in respect to devotion, the more noble in respect to understanding, and the holier in regard to what it contains,' for it contains Christ Himself and is 'as it were the perfection of the spiritual life and the goal of all the sacraments'" (*MF* 38). This presence, he said, is called real not because the others are unreal but because it is real par excellence (*MF* 39). As a substantial presence of the whole and complete Christ, the Eucharist surpasses his transitory and virtual presence in the waters of baptism, in the other sacraments, in the proclamation of the word, and in the minister who represents Christ in these actions.

As if this were not authority enough, one could note that Vatican II in its Constitution on the Liturgy, said that Christ is present "especially (*maxime*) under the eucharistic species" (SC 7). And Pope John Paul II, in his 2003 encyclical on the Eucharist, says that we should be able "to recognize Christ in his many forms of presence, but above all in the living sacrament of his body and blood."[13]

There is a vast difference between Christ's presence in the Eucharist and in the assembly or its members. The worshipers, if they have the proper dispositions, are mystically united to God by grace. The Holy Spirit dwells in them, but they retain their own personal identity. They are not transubstantiated; they do not cease to be themselves and turn into Christ the Lord. The Church as Mystical Body can never rise to the dignity of Christ in his individual body, which was born of the Virgin Mary, died on the Cross, and is gloriously reigning in heaven. That body is present substantially in the Eucharist but not in the Christian community. There is a vast difference between the adoration we give to Christ in the Eucharist and the veneration we offer to the saints.

Some of these minimizing theologians argue that because the purpose of the Eucharist is to form the Church as the body of Christ, his ecclesial presence is more intense and more important than that in the consecrated elements.[14] The error in this logic can be exposed if one thinks of the Incarnation. Jesus became man and died on the Cross for the sake of our redemption, but it does not follow that God is more intensely present in the community of the redeemed than in the Incarnate Son, or that our devotion should focus more on our fellow Christians than on Christ the Lord.

A second argument sometimes used to exalt the Church above the Eucharist is that the Church as a general sacrament produces the seven special sacraments, including the Eucharist. The Church, it is said, cannot give what she does not have. But this argument overlooks the fact that the Church does not produce the sacraments by her own power. The Eucharist, like the other sacraments, is God's gift. In producing it, the Church is subordinate to Christ, the principal minister. The Church, moreover, is built up by the Eucharist. The faithful are one body because they partake of the one bread, which is Christ the Lord (1 Cor 10:17). And so we can truly say, as Pope John Paul does in his encyclical, that if the Church makes the Eucharist, it is no less true that the Eucharist makes the Church (*EE* 26).

A third line of thinking that tends to minimize the reality of Christ's presence in the Eucharist comes from the personalist phenomenology that was in fashion around the time of Vatican II. Concentrating as it does on interpersonal relations, this school of thought equates personal existence with human relationships. Theologians of this tendency rejected the idea of substance, especially as applied to the Eucharist, which they treated as a communal meal. Even on the natural level, they said, a meal with friends is much more than food and drink; it is a social occasion for expressing and cementing human relationships. So too, they say, with the Eucharist. In inviting us to his Supper, the Lord gives the bread and wine a new meaning and a new purpose, as effective symbols of his redemptive love.

The elements are changed insofar as they acquire new significance and a new finality. For this reason, they maintained, we should speak of "transignification" and "transfinalization" rather than "transubstantiation."[15]

These novel terms are ugly and cumbersome, and thus rhetorically no improvement on "transubstantiation." But in what they positively express, the terms are harmless. In the Eucharist the significance and purpose of the bread and wine are indeed changed: they indicate and bring about spiritual nourishment and joyful communion with Christ and with fellow Christians. But the alternative terminology is deficient because it tells us nothing about what happens to the consecrated elements in themselves.

Paul VI points out in his encyclical the *Mystery of Faith* that the bread and wine are able to take on a radically new significance and finality because they contain a new reality. The change of meaning and purpose depend on a prior ontological change (*MF* 46). We can relate personally to Christ in the sacrament, and he to us, because he is really there. His presence in the sacrament is real and personal whether or not anyone believes or perceives it. The Eucharist is not just a sign, but a person who subsists in his own right, as all persons do.

A Dutch theologian of the 1960s put the question whether the real presence would remain in consecrated hosts if everyone in the world were suddenly killed by some extraordinary disaster. He answered the question in the negative on the ground that personal presence cannot exist except in a mutual encounter between free and conscious subjects.[16]

This theologian seems to confuse two meanings of "presence." It can mean *presence in*, as the soul is present in the body or as Christ is present in the eucharistic elements. Or it can mean *presence to* others. Of the two, *presence in* is the more fundamental. To reduce the real presence to the latter is reductionist. It departs from the faith of the Catholic Church, which holds that Christ's real presence in the Eucharist is objective and independent of anyone's perception of it.

Questions continue to be raised about the term "substance," mainly because the classical concept of substance, common to realist thought, is not widely accepted today. Since the time of Descartes and Locke the term has come to stand for something self-enclosed and inert, whereas formerly it meant an active, relation-generating center, which through its accidents entered into dynamic relations with other creatures. Understandably, today, many people find it strange to call a person a substance.

But if the classical concept is abandoned, some other term must be found to designate what a thing is in its own fundamental reality. In calling the eucharistic presence of Christ substantial, the Church means that the Eucharist in its own reality is nothing other than Christ.

"Transubstantiation," as I have explained, is the process by which one substance, that of the bread or wine, becomes another substance, that of Christ's body and blood, without any change in its physico-chemical aspects. Trent taught that the term was very apt (DS 1652). Paul VI, in 1965, said that it was still "fitting and accurate" and, as I have mentioned, found it superior to other terms that had been proposed (*MF* 46). But the Church is not definitively wedded to any particular vocabulary. A change in the terminology remains theoretically possible.

PRACTICAL CONSEQUENCES

Partly as a result of the new eucharistic theologies proposed during and shortly after Vatican II, there was a temporary loss of interest in the reserved sacrament. All attention came to be focused on the actual celebration of Mass. In many parishes and religious houses Benediction of the Blessed Sacrament was suddenly abandoned. In some churches the Blessed Sacrament was reserved in an inconspicuous place more like a closet than a chapel. The faithful were incessantly being told by avant-garde religious educators that the purpose of the sacrament was to be received in communion, not to be adored, as if the two were mutually exclusive.

The ecclesiastical magisterium has constantly resisted and countered this negative trend. While agreeing that the primary purpose of the Eucharist is to make the sacrifice of the Cross present and to give spiritual nourishment to the faithful, the Council of Trent insisted that the Blessed Sacrament is to be honored and adored after the liturgy of the Mass has been completed (DS 1643, 1656). To deny this is tantamount to a denial of the substantial presence of Christ in the sacrament.

In 1965, Pope Paul VI spoke out forcefully in favor of the reservation of the Blessed Sacrament in a place of honor in the church. He exhorted pastors to expose the sacrament for solemn veneration and to hold eucharistic processions on suitable occasions; he urged the faithful to make frequent visits to it (*MF* 55, 66–68).

Pope John Paul II, in his many writings as pope, has sought to promote the worthy celebration of the Eucharist and devotion to the Eucharist outside of the Mass. In his encyclical of 2003 he expresses satisfaction that in many places adoration of the Blessed Sacrament is fervently practiced but laments that elsewhere the practice has been almost completely abandoned (*EE* 10). Worship of the sacrament outside of the Mass, he writes, "is of inestimable value for the life of the Church. This worship is strictly linked to the celebration of the eucharistic sacrifice. . . . It is the responsibility of pastors to encourage, also by their personal witness, the practice of eucharistic adoration and exposition of the Blessed Sacrament in particular, as well as prayer of adoration before Christ present under the eucharistic species" (*EE* 25).

The pope himself spends long hours before the Blessed Sacrament and receives many of his best insights from these times of prayer. Like St. Alphonsus Liguori, whom he quotes on the point, he is convinced of the religious value of adoring Jesus in the Blessed Sacrament. Prayer before the Eucharist outside of Mass, he writes, enables us to make contact with the very wellspring of grace (*EE* 25).

Thanks in great part to this papal encouragement, there has been a striking resurgence in the practice of exposition and holy hours of adoration. In the year 2000 it was reported that more than a thousand parishes in the United States sponsored perpetual eucharistic adoration, while another thousand provided opportunities for adoration during a substantial portion of the day.[17] These practices, far from undermining the hunger for Holy Communion, stimulate it. They prolong and increase the fruits of active participation in the Mass. They also express and fortify the faith of Catholics in the full meaning of the real presence. By abiding in our midst in this sacramental form, the Lord keeps his promise to be with his Church "always, to the close of the age" (Mt 28:20).

Although the mystery of the real presence certainly stretches our powers of comprehension to the utmost, it is not simply a puzzle. It is a consoling sign of the love, power, and ingenuity of our Divine Savior. He willed to bring himself into intimate union with believers of every generation, and to do so in a way that suits our nature as embodied spirits. The forms of food and drink, deeply charged with memories from the history of ancient Israel, are meaningful even to the unlearned throughout the ages. They aptly symbolize the spiritual nourishment and refreshment conferred by the sacrament. On another level, they call to mind the crucifixion of Christ, who shed his blood for our redemption. And finally, they prefigure the everlasting banquet of the blessed in the heavenly Jerusalem. The many-layered symbolism of the Eucharist is not separable from the real presence. The symbolism has singular power to recapture the past, transform the present, and anticipate the future because it contains the Lord of history truly, really, and substantially.

NOTES

1. For an exposition of these three terms, see Max Thurian, *The Mystery of the Eucharist: An Ecumenical Approach* (Grand Rapids, Mich.: Eerdmans, 1984), 55–58.

2. Vatican II, *Presbyterorum Ordinis* 5, citing Thomas Aquinas, *Summa theologiae*, part III, qu. 65, art. 3, ad 1; cf. qu. 79, art. 1c and ad 1.

3. See Thomas Aquinas, *Summa theologiae*, part III, qu. 77, art. 6, "Can the species nourish?" St. Thomas refers to 1 Cor 11:21 and the standard commentaries to show that the species, taken in sufficient quantities, can satisfy hunger and inebriate.

4. This line of thinking, stemming from Paschasius Radbertus, is represented by Lanfranc and Guitmund of Aversa. See Mark G. Vaillancourt, "Guitmund of Aversa and the Eucharistic Theology of St. Thomas," *The Thomist* 68 (2004): 577–600.

5. Jean Borella, *The Sense of the Supernatural* (Edinburgh: T & T Clark, 1998), 71–77. He finds the doctrine of the "threefold body of Christ" in Ambrose, Paschasius Radbertus, and Honorius of Autun. Henri de Lubac speaks of Amalarius of Metz and Gottschalk of Orbais as representatives of this medieval doctrine. See his *Corpus mysticum: L'Eucharistie et l'Église au Moyen Âge*, 2d ed. (Paris: Aubier, 1949), 37. These theologians did not deny the real identity between the natural and eucharistic bodies of Christ.

6. Thomas Aquinas, *Summa theologiae* part III, qu. 76, art. 6. For a lucid commentary, see Abbot Anscar Vonier, *A Key to the Doctrine of the Eucharist* (1923; reprinted Bethesda, Md.: Zaccheus Press, 2003), 132–33.

7. Thomas Aquinas, *Summa theologiae*, part III, art. 8, ad 2 and ad 3.

8. Ibid., part III, qu. 76, a. 3.

9. Ibid., qu. 76, art. 7.

10. Judith Marie Kubicki attributes to Karl Rahner, Edward Schillebeeckx, and Piet Schoonenberg the position that the Church as sacrament is "the primary location of Christ's presence in the world." See her article "Recognizing the Presence of Christ in the Liturgical Assembly," *Theological Studies* 65 (2004): 817–37, at 821.

11. Pius XII, encyclical *Mediator Dei*, 20.

12. Paul VI, encyclical *Mysterium Fidei*, 36.

13. John Paul II, encyclical *Ecclesia de Eucharistia*, 6.

14. Typical of this point of view is the brief article "Changing Elements of People?" by F. Gerald Martin in *America* 182 (March 4, 2000): 22. Reacting against the tendency to separate the real presence from Holy Communion, he falls into the opposite error, belittling devotion to the reserved sacrament, as if it interfered with frequent reception.

15. The term "transfinalization" was apparently coined by the French Marist Jean de Baciocchi but was used by many others. The term "transignification" is associated in particular with the Dutch Jesuit Piet Schoonenberg. For good accounts of these trends, see Joseph M. Powers, *Eucharistic Theology* (New York: Seabury, 1967), 111–79, and Colman O'Neill, *New Approaches to the Eucharist* (Staten Island, N.Y.: Alba House, 1967), 103–26.

16. Piet Schoonenberg, "The Real Presence in Contemporary Discussion," *Theology Digest* 15 (Spring 1967): 3–11, at 10.

17. I take these figures from Amy L. Florian, "Adore Te Devote," *America* 182 (March 4, 2000): 18–21, at 18.

34

Benedict XVI

Interpreter of Vatican II

October 25, 2005

L ike his predecessor John Paul II, Benedict XVI was present at all four sessions of the Second Vatican Council from 1962 to 1965. Whereas Karol Wojtyla, the future John Paul, took part as a bishop, the young Joseph Ratzinger did so as a theological expert. During and after the council he taught successively at the universities of Bonn (1959–63), Münster (1963–66), Tübingen (1966–69), and Regensburg, until he was appointed archbishop of Munich in 1977. In 1981 he became prefect of the Congregation for the Doctrine of the Faith, a post he held until the death of John Paul II in April 2005.

In his many publications, Ratzinger has continued to debate questions that arose during the council, and in some cases has expressed dissatisfaction with the council's documents. In this respect he differs from Pope John Paul, who consistently praised the council and never to my knowledge criticized it. For this reason, Ratzinger's comments on Vatican II are particularly intriguing. We may conveniently divide the material into three stages: his participation at the council, his early commentaries on the council documents, and his later reflections on the reception of the council. After surveying these three areas, I shall examine his changing reactions to the four great Constitutions: those on the Liturgy (*Sacrosanctum Concilium*), on Revelation (*Dei Verbum*), on the Church (*Lumen gentium*), and on the Church in the Modern World (*Gaudium et spes*).

A Theologian at Vatican II

At the council, Ratzinger was much sought after as a rising theological star. He worked very closely with senior Jesuits, including Karl Rahner, Alois Grillmeier, and Otto Semmelroth, all of whom kept in steady communication with the German bishops. The German Cardinals Josef Frings of Cologne and Julius Döpfner of Munich and Freising, strongly supported by theologian-bishops such as the future Cardinal Hermann Volk, exercised a powerful influence, generally opposing the schemas drawn up by the Preparatory Commission under the guidance of Cardinal Alfredo Ottaviani and Father Sebastian Tromp, S.J.

Late in the first session, Ratzinger was named a theological adviser to Cardinal Frings, a position he held until the end of the council. Many of his biographers suspect that he drafted Frings's speech of November 8, 1963, vehemently attacking the procedures of the Holy Office. In combination with other events, this speech probably influenced Paul VI to restructure the Holy Office and give it a new name, the Congregation for the Doctrine of the Faith.

During the first session, several official schemas were distributed by the Preparatory Commission with the expectation that the council fathers would accept them, at least in revised form. The German contingent were generally content with the proposed document on the liturgy, but reacted adversely to those on revelation and the Church and sought to replace them.

With regard to revelation, Ratzinger agreed that the preliminary schema was unacceptable and should be withdrawn.[1] At the request of Cardinal Frings, he wrote an alternative text, which was then reworked with the help of Rahner. To the annoyance of Ottaviani, three thousand copies of this text were privately circulated among the council fathers and experts. Yves Congar, though generally sympathetic, calls the Rahner-Ratzinger paper far too personal to have any chance of being adopted.[2] He also criticizes it for taking too little account of the good work in the preparatory schemas.[3] Gerald Fogarty calls it a barely mitigated synthesis of Rahner's systematic theology.[4]

Notwithstanding the rejection of their schema, Rahner and Ratzinger had some input into the new text prepared by the Mixed Commission named by Pope John XXIII. Both were appointed as consultors to the subcommission revising the new text.[5] Rahner strongly advocated his personal position on the relationship between Scripture and tradition.[6] Ratzinger helped in responding to proposed amendments to the chapter dealing with tradition; he also had an opportunity to introduce modifications in the chapter dealing with the authority and interpretation of Scripture.[7]

On the Church, Ratzinger joined with the German bishops and with his fellow experts in getting the idea of the Church as sacrament deeply inscribed into the Constitution—a concern to which Frings spoke on the council floor.[8] Both Ratzinger and Rahner served on the subcommission that revised the formulations on collegiality in articles 22 and 23.[9]

Ratzinger was also appointed to a team for redrafting the schema on the Church's Missionary Activity for the last session of the council. He worked closely with Congar in defining the theological foundation of missions, a theme on which the two easily found agreement.[10] Congar, in his diary, characterizes Ratzinger as "reasonable, modest, disinterested, and very helpful."[11] He credits Ratzinger with coming up with the definition of missionary activity that was accepted and also with proposing the inclusion of a section on ecumenism in the document.[12] Others credit him with devising a footnote that allowed Latin America to be included as a missionary region even though its people had been previously evangelized.[13]

At discussions of the pastoral constitution *Gaudium et spes* in September 1965, Ratzinger voiced many of the criticisms that would later appear in his books and articles: the schema was too naturalistic and unhistorical; it took insufficient notice of sin and its consequences, and was too optimistic about human progress.[14]

All in all, we may say that Ratzinger belonged to the inner circle of theologians whose thinking prevailed at Vatican II. Still in his thirties, he as yet lacked the public standing of Congar, Rahner, and Gérard Philips. In the early sessions he collaborated very closely with Rahner and the German Jesuits in opposition to the Roman school, though he spoke with moderation. Some of the anti-Roman leaders, Congar surmises, spoke harshly because they were seeking revenge for not having been named to the Preparatory Commission.[15]

As the council progressed, Ratzinger became more independent. He made an original and important contribution to the document on missions and mounted a highly personal critique of the Pastoral Constitution on the Church in the Modern World that reflected his preference for Augustine over Aquinas and his sensitivity to Lutheran concerns.

LATER COMMENTS ON THE COUNCIL

During the council and the first few years after its conclusion, Ratzinger wrote a number of commentaries on the conciliar documents.[16] While making certain criticisms, they express his agreement with the general directions of Vatican II and his acceptance of the three objectives named by John XXIII: renewal of the Church, unity among Christians, and dialogue with the world of today.[17] He welcomed the rejection of some of the preparatory schemas, chiefly because they were phrased in abstract Scholastic terms and failed to speak pastorally to the modern world. He appreciated the council's freedom from Roman domination and the openness and candor of its discussions.[18]

As a member of the progressive wing at the council, Ratzinger taught at Tübingen with Hans Küng and joined the editorial board of the progressive review *Concilium*, edited from Holland. In 1969, after the academic uprisings at Tübingen, he moved to the more traditional faculty of Regensburg. Then, in 1972, he became one of the founding editors of the review *Communio*, a more conservative counterpart of *Concilium*. His theological orientation seemed to be shifting.

In 1975, Ratzinger wrote an article on the tenth anniversary of the close of Vatican II. He there differed from the progressives who wanted to go beyond the council and from the conservatives who wanted to retreat behind the council. The only viable course, he contended, was to interpret Vatican II in strictest continuity with previous councils such as Trent and Vatican I, since all three councils are upheld by the same authority: that of the pope and the college of bishops in communion with him.[19]

Two years later, Ratzinger became an archbishop and a cardinal, and then in 1981 Cardinal Prefect of the Congregation for the Doctrine of the Faith. In an interview published in 1985 he denied that Vatican II was responsible for causing the confusion of the postconciliar period. The damage, he said, was due to the unleashing of polemical and centrifugal forces within the Church and the prevalence, outside the Church, of a liberal-radical ideology that was individualistic, rationalistic, and hedonistic.[20] He renewed his call for fidelity to the actual teaching of the council without reservations that would truncate its teaching or elaborations that would deform it.[21]

The misinterpretations, according to Ratzinger, must be overcome before an authentic reception can begin. Traditionalists and progressives, he said, fell into the same error: they failed to see that Vatican II stood in fundamental continuity with the past. In rejecting some of the early drafts, the council fathers were not repudiating their doctrine, which was solidly traditional, but only their style, which they found too Scholastic and insufficiently pastoral.[22] Particularly harmful was the tendency of progressives to contrast the letter of the council's texts with the spirit. The spirit is to be found in the letter itself.[23]

Some consider that the Pastoral Constitution on the Church in the Modern World, composed in the final phase, should be seen as the climax of the council, for which the other Constitutions are preparatory. Ratzinger takes the opposite view. The Pastoral Constitution is subordinate to the two Dogmatic Constitutions—those on revelation and the Church—that orient the interpreter toward the source and center of the Christian life. The Constitution on the Liturgy, though not strictly dogmatic, was the most successful of the four Constitutions; the Pastoral Constitution *Gaudium et spes* was a tentative effort to apply Catholic doctrine to the current relationship of the Church to the world.[24]

In light of these principles, it may be of interest to examine some of Ratzinger's specific comments on the four Constitutions: those on Liturgy, Revelation, the Church, and the Church in the Modern World. For the sake of brevity I shall bypass his occasional comments on other Vatican II documents.

On the Liturgy

The first document debated in the session of 1962 was on liturgy. In his early commentaries Ratzinger praises it highly. He applauds its efforts to overcome the isolation of the priest celebrant and to foster active participation by the congregation.[25] He agrees with the Constitution on the need to attach greater importance to the word of God in Scripture and in proclamation.[26] He is pleased by the Constitution's provision for Holy Communion to be distributed under both species[27] and its encouragement of regional adaptations regulated by episcopal conferences,[28] including the use of the vernacular.[29] "The wall of Latinity," he wrote, "had to be breached if the liturgy were again to function either as proclamation or as invitation to prayer."[30] He also approved of the council's call to recover the simplicity of the early liturgies and remove superfluous medieval accretions.[31]

In subsequent writings as Cardinal, Ratzinger seeks to dispel current misinterpretations. The council fathers, he insists, had no intention of initiating a liturgical revolution. They intended to introduce a moderate use of the vernacular alongside of the Latin, but they had no thought of eliminating Latin, which remains the official language of the Roman rite. In calling for active participation, the council did not mean the incessant commotion of speaking, singing, reading, and shaking hands; prayerful silence could be an especially deep manner of personal participation. He particularly regrets the disappearance of traditional sacred music, contrary to the intention of the council. Nor did the council wish to initiate a period of feverish liturgical experimentation and creativity. It strictly forbade both priests and laity to change the rubrics on their own authority.[32]

Ratzinger in several places laments the abruptness with which the Missal of Paul VI was imposed after the Council, with its summary suppression of the so-called Tridentine Mass. This action contributed to the impression, all too widespread, that the council was a breach rather than a new stage in a continuous process of development.[33] For his part, Ratzinger seems to have nothing against the celebration of Mass according to the Missal that was in use before the council.[34]

ON REVELATION

In his earliest comments on the Constitution on Divine Revelation, the young Ratzinger spoke very positively. The first sentence appealed to him because it placed the Church in a posture of reverently listening to the Word of God.[35] He also welcomed the council's effort to overcome the neurotic antimodernism of the neo-Scholastics[36] and to adopt the language of Scripture and contemporary usage.[37] He was pleased with the council's recognition of the process by which Scripture grows out of the religious history of God's people.[38]

In his chapters on *Dei Verbum* for the Vorgrimler commentary, Ratzinger again praises the preface as opening the Church upward to the Word of God and for emphasizing the value of proclamation. While continuing to note the success of the first chapter in emphasizing revelation through history, he faults its survey of Old Testament history for excessive optimism and for overlooking the prevalence of sin. Some attention to the Lutheran theme of law and gospel, he remarks, would have enriched the text.[39] The theology of faith in the Constitution, in his estimation, is consonant with, yet richer than, that of Vatican I.

Ratzinger's discussion of tradition in chapter 2 shows a keen appreciation of the difficulties raised by Protestant commentators. He interprets this chapter as giving a certain priority to Scripture over tradition and praises it for subordinating the Church's teaching office to the Word of God. But he faults it for failing to recognize Scripture as a norm for identifying unauthentic traditions that distort the gospel.[40]

The elder Ratzinger speaks from a different perspective, more confessionally Catholic. While still regarding the Constitution on Divine Revelation as one of the outstanding texts of the council, he holds that it has yet to be truly received. In the prevalent interpretations he finds two principal defects. In the first place, it is misread as though it taught that all revelation is contained in Scripture. Ratzinger now makes the point that revelation, as a living reality, is incapable of being enclosed in a text. Tradition is "that part of revelation that goes above and beyond Scripture and cannot be comprehended within a code of formulas."[41]

The neglect of living tradition, according to the Cardinal Prefect, was one of the most serious errors of postconciliar exegesis. The other was the reduction of exegesis to the historical-critical method. In an article about contemporary biblical interpretation, he comments on the seeming impasse between exegetes and dogmatic theologians. Offering a way out of the dilemma, the council teaches that historical-critical method is only the first stage of exegesis. It helps to illuminate the text on the human and historical level, but to find the word of God the exegete must go further, drawing on the Bible as a whole, on tradition, and on the whole system of Catholic dogma. "I am personally persuaded," he writes, "that a careful reading of the whole text of *Dei Verbum* can provide the essential elements of a synthesis between historical method and theological hermeneutics." But unfortunately, the postconciliar reception has practically discarded the theological part of the council's statement as a concession to the past, thus allowing Catholic exegesis to become almost undistinguishable from Protestant.[42]

In combination with the virtual monopoly of historical-critical exegesis, the neglect of tradition leads many Christians to think that nothing can be taught in the Church that does not pass the scrutiny of historical-critical method. In practice this meant that the shifting hypotheses of exegetes became the highest doctrinal authority in the Church.[43]

ON THE CHURCH

Over the years, Ratzinger has had a great deal to say about the Dogmatic Constitution on the Church. In his earliest observations he contends that it did well to subordinate the image of Mystical Body to that of People of God. The Mystical Body paradigm, much in favor under Pius XII, makes it all but impossible to give any ecclesial status to non-Catholics and leads to a false identification of the Church with Christ her Lord.[44] The image of People of God, he contends, is more biblical; it gives scope for recognizing the sins of the Church, and it indicates that the Church is still on pilgrimage under the sign of hope.[45] For similar reasons, he supports the theme of Church as sacrament. As a sign and instrument, the Church is oriented to a goal that lies beyond herself.[46]

In his early commentaries, Ratzinger shows special interest in episcopal collegiality. The apostles, he believes, constituted a stable group or college under Peter as their head, as do the bishops of later generations under the primacy of Peter's successor.[47] Collegiality, in his view, favors horizontal communication among bishops.[48] Behind collegiality lies the vision of the Church as made up of relatively autonomous communities under their respective bishops.[49] The rediscovery of the local church makes it clear that multiplicity belongs to the structure of the Church.[50] According to the New Testament, Ratzinger observes, the Church is a communion of local churches, mutually joined together through the Body and the Word of the Lord, especially when gathered at the Eucharist.[51] Bishops, as heads of particular churches, must collaborate with one another in a ministry that is essentially communal.[52] Not all initiative has to rest with the pope alone; he may simply accept what the body of bishops or some portion of it decrees.[53]

Ratzinger was less upset than some of his fellow theologians by the "Prefatory Note of Explanation" appended to the third chapter of *Lumen gentium* to clarify the doctrine of collegiality. This note supplied a number of necessary elucidations, even while tipping the scales somewhat in favor of papal primacy.[54] Its importance should not be exaggerated, because it is neither a conciliar document nor one signed by the pope.[55] Although the pope evidently approved of it, it was signed only by the Secretary General of the Council.[56]

Ratzinger, at this stage of his career, contends that the Synod of Bishops established by Paul VI in September 1965 is in some respects collegial. The majority of the members are elected by the bishops, and it is called a synod, a term evoking the structures of the ancient Church.[57] The Synod, he says, is "a permanent council in miniature."[58] He likewise characterizes episcopal conferences as quasi-synodal intermediate agencies between individual bishops and the pope, possessing legislative powers in their own right.[59] Writing for *Concilium* in 1965, he calls the conferences partial realizations of collegiality and asserts that they have a genuinely theological basis.[60]

At Vatican II there was a division of opinion about whether or not to treat Mariology in a separate document. With the general body of German theologians, Ratzinger supported the inclusion of Mary in the Constitution on the Church, as finally took place.[61] Unlike Bishop Wojtyla, he was wary of Marian maximalism and apparently averse to new titles such as "Mother of the Church." Moved partly by ecumenical considerations, he praised the restraint of the council in its references to Mary as Mediatrix and Co-Redemptrix.[62]

Ratzinger in these early commentaries praised the Constitution on the Church for its ecumenical sensitivity. It overcomes the impression that non-Catholic Christians are connected to the Church only by some kind of implicit desire, as Pius XII had seemed to teach. Read in conjunction with the Decree on Ecumenism, *Lumen gentium* gives positive ecclesial status to Protestant and Orthodox communities.[63] For Ratzinger, only the Catholic Church is *the* Church, but it is possible for particular churches or ecclesial communities to exist irregularly outside her borders.[64] Some, such as the Eastern Orthodox communities, deserve to be called churches in the theological sense of the word.[65]

Throughout his later career, Ratzinger has continued to write extensively on the issues raised by Vatican II's Constitution on the Church. He frequently returns to the theme of the Church as "people of God," which had been a topic in his doctoral dissertation. In calling the Church by that title, he now says, the council was not using the term "people" in a sociological sense. From an empirical point of view, Christians are not a people, as may be shown from any sociological analysis. But the non-people of Christians can become the people of God through inclusion in Christ, by sacramental incorporation into his crucified and risen body. In other words, the Church is the people of God because it is, in Christ, a sacrament. Here, too, we must note a serious failure of reception: since the council, "the idea of the Church as sacrament has hardly entered people's awareness."[66]

Ratzinger is not opposed to the ecclesiology of communion that came to the fore at the 1985 Synod session on the interpretation of Vatican II. Thanks to the Eucharist, the Church is communion with the whole Body of Christ.[67] But he notes that communion has become in some measure a buzzword and is frequently distorted by a unilateral emphasis on the horizontal dimension to the neglect of the divine; it is also misused to promote a kind of egalitarianism within the Church.[68]

The early Ratzinger attached great importance to the council's retrieval of the theology of the local church. Since 1992, however, he has contended that the universal Church has ontological and historical priority over the particular churches. It was not originally made up of local or regional churches. Those who speak of the priority of the particular church over the universal, he says, misinterpret the council documents.[69]

Turning to collegiality, the elder Ratzinger points out that according to Vatican II the bishop is first of all a member of the college, which is by nature universal. He is a successor of the apostles, each of whom, with and under Peter, was jointly responsible for the universal Church. Bishops who are assigned to dioceses participate in the direction of the universal Church by governing their own churches well, keeping them in communion with the Church Catholic. The Synod of Bishops, in Ratzinger's later theology, is no longer seen as a collegial organ or as a council in miniature; it is advisory to the pope as he performs his primatial task. In so doing it makes the voice of the universal Church more clearly audible in the world of our day.[70]

A similar shift is apparent in Ratzinger's view of episcopal conferences, which he had earlier characterized as collegial organs with a true theological basis. But by 1986 he says: "We must not forget that the episcopal conferences have no theological basis, they do not belong to the structure of the Church as willed by Christ, that cannot be eliminated; they have only a practical, concrete function."[71] It is difficult to deny that on episcopal conferences, as on the Synod of Bishops, the Cardinal has retracted his own earlier positions.

One of the most contentious issues in the interpretation of *Lumen gentium* is the meaning of the statement that the Church of Christ "subsists in" the Roman Catholic Church (*LG* 8). Some have interpreted it as an admission that the Church of Christ is found in many denominational churches, none of which can claim to be the one true Church. Ratzinger asserts the opposite. For him, "subsists" implies integral existence as a complete, self-contained subject. Thus the Catholic Church truly is the Church of Christ. But the term "subsists" is not exclusive; it allows for the possibility of ecclesial entities that are institutionally separate from the one Church. This dividedness, however, is not a desirable mutual complementarity of incomplete realizations; it is a deficiency that calls for healing.[72]

In the sphere of Mariology, Ratzinger laments what he sees as another misunderstanding of the council. The inclusion of a chapter on Mary as the culmination of the Constitution on the Church, he believes, should have given rise to new research rather than to neglect of the mystery of Mary. He himself has overcome certain reservations about Marian titles that he had expressed at the time of the council. It is imperative to turn to Mary, he believes, in order to learn the truth about Jesus Christ that is to be proclaimed.[73]

On the Church in the Modern World

The Pastoral Constitution *Gaudium et spes* in final form was primarily the work of French theologians. The German group did not control the text. At the time of the council Ratzinger already noted many difficulties, beginning with the problem of language. In opting for the language of modernity, the text inevitably places itself outside the world of the Bible, so that as a result the biblical citations come to be little more than ornamental.[74] Because of its stated preference for dialogue, the Constitution makes faith appear not as an urgent demand for total commitment but as a conversational search into obscure matters. Christ is mentioned only at the end of each section, almost as an afterthought.[75] Instead of replacing dogmatic utterances with dialogue, Ratzinger contends, it would have been better to use the language of proclamation, appealing to the intrinsic authority of God's truth.[76]

The Constitution, drawing on the thought of Teilhard de Chardin, links Christian hope too closely to the modern idea of progress.[77] Material progress is ambivalent because it can lead to degradation as well as to true humanization.[78] The cross teaches us that the world is not redeemed by technological advances but by sacrificial love.[79] In the section on unification, *Gaudium et spes* approaches the world too much from the viewpoint of function and utility rather than that of contemplation and wonder.[80]

Ratzinger's Commentary on Chapter 1 of *Gaudium et spes* contains still other provocative comments. The treatment of conscience in article 16, in his view, raises many unsolved questions about how conscience can err and about the right to follow an erroneous conscience. The treatment of free will in article 17 is in his judgment "downright Pelagian."[81] It leaves aside, he complains, the whole complex of problems that Luther handled under the term "*servum arbitrium*," although Luther's position does not itself do justice to the New Testament.[82]

Ratzinger is not wholly negative in his judgment. He praises the discussion of atheism in articles 19–21 as "balanced and well-founded."[83] He is satisfied that the document, while "reprobating" atheism in all its forms, makes no specific mention of Marxist Communism, as some cold warriors had desired.[84] He is enthusiastic about the centrality of Christ and the Paschal mystery in article 22, and finds here a statement on the possibilities of salvation of the unevangelized far superior to the "extremely unsatisfactory" expressions of the Dogmatic Constitution on the Church, article 16, which seemed to suggest that salvation is a human achievement rather than a divine gift.[85]

With regard to this Constitution, the senior Ratzinger does not seem to have withdrawn his early objections, notwithstanding his exhortations to accept the entire teaching of Vatican II. But he finds that the ambiguities of *Gaudium et spes* have been aggravated by secularist interpretations.

The council was right, Ratzinger maintains, in its desire for a revision of the relations between the Church and the world. There are values that, having originated outside the Church, can find their place, at least in corrected form, within the Church. But the Church and the world can never meet each other without conflict.[86] Worldly theologies too easily assimilate the gospel to secular movements. In scattered references here and there in his interviews, Ratzinger mentions at least three specific deviations in the interpretations.

In the first place, *Gaudium et spes* did make reference to signs of the times, but it stated that they need to be discerned and judged in the light of the gospel (*GS* 4). Contemporary interpreters treat the signs of the times as a new method that finds theological truth in current events and makes them normative for judging the testimony of Scripture and tradition.[87]

Second, the Pastoral Constitution may have erred in the direction of optimism, but it did speak openly of sin and evil. In no less than five places it made explicit mention of Satan. Postconciliar interpreters, however, are inclined to discount Satan as a primitive myth.[88]

Third, *Gaudium et spes* refers frequently to the kingdom of God. Secularist readers prefer to speak simply of the kingdom (without reference to any King) or, even more vaguely, to the "values" of the kingdom: peace, justice, and conservation.

Can this trio of values, asks Ratzinger, take the place of God? Values, he replies, cannot replace truth, nor can they replace God, for they are only a reflection of him. Without God, the values become distorted by inhuman ideologies, as has been seen in various forms of Marxism.[89]

RATZINGER'S CONSISTENCY

Undeniably, there have been some shifts in Ratzinger's assessment of Vatican II. Still finding his own theological path, he was in the first years of the council unduly dependent on Karl Rahner as a mentor. Only gradually did he come to see that he and Rahner lived, theologically speaking, on different planets. Whereas Rahner found revelation and salvation primarily in the inward movements of the human spirit, Ratzinger finds them in historical events attested by Scripture and the Fathers.[90]

Ratzinger's career appears to have affected his theology. As an archbishop and a cardinal he has had to take increasing responsibility for the public life of the Church and has gained a deeper realization of the need for universal sacramental structures to safeguard the unity of the Church and her fidelity to the gospel. He has also had to contend with interpretations of Vatican II that he and the council fathers never foresaw. His early hopes for new mechanisms such as episcopal conferences have been tempered by the course of events.

Notwithstanding the changes, Benedict XVI has shown a fundamental consistency. As a personalist in philosophy and as a theologian in the Augustinian tradition, he expects the Church to maintain a posture of prayer and worship. He is suspicious of technology, of social activism, and of human claims to be building the kingdom of God. For this reason he most appreciates the council documents on the Liturgy and Revelation, and he has reservations about the Constitution on the Church in the Modern World, while giving it credit for some solid achievements.

The contrast between Pope Benedict and his papal predecessor is striking. John Paul II was a social ethicist, anxious to involve the Church in shaping a world order of peace, justice, and fraternal love. Among the documents of Vatican II, John Paul's favorite was surely the Pastoral Constitution *Gaudium et spes*. Benedict XVI, who looks upon *Gaudium et spes* as the weakest of the four Constitutions, shows a clear preference for the other three.

Although the Polish philosopher and the German theologian differ in outlook, they agree that the council has been seriously misinterpreted. It needs to be understood in conformity with the constant teaching of the Church. The true spirit of the council is to be found in, and not apart from, the letter. When rightly interpreted, the documents of Vatican II can still be a powerful source of renewal for the Church.

NOTES

1. Yves Congar, *Mon Journal du Concile* (Paris: Cerf, 2002), 1:123.

2. Ibid., 1:201.

3. Ibid., 1:156–57.

4. Gerald P. Fogarty, "The Council Gets Underway," in *History of Vatican II*, ed. Giuseppe Alberigo, 5 vols. (Maryknoll, N.Y.: Orbis, 1995–2006), 2:69–106, at 88.

5. Joseph Ratzinger, "Dogmatic Constitution on Divine Revelation: Origin and Background," in *Commentary on the Documents of Vatican II*, 5 vols., ed. Herbert Vorgrimler (New York: Herder and Herder, 1967–69), 3:155–66, at 162.

6. Riccardo Burigana, *La Bibbia nel Concilio* (Bologna: Il Mulino, 1998), 186–67.

7. Evangelista Vilanova, "The Intersession (1963–1964)" in Alberigo, *History*, 3:347–490, at 375–76.

8. Günther Wassilovwky, *Universales Heilssakrament Kirche* (Innsbruck: Tyrolia, 2001), 386; cf. Alberto Melloni, "The Beginning of the Second Period," in Alberigo, *History*, 3:1–115, at 44.

9. Melloni, "Beginning," 113.

10. Suso Brechter, "Decree on the Church's Missionary Activity," in Vorgrimler, *Commentary*, 4:87–181, at 101–2; cf. Riccardo Burigana and Giovanni Turbandi, "The Intersession," in Alberigo, *History*, 4:453–615, at 576.

11. Congar, *Mon Journal*, 2:355–56.

12. Ibid., 356, 462.

13. Decree *Ad gentes* 6, note 37; cf. Burigana and Turbanti, "Intersession" 582 n. 302.

14. Congar, *Mon Journal*, 2:395.

15. Ibid., 1:181.

16. Ratzinger's basic commentary on Vatican II consists of a set of four articles published after each of the four sessions and then collected into a book, *Theological Highlights of Vatican II* (New York: Paulist, 1966). For the French Unam Sanctam series *L'Église de Vatican II*, ed. by G. Baraúna (Paris: Cerf, 1967), he wrote an article on the theology of collegiality (763–90). For the five-volume *Commentary on the Documents of Vatican II*, edited by Herbert Vorgrimler, he contributed an article on the Prefatory Note of Explanation (1:297–305), commentaries on chapters 1,2, and 6 of the Constitution on Revelation (3:155–98), and a commentary on chapter 1 of the Pastoral Constitution *Gaudium et spes* (5:115–63).

17. Ratzinger, *Highlights*, 42.

18. Ibid., 11.

19. This article is summarized in Joseph Ratzinger and Vittorio Messori, *The Ratzinger Report* (San Francisco: Ignatius, 1985), 27–28.

20. Ibid., 30.

21. Ibid., 31.

22. Ibid., 41.

23. Ibid., 40.

24. Joseph Ratzinger, *Principles of Catholic Theology* (San Francisco: Ignatius, 1987), 378–79, 390.

25. Ratzinger, *Highlights*, 15.

26. Ibid.

27. Ibid., 16.

28. Ibid., 16, 76.

29. Ibid., 17.

30. Ibid., 87.

31. Ibid., 14, 87.

32. *Ratzinger Report*, 126–29.

33. Joseph Ratzinger, *The Feast of Faith: Approaches to a Theology of the Liturgy* (San Francisco: Ignatius, 1986), 79–87.

34. *Ratzinger Report*, 123–25.

35. Ratzinger, *Highlights*, 149.

36. Ibid., 23.

37. Ibid., 24.

38. Ibid., 98–99.

39. Ratzinger, Commentary on Chapter I of *Dei Verbum* in Vorgrimler, *Commentary*, 3:174.

40. Ratzinger, Commentary on Chapter II of *Dei Verbum*, in Vorgrimler, *Commentary*, 3:193.

41. Joseph Ratzinger, *Milestones: Memoirs 1927–1977* (San Francisco: Ignatius, 1998), 127.

42. Joseph Ratzinger, ed., *Schriftauslegung im Widerstreit*, Quaestiones Disputatae 117 (Freiburg: Herder, 1989), 20–21. This passage is lacking in the English version of Ratzinger's essay in *Biblical Interpretation in Crisis*, ed. Richard John Neuhaus (Grand Rapids, Mich.: Eerdmans, 1989).

43. Ratzinger, *Milestones*, 125–26.

44. Ratzinger, *Highlights*, 45, 90.

45. Ibid., 45–47.

46. Ibid., 48–49.

47. Ibid., 49–52.

48. Ibid., 52.

49. Ibid., 91.

50. Ibid., 121.

51. Ibid., 123; Ratzinger, *Principles of Catholic Theology*, 288–89.

52. Ratzinger, *Highlights*, 111, 122.

53. Ibid., 113–14.

54. Ibid., 115.

55. Ibid., 116.

56. For a more detailed and technical discussions of the NEP, see the Ratzinger articles in Vorgrimler, *Commentary*, 1:297–305, and Baraúna, *L'Église*, 781–87, where he praises the text for clearing up certain common misunderstandings. He faults it, however, for seemingly restricting collegial acts to those performed by the entire college when summoned into action by the pope. He thinks that the practical significance of collegiality lies in giving ecclesial value to episcopal actions of groups of bishops on the national, provincial, and diocesan levels.

57. Ratzinger, *Highlights*, 141.

58. Ibid., 142.

59. Ibid., 16.

60. Ratzinger, "Pastoral Implications of Episcopal Collegiality," Concilium 1, *The Church and Mankind* (New York: Paulist, 1965), 39–67, at 64.

61. Ratzinger, *Highlights*, 54, 59–60.

62. Ibid., 93–95.

63. Ibid., 67.

64. Ibid., 74.

65. Ibid., 75.

66. Joseph Ratzinger, *Church, Ecumenism, and Politics* (New York: Crossroad, 1988), 19.

67. Joseph Ratzinger, *Called to Communion: Understanding the Church Today* (San Francisco: Ignatius, 1996), 82.

68. Joseph Ratzinger, *Pilgrim Fellowship of Faith* (San Francisco: Ignatius, 2005), 132.

69. Ibid., 133–44.

70. Ratzinger, *Church, Ecumenism, and Politics*, 46–62.

71. *Ratzinger Report*, 59.

72. Ratzinger, *Pilgrim Fellowship*, 144–49.

73. *Ratzinger Report*, 104–6.

74. Ratzinger, *Highlights*, 152–53.

75. Ibid., 155.

76. Ibid., 156–57.

77. Ibid., 157–60.

78. Ibid., 164.

79. Ibid., 159.

80. Ibid., 162.

81. Ratzinger, "Commentary on Pastoral Constitution on the Church in the Modern World," part 1, chapter 1, in Vorgrimler, *Commentary*, 5:138.

82. Ibid., 138–40.

83. Ibid., 145.

84. Ibid., 150.

85. Ibid., 163.

86. *Ratzinger Report*, 36.

87. Ibid., 177.

88. Ibid., 139.

89. Ratzinger, *Pilgrim Fellowship*, 288–89; cf. *Milestones*, 137.

90. Ratzinger, *Milestones*, 128.

35

The Mission of the Laity

March 29, 2006

I n some past centuries it might almost have seemed that the laity had no mission. The Lord, it was said, had assigned the mission to evangelize the world to the apostles and their successors. Since the word *apostle* means someone sent, a herald, an emissary, it might seem that persons not in the apostolic succession could not be sent. Throughout the Middle Ages and early modern times, laypeople were active in the world, but ordinarily played a rather passive role in the Church. Saints like King Louis IX and Thomas More applied their faith admirably to the world of politics, but did not meddle in ecclesiastical affairs. Other laypersons were scholars and apologists for the faith, but official documents of the Church did not speak of them as having a mission or ministry, terms that were commonly applied to the Church and to the clergy but not to the laity.

THE LAY APOSTOLATE

Sensing the advent of a new situation, the popes at the beginning of the twentieth century began to involve the laity in the ministry of the Church. Pius X established Catholic Action, and Pius XI assiduously fostered its growth. In 1928 he wrote, "Catholic Action has no other purpose than the participation of the laity in the apostolate of the hierarchy."[1] But Catholic Action made no provision for the laity to exercise an apostolate of their own.

With Pius XII (1939–58) we see a further positive development. In an address of 1946 he declared, "The faithful, more precisely the lay faithful, find themselves on the front lines of the Church's life; for them the Church is the animating principle for human society. Therefore, they in particular, ought to have an ever-clearer consciousness not only of belonging to the Church, but of being the Church. . . . These are the Church."[2]

Pius XII modified the statements of his predecessors about the dependence of the lay apostolate on the hierarchy. That dependence, he said, admits of degrees. It is strictest in the case of Catholic Action, which is an instrument in the hands of the hierarchy. But other works of the lay apostolate, he observed, could be left more or less to the free initiative of laypersons, while of course being conducted within the limits allowed by competent ecclesiastical authorities.[3]

Here in the United States, Catholic Action had only limited success, except perhaps in the well-attended Summer School for Catholic Action, which drew large crowds of students until the time of Vatican II. The period between the two world wars nevertheless witnessed a prodigious growth of lay activity on the part of Catholics. In 1917 the National Catholic Welfare Conference set up the National Council of Catholic Men and the National Council of Catholic Women. Also in 1917 David Goldstein, a Jewish convert to Catholicism, took to preaching on the streets as a lay evangelist. Several years later, he and Martha Moore Avery established the Catholic Campaigners for Christ. Likewise in 1917 Thomas Wyatt Turner, a lay professor at Howard University, organized the Federation of Colored Catholics, which eventually blended into the Catholic Interracial Council. In 1924, Michael Williams founded the lay Catholic magazine *Commonweal*. In 1933, Peter Maurin and Dorothy Day launched the Catholic Worker movement. About 1940, Catherine de Hueck established Friendship House, while another group of lay Catholics founded the magazine *Integrity*. Pat and Patty Crowley started the Christian Family Movement in 1947. Thus there was no lack of vigorous Catholic lay movements.[4]

The Second Vatican Council did much to bring official Catholic teaching abreast of the de facto situation, but the council can hardly be said to have made revolutionary changes in the theology of the laity. Its treatment of the laity in the Constitution on the Church and in the Decree on the Apostolate of the Laity reflected predominantly the work of Yves Congar, whose classic work on the laity had been published ten years earlier.[5]

The council wrestled with the question how to define the lay faithful. From a canonical point of view, they were baptized Christians who had not received the sacrament of orders. Seeking a more positive definition, the council fathers taught that lay Christians were incorporated in the Body of Christ by virtue of their baptism and therefore shared in their own way in Christ's threefold office as priest, prophet, and king. As a result they partook in the mission of the Church. What was specific to the laity as such, according to the council, was their secular calling— namely, to engage in temporal affairs, seeking to order them according to the plan of God. "They live in the world," said the council, "that is, in each and in all of the secular professions and occupations. They live in the ordinary circumstances of family and social life, from which the very web of their existence is woven" (*LG* 31). From this it followed that they "are called in a special way to make the Church present and operative where only through them can she become the salt of the earth" (*LG* 33).

As a general description of what the lay faithful are to do, the council selected the term "apostolate," perhaps because it had been used in the documents on Catholic Action. It defined the apostolate as the sum total of the activity whereby the Mystical Body spreads the kingdom of Christ and thereby brings the world to share in Christ's saving redemption (*AA* 2). Vatican II made an important further advance, in the spirit of Pius XII. It stated that while laypersons can be called to participate in the apostolate of the hierarchy, as is the case in Catholic Action, this is not their sole way of exercising the apostolate. Before receiving any mandate from the hierarchy, they already participate in the saving mission of the Church through their baptism and confirmation. Through these sacraments the Lord himself commissions them to the apostolate. Far from being merely passive recipients of the ministrations of the hierarchy, all the lay faithful have a positive role to play; they are called to make their own contribution to the growth and sanctification of the Church (*LG* 33; *AA* 2–3).

The council was quite aware that its "secular" characterization of the mission of the laity was not a rigorous definition: it did not apply to all members of the laity nor exclusively to them. Together with laypersons, some priests and religious were engaged in the temporal sphere, and thus were doing what the council depicted as proper to the laity. Nevertheless, said the council, Christians in sacred orders were by their particular vocation chiefly and professedly ordained to the sacred ministry. Religious, for their part, were called to give striking testimony to the transfiguration of the world in the spirit of the beatitudes. Thus the clergy and religious were distinguished from the laity by their specific vocation (*LG* 31).

Conversely, it could be said that some members of the laity were working in ecclesiastical rather than secular tasks, but since they did so without ordination, they remained laymen. In seeking a strict definition of the laity, therefore, one had to fall back in the end on the negative marks of not being ordained and not being vowed religious.

At various points in its documents, Vatican II sought to clarify the respective competences of the hierarchy and the laity, making several important distinctions.[6] All Christians, it taught, are called by virtue of their baptism to be active in extending and sanctifying the Church, though always under the supervision of the hierarchy. The laity in particular are called to make the Church present and operative in secular environments where it is difficult for clergy and vowed religious to penetrate. Over and above this general call, some members of the laity receive a special mandate from the hierarchy to cooperate in a more immediate way in the apostolate of the hierarchy, as did the co-workers in the gospel to whom Paul refers in his letters (Rom 16:3ff; Phil 4:3). Catholic Action, I suppose, would fit into this category. And finally, a few may be commissioned to supply for certain sacred functions ordinarily reserved to the clergy because of a shortage of priests or some persecution that prevents priests from performing their tasks. Laypersons cannot, of course, perform functions reserved to the ordained by divine law, such as saying Mass and giving sacramental absolution in the sacrament of Penance. But they can receive the deputation, for example, to baptize, to witness marriages, to preach, and to distribute Holy Communion.

Lay Ministry in Authoritative Teaching

In the documents of Vatican II, the distinction is often made between the sacred ministry of the ordained and the apostolate of the laity. With its predilection for the term "apostolate," the council applied the term "ministry" only rarely to laypersons, but these instances, though few in number, are significant in view of later developments. The Constitution on the Liturgy speaks of servers, lectors, commentators, and choir members as performing a true ministry (*SC* 29; cf. 35, 112, 122). The Decree on Christian Education speaks of religious instruction carried out by laypersons as a true ministry (*GE* 7, 8). The Decree on the Church's Missionary

Activity characterizes missionary work, whether performed by clergy, religious, or laity, as a ministry (*AG* 26). It speaks of the ministry of those who without ordination perform works proper to deacons such as teaching catechism, presiding over communities in the name of the pastor, or practicing charity in social or relief work (*AG* 16). The Pastoral Constitution on the Church in the Modern World uses the term *ministerium* rather loosely to indicate any kind of service, including work on behalf of peace, justice, and the defense of human life (*GS* 38, 51, 79), which are normally the task of laypersons.[7]

The question of terminology is important because it has become a matter of controversy. The Holy See in 1997 published a document forbidding laypersons to assume titles such as "pastor" and "chaplain," but not excluding a discriminating use of the word "minister."[8] Some, going beyond this instruction, contend that the terms "minister" and "ministry" should be reserved to the ordained and never applied to laypersons. Others object that the term "ministry" should be restricted to the exercise of an established office in the Church. But neither of these positions seems to be warranted by official Catholic teaching; still less by Scripture and tradition.

Biblically, the term most closely corresponding to ministry seems to be *diakonia*, which is translated into Latin as *ministerium* or *ministratio*. This term has a range of meanings extending all the way from service to office. So, likewise, the term *diakonos* or *minister* can mean a servant, a helper, a minister, or a deacon. In First Corinthians, chapter 12—a passage that is of great interest for our purposes—Paul speaks of varieties of charisms (*charismatōn*), ministries (*diakoniōn*), and activities (*energēmatōn*), all proceeding from the same God, who is Father, Son, and Holy Spirit. In his first list of gifts, services, or works, Paul mentions healing, miracle working, prophesying, speaking in tongues, and interpreting tongues, which do not seem to require any office, but a little later in the chapter he mentions the offices of apostle, teacher, and administrator as forms of *diakonia*. Thus biblically the term most closely corresponding to ministry embraces both official and unofficial activities dedicated to the upbuilding of the Christian community.[9]

In official Catholic documents since Vatican II there has been a growing tendency to apply the term "ministry" to lay activities, where the council would probably have used "apostolate." "Ministry" is used in particular for services intended to build up the Church from within, whereas "apostolate," to the extent that it is still used, connotes activities directed outward to the world.

In 1972, Pope Paul VI established the offices of lector and acolyte as lay ministries. In so doing he declared: "Ministries may be committed to lay Christians. They are no longer regarded as reserved to candidates for the sacrament of orders."[10] When establishing these two ministries he invited episcopal conferences to submit requests for other official lay ministries to be acknowledged. This papal invitation has been generally ignored, probably because laypersons find the concept of installed ministries too clerical for their taste. But the pope's declaration that ministry should be open to lay Catholics has been gladly accepted.

Several years later, in his apostolic exhortation on evangelization, Paul VI taught: "The laity can also feel called, or in fact be called, to cooperate with their pastors in the service of the ecclesial community, for the sake of its growth and life. This can be done through the exercise of different kinds of ministries according to the grace and charisms which the Lord has been pleased to bestow on them."[11]

Pope John Paul II spoke of lay ministries on many occasions. For example, in his apostolic exhortation *Familiaris Consortio* he devoted four paragraphs to the ministry of evangelization and catechesis carried out by Christian parents. "The ministry of evangelization carried out by Christian parents," he wrote, "is original and irreplaceable" (*FC* 53).

In his apostolic exhortation on the laity, published in 1988, Pope John Paul expressed satisfaction with the progress made since Vatican II in achieving greater collaboration among priests, religious, and lay faithful in the proclamation of the word of God, in catechesis, and in the great variety of services entrusted to the lay faithful, including women. In a special section on lay ministries the pope strongly urged pastors to "acknowledge and foster the ministries, offices, and roles of the lay faithful that find their foundation in the Sacraments to Baptism and Confirmation" (CL 23). But at the same time he cautioned against "a too-indiscriminate use of the word 'ministry,'" which is sometimes overextended to include merely casual or occasional activities. The pope also warns against "clericalization" of the lay faithful, which would overlook the distinction between their functions and those of the ordained.

In his apostolic letter *Novo millennio ineunte*, published at the close of the great jubilee of the year 2000, John Paul II stated that in addition to ordained ministries, "other ministries, whether formally instituted or simply recognized, can flourish for the good of the whole community . . . from catechesis to liturgy, from education of the young to the widest array of charitable works" (NMI 46).

THE UNITED STATES BISHOPS ON LAY MINISTRY

Here in the United States, the Conference of Catholic Bishops in its annual meetings of 1980, 1995, and 2005 has published three significant documents on lay ministry. The first of them, entitled "Called and Gifted,"[12] recalled that the Second Vatican Council encouraged the laity to use their gifts both for the service of humankind and for building up the Church, that is to say, for ecclesial ministry. The document noted that lay ministries of this second kind were relatively new in the Church. The development was to be welcomed, said the bishops, not least because it permitted the Church to avail herself of the manifold talents of women, some of which had not been sufficiently utilized in the past.

The 1995 document, titled "Called and Gifted for the New Millennium,"[13] distinguished still more clearly between the two areas of lay activity: their witness and service in secular society and their service to the Church, calling only the latter "ecclesial lay ministry." Lay ministry, it stated, is not just a job but a true call from God, and is vitally important for renewing the Church as a community. The study also pointed out the many varieties of lay ministry being exercised today in parishes and other settings, such as marriage tribunals, schools, shelters for the homeless, peace and justice networks, and healthcare facilities.

The 2005 statement, much longer than its two predecessors, bears the title "Co-Workers in the Vineyard" and the subtitle "A Resource for Guiding the Development of Lay Ecclesial Ministry."[14] It is called a *lay* ministry, says the document, because it is founded on the sacraments of initiation (baptism, confirmation, and Eucharist) rather than the sacrament of orders, which grounds the sacred ministry of the clergy. It is *ecclesial* because it is approved and supervised by Church authority and because it aims at building up the Church. It is a *ministry* because it is a participation in the threefold ministry of Christ as prophet, priest, and king.

"Co-Workers" deals at some length with four main points: the call to lay ecclesial ministry and its discernment; formation for such ministry;

the authorization, appointment, and induction of ministers; and finally, the workplace in which ministry is conducted. Justly described as a "landmark document,"[15] it should greatly help to assure that lay ministers are competent, that their ministries are duly authorized, and that their functions are not confused with the sacred ministries reserved to the ordained. Without making a class out of lay ministers, it does give them the kind of recognition they so richly deserve.

LAY MINISTRIES SINCE VATICAN II

A recent study, *Lay Parish Ministers*, published by the National Pastoral Life Center here in New York City, impressively documents the exponential growth of lay ministries in Catholic parishes in the United States.[16] Outnumbering priests, lay ministers who work more than twenty hours a week now number more than 30,000. Ninety-three percent of them are paid for their work, while a little over 6 percent are volunteers. About 80 percent are women, 20 percent men.

The activities of these parish ministers are almost as diverse as parish life itself. They may be broken down under headings such as the following. About one-quarter are general parish ministers, a category that includes parish life coordinators. About 40 percent are in religious education. About 10 percent are youth ministers. The rest are in fields such as music ministry, liturgy, and various kinds of social outreach. Among the kinds of work done by lay ministers we may think of ministry to the sick and elderly, evangelization, instruction of catechumens, preparation for first communion, marriage preparation, spiritual direction, and counseling the bereaved.

The study I am summarizing records an extremely high level of satisfaction on the part of lay ministers in their work. Well over 90 percent describe their work as meaningful and spiritually rewarding; 87 percent say that they would encourage others to enter lay ministry. Conversely, parishioners generally report that they are content with the competence and dedication of the lay ministers. Such resistance as there might have been a decade or two ago seems to be crumbling.

Recent reviews of the current situation call attention to a number of areas of concern, both practical and theoretical.[17] Among the practical concerns, they mention the relatively low salaries, which make it difficult for heads of families to take on lay ministries. Also in this category of practical concerns, they mention the need for adequate training, especially in areas of theology, church administration, and canon law. If lay ministers sometimes deviate from sound doctrine or sound ecclesial practice, it is often because the ministers are poorly instructed and perhaps unaware of official directives. Still another concern is that some priests are not at ease in working collaboratively with laypersons. It is a difficult art to exercise authority and at the same time avoid any taint of authoritarianism.

Among the more theoretical concerns are questions concerning the proper line of demarcation between the responsibilities of the hierarchy and laypeople in the Church. Two opposite excesses are possible: laicism and clericalism. Laicism so emphasizes baptism as to imagine that it confers all rights and powers in the Church, so that ordination would not be understood as giving any new sacramental and hierarchical powers. The clericalist deviation overemphasizes the value of ordination, with the result that the active powers conferred by baptism, confirmation, and matrimony are unduly minimized. Some Protestant Reformers of the sixteenth century gravitated toward laicism; Catholics in the Counter-Reformation era tended toward clericalism. Each of the two errors survives to some extent and could be documented in current Catholic literature.

The Second Vatican Council showed a viable path between the two extremes. In continuity with earlier councils, it taught that the powers of presiding at liturgical worship, teaching obligatory doctrine, and governing the people of God belong by divine right to the pope and the bishops, assisted by other members of the clergy. The laity, by virtue of their sacramental incorporation in the body of Christ, have a ministry to build up the Church under the supervision of the hierarchy, to bear witness to their faith, and to engage in the sanctification of the world. The council characterized the split between faith and daily life as one of the most serious errors of our time (*GS* 43). To correct this error, laypersons who live in the ordinary circumstances of the world must be made conscious of their Christian responsibilities.

Pope John Paul II gave special attention to the role of the laity in connection with missionary activity, re-evangelization, and the evangelization of cultures. "Their responsibility, in particular," he wrote, "is to testify how the Christian faith constitutes the only fully valid response—consciously perceived and stated by all in varying degrees—to the problems and hopes that life poses to every person and society. This will be possible if the lay faithful will know how to overcome in themselves the separation of the Gospel from life to take up again in their daily activities in family, work, and society, an integrated approach to life that is fully brought about by the inspiration and strength of the Gospel" (*CL* 34).

Although Vatican II has led to a gratifying expansion of lay ministries within the Church, the council's hopes that the lay faithful would find new motivation for evangelizing the world and transforming the temporal order according to the plan of God remain largely unfulfilled. Indeed, Catholic lay organizations are perhaps less vigorous today than they were before the council. Seeking to overcome any confessional isolation, all too many Catholics have become reluctant to support distinctively Christian and Catholic organizations.

Some authors contend that overemphasis on lay ministries is partly responsible for obscuring the secular mission of the laity, which the Second Vatican Council regarded as primary. In 1977 a group of Catholics based in Chicago issued a "Declaration of Concern" in which they complained that lay ministry since Vatican II had come to mean involvement in Church-related activities, such as religious education, pastoral care, and liturgical functions, with the result that the responsibility of the laity to transform political, economic, and social institutions had been devalued.[18] During the past few years, Mr. Russell Shaw has taken the same position in several books. The unwarranted attention given to lay ecclesial ministries, he says, in combination with other factors, has distracted the laity from what Vatican II described as their main function.[19]

It would be a mistake, I believe, to make a sharp dichotomy between ministry in the Church and apostolate in the world, as if it were necessary to choose between them. Lay ministries in the Church, properly conducted, can greatly help to offset the forces of secularism; they can form a Catholic people sufficiently united to Christ in prayer and sufficiently firm and well instructed in their faith to carry out the kinds of apostolate that Vatican II envisaged. Only if they are thoroughly imbued with Catholic values and properly informed about Catholic doctrine can lay Catholics be expected to bear witness confidently to the gospel in the complex world of our day. Lay ministers are desperately needed to enable our Catholic schools and parishes to fulfill their mission and to give quality service to the growing Catholic population. They can help fathers and mothers to live up to their duties in the Christian family; they can help Catholics in business, politics, and the professions to understand their religious opportunities and responsibilities. Well-trained ministers are needed to produce lay apostles, and likewise to foster vocations to the priesthood and the religious life, which are in short supply.

Ours is not a time for rivalry between clergy and laity, or between lay ministers and apostles to the world, as if what was given to the one were taken away from the other. Only through cooperation among all her members can the Church live up to her divine calling. Just as the eye cannot say to the ear, "I have no need of you," so the lay minister and the social reformer, the contemplative religious and the parish priest must say to each other: I need your witness and assistance to discern and live up to my own vocation in the Body of Christ. Because the lay faithful constitute the overwhelming majority of Catholics, the future of the Church lies predominantly in their hands. The recognition recently given to lay ecclesial ministries should help the laity to rise to the challenges and opportunities that are theirs today.

NOTES

1. Letter of Pius XI to Cardinal Bertram, November 13, 1928, in *Clergy and Laity: Official Catholic Teachings*, ed. Odile M. Liebard (Wilmington, N.C.: Mc-Grath, 1978), 30–34, at 31.

2. Pius XII, Address to New Cardinals, February 20, 1946; AAS 38 (1946): 149; quoted by John Paul II, apostolic exhortation *Christifideles laici*, 9.

3. Pius XII to World Congress of the Lay Apostolate, October 14, 1951, §29; ibid., 88–97, at 94.

4. Patrick Carey, "Lay Catholic Leadership in the United States," *U.S. Catholic Historian* 9 (1990): 223–47.

5. Yves Congar, *Lay People in the Church* (Westminster, Md.: Newman, 1957); French original: *Jalons pour une théologie du laïcat* (Paris: Cerf, 1953). Congar reports that the schema on the laity drawn up by Gérard Philips, and accepted by the Council, agreed with his own thinking. See Yves Congar, *Mon Journal au Concile* 1 (Paris: Cerf, 2002), 57.

6. Louis Ligier " 'Lay Ministries' and Their Foundations in the Documents of Vatican II," in *Vatican II: Assessments and Perspectives*, ed. René Latourelle, 3 vols. (New York: Paulist, 1989), 2:160–76.

7. Elissa Rinere, "Conciliar and Canonical Applications of 'Ministry' to the Laity," *Jurist* 47 (1987): 204–27.

8. Congregation of the Clergy and seven other Roman dicasteries, *Ecclesiae de Mysterio*; trans. "Some Questions Regarding Collaboration of Nonordained Faithful in Priests' Sacred Ministry," *Origins* 27 (November 27, 1997): 397–409, esp. 402–3.

9. For a thorough study, see John N. Collins, *Diakonia* (New York: Oxford University Press, 1990). Commenting on 1 Cor 12:4–5, he remarks that the ministries in question were either commissions handed out by church authorities or gifts received directly from God and recognized by the community or its leaders. Paul was not implying that anything a Christian undertook was, and should be recognized as, ministry (258–59).

10. Paul VI, apostolic letter *Ministeria quaedam* (1972) in *Vatican Council II: The Conciliar and Post Conciliar Documents*, ed. Austin Flannery (Northport, N.Y.: Costello, 1975), 427–32, at 429.

11. Paul VI, apostolic exhortation *Evangelii nuntiandi*, 73.

12. United States Bishops, "Called and Gifted: Catholic Laity 1980," *Origins* 10 (November 27, 1980): 369–73.

13. United States Bishops, "Called and Gifted for the Third Millennium," *Origins* 25 (November 30, 1995): 409–15.

14. United States Bishops, "Co-Workers in the Vineyard of the Lord: A Resource for Guiding the Development of Lay Ecclesial Ministry," *Origins* 35 (December 1, 2005): 404–27.

15. H. Richard McCord, "Lay Ecclesial Ministry: An Overview," *Origins* 35 (March 9, 2006): 625–29.

16. David DeLambo, *Lay Parish Ministers: A Study of Emerging Leadership* (New York: National Pastoral Life Center, 2005).

17. For two recent reactions to the National Pastoral Life Center Study, see Karen Sue Smith, "The Francis Next Door," *America* 194 (February 27, 2006): 8–11, and Paul Wilkes, "A Prediction Fulfilled," ibid., 12–14.

18. Chicago Declaration of Concern "On Devaluing the Laity," *Origins* 7 (December 29, 1977): 440–42.

19. Russell Shaw, *To Hunt, to Shoot, to Entertain* (San Francisco: Ignatius, 1993); *Ministry or Apostolate?* (Huntington, Ind.: Our Sunday Visitor, 2002); "What Should the Laity Be Doing?" *Crisis* 23 (December 2005): 23–25.

36

The Ignatian Charism at
the Dawn of the
Twenty-first Century

November 29, 2006

This lecture is intended to complete a series of four on the Jesuit founders whose jubilees are being celebrated this year. At Fordham we have had in 2006 one lecture on Saint Ignatius, one on Peter Faber, one on Francis Xavier, and now, to complete the series, a lecture on the Ignatian charism today.

The notion of the Ignatian charism requires some explanation. A charism is a gift of grace, conferred not for one's personal sanctification but for the benefit of others. Saint Paul has a famous list of charisms in the twelfth chapter of First Corinthians. They include the gifts of prophecy, speech, miracle-working, and speaking in tongues. If these are charisms bestowed on some members of the Church, what, if any, are charisms given to Saint Ignatius of Loyola? Who are the beneficiaries? Are these charisms still bestowed today? And if so, who are the recipients?

In what follows I shall speak principally of the gifts that Saint Ignatius possessed in an eminent way and that he expected to be applied and handed down with God's help in the Society he founded.

THE IGNATIAN VISION: THREE FOCI

The life of Saint Ignatius was remarkably focused. Beginning with his long convalescence at Loyola after being wounded at Pamplona, he was

---

led by God through a series of stages culminating in the foundation and organization of the Society of Jesus. The Society, when first officially established in 1540, had only ten members, including the inner circle of the three whose anniversaries we celebrate this year. All of them recognized without a shadow of doubt that the true founder of the Society of Jesus, under God, was none other than Ignatius. He was endowed with an extraordinary gift—a charism, one may say—of leadership. His primary achievement was the founding of a new religious order in many ways quite unlike any order that had previously existed. It was an order of men vowed to live in the midst of the world with their eyes continually focused on God, on Jesus Christ, and on the needs of the Church.

These three foci of the Ignatian vision are compactly expressed in the bull of Pope Paul III in 1540, confirmed by a similar bull of Julius III in 1550. Both these documents quoted in full the "Formula of the Institute" composed by Ignatius himself. The Formula begins with these lapidary words: "Whoever desires to serve as a soldier of God beneath the banner of the cross in our Society, which we desire to be designated by the name of Jesus, and to serve the Lord alone and the Church his Spouse, under the Roman pontiff, the vicar of Christ on earth, should, after a vow of perpetual chastity, poverty, and obedience, keep the following in mind."

The first feature of the Jesuit in this description is to be a soldier of God. Anyone who enters the Society, says the Formula, must "first of all keep before his eyes God and then the nature of this Institute which he has embraced and which is, so to speak, a pathway to God." According to his custom Ignatius here distinguishes between the means and the end. The end for which the Jesuit order exists is the greater glory of God. In the Constitutions he composed for the Society, Ignatius repeats the phrase *ad maiorem Dei gloriam* in the same or similar words 376 times. Because God is God, he deserves all the praise and service we can give him. The use of the comparative "greater" (*maiorem*) is significant. It signifies the desire to excel, to seek ever more (*magis*). What we have done and are presently doing is never enough.

The life of the Jesuit according to the Institute is in the second place centered on Jesus Christ, who is, in the phrase of Saint Ignatius, the way that leads to life.[1] The "Formula of the Institute" specifies that the Society is to be designated by the name of Jesus. Saint Ignatius never thought of himself as the head of the Jesuits. He wanted only to be a companion in the following of Jesus, the true head of the Society.

Saint Ignatius received a remarkable grace while praying at the chapel of La Storta, just outside Rome, in October 1537, together with Peter Faber and Diego Lainez. He was, as he declares, "very specially visited by the Lord" whom he saw carrying his cross on his shoulder in the presence of his Father, who said to Ignatius, "I want you to serve us." From that moment forth, Saint Ignatius never doubted that the Father had placed him with the Son; he insisted adamantly that the new Congregation ought to be called the Society of Jesus.[2]

Already in the meditation on the Two Standards in the *Spiritual Exercises*, written some years earlier, Ignatius had the retreatant ask for the grace to be received under the standard of Christ. And so in the "Formula of the Institute" he has those entering the Society express the desire to fight under the banner of the cross. This is a commitment to struggle ceaselessly against great odds and to fight bravely, not heeding the wounds, imitating the example of Christ, who embraced the cross to accomplish our redemption.

The third component is the ecclesial. Totally and unequivocally a man of the Church, Ignatius writes in the "Formula of the Institute" that the prospective Jesuit must be resolved to serve "the Lord alone and the Church his spouse." Here we may detect an echo of Ignatius's famous "Rules for Thinking with the Church," at the conclusion of the *Spiritual Exercises*, where he refuses to admit any discrepancy between the service of Christ and the Church. "I must be convinced," he writes, "that in Christ our Lord, the bridegroom, and in His spouse the Church, only one Spirit holds sway, which governs and rules for the salvation of souls."[3] The hierarchical and Roman Church, he says, is "the true Spouse of Christ our Lord, our holy Mother."[4]

Saint Ignatius's allegiance is not to some abstract idea of the Church but to the Church as it concretely exists on earth, with the Roman pontiff at its summit. The popes of Saint Ignatius's day may not have been the holiest and the wisest of men, but he looked upon them with the eyes of faith and saw in each of them the Vicar of Christ for the teaching and government of the universal Church. As early as 1534, when the original seven companions took their vows at Montmartre, they had the idea of placing themselves at the disposal of the pope, asking him to assign them to the missions he considered most pressing.[5] After the papal approval of the Institute in 1540, Ignatius established himself at Rome, where he spent the rest of his life in order to be available to the pope.

As yet I have stated the goal of the Society of Jesus in only the most general terms—the glory of God, the service of Christ, and availability to the pope. Ignatius still had to specify what kind of service his order would be prepared to offer. This too is mentioned in the "Formula of the Institute." In the sentence following the one I have quoted, Saint Ignatius writes that whoever wishes to enter should know he is asking to be "a member of a Society founded chiefly for this purpose: to strive especially for the defense and propagation of the faith and for the progress of souls in Christian life and doctrine." And then he mentions various means whereby these goals are to be achieved: "public preaching, other ministries of the word of God, spiritual exercises, education in Christianity, hearing confessions, and administering other sacraments." And then in the next sentence the Formula speaks of certain works of charity: reconciling the estranged, ministering to persons in prisons and hospitals, and similar services.

Principles for the Society of Jesus

A number of attempts have been made in recent years to gather up certain principles that shine through the writings of Saint Ignatius and are envisaged as permanent features of the Society he founded.[6] Any such list presupposes, of course, the common elements of all religious orders in the Catholic Church, including the faithful observance of the usual vows of religion: poverty, chastity, and obedience. The following ten features may serve as a summary of what is more specific to the spirit of Saint Ignatius.

1. Dedication to the glory of God, the "ever greater God," whom we can never praise and serve enough. This gives the Jesuit a kind of holy restlessness, a ceaseless effort to do better, to achieve the more or, in Latin, the *magis*. Ignatius may be said to have been a God-intoxicated man in the sense that he made "the greater glory of God" the supreme norm of every action, great or small.

2. Personal love for Jesus Christ and a desire to be counted among his close companions. Repeatedly in the *Exercises*, Jesuits pray to know Christ more clearly, to love him more dearly, and to follow him more nearly. Preaching in the towns of Italy, the first companions deliberately imitated the style of life of the disciples whom Jesus had sent forth to evangelize the towns of Galilee.

3. To labor with, in, and for the Church, thinking at all times with the Church in obedience to its pastors. Throughout the Constitutions, Ignatius insists on the teaching of the doctrine that is "safer and more approved," so that students may learn the "more solid and safe doctrine."[7]

4. Availability. To be at the disposal of the Church, ready to labor in any place, for the sake of the greater and more universal good. Regarding the Society as the spiritual militia of the pope, Saint Ignatius sees the whole world, so to speak, as his field of operations. Inspired by this cosmic vision, he admits no divisions based on national frontiers or ethnic ties.

5. Mutual union. Jesuits are to see themselves as parts of a body bound together by a communion of minds and hearts. In the Constitutions, Saint Ignatius asserted that the Society could not attain its ends unless its members were united by deep affection among themselves and with the head.[8] Many authors quote in this connection the term Ignatius used of his first companions: "friends in the Lord."

6. Preference for spiritual and priestly ministries. The Jesuits are a priestly order, all of whose professed members must be ordained, although the cooperation of spiritual and lay coadjutors is highly valued. In the choice of ministries, Ignatius writes, "spiritual goods ought to be preferred to bodily," since they are more conducive to the "ultimate and supernatural end."[9]

7. Discernment. Ignatius was a master of the practical life and the art of decision making. He distinguished carefully between ends and means, choosing the means best suited to achieve the end in view. In the use of means he consistently applied the principle *tantum . . . quantum*, meaning "as much as helps," but not more. In this connection he teaches the discipline of indifference in the sense of detachment from anything that is not to be sought for its own sake.

8. Adaptability. Ignatius always paid close attention to the times, places, and persons with which he was dealing. He took care to frame general laws in such a way as to allow for flexibility in application.

9. Respect for human and natural capacities. Although he relied primarily on spiritual means, such as divine grace, prayer, and sacramental ministry, he took account of natural abilities, learning, culture, and manners, as gifts to be used for the service and glory of God. For this reason he showed a keen interest in education.

10. An original synthesis of the active and the contemplative life. Jerome Nadal spoke of the Jesuit practice "of seeking a perfection in our

prayer and spiritual exercises in order to help our neighbor, and by means of that help of neighbor acquiring yet more perfection in prayer, in order to help our neighbor even more." According to Nadal, it is a special grace of the whole Society to be contemplative not only in moments of withdrawal but also in the midst of action, thus "seeking God in all things."[10]

DIRECTIVES OF RECENT POPES

In view of my assignment to speak of the Ignatian charism today, I shall shift immediately to the twentieth century and to the years since the Second Vatican Council. The popes, as the highest superiors of all Jesuits, have given us wise directives regarding the application of our Jesuit charism to the needs of the day. They have addressed each of the four General Congregations held since 1965. On the theory that the charism of the Society is correlative with its mission, I shall particularly examine the injunctions of recent popes.

Addressing the Thirty-first General Congregation on May 7, 1966, Pope Paul VI congratulated the Society for being "the legion ever faithful to the task of protecting the Catholic faith and the Apostolic See." He took the occasion to charge the Jesuits with a new mission: to make a "stout, united stand against atheism," which was rapidly spreading at the time, "frequently masquerading as cultural, scientific, or social progress."

In an address to the second session of the same congregation on November 16, 1966, Paul VI raised questions about whether some Jesuits were accepting naturalistic norms for their apostolate and weakening in that traditional loyalty to the Holy See which had been so dear to Saint Ignatius. In its Decree on the Mission of the Society today, General Congregation 31 accepted the mandate to confront atheism and offered the Society completely to the Church under the direction of the pope.

In his address to the Thirty-second General Congregation on December 3, 1974, Pope Paul VI referred to the "vocation and charism proper to Jesuits," transmitted by an unbroken tradition, which includes conformity to the will of God and that of the Church. In a valuable analysis, he reminded Jesuits of their fourfold vocation: to be religious, to be apostolic, to be priests, and to be united with the bishop of Rome. He admonished them not to be seduced by the dazzling perspective of worldly humanism and the pursuit of novelty for its own sake. In subsequent correspondence he renewed his earlier warnings that the Society of Jesus should retain its religious and priestly character and avoid ways of action more appropriate to secular institutes and lay movements. The role of ordained Jesuits, he said, should be clearly distinct from the role of laity.

In response, the Thirty-second General Congregation strongly reaffirmed the Society's reverence and loyalty to the Holy See and to the magisterium of the Church. It underlined the sacerdotal (or priestly) character of the Society, while recognizing the value of the contribution of lay coadjutors.

Pope John Paul II on September 2, 1983, delivered a homily to the Thirty-third General Congregation. The Ignatian spirit, he said, is a special charism that makes the Society of Jesus a privileged instrument of the Church's action at all levels. After repeating the mandate of Paul VI to resist atheism, he spoke of the danger of confusing the tasks proper to priests with those of the laity. "Intimate knowledge, strong love, and closer following of the Lord," he said, "are the soul of your vocation" (83).

John Paul II in his allocution to General Congregation 34 on January 5, 1995, spoke of the singular charism of fidelity to the Successor of Peter, which marks out the Society of Jesus as being "totally and without reservation of the Church, in the Church, and for the Church." The charism of the Society, he said, should make Jesuits witnesses to the primacy of God and his will, which points to the primacy of spirituality and prayer. He asked that Jesuits, seeking to follow the leadership of Saint Francis Xavier in missionary evangelization, be in the forefront of the new evangelization, promoting a deep interior relationship with Jesus Christ, the first evangelizer. In their universities, His Holiness said, Jesuits should teach clear, solid, organic knowledge of Catholic doctrine. They should be very attentive not to confuse their students by questionable teachings at variance with the Church's doctrine on faith and morals.

Benedict XVI in a speech of April 22, 2006, celebrating the current jubilee year, exhorted the Society to continue in its tradition of imparting solid training in philosophy and theology as a basis for dialogue with modern culture. The Society of Jesus, he said, enjoys an extraordinary legacy in the holiness of Saint Ignatius, the missionary zeal of Francis Xavier, and the apostolate of Peter Faber among leaders of the Reformation. In many of his addresses this pope has aligned himself with Paul VI and John Paul II by insisting that the primary and indispensable task of the priest is to be an expert in the spiritual life and a witness to the truth of revelation. The promotion of justice in society, he believes, is primarily a responsibility of the laity.

CONTEMPORARY CHALLENGES

The challenges of our day are certainly different from those of the sixteenth century, but they are, I believe, analogous, and for this reason, I would contend, the Society is well positioned to deal with them. Its charism is by no means outdated.

The sixteenth century, like our own, was a time of rapid and radical cultural change. That time witnessed the rise of anthropocentric humanism, the birth of the secular State, and the autonomy of the social and physical sciences. Jesuits who have studied their own tradition have stellar examples of scholars who equipped themselves to enter into these new fields and show the coherence between the new learning and the Catholic heritage of faith. We have only to think of the economic and legal philosophy of Luis de Molina and Juan de Lugo, the astronomical achievements of Christopher Clavius, the atomic theories of Roger Boscovich, and the pioneering ideas of so many other Jesuit experts in the physical and social sciences. They spoke incisively to the problems of their day, building bridges between faith and reason, between theology and science. In our day some Jesuits are venturing into questions concerning cosmic and human origins and into complex problems of biochemistry and genetic engineering, all of which are so vital for the future of faith and morals.

The sixteenth century, as the great age of discovery, had early experiences of globalization. Eager to evangelize the whole world, Jesuits were leaders in the missionary apostolate to the Americas, to parts of Africa, to India and the Far East. They not only sent missionaries but also trained them to present the gospel in a manner suited to the cultures of various peoples. Francis Xavier is the most famous, but he was by no means alone. Matteo Ricci and Roberto de Nobili are only two of dozens of outstanding missionaries who preached the gospel in an inculturated form, inspired by the principles of Saint Ignatius.

Proclamation in an accommodated style is not less needed today than in the past. The fields are white for the harvest, but the laborers are few.

Who can better fill the urgent demand for priests to proclaim the gospel and administer the sacraments in continents like Africa, where conversions to Christianity are so numerous and so rapid? Indigenous Jesuits in the young churches, if they are well trained, can take up the task left to them by foreign missionaries.

The age of Ignatius was no stranger to the clash of civilizations. The Muslim world and the Christian world were engaged in incessant warfare. Jews were being mistreated and persecuted in many countries. Jesuit missionaries protested against the injustices of colonial powers and encountered fierce opposition from the existing religious establishment in practically every country they evangelized. In the course of time, they became leaders in interreligious dialogue. Missionaries learned to respect the good things in native cultures while sifting out the chaff. That is still a task of great urgency today. Jesuits have in their tradition rich resources for learning how and how not to deal with non-Christian religions. Bloody conflict and useless provocation must be avoided, while, on the other hand, Christians must frankly oppose elements in every religion and every culture that promote superstition or injustice.

The sixteenth century saw the division of Western Christianity between the Protestant nations of northern Europe and the Catholic nations of the south. The Jesuits, few though they were in number, accomplished great things by their energy and heroism. Peter Faber did extraordinary work to stem the tide of heresy in Germany and the Low Countries. He inspired Peter Canisius and a host of others to go forward in his footsteps. One wonders what the Jesuits of those days would do if they were alive today to see the defection of so many Latino Catholics from the Church in the United States and in Central and South America. The need is evident; the principles are clear, but there are all too few talented candidates to take up the task.

Centralization of the Church was imperative in the days of Saint Ignatius. He himself clearly perceived the need for the papacy as the headquarters of the universal Church. He saw that Catholicism must be universal and that nationalism and ethnocentrism could have no place in it. He founded a Society made up of Spaniards, Portuguese, Frenchmen, Germans, Italians, Englishmen, and many others who worked together in an undivided apostolate under the direction of a single general superior. One of the great blessings of the Society of Jesus, today as in the past, is its worldwide horizon. Jesuits are "friends in the Lord" undivided by distinctions of nationality, ethnic origin, or social class.

A great weakness of the Church in the Europe of Saint Ignatius's day was ignorance of the faith. Many priests were barely literate, and the laity in some countries did not know the basic elements of the creed. Rather than complain and denounce, Ignatius preferred to build. Popular education, he perceived, was on the rise. Taking advantage of the new desire for learning, Ignatius quickly set about founding schools, colleges, and seminaries. The pedagogical efforts of the Jesuits in the past count among their greatest services to the Church. Their educational institutions, I believe, are still among the major blessings that the Society of Jesus offers to the Church and to the culture at large.

Jesuits in the past have entered deeply into the intellectual apostolate. Many were leaders in practical sciences such as political theory. They can look back on a great tradition extending from Francisco Suárez in the sixteenth century to John Courtney Murray in the twentieth. Nothing suggests that this type of research has lost its relevance. The Church needs loyal and devoted scholars who will carry this kind of reflection further, in view of new and developing situations. Here again the Society has much to contribute if sufficient numbers will hear the call.

In the sixteenth century, the Society of Jesus was at the vanguard of the Church in dealing with the problems posed by the Protestant Reformation, by the new science, and by access to new continents which had been beyond the awareness of Europeans in the past. Today the Church is confronted with mounting secularism, dramatic advances in technology, growing globalization, and multiple clashes of cultures. If anyone should ask whether these developments render the Ignatian charisms obsolete, I would reply with an emphatic No.

The Society can be abreast of the times if it adheres to its original purpose and ideals. The term *Jesuit* is often misunderstood. Not to mention enemies for whom *Jesuit* is a term of opprobrium, friends of the Society sometimes identify the term with independence of thought and corporate pride, both of which Saint Ignatius deplored. Others reduce the Jesuit trademark to a matter of educational techniques, such as the personal care of students, concern for the whole person, rigor in thought, and eloquence in expression. These qualities are estimable and have a basis in the teaching of Saint Ignatius. But they omit any consideration of the fact that the Society of Jesus is an order of vowed religious in the

Catholic Church. They are bound by special allegiance to the pope, the bishop of Rome. And above all, it needs to be mentioned that the Society of Jesus is primarily about a person: Jesus, the Redeemer of the world. If the Society were to lose its special devotion to the Lord (which, I firmly trust, will never happen) it would indeed be obsolete. It would be like salt that had lost its savor.

The greatest need of the Society of Jesus, I believe, is to be able to project a clearer vision of its purpose. Its members are engaged in such diverse activities that its unity is obscured. In this respect the recent popes have rendered great assistance. Paul VI helpfully reminded Jesuits that they are a religious order, not a secular institute; that they are a priestly order, not a lay association; that they are apostolic, not monastic, and that they are bound to obedience to the pope, not wholly self-directed.

Pope John Paul II, in directing Jesuits to engage in the new evangelization, identified a focus that perfectly matches the founding idea of the Society. Ignatius was adamant in insisting that it be named for Jesus, its true head. The *Spiritual Exercises* are centered on the Gospels. Evangelization is exactly what the first Jesuits did as they conducted missions in the towns of Italy. They lived lives of evangelical poverty. Evangelization was the sum and substance of what Saint Francis Xavier accomplished in his arduous missionary journeys. And evangelization is at the heart of all Jesuit apostolates in teaching, in research, in spirituality, and in the social apostolate. Evangelization, moreover, is what the world most sorely needs today. The figure of Jesus Christ in the Gospels has not lost its attraction. Who should be better qualified to present that figure today than members of the Society that bears his name?

NOTES

1. *The First and General Examen*, §101, in *The Constitutions of the Society of Jesus*, by George E. Ganss, S.J. (St. Louis: Institute of Jesuit Sources, 1970), 75–109, at 108.

2. Pedro Arrupe, "Our Way of Proceeding," in *The Spiritual Legacy of Pedro Arrupe, S.J.* (Rome: Jesuit Curia, 1985), 43–85, at 105–6.

3. Ignatius of Loyola, *Spiritual Exercises*, §365.

4. Ibid., §353.

5. Paul Dudon, Saint *Ignatius of Loyola* (Milwaukee: Bruce, 1949), 154.

6. For example, General Congregation 34, Decree 26, "Characteristics of Our Way of Proceeding"; also Arrupe, "Our Way of Proceeding."

7. Constitutions, §358, §464.
8. Ibid., §655.
9. Ibid., §623b, §813.
10. Arrupe, "Our Way of Proceeding," 50; GC 34, Decree 26, §6.

37

Evolution, Atheism, and Religious Belief

April 17, 2007

John Paul II: From Conflict to Dialogue

During the second half of the nineteenth century, it became rather common to speak of a warfare between science and religion.[1] In the course of the twentieth century, the hostility gradually subsided. At the beginning of his pontificate, John Paul II, following in the footsteps of the Second Vatican Council, established a commission to review and correct the condemnation of Galileo at his trial of 1633. In 1983 he held a conference celebrating the 350th anniversary of the publication of Galileo's *Dialogues Concerning Two New Sciences*, at which he remarked that the experience of the Galileo case had led the Church "to a more mature attitude and a more accurate grasp of the authority proper to her," enabling her better to distinguish between "essentials of the faith" and the "scientific systems of a given age."[2]

On September 21–26, 1987, the pope sponsored a study week on science and religion at Castel Gandolfo. On June 1, 1988, reflecting on the results of this conference, he sent a very positive and encouraging letter to the director of the Vatican Observatory steering a middle course between a separation and a fusion of the disciplines. He recommended a program of dialogue and interaction, in which the disciplines would neither seek to supplant each other nor would they ignore each other. They should search together for a more thorough understanding of one another's competencies and limitations and especially for common ground. Science should not try to become religion, nor should religion seek to take the place of science. Science can purify religion from error and superstition, while religion purifies science from idolatry and false absolutes. Each discipline should therefore retain its integrity and yet be open to the insights and discoveries of the other.[3]

In a widely noticed message on evolution to the Pontifical Academy of Sciences, sent on October 22, 1996, John Paul II noted that, while there are several theories of evolution, the fact of the evolution of the human body from lower forms of life is "more than a hypothesis." But human life, he insisted, was separated from all that is less than human by an "ontological difference." The spiritual soul, said the pope, does not simply emerge from the forces of living matter nor is it a mere epiphenomenon of matter. Faith enables us to affirm that the human soul is immediately created by God.[4]

SCHÖNBORN'S INTERVENTION

The pope was interpreted in some circles as having accepted the neo-Darwinian view that evolution is sufficiently explained by random mutations and natural selection (or "survival of the fittest") without any kind of governing purpose or finality. Seeking to offset this misreading, Cardinal Christoph Schönborn, the archbishop of Vienna, published on July 7, 2005, an op-ed piece in the *New York Times* in which he quoted a series of pronouncements of John Paul II to the contrary. For example, the pope declared at a general audience of July 19, 1985, "The evolution of human beings, of which science seeks to determine the stages and discern the mechanism, presents an internal finality which arouses admiration. This finality, which directs beings in a direction for which they are not responsible, obliges one to suppose a Mind which is its inventor, its creator." In this connection the pope said that to ascribe human evolution to sheer chance would be an abdication of human intelligence.[5]

Cardinal Schönborn was also able to cite Pope Benedict XVI, who stated in his inauguration Mass as pope on April 24, 2005: "We are not some casual and meaningless product of evolution. Each of us is the result of a thought of God. Each of us is willed, each of us is loved, each of us is necessary."[6]

Many readers interpreted Cardinal Schönborn's article as a rejection of evolution. Some letters to the editor accused him of favoring a retrograde form of creationism and contradicting John Paul II. They seemed unable to grasp the fact that he was speaking the language of classical philosophy and was not opting for any particular scientific position. His critique was directed against those neo-Darwinists who pronounced on philosophical and theological questions by the methods of natural science.

Several Catholic experts on biology, such as Kenneth R. Miller and Stephen M. Barr, in their replies to Schönborn, insisted that one could be a neo-Darwinist in science and an orthodox Christian believer. Distinguishing different levels of knowledge, they contended that what is random from a scientific point of view is included in God's eternal plan. God, so to speak, rolls the dice but is able by his comprehensive knowledge to foresee the result from all eternity.

This combination of Darwinism in science and theism in theology may be sustainable, but it is not the position Schönborn intended to attack. As he made clear in a subsequent article for *First Things* (January 2006), he was taking exception only to those neo-Darwinists—and they are many—who maintain that no valid investigation of nature could be conducted except in the reductive mode of mechanism, which seeks to explain everything in terms of quantity, matter, and motion, excluding specific differences and purpose in nature.[7] He quoted one such neo-Darwinist as stating: "Modern science directly implies that the world is organized strictly in accordance with deterministic principles or chance. There are no purposive principles whatsoever in nature. There are no gods and no designing forces rationally detectable."[8]

Cardinal Schönborn shrewdly observes that positivistic scientists begin by methodically excluding formal and final causes. Having then described natural processes in terms of merely efficient and material causality, they turn around and reject every other kind of explanation. They simply disallow the questions about why anything (including human life) exists, how we differ in nature from irrational animals, and how we ought to conduct our lives.

THE ATHEIST ASSAULT

During the past few years there has been a new burst of atheistic literature that claims the authority of science, and especially Darwinist theories of evolution, to demonstrate that it is irrational to believe in God. The titles of some of these books are very revealing: *The End of Faith*, by Sam Harris; *Breaking the Spell: Religion as a Natural Phenomenon*, by Daniel Dennett (2006); *The God Delusion*, by Richard Dawkins (2006); *God: the Failed Hypothesis*, by Victor J. Stenger (2007); and *God Is Not Great: How Religion Poisons Everything*, by Christopher Hitchens (2007). The new atheists are writing with the enthusiasm of evangelists propagating the gospel of irreligion.

These writers generally agree in holding that evidence, understood in the scientific sense, is the only valid ground for belief. Science performs objective observations by eye and by instrument; it builds models or hypotheses to account for the observed phenomena. It then tests the hypotheses by deducing consequences and seeing whether they can be verified or falsified by experiment. All worldly phenomena are presumed to be explicable by reference to inner-worldly bodies and forces. Unless God were a verifiable hypothesis tested by scientific method, they hold, there would be no ground for religious belief.[9]

Richard Dawkins, a leading spokesman for this new antireligion, may be taken as representative of the class. The proofs for the existence of God, he believes, are all invalid, since among other defects they leave unanswered the question "Who made God?"[10] "Faith," he writes, "is the great cop-out, the great excuse to evade the need to think and evaluate evidence. . . . Faith, being belief that isn't based on evidence, is the principal vice in any religion."[11] Carried away by his own ideology, he speaks of "the fatuousness of the religiously indoctrinated mind."[12] He makes the boast that in the quest to explain the nature of human life and of the universe in which we find ourselves, religion "is now completely superseded by science."[13]

Dawkins's understanding of religious faith as an irrational commitment strikes the Catholic as very strange. The First Vatican Council condemned fideism, the doctrine that faith is irrational. It insisted that faith is and must be in harmony with reason. John Paul II developed the same idea in his encyclical on *Faith and Reason*, and Benedict XVI, in his Regensburg academic lecture of September 12, 2006, insisted on the necessary harmony between faith and reason. In that context he called for a recovery of reason in its full range, offsetting the tendency of modern science to limit reason to the empirically verifiable.[14]

CHRISTIAN DARWINISM

Catholics who are expert in the biological sciences take several different positions on evolution. As I have already indicated, one group, while explaining evolution in terms of random mutations and survival of the fittest, accepts the Darwinist account as accurate on the scientific level, but rejects Darwinism as a philosophical system. This first group holds that God, eternally foreseeing all the products of evolution, uses the natural process of evolution to work out his creative plan. Following Fred Hoyle, some members of this group speak of the "anthropic principle," meaning that the universe was "fine-tuned" from the first moment of creation to allow the emergence of human life.[15]

A recent example of this point of view may be found in the 2006 book of Francis S. Collins, *The Language of God.* Collins, a world-renowned expert on genetics and microbiology, was raised without any religious belief and became a Christian after finishing his education in chemistry, biology, and medicine. His professional knowledge in these fields convinced him that the beauty and symmetry of human genes and genomes strongly testifies in favor of a wise and loving Creator. But God, he believes, does not need to intervene in the process of bodily evolution. Collins holds for a theory of theistic evolutionism which he designates as the "BioLogos" position. Although he is not a Catholic, he approvingly refers to the views of Pope John Paul II on evolution in his 1996 message to the Pontifical Academy of Sciences, to which I have already referred. He builds on the work of the Anglican priest Arthur Peacock, who has written a book with the title *Evolution: the Disguised Friend of Faith.* He quotes with satisfaction the words of President Bill Clinton, who declared at a White House celebration of the Human Genome Project in June 2000, "Today we are learning the language in which God created life. We are gaining ever more awe for the complexity, the beauty, and the wonder of God's most divine and sacred gift."[16]

Theistic evolutionism, like classical Darwinism, refrains from asserting any divine intervention in the process of evolution. It concedes that the emergence of living bodies, including the human, can be accounted for on the empirical level by random mutations and survival of the fittest. But theistic evolutionism rejects the atheistic conclusions of Dawkins and his cohorts. The physical sciences, it maintains, are not the sole acceptable source of truth and certitude. Science has a real though limited competence. It can tell us a great deal about the processes that can be observed or controlled by the senses and by instruments, but it has no way of answering deeper questions involving reality as a whole. Far from being able to replace religion, it cannot begin to tell us what brought the world into existence, nor why the world exists, nor what our ultimate destiny is, nor how we should act in order to be the kind of persons we ought to be.

Viewed as a scientific system, Darwinism has some attractive features. Its great advantage is its simplicity. Ignoring the specific differences between different types of being and the purposes for which they act, Darwinism of this type reduces the whole process of evolution to matter and motion. On its own level it produces plausible explanations that seem to satisfy many practicing scientists.

INTELLIGENT DESIGN

Notwithstanding these advantages, Darwinism has not triumphed, even in the scientific field. An important school of scientists supports a theory known as intelligent design. Michael Behe, a professor at Lehigh University, contends that certain organs of living beings are "irreducibly complex." Their formation could not take place by small random mutations, because something that had only some but not all the features of the new organ would have no reason for existence and no advantage for survival. It would make no sense, for example, for the pupil of the eye to evolve if there were no retina to accompany it, and vice versa, it would be nonsensical for there to be a retina with no pupil. As a showcase example of a complex organ all of whose parts are interdependent, Behe proposes the bacterial flagellum, a marvelous swimming device used by some bacteria.[17]

At this point we get into a very technical dispute among microbiologists that I will not attempt to adjudicate. In favor of Behe and his school, we may say that the possibility of major sudden changes effected by a higher intelligence should not be antecedently ruled out. But we may take it as a sound principle that God does not intervene in the created order without necessity. If the production of organs such as the bacterial flagellum can be explained by the gradual accumulation of minor random variations, the Darwinist explanation should be preferred. As a matter of policy, it is imprudent to build one's case for faith on what science has not yet explained, because tomorrow it may be able to explain what it cannot explain today. History teaches us that the "God of the gaps" often proves to be an illusion.

THE RECOVERY OF TELEOLOGY

Darwinism is criticized by yet a third school of critics, including philosophers such as Michael Polanyi, who builds on the work of Henri Bergson and Pierre Teilhard de Chardin. Philosophers of this orientation, notwithstanding their mutual differences, agree that biological organisms cannot be understood by the laws of mechanics alone. The laws of biology, without in any way contradicting those of physics and chemistry, are more complex. The behavior of living organisms cannot be explained without taking into account their striving for life and growth. Plants, by reaching out for sunlight and nourishment, betray an intrinsic aspiration to live and grow. This internal finality makes them capable of success and failure in ways that stones and minerals are not. Because of the ontological gap that separates the living from the nonliving, the emergence of life cannot be accounted for on the basis of purely mechanical principles. In tune with this school of thought, the English mathematical physicist John Polkinghorne holds that Darwinism is incapable of explaining why multicellular plants and animals arise when single cellular organisms seem to cope with the environment quite successfully.[18] There must be in the universe a thrust toward higher and more complex forms.

The Georgetown professor John F. Haught, in a recent defense of the same point of view, points out that natural science achieves exact results by restricting itself to measurable phenomena, ignoring deeper questions about meaning and purpose. By its method it filters out subjectivity, feeling, and striving, all of which are essential to a full theory of cognition. Materialistic Darwinism is incapable of explaining why the universe gives rise to subjectivity, feeling, and striving.[19]

The Thomist philosopher Étienne Gilson vigorously contended in his book *From Aristotle to Darwin and Back Again* that Francis Bacon and others perpetrated a philosophical error when they eliminated two of Aristotle's four causes from the purview of science. They sought to explain everything in mechanistic terms, referring only to material and efficient causes and discarding formal and final causality.[20]

Without the form, or formal cause, it would be impossible to account for the unity and specific identity of any substance. In the human composite the form is the spiritual soul, which makes the organism a single entity and gives it its human character. Once the form is lost, the material elements decompose, and the body ceases to be human. It would be futile, therefore, to try to define human beings in terms of their bodily components alone.

Final causality, as I have already suggested, is particularly important in the realm of living organisms. The organs of the animal or human body are not intelligible except in terms of their purpose or finality. The brain is not intelligible without reference to the faculty of thinking that is its purpose, nor is the eye intelligible without reference to the function of seeing.

These three schools of thought are all sustainable in a Christian philosophy of nature. Although I incline toward the third, I recognize that well qualified experts profess theistic Darwinism and intelligent design, respectively.

The Hand of God

All three of these Christian perspectives on evolution affirm that God plays an essential role in the process, but they conceive of God's role in different ways. According to the first view, theistic Darwinism, God initiates the process by producing from the first instant of creation (the "Big Bang") the matter and energies that will gradually develop into vegetable, animal, and eventually human life on this earth and perhaps elsewhere. According to the second view, intelligent design, the development does not occur without divine intervention at certain stages, producing irreducibly complex organs. According to the third view, the teleological, the forward thrust of evolution and its breakthroughs into higher grades of being depend on the dynamic presence of God to his creation. Many adherents of this school would say that the transition from physico-chemical existence to biological life, and the further transitions to animal and human life, require a new exercise of divine creative causality.

Much of the scientific community seems to be fiercely opposed to any theory that would bring God actively in the process of evolution, as the second and third theories do. Christian Darwinists run the risk of conceding too much to their atheistic colleagues. They may be overinclined to grant that the whole process of emergence takes place without the involvement of any higher agency. Theologians must ask whether it is acceptable to banish God from his creation in this fashion.

Several centuries ago, a group of philosophers known as deists excogitated a theory that God had created the universe and ceased at that point to have any further influence. Most Christians firmly disagreed, holding that God continues to act in history. In the course of centuries he gave revelations to his prophets; he worked miracles; he sent his own Son to become a man; he raised Jesus from the dead. If God is so active in the supernatural order, producing effects that are publicly observable, it is difficult to rule out on principle all interventions in the process of evolution. Why should God be capable of creating the world from nothing but incapable of acting within the world he has made? The tendency today is to say that creation was not complete at the origins of the universe but continues as the universe develops in complexity.

Phillip Johnson, a leader in the intelligent design movement, accused the Christian Darwinists of falling into an updated deism, exiling God "to the shadowy realm before the Big Bang," where he "must do nothing that might cause trouble between theists and scientific naturalists."[21]

The Catholic Church has consistently maintained that the human soul is not a product of any biological cause, but is immediately created by God. This doctrine, to my mind, raises the question whether God is not necessarily involved in the fashioning of the human body, since the human body comes to be when the soul is infused. The advent of the human soul makes the body correlative with it and therefore human. Even though it may be difficult for the scientist to detect the point at which the evolving body passes from the anthropoid to the human, it would be absurd for a brute animal—say, a chimpanzee—to possess a body perfectly identical with the human.[22]

SOURCES OF RELIGIOUS BELIEF

Atheistic scientists often write as though the only valid manner of reasoning is that current in modern science: to make precise observations and measurements of phenomena, to frame hypotheses to account for the data, and to confirm or disconfirm the hypotheses by experiments. I find it hard to imagine anyone coming to belief in God by this route.

It is true, of course, that the beauty and order of nature has often moved people to believe in God as creator. The eternal power and majesty of God, says St. Paul, is manifest to all from the things God has made (Rom 1:20). To the people of Lystra, Paul proclaimed that God has never left himself without witness, "for he did good and gave you from heaven rains and fruitful seasons, satisfying your hearts with food and gladness" (Acts 14:17). Christian philosophers have fashioned rigorous proofs based on these spontaneous insights. But these deductive proofs do not rely upon modern scientific method.

It may be of interest that the scientist Francis Collins came to believe in God not so much from contemplating the beauty and order of creation—impressive though it is—as because of moral and religious experience. His reading of C. S. Lewis convinced him that there is a higher moral law to which we are unconditionally subject, and that the only possible source of that law is a personal God. Lewis also taught him to trust the natural instinct by which the human heart reaches out ineluctably to the infinite and the divine. Every other natural appetite—such as those for food, sex, and knowledge—has a real object. Why, then, should the yearning for God be the exception?

To believe in God is natural, and the belief can be confirmed by philosophical proofs. Yet Christians generally believe in God, I suspect, not because of these proofs but rather because they revere the person of Jesus, who teaches us about God by his words and actions. It would not be possible to be a follower of Jesus and an atheist.

Critics of theism, such as Dawkins, Harris, Stenger, and Hitchens seem to know very little of the spiritual experience of believers. As Terry Eagleton wrote in his review of Dawkins's *The God Delusion*:

> Imagine someone holding forth on biology whose only knowledge is the *Book of British Birds*, and you have a rough idea of what it feels like to read Richard Dawkins on theology. . . . If card carrying rationalists like Dawkins [were asked] to pass judgment on the geopolitics of South Africa, they would no doubt bone up on the question as assiduously as they could. When it comes to theology, however, any shoddy old travesty will pass muster.[23]

Some contemporary scientific atheists are so caught up in the methodology of their discipline that they imagine it must be the only method for solving every problem. But other methods are needed for grappling with questions of another order. Science and technology, which is its offspring, are totally inadequate in the field of morality. While science and technology vastly increase human power, power is ambivalent. It can accomplish good or evil; the same inventions can be constructive or destructive. The tendency of science, when it gains the upper hand, is to do whatever lies within its capacity, without regard for any moral constraints. As we have experienced in recent generations, technology uncontrolled by moral standards, has visited untold horrors on the world. To distinguish between the right and wrong use of power, and to motivate human beings to do what is right even when it does not suit their convenience, requires recourse to moral and religious norms. The biddings of conscience make it clear that we are inescapably under a higher law that requires us to behave in certain ways, and judges us guilty if we disobey it. We would turn in vain to scientists to inform us about this higher law.

Some evolutionists contend that morality and religion arise, evolve, and persist according to Darwinian principles. Religion, they say, has survival value for individuals and communities. But this alleged survival value, even if it be real, tells us nothing about the truth or falsity of any moral or religious system. Since questions of this higher order cannot be answered by science, philosophy and theology still have an essential role to play.

Justin Barrett, an evolutionary psychologist now at Oxford, is also a practicing Christian. He believes that an all-knowing, all-powerful, and perfectly good God crafted human beings to be in loving relationship with him and with one another. "Why wouldn't God," he asks, "design us in such a way as to find belief in divinity quite natural?" Even if these mental phenomena can be explained scientifically, the psychological explanation does not mean that we should stop believing. "Suppose that science produces a convincing account for why I think my wife loves me," he writes, "should I then stop believing that she does?"[24]

A metaphysics of knowledge can take us further in the quest for religious truth. It can give reasons for thinking that the natural tendency to believe in God, manifest among all peoples, does not exist in vain. Biology and psychology can examine the phenomena from below. But theology sees them from above, as the work of God calling us to himself in the depths of our being. We are, so to speak, programmed to seek eternal life in union with God, the personal source and goal of everything that is true and good. This natural desire to gaze upon him, while it may be suppressed for a time, cannot be eradicated.

CONCLUSION

Science can cast a brilliant light on the processes of nature and can vastly increase human power over the environment. Rightly used, it can notably improve the conditions of life here on earth. Future scientific discoveries about evolution will presumably enrich religion and theology, since God reveals himself through the book of nature as well as through redemptive history. Science, however, performs a disservice when it claims to be the only valid form of knowledge, displacing the esthetic, the interpersonal, the philosophical, and the religious. The recent outburst of atheistic scientism is an ominous sign. If unchecked, this arrogance could lead to a resumption of the senseless warfare that raged in the nineteenth century, thus undermining the harmony of different levels of knowledge that has been foundational to our Western civilization. By contrast, the kind of dialogue between evolutionary science and theology proposed by Pope John Paul II can overcome the alienation and lead to authentic progress both for science and for religion.

NOTES

1. John William Draper, *History of the Conflict between Religion and Science* (New York: D. Appleton, 1874); Andrew Dickson White, *The Warfare of Science and Theology in Christendom* (New York: D. Appleton, 1896).

2. John Paul II, "A Papal Address on the Church and Science," *Origins* 13 (June 2, 1983): 49–53, quotation from 51.

3. John Paul II, "A Dynamic Relationship of Theology and Science," *Origins* 18 (November 17, 1988): 375–78.

4. John Paul II, "Message to the Pontifical Academy of Sciences on Evolution," *Origins* 26 (December 5, 1996): 414–16.

5. John Paul II, *God, Father and Creator* (Boston: Pauline Books & Media, 1996), 103–5.

6. Benedict XVI, "The Inauguration Homily," *Origins* 34 (May 5, 2005): 733, 735–37, at 736.

7. Christoph Schönborn, "The Designs of Science," *First Things* 159 (January 2006), 34–38, at 37.

8. Ibid., 35. The quotation from Will Provine is given without reference.

9. This is approximately the method described by Victor J. Stenger, *God: The Failed Hypothesis* (Amherst, N.Y.: Prometheus Books, 2007), preface and chapter 1.

10. Richard Dawkins, *The God Delusion* (New York: Houghton Mifflin, 2006), 109; cf. 158.

11. Richard Dawkins, "Is Science a Religion?" *The Humanist* 57 (1997): 26–29, quoted by Francis S. Collins, *The Language of God* (New York: Free Press, 2006), 2; also by Alister McGrath, *Dawkins' God* (Oxford: Blackwell, 2005): 84.

12. Dawkins, *God Delusion*, 314.

13. Ibid., 347.

14. Benedict XVI, "The Regensburg Academic Lecture," *Origins* 36 (September 28, 2006): 248–52.

15. For an exposition of the "Anthropic Principle" and "fine tuning," see Terence L. Nichols, *The Sacred Cosmos* (Grand Rapids, Mich.: Brazos Press, 2003), 78–82.

16. Francis S. Collins, *Language of God*, 2.

17. Michael J. Behe, *Darwin's Black Box: The Biochemical Challenge to Evolution* (New York: Free Press, 1996), 70–75.

18. John Polkinghorne, *The Faith of a Physicist* (Princeton, N.J.: Princeton University Press, 1994), 17

19. John F. Haught, *Is Nature Enough?* (New York: Cambridge University Press, 2007), 15, 78–88.

20. Étienne Gilson, *From Aristotle to Darwin and Back Again: A Journey in Final Causality, Species, and Evolution* (Notre Dame, Ind.: University of Notre Dame, 1984). See especially chapter 2, "The Mechanist Objection."

21. See Phillip E. Johnson and Howard J. Van Till, "God and Evolution: An Exchange," *First Things* 34 (1993): 32–41; quotation from Johnson's response, 40.

22. On the material in this paragraph, the reflections of St. Thomas are still valuable. See his *Summa contra Gentiles*, Book II, qq. 80–81, 83, and 87.

23. Terry Eagleton, review of Dawkins, *The God Delusion*, in *The London Review of Books*, October 2006. I cite the review as quoted by Peter Steinfels, "Beliefs," *New York Times*, 3 March 2007, p. B5. Alister McGrath, in his previously cited *Dawkins' God*, likewise censures Dawkins for his superficial and inaccurate engagement with theology.

24. Justin Barrett, quoted without source by Robin Marantz Henig, "Darwin's God," *New York Times Magazine*, 4 March 2007, 78.

38

Who Can Be Saved?

November 7, 2007

Nothing is more striking in the New Testament than the confidence with which it proclaims the saving power of belief in Christ. Almost every page confronts us with a decision of eternal consequence: Will we follow Christ or the rulers of this world? The gospel is, according to Paul, "the power of God for salvation to everyone who has faith" (Rom 1:16). The apostles and their associates are convinced that in Jesus they have encountered the Lord of life and that he has brought them into the way that leads to everlasting blessedness. By personal faith in him and by baptism in his name, Christians have passed from darkness to light, from error to truth, and from sin to holiness.

Paul is the outstanding herald of salvation through faith. To the Romans he writes: "If you confess with your lips that Jesus is Lord and believe in your heart that God raised him from the dead, you will be saved" (Rom 10:9). Faith, for him, is inseparable from baptism, the sacrament of faith. By baptism the Christian is immersed in the death of Christ so as to be raised with him to newness of life (Rom 6:3–4).

The Book of Acts shows the Apostles preaching faith in Christ as the way to salvation. Those who believe the testimony of Peter on the first Pentecost ask him what they must do to be saved. He replies that they must be baptized in the name of Jesus Christ for the forgiveness of their sins and thereby save themselves from the present crooked generation (Acts 2:37–40). When Peter and John are asked by the Jewish religious authorities by what authority they are preaching and performing miracles, they reply that they are acting in the name of Jesus Christ and that "there is no other name under heaven given among men by which we must be saved" (Acts 4:12). Paul and his associates bring the gospel first of all to the Jews because it is the fulfillment of the Old Testament promises. When the Jews in large numbers reject the message, Paul and Barnabas announce that they are turning to the Gentiles in order to bring salvation to the uttermost parts of the earth (Acts 13:46–47).

A few chapters later in Acts we see Paul and Silas in prison at Philippi. When their jailer asks them, "What must I do to be saved?" they reply, "Believe in the Lord Jesus and you will be saved." The jailer and his family at once accept baptism and rejoice in their newfound faith (Acts 16:30–34).

The same doctrine of salvation permeates the other books of the New Testament. Mark's Gospel ends with the missionary charge: "Go into all the world and preach the gospel to the whole of creation. He who believes and is baptized will be saved; but he who does not believe will be condemned" (Mk 16:15–16). John in his Gospel speaks no less clearly. Jesus at one point declares that those who hear his word and believe in him do not remain in darkness, whereas those who reject him will be judged on the last day (Jn 12:44–50). At the Last Supper Jesus declares, "This is eternal life, that they may know thee, the only true God, and Jesus Christ whom thou hast sent" (Jn 17:3). John concludes the body of his Gospel with the statement that he has written his account "so that you may believe that Jesus is the Christ and that believing you may have life in his name" (Jn 20:31). From these and many other texts I draw the conclusion that according to the primary Christian documents salvation comes through personal faith in Jesus Christ, followed and signified by sacramental baptism. The New Testament is almost silent about the eternal fate of those to whom the gospel has not been preached. From the texts already discussed it seems apparent that those who became believers did not think they had been on the road to salvation before they heard the gospel. In his sermon at Athens Paul says that in times past God overlooked the ignorance of the pagans, but he does not say that these pagans were saved. In the first chapter of Romans, Paul says that the Gentiles have come to a knowledge of God by reasoning from the created world but that they are guilty because by their wickedness they have suppressed the truth and fallen into idolatry. In the second chapter of Romans, Paul indicates that Gentiles who are obedient to the biddings of conscience can be excused for their unbelief, but he indicates that they fall into many sins. He concludes that "all have sinned and fall short" of true righteousness (Rom 3:23). For justification, Paul asserts, both Jews and Gentiles must rely on faith in Jesus Christ, who expiated the sins of the world on the Cross.

THE PATRISTIC AGE

Animated by vibrant faith in Christ the Savior, the Christian Church was able to conquer the Roman Empire. No opposition, no threats, no persecutions could prevent the heralds of the gospel from proclaiming the glad tidings to every people. The converts were convinced that in embracing Christianity they were escaping from the darkness of sin and superstition and entering into the realm of salvation. For them Christianity was the true religion, the faith that saves. It would not have occurred to them that any other faith could save them.

It was not long before theologians had to face the question whether anyone could be saved without Christian faith. They did not give a wholly negative answer. They agreed that the patriarchs and prophets of Israel, because they looked forward in faith and hope to the Savior God would send, could be saved by adhering in advance to Him who was to come.

The apologists of the second and third centuries made similar concessions with regard to certain Greek philosophers.[1] The prologue to John's Gospel taught that the eternal Word enlightens all men who come into the world. Justin Martyr speculated that philosophers such as Socrates and Heraclitus had lived according to the Word of God, the Logos who was to become incarnate in Christ, and could therefore be reckoned as being in some way Christians. Irenaeus, Clement of Alexandria, and Origen held that the Wisdom of God gave graces to people of every generation, both Greeks and barbarians.

It should be noted, however, that the saving grace of which these theologians were speaking was given only to pagans who lived before the time of Christ. It was given by the Word of God who was to become incarnate in Jesus Christ. There was no doctrine that pagans could be saved since the promulgation of the gospel without embracing the Christian faith.

Origen and Cyprian, in the third century, formulated the maxim that has come down to us in the expression "outside the Church no salvation" (*extra Ecclesiam nulla salus*). They spoke these words with heretics and schismatics primarily in view, but they do not appear to have been any more optimistic about the prospects of pagans for salvation. Assuming that the gospel had been promulgated everywhere, writers of the high patristic age considered that Christians alone could be saved in the Christian era. In the East this view is represented by Gregory of Nyssa and John Chrysostom. The view attributed to Origen that hell would in the end be evacuated and that all the damned would eventually be saved was condemned in the sixth century.[2]

In the West, Augustine, following Ambrose and others, taught that, because faith comes by hearing, those who had never heard the gospel would be denied salvation. They would be eternally punished for original sin as well as for any personal sins they had committed. Augustine's disciple Fulgentius of Ruspe exhorted his readers: "Firmly hold and by no means doubt that not only all pagans, but also all Jews, and all heretics and schismatics who are outside the Catholic Church, will go to the eternal fire that was prepared for the devil and his angels."

THE MIDDLE AGES

The views of Augustine and Fulgentius remained dominant in the Christian West throughout the Middle Ages. The Fourth Lateran Council (1215) reaffirmed the formula "outside the Church no salvation," as did Pope Boniface VIII in 1302. At the end of the Middle Ages the Council of Florence (1442) repeated the formulation of Fulgentius to the effect that no pagan, Jew, schismatic, or heretic could be saved.

On one point the medieval theologians diverged from rigid Augustinianism. On the basis of certain passages in the New Testament they held that God seriously wills that all may be saved. They could cite the statement of Peter before the household of Cornelius: "Truly I perceive that God shows no partiality, but in every nation anyone who fears him and does what is right is acceptable to him" (Acts 10:34–35). The First Letter to Timothy, moreover, declares that God "desires all men to be saved and come to the knowledge of the truth" (1 Tim 2:4). These assurances made for a certain tension in Catholic teaching on salvation. If faith in Christ was necessary for salvation, how could salvation be within reach of those who had no opportunity to learn about Christ?

Thomas Aquinas, in dealing with this problem, took his departure from the axiom that there was no salvation outside the Church. To be inside the Church, he held, it was not enough to have faith in the existence of God and in divine providence, which would have sufficed before the coming of Christ. God now required explicit faith in the mysteries of the Trinity and the Incarnation. In two of his early works (his *De Veritate* and his *Commentary on Romans*) he discusses the hypothetical case of a man brought up in the wilderness, where the gospel was totally unknown. If this man lived an upright life with the help of the graces given him, Thomas reasoned, God would make it possible for him to become a Christian believer, either through an inner illumination or by sending a missionary to him. Thomas referred to the biblical example of the centurion Cornelius who received the visitation of an angel before being evangelized and baptized by Peter (Acts, chapter 10). In his great *Summa theologiae*, however, Saint Thomas omits any reference to miraculous instruction; he goes back to the Augustinian theory that those who had never heard the gospel would be eternally punished for original sin as well as their personal sins.

The Reformation and Counter-Reformation

A major theological development occurred in the sixteenth and seventeenth centuries. The voyages of discovery had by this time disclosed that there were huge populations in North and South America, Africa, and Asia who had lived since the time of Christ and had never had access to the preaching of the gospel. The missionaries found no sign that even the most upright among these peoples had learned the mysteries of the Trinity and the Incarnation by interior inspirations or angelic visitations.

Luther, Calvin, and the Jansenists professed the strict Augustinian doctrine that God did not will to save everyone, but the majority of Catholic theologians rejected the idea that God had consigned all these unevangelized persons to hell without giving them any possibility of salvation. A series of theologians proposed more hopeful theories that they took to be compatible with Scripture and Catholic tradition.

The Dominican Melchior Cano argued that these populations were in a situation no different from that of the pre-Christian pagans praised by

Justin and others. They could be justified in this life (but not saved in the life to come) by implicit faith in the Christian mysteries. Another Dominican, Domingo de Soto, went further, holding that, for the unevangelized, implicit faith in Christ would be sufficient for salvation itself. Their contemporary, Albert Pighius, held that for these unevangelized persons, and for all who had not heard the gospel credibly proclaimed, the only faith required would be that mentioned in Hebrews 11:6, which states: "Without faith it is impossible to please him [God]. For whoever would draw near to God must believe that he exists and that he rewards those who seek him." They could therefore be saved by general revelation and grace even though no missionary came to evangelize them.

Francisco Suárez, S.J., following these pioneers, argued for the sufficiency of implicit faith in the Trinity and the Incarnation together with an implicit desire for baptism on the part of the unevangelized. Juan de Lugo, S.J., agreed, but he added that such persons could not be saved if they had committed serious sins, unless they obtained forgiveness by an act of perfect contrition.

Modern Catholic Doctrine

In the mid-nineteenth century the Jesuits of the Gregorian University followed in the tradition of Suárez and de Lugo, with certain modifications that need not concern us here. Pope Pius IX incorporated some of their ideas in two important statements, issued in 1854 and 1863 respectively. In the first he said that, while no one can be saved outside of the Church, God would not punish people for their ignorance of the true faith if their ignorance was invincible. In the second statement Pius IX went further. He declared that persons invincibly ignorant of the Christian religion who observed the natural law and were ready to obey God would be able to attain eternal life, thanks to the workings of divine grace within them. In the same letter the pope reaffirmed that no one could be saved outside the Catholic Church. He did not explain in what sense such persons were, or would come to be, in the Church. He could have meant that they would receive the further grace needed to join the Church, but nothing in his language suggests this. More probably he thought that such persons would be joined to the Church by implicit desire, as some theologians were teaching by his time.

In 1943, Pope Pius XII did take this further step. In his encyclical on the Mystical Body he distinguished between two ways of belonging to the Church: in actual fact (*in re*) or by desire (*in voto*). Those who belonged *in voto*, however, were not really members. They were ordered to the Church by the dynamism of grace itself, which related them to the Church in such a way that they were in some sense in it. The two kinds of relationship, however, were not equally conducive to salvation. Those adhering to the Church by desire could not have a sure hope of salvation because they lacked many spiritual gifts and helps available only to those visibly incorporated in the true Church.

Mystici Corporis represents a forward step in its doctrine of adherence to the Church through implicit desire. From an ecumenical point of view that encyclical is deficient since it does not distinguish between the status of non-Christians and non-Catholic Christians—a deficiency that would be remedied by Vatican II.

The next important document on our subject came from the Holy Office in its letter to Cardinal Richard Cushing of Boston in 1949. The letter pointed out, in opposition to Father Leonard Feeney, S.J., and his associates at St. Benedict Center, that, although the Catholic Church was a necessary means for salvation, one could belong to it not only by actual membership but by desire, even an unconscious desire.[3] If that desire was accompanied by faith and perfect charity, it could lead to eternal salvation.

Neither the encyclical *Mystici corporis* nor the letter of the Holy Office specified the nature of the faith required for *in voto* status. Did the authors mean that the virtue of faith or the inclination to believe would suffice, or did they require actual faith in God and divine providence, or actual faith in the Trinity and Incarnation? The documents we are studying did not deal with these questions.

VATICAN COUNCIL II

Vatican II in its Dogmatic Constitution on the Church and its Decree on Ecumenism made some significant departures from the teaching of Pius XII. It avoided the term *member* and said nothing of an unconscious desire for incorporation in the Church. It taught that the Catholic Church was the all-embracing organ of salvation and was equipped with the fullness of means of salvation (*UR* 2). Other Christian churches and communities possessed certain elements of sanctification and truth that were, however, derived from the one Church of Christ that subsists in the Catholic Church today. For this reason God could use them as instruments of salvation (*UR* 2). God had, however, made the Catholic Church necessary for salvation, and all who were aware of this had a serious obligation to enter the Church in order to be saved (*LG* 14). God uses the Catholic Church not only for the redemption of her own members but as an instrument for the redemption of all (*LG* 9). The witness and prayers of Christians, together with the eucharistic sacrifice, have an efficacy that goes out to the whole world (*LG* 10; *SC* 10).

In several important texts Vatican II took up the question of the salvation of non-Christians. Although they were related to the Church in various ways, they were not incorporated in her. God's universal salvific will, it taught, means that he gives non-Christians, including even atheists, sufficient help to be saved. Whoever sincerely seeks God and, with his grace, follows the dictates of conscience is on the path to salvation (*LG* 16). The Holy Spirit in a manner known only to God makes it possible for each and every person to be associated with the Paschal mystery (*GS* 22). "God, in ways known to himself, can lead those inculpably ignorant of the gospel to that faith without which it is impossible to please him (Heb 11:6)" (*AG* 7). The council does not indicate whether it is necessary for salvation to come to explicit Christian faith before death, but the texts give the impression that implicit faith may suffice.

Vatican II leaves open the question whether non-Christian religions contain revelation and are means that can lead their adherents to salvation. It does say, however, that other religions contain elements of truth and goodness, that they reflect rays of the Truth that enlightens all men, and that they can serve as preparations for the gospel (*NA* 2; *AG* 3). Christian missionary activity serves to heal, ennoble, and perfect the seeds of truth and goodness that God has sown among non-Christian peoples, to the glory of God and the spiritual benefit of those evangelized (*AG* 9 and 11).

While repeatedly insisting that Christ is the one Mediator of salvation, Vatican II shows forth a generally hopeful view of the prospects of non-Christians for salvation. Its hopefulness, however, is not unqualified. "Rather often," it states, "men, deceived by the evil one, have become caught up in futile reasoning and have exchanged the truth of God for a lie, serving the creature rather than the Creator (Rom 1:21, 25). Or, some there are who, living and dying in a world without God, are subject to utter hopelessness" (*LG* 16). The missionary activity of the Church is urgent for bringing such persons to salvation.

POSTCONCILIAR DEVELOPMENTS

After the council, Paul VI in his great pastoral exhortation "Evangelization in the Modern World" and John Paul II in his encyclical *Redemptoris missio* reiterated and interpreted the teaching of Vatican II in relation to certain problems and theological trends arising since the council. Both popes were on guard against political and liberation theology, which would seem to equate salvation with formation of a just society on earth, and against styles of religious pluralism that would attribute independent salvific value to non-Christian religions. Toward the end of John Paul's pontificate, the Congregation for the Doctrine of the Faith issued the declaration *Dominus Iesus*, which emphatically taught that all grace and salvation must come through Jesus Christ, the one Mediator. The positive elements of non-Christian religions may, however, fall within the divine plan of salvation.

Wisely, in my opinion, the popes and councils have avoided talk about implicit faith, a term that is vague and ambiguous. They do speak of persons who are sincerely seeking for the truth and of others who have found it in Christ. They make it clear that sufficient grace is offered to all and that God will not turn away those who do everything within their power to find God and live according to his law. We may count on him to lead such persons to the faith needed for salvation.

One of the most interesting developments in postconciliar theology has been Karl Rahner's idea of "anonymous Christians." He taught that God offers his grace to everyone and reveals himself in the interior offer of grace. Grace, moreover, is always mediated through Christ and tends to bring its recipients into union with him. Those who accept and live by the grace offered to them, even though they have never heard of Christ and the gospel, may be called anonymous Christians.

Although Rahner denied that his theory undermined the importance of missionary activity, it was widely understood as depriving missions of their salvific importance. Some readers of his works understood him as teaching that the unevangelized could possess the whole of Christianity except the name. Saving faith, thus understood, would be a subjective attitude without any specifiable content. In that case, the message of the gospel would have little to do with salvation.

Two Perspectives to Be Reconciled

The history of the doctrine of salvation through faith has gone through a number of stages since the high Middle Ages. Using the New Testament as their basic text, the Church Fathers regarded faith in Christ and baptism as essential for salvation. On the basis of his study of the New Testament and Augustine, Thomas Aquinas held that explicit belief in the Trinity and the Incarnation was necessary for everyone who lived since the time of Christ, but he granted that in earlier times it was sufficient to believe explicitly in the existence and providence of God. In the sixteenth century, theologians speculated that the unevangelized were in the same condition as pre-Christians, and were not held to believe explicitly in Christ until the gospel was credibly preached to them. Pius IX and the Second Vatican Council taught that all who followed their conscience, with the help of the grace given to them, would be led to the faith that was necessary for them to be saved. During and after the council, Karl Rahner maintained that saving faith could be had without any definite belief in Christ or even in God. We seem to have come full circle from the teaching of Paul and the New Testament that belief in the message of Christ is the source of salvation.

Reflecting on the development, one can see certain gains and certain losses. The New Testament and the theology of the first millennium give little hope for the salvation of those who, since the time of Christ, have had no chance of hearing the gospel. If God has a serious salvific will for all, this lacuna needed to be filled, as it has been by theological speculation and Church teaching since the sixteenth century. Modern theology, preoccupied with the salvation of non-Christians, has tended to neglect the importance of explicit belief in Christ, so strongly emphasized in the first centuries. It should not be impossible, however, to reconcile the two perspectives.

Scripture itself assures us that God has never left himself without witness to any nation (Acts 14:17). His testimonies are marks of his saving dispensations toward all. The inner testimony of every human conscience bears witness to God as lawgiver, judge, and vindicator. In ancient times the Jewish Scriptures drew on literature that came from Babylon, Egypt, and Greece. The book of Wisdom and Paul's Letter to the Romans speak of God manifesting his power and divinity through his works in nature. The religions generally promote prayer and sacrifice as ways of winning God's favor. The traditions of all peoples contain elements of truth imbedded in their cultures, myths, and religious practices. These sound elements derive from God, who speaks to all his children through inward testimony and outward signs.

The universal evidences of the divine, under the leading of grace, can give rise to a rudimentary faith that leans forward in hope and expectation to further manifestations of God's merciful love and of his guidance for our lives. By welcoming the signs already given and placing their hope in God's redeeming love, persons who have not heard the tidings of the gospel may nevertheless be on the road to salvation. If they are faithful to the grace given them, they may have good hope of receiving the truth and blessedness for which they yearn.

The search, however, is no substitute for finding. To be blessed in this life, one must find the pearl of great price, the treasure hidden in the field, which is worth buying at the cost of everything one possesses. To Christians has been revealed the mystery hidden from past ages, which the patriarchs and prophets longed to know. By entering through baptism into the mystery of the Cross and Resurrection, Christians undergo a radical transformation that sets them unequivocally on the road to salvation. Only after conversion to explicit faith can one join the community that is nourished by the word of God and the sacraments. These gifts of God, prayerfully received, enable the faithful to grow into ever greater union with Christ.

In Christ's Church, therefore, we have many aids to salvation and sanctification that are not available elsewhere. Cardinal Newman expressed the situation admirably in one of his early sermons:

> The prerogative of Christians consists in the possession, not of exclusive knowledge and spiritual aid, but of gifts high and peculiar; and though the manifestation of the Divine character in the Incarnation is a singular and inestimable benefit, yet its absence is supplied in a degree, not only in the inspired record of Moses, but even, with more or less strength, in those

various traditions concerning Divine Providences and Dispositions which are scattered through the heathen mythologies.[4]

We cannot take it for granted that everyone is seeking the truth and is prepared to submit to it when found. Some, perhaps many, resist the grace of God and reject the signs given to them. They are not on the road to salvation at all. In such cases the fault is not God's but theirs. The references to future punishment in the Gospels cannot be written off as empty threats. As Paul says, God is not mocked (Gal 6:7).

CONCLUSION

We may conclude with certitude that God makes it possible for the un-evangelized to attain the goal of their searching. How that happens is known to God alone, as Vatican II twice declares. We know only that their search is not in vain. "Seek, and you will find," says the Lord (Mt 7:7). If non-Christians are praying to an unknown God, it may be for us to help them find the One they worship in ignorance. God wants everyone to come to the truth. Perhaps some will reach the goal of their searching only at the moment of death. Who knows what transpires secretly in their consciousness at that solemn moment? We have no evidence that death is a moment of revelation, but it could be, especially for those in pursuit of the truth of God.

Meanwhile it is the responsibility of believers to help these seekers by word and by example. Whoever receives the gift of revealed truth has the obligation to share it with others. Christian faith is normally transmitted by testimony. Believers are called to be God's witnesses to the ends of the earth.

Who, then, can be saved? Catholics can be saved if they believe the word of God as taught by the Church and if they obey the commandments. Other Christians can be saved if they submit their lives to Christ and join the community where they think he wills to be found. Jews can be saved if they look forward in hope to the Messiah and try to ascertain whether God's promise has been fulfilled. Adherents of other religions can be saved if, with the help of grace, they sincerely seek God and strive to do his will. Even atheists can be saved if they worship God under some other name and place their lives at the service of truth and justice. God's saving grace, channeled through Christ the one Mediator, leaves no one unassisted. But that same grace brings obligations to all who receive it. They must not receive the grace of God in vain. Much will be demanded of those to whom much is given.

NOTES

1. For the history of Church doctrine and theological speculation on the requirements for salvation see the classic work of Louis Capéran, *Le problème du salut des infidèles* (Toulouse: Grand Séminaire, 1934); Avery Dulles, *The Assurance of Things Hoped For* (New York: Oxford University Press, 1994), and Francis A. Sullivan, *Salvation Outside the Church?* (New York: Paulist, 1992). Sullivan's treatment of the question has been especially useful for this article.

2. The Synod of 543, in which the errors of the "Origenists" were condemned, had been called by the Emperor Justinian and was apparently approved by Pope Vigilius. The error in question is in Denzinger-Schönmetzer, *Enchiridion symbolorum*, 411.

3. The position attributed to Father Feeney is most fully stated in "Reply to a Liberal," by Raymond Karam, in *From the Housetops* 3 (Spring 1949): 1–70.

4. John Henry Newman, *University Sermons Preached at Oxford*, 3d ed., sermon III, no. 28 (London: Longmans, Green, 1871), 31.

McGINLEY LECTURES
PREVIOUSLY PUBLISHED

Fall 1988   "University Theology as Service to the Church"
             Modified version in *The Craft of Theology*, chapter 10,
             1995 ed. (New York: Crossroad): 149–64.

Spring 1989 "Teaching Authority in the Church"
             Previously unpublished

Fall 1989   "Catholicism and American Culture: The Uneasy
             Dialogue"
             Published: "Catholicism and American Culture: The
             Uneasy Dialogue," *America* 162 (January 27, 1990):
             54–59.

Spring 1990 "Faith and Experience: Strangers? Rivals? Partners?"
             Published: "Faith and Experience: Strangers? Rivals?
             Partners?" *The Priest* 46 (September 1990): 19–22.

Fall 1990   "Newman, Conversion, and Ecumenism"
             Published: "Newman, Conversion, and Ecumenism,"
             Theological Studies 51 (December 1990): 717–31.

Spring 1991 "The Uses of Scripture in Theology"
             Incorporated into *The Craft of Theology*, chapter 5,
             1995 ed. (New York: Crossroad): 69–86.

Fall 1991   "John Paul II and the New Evangelization"
             Published: "John Paul II and the New Evangelization,"
             America 166 (February 1, 1992): 52–59, 69–72.

Spring 1992 "Historical Method and the Reality of Christ"
             Incorporated into *The Craft of Theology*, chapter 14, 1995
             ed. (New York: Crossroad): 211–24.

Fall 1992   "Religion and the Transformation of Politics"

Published: "Religion and the Transformation of Politics," *America* 167 (October 24, 1992): 296–301.

Spring 1993   "The Church as Communion"

Published in: *Historical Theology and the Unity of the Church : Consistency and Continuity in the Christian Tradition. Essays in Honor of John Meyendorff,* ed. Bradley Nassif (Grand Rapids, Mich.: Eerdmans, 1996), 125–39.

Fall 1993   "The Prophetic Humanism of John Paul II"

Published: "The Prophetic Humanism of John Paul II," *America* 169 (October 23, 1993): 6–11.

Spring 1994   No lecture given.

Fall 1994   "The Challenge of the Catechism"

Published: "The Challenge of the Catechism," *First Things* 49 (January 1995): 46–53.

Spring 1995   "Crucified for Our Sake: Love, Violence, and Sacrifice"

Published: The Death of Jesus as Sacrifice," *Josephinum Journal of Theology* 3 (Summer/Fall 1996): 4–17.

Fall 1995   "John Paul II and the Advent of the New Millennium"

Published: "John Paul II and the New Millennium," *America* 173 (December 9, 1995): 9–15.

Spring 1996   "Priesthood and Gender: Issues in the Debate"

Published: "Gender and Priesthood: Examining the Teaching," *Origins* 25 (May 2, 1996): 778–84.

Fall 1996   "The Limits of Dialogue"

Published in part: "The Travails of Dialogue," *Crisis* (February 1997): 16–19.

Spring 1997   "The Ignatian Charism and Contemporary Theology"

Published: "The Ignatian Charism and Contemporary Theology," *America* 176 (April 26, 1997): 14–22.

Fall 1997   "Mary at the Dawn of a New Millennium"

Published: "Mary at the Dawn of a New Millennium," *America* 178 (January 31-Februaty 7, 1998): 8–10, 12–16, 18–19.

Spring 1998   "Should the Church Repent?"
               Published: "Should the Church Repent?" *First Things* 88
               (December 1998): 36–41.

Fall 1998   "Human Rights: The United Nations and Papal
               Teaching"
               Published: "Human Rights: The United Nations and
               Papal Teaching," *America* 179 (December 5, 1998): 14–19.

Spring 1999   "Can Philosophy Be Christian?"
               Published: "Can Philosophy Be Christian?" *First Things*
               102 (April 2000): 24–29.

Fall 1999   "Justification Today: A New Ecumenical Breakthrough"
               Published: "Two Languages of Salvation," *First Things*
               98 (December 1999): 25–30.

Spring 2000   "The Papacy for a Global Church"
               Published: "The Papacy for a Global Church," *America*
               183 (July 15–22, 2000): 6–11.

Fall 2000   "The Death Penalty: A Right to Life Issue?"
               Published: "Catholicism and Capital Punishment," *First
               Things* 112 (April 2001): 30–35.

Spring 2001   "Religious Freedom: A Developing Doctrine"
               Published: "Religious Freedom: Innovation and
               Development," *First Things* 118 (December 2001): 35–39.

Fall 2001   "Christ Among the Religions"
               Published: "Christ Among the Religions," *America* 186
               (February 4, 2002): 8–15.

Spring 2002   "When to Forgive"
               Published: "When to Forgive," *America* 187 (October 7,
               2002): 6–10.

Fall 2002   "The Population of Hell"
               Published: "The Population of Hell," *First Things* 133
               (May 2003): 36–41.

Spring 2003   "True and False Reform of the Church"
               Published: "True and False Reform," *First Things* 135
               (August/September 2003): 14–19.

Fall 2003   "John Paul II and the Mystery of the Human Person"
             Published: "John Paul II and the Mystery of the Human
             Person," *America* 190 (February 2, 2004): 10–14.

Spring 2004 "The Rebirth of Apologetics"
             Published: "The Rebirth of Apologetics," *First Things*
             143 (May 2004): 18–23.

Fall 2004   "A Eucharistic Church: The Vision of John Paul II,"
             Published: "A Eucharistic Church: The Vision of John
             Paul II," *America* 191 (December 20–27, 2004), 8–12.

Spring 2005 "How Real Is the Real Presence?"
             Published: "How Real Is the Real Presence?" *Origins* 34
             (March 17, 2005): 627–31.

Fall 2005   "Pope Benedict—Interpreter of Vatican II"
             Published: "From Ratzinger to Benedict," *First Things*
             160 (February 2006): 24–29

Spring 2006 "The Mission of the Laity"
             Published: "Can Laity Properly Be Called 'Ministers'?"
             Origins 35 (April 20, 2006): 725–31.

Fall 2006   "The Ignatian Charism at the Dawn of the Twenty-First
             Century"
             Published: "What Distinguished the Jesuits? The
             Ignatian Charism at the Dawn of the Twenty-First
             Century," *America* 196 (January 15–22, 2007): 20–25.

Spring 2007 "Evolution, Atheism, and Religious Belief"
             Published: "God and Evolution," *First Things* 176
             (October 2007): 19–24.

Fall 2007   "Who Can Be Saved?"
             Published: "Who Can Be Saved?" *First Things* 180
             (February 2008): 17–22.

INDEX